KT-522-960

Corporate Finance
and Investment

Corporate Finance and Investment
Decisions and Strategies

Richard Pike
and
Bill Neale

Prentice Hall
New York   London   Toronto   Sydney   Tokyo   Singapore

First published 1993 by
Prentice Hall International (UK) Ltd
Campus 400, Maylands Avenue
Hemel Hempstead
Hertfordshire, HP2 7EZ
A division of
Simon & Schuster International Group

© Prentice Hall International (UK) Ltd, 1993

All rights reserved. No part of this publication may be
reproduced, stored in a retrieval system, or transmitted,
in any form, or by any means, electronic, mechanical,
photocopying, recording or otherwise, without the prior
permission, in writing, from the publisher.
For permission within the United States of America
contact Prentice Hall Inc., Englewood Cliffs, NJ 07632

Typeset in 10/12pt Ehrhardt
by Vision Typesetting, Manchester

Printed and bound in Great Britain by
Redwood Books, Trowbridge, Wiltshire

Library of Congress Cataloging-in-Publication Data

Pike, Richard.
    Corporate finance and investment : decisions and strategies /
Richard Pike and Bill Neale.
        p.   cm.
    Includes bibliographical references and index.
    ISBN 0-13-853144-7 (pbk.)
    1. Coporations – Great Britain – Finance.   2. Investments – Great
Britain.   3.Corporations – Europe – Finance.   I. Neale, Bill.
II. Title.
HG4135.P35   1993   92–2397
658.15'0941 – dc20   CIP

British Library Cataloguing in Publication Data

A catalogue record for this book is available from
the British Library

ISBN 0-13-853144-7

    3   4   5   97   96   95   94

Contents

Preface

Corporate Finance and Investment: Decisions and Strategies has been written to address the main challenges in finance of the 1990s. A book of this length must of necessity limit its attention to a defined area of finance, and the field covered by this text has a distinctly corporate focus, examining issues primarily from the viewpoint of a manager in a company.

The book has been written with both newcomers to finance and students with a prior knowledge of the subject in mind. Some prior knowledge of accounting, economics and statistics is helpful. It is relevant to MBA and other post-graduate courses, undergraduate and diploma courses, and post-experience programmes. Students seeking a professional qualification will also find it very relevant, especially those taking the financial management papers for the Chartered Association of Certified Accountants, and the Certified Diploma in Finance and Accounting, Chartered Institute of Management Accountants and Institute of Chartered Accountants of England and Wales. In particular, we believe that this book is highly compatible with the recent syllabus revision by CACA, which now involves the study of Financial Management at two levels, Paper 8, 'Managerial Finance' and Paper 14, 'Financial Strategy'.

Distinctive features

This text possesses a number of distinctive features:

1. *A strategic focus.* Students often regard financial management as a subject quite distinct from management and business policy. We attempt to relate the subject to the practice of management and business policy, choosing to emphasize the strategic, rather than the operational, aspects. This focus lends itself particularly well to MBA and business/ management and undergraduate programmes.

2. *A practical and 'common-sense' approach.* Some texts are dominated by increasingly mathematical financial theory. Theory has its place, and this text covers a good deal of financial theory but in as 'user-friendly' a way as possible. We seek to blend theory and practice; to ask why they sometimes differ; and to assess the role of less sophisticated

financial approaches in the world of business. In other words, although academics, we do not elevate theory above common sense and intuition!

3. *A 'readable' text.* This, of course, is a matter of opinion! Our experience is that many of our target audience prefer a more descriptive approach using worked examples and diagrams, rather than a heavily mathematical approach. There is a place for formulae, proofs and quantitative analysis but, where possible, the reader is offered an alternative narrative explanation. Appendices are often used to deal with proofs and derivations, and readers are referred to texts with more mathematical approaches.

4. *A European focus.* The book draws primarily on British financial management, but also has regard to its application to much of the rest of Europe. It is our view that it is no longer appropriate to expect MBA, undergraduate or professional students to read otherwise excellent American finance texts which frequently have somewhat limited relevance to the European setting.

Aids to learning

We introduce a host of pedagogic devices to aid student learning:

1. *Learning objectives* spelling out what the reader should have achieved, in terms of concepts, terminology and skills, are specified early in each chapter.

2. *Topical 'hors d'oeuvres'* are served up at the start of each chapter as a relish prior to the reader tucking into the 'meat' of the chapter.

3. *Key learning points* are presented in summary form throughout each chapter, along with practical worked examples and mini-cases.

4. *Key revision points* at the end of each chapter summarize the main concepts covered.

5. *End of chapter questions* take three forms:
   (a) Short self-test questions.
   (b) Exercises of varying levels of complexity. Some have solutions at the end of the book, while others are suitable for tutorial use. A *Lecturer's Guide* with fully worked solutions is available to those lecturers adopting the text.
   (c) Practical assignments. Case studies and assignments (including in-company assignments) suitable for courses where assessed coursework is set.

6. *Structure of the book.* This text is structured into four distinct parts:

   Part I   A framework for financial decisions.
   Part II   Investment decisions and strategies.
   Part III Financing decisions and policy.
   Part IV Integrated topics.

Acknowledgements

We wish to acknowledge the considerable help and advice received from colleagues and others.

1. People who have read and offered helpful comments on sections of the book include: Chris Guilding, Chris Parkinson, Jon Robinson, Steven Fraser and Stuart Sanderson; and particularly Iain Bowie and Gerry Gannon for commenting on the whole manuscript. Also, the various groups of students who have been exposed to much of the material and offered (usually) helpful observations.

2. People/organizations who have consented to use of material include:

    *   Chris Pass, Johannes Meerjanssen
    *   Chartered Institute of Management Accountants and Chartered Institute of Certified Accountants
    *   London Business School (Risk Measurement Service)
    *   Hoare Govett Investment Research
    *   *The Financial Times*
    *   3i
    *   Graham Quick, of Extel Financial
    *   Various companies which have agreed to the use of extracts from their respective annual reports
    *   We are particularly grateful to Tom McRac for contributing a significant element of Chapter 19.

Finally, our thanks to Jean Lister and Lorna Pickersgill who had the unenviable task of typing our endless drafts of the book.

PART I

A Framework for Financial Decisions

A good grasp of the framework for financial decisions is important if the reader is to appreciate the issues discussed in subsequent chapters of the book.

Part I provides an introduction to the scope and the fundamental concepts of financial management. A broad picture of the topic and the important role it plays in business is provided in Chapter 1, which examines the nature of financing and investment decisions, the role of the financial manager and the fundamental objective for corporate financial management. This then leads on, in chapter 2, to introduce the reader to the financial and tax environment in which businesses operate.

Central to financial management are the time-value of money and present value concepts discussed in Chapter 3. These and other concepts are developed in Chapter 4 to provide an understanding of valuation. Subsequent parts of the book then go on to apply these valuation concepts to investment, financing and other decisions.

CHAPTER 1
An overview of financial management

CORPORATE FINANCE IN PRACTICE

In the 1990 annual report of The Quaker Oats Company, the chairman stated:

'Our objective is to maximize value for shareholders over the long term. As a worldwide marketer of grocery products, value is embodied in our strong portfolio of brands. Management is empowered to oversee the investment in, and maintenance of, our brands to maximize their growth and profit potential. In all lines of business, Quaker managers must weigh the impact of strategic issues on investment decisions. Ultimately, our goal is the goal of all professional investors – to maximize value by generating the highest cash flow possible.

There are two challenges created by this goal. The first is to pursue business strategies that strike the proper balance between profitability and growth in each of our brands. The second challenge is to invest in projects that will allow us to consistently deliver cash flows to shareholders at rates in excess of our cost of capital and better than our competitors.'

1.1 Introduction

The reader of Quaker's annual report is left in little doubt that the company has a clear idea of its purpose and how it intends to achieve it. Its mission is to maximize value for its shareholders by successfully marketing leading consumer brands. An organization like Quaker, with such a strong portfolio of brands, understands the importance of meeting the requirements of its existing and potential customers. But it also recognizes that the most important 'customers' whose requirements must be satisfied are the shareholders – the owners of the business. Its objectives, strategies and decisions are all directed towards creating value for the shareholders.

3

One of the challenges referred to by Quaker's chairman is to invest in projects that consistently deliver cash flows to shareholders yielding rates of return that are in excess of the cost of financing those projects and better than the competition. The primary focus of this book centres on this very issue: *How can firms create value through sound investment decisions and financial strategies?*

Outline of the book

This book aims to provide the reader with a clear understanding of the more important or strategic issues in corporate financial management. It does not pretend to offer a fully comprehensive text on either corporate strategy or corporate finance – to do so would require a much lengthier and bulkier text; nor does it over-emphasize theoretical developments which appear, as yet, to have only limited practical value.

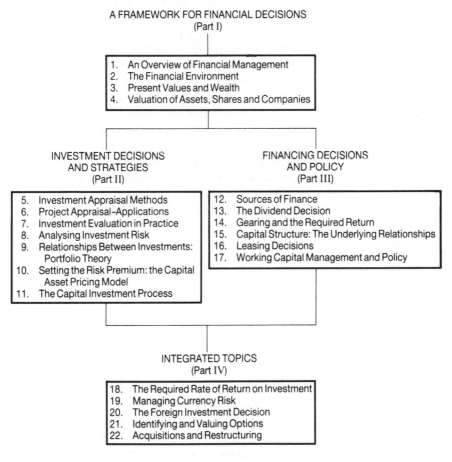

A FRAMEWORK FOR FINANCIAL DECISIONS
(Part I)

1. An Overview of Financial Management
2. The Financial Environment
3. Present Values and Wealth
4. Valuation of Assets, Shares and Companies

INVESTMENT DECISIONS
AND STRATEGIES
(Part II)

5. Investment Appraisal Methods
6. Project Appraisal–Applications
7. Investment Evaluation in Practice
8. Analysing Investment Risk
9. Relationships Between Investments: Portfolio Theory
10. Setting the Risk Premium: the Capital Asset Pricing Model
11. The Capital Investment Process

FINANCING DECISIONS
AND POLICY
(Part III)

12. Sources of Finance
13. The Dividend Decision
14. Gearing and the Required Return
15. Capital Structure: The Underlying Relationships
16. Leasing Decisions
17. Working Capital Management and Policy

INTEGRATED TOPICS
(Part IV)

18. The Required Rate of Return on Investment
19. Managing Currency Risk
20. The Foreign Investment Decision
21. Identifying and Valuing Options
22. Acquisitions and Restructuring

Figure 1.1 Outline of book

The book is divided into four parts as illustrated in Figure 1.1. Part I considers the underlying concepts of managerial finance and the financial environment within which decisions are made. Central to this section is the valuation concept and the time-value of money.

Part II considers investment decisions and related aspects. Emphasis is placed on evaluation mechanics and their practical application. Because future benefits are not known with any degree of certainty, investment appraisal necessarily requires analysis of risk. Three chapters are devoted to handling risk: the first considers the project in isolation, while the others view risk more from a shareholder perspective. Part II concludes with an examination of the total investment process for planning and controlling strategic decisions.

Part III examines the main strategic financing decisions. It outlines the main sources of finance available to companies, and addresses the question of whether, and if so how, corporate managers can create value through dividend policy and capital structuring. A related issue is the decision to lease, rather than acquire, capital assets. Working capital management and policy are key topics addressed in this section.

Finally, Part IV addresses integrated topics in finance and investment. Fundamental to the whole of financial management is the rate of return required by shareholders. Various approaches are considered for its estimation.

Business operations increasingly have an international dimension. Companies trading overseas need to consider how they can obtain protection against the risk of foreign exchange movements. Many UK household names now produce the bulk of their output from overseas-located plants. The evaluation of this foreign investment and the safeguarding of resulting cash flows from exposure to exchange risk present further complications.

Analysis and valuation of businesses for acquisition, corporate restructuring and options have both investment and financing implications, so we address them in the latter part of the book.

Finance and planning

This first chapter provides a broad picture of the subject matter of financial management and of the important role it plays in achieving financial objectives and operating successful businesses. First, we consider where financial management fits into the strategic planning process for a new business. This leads to an outline of the finance function and to the role of the financial manager, and what objectives he may follow. Central to the subject is the nature of these financial objectives and how they affect shareholders' interests. Finally, we provide an outline of the development of the book and the strategic focus which we aim to provide.

Ken Brown, a recent business graduate, decides to set up his own small bakery business. He recognizes that a clear business strategy is required, giving a broad thrust to be adopted in achieving his objectives, and that the main issues are market identification, competitor analysis and business formation. He identifies a suitable market with room for a new entrant and develops a range of bakery products which are expected to stand up well, in terms of price and quality, with the existing competition.

Brown and his wife become the directors of a newly-formed *limited company*, Brownbake Ltd. Such a company is an entity which, in law, is quite separate from its owners or managers.

LEARNING OBJECTIVES

By the end of this first chapter the reader should have gained a better appreciation of:

- What corporate finance and investment decisions involve.
- How financial management has evolved.
- The finance function and how it relates to its wider environment and to strategic planning.
- The central role of cash in business.
- The central goal of shareholder wealth-creation and how investors can encourage managers to adopt this goal.

A particular advantage of such an entity is that the financial liability of the owners is limited to the amount they have paid in, or have agreed to pay in. Should the company become insolvent, those with outstanding claims on the company cannot compel the owners (shareholders) to pay in further capital.

Brown must now concentrate on how the business strategy is to be implemented. This requires careful planning of the decisions to be taken and their effect on the business. Planning requires answers to some important questions. What resources are required? Does the business require premises, equipment, vehicles and material to produce and deliver his product? Once these issues have been addressed, an equally important question is: How will such plans be funded? However sympathetic his bank manager, Brown will probably need to find other investors who are willing to carry a large part of the business risk. Eventually, these operating plans must be translated into financial plans giving a clear indication of the investment required and the intended sources of finance. Financial management is primarily concerned with such issues and applies equally to small businesses (like Brown's) and the large multinational corporations.

1.2   The finance function

In a well-organized business, each section should arrange its activities so as to maximize its contribution towards the attainment of corporate goals. The finance function is a very sharply focused function, its activities being specific to the financial aspects of management decisions.

It is the *task of those involved within the finance function to plan, raise and use funds in an efficient manner to achieve corporate financial objectives.* Two central activities are:

1.   Providing the link between the business and the wider financial environment.
2.   Investment and financial analysis and decision-making.

Link with financial environment

The finance function provides the link between the firm and the financial markets in which funds are raised and the company's shares and other financial instruments are traded. The financial manager, whether a corporate treasurer in a multinational company or the sole trader of a small business, performs a vital function by acting as an *intermediary* between financial markets and the firm. This is the subject of Chapter 2.

Investment and financial decisions

Financial management is primarily concerned with *investment and financing decisions* and their interactions in business organizations. These two broad areas for decision-making lie at the heart of financial management theory and practice. Let us first be clear what we mean by these decisions.

The *investment decision*, sometimes referred to as the capital budgeting decision, is the decision to acquire assets. Most of these assets will be *real assets* employed within the business to produce goods or services to satisfy consumer demand. Real assets may be tangible, such as land and buildings, plant and equipment, and stocks, or intangible, such as patents, trademarks and 'know-how'. Sometimes a firm may choose to invest in *financial assets* outside the business in the form of short-term securities and deposits. The basic problems facing management concerning investments are:

1. *How much* should the firm invest?
2. *In which projects* should the firm invest?

A considerable part of this book is devoted to these very issues.

The *financing decision* addresses the problems: how much capital should be raised to fund the firm's operations (both existing and proposed), and what is the best mix of financing? In the same way that a firm can hold financial assets such as shares and loan deposits, it can also sell claims on its own real assets, by issuing shares, raising loans, undertaking lease obligations, and so on.

1.3   Cash – the lifeblood of the business

Central to the whole of finance is the generation and management of cash. Figure 1.2 illustrates the flow of cash for a typical manufacturing concern. Rather like the bloodstream in a living body, cash is viewed as the 'lifeblood' of the business flowing to all essential parts of the corporate body. If at any point the cash fails to flow properly, a 'clot' occurs which can damage the business and, if not addressed in time, can prove fatal!

Good cash management lies at the heart of a healthy business. Let us now consider the major sources and uses of cash for a typical business concern.

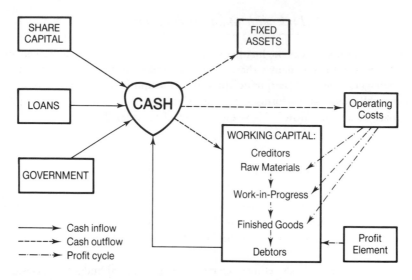

Figure 1.2   Cash – the lifeblood of a business

Sources of cash

Shareholders' funds

The largest proportion of long-term finance is usually provided by shareholders and is termed *equity capital*. Share ownership lies at the heart of modern capitalism. By purchasing a portion of, or shares in, a company, almost anyone can become a shareholder with some degree of control over a company.

Ordinary share capital is the main source of new money from shareholders. They are entitled both to participate in the business through voting in a general meeting and to receive dividends out of profits. As owners of the business, the ordinary shareholders bear the greatest risk, but enjoy the main fruits of success in the form of higher dividends and capital gains.

Retained profits

For an established business the main source of equity funds will be internally generated from successful trading. Any profits remaining after all operating costs, interest payments, taxation and dividends are reinvested in the business (i.e. ploughed back) and regarded as part of the equity capital.

Loan capital

Money lent to a business by third parties is termed debt finance or loan capital. Most companies borrow money on a long-term basis by issuing loan stocks (or debentures). The terms of the loan will specify the amount of the loan, rate of interest and date of payment, redemption date and method of repayment. Loan stock typically carries a lower risk than equity capital and, hence, a lower return.

The finance manager will monitor the long-term financial structure by examining the relationship between loan capital, where interest and loan repayment are contractually obligatory, and ordinary share capital, where dividend payment is at the discretion of directors. This relationship is termed *gearing* (better known in the United States as *leverage*).

Government

Governments and the European Community provide various financial incentives and grants to the business community. A major cash payment for successful businesses will be taxation. A fuller discussion on types of finance is found in Chapter 12.

Uses of cash

In our simple diagram, there are three major uses of finance.

1. As has already been indicated, cash is used to service the main sources of finance. Dividends (interim and final) are declared and paid to shareholders; interest is paid to lenders along with any repayment of loan due; and taxation is paid on profits earned.
2. Cash is invested in long-term assets, such as buildings and plant, to produce goods or services. Such investment decisions require careful analysis as they are largely irreversible and costly to abandon.
3. Cash is used to pay for materials, labour, overhead expenses and other costs incurred in producing the goods or services offered to customers. At any point in time, there will be a given level of investment in stocks of raw materials, work-in-progress, finished goods and debtors (i.e. goods invoiced but not yet paid for), these *current assets* being partly offset by *current liabilities*, i.e. amounts owing to suppliers of goods and services (creditors). The net investment (current assets less current liabilities) is termed *working capital*, which needs careful management.

1.4   The emergence of financial management

Early developments

While aspects of finance, such as the use of compound interest in trading, can be traced back to the Old Babylonian period (*c*.1800 BC), the emergence of financial management as a key business activity is a far more recent development. Looking back over the twentieth century, we can observe that financial management has evolved from a peripheral to a central aspect of corporate life, and that this change has been brought about largely through the need to respond to the changing economic climate.

In the first half of the century, business finance was viewed as essentially a descriptive, external operation, whereas in the second half, financial management became more of an internal analytical activity – the financial manager being an intermediary between internal operations and the external financial environment. With continuing industrialization in the United Kingdom and much of Europe in the first quarter of the century, the key financial issues centred around forming new businesses and raising capital for expansion. The legal and descriptive considerations of the types of securities issued, company formations and mergers are examples of the subject's development during this period.

As business activity moved from growth to survival during the depression of the 1930s, not unnaturally, finance evolved by focusing more on business liquidity, reorganization and insolvency.

More recent developments

In the post-war years, a succession of Companies Acts and Accounting Standards have been designed to increase investors' confidence in published financial statements. This, together with improvements in the efficiency and regulation of financial markets, has provided a better basis for the development of financial theory and its practical application (although the reader will probably find no difficulty in recalling one or two financial scandals where the quality of financial reporting was brought into question).

In recent years, we have seen the emergence of financial management as a major contributor to corporate prosperity and growth in the analysis of investment and financing decisions. The subject continues to respond to external economic and technical developments:

1. The move to floating exchange rates, relative interest rates and high levels of inflation experienced during the 1970s focused attention on interest rate and currency management, and the impact of inflation on business decisions. For example, in September 1992, following intense pressure by currency speculators, the British Government was forced to suspend its membership of the European Exchange Rate Mechanism, leading to an effective devaluation of sterling. New ways of coping with these uncertainties have been developed to allow investors to hedge or cover such risks, where possible.
2. Successive waves of merger activity in the 1960s, 1970s and 1980s increased our understanding of valuation and takeover tactics. In the 1980s, with the government committed to freedom of markets and financial liberalization, came the mega-merger. Rowntree was swallowed up by the Swiss, ICL by the Japanese and Jaguar by the Americans.
3. Technological progress in communications has led to the globalization of business. The single European market has created a major financial market where there is, in the main, unrestricted capital movement. A businessman based in Glasgow can raise finance in Zurich or Tokyo to finance a new project in Stockholm or Chicago.
4. Modern computer technology not only makes globalization of finance possible, it also brings complex financial calculations and financial data bases within easy reach of every manager.

5. Complexities in taxation and the enormous growth in new financial instruments for raising money has made some aspects of financial management a highly specialized activity.

6. Greater awareness of the need to view all decision-making within a strategic framework is moving the focus away from purely technical to more strategic issues. For example, a good deal of corporate restructuring has taken place, breaking down large organizations into smaller, more strategically compatible businesses.

1.5 The finance department in the firm

The organization structure for the finance department will vary with company size and other factors. A simplified structure for a fairly large organization is given in Figure 1.3.

The board of directors is appointed by the shareholders of the company. Virtually all business organizations of any size are formed into limited liability companies, thereby reducing the risk borne by shareholders and, for companies whose shares are listed on a Stock Exchange, giving investors a ready market for disposal of their holdings or further investment.

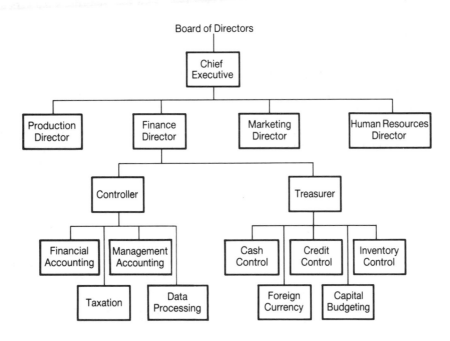

Figure 1.3 The Finance Department in the firm

Corporate finance staff responsibilities

The finance director, reporting to the chief executive, has two broad responsibilities:

1. *Providing financial information and advice* for internal and external users. The financial accountant prepares the statutory financial accounts and deals with the auditors; the management accountant seeks to provide information for decision-making, planning and control. Other departments, such as taxation and data processing, may also report to the controller (or chief accountant).

2. *Managing cash and providing funds* at the best possible rate is the responsibility of the treasurer or financial manager. Typical functions within the treasury area also include the management of cash, credit and inventory, co-ordination of the capital budgeting process (sometimes within the controller's department) and foreign currency management.

We may characterize the responsibilities of the financial manager as the enhancement of corporate objectives by involvement in the following:

1. *Strategic investment and financing decisions.* As already discussed, the financial manager must raise the finance to fund growth and assist in the appraisal of key capital projects.

2. *Dealing with the capital markets.* The financial manager, as the intermediary between the markets and the company, must develop good links with the company's bankers and other major financiers and be aware of the appropriate sources of finance for corporate requirements.

3. *Managing the exposure to risk.* Interest rates and exchange rates can vary considerably. The finance manager should take steps to ensure that exposure to adverse movements is adequately managed. Various techniques for *hedging* (a term for reducing exposure to risk) are available in this regard.

4. *Forecasting, co-ordination and control.* Virtually all important business decisions have financial implications. The financial manager should assist in and, where appropriate, co-ordinate and control activities which have a significant impact on cash flow.

1.6   The financial objective

We have already seen that for any company there are likely to be a number of corporate goals, some of which may, on occasions, conflict. In finance, we assume that *the objective of the firm is to maximize the value of the firm's shares.* Put simply, this means that managers should create as much wealth as possible for the shareholders. Given this objective, any financing or investment decision expected to improve the value of the shareholders' stake in the firm is acceptable.

Let it be said at the outset that the above goal may not be entirely consistent with the reader's views and, indeed, with the views of many practising managers. In recent years, a wide variety of goals has been suggested for the firm, from the traditional goal of

Table 1.1 Importance of financial objectives: 100 large UK firms viewing objectives as 'very important'

	1980 (%)	1986 (%)	1992 (%)
Short-term (1–3 years)			
Profitability (e.g. return on investment)	54.7	71.7	69.0
Earnings	42.2	56.1	58.0
Long-term (over 3 years)			
Sales growth	20.7	9.5	14.1
Earnings per share growth	9.0	56.3	55.1
Growth in shareholders' wealth	19.8	45.7	52.6

Sources: Pike (1988, 1992).

profit-maximization to the inclusion of goals relating to earnings per share, sales, employee welfare, manager satisfaction, survival, and the good of society. It has also been questioned whether management attempts to *maximize* by seeking optimal solutions, or to '*satisfice*', by seeking merely satisfactory solutions.

One objective pursued by managers is that of sales revenue maximization, subject to a minimum profit constraint. As long as a company matches the average rate of return for the industry sector, the shareholders are likely to be content to stay with their investment. Thus, once this level is attained, managers will be tempted to pursue other goals. As sales levels are frequently employed as a basis for managerial salaries and status, managers may adopt goals which maximize sales subject to a minimum profit constraint.

Empirical evidence suggests that maximization of shareholders' wealth is not the only goal of management, nor is it necessarily the most important. Managers are more interested in profitability than in wealth-creation.

A recent survey by Pike (1988) asked finance directors in the largest UK companies to rank specified goals in order of importance. A summary of results is provided in Table 1.1.

A number of observations can be drawn. First, between 1980 and 1992 there was a much stronger emphasis on financial goals, particularly those relating to profit and growth. Second, while profitability measures (e.g. return on investment) are still seen within firms as the most important financial goals, an enormous increase occurred in investor-related goals, such as growth in earnings per share and shareholder wealth.

The financial manager has the specific task of advising management on the financial implications of the plans and activities of the firm. The shareholder wealth objective should underlie all such advice. Of course, the chief executive may on occasions allow non-financial considerations to take precedence over financial ones. It is not possible to translate this objective directly to the public sector or not-for-profit organizations. However, in seeking to create wealth in such organizations, the 'value for money' goal is perhaps nearest.

1.7 The agency problem

Potential conflict arises when there is a separation of ownership from management. The ownership of most larger companies is widely spread, while the day-to-day control of the business rests in the hands of a few managers who usually have a relatively small proportion of the total shares issued. This can give rise to what is termed *managerialism* – self-serving behaviour by managers at the shareholders' expense. Accordingly, managers may be more concerned with their own welfare than that of their shareholders, doing just enough for the shareholders to prevent awkward questions at Annual General Meetings. Examples of managerialism include pursuing more perquisites (splendid offices and company cars, etc.) and adopting low-risk survival strategies and 'satisficing' behaviour. This conflict has been explored by Jensen and Meckling (1976), who developed a theory of the firm under agency arrangements. Managers are, in effect, agents for the shareholders and are required to act in their best interests. However, they have operational control of the business and the shareholders receive little information on whether the managers are acting in their best interests.

Managing the agency problem

To attempt to deal with such agency problems, various incentives and controls have been recommended, all of which incur costs. Incentives frequently take the form of bonuses tied to profits and share options as part of a remuneration package scheme.

Managerial incentives: Blanco plc

Relating managers' compensation to achievement of company owner-oriented targets is an obvious way in which the interests of both managers and shareholders are brought closer together. A group of major institutional shareholders of Blanco plc has expressed concern to the chief executive that management decisions do not appear to be fully in line with shareholder requirements. They suggest that a new remuneration package is introduced to help solve the problem.

Remuneration package schemes have increasingly been introduced as a method to encourage managers to take decisions which are consistent with the objectives of the shareholders. The main factors to be considered in the Blanco plc case might include:

1. Linking management compensation to changes in shareholder wealth, where possible reflecting managers' contribution to increased shareholder wealth.
2. Rewarding managerial efficiency not managerial luck.
3. Matching the time-horizon for decisions of managers with that of shareholders. Many managers will look towards maximizing short-term profits rather than long-term shareholder wealth.
4. Making the scheme easy to monitor, inexpensive to operate, clearly defined and incapable of managerial manipulation. A number of cases have arisen where poorly devised schemes have 'backfired', giving senior managers huge bonuses. For example, a share option scheme for The Burton Group had to be amended in 1987 after protests from institutional investors who realized that the chief executive stood to make £8 million on top of his salary.

Two performance-based incentive schemes which Blanco plc might consider are discussed below.

(1) *Executive share option schemes* are long-term compensation arrangements which permit managers to buy shares at a given price at some future date. Subject to certain provisos and tax rules, a share option scheme usually entitles managers to acquire a fixed number of shares over a fixed period of time for a fixed price. The shares need not be paid for until the option is exercised, which is normally somewhere between three and ten years after the granting of the option. Such options only have value when the actual share price exceeds the option price; managers are thereby encouraged to pursue policies which enhance long-term wealth-creation. At least a quarter of British companies now operate share option schemes which are spreading to managers well below board level. The figure is far higher for companies recently coming to the Stock Market, where virtually all have had executive share option schemes and around 25 per cent of those operate some form of all-employee scheme. However, a major problem with these approaches is that general stock market movements, due mainly to macro-economic events, are sometimes so large as to dwarf the efforts of managers. No matter how hard a management team may seek to make wealth-creating decisions, the effects on share price in a given year may be undetectable if general market movements are downward. *A good incentive scheme is one where managers have a large degree of control over achieving targets.*

(2) This has led to the *performance share incentive scheme*, where shares are allotted to managers on attaining performance targets which are less loosely linked to share prices. Commonly employed performance measures are growth in earnings per share, return on equity and return on assets. Managers are allocated a certain number of shares to be received on attaining prescribed targets. While this incentive scheme offers managers greater control, there is the danger that the performance measures may not be entirely consistent with shareholder goals. For example, adoption of return on assets as a measure, which is based on book values, can prohibit investment in wealth-creating projects with heavy depreciation charges in early years.

Executive compensation schemes, such as those outlined above, are imperfect, but useful, mechanisms for retaining able managers and encouraging them to pursue goals which promote shareholder value.

The other way of attempting to overcome the 'agency' problem of managers pursuing their own, rather than shareholders', interests is by incurring *agency costs*. Agency costs include:

1. *Costs of monitoring* managers' behaviour, e.g. by instituting management audits or by introducing additional reporting requirements; and

2. *Bonding costs* to gain assurances from managers that shareholders' interests will be paramount in their decision-making.

To what extent does the agency problem invalidate the goal of maximizing the value of the firm? If in a large, publicly quoted company senior managers were pursuing goals not fully compatible with shareholders' interests, it is likely that this would in time come to light and be controlled by the following mechanism. As we shall discuss in Chapter 2, in an efficient, highly competitive stock market, the share price is a 'fair' reflection of investors' perceptions of the company's expected future performance. Agency problems will, before long, be reflected in a lower than expected share price. This could lead to an *internal* response, the shareholders replacing the board of directors with others more committed to their goals, or to an *external* response, the company being acquired by a better-performing company where shareholder interests are pursued to a greater extent.

1.8   The corporate governance debate

In recent years, there has been considerable concern in the UK about the standards of corporate governance. While in Company Law directors are obliged to act in the best interests of shareholders, there have been many instances of boardroom behaviour difficult to reconcile with this ideal.

For example, there have been numerous examples of spectacular collapses of companies like British and Commonwealth Holdings, Polly Peck and Maxwell Communications Corporation, often the result of excessive debt financing in order to finance ill-advised takeovers, and sometimes laced with fraud. Many companies have been criticized for the generosity with which they reward their leading executives. In this respect, the procedures for remunerating executives have been less than transparent, and many compensation schemes involve payment by results in one direction alone. Many chief executives have been criticized for receiving pay increases in proportionate terms several times greater than the increases awarded to less exalted staff. This has been noticeable in the newly privatized companies (although there has clearly been an element of 'catching-up' with boardroom pay levels elsewhere).

The most spectacular example of boardroom misbehaviour was the collapse of Robert Maxwell's empire in 1991 when, following his death at sea, it became clear that millions of pounds had been fraudulently converted. In particular, the pension fund of Mirror Group Newspapers had been ransacked in order to finance an illegal scheme for supporting the share price of Maxwell Communications Corporation. There was no doubt that the excessive degree of control which Robert Maxwell was able to wield in his combined position of chairman of the board and chief executive was a contributory factor to the abuses which resulted in substantial losses for both shareholders and pensioners.

In the train of these and similar scandals, the Committee on The Financial Aspects of Corporate Governance, chaired by Sir Adrian Cadbury, was set up by The Financial Reporting Council, the Stock Exchange and the accountancy profession. Its brief was to examine, and make recommendations on, the role of directors, executive and non-executive, and auditors. Its draft report, issued in May 1992, made the following recommendations:

- No one individual on the board should have 'unfettered powers of decision', i.e. the roles of chairman and chief executive should be split.
- Non-executive directors should bring an independent judgement to bear on issues of strategy, performance, resources and standards of conduct.

- The majority of non-executive directors should be free of any business or financial connection with the company.
- Directors' service contracts should not exceed three years without shareholders' approval.
- Directors' emoluments should be fully disclosed and split into their salary and performance-related elements.
- Executive directors' pay should be subject to the recommendations of a remuneration committee made up wholly or mostly of non-executives.
- Interim company reports should contain balance sheet information and be reviewed by the auditors.
- The operation of a company's pension fund should be separate and distinct from that of the company itself.
- The relationship between boards and directors should be 'professional and objective'.
- There should be full disclosure of non-audit fees to reveal conflicts of interests and there should be regular rotation of auditors.

At the time of writing, these are only draft proposals, but have been generally received as steps in the right direction. The main reservations which have been expressed centre on the issues of compliance and enforcement. It is proposed that these changes in the rules and responsibilities of directors and auditors be non-statutory. The Stock Exchange does not intend to withdraw the listings of companies which fail to comply although it hopes that any adverse publicity will whip offenders into line. This 'lack of teeth' has raised suspicions that determined wrong-doers will still be able to exert their influence on weak boards of directors, to the detriment of the relatively ill-informed private investor in particular. Much will depend on the quality of non-executive directors whom, it is to be hoped, will not simply be members of an interlocking clique. If the chairman of Company X is a non-executive director of Company Y, whose chairman is also a non-executive director of Company X's board, it is difficult to see how shareholder interests can be adequately protected.

1.9 The risk dimension

Some financial decisions incur very little risk – for instance, the interest from investing in government stocks is known; others may carry far more risk, such as the return on the decision to acquire shares. In business life, as in other aspects of life, *risk and expected return tend to be related: the greater the perceived risk, the greater the return required by investors*. This is seen in Figure 1.4.

When the finance manager of a company seeks to raise funds, potential investors take a view on the risk related to the intended use of the funds. This can best be measured in terms of a *risk premium* above the risk-free rate (R_f) obtainable from, say, government stocks to compensate them for taking risk. The capital market offers a host of investment opportunities for private and corporate investors, but in all cases, there exists a clear relationship between the perceived degree of risk involved and the expected return. For example, R_f in Figure 1.4 represents the return on 3-month Treasury Bills, point A represents an investment in a

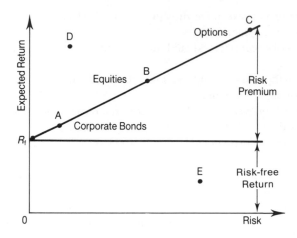

Figure 1.4 Risk–return trade-off

long-term fixed interest corporate bond, point B – a typical share in a listed company; and point C – an investment in the more speculative options or futures markets.

   One task of the financial manager is to *raise funds in the capital markets at a cost consistent with the perceived risk and to invest such funds in wealth-creating opportunities within the business.* Here it is quite possible – because of a firm's competitive advantage, or possession of superior brand names – to make highly profitable capital projects with relatively little risk (see D in diagram). It is also possible to find the reverse, such as project E. Now recall, from the start of this chapter, that Quaker Oats' goal is to deliver cash flows to shareholders at rates in excess of their cost of capital. In effect, this means that they seek to invest in projects, such as D, that offer returns better than obtainable on the capital market for the same degree of risk.

1.10   The strategic dimension

To enhance shareholder value, managers could adopt a wide range of strategies. Strategic management may be defined as a systematic approach to positioning the business in relation to its environment to ensure continued success and offer security from surprises. While no approach can guarantee continuous success and total security, an integrated approach to strategy formulation, involving all levels of management, can go some way in this direction.

   Strategy can be developed at three levels:

1.   *Corporate strategy* is concerned with the broad issues, such as which types of business the company should be in. Strategic finance has an important role to play here. For example, the decision to enter or exit from a business – whether through corporate acquisitions, organic growth, divestment or buy-outs – requires sound financial analysis. Similarly, the decision as to the appropriate capital structure and dividend policy form part of strategic development at the corporate level.

2. *Business or competitive strategy* is concerned with how strategic business units (SBUs) compete in particular markets. Business strategies are formulated which influence the allocation of resources to these units. This allocation may be based on the attractiveness of the markets in which SBUs operate and the firm's competitive strengths. Porter (1985) identifies five competitive forces determining the profitability of an industry.

   (a) *Threat of potential entrants.* New entrants to the industry will increase total productive capacity and this can result in price wars and reduced profitability. The size of the threat is determined by the entry barriers created by such things as differentiation of products, the capital requirement and economies of scale.

   (b) *Competition among existing companies.* Intensive rivalry is the result of factors such as numerous or equally balanced competitors, slow industry growth and a high level of fixed charges in the cost structure, i.e. *operational gearing.*

   (c) *Pressure from substitutes.* While firms compete within an industry, the industry itself also competes in the sense that other industries can often deliver substitute products. For example, the oil industry offers a substitute product for the coal industry. In the case of a price increase, customers may shift from one to the other.

   (d) *Bargaining power of buyers.* Buyers create a competitive force by exerting a downward pressure on prices, negotiating for higher quality or better service, and playing off one competitor against another, all at the expense of the industry's profitability.

   (e) *Bargaining power of suppliers.* Suppliers can exert considerable pressure on an industry by threatening to raise prices or to cut the quality of the goods and services delivered.

   Careful analysis of the above factors enables managers to understand better the major competitive forces which shape the industry structure and, thereby, determine the levels of profitability a company can expect to earn. A business strategy stands little chance of success unless developed with a clear understanding of the firm's competitive setting. Each of the five competitive forces will vary in intensity and importance according to the industry in which the firm operates. For example, the newly privatized UK water industry is virtually free from these competitive forces, whereas another former publicly-owned company, Rolls–Royce, is intensely affected by most of them since it operates in a global market.

3. *Operational strategy* is concerned with how functional levels contribute to corporate and business strategies. For example, the finance function may formulate strategies to achieve the new dividend policy identified at the corporate strategy level. Similarly, a foreign currency exposure strategy may be developed to reduce the risk of loss through currency movements. A typical strategic planning process will encompass the elements outlined in Figure 1.5.

Strategic planning and shareholder value

The importance of the five competitive forces in determining shareholder wealth cannot be underestimated. They largely determine the price at which goods and services can be sold,

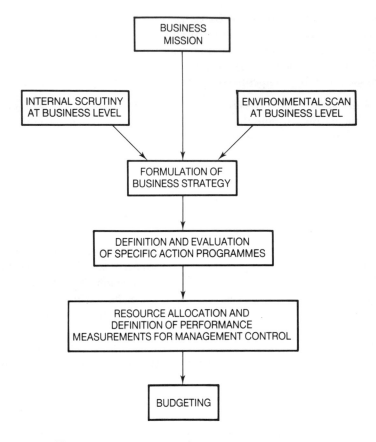

Figure 1.5   Main elements in strategic planning

the quantities sold, the cost of production, the level of required investment and the risks inherent in the business. However, individual companies can develop strategies which lead to long-term financial performance well above the industry average. A recent study (Gale and Swire 1988) of over 600 business units which tracked the consequences of business strategies over a long period of time on financial performance concluded that market share, quality, capacity utilization and capital investment strategies had the greatest impact on shareholder wealth.

Figure 1.6 illustrates the *linkage between strategic planning and shareholder value creation*. The diagram illustrates that to enhance shareholder value – the primary objective of financial management – management should focus specifically on two vital tasks. The first task, which the whole management team will contribute to, is to maximize cash flow from trading operations. To this end, management should devote much of its attention to the main *value drivers*:

1.   *The rate of growth in sales and profit margins* for the planning period specified (i.e. implementing the business strategy).

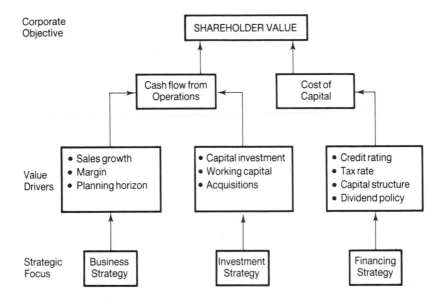

Figure 1.6 Shareholder value analysis framework

2. *Making sound investment decisions* compatible with the company's investment strategy.
3. In addition to increasing operating cash flow, corporate management – particularly the financial manager – should seek to *reduce the cost of capital*. Part III of this book assesses the various financial strategies which may reduce the cost of capital and, hence, increase shareholder value; in particular, capital structure, dividend policy and taxation issues are addressed. Shareholder value analysis is further developed in Chapter 4.

1.11 Making strategic finance decisions

We have already stated that this book concentrates on strategic investment and financial decisions, together with their interactions. While, in practice, some decisions appear to be 'inspired' and lacking in any rational process, most approaches to decisions of a financial nature have five common elements.

1. *Clearly defined goals.* It is particularly noticeable how, in recent years, corporate managements have realized the importance of defining and communicating their declared mission and goals. One such example is Dalgety plc, whose Annual Report for 1990 states:

> Quality is at the heart of our management philosophy – the quality of our products and services. We play a responsible role in the communities in which we work. We aim to provide our shareholders with increased earnings and dividends, our customers with high quality products and services and our employees with rewarding careers.

It can be seen that a range of goals is expressed, some more quantifiable than others, some more relevant to financing decisions, each on occasions in conflict with other goals.

2. *Identify possible courses of action* to achieve these objectives. This requires the development of business strategies from which individual decisions emanate. Returning to Dalgety plc:

> Our strategy is clearly focused on strengthening our market positions in agri-business and food. Our products are backed by excellent research and technical skills. We invest in areas that we know well and where we see attractive and sustainable returns. We practise a decentralised style which allows our management to operate effectively subject to sound financial control and strategic direction.

An even clearer picture of the relationship between the business mission, financial goals and operating strategies is provided by The Quaker Oats Company taken from its 1990 Annual Report (Table 1.2).

   The search for new investment and financing opportunities for any organisation is far better focused and cost-effective when viewed within well-defined financial objectives and strategies. Most decision opportunities have more than one possible solution. For instance, the requirement for an additional source of finance to fund a new product launch can be satisfied by a multitude of possible financial options.

3. *Assemble relevant information* to the decision. The financial manager must be able to identify what information is relevant to the decision and what is not. Data gathering can

---

Table 1.2   The Quaker Oats Company's goals and strategies

Business Mission
To maximize value for our shareholders as a successful, independent marketer of leading consumer brands.

Business Strategy
To maximize value by generating the highest cash flow possible through internal product development and acquisitions and making strategic decisions to invest where growth and returns are most attractive.

Financial Goals
1. Achieve return on equity of 25 per cent or more.
2. Achieve 'real' earnings growth of 7 per cent p.a. over time.
3. Increase dividends, consistent with earnings growth, in 'real' terms.
4. Maintain a strong financial position as represented by Quaker's current bond and commercial paper ratings.

Operating Strategies
1. Continue to be a leading marketer of strong consumer brands.
2. Achieve profitable, better-than-average 'real' volume growth in our worldwide grocery business.
3. Improve the profitability of low-return business or divest them.

Source: Quaker Oats Company Annual Report, 1990.

be costly, but good, reliable information greatly facilitates decision analysis and confidence in the decision outcome.

4. *Evaluation*. Analysing and interpreting assembled information lies at the heart of financial analysis and a good part of this book is devoted to techniques and approaches to appraising financial decisions.

5. *Monitor the effects of the decision taken*. However sophisticated a firm's financial planning system, there is no real substitute for experience. Feedback on the performance of past decisions provides vital information on the reliability of data gathered, the efficacy of the method employed in decision appraisal and the judgement of decision-makers.

1.12   Financial theory and practice

To what extent is financial theory directly applicable to the world of commerce and industry? It is said that a good theory should be empirical rather than speculative. So, can the student of finance apply the theory to develop successful investment and financing strategies? The extent to which financial theory will prove useful in practice rests partly on the degree of realism in the assumptions underlying the theory. Ultimately, the realism of a theory's assumptions are judged by the extent to which the theory offers meaningful and useful explanations and predictions. None the less, it is beneficial to consider some of the rather restrictive assumptions sometimes made in developing financial models.

1. All markets – not just capital markets – are perfectly competitive.
2. Information is perfect and costless and transaction costs are zero.
3. No taxes exist.

These assumptions lead naturally to certain propositions. First, only shareholders are interested in the firm. A perfect labour market implies that managers and workers can always find another equally attractive job. Second, shareholders are only interested in maximizing the market value of their shareholdings. Given perfect, costless information, managers are perfectly controlled by the shareholders to implement value-maximizing strategies. Thirdly, as will be discussed in subsequent chapters, the pursuit of shareholder wealth is achieved by instructing managers to invest only in those projects which are worth more than they cost. Financing strategies, whether concerning dividends, capital structure or leasing, are largely irrelevant as they do little to increase shareholders' wealth.

   Most people would agree that the assumptions underlying the theory of finance appear to be at odds with reality. Information is imperfect; transaction costs and information costs may be sizeable. Markets are frequently highly imperfect; management will usually have a good deal of interest in the firm – interest which may well conflict with that of shareholders. Managers have far from complete knowledge on such things as the set of feasible financing strategies available, their cash flow patterns and impact on market values. Shareholders are even less well informed. Taxation policy, bankruptcy costs and other factors can have a major influence on financial strategies. Throughout this book, we shall attempt to allow for such practical, real-world considerations when considering appropriate financial policy decisions. However, we hope that a clearer understanding of the concepts, together with an awareness of the degree of realism in their underlying assumptions, will enable the reader to make sound and successful investment and financial decisions in practice.

1.13   Summary

This chapter provides an overview of strategic financial management and the critical role it plays in corporate survival and success.

Key points

- It is the task of the financial manager to plan, raise and use funds in an efficient manner to achieve corporate financial objectives. This implies (1) involvement in investment and financing decisions, (2) dealing with the financial markets, and (3) forecasting, co-ordinating and controlling cash flows.
- Cash is the lifeblood of any business. Financial management is concerned with cash generation and control.
- Financial management has evolved rapidly over this century, largely in response to economic and other external events (e.g. inflation and technological developments), making globalization of finance a reality and the need to concentrate on more strategic issues essential.
- The distinction should be drawn between accounting – the mere provision of relevant financial information for internal and external users – and financial management – the utilization of financial and other data to assist financial decision-making.
- In finance, we assume that the primary corporate goal is to maximize value for the shareholders.
- The agency problem – managers pursuing actions not totally consistent with shareholders' interests – can be reduced both by managerial incentive schemes and also by closer monitoring of actions.
- A fundamental premise of finance is that investors require compensation for taking risks in the form of enhanced potential returns.
- Most of the assumptions underlying pure finance theory are not particularly realistic. In practice, market and other imperfections must also be considered in practical financial decision-making.
- Financial management has an essential role in strategic development and implementation at strategic, business and operational levels. Competitive forces, together with business strategy, influence the value drivers which impact on shareholder value.

Further reading

Most finance texts have helpful introductory chapters, for example Brealey and Myers (1991) and McLaney (1991). For a fuller discussion on managerial compensation, see Lambert and Larcker (1985). Details on these and other references are provided in the bibliography.

Questions

Self-test questions

1. What do you understand by *investment* decisions and *financing* decisions? Provide two examples of each.
2. What are the financial manager's primary tasks?
3. The past ten years have seen a much greater emphasis on investor-related goals, such as earnings per share and shareholder wealth. Why do you think this has arisen?
4. The goal of the firm should be to create wealth for the owners. How realistic is it to adopt this single objective? What else might be considered?
5. Identify some potential agency problems that may arise between shareholders and managers.

Exercises

1. Why is the goal of maximizing owners' wealth helpful in analyzing capital investment decisions? What other goals should also be considered? (Solution in Appendix A.)
2. (a) A group of major shareholders of Zedo plc wishes to introduce a new remuneration scheme for the company's senior management.

      Explain why such schemes might be important to the shareholders. What factors should the shareholders consider when devising such schemes?

   (b) Eventually a short-list of three possible schemes is agreed. All pay the same basic salary plus:
      (i) A bonus based upon at least a minimum pre-tax profit being achieved.
      (ii) A bonus based upon turnover growth.
      (iii) A share option scheme.
      Briefly discuss the advantages and disadvantages of each of these three schemes.
      (ACCA Level 3, June 1990)

3. The 1991 Annual Report for Marks & Spencer states the following:

   The Group's Treasury operates as a profit centre, but within strict risk limits and with a prohibition on speculative activity. The department contributed to profits at a higher rate than last year, through the management of cash resources, borrowings and foreign exchange.... Group capital expenditure during the year amounted to £300 million (last year £280 million) and this was financed from Group cash resources. As a result of the strong cash flow, the gearing ratio (net debt to shareholders' funds) has fallen further from 17 per cent to 14 per cent.

From this statement, what impression do you gain as to its attitude towards financial risk and its competence in financial management?

Practical assignment

1. Examine the annual report for a well-known company, particularly the chairman's statement. Are the corporate goals clearly specified? What specific references are made to financial management?
2. Document the organization chart for the finance department in your company. How does it differ from that given in the chapter? Is there a clear distinction between finance and accounting?

CHAPTER 2
The financial environment

NOT SO PRETTY POLLY

In August 1990, Polly Peck, the food and electronics group, was sitting pretty. The darling of the stock market, its shares had just peaked at 457p, valuing the company at nearly £1.8 billion. Interim profits were well up on the previous year and, to most investors, prospects looked good.

Yet within a month Polly Peck's shares were suspended after plummeting to 108p, and were well on their way to becoming almost worthless. How could this change occur so rapidly? The specific reason was that a company connected with the chairman, Asil Nadir, was being investigated by the Serious Fraud Office, and the news was looking very bleak for the company.

Some might argue that this is a good example of market efficiency in action: the stock market reacting rapidly to new information. But closer analysis of the published accounting statements by investors would have raised suspicions much earlier – and saved some a fortune!

Just how efficient are the financial markets in Europe, and what are the implications for corporate management?

2.1 Introduction

The corporate financial manager (or treasurer) has the important task of ensuring that there are sufficient funds available to meet all the likely needs of the business. To do this properly, the financial manager requires both a clear grasp of the future financial requirements of the business and of the workings of the financial markets. This chapter provides an overview of the financial markets, and the major institutions within them, paying particular attention to the nature of the capital market. As taxation has an important impact on financial management, a summary of the main tax considerations is also provided.

27

LEARNING OBJECTIVES

By the end of this chapter the reader should appreciate the nature of financial markets and the main players within it. A clear understanding is required of the following topics:

- The function of the Stock Exchange.
- The extent to which the capital market is efficient.
- How taxation affects corporate finance.

Improved skills in reading the financial pages in a newspaper should also be achieved.

2.2   Financial markets

A financial market is any mechanism for trading financial assets or claims. Frequently, there is no physical marketplace, transactions being conducted by telephone. London is regarded as the leading European financial centre whose main financial markets are:

1. The *money market* channels wholesale funds, usually for less than one year, from lenders to borrowers. The market is largely dominated by the major banks and other financial institutions.

2. The *securities or capital market* deals with long-dated securities such as shares and loan stock. The Stock Exchange is the best-known institution in the capital market, but there are other markets, such as the Eurobond market.

3. The *foreign exchange market* is a market for buying and selling one currency against another. Deals are either on a *spot* basis (i.e. at current rates) or on a *forward* basis.

4. The *London traded options market* (LTOM) provides investors with the opportunity to buy or sell securities at a specified price and at a specific future time.

5. The *London International Financial Futures Exchange* (LIFFE) provides a means of hedging (i.e. protecting) or speculating against movements in currencies and interest rates. (The LTOM and LIFFE have now merged.)

Collectively, financial markets provide a mechanism through which the corporate financial manager has access to a wide range of sources of finance and instruments for managing finance.

Capital markets have two important elements:

1. A *primary function* – providing new capital for business and other activities, usually in the form of share issues to new or existing shareholders (equity) or loans.

2. A *secondary function* – trading securities already in issue, thus enabling share or bond
    holders to dispose of their holdings whenever they wish. A strong secondary market is
    therefore a necessary condition for an effective primary market as no investor wants to
    feel 'locked in' to an investment which cannot be realized when the need arises.

Imagine what business life would be like if these capital markets were not available to
companies. New businesses could only start up if the owners had sufficient personal wealth to
fund the initial capital investment; existing businesses could develop only through
reinvesting profits generated; and investors could not easily dispose of their shareholdings. In
fact, in many parts of the world where financial markets are extremely basic or even
non-existent, this is exactly what does happen. *The development of a strong and healthy
economy rests very largely on efficient, well-developed financial markets.*

Financial markets promote savings and investment by providing a mechanism by which
the financial requirements of lenders (typically personal savers) and borrowers (typically
businesses and governments) can be met. Figure 2.1 provides a simple diagram of how
businesses finance their operations.

Financial institutions (such as pension funds, insurance companies, banks, building
societies, unit trusts and specialist investment institutions) act as *financial intermediaries*,

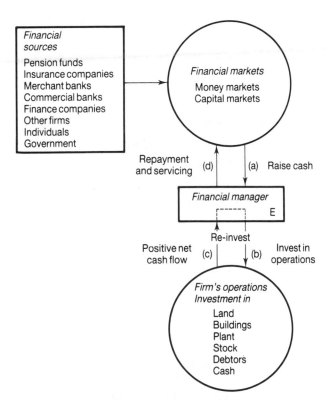

Figure 2.1   The Financial Manager as an intermediary

collecting funds from savers to lend to their corporate and other customers through the *money* and *capital markets.*

   The financial manager raises cash ((a) in Figure 2.1) by selling claims in the company's existing or future assets (e.g. by issuing shares). The cash is then used to acquire fixed and current assets (b). If those investments are successful, they will generate positive cash flows (c) from business operations. This cash surplus is used to service existing financial obligations in the form of dividends, interest, lease payments, etc. and to make repayments (d). Any residue is reinvested in the business to replace existing assets or expand operations.

Financial institutions provide a useful service

The needs of lenders and borrowers rarely match. These differences in requirements between lenders and borrowers mean that there is an important role for financial intermediaries, such as banks, if the financial markets are to operate efficiently:

1. *Re-packaging finance:* gathering small amounts of savings from a large number of individuals and re-packaging them into larger bundles for lending to businesses. The banks are a good example here.

2. *Risk-reduction:* placing small sums from individuals in large, well-diversified investment portfolios, e.g. unit trusts.

3. *Liquidity transformation:* bringing together short-term savers and long-term borrowers (e.g. building societies and banks). Borrowing 'short' and lending 'long' is only acceptable where relatively few savers will want to withdraw funds at any given time. The history of banking and building society failures (e.g. the Savings and Loan Associations in the United States) shows that this is not always the case.

4. *Cost reduction:* minimizing transaction costs by providing convenient and relatively inexpensive services for linking small savers to larger borrowers, e.g. government savings certificates.

5. *Financial advice:* giving advisory and other services to both lender and borrower.

2.3   The financial services sector

The financial services sector can be divided into three groups: institutions engaged in (1) deposit-taking, (2) contractual savings, and (3) other forms of savings.

1.   Deposit-taking institutions

Clearing banks have three important roles: they operate nationwide networks (high street banks); they effect a national payments system by clearing cheques and by taking in and paying out notes and coins; and they accept deposits in very small as well as large amounts. Hence, these operations are often called *retail banking*. As well as being the dominant force in retail banking, the clearing banks have diversified into wholesale banking and are continuing to expand their international activities.

A glance at the Balance Sheet of any clearing bank reveals that the main sterling assets are advances to the private sector, other banks, the public sector in the form of treasury bills and government securities, local authorities, and private households. The main instrument of lending is the overdraft, though there has been a substantial growth of term loans in recent years.

Wholesale banks

Wholesale banking or merchant banking developed out of the enormous growth in trade, and its need for finance. *Accepting houses* were formed whose main business was to accept bills of exchange (promising to pay a sum of money at some future date) from less well-known traders, and from *discount houses* which provided cash by discounting such bills. *Merchant banks* nowadays have three major activities which are frequently organized into separate divisions: corporate finance, mergers and acquisitions, and fund management.

Merchant banks' activities include giving *financial advice to companies and arranging finance* through syndicated loans and new security issues. Merchant banks are also members of the Issuing Houses Association, an organization responsible for the *flotation of shares* subsequently traded on the Stock Exchange. This not only involves advising a company upon the correct mix of financial instruments to be issued but also on the drawing up of a prospectus and underwriting the issue. They also play a leading role in the *development of new financial products* like swaps, options and other derivative products (discussed later) which became very popular during the 1980s.

Another area of activity for wholesale banks is advising companies on *mergers and acquisition issues*. This involves not only assisting in the negotiations of a 'friendly' merger of two independent companies but also developing strategies for 'unfriendly' takeovers or acting as adviser for a company defending against an acquisitive aggressor.

Finally, merchant banks fulfil a major role as *managers of the investment portfolios* of some pension funds, insurance companies, investment and unit trusts and various charities. Whether in arranging finance, advising on takeover bids or managing the funds of institutional investors, merchant banks exert considerable influence on both corporate finance and the capital market.

The growth of *overseas banking* has been closely linked to the development of Euro-currency markets and to the growth of multinational companies. Over 300 foreign banks are currently listed by the Bank of England. A substantial amount of their business consists of providing finance to branches or subsidiaries of foreign companies.

Building societies are a form of savings bank specializing in the provision of finance for house purchase in the private sector. As a result of deregulation of the financial services industry, building societies were the fastest growing financial institutions during the 1980s. They now offer almost a complete set of private banking services.

2.   *Institutions engaged in contractual savings*

Pension funds are institutions which accumulate funds in order to meet the future pension liabilities of a particular organization to its employees. Funds are normally built up from contributions paid by the employer and employees. They can be divided into *self-administered schemes*, where the funds are invested directly in the financial markets; and *insured schemes*, where the funds are invested by, and the risk is covered by, a life assurance company. Pension schemes have enormous and rapidly growing funds available for investment in the securities markets. Together with insurance companies, they comprise the major purchasers of company securities.

Insurance companies' activities can be divided into long-term and general insurance. Long-term insurance business consists mainly of *life assurance and pension provision*. Policyholders pay premiums to the companies and are guaranteed either a lump sum in the event of death, or a regular annual income for some defined period. With a guaranteed premium inflow and predictable aggregate future payments there is little need for liquidity, so life assurance funds are able to invest heavily in long-term assets.

General insurance business (e.g. fire, accident, motor, marine and other insurance) consists of contracts to cover losses within a specified period, normally twelve months. As liquidity is important here, a greater proportion of funds is invested in short-term assets, although a considerable proportion of such funds is invested in securities and property.

Other financial institutions

Investment trust companies are limited liability companies which invest mainly in the ordinary shares of other companies. The funds at their disposal are 'closed', being restricted to the shares and loans issued and profits retained by the company.

Unit trusts also invest in the shares of companies. They, however, are 'open-ended'; the resources at their disposal can vary greatly over time, depending on whether cash is going into the trust from the sale of 'units' or is going out because subscribers are selling their units back to the trust.

The main function of both investment and unit trusts is to provide vehicles for smaller investors to achieve much more diversified portfolios than they could hold for themselves. Such diversification can lead to significant risk reduction.

Stockbrokers are the intermediaries between the two parties involved in a stock market transaction. Since deregulation in 1986, and the abolition of fixed commission fees, most stock broking firms have linked up with other institutions to become *market makers*. In much the same way as a stall-holder in a street market, market makers trade in shares with their own money in the hope they can make a profit on their transactions.

Finance houses originally specialized in hire-purchase finance of railway wagons and then moved on to commercial vehicles, cars and then consumer durables. They have more recently moved into other forms of financing such as leasing and factoring (discussed in later chapters).

Disintermediation and securitization

While financial intermediaries play a vital role in the financial markets, there has been a new development termed *disintermediation*. This is the process by which companies borrow and lend funds directly between themselves *without* recourse to financial intermediaries such as banks and other institutions. Allied to this is the process of *securitization*, the development of new financial instruments to meet ever-changing corporate needs (i.e. financial engineering).

Securitization and disintermediation have permitted larger companies to create alternative, more flexible forms of finance than was traditionally available through the banking system. This, in turn, has forced banks to become more competitive in the services offered to larger companies.

2.4 The securities or capital market

The capital market is the market where long-term capital is raised and traded. *The Stock Exchange is the principal trading market for long-dated securities in the United Kingdom.* The markets in the United Kingdom can be categorized as follows:

1. The *International Stock Exchange (ISE)*, dealing with listed securities, unlisted securities, and traded options.
2. The *'Eurobond' market* (explained in Chapter 12).
3. The *Over-The Counter (OTC) market*.

A stock exchange has two principal economic functions. These are to enable companies to *raise capital* (the primary market), and to *facilitate the trading of shares* through the negotiation of a price at which ownership of a company is transferred between investors. Turnover on the ISE secondary market totalled £234 billion in 1991, while only £18 billion was raised in the primary market during that period.

The ISE currently has two tiers. The main market is the *Official List*, which comprises about 1,900 UK equity securities with a total market capitalization as at Autumn 1992 of £580 billion. Companies operating in this market are *listed* companies, having to satisfy a large number of requirements of the Stock Exchange concerning size, history and disclosure of information.

The second tier is the *Unlisted Securities Market* (USM) which was established in 1980 to encourage growing enterprises to become public companies. The entry requirements are less stringent than for listed companies. In Autumn 1992 there were some 312 companies which were designated members of the USM and their total capitalization amounted to about £6 billion.

In 1987 the *Third Market* was established to meet the needs of companies wishing to see their shares traded publicly but which did not have the required three-year trading record necessary to join the USM. However, EC legislation to harmonize listing requirements blurred the distinction between the Third Market and USM, leading to its closure at the end of 1990.

While the vast majority of share trading takes place through the Stock Exchange, it is not the only trading method. For some years there has been a small, but active *Over-The-Counter* (OTC) market, where organizations trade their shares, usually through an intermediary on a 'matched bargain' basis.

Obtaining a USM quotation

Majestic plc, a manufacturer of office furniture, was formed in 1990 and has shown strong growth in sales and earnings over the past three years, producing after-tax profits of £1 million in 1993. The directors are now looking to expand their business into other parts of Europe and require an additional £2 million. At the same time they would like to realize a proportion of their investment holding. They decide to obtain a quotation on the Unlisted Securities Market and to allow up to 25 per cent of the equity to be traded. A number of steps are required to be taken for Majestic plc to gain USM status:

1. *Review of current position.* Before going further, the company needs to be sure that it has the appropriate management team, particularly that the financial expertise is available to meet the demands of being a public company.

2. *Appoint a professional team* to take the company to the USM. Typically, this involves a sponsoring broker, solicitor and accountant.

3. *Gather and present information.* A report on the company's activities, accounts and prospects will be prepared, involving a detailed review of the financial records. This information will then be used to prepare the *prospectus* and other documentation required by the Stock Exchange.

Majestic plc may well obtain a USM quotation as it meets the main requirements:

1. At least three years' trading.
2. No minimum market capitalization, but a minimum of £3 million is normally expected.
3. Over 10 per cent of the shares must be in the hands of the public.

Unquoted companies

Not all companies seek a stock market quotation for their shares; the vast majority are unquoted.

WHY COMPANIES REMAIN PRIVATE

- Unable to achieve a quotation (e.g. insufficient size or trading record).
- Avoid pressures of stock market investors demanding earnings and dividend growth.
- Retain control over the company and avoid widespread share ownership, thus being less vulnerable to takeover.
- No requirement for a large-scale increase in equity.
- Avoid the stringent stock market regulations and monitoring.

Some companies have decided to revert from a quoted status company to an unquoted company. Reasons for this change have been to avoid the threat of takeover and the pressure from investors for short-term financial performance.

Stock market operational procedures

Prior to the so-called 'Big Bang' in October 1986, there was a rigid distinction between *jobbers* and *brokers*, with jobbers buying and selling shares in the market and brokers acting as agents for their clients. This system, together with the fixed commissions for the brokers, was abolished and under the new 'dual capacity' system *market-makers* and *broker-dealers* are now able to buy and sell both as principals and as agents.

In anticipation of this event there was a crescendo of activity in the City with the merging of merchant banks, stockbrokers and jobbers in order to combine their special skills and prepare for the new opportunities and competition which came with deregulation.

Simultaneously there was an unprecedented technological build-up. A new electronic marketplace called *Stock Exchange Automated Quotation System (SEAQ)* was introduced. It includes the display of market information and a complete recording of all trading done on the Stock Exchange. The introduction of the new trading arrangements, and in particular SEAQ, was accompanied by a movement of business away from the Exchange floor to dealing rooms, where transactions are now made by telephone on the basis of information carried on screens.

The force behind the reforms in the Stock Exchange was the need to increase the efficiency and liquidity of its markets – not only to improve the service available to domestic investors and borrowers but also to exhance the competitiveness of London as an international financial centre. A paperless settlement system, called TAURUS, is expected to further improve efficiency and competitiveness.

Share ownership in Great Britain

In 1963, almost 60 per cent of all UK equities were held by private individuals. Today the situation is radically changed; nearly two-thirds of all shares in British companies are held by the investing institutions, the pension funds, insurance groups and investment and unit trusts. This is illustrated in Table 2.1. These impersonal bodies, acting for millions of pensioners and employees, policyholders and small investors, are today's market mammoths with, between them, vast potential power to influence the market and the companies they invest in.

Altogether, the market worth of UK pension fund assets rocketed from only £4.5bn in 1963 to £200bn by the end of 1989, over 50 per cent being invested in UK equities.

2.5 The Efficient Market Hypothesis

If financial managers are to achieve corporate goals they require well-developed financial markets where transfers of wealth from savers to borrowers is efficient both in pricing and operational cost. To what extent are the major capital markets efficient?

Table 2.1 Share of ownership of UK equities, 1975–89

	1975 (%)	1981 (%)	1989 (%)
Pension Funds	16.8	26.7	29
Insurance Companies	15.9	20.5	25
Investment Trusts	10.1	7.1	3
Unit Trusts	4.1	3.6	6
Institutions	46.9	57.9	63
Persons	37.5	28.2	18
Charities	2.3	2.2	2
Industry	4.1	5.1	4
Government	3.6	3.0	5
Overseas	5.6	3.6	8
Total	100	100	100
Total Value (£bn)	45	92	460

Source: UBS Phillips & Drew (1990).

We often talk of the shares of a particular company being under- or over-valued, the implication being that the stock market pricing mechanism has got it wrong and that investors know better. An efficient share market is one where shares are always correctly priced and where it is not possible to outperform the market consistently, except by luck. *In an efficient capital market, current market prices fully reflect available information.*

Consider any of the major European stock markets. On any given trading day there may be hundreds of analysts – representing the powerful financial institutions which dominate the market – closely tracking on their computer terminals the daily performance of the share price of, say, Rolls-Royce. They each receive at the same time new information from the company – a major order, a labour dispute, or a revised profits forecast. This information is rapidly evaluated and reflected in the share price by their decisions to buy or sell Rolls-Royce shares. *The measure of efficiency is seen in the extent to which the market reflects new information rapidly in the share price.*

Market efficiency, as viewed within the Efficient Market Hypothesis (EMH), may be defined at *three* levels:

1. *The weak form of the EMH* states that current share prices fully reflect *all information contained in past price movements.* If this level of efficiency holds, there is no value in trying to predict future price movements by analyzing trends in past price movements. If the share price for Rolls-Royce over the past four days has risen from 170p to 180p, the weak form of the EMH argues that this trend offers no clues as to tomorrow's price – the stock market has no memory. Efficient stock market prices approximate a *random walk*, meaning they will fluctuate more or less randomly, any departure from randomness being too expensive to determine.

2. *The semi-strong form of the EMH* states that current market prices reflect *all publicly available information.* In other words, there is no benefit in analyzing existing

information, such as may be given in published accounts, some time after the information has been released; the stock market has already captured this information in the current share price. Only those with access to information prior to its general release (such as managers in the particular company) can earn superior or abnormal returns over the normal return expected for the associated degree of risk.

3. *The strong form of the EMH* goes beyond the previous two by stating that current market prices reflect *all relevant information* – evenly if privately held. The implications of such a level of market efficiency are clear: *no one* can consistently beat the market, i.e. earn abnormal returns.

To what extent are the major stock markets efficient as described in the three forms of the EMH? Considerable empirical tests on market efficiency conducted over many years suggest the following:

1. *There is little benefit in attempting to forecast future share price movements by analysing past price movements. Chartists* are analysts who devise systems aimed at spotting trends in share prices, or critical points of change. This mostly involves the use of charts of past price movements. For example, charts are used to predict 'floors' and 'ceilings', marking the end of a share price trend. In between, charts are used to detect patterns of 'resistance' (for shares on the way up) and 'support' (for shares on the way down). As the EMH seems to hold in its weak form, the value of such charts must be questioned.

2. For quoted companies which are regularly traded on the stock market, it is *unlikely that analysts will be able to find significantly over- or under-valued shares through studying information which is publicly held*. However, analysts with specialist knowledge, paying careful attention to smaller, less well-traded shares, may be more successful in this regard. Equally, analysts able to respond to new information a little ahead of the market as a whole may make further gains. The semi-strong form of the EMH seems, therefore, to hold fairly well for the majority of quoted shares.

3. The strong form of the EMH does not hold, so superior returns can be achieved by those with 'inside knowledge'. However, it is the duty of directors to act in the shareholders' best interests, and it is a criminal offence to engage in insider trading for personal gain. The fact that several notable cases of insider trading have led to the conviction of senior executives is testimony to the fact that market prices do not fully reflect unpublished information!

Criticisms of market efficiency

Much of the criticism of the EMH is misplaced because it is based on a misconception of what the hypothesis actually says. For example, it does not mean that financial expertise is of no value in stock markets and that selecting a share portfolio may just as well be achieved by sticking a pin in the financial pages. This is clearly not the case, and we will discuss in a later chapter how diversification can significantly reduce investor risk. It does suggest, however, that in an efficient market there is 'no free lunch'; after adjusting for portfolio risk, fund managers will not, on average, achieve returns higher than that of a randomly selected portfolio. Roll (1991) makes the point that it is not essential that *all* publicly available information is reflected in share prices. Instead, it means that the link 'between unreflected information and prices is too subtle and tenuous to be easily or costlessly detected'.

Market efficiency also suggests that share prices are 'fair' in the sense that they reflect the value of that stock given the available information. Shareholders need not therefore be unduly concerned with whether they are paying too much for a particular share.

The fact that a lot of investors have done very well through investing on the stock market should not surprise us. For much of this century the market has generated positive returns. Most investment advice, if followed over a long period of time, is likely to have done well; the point is, however, that, in efficient markets, investors cannot consistently achieve above-average returns other than by chance. Market efficiency seems to be less in evidence among smaller firms. Shares of small companies tend to yield higher average returns than those of larger companies of comparable risk. But these and other mysteries seem to be the exceptions that prove the rule.

Black Monday

In October 1987, on 'Black Monday', there was a sudden and dramatic fall in share prices on most of the world's stock markets, share prices falling by 30 per cent or more. Had this collapse been triggered by some cataclysmic event, shareholders' reactions could be easily explained as the efficient market reacting to new information. The problem, however, was that Black Monday was not a reaction to external events, rather a recognition that the prolonged rising ('bull') market had ended and that the speculative share price bubble had burst. This brings into question the validity of the simple EMH which implies that share prices cannot rise to the artificially high levels observed prior to the 1987 crash.

This enigma has led to a re-evaluation of the simple EMH and the assumption that there is a single 'true'-value for the level of shares, to a view that there is a very wide range of plausible values.

Implications of market efficiency for corporate managers

The overall message for corporate finance managers in quoted companies is that managers and investors are directly linked through stock market prices, corporate actions being rapidly reflected in share prices. This indicates that:

1. Investors are not easily fooled by glossy financial reports or 'creative accounting' techniques, which boost corporate reported earnings but not underlying cash flows.
2. Corporate management should endeavour to make decisions which maximize shareholder wealth.
3. There is little point in bothering with the *timing of new issues*. Market prices are a 'fair' reflection of the information available and rationally evaluate the degree of risk in shares.
4. Where corporate managers possess information not yet released to the market (termed

'information asymmetry'), it has some opportunity for influencing prices. For example, it may 'keep up its sleeve' information so that, in the event of an unwelcome takeover bid, it can release some information offering positive signals.

2.6   A new perspective – Chaos Theory

The EMH is based on the assertion that rational investors rapidly absorb new information about a company's prospects which then is impounded into the share price. Any other price variations are attributable to random 'noise'. This implies that the market has no memory – it simply reacts to the advent of each new information snippet, registers it accordingly and settles back into equilibrium; in other words, all price-sensitive events are random and independent of each other.

The crash of 1987, possibly attributed to the market's realization that shares were overvalued and triggered by the collapse of a relatively minor management buy-out deal, has provoked more detailed scrutiny of the pattern of past share prices. This has uncovered evidence that share price movements do not always conform to a 'random walk'. For example, significant downturns happened more frequently than significant upturns.

A new branch of mathematics, *Chaos Theory*, has been harnessed to help explain such features. Chaos Theory is based on the study of natural systems such as weather patterns and river systems. Observations of these systems often give a chaotic appearance – they seem to lurch wildly from one extreme to another. Chaos theorists suggest that apparently random, unpredictable patterns are governed by sets of complex sub-systems which react interdependently. These systems can be modelled, and their behaviour forecast, but predictions of the behaviour of chaotic systems are very sensitive to the precise conditions specified at the start of the estimation period. Therefore, an apparently small error in the specification of the model can lead to major errors in the forecast.

Edgar Peters (1991) has suggested that stock markets are chaotic in this sense. Markets *do* have memories, *are* prone to major price swings and *do not behave entirely randomly*. For example, in the United Kingdom, he found that today's price movement is affected by price changes which occurred several years previously. The most recent changes, however, have the biggest impact, the effect reducing the further backwards it is traced. In addition, he found that price moves were persistent, i.e. if previous moves in price had been upwards, then the subsequent price move was more likely to be up than down. Yet, Chaos Theory also suggests that persistent trends are also more likely to result in major reversals!

Peters' work suggests that world stock markets do exhibit patterns which are overlaid with substantial random noise. The more noise, the less efficient the market. In this respect, the US markets appear to be more efficient than those in the United Kingdom and Japan. Other observers suggest that markets are essentially rational and efficient, but succumb to chaos on occasions, with bursts of chaotic frenzy being attributed to speculative activity, suggesting some scope for informed insiders to outperform the market during such periods.

Which view is right? Are stock markets efficient, chaotic or somewhere in between? At present, we simply do not know, pending the results of further research. It seems that corporate financial managers cannot necessarily regard *today's* market price as a fair assessment of company value, but that the market may well correctly value a company over a period of years. As in many other things, examination of long-term trends gives more insight than consideration of short-term oscillations. For example, if a company's share price persistently underperforms the market, then something appears to be wrong – its profitability really is low, its management poor, or perhaps it has failed to release the right amount of information to the market. It would be folly to disregard the market, however irrational one suspects it might be at times.

2.7   Short-termism in the City

The pressure to perform well has not only led fund managers to increase their activity in managing funds, but may also have led to a more short-term perspective regarding investment. The argument is that fund managers focus on the short-term performance of companies in arriving at a valuation of companies' worth. This takes the form of an assertion that excessive emphasis is placed on current profit performance and dividend payments. Such apparent behaviour is said to have a number of consequences. One is that management, in order to keep up the price of their stock and so keep down their cost of capital, will tend to focus on producing the short-term results that it thinks the market wants to see. This results in neglect of the long term by management failing to undertake important long-term investments in resources and research and development. The second consequence is that the volatility of short-term corporate results will be exaggerated in securities markets, producing unacceptable fluctuations in stock prices.

This chain of argument gained support from a survey carried out by the Department of Trade and Industry's Innovation Advisory Board (1990) which suggested that:

1.   The corporate/City interface has resulted in too high a priority for short-term profits and dividends at the expense of R & D and other innovative investment; and that
2.   Particular practices of key financial institutions have helped to sustain such priority for the short term.

The argument is further supported by a CBI survey of 109 major companies in 1987, in which 35 per cent expressed doubt that financial institutions take a long-term and strategic evaluation of their companies. As a result of the CBI's concern, it set up a taskforce to investigate the whole issue. Its report concluded, however, that many British companies have given insufficient weight to long-term development, but that this does not arise primarily from City pressure. It arises mainly from underlying economic and political factors, including inadequate profitability (Ferguson 1989).

The problem of short-termism has also been addressed by American researchers (e.g. Graves 1988) arguing that the increasing shareholder power of institutional investors has had a damaging effect on R & D expenditure among US firms.

Efficient Market Theory argues that rational investors will approve of any long-term investments that make sound economic sense. They will not sell the stock of a fundamentally sound firm undertaking productive long-term investments that promise excessive future cash flows just because that firm has reported one bad trading period. Any such short-term stock shuttling is viewed as irrational behaviour.

The City rejects most of the criticism of short-termism, arguing that much of the responsibility for the lack of long-term innnovative investment is attributable to managers, to their preference for growth by acquisition, their poor record of commercial development and their reward systems based on short-term targets. This view is advocated by Marsh (1991), who claims that

> There is no evidence that shares are priced in a way which emphasises their short- rather than long-run prospects. Nor is there any evidence that the market penalises long-term investments or expenditure on R & D by awarding the shares of the company in question a lower rating – indeed quite the contrary.

He identifies 'managerial short-termism' as a key force behind poor investment in the United Kingdom. When it comes to making plans for the future, managers' perceptions will be influenced by their organizational systems and contexts, including the way they are remunerated and rewarded; their time-horizons within their job; the role played by the internal performance measurement and management accounting systems; and the internal capital budgeting and project appraisal systems.

Whatever the merit of the respective arguments there is broad consensus among all parties to the debate that action is required to improve communication between the City and industry. It emerges very clearly from the debate on short-termism that UK companies will need to improve the information they provide to the capital markets on their R & D activity and other strategic investments if they are to achieve a market rating appropriate to their future expected profitability.

According to Ball (1991) the whole debate about short-termism takes place for two reasons:

> Firstly, the debate reflects a discussion between people who are on opposite sides of the street. The parties concerned find themselves on the one side or the other of the line that divides the suppliers and the demanders of funds. Secondly, within the 'mass' and the 'average' are individual firms and people who both gain and suffer from their experience. On the whole the losers tend to be more vociferous and usually better organised than the winners, who keep quiet.

2.8 Reading the financial pages

Corporate finance is changing at such a rate that it is essential for students of finance to read the financial pages in newspapers on a regular basis. In this section we explain the London Share Service pages in *The Financial Times*, although many other newspapers provide a similar service.

The FT-SE Index

Every day shares move up or down with the release of information from within the firm, such as a revised profits forecast, or from an external source, such as the latest government statistics on inflation or unemployment. To indicate how the whole share market has performed a share index is used, the most common being the FT-SE Index – more familiarly known as 'Footsie'. This index is based on the prices of the hundred most valuable British quoted companies, each company being weighted in proportion to its total market value. All the world's major stock markets have similar indices, for example the Nikkei index in Japan, the Dow Jones index in the United States, and the CAC-40 in France.

Every share index is constructed on a base date and base value. The FT-SE 100 started with a base value of 1,000 at the end of 1983. On 26 February 1992, the Index was reporting a value of 2,546, which means that in just over eight years the value of the market represented by the index has increased by two and a half times, an average annual increase of 11 per cent, well above the rate of inflation over the same period.

The FT-Actuaries Share Indices, as shown in Table 2.2, provide indices of share movements by sector and total to give the All-Share Index, representing 500 of the more commonly traded quoted industrial companies plus 154 financial services companies. Financial managers will study how the performance of their shares compares with the appropriate sector and its competitors within the sector. In particular, the earnings yield, dividend yield and price/earnings ratio are important indicators.

Earnings yield

This is the total earnings (profit after tax) over the previous year of companies in the index for each sector, expressed as a percentage of the sector's market value. Take a look at the Brewers and Distillers sector where the earnings yield is 7.59 per cent. This is lower than, say, the Engineering sector yield of 9.44 per cent because the United Kingdom was in the midst of a recession at the time we are considering and stock prices of brewery companies tend to be less affected by economic downturns than engineering companies.

Dividend yield

This is the gross, or pre-tax, dividends of the companies in the sector in the last year as a percentage of the total value of the sector. Generally, sectors with low dividend yields are those with companies where the market expects high growth. The gross dividend yield for all industrial companies in the index is just 4.44 per cent – well below the 10 per cent return investors could currently earn on a safe investment in Treasury Bills. Obviously, shareholders are looking to a capital gain on top of the dividend yield to recompense them for the higher risks involved.

Price: Earnings ratio

The P:E ratio is a much used performance indicator. It is the share price divided by the current earnings per share. So for the sector, it is the total market value of the companies

Table 2.2 FT-Actuaries Share Indices

Equity Groups & Sub-sections — Figures in parentheses show number of stocks per section	Index No.	Day's Change %	Est. Earnings Yield % (Max.)	Gross Div Yield % (Act at (25%)	Est. P/E Ratio (Net)	xd adj. 1992 to date
1 **CAPITAL GOODS (178)**	795.14	−0.4	8.28	6.00	15.45	1.41
2 Building Materials (23)	981.29	...	7.12	6.34	18.92	0.44
3 Contracting, Construction (28)	887.23	+0.1	8.98	8.23	16.07	1.32
4 Electricals (7)	2438.73	−0.8	10.13	6.15	12.42	1.47
5 Electronics (26)	1820.80	−0.2	10.06	4.70	12.60	1.86
6 Engineering-Aerospace (8)	327.57	−0.3	12.49	7.93	9.73	5.78
7 Engineering-General (43)	490.82	−0.6	9.44	4.81	13.08	1.21
8 Metals and Metal Forming (10)	326.39	−0.7	2.12	10.59	—	0.00
9 Motors (14)	316.45	−1.0	8.03	7.48	16.55	0.00
10 Other Industrial Materials (19)	1602.57	−0.6	7.51	5.12	15.85	0.69
21 **CONSUMER GROUP (188)**	1668.96	−0.7	6.95	3.34	17.69	4.74
22 Brewers and Distillers (23)	2117.13	−0.4	7.59	3.35	15.89	7.92
25 Food Manufacturing (18)	1265.80	−1.2	8.53	4.04	14.46	2.11
26 Food Retailing (17)	2617.42	−0.1	8.43	3.17	15.41	4.06
27 Health and Household (24)	4363.25	−1.3	5.34	2.36	21.37	15.12
29 Hotels and Leisure (23)	1299.25	+0.3	7.16	5.19	17.40	8.54
30 Media (24)	1542.18	−0.4	6.34	3.54	19.85	2.97
31 Packaging, Paper & Printing (17)	751.95		7.04	4.41	17.23	0.22
34 Stores (32)	1053.28	−0.9	7.01	3.43	18.90	1.91
35 Textiles (10)	635.51	−0.2	7.23	4.87	17.66	0.53
40 **OTHER GROUPS (116)**	1228.23	−0.3	9.82	5.40	12.84	6.41
41 Business Services (16)	1393.65	−0.7	7.20	4.71	17.67	0.27
42 Chemicals (21)	1515.35	−0.2	6.62	4.83	18.68	0.59
43 Conglomerates (11)	1334.84	+0.6	10.85	7.58	11.22	3.18
44 Transport (14)	2415.92	+0.1	5.25	4.69	25.14	2.46
45 Electricity (16)	1198.24	−0.5	15.13	6.20	8.60	17.21
46 Telephone Networks (4)	1400.53	−0.7	11.20	4.48	11.65	16.02
47 Water (10)	2419.41	−0.4	17.63	6.57	6.25	0.00
48 Miscellaneous (24)	1843.83	−0.2	5.56	5.29	24.57	1.18
49 **INDUSTRIAL GROUP (482)**	1308.62	−0.5	8.07	4.44	15.49	4.43
51 Oil & Gas (18)	2015.81	−0.3	9.48	6.99	13.92	36.07
59 **500 SHARE INDEX (500)**	1376.04	−0.5	8.21	4.70	15.32	6.70
61 **FINANCIAL GROUP (87)**	727.86	...	...	6.40	-	2.61
62 Banks (9)	907.83	+0.4	4.49	5.91	44.53	6.20
65 Insurance (Life) (6)	1429.81	−0.2	—	5.97	—	0.00
66 Insurance (Composite) (7)	484.91	+0.4	—	8.99	—	0.00
67 Insurance (Brokers) (10)	965.23	+0.4	8.01	6.92	16.42	2.37
68 Merchant Banks (7)	479.68	+0.2	—	4.47	—	0.00
69 Property (33)	738.41	−2.0	7.79	6.14	17.57	0.93
70 Other Financial (14)	246.11	+0.1	8.08	7.09	16.35	0.89
71 Investment Trusts (68)	1177.88	...	—	3.73	—	4.11
99 **ALL-SHARE INDEX (654)**	1221.30	−0.4	—	4.88	—	5.72

	Index No.	Day's Change	Day's High (a)	Day's Low (b)	Feb 24	Feb 21
FT-SE 100 SHARE INDEX*	2546.8	−12.9	2572.8	2544.1	2559.7	2542.3

A Framework for Financial Decisions

Table 2.3 Financial Times London Share Service

Food Retailing	Notes	Price	+ or −	1991/92 high	low	Mkt Cap £m	Yld Gr's	P/E
■ASDA	§	39xd	...	*123	26	869.7	7.2	9.5
■AlbertFisher		59	−3	135	57	354.0	8.5	5.7
★Appleby W'ward		225	...	270	223	12.5	5.0	8.8
■Argyll	†g	323	−4	329	$234\frac{7}{8}$	3,591	3.6	14.7
■Ashley		$35\frac{1}{2}$	...	119	32	50.0	7.3	4.9
$8\frac{1}{4}$p Net Cv Pf		75xd	...	154	75	10.5	14.7	—
Brake Bros	†	435	...	436	266	197.5	1.6	19.0
■Budgens		41	...	58	26	66.6	—	—
Cullen's		38	...	41	28	9.94	1.8	11.6
Dairy Farm $		78	...	92	$65\frac{1}{2}$	1,275	3.3	14.9
★Dumas		23	...	26	21	2.67	—	56.8
★Farepak 10p	†	265	...	275	124	63.1	1.9	24.2
Fyffes I£	g	88	...	*105	81	245.7	1.6	Φ
■Geest	†	343	...	363	258	239.4	2.7	13.7
Greggs	†	398	...	455	395	44.1	4.5	10.0
Hunter Saphir	‡	54	−3	85	46	13.3	‡	5.8
■Iceland	†	437	...	448	265	375.6	2.2	13.8
■KwikSave		558	+5	639	464	858.9	3.5	12.6
■Low(Wm)		239	...	343	218	127.0	4.7	7.6
M & W		100	...	123	84	15.3	3.0	11.3
■MerchantRetl	†g	19	$-\frac{1}{2}$	*$46\frac{1}{2}$	$13\frac{1}{2}$	17.2	16.8	7.4
■Morrison(W)	M	299	+2	*299	186	699.7	0.8	16.7
$5\frac{1}{4}$ pc Cv Pf		180	...	183	123	84.0	3.9	—
■NurdinP"k	†	182	−1	202	152	222.7	3.8	11.6
■ParkFood	M	112	...	114	37	58.7	15.5	3.4
■Sainsbury(J)	†g	$391\frac{1}{2}$	$+1\frac{1}{2}$	396	$300\frac{1}{2}$	6,878	2.5	16.8
Shoprite		305xd	...	401	102	42.5	1.7	51.0
■Tesco	†	$260\frac{1}{2}$	$+\frac{1}{2}$	*299	205	5,053	2.7	15.4
■Thorntons		196	...	198	138	123.3	2.4	15.8
★Wardell Robts I£	†g	$104\frac{1}{4}$	$+2\frac{1}{2}$	115	77	23.2	3.9	11.2
Watson & Phlp		335	...	361	225	115.1	5.1	13.4

represented divided by total sector earnings. The P:E ratio is a measure of the market's confidence in a particular company or industry. A high P:E usually indicates that investors have confidence that profits will grow strongly in future, although irregular events like a rumoured takeover bid will raise the P:E ratio if it leads to higher share price.

Let us now turn to the performance of individual companies. Table 2.3 is an extract from the London Share Service pages in *The Financial Times* giving the Food Retailing sector. We will focus on the major supermarket chain, ASDA Group.

Indication that ASDA shares are actively traded is given by the block symbol. Transactions and prices of such stocks are published continuously through the Stock Exchange Automated Quotation system (SEAQ). ASDA is one of the top 100 companies (termed alpha stocks). As we move down in trading activity and company size we come to the 500 or so beta stocks through to the gamma and, lastly, delta stocks. Stocks operating in thin markets (typically of gamma and delta status) tend to have wider *spreads* – the difference between the bid (buying) price and offer (selling) price.

The share price for ASDA, based on the mid-price at the close of the previous day, is reported as 39xd, with a range over the previous year of between 123p and 26p. Prices quoted assume that shareholders buying a share are entitled to the forthcoming dividend unless they specifically exclude it. The share is then quoted 'ex div' (or xd) as in ASDA's case. This means that because a dividend is shortly to be declared, new investors will not receive the next dividend, it being received by the seller. The high–low price variation over the previous year indicates the considerable volatility ASDA has experienced. As the cost of finance is a function of the risk perceived by the capital market, corporate finance managers should seek to keep share price volatility to a minimum.

The next column shows the market capitalization of the company, calculated by multiplying the number of ordinary shares in issue by the current share price. We have earlier defined the gross dividend yield and P:E ratio. In ASDA's case, the dividend yield is well above the sector average and the P:E ratio well below average, both statistics indicating the current low price of its shares.

2.9   Taxation and financial decisions

Few financial decisions are unaffected by taxation considerations. *Corporate and personal taxation affect both the cash flows received by companies and the dividend income received by shareholders.* Consequently, financial managers need to understand the tax consequences of investment and financing decisions. Taxation is a particularly important consideration in three key areas of financial management: raising finance, investing in fixed assets and payment of dividends.

Raising finance

There are clear tax benefits in raising finance by issuing debt rather than capital. Interest on borrowings attracts tax relief, thereby reducing the company's tax bill, while a dividend payment on equity capital does not attract tax relief. The tax system is thereby biased strongly in favour of debt finance.

Investing in fixed assets

Certain types of fixed assets attract a form of tax relief termed *capital allowances*. These are tax incentives to stimulate certain types of investment such as in industrial plant and machinery. The taxation implications of an investment decision can be very important.

Paying dividends

At one time in the United Kingdom company profits were effectively taxed twice – first on the profits achieved and then again on those profits paid to shareholders in the form of dividends. Such a tax system (which still exists in certain countries, including the United States) is clearly biased in favour of retaining profits rather than paying out large dividends. The UK taxation system is more neutral, the same tax bill being paid (for companies making profits) regardless of the dividend policy. However, retentions are still slightly more attractive because the *timing of the tax payment is affected by dividend policy*. Advance Corporation Tax (ACT) is paid at the time of the dividend which, for companies making large dividend payments, brings forward a significant proportion of the total tax bill. Where a company has insufficient taxable profits to recover the ACT paid, the taxation aspects become particularly important.

The corporate financial manager should not only understand how taxation affects the company, but also how it affects the company's shareholders. For example, some financial institutions (e.g. pension funds) pay no tax; some shareholders pay standard rate income tax, while others pay higher-rate income tax. Some may prefer capital gains to dividends.

The Appendix to this chapter provides further information on Income Tax, Capital Gains Tax and Corporation Tax (including capital allowances), which readers of this text in the United Kingdom are encouraged to study.

2.10   Summary

This chapter has introduced readers to the financial and tax environment within which financial and investment decisions take place.

Key points

- Financial markets consist of numerous specialist markets where financial transactions occur (e.g. the money market, capital market, foreign exchange market, options and futures markets).
- Financial institutions (e.g. banks, building societies, pension funds, etc.) provide a vital service by acting as financial intermediaries between savers and borrowers.
- Securitization and disintermediation have permitted larger companies to create alternative, more flexible forms of finance.
- The Stock Exchange operates two tiers: the Official List for larger established companies, and the Unlisted Securities Market for smaller companies unable or unwilling to fulfil the stringent requirement for a full listing.
- Financial institutions hold around two-thirds of UK equities, the largest investors being pension funds and insurance companies.
- An efficient capital market is one where investors are rational and share prices reflect all available information. The Efficient Market Hypothesis (EMH) has been examined in its various forms (weak, semi-strong and strong) and, in all but the strong form, seems to hold up reasonably well (although some would dispute this).
- The problem of 'short-termism' may stem more from managerial attitudes than those of investors.

- Taxation plays a key role in financial management, particularly in the areas of raising finance, investing in fixed assets and paying dividends.

Appendix
UK taxation

Taxation can have a significant impact on financial management decisions. In this appendix we outline the main forms of taxation relevant to the topic.

Unfortunately for students and authors of financial texts, the tax system is constantly changing, motivated partly by efforts of governments to seek short-term political advantage, and partly by genuine attempts to reform the system, as in the introduction of the imputation system of Corporate Taxation in 1973 in the United Kingdom. The vehicle for making tax changes is the annual Budget, which, after suitable debate, is ratified in the subsequent Finance Act. It is not a true budget since expenditure decisions are announced in the preceding Autumn Statement – it is an announcement of how the government intends to finance predetermined expenditure plans.

It follows that finance managers and individual investors should keep fully abreast of any alterations in the tax system and consider their consequences for financial decisions under their control. However, a full treatment of personal and corporate taxation is outside the scope of this book – of necessity, we are forced to confine ourselves to a brief discussion of those elements of the UK tax system of most relevance to the financial decisions discussed in this book.

Personal taxation

All individuals earning incomes above a certain level (£3,445 in 1992–3) are liable to income tax on both *earned income* (essentially wages and salaries from employment and income from self-employment) and *investment income* received from holdings of stocks and shares and bank and building society accounts. In the 1992–3 tax year this taxable income was taxed at a basic or standard rate of tax of 25 per cent up to £23,700 and at 40 per cent thereafter. Husbands and wives are now taxed separately and independently, the former married couples' allowance having been abolished for all people below pension age. There are allowances available for special cases such as the blind person's allowance and an additional personal allowance for single parents. Relief on mortgage interest payments is available at the basic rate only for the first £30,000 of the mortgage. For a mortgage interest rate of 11 per cent, this results in an annual tax subsidy of $(11\% \times £30,000 \times 25\%) = £825$. Relief is obtainable at source – the mortgagor (the borrower) makes a payment to the mortgagee (the lender) net of tax relief, a system known as MIRAS – Mortgage Interest Relief at Source. The generosity of the tax system in this respect has arguably distorted the pattern of investment in the United Kingdom. So long as house prices continued to rise, individuals had an extra incentive to invest in housing rather than in the corporate sector.

This partly explains the introduction by the government of a range of schemes designed to promote wider and deeper share ownership such as Personal Equity Plans (PEPs) (see Chapter 13), Tax Exempt Special Savings Accounts (TESSAs) and the Business Expansion Scheme (BES). A PEP is a scheme whereby individuals can place equity investments into a tax-free fund, i.e. the dividend income and any capital gains are free of any tax. A TESSA is an income tax-free savings account operated by a bank or building society for individuals prepared to tie up their savings for five years. The BES is a device to encourage equity investment in small, unquoted, often newly formed companies. These holdings, subject to an upper limit of £40,000 p.a., qualify for relief from both income tax (making the *effective* investment for a 40 per cent tax payer only 60 per cent of the value of the shares purchased) and capital gains tax on disposal if held for five years. This scheme is due to be abolished in 1993 although existing investments will be unaffected.

Capital Gains Tax

Individuals are liable to tax on any capital gains arising from the disposal of real assets or securities. Such capital gains are taxable as income above an exempt amount of £5,800 (1992–3). Any unused relief cannot be carried forward to subsequent years, although realized losses can be set against gains, and in most cases, an indexation allowance is available to remove the portion of the gain attributable solely to price inflation over the holding period. Although the *rates* of tax applicable to income from dividend payments and income from capital gains are equal, capital appreciation may be more preferable to some investors than other income. The CGT exemption together with the element of investor choice as to *when* to realize capital gains, makes capital appreciation potentially more attractive to the higher rate income tax payer.

Corporation Tax

Two major changes have occurred in UK corporate taxation in the past two decades: first, the move from a 'classical' to an 'imputation' system in 1973; and second, the abolition in 1984 of generous investment incentives, coupled with a substantial reduction in the rate of Corporation Tax.

A 'classical' corporation tax system, as applies for example in the United States, involves a *'double taxation of dividends'*. Corporate income, if paid as dividend, is effectively taxed twice – initially, as corporate profits tax is applied, and second, as personal income tax is applied. For example, with rates of corporate and personal tax both set at 40 per cent, each £1 of pre-tax corporate income which is paid as dividend, is worth only $(1–40\%)$ $(1–40\%) = £0.36$ in the hands of shareholders. The company could choose its own effective average tax rate, depending on its distribution policy, ranging from 40 per cent with no retention to 64 per cent for 100 per cent distribution (i.e. 40 per cent on profits plus 40 per cent income tax on the remaining 60 per cent fully distributed to shareholders). The system is supposed to encourage retention to enable companies to fund reinvestment, but there was widespread agreement that excessive retentions could, and did, distort the pattern of investment into low-yielding projects or quick pay-off investments.

An Imputation System gives credit to shareholders for tax already paid on corporate income. Any dividends subsequently paid out of taxed corporate income are treated as net-of-standard rate income tax. In other words, the rate of Corporation Tax, currently (1992–3) 33 per cent, is deemed to contain an element of personal income tax. This is intended to make the dividend decision largely tax-neutral, in so far as dividend recipients will face no further tax liability (unless they lie in the higher rate bracket).

For example, each £1 of corporate income is now taxed at 33 per cent, leaving post-tax income of £0.67. If the company declares a dividend of, say, 15p, this is deemed to have already borne income tax of 25 per cent. The net-of-tax income is thus equivalent to a pre-tax dividend 'grossed up' at the standard rate, i.e. $\dfrac{15p}{(1-25\%)} = 20p$. In other words, the dividend recipient is deemed to have paid income tax of $(20p - 15p) = 5p$. This 5p is called a *tax credit*, and can be reclaimed by a non-taxpayer, whereas higher rate taxpayers would face a supplementary tax charge, based on the gross dividend of $(40\% - 25\%) \times 20p = 3p$.

Advance Corporation Tax

Despite the intention of its designers, the present tax regime is not actually neutral in its impact on the dividend decision, because payment of a dividend triggers off a liability to Advance Corporation Tax (ACT). The rate of ACT is set to ensure that the Inland Revenue has received monies equal to the tax credit, thus freeing dividend payments of any further (standard rate) tax liability. The rate of ACT depends on the ruling rate of basic rate tax. Take the preceding example where the tax credit was 5p. Using the present 25 per cent basic rate, ACT is applied to the *net* dividend using the fraction 25/75 i.e. ACT = $25/75 \times 15p = 5p =$ tax credit. ACT is paid at the end of the calendar quarter in which the dividend is paid and typically precedes the payment of the main Corporation Tax liability, which becomes payable nine months after the end of the company's financial year.

If a company makes a dividend payment, thus incurring an ACT liability, it is given suitable credit or 'relief' when making its so-called Mainstream Corporation Tax (MCT), based on profits. There are thus important delays in the phasing of a company's tax payments.

Consider the following example. A company makes pre-tax profits of £100m in the year ended 31 December 1991. Its total Corporation Tax liability is thus $(33\% \times £100m) = £33m$, payable on 30 September 1992. It declares a net dividend of £12m, payable on 10 April 1992. This triggers an ACT liability of $25/75 \times £12m = £4m$, payable by the end of June 1992. Mainstream Corporation Tax is thus $(£33m - ACT) = £29m$.

	£12m	£4m	£29m
	Dividend	ACT	MCT
£100m	Paid	Payable	Payable
←————PROFITS EARNED————→			

1.1.92	FINANCIAL YEAR	31.12.92	10.4.93	30.6.93	30.9.93

It is clear that for profits earned very early in the firm's 1992 financial year, the delay in the subsequent tax impact can extend to 21 months, and generally the tax delay period varies between 9 and 21 months. (The reader will find that in subsequent examples, we have usually assumed a tax delay period of one year, although 15 months would perhaps be more typical.)

It must be stressed that ACT is a tax on dividend payment not a tax on corporate profit. It is the payment of a dividend that prompts the tax liability, regardless of the company's profitability. This means that financial managers in *unprofitable* companies could bestow on the Inland Revenue an interest-free loan if they pay a dividend which triggers off an ACT liability which cannot be relieved (i.e. set off) against MCT. Unrelieved ACT can be carried forward for up to six years before it is written off – this is referred to as *'overhang'*.

Investment incentives

Not all depreciation can be regarded as an allowable expense for tax purposes. The Inland Revenue operates a system of *capital allowances*. In 1984, the United Kingdom moved from a system of First Year Allowances (FYAs) to Annual or *Writing Down Allowances* (WDAs). Until 1984, expenditure on plant, equipment and industrial buildings qualified for 100 per cent relief against Corporation Tax in the first year of the project. Each £1 of expenditure could be set against profits for tax purposes, thus reducing the Corporation Tax payable. For a profitable company, this was equivalent to payment of a grant because it assisted cash flow by the tax saving (subject to an official approval delay). At the rate of Corporation Tax applicable up to 1984, this was equivalent to a grant of $(52\% \times 100\%) = 52\text{p}$ per £1 of capital expenditure, (ignoring any tax delays).

The present system allows companies to set against profits 25% of their qualifying capital expenditure on plant and equipment in each year of the project, based on a reducing balance. So for an expenditure of £1,000, the allowances behave as in Table 2.4.

Clearly, the tax allowances also diminish over time. Companies are allowed to write assets down for tax purposes to their disposal values. Any discrepancy between written down value (WDV) and disposal value may trigger a tax liability or qualify for tax relief. For example, in the above example, disposal of the asset for £500 after three years, i.e. for £78 above the WDV, would trigger a *Balancing Charge* and the company would be liable for capital gains tax on the £78. Disposal for, say, £300, would qualify the company for a Balancing Allowance of $(£422 - £300) = £122$, a loss which would be set against any capital gains elsewhere.

The present system allows companies to write off fully their assets for tax purposes, but over a considerably longer period than was possible under the system of FYAs. Coupled with a lower rate of Corporation Tax (33 per cent in 1992–3 compared to 52 per cent up to 1984),

Table 2.4 Calculating tax allowances

Year of Project	Tax Allowance (£)	Written-Down Value at Year-end (£)
1	$25\% \times 1,000 = 250$	750
2	$25\% \times 750 = 187.5$	562.5
3	$25\% \times 562.5 = 140.6$	421.9, etc.

the value of the tax allowances has been considerably reduced, thus dampening the incentive to invest, although, according to the proponents of WDAs, this reduces the extent to which investment decisions are driven by tax-saving motives rather than purely commercial considerations.

A further point to grasp is that incentive systems like these are designed to accelerate the rate of tax-allowable depreciation which usually bears little relationship to the depreciation figures recorded in published company accounts. In other words, company accountants compute two sets of depreciation figures, one for reporting purposes, based on notions of cost and prudence, and a second for tax purposes.

Further reading

Clear and more thorough introductions to capital markets are found in Foley (1991), Weston and Copeland (1988), O'Shea (1986) and Redhead (1990).

The Stock Exchange Fact Book is published annually by The Stock Exchange. A classic review article on market efficiency is Fama (1970), while Rappaport (1987) examines the implications for managers. Tests on capital market efficiency are found in Copeland and Weston (1988), while some exceptions to efficiency are found in the June 1977 special issue of *Journal of Financial Economics*. Peters (1991) applies chaos theory to stock markets. Discussion on short-termism in the City is found in Marsh (1991) and Ball (1991).

Questions

Self-test questions

1. What are financial intermediaries and what economic service do they perform?
2. To what extent does an effective primary capital market depend on a healthy secondary capital market?
3. What type of company would be most likely to trade on:
   (a) the Listed Securities market?
   (b) the Unlisted Securities Market?
   (c) the Over-the-Counter Market?
4. List three important changes to the International Stock Exchange brought about by 'Big Bang' in 1986.

Exercises

1. In what ways can taxation policy influence financial management decisions? (Answer in Appendix A.)

2. Discuss the implications of market efficiency for corporate financial management.

Practical assignment

Select two companies from one sector in *The Financial Times* share information service. Analyse the share price and other data provided and compare with the FT All-Share Index data for the sector. Suggest why the P:E ratios for the companies differ.

CHAPTER 3
Present values and wealth

A SMART MOVE?

Soldem Pathetic Football Club has recently been bought out by a wealthy property dealer who, as chairman, intends to return the club to its First Division glory days and pay a good dividend each year to the shareholders of the newly formed quoted company, by making sound investments in quality players. Wonder goal scorer, Gary Spinnaker, has a £3 million price tag and is looking for a move. The chairman reckons that, quite apart from the extra income at the turnstiles from buying Gary, he could be sold for £4 million by the end of the year to a wealthy overseas club, given the way transfer prices are moving, even ignoring inflation. Should he bid for Spinnaker? Later in the chapter we use present value analysis to assess whether this would be a smart move for Soldem Pathetic FC.

3.1 Introduction

If football club or business managers are to make decisions and manage resources in the best interests of the owners, they need to be able to evaluate whether their proposed actions, which probably have financial implications spreading over many years, are *wealth-creating*. To do this, a clear understanding of *cash flow* and the *time-value of money* is essential. Capital investment decisions, security and bond value analyses, financial structure decisions, lease vs. buy decisions and the tricky question of the required rate of return can only be addressed once the reader has understood exactly what the old expression 'time is money' really means.

To do this we will consider in this chapter the measurement of wealth and the fundamental role it plays in the decision-making process, the time-value of money which underlies the discounted cash flow concept, and the net present value approach for analysing investment decisions.

LEARNING OBJECTIVES

Having completed this chapter students should have a sound grasp of the time-value of money and discounted cash flow concepts. In particular students should appreciate:

- Why the value of money changes with time.
- Present value formulae for single amounts, annuities and perpetuities.
- The net present value approach and why it is consistent with shareholder goals.

Skills developed in discounted cash flow analysis, using both formulae and tables, will help the reader enormously in subsequent chapters.

3.2   Measuring wealth-creation

'Cash flow is King!' pronounced City analysts, UBS-Phillips and Drew in 1991. The recession experienced in much of Europe at the time focused attention on companies' power to generate cash. Spectacular business collapses, such as those experienced recently by Coloroll, Polly Peck and Brent Walker, demonstrate that reliance on profits or earnings per share as predictors of performance can be dangerous.

The chairman of Rockwood Holdings stated in the Annual Report for 1988: 'Last year we delivered a 425% increase in turnover from £19.9m to £109.8m.' When Rockwood was placed into the hands of the receiver the following year, it was not the lack of sales or even profits that put it there. It was the lack of cash. Businesses go bust because they run out of cash. Of course, there are always reasons behind why the cash disappeared – the effects of recession, the over-ambitious investment programme, the rapid growth without adequate long-term finance – but basically corporate survival and success all comes down to cash flow and value-creation.

Recall from Chapter 1 that the assumed objective of the firm is to create as much wealth as possible for its shareholders. A successful business is one that creates value for its owners. Wealth is created when the market value of the outputs exceeds the market value of the inputs, i.e. the benefits are greater than the costs. Expressed mathematically:

$$V_j = B_j - C_j$$

The value (V_j) created by decision j is the difference between the benefits (B_j) and the costs (C_j) attributable to the decision. This leads to an obvious decision rule: *Accept only those investment or financing proposals that enhance the wealth of shareholders*, i.e. accept if $B_j - C_j > 0$.

This, in a nutshell, is what good investment and financial decision-making is all about. Nothing could be simpler in concept – the problems emerge only when we probe more deeply into how the benefits and costs are measured and evaluated. One obvious problem is that benefits and costs usually occur at different times and over a number of years. This leads us to consider the *time-value of money*.

3.3 Time-value of money

An important principle in financial management is that the value of money depends on *when* the cash flow occurs – £100 *now* is worth *more* than £100 at some *future* time. Why should this be? There are at least four good reasons:

- *Risk*   £100 now is certain, whereas £100 receivable next year is less certain. This 'bird-in-the-hand' principle affects many aspects of financial management.

- *Inflation*   Under inflationary conditions the value of money, expressed in terms of its purchasing power over goods and services, declines.

- *Personal Consumption Preference*   Most of us have a strong preference for immediate rather than delayed consumption. As generations of politicians have found to their cost, the promise of jam tomorrow comes a poor second to jam today.

- *Investment Opportunities*   Even when the above reasons are ignored, the fact still remains that money – like any other desirable commodity – has a price. Given the choice of £100 now or the same amount in one year's time, it is always preferable to take the £100 now because it could be invested over the next year at, say, a 10 per cent interest rate to produce £110 at the end of one year. If 10 per cent is the best available annual rate of interest, then one would be indifferent to (i.e. attach equal value to) receiving £100 now or £110 in one year's time. Expressed another way, the *present value* of £110 receivable one year hence is £100.

How did we obtain the present value? Simply by multiplying the future cash flow by the reciprocal of 1 plus the rate of interest, i,

$$\text{i.e. } \frac{1}{(1+i)} = \frac{1}{(1+0.10)} = \frac{1}{(1.1)} \text{ or } 0.9091$$

The present value of the investment is, therefore, the future cash flow multiplied by a *discount factor*:

$$£110 \times \frac{1}{(1.1)} = £100$$

Discounting is the process of adjusting future cash flows to their present values. It is, in effect, compounding in reverse.

Let us now return to the problem facing the management of Soldem Pathetic FC raised at the start of this chapter. Will buying Gary Spinnaker for £3 million create wealth for the club's shareholders and, at the same time, keep the fans happy? One way of assessing this is to assume the star is sold after one year for £4 million.

The present value (PV) of £4 million receivable one year hence, assuming a 10 per cent rate of interest as the reward that the shareholders demand for accepting the delayed pay-off, is:

$$PV = \text{discount factor} \times \text{future cash flow} = \frac{1}{1.10} \times £4 \text{ million}$$

$$= £3.636 \text{ million}$$

How much better off will the club be if it buys Spinnaker? The answer is, *in present value* terms:

$$(£3.636 \text{ million} - £3 \text{ million}) = £636{,}000.$$

This we call the *net present value* (NPV). The decision to buy the player makes economic sense; it promises to create wealth for the club and its shareholders, even excluding the likely additional gate receipts. Of course, nothing is certain in this world. Gary Spinnaker could break a leg in the very first game for his new club and never play again. In such an unfortunate situation, the club would achieve a negative NPV of £3 million, the initial cost. Alternatively, he could be insured against such injury, in which case there would be premiums to pay, resulting in a lower net present value.

Another way of looking at this issue is to ask whether the investment offers a return greater than could have been achieved by investing in financial, rather than human, assets. The return over one year from acquiring Spinnaker's services is:

$$\text{Return} = \frac{\text{profit}}{\text{investment}} = \frac{£4 \text{ million} - £3 \text{ million}}{£3 \text{ million}} = 33.3\%$$

If the available rate of interest is 10 per cent, the investment in Spinnaker is a considerably more rewarding prospect.

In this highly simplified example, we assumed that the future value was certain and the interest rate known. There is, of course, a spectrum of interest rates to be found listed in the financial press. This variety of rates of interest arises predominantly because of uncertainty surrounding the future and imperfections in the capital market. To simplify our understanding of the time-value of money concept, let us 'assume away' these realities. In our make-believe world, the lender knows with certainty the future returns arising from the proposal for which finance is sought, and can borrow or lend on a *perfect capital market*. The latter assumes that:

1. Relevant information is freely available to all participants in the market.
2. No transaction costs or taxes are involved in using the capital market.
3. No participant (borrower or lender) can influence the market price for funds by the scale of his activities.
4. All participants can lend and borrow at the same rate of interest.

Under such conditions, the corporate treasurer of a major company like Shell cannot raise funds any more cheaply than the chairman of Soldem Pathetic or any other firm. A single market rate of interest prevails. Borrowers and lenders will base time-related decisions on this unique market rate of interest. The impact of uncertainty will be discussed in later chapters; for the present these over-simplistic assumptions will help us to grasp the basics of financial management.

3.4   Compounding and discounting

The process of *compounding* provides a convenient way of adjusting for the time-value of money. An investment made now in the capital market of $£V_0$ gives rise to a cash flow of $£V_0(1+i)^2$ after two years, and so on. In general, the *terminal or future value* (FV) of $£V_0$ invested today at a compound rate of interest of $i\%$ for n years will be:

$$FV_{(i,n)} = £V_0(1+i)^n \tag{3.1}$$

Notice the use of the terms i and n. These will be applied consistently to indicate the relevant rate of interest and the relevant year, respectively.

Now try this example: find the future value of $£100$ invested for three years at a compound rate of interest of 10 per cent. Applying Equation (3.1):

$$FV_{(10\%, \, 3 \, yrs)} = £100 \, (1+0.10)^3$$
$$= £100 \times 1.331 = £133.10$$

The future value of $£100$ invested at 10 per cent for three years is $£133.10$, found by multiplying the investment of $£100$ by the *future value interest factor* (FVIF), in this case 1.331. Equation (3.1) can therefore be rewritten:

$$FV_{(i,n)} = £V_0 \times FVIF_{(i,n)}$$

The *present value interest factor* (PVIF) works in the opposite direction.

Taking the formula $FV_{(i,n)} = V_0(1+i)^n$ in Equation (3.1) and dividing both sides by $(1+i)^n$, we derive:

$$PV_{(i,n)} = \frac{FV_n}{(1+i)^n} \tag{3.2}$$

which can be read as the present value of cash flow FV receivable in n years' time given a rate of interest i. This is the process of *discounting* future sums to their present values. Applying the present value formula to check the previous example, the present value of $£133.10$ receivable three years hence, discounted at 10 per cent, would be $£100$:

$$PV_{(10\%, \, 3 \, yrs)} = \frac{£133.10}{(1+0.10)^3} = \frac{£133.10}{1.331} = £100$$

The message is: do not pay more than $£100$ today for an investment offering a certain return of $£133.10$ after three years, assuming a 10 per cent market rate of interest.

The effect of discounting

It is useful to see how the discounting process affects present values at different rates of interest. This is seen in Figure 3.1 using interest rates of between zero and 20 per cent. It will

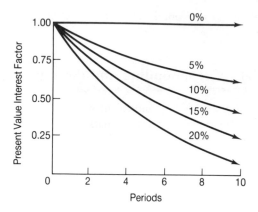

Figure 3.1   The relationship between present value interest factor and
interest over time

be seen that the value of £1 decreases very significantly as the rate and period increase. Indeed after, say, ten years for an interest rate of 20 per cent, the present value of a cash flow is worth only a small fraction of its nominal value.

Much of the tedium of using formulae and power functions can be eased by using discount tables or computer-based spreadsheet packages. Discount tables are provided in Appendix B, giving the present value of a future single sum, while Appendix C gives the present value of a constant annual sum (i.e. an annuity).

Table 3.1 summarizes the discount factors for three key rates of interest. Readers are recommended to have a 'feel' for how money changes with time for these rates of interest. The 15 per cent discount rate is particularly useful, because investment surveys (e.g. Pike 1988) suggest that this is the most popular discount rate used in evaluation of capital projects. It also happens to be easy to remember: every five years the discounted value halves. Thus, after five years the value of £1 is 50p, after 10 years, 25p, and so forth.

Many managers today enter into what appear to be profitable long-term contracts without fully recognizing the time-value of money.

Example

Robbie Dobson, a well-known soccer manager with a leading Dutch club, is nearing the end of his contract and has been offered a lucrative contract worth £75,000 for each of the next three years to manage the Swedish national team. If he took up such an appointment, he would lose in the region of £60,000 a year, being the new four-year contract offered by his present club. He also estimates that if he takes the new post, it would take about a year to find a club offering at least as good a salary as his present one. Assuming the market rate of interest is 10 per cent, would the move be economically sensible?

Dobson has a straight financial choice between 'staying put' or taking up the new appointment.

Table 3.1 Present value of a single future sum

Year	10%	15%	20%
0	£1.00	£1.00	£1.00
5	0.60	0.50	0.40
10	0.40	0.25	0.16
15	0.24	0.12	0.06
20	0.15	0.06	0.03
25	0.09	0.03	0.01

Option 1: stay put

$$PV = \frac{£60,000}{1.1} + \frac{£60,000}{(1.1)^2} + \frac{£60,000}{(1.1)^3} + \frac{£60,000}{(1.1)^4}$$

$$= \frac{£60,000}{1.1} + \frac{£60,000}{1.21} + \frac{£60,000}{1.331} + \frac{£60,000}{1.464}$$

$$= £190,194$$

Option 2: new appointment

$$PV = \frac{£75,000}{1.1} + \frac{£75,000}{(1.1)^2} + \frac{£75,000}{(1.1)^3} + \frac{0}{(1.1)^4}$$

$$= £186,514$$

In economic terms, Dobson would do better to stay where he is (although you may wish to question the assumption that it would take Dobson a year longer to find a job after being Swedish team manager!).

You will have observed that the annual income within each option was constant over the contract period. In such circumstances, the process of finding the present value can be greatly simplified by finding the present value of an annuity using the tables in Appendix C. These are simply the addition of the relevant single year factors.

From the table, the *present value interest factor for an annuity* (PVIFA) for 10 per cent for four years is 3.1699 and for three years is 2.4868. We simply multiply the constant income received each year by this factor:

$$Option\ 1\ £60,000 \times PVIFA_{(10,4)} = £60,000 \times 3.1699 = £190,194$$
$$Option\ 2\ £75,000 \times PVIFA_{(10,3)} = £75,000 \times 2.4868 = £186,510$$

It is standard practice to write interest factors as: Interest factor (rate, period).
Examples:
$PVIF_{(8,10)}$ is the present value interest factor at 8 per cent for ten years.
$PVIFA_{(10,4)}$ is the present value interest factor for an annuity at 10 per cent for four years.

3.5   Present value formulae

We have already seen that the present value of a future cash flow is found by multiplying the cash flow by the present value interest factor. The present value concept is not difficult to apply in practice. This section is devoted to explaining the various present value formulae, and illustrating how they can be applied to investment and financing problems. Throughout, we shall use the symbol £X to denote annual cash flow and i to denote the interest, or discount, rate (expressed as a percentage).

Present value

Equation (3.2) told us that the present value of £X receivable in n years is calculated from the expression:

$$PV_{(i,n)} = \frac{X_n}{(1+i)^n}$$
$$= X \text{ times } PVIF_{(i,n)}$$

Example

Calculate the present value of £1,000 receivable in ten years' time, assuming a discount rate of 14 per cent:

$$PVIF_{(14,10)} = \frac{1}{(1.14)^{10}} = 0.26974$$

Alternatively, the table in Appendix B provides the discount factor of 0.26974 for $n = 10$ and $i = 14$ per cent:

$$PV = 1000 \times 0.26974 = £269.74$$

The present value of £1,000 receivable ten years hence, discounted at 14 per cent, is thus £269.74.

Valuing perpetuities

Frequently, an investment pays a fixed sum each year for a specified number of years. A series of annual receipts or payments is termed an *annuity*. The simplest form of annuity is the infinite series or *perpetuity*. For example, certain government stocks offer a fixed annual income, but there is no obligation to repay the capital. The present value of such stocks (called *irredeemables*) is found by dividing the annual sum received by the annual rate of interest:

$$PV \text{ perpetuity} = \frac{X}{i} \qquad (3.3)$$

Example

Uncle George wishes to leave you in his will an annual sum of £10,000 a year starting next year. Assuming an interest rate of 10 per cent, how much of his estate must be set aside for this purpose? The answer is:

$$\text{PV perpetuity} = \frac{£10,000}{0.1} = £100,000$$

Suppose that your benevolent uncle now wishes to compensate for inflation estimated to be at 5 per cent per annum. The formula can be adjusted to allow for growth at the rate of g per cent p.a. in the annual amount. (The derivation for the present value of a growing perpetuity is found in Appendix II at the end of the chapter.)

$$\text{PV} = \frac{X}{i-g}$$

As long as the growth rate is less than the interest rate, we can compute the new present value required. In this case, it is:

$$\text{PV} = \frac{£10,000}{0.10 - 0.05} = £200,000$$

We will find in later chapters that this formula plays a key part in analysing financial decisions.

Valuing annuities

An annuity is an investment paying a fixed sum each year for a specified period of time. Examples of annuities include many credit agreements and house mortgages.

Because the life of the annuity is less than that for a perpetuity, its value will also be somewhat less. In fact, the formula for calculating the present value of an annuity of £A is found by calculating the present value of a perpetuity and deducting the present value of that element falling beyond the end of the annuity period. This gives the formula (see Appendix II at the end of chapter for the derivation) for the present value of an annuity (PVA):

$$\text{PVA}_{(i,n)} = A\left(\frac{1}{i} - \frac{1}{i(1+i)^n}\right) \tag{3.4}$$
$$= A \times \text{PVIFA}_{(i,\ n)}$$

In words, *the present value of an annuity for* n *years at* i *per cent is the annual sum multiplied by the appropriate present value interest factor for an annuity.*

Suppose an annuity of £1,000 is issued for twenty years at 10 per cent. Using the table in Appendix C, we find the present value as follows:

$$\text{PVA}_{(10,20)} = £1,000 \times \text{PVIFA}_{(10,20)}$$
$$= £1,000 \times 8.5136 = £8,513.60$$

Calculating interest rates

Sometimes, the present values and future cash flows are known, but the rate of interest is not given. A credit company may offer to lend you £1,000 today on condition that you repay £1,643 at the end of three years. To find the compound rate of interest on the loan, we solve the present value formula for i:

$$PV_{(i,n)} = PVIF_{(i,n)} \times FV$$

$$PVIF_{(i,3)} = \frac{PV}{FV} = \frac{£1000}{£1643} = 0.60864$$

Turning to the tables in Appendix B and looking for 0.6086 under the year 3 column, we find the rate of interest is 18 per cent.

Annual percentage rates (APR)

Unless otherwise stated, it is always assumed that discounting is an annual process; cash payments or benefits arise either at the start or the end of the year. Frequently, however, the contractual payment period is less than one year. Building societies and government bonds pay interest semi-annually or quarterly. Interest charged on credit cards is often applied monthly, or even daily. To compare the true costs or benefits of such financial contracts, it is necessary to determine the effective rate of interest, termed the annual percentage rate (APR). We can calculate the APR by applying the formula:

Annual Percentage Rate:

$$APR = \left(1 + \frac{i}{q}\right)^q - 1$$

where q is the payment frequency within each year and i is the specified annual rate of interest.

Table 3.2 Annual percentage rate for a loan with interest payable

Annually	$(1 + 0.22)$	$-1 = 0.22$ or 22%
Semi-annually	$\left(1 + \dfrac{0.22}{2}\right)^2$	$-1 = 0.232$ or 23.2%
Quarterly	$\left(1 + \dfrac{0.22}{4}\right)^4$	$-1 = 0.239$ or 23.9%
Monthly	$\left(1 + \dfrac{0.22}{12}\right)^{12}$	$-1 = 0.244$ or 24.4%
Daily	$\left(1 + \dfrac{0.22}{365}\right)^{365}$	$-1 = 0.246$ or 24.6%

What, then, is the APR for a 22 per cent p.a. loan payable on a variety of possible terms ranging from annually to daily? Table 3.2 calculates these APRs.

It can be seen that by charging compound interest on a daily basis, the effective annual charge is 24.6 per cent, some 2.6 per cent higher than on an annual basis. It is now a legal requirement for many financial contracts that the lender clearly states the APR.

3.6 Net present value

We have assumed that the paramount objective of the firm is to create as much wealth as possible for the owners through the efficient use of existing and future resources. To create wealth, the present value of all future cash inflows must exceed the present value of all anticipated cash outflows. Quite simply, *an investment with a positive net present value increases the owners' wealth.*

Most decisions involve both costs and benefits. Usually, the initial expenditure incurred on an investment undertaken is clear-cut: it is what we pay for it. This includes the cash paid to the supplier of the asset plus any other costs involved in making the project operational. The problems really start in measuring the worth of the investment project. What an asset is worth has little to do with what it cost or what value is placed on it in the firm's balance sheet. A machine standing in the firm's books at £20,000 may be worth far more if it is essential to the manufacture of a highly profitable product, or far less than this if rendered obsolete through the advent of new technology. In order to measure its worth, we need to consider the *value of the current and future benefits less costs* arising from the investment. Wherever possible, these benefits should be expressed in terms of *cash flows*. Sometimes (as will be discussed later) it is impossible to quantify benefits so conveniently. Typically, investment decisions involve an initial capital expenditure followed by a stream of cash receipts and disbursements in subsequent periods. The net present value (NPV) method is applied to evaluate the desirability of investment opportunities. NPV is defined as:

$$NPV = \frac{X_1}{(1+k)} + \frac{X_2}{(1+k)^2} + \frac{X_3}{(1+k)^3} + \ldots + \frac{X_n}{(1+k)^n} - I$$

which may be summarized as:

$$NPV = \sum_{t=1}^{n} \frac{X_t}{(1+k)^t} - I$$

Where:

X_t = the net cash flow arising at the end of year t
I = the initial cost of the investment
n = the project's life
k = the minimum required rate of return on the investment or discount rate.

(The Greek letter Σ, or sigma, denotes the sum of all values in a particular series.)

Note that we have introduced a subtle change in notation, replacing i, which denoted the general market rate interest, by k, which refers to the rate of return that must be achieved by the firm in question. As we shall see, k may vary significantly from firm to firm.

A project's net present value (NPV) is determined by summing the net annual cash flows discounted at a rate which reflects the cost of an investment of equivalent risk on the capital market, and deducting the initial outlay.

THE NET PRESENT VALUE RULE

Wealth is maximized by *accepting all projects that offer positive net present values* when discounted at the required rate of return for each investment.

Examination of the NPV formula reveals that most of the main elements are largely externally determined. For example, in the case of investment in a new piece of manufacturing equipment, management has relatively little influence over the price paid, the life expectancy or the discount rate. These elements are determined, respectively, by the price of capital goods, the rate of new technological development and the returns required by the capital market. Management's main opportunity for wealth-creation lies in its ability to implement and manage the project so as to generate positive net cash flows over the project's economic life.

An NPV example: Gazza Ltd

The management of Gazza Ltd is currently evaluating an investment costing £10,000. Anticipated net cash inflows are £6,000 received at the end of Year 1, and £6,000 received at the end of Year 2. The firm operates in a low-risk industry and divides its various projects into three categories: (1) low-risk, where the required rate of return is 10 per cent; (2) medium-risk, where the required rate of return is 13 per cent; and (3) high-risk, where the required rate of return is 16 per cent. Using the NPV formula given above will provide the estimates illustrated in Table 3.3, which shows the NPV of the project under each of the three risk classifications.

Starting with the low-risk assumption, the cash flows are discounted at a rate of 10 per cent. The Year 1 cash flow has a present value of £5,400 and the Year 2 cash flow has a present value of £5,000. The present value of the inflows is therefore £10,400 and, after deducting the initial outlay which has a present value of £10,000, the project has a net present value of

Table 3.3 Gazza Ltd: net present value of a project

Risk Class	Discount Rate	Present Value of Cash Inflows Year 1	Year 2	Cost	NPV
Low	10%	£5,400	£5,000	£10,000	£400
Medium	13%	£5,300	£4,700	£10,000	nil
High	16%	£5,200	£4,400	£10,000	−£400

£400. The project should be accepted; it has a positive NPV. It does in fact create wealth. If the projected cash flows are generally expected to be achieved, the market value of the firm should rise by £400. On the other hand, if the project is classified as high-risk, the cash inflows are discounted at a rate of 16 per cent and the NPV is estimated at −£400. The project is unacceptable; it has a negative NPV. Its acceptance would have the effect of reducing the firm's market value by £400. Clearly, it would not be wise to exchange £10,000 today for future cash flows having a present value today of only £9,600. If the project is classified as average risk, the discount rate used is 13 per cent, yielding an NPV of zero. The project is just acceptable; it yields 13 per cent which is the required rate of return. From this simple example, we can draw two important conclusions:

1. Project acceptability depends upon cash flows and risk.
2. The higher the risk of a given set of expected cash flows (and the higher the applied discount rate), the lower will be its present value, that is, the assessment of the value by the recipient of a given expected cash flow decreases as its risk increases.

NPV break-even analysis

The present value approach for annuities referred to in an earlier section is also useful in NPV analysis.

Barnes plc is considering a new investment costing £32,500 and expected to produce net cash receipts of £10,000 p.a. for the next five years. Assuming a 10 per cent discount rate, is the investment worthwhile?

$$
\begin{aligned}
\text{PVA} &= £10,000 \times \text{PVIFA}_{(10.5)} \\
&= £10,000 \times 3.7908 = £37,908 \\
\text{NPV} &= \text{PV of annuity} - \text{Investment cost} \\
&= £37,908 - £32,500 = £5,408
\end{aligned}
$$

The project offers a positive NPV of £5,410 and should be accepted.

Suppose Barnes now wants to determine the minimum annual cash flow that will be necessary to make the project acceptable, sometimes termed the break-even NPV. In effect, this means that the present value of the annuity to give a zero NPV (termed A_{min}) minus the initial outlay must equal zero:

$$
[A_{min} \times \text{PVIFA}_{(10.5)}] - I = 0
$$

Therefore,

$$
A_{min} = \frac{I}{\text{PVIFA}_{(10.5)}} = \frac{£32,500}{3.791} = £8,573
$$

The annual cash flow could fall as low as £8,573 before the investment ceases to be viable. The minimum annual cash benefit receivable each year to break even is therefore found by dividing the initial investment outlay by the present value annuity interest factor.

Why NPV makes sense

We examine in the appendix to this chapter, at a more rigorous level, the rationale for the NPV approach and how the net present value concept permits efficient separation of ownership and corporate management.

The main rationale for why the net present value approach makes sense may be summarized as follows:

1. Managers are assumed to act in the best interest of the owners or shareholders. This they can do by seeking to increase shareholders' wealth in the form of maximizing cash flows through time. There is a market rate of exchange between current and future wealth, which is reflected in the current rate of interest.

2. Managers should undertake all projects up to the point at which the marginal return on the investment is equal to the rate of interest on equivalent financial investments in the capital market. This is exactly the same as the net present value rule: accept all investments offering positive net present values when discounted at the equivalent market rate of interest. The result is an increase in the market value of the firm and thus in the market value of the shareholders' stake in the firm.

3. Management need not concern itself with shareholders' particular time patterns of consumption or risk preferences. In well-functioning capital markets, shareholders can borrow or lend funds to achieve their personal consumption requirements. Further-more, by carefully combining risky and safe investments they can achieve the desired risk characteristics for those consumption requirements.

3.7 Summary

In this chapter, we have examined the meaning of wealth and its fundamental importance in financial management. Given that for most capital projects there is a time-lag between the initial investment outlay and the receipt of benefits, consideration must be given to both the timing and size of the costs and benefits. Whenever there is an alternative opportunity to use funds committed to a project (e.g. to invest in the capital market or in other capital projects) cash today is worth more than cash received tomorrow.

Key points

- Money, like any other scarce resource, has a cost. We allow for the time-value of money by the process of discounting. The higher the interest cost for a future cash flow, the lower its present value.
- Discount tables take away much of the tedium of discounting – but computer spreadsheets eliminate it altogether!

- Standard discount factors are:
  PVIF = the present value interest factor
  PVIFA = the present value interest factor for an annuity
  Conventional shorthand is:
    Interest factor (rate of interest, number of years)
    e.g. $\text{PVIFA}_{(10,3)}$ reads 'the present value interest factor of an annuity at 10 per cent for three years'.
- The net present value (NPV) of a project is found by (1) discounting a project's future net cash flows at the minimum required rate of return for the project; and (2) deducting the initial investment outlay from the total present values over the project's life.
- Where the corporate goal is to maximize the wealth of its shareholders, the simple decision rule is:
    When the NPV is positive, accept the investment.
    When the NPV is negative, reject the investment.

Appendix I

The investment–consumption decision

Theoretical case for NPV

We suggested earlier in this chapter that managers should base investment decisions on the net present value criterion: accept all projects which offer a positive net present value. It is now necessary to justify this claim by presenting the theoretical case as to why the NPV rule makes sense both for the firm and its owners.

There are fundamentally three financial decisions facing individuals and shareholders.

1. *Consumption decisions:* How much of the resources available should I spend on immediate consumption?

2. *Investment decisions:* How much of the resources available should I forgo *now* in the expectation of *increased* resources at some time in the future? How should such decisions be made?

3. *Financing decisions:* How much cash should I borrow or lend to enable me to carry out the above investment and consumption decisions?

Clearly, these decisions are interrelated and should not, therefore, be viewed in isolation.

Individuals are faced with the choice of how much of their wealth should be *consumed* immediately, and how much should be *invested* for consumption at a later date. This applies equally to the young child with his or her pocket money, the undergraduate with his or her grant, the professional with his or her capital, and the shareholder with his or her investment portfolio. All these cases involve a trade-off between immediate and delayed consumption.

We are primarily concerned with how managers should reach investment decisions.

Cash generated from business operations can be utilized in two ways: it can be distributed to the shareholders in the form of a dividend, or reinvested within the business. At least once each year the directors decide how much of the shareholders' wealth to distribute in the form of dividends and how much to withhold for investment purposes, such as building up stock levels or purchasing new equipment. The shareholders will only be willing to forgo a higher *present* level of consumption (in the form of dividends) if they expect an even greater *future* level of consumption. It is this willingness to give up consumption now with the aim of increasing future consumption which characterizes investment decisions.

Graphical example

David Platt is the sole proprietor of Platt Enterprises, a new business with just one asset of £4 million in cash. He has a number of interesting investment ideas (all lasting just a year) but before investing his capital within the business, he asks the following key questions:

1. What is the return I could earn by investing my capital (or some part of it) in the capital market?
2. How much should I invest within the business?
3. What is the net present value of the business?

Before addressing these issues and in order to present a conceptual framework for the NPV rule, it is first necessary to make certain simplifying assumptions that allow us to portray in two-dimensional form the essential features of the investment-consumption decision model. The basic assumptions are:

1. Investors are wealth-maximizers.
2. Only two periods are considered – the present period (t_0) and the next period (t_1). This two-period model implies that investments involve an immediate cash outlay in t_0 in return for a cash benefit in the following period, t_1.
3. All information for decision-making is known with certainty.
4. Investment projects are entirely independent of each other and are divisible.

The reader will recognize that these assumptions are clearly unrealistic in the actual setting within which investment decisions are taken in practice. None the less, unless the logic of the net present value approach is first understood within this highly simplified setting, it is doubtful whether its relevance and limitations can be fully grasped within the complex real world of business.

Figure 3.2 illustrates the investment opportunities for Platt Enterprises. The curve is the *investment opportunities line*, representing all the capital projects available to the firm, ranked in order of profitability. At one extreme, Platt may decide to pay himself a massive dividend by liquidating the business and receiving £4 million today. At the other extreme, he could invest the whole £4 million in one-year capital projects to obtain £4 million next year.

How should he proceed to make investment decisions under the assumptions laid down? He requires a criterion for judging between cash today and cash receivable next year. In

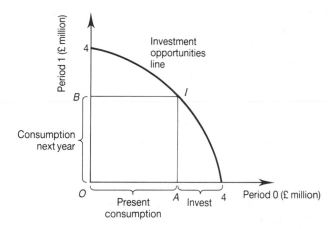

Figure 3.2   Investment opportunities for Platt Enterprises

effect, he requires a rate of exchange for the transfer of wealth across time. Suppose he requires a minimum of £115 receivable next year to induce him to give up £100 now, the rate of exchange would be £115$_{t0}$:£100$_{t1}$, or £1.15:£1. This represents a premium for delayed consumption of one year of

$$\frac{£115}{£100} - 1 = 0.15, \text{ or } 15\%$$

This exchange rate between today's money and tomorrow's money varies with the level of present consumption sacrificed. Platt may be willing to forgo the first £100 of potential dividend in return for an additional 15 per cent next year, but to persuade him to delay the consumption of a further £100 will probably require something in excess of 15 per cent. This variable exchange rate for the transfer of wealth across time at various levels of investment is termed the *Marginal Rate of Time Preference*, and will differ from individual to individual.

It will be observed that the investment opportunities line is *concave* to the origin rather than a straight line. This shape indicates the decreasing returns to scale of each subsequent investment opportunity. As a wealth-maximizer, Platt will first select those investment projects offering the greatest return and work down towards those offering the least return. Somewhere along the line (project I in Figure 3.2) the owner-manager will stop. Why should Platt not wish to undertake further investment? Point I represents the marginal project beyond which it ceases to be worthwhile to invest – the marginal return from the next £1 in investment would not be sufficient to compensate for the sacrifice involved in giving up a further £1 in dividends. For Platt, I represents the point where the *marginal return on investment equals his marginal rate of time preference*.

Borrowing and lending opportunities

So far, under our highly simplistic assumptions, our owner-manager, Platt, is given only two decisions – consumption and investment decisions. The more he invests, the less he can consume now, and vice versa. This ignores the third choice open to him, namely the _financing decision_. Where capital markets exist, individuals and firms can buy and sell not only _real_ assets (i.e. fixed and current) but also _financial_ assets. As we saw earlier in this chapter, when perfect capital markets are introduced (i.e. no borrower can influence the interest rate, all traders have equal and costless access to information, no transaction costs or taxes), there will be a single market rate of interest for both borrowing and lending.

The existence of a capital market permits owners to transfer wealth across time in a manner different from the investment-consumption pattern of the firm. This is depicted in our example by the interest rate line in Figure 3.3 which represents the exchange rate between current and future cash flows under perfect capital market conditions. Its slope is $(1 + i)$, where i denotes the single period rate of interest.

In our example, the interest rate is found by relating present wealth to next year's wealth at any point on the graph. At the extremes this is £6 million/£5 million = 1.20. The interest rate is therefore 20 per cent.

With the introduction of financing opportunities afforded by the capital market, Platt can now identify the appropriate level of corporate investment. He should continue to invest until project M – where the interest rate line is tangential to the investment opportunities line. At this point, all investments offering a return at least as high as the market rate of interest are accepted. They all offer positive net present values. Reading off the graph in Figure 3.3, we find that investment as far as M would mean a dividend of £3 million today and an investment of £1 million (i.e. £4 million − £3 million). Quite simply, it is not worth investing further as the projects offer negative NPVs. To put it another way, it would be more beneficial for Platt to withdraw the £3 million from the business and to invest it in the capital market at 20 per cent p.a.

What then is the net present value of the £1 million investment programme envisaged by

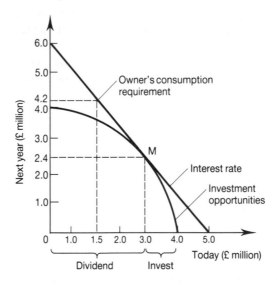

Figure 3.3 Investment and financing opportunities for Platt Enterprises

Platt? Reading off the investment opportunities curve, we find that the capital outlay will produce cash flows of £2.4 million next year. The NPV is therefore £1 million:

$$\text{NPV} = \frac{£2.4\text{m}}{1.2} - £1\text{m} = £2\text{m} - £1\text{m} = £1\text{m}$$

The new value of the business becomes £5 million (starting capital of £4 million plus NPV of investment programme).

We suggested earlier that the £3 million not invested by the firm would be paid out as a dividend. An alternative would be for the firm to invest all or part of it on behalf of the owners in the capital market until such time as investment opportunities offering positive NPVs arise. Suppose Platt is only looking for a dividend of £1.5 million. The extra £1.5 million can be invested in the capital market to earn £1.8 million next year (i.e. £4.2m − £2.4m, or £1.5m × 1.20). Platt's cash flow next year will then be the £2.4m from capital investments plus the £1.8m from financial investments.

Separating ownership from management

Most firms are characterized by a large number of shareholders (owners), few of whom are actively involved in the management of the firm. It would obviously be an impossible task for managers to evaluate investment decisions on the basis of the personal investment-consumption preferences of all the shareholders. Happily, the existence of capital markets renders any such foolhardy attempt unnecessary. Managers do not need to select an investment programme whose cash flows exactly match shareholders' preferred time patterns of consumption. The task of the manager is to maximize present value by accepting all investment proposals offering a return at least as good as the market rate of interest.

This criterion maximizes the current wealth of the shareholders who can then transform that wealth into whatever time pattern of consumption they require. This they can do by lending or borrowing on the capital market until their marginal rate of time preference equals the capital market rate of interest. This *Separation Theorem*, as it is usually termed, leads to the following decision rules:

1. Corporate management should invest in projects offering positive net present values when discounted at the capital market rate.
2. Shareholders should borrow or lend on the capital market to produce the wealth distribution which best meets their personal time pattern of consumption requirements.

Capital market imperfections

Based on the assumptions laid down at the start of the chapter, we have shown that managers should undertake investments up to the point at which the marginal return on investment is equal to the rate of return in the capital market. It will be recalled that two important assumptions were the existence of *perfect* capital markets and the absence of risk. When these assumptions are relaxed, the argument in favour of the net present value rule becomes

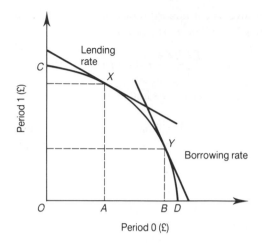

Figure 3.4   Investment decisions in imperfect capital markets

weaker. For one thing, there is no longer a unique rate of interest in the capital market, but a range of interest rates varying with the status of borrower, the amount required and the perceived riskiness of the investment. A detailed analysis of investment under risk is the subject of subsequent chapters, but at this stage, we can say that a project's return should be compared with the rate of return on investments in the capital market of *equivalent risk* – the greater the investment risk, the higher the required rate of return.

A major concern involves the particular capital market imperfections where the borrowing rate is substantially higher than the lending rate. When this is the case the two-period investment model will resemble Figure 3.4. The steeper line represents the interest rate for the borrower and the flatter line represents the lending rate. The existence of two different interest rates gives rise to two different points on the investment opportunities line CD. Prospective borrowers, having to pay a higher rate of interest for funds, would prefer the company to invest only £BD this year (i.e. up to project Y). However, prospective lenders will require the company to discount at the lower lending rate leading to a much greater investment of £AD, with investment X being the marginal project.

There is no simple solution to the investment–consumption decision when capital market imperfections prevail. Fortunately, in the United Kingdom, United States, Japan and much of Western Europe, capital markets are highly competitive and function fairly well so that differences between lending and borrowing rates are minimized, but significant differentials can be found in emerging capital markets such as that in Hungary.

We have examined, with the aid of two-period investment-consumption models, why the net present value approach makes sense. This logic can be summarized as follows:

1. Managers are assumed to act in the best interest of the owners or shareholders. This they can do by seeking to increase shareholders' wealth in the form of maximizing cash flows through time. There is a market rate of exchange between current and future wealth which is reflected in the current rate of interest.

2. Managers should undertake all projects up to the point at which the marginal return on

the investment is equal to the rate of interest on equivalent financial investments in the capital market. This is exactly the same as the net present value rule: accept all investments offering positive net present values when discounted at the equivalent market rate of interest. The result is an increase in the market value of the firm and thus in the market value of the shareholders' stake in the firm.

3. Management need not concern itself with shareholders' particular time patterns of consumption or risk preferences. In well-functioning capital markets, shareholders can borrow or lend funds to achieve their personal consumption requirements. Furthermore, by carefully combining risky and safe investments they can achieve the desired risk characteristics for those consumption requirements.

Appendix II   Present value formulae

1. *Formula for the present value of a perpetuity*

This formula derives from the present value formula:

$$PV = \frac{X}{1+i} + \frac{X}{(1+i)^2} + \frac{X}{(1+i)^3} + \dots$$

Let $X/(1+i) = a$ and $1/(1+i) = b$. We now have:

(i) $PV = a(1 + b + b^2 + \dots)$

Multiplying both sides by b gives us:

(ii) $PVb = a(b + b^2 + b^3 + \dots)$

Subtracting (ii) from (i) we have:

$$PV(1-b) = a$$

Substituting for a and b,

$$PV\left(1 - \frac{1}{1+i}\right) = \frac{X}{1+i}$$

Multiplying both sides by $(1+i)$ and rearranging, we have:

$$PV = \frac{X}{i}$$

2. *Formula for the present value of a growing perpetuity*

In note 1 we obtained:

$$PV(1-b) = a$$

Redefining $b = (1+g)/(1+i)$ and keeping $a = X/(1+i)$:

$$PV\left(1 - \frac{1+g}{1+i}\right) = \frac{X}{1+i}$$

Multiplying both sides by $(1+i)$ and rearranging, we have:

$$PV = \frac{X}{i-g}$$

3. *The present value of annuities*

The above perpetuities were special cases of the annuity formula. To find the present value of an annuity, we can first use the perpetuity formula and deduct from it the years outside the annuity period. For example, if an annuity of £100 is issued for twenty years at 10 per cent, we would find the present value of a perpetuity of £100 using the formula:

$$PV = \frac{X}{i} = \frac{100}{0.10} = £1,000$$

Next, find the present value of a perpetuity for the same amount, *starting* at Year 20 using the formula:

$$PV = \frac{X}{i(1+i)^t} = \frac{£100}{0.10(1+0.10)^{20}} = £148.64$$

The difference will be:

$$PV \text{ of annuity} = \frac{X}{i} - \frac{X}{i(1+i)^t}$$
$$= £1,000 - £148.64 = £851.36$$

The present value of an annuity of £100 for twenty years discounted at 10 per cent is £851.36.

The formula may be simplified to:

$$PV \text{ of annuity} = X\left(\frac{1}{i} - \frac{1}{i(1+i)^t}\right)$$

Further reading

Brealey and Myers (1991) and Lumby (1991) provide a good theoretical case for net present value. Levy and Sarnat (1990) give perhaps the best treatment of discounted cash flow analysis. The work of Hirshleifer (1958) provides the background to the approach adopted in the appendix.

Questions

Self-test questions

1. Define the main elements in the capital budgeting decision.
2. Give four reasons why £1 now is worth more than £1 tomorrow.
3. Why should managers seek to maximize net present value? Is business not about maximizing profit?
4. Explain the difference between accounting profit and cash flow.
5. Calculate the present value of £1,000 receivable twelve years hence, assuming the discount rate (cost of capital, percentage interest rate, discount factor, capitalization rate) to be 12 per cent.

Exercises (Answers to questions 1–5 in Appendix A)

1. Calculate the present value of £623 receivable in eight years' time plus £1,092 receivable eight years after that, assuming an interest rate of 7 per cent.
2. Calculate the present value of a ten-year annuity of £100, assuming an interest rate of 20 per cent.
3. Calculate the present value of £250 receivable annually for twenty-one years plus £1,200 receivable after twenty-two years, assuming an interest rate of 11 per cent.
4. A firm is considering the purchase of a machine which will cost £20,000. It is estimated that annual savings of £5,000 will result from the machine's installation, that the life of the machine will be five years, and that its residual value will be £1,000. Assuming the required rate of return to be 10 per cent, what action would you recommend?
5. (Based on the appendix to this chapter) Ron Bratt decides to commence trading as a sportswear retailer, with initial capital of £6,000 in cash. The capital market and investment opportunities available are shown below:

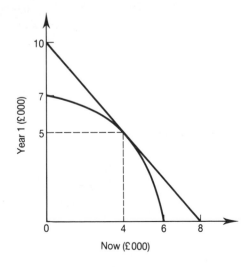

You are required to calculate:
(a) How much the firm should invest in real assets.
(b) The market rate of interest for the business.
(c) The average rate of return on investment.
(d) The net present value of the investment.
(e) The value of the firm after this level of investment.
(f) Next year's dividend if Bratt only requires a current dividend of £3,000.

6. Calculate the net present value of projects A and B, assuming discount rates of 0 per cent, 10 per cent and 20 per cent.

	A £	B £
Initial outlay	1,200	1,200
Cash receipts:		
Year 1	1,000	100
Year 2	500	600
Year 3	100	1,100

Which is the superior project at each level of discount rate? Why do they not all produce the same answer?

7. The directors of Yorkshire Autopoints are considering the acquisition of an automatic car-washing installation. The initial cost and setting-up expenses will amount to about £140,000. Its estimated life is about seven years, and estimated annual accounting profit is as follows:

Year	1	2	3	4	5	6	7
Operational cash flow (£)	30,000	50,000	60,000	60,000	30,000	20,000	20,000
Depreciation (£)	20,000	20,000	20,000	20,000	20,000	20,000	20,000
Accounting profit (£)	10,000	30,000	40,000	40,000	10,000	—	—

At the end of its seven-year life, the installation will yield only a few pounds in scrap value. The company classifies its projects as follows:

	Required rate of return
Low risk	20 per cent
Average risk	30 per cent
High risk	40 per cent

Car-washing projects are estimated to be of average risk.

(a) Should the car-wash be installed?
(b) List some of the popular errors made in assessing capital projects.

Work-based assignment

List three decisions in your business where cash flows arise over a lengthy time-period and where discounted cash flow may be beneficial. To what extent is DCF applied (formally or intuitively)? What are the dangers of ignoring the time-value of money in these particular cases?

CHAPTER 4
Valuation of assets, shares and companies

A VALUATION POSER

In 1989, US investment house, Kohlberg-Kravis-Roberts (KKR), the acknowledged 'champs' in organizing and mounting 'leveraged buy-outs' (in essence, these involve buying companies with borrowed capital to be repaid by selling at a profit some or all of the acquired assets), bought the giant food group RJR Nabisco for $25 bn, in what was then the world's largest ever takeover. In order to repay borrowings, KKR swiftly launched a disposal programme, including the sale of a package of assets to the French food company, BSN, for a total of $2.5 bn, in June 1989. The following month, BSN sold the Walkers and Smiths crisps companies to the US firm Pepsico for $860m. This figure was greeted with some surprise by many City analysts who reckoned it at $300m higher than the value placed on the firms in the sale to BSN, reflecting a profit of over 50 per cent in less than a month. Did someone boob at KKR or were the City experts wrong?

4.1 Introduction

The financial manager controls capital flows into, within and out of the enterprise to achieve maximum value for shareholders. The acid test of effectiveness is the extent to which these operations enhance shareholder wealth. As an action guide, the financial manager needs a thorough understanding of the determinants of value to anticipate the consequences of alternative decisions. If there is an active and efficient market in the company's shares, the market itself should provide a reliable indication of value. However, managers may feel that the guidelines provided by the market are biased or incomplete, and may wish to undertake their own valuation exercises. Indeed, some managers behave as though they do not accept the Efficient Markets Hypothesis (EMH) outlined in Chapter 2. In addition, there are specific cases where financial managers must undertake valuations, for example, when valuing a proposed acquisition, or when assessing the value of their own companies when defending against takeover raiders.

Valuation skills thus have an important strategic dimension. In order to advise on the desirability of alternative financial strategies, the financial manager needs to assess the value to the firm of pursuing each option. This chapter examines the major difficulties in valuation and explains the main methods available.

LEARNING OBJECTIVES

The ultimate effectiveness of financial management is judged by its contribution to the value of the enterprise. This chapter aims to:

- Provide the reader with an understanding of the main ways of valuing companies and shares, and the limitations of these.
- Stress that valuation is an imprecise art.
- Offer an understanding of the dividend valuation model, an important underpinning of the analysis of dividend policy in Chapter 13.

A sound grasp of the principles of valuation is essential for many other areas of financial management.

4.2 The valuation problem

Valuation is far from an exact science. Anyone who has ever attempted to buy or sell a second-hand car or house will appreciate that value, like beauty, is in the eye of the beholder. The value of any tradeable item is whatever the highest bidder is prepared to (genuinely) offer. With a well-established market in the asset concerned, and if the asset is fairly homogeneous, valuation is relatively simple. *So long as the market can be accepted as being reasonably efficient, then the market price can be trusted as a fair assessment of value.*

Problems arise in valuing unique assets, or assets which have no recognizable market, such as the shares of unquoted companies. Even with a ready market, valuation may be complicated by a change of use or ownership. For example, the value of an incompetently managed company may be less than the same enterprise when shaken up by replacement managers wielding new brooms. But by how much would value increase? Valuing the firm under new management would require access to key financial data not readily available to outsiders. Similarly, a conglomerate which has grown haphazardly may be worth more when broken up and its individual components sold off to the highest bidders. But who are the prospective bidders, and how much might they offer? Undoubtedly, valuation in practice involves considerable informed guesswork.

Returning to the KKR/BSN case, we do not know how the valuations were arrived at. All we know is that there was no consistent assessment of value between two sets of financial experts. Indeed, this illustrates the paramount lesson of the hazardous activity of valuation – about the only certain aspect of a valuation is that it will be wrong! However, this is no excuse for hand-wringing. A key question in such cases is whether the valuations were reasonable in the light of the information available at the time. The advisers to the British government in its privatization programme have been frequently criticized for underpricing issues like British Gas, British Airways and the Water Authorities, and there is little doubt that much of this criticism is well justified. On the other hand, the difficulties of setting a value on unique enterprises, often very large ones, should not be ignored. It should be noted, moreover, that few 'hindsight critics' offered their own valuations before the event.

Several analytical techniques are available to assist the financial manager, but none is totally fool-proof. The three basic valuation methods are net asset value, the dividend valuation model and earnings valuation, which often give different answers. Different approaches may be required when valuing whole companies from those appropriate to valuing part shares of companies.

4.3   Valuing a company using published accounts

A tempting starting point in trying to value a company is the asset value stated in the accounts. This approach to valuation has obvious appeal for those who are impressed by the apparent objectivity of published accounting data. The Balance Sheet shows the recorded value for the total of fixed assets, both tangible and intangible, and current assets, stocks and work-in-progress, debtors and any holdings of liquid assets such as cash and marketable securities. After deducting the debts of the company, both long- and short-term creditors (including trade creditors), from the total asset value, the residual figure is the *Net Asset Value (NAV)*, i.e. the value of the company's net assets or the book value of the owners' stake in the company, sometimes called 'owners' equity'.

The last published Balance Sheet for Braythorn plc, prepared in vertical form, and shown in Table 4.1, pinpoints its NAV. The NAV is simply the net assets figure, £42m,

Table 4.1   Balance Sheet for Braythorn plc as at 31 December 1991

		£m
Assets employed:		
Fixed assets (net)		48
Current assets:		
stocks	12	
debtors	8	
cash	3	
Creditors falling due within one year:	(19)	
Net current assets		4
Total assets less total liabilities		52
Creditors falling due after one year		(10)
Net assets		42
Financed by:		
Called up share capital		25
Reserves		17
Shareholder funds		42

which, by definition, must coincide with shareholder funds, i.e. the value of the shareholders' equity stake net of all liabilities. However, for a variety of reasons, the NAV is a very unreliable indicator of company value in most circumstances. Most crucially, it is based on a valuation of the separate assets of the enterprise, although the accountant will assert that the valuation has been made on a 'going concern basis', i.e. as if the bundle of assets will continue to operate in their current use. However, such a valuation usually understates the earning power of the assets.

The market value of Braythorn will probably exceed the £42m balance sheet value because its assets, when combined with its workforce and strategies, are worth more than the bare assets alone. If the profit potential of the company is suspect, however, then break-up value assumes greater importance. The value of the assets in their best alternative use (e.g. selling them off) might then exceed the current value of the business, providing a signal to the owners to disband the enterprise and shift the resources into alternative uses.

Problems with asset valuation

The NAV, even as a measure of break-up value, is usually seriously defective for three main reasons.

Fixed asset values are usually out-of-date

Book values of equipment, e.g. £48m for Braythorn, are expressed net of depreciation, the result of a concern to write off assets over their assumed useful lives. Depreciating an asset, however, is not an attempt to arrive at a market-oriented assessment of value. Most commonly, companies use historic cost as a basis for depreciation. It would be an amazing coincidence if the historic cost less accumulated depreciation were an accurate measure of the value of equipment to the owners especially at times of generally rising prices. Some companies try to overcome this problem by periodic revaluations of assets, especially freehold property. However, few companies do this annually, and even when they do, the resulting estimate is only valid at the Balance Sheet date.

A more sophisticated approach (but stoutly resisted by the accounting profession) is to adopt current cost accounting (CCA). Under CCA, assets are valued at their replacement cost, i.e. what it would cost the firm now to obtain assets of similar vintage. For example, if a machine cost £1m five years ago, and asset prices have inflated at 10 per cent p.a., the cost of a new asset would be about £1.6m. The historic cost less five years' depreciation on a straight-line basis, and assuming a ten-year life, would be £0.5m. However, the replacement cost, allowing for depreciation, would be around £0.8m.

There are obvious problems in applying CCA. For example, estimating current cost requires knowledge of the rate of inflation of identical assets, and of the impact of changing technology on replacement values. Nevertheless, the replacement cost measure is often far closer to a market value than historic cost less depreciation. Ideally, companies should revalue assets annually but the time and costs involved are generally considered prohibitive.

Stock values are often unreliable

Accepted accounting practice (SSAP 9) values stocks at the lower of cost or net realizable value. Such a conservative figure may hide appreciation in the value of stocks, e.g. when raw material and fuel prices are rising. Conversely, in some activities, fashions and tastes change rapidly, and although the recorded stock value might have been reasonably accurate at the Balance Sheet date, it may look inflated some time later.

The debtors figure may be suspect

Similar comments apply to the recorded figure for debtors. Not all debtors can be easily converted into cash since debtors may include certain dubious or bad debts, although these should have been provided for. Numerous 'phantom' debtors were found by the electronics and defence contractor Ferranti, when it consolidated the accounts of its 1988 acquisition, US armaments manufacturer International Signal Corporation. ISC had carried some highly questionable debtors in its accounts for several years. As a result of this revelation, and allowing also for significant over-valuation of work-in-progress, Ferranti was forced, in 1990, to write off £215m of shareholder funds, when it finally realized the magnitude of the problem within its new subsidiary. The debtor collection period, supplemented by an ageing profile of outstanding debts, should have provided clues to the reliability of the debtors position.

A further problem: valuation of intangible assets

Unfortunately, even if these problems can be overcome, the resulting asset valuation is often less than the market value of the firm. A good example of this is the case of many 'people businesses', which typically have few fixed assets and low stock levels. Based on the accounts, several leading quoted advertising agencies and consultancies have tiny or even negative NAVs. Why then do they often have substantial market values? The answer is simple. The 'people' they employ are 'assets' whose interactions confer earning power, the quality which ultimately determines value. However, like professional footballers, they do not appear on Balance Sheets. Some companies have attempted to close the gap between economic value and NAV by valuing certain intangible assets under their control, such as brand names.

Valuation of brands

The brand valuation issue came to the fore in 1988 when the Swiss confectionery and food giant Nestlé offered to buy Rowntrees, the UK chocolate manufacturer, for more than double its market value. This event generated considerable discussion about whether and why the market had undervalued Rowntrees and perhaps other companies which had invested heavily in brands, either via internal product development or by acquisition. Later that year, Grand Metropolitan Hotels decided to capitalize acquired brands in their accounts, and were followed by several other owners of 'household name' brands.

Decisions to enter the value of brands in Balance Sheets seemed a direct consequence of the prevailing official accounting guidelines, relating to the treatment of assets acquired at prices above book value. These have enabled firms to write off goodwill to reserves, thus reducing capital, rather than carry it as an asset to be depreciated against income in the Profit and Loss Account, as in most European economies. UK regulations allowed companies to report higher earnings per share, but with reduced shareholder funds thus raising the return on capital, especially so for merger-active companies.

The impact of brand valuation is to raise the intangible assets in the Balance Sheet and thus the NAV. Some chairmen have presented the policy as an effort to make the market more aware of the 'true value' of the company. Under *strong-form* capital market efficiency, the effect on share price would be negligible since the market would already be aware of the economic value of brands which would account for the market value exceeding the asset value in the first place!

However, under weaker forms of market efficiency, if placing a Balance Sheet value on brands provides genuinely new information, it may become an important vehicle for improving the stock market's ability to set 'fair' prices.

AN ILLUSTRATION OF BRAND VALUATION: CADBURY SCHWEPPES

In February 1990, Cadbury Schweppes, the confectionery and soft drinks group, placed a Balance Sheet value of £307m on the main brands acquired during the previous five years. These included Canada Dry, Bassetts and Trebor. Its finance director argued that the prior practice of writing off goodwill acquired when companies were acquired at prices above asset values and of writing off to Profit and Loss Account the ongoing expenditure on 'nurturing and succouring' brands 'to make them grow and be more valuable' had led to serious understatement of shareholder funds in the accounts. The valuation was based on the cost of the brands, assessed by their imputed earning power at the time of acquisition. The effect was to double the Balance Sheet value of shareholder funds. However, the market was indifferent. On the announcement day, Cadbury shares actually fell by 2p from 317p to 315p (less than 1 per cent) against a similar fall in the market. But had the market anticipated this announcement after other brand-owners had previously adopted similar policies?

Generally speaking, the NAV, even at its most reliable, only really offers a guide to the lower limit of company value. Even then, some form of adjustment for the issues raised above is required.

The take-over defence tactic of revaluing assets is fairly common. The motive is to raise the market value of the firm and thus make the bid more expensive and more difficult to finance (possibly a motive in Cadbury's case, since the US conglomerate, General Cinema, held over 20 per cent of the equity). However, the impact on share price will be minimal unless the re-valuation provides new information, and this largely depends on the perceived quality and objectivity of the 'expert valuation'.

From this discussion of the accounts-based approach to valuation, we are forced to conclude that while the NAV may provide a useful reference point, it is unlikely to be a reliable guide to valuing firms. In the rest of this chapter, we rely mainly on the general theory of value, introduced in Chapter 3.

4.4   Company value: the theory and a simple case

The value of any item depends upon the stream of benefits which the owner expects to enjoy from his ownership. Sometimes these benefits are intangible, as in the case of Van Gogh's 'Irises' – the benefits are the aesthetic delights one might enjoy from viewing the painting (if one dared to remove it from the bank vault!). In the case of financial assets, the benefits are less subjective. Ownership of ordinary shares, for example, entitles the holder to receive a stream of future cash flows in the form of dividends plus a lump sum when the shares are sold on to the next purchaser, and perhaps a liquidating dividend when the company is finally wound up. Benefits separated by time should be compared on an equivalent basis by discounting them at the minimum rate of return required by shareholders, the *equity cost of capital*, which we now denote as k_e.

Valuing a newly-created company: Navenby plc

Let us take a simple example. Navenby plc is to be formed by public issue of one million £1 shares. It proposes to purchase and let out residential property, an activity known to be lucrative. It has been agreed that after five years, the company will be liquidated and the proceeds returned to shareholders. The fully subscribed book value of the company is £1m, the amount of cash offered for the shares. However, this takes no account of the investment returns likely to be generated by Navenby. In the prospectus inviting investors to subscribe, the company announced details of its £1m investment programme. It has concluded a deal with a builder to purchase a block of properties on very attractive terms, as well as instructing a letting agency to rent out the properties at a guaranteed income of £130,000 p.a. Based upon recent property price movements, Navenby's management reckon that a 70 per cent capital appreciation over the five-year period is a reasonable estimate. All net income flows (after management fees of £30,000 p.a.) will be paid out as dividends.

Navenby is easy to value. Its value is the sum of discounted future expected cash flows from the projected activity:

Year	1	2	3	4	5
Net rentals p.a. (£m)	+0.1	+0.1	+0.1	+0.1	+0.1
Sale proceeds (£m)					+1.7

If shareholders require a 12 per cent return for an activity of this degree of risk, the PV of the project is found using the relevant annuity (PVIFA) and single payment (PVIF) discount factors as follows:

$$PV = £0.1\text{m}.\text{PVIFA}_{(12.5)} + £1.7\text{m}.\text{PVIF}_{(12.5)}$$
$$= £0.361\text{m} + £0.964\text{m} = £1.325\text{m}$$

The value of the company is £1.325m and shareholders are better off by £0.325m. In effect, the managers of Navenby are offering to convert subscriptions of £1m into cash flows worth £1.325m. If there is general consensus that these figures are reasonable estimates, and if the market efficiently processes new information, then Navenby's share price should be £1.33. If so, Navenby has created wealth of £0.325m.

The general valuation model

In analysing Navenby, we applied the general valuation model which states that the value of any asset is the sum of all future discounted net benefits expected to flow from the asset:

$$V_0 = \sum_{t=1}^{N} \frac{X_t}{(1+k_e)^t}$$

Where:

X_t = net cash inflow or outflow in year t
k_e = rate of return required by shareholders

THE VALUE OF NAVENBY

It should be noted that for this newly-formed company, the valuation expression can be written in two ways. Value is expressed as:

value = cash subscription + NPV of proposed activities; or
value = present value of all future cash inflows less outflows

---

A moment's thought should convince the reader that these are equivalent expressions. The value of Navenby is £1.325m, and the value of the investment is £0.325m, i.e. it would be rational to pay up to £0.325m to be allowed to undertake the investment opportunity. Valuation of Navenby is a relatively straightforward exercise partly because the company has only one activity but primarily because most key factors are known with a high degree of precision. In practice, future company cash flows and dividends are far less certain.

The oxygen of publicity

Many corporate managers are somewhat parsimonious in their release of information to the market – the international trading and mining company Lonrho is often accused of this. Their motives are often understandable, such as reluctance to divulge commercially sensitive intelligence. As a result, many valuations are based on inspired guesswork. The value of a company quoted on a semi-strong efficient share market can only be the product of what information has been released.

Yet company chairmen are fond of complaining that the market persistently undervalues their companies. Some, for example, Richard Branson (Virgin), Andrew Lloyd-Webber (Really Useful Group) and Harry Goodman (International Leisure Group), have, in exasperation, even mounted buy-back operations to repurchase publicly-held shares to return 'their' enterprises into private hands. The 'problem', however, is often of their own making. The market can only absorb and process the information offered to it. Indeed, information-hoarding may even be interpreted adversely. If information about company performance and future prospects is jealously guarded, we should not be surprised if the valuation, even of quoted companies, appears somewhat haphazard.

4.5   Valuing shares

The Navenby example demonstrates explicitly why investors purchase and hold ordinary shares. Shareholders attach value to shares because they expect to receive a stream of dividends and possibly an eventual capital gain. However, Navenby was a special case in so far as it proposed to pay out all its earnings as dividend – few companies do this in reality. Although shareholders are legally entitled to the earnings of a company, in the case of a company with a dispersed ownership body, their influence on the dividend payout is limited by their ability to exert their voting power on the directors. Other things being equal, shareholders prefer higher to lower dividends but as shown in a later chapter, issues such as capital investment strategy and taxation may cloud the relationship between company dividend policy and share value. With this reservation in mind, we now develop the so-called *Dividend Valuation Model (DVM)*, which is more appropriate to valuing part shares of companies rather than whole enterprises.

The dividend valuation model

The DVM states that the value of a share now, P_0, is the sum of the stream of future discounted dividends plus the value of the share as and when sold, in some future year n:

$$P_0 = \frac{D_1}{(1+k_e)} + \frac{D_2}{(1+k_e)^2} + \frac{D_3}{(1+k_e)^3} + \dots + \frac{D_n}{(1+k_e)^n} + \frac{V_n}{(1+k_e)^n}$$

However, since the new purchaser will, in turn, value the stream of dividends after year n, we can infer that the *value of the share at any time may be found by valuing all future expected dividend payments over the lifetime of the company*. If the life-span is assumed infinite and the annual dividend is constant, we have:

$$P_0 = \sum_{t=1}^{\infty} \frac{D_t}{(1+k_e)^t} = \frac{D_1}{k_e} \quad \text{where } D_1 = D_2 = D_3, \text{ etc.}$$

(This is an example of valuing a perpetuity, the mathematics of which is explained in Chapter 3.)

For example, a company whose shareholders require a return of 15 per cent, and which is expected to pay a constant dividend of £3m through time would be valued thus:

$$P_0 = \frac{£3m}{0.15} = £20m$$

In reality, the informational requirements of this basic model are daunting. The annual dividend is unlikely to remain unchanged indefinitely, and it seems somewhat heroic to pretend an ability to forecast a varying stream of future dividend flows. To a degree, the forecasting problem is moderated by the effect of applying a risk-adjusted discount rate because more distant dividends are more heavily discounted. For example, using a 20 per cent discount rate, the present value of a dividend of £1 in fifteen years' time is only 6p, while £1 received in twenty years adds only 3p to the value of a share. In other words, for a realistic cost of equity capital, we lose little by assuming a time-horizon of, say, fifteen years. Even so, reliable valuations still require estimates of dividends over the intervening years, and by the same logic, any errors will have a magnified effect during this period!

Allowing for future dividend growth

Dividends fluctuate over time for various reasons, largely due to variations in the company's fortunes, although most firms attempt to grow dividends more or less in line with the company's longer-term earnings growth rate. For reasons explained in Chapter 13, financial managers attempt to 'smooth' the stream of dividends. For companies operating in mature industries, this growth rate will roughly correspond to the underlying growth rate of the whole economy. For companies operating in activities with attractive growth opportunities, dividends are likely to grow at a faster rate, at least over the medium term.

ALLOWING FOR DIVIDEND GROWTH

The DVM extended to include a *constant* rate of growth becomes the Dividend Growth Model (DGM). This values a share as the sum of all discounted dividends, growing at the annual rate g:

$$P_0 = \frac{D_0(1+g)}{(1+k_e)} + \frac{D_0(1+g)^2}{(1+k_e)^2} + \frac{D_0(1+g)^3}{(1+k_e)^3} + \ldots + \frac{D_0(1+g)^n}{(1+k_e)^n}$$

Where:

D_0 = the current year's dividend,

so that:

$D_0(1+g)$ = the dividend to be paid in one year's time, etc.

A Framework for Financial Decisions

The notes to Chapter 3 show that, so long as $k_e > g$, such a series growing to infinity has a present value of:

$$P_o = \frac{D_o(1+g)}{(k_e - g)} = \frac{D_1}{(k_e - g)}$$

where D_1 = next year's dividend.

Although this version of the model is often used in practice by security analysts, at least as a reference point, we must stress its reliance upon some key assumptions. Dividend growth results from earnings growth, generated solely by new investment financed by retained earnings. Such investment is, of course, only worthwhile if the anticipated rate of return, R, is in excess of the cost of equity, k_e. Furthermore, it is assumed that the company will retain a constant fraction of earnings and invest these in a continuous stream of projects all offering a return of R.

Navenby again

To illustrate the model, we return to the Navenby example. Removing the asset sale, we now allow Navenby to operate over an infinite life. Suppose further that at the end of the first year, it will retain 50 per cent of its earnings and reinvest these at an expected annual return of 20 per cent, comfortably above the required 12 per cent. In the following year, earnings will grow at 10 per cent to reach a new level of:

'old' cash flow + return on reinvested earnings = new earnings level
£100,000 + 20%(50% × £100,000) = £100,000 + £10,000 = £110,000

If further retentions of 50 per cent are made at the end of the second year and also reinvested in projects offering annual returns of 20 per cent, earnings after three years will be:

£110,000 + 20%(50% × £110,000) = £110,000 + £11,000 = £121,000

and so on. The policy of retention and reinvestment has launched Navenby on an exponential growth path. The growth rate of 10 per cent is a compound of the retention ratio, denoted by b, and the return on reinvested earnings, R:

$$g = (b \times R) = 50\% \times 20\% = 10\%.$$

Table 4.2 shows the future behaviour of both earnings and dividends on the assumptions of constant b and R. Clearly, both magnitudes grow in tandem, so long as the company maintains the same retention ratio (50 per cent), corresponding to a dividend cover of 2.0.

Table 4.2 How earnings and dividends grow in tandem

Year	1	2	3	4	etc.
Earnings	£0.1m	£0.11m	£0.121m	£0.1331m	etc.
Dividends (50%)	£0.05m	£0.055m	£0.0605m	£0.6655m	etc.

In Chapter 13, we examine more fully the issues of whether and how a change in dividend policy can be expected to alter company value. For the moment, we are mainly concerned with the mechanics of the DGM and rely simply on the assumption that any retained earnings are used for worthwhile investment. If this applies, the value of the company will be higher with retentions-plus-re-investment than if the investment opportunities were neglected, i.e. the decision to retain benefits shareholders because of company access to projects offering returns higher than they could otherwise obtain.

4.6 Problems with the dividend growth model

The dividend growth model, while possessing some convenient properties, has some major limitations, which we now consider.

What if a company pays no dividend?

The company may be faced with highly attractive investment opportunities which cannot be financed in other ways. According to the model, such a company would have no value at all! Total retention is fairly common, either because the company has suffered an actual or expected earnings collapse, or because, as in some European economies, e.g. Switzerland, it is not uncommon to encounter firms whose expressed policy is to pay no dividends at all. In both situations, we observe that such companies do not have zero values.

In the former case, the company would have a positive value so long as the management were thought capable of staging a corporate recovery, in other words, the market is valuing more distant dividends on hopes of a turn-around in earnings. If recovery is thought unlikely, market value will be positive so long as the net asset value is positive, i.e. the company is valued at its break-up value.

In the second situation, the market is implicitly valuing the liquidating dividend when the company is ultimately wound up. Until this happens, the company is adding to its reserves as it reinvests, and continually enhancing its earning power and hence its value. In effect, the market is valuing the stream of future earnings which are legally the property of the shareholders.

Will there always be enough worthwhile projects in the future?

The DGM implies sufficient supply of positive NPV projects to match the available earnings. It is most unlikely that there will always be sufficient attractive projects available, each offering a constant rate of return, R, sufficient to absorb a given fraction, b, of earnings in each future year. While a handful of firms do have very lengthy life-spans, corporate history typically parallels the marketing concept of the Product Life Cycle – Introduction, (Rapid) Growth, Maturity, Decline and Death, with paucity of investment opportunities a very common reason for corporate demise. It is thus rather hopeful to value a firm over a perpetual life-span. However, the reader should recall our earlier point that the discounting process accounts for most of the value over a life-span of, say, fifteen years.

What if the growth rate exceeds the discount rate?

The arithmetic of the model shows that if $g > k_e$, the denominator becomes negative and value is infinite! Again, this appears nonsensical, but many companies do experience periods of very rapid growth in practice. Usually, however, company growth settles down to a less dramatic pace after the most attractive projects are exploited, and once the firm's markets mature and competition emerges. There are two ways of redeeming the model in these cases. First, we may regard g as a long-term average or 'normal' growth rate. This is not totally satisfactory as rapid growth often occurs early in the life-cycle, and the value computed would thus understate the worth of near-in-time dividends. Alternatively, we could segment the company's life-span into periods of varying growth and value these separately. For example, if we expect 25 per cent growth in the first five years and 7 per cent growth thereafter, the expression for value is:

P_o = Present value of dividends during years 1–5 + Present value of all further dividends

Note that the second term is a perpetuity beginning in year 6, but we have to find its present value. Hence it is discounted down to year zero as in the following expression.

$$P_o = \frac{D_o(1.25)}{(1+k_e)} + \frac{D_o(1.25)^2}{(1+k_e)^2} + \frac{D_o(1.25)^3}{(1+k_e)^3} + \ldots + \frac{D_o(1.25)^5}{(1+k_e)^5} + \left(\frac{D_6}{(k_e - 7\%)} \times \frac{1}{(1+k_e)^5} \right)$$

$$= \sum_{t=1}^{5} \frac{D_o(1+g_f)}{(1+k_e)^t} + \sum_{t=6}^{\infty} \frac{D_5(1+g_s)}{(1+k_e)^t}$$

Where:

g_f = rate of fast growth during years 1–5
g_s = rate of slow growth from year 6 onwards.

The model can be enhanced by assuming that the return on re-invested funds, R, declines as the amount of investment increases, thus setting a limit to worthwhile investment. This in turn helps fix the optimal retention ratio which would otherwise be zero, if $(R < k_e)$, or 100 per cent (if $R > k_e$). This adjustment accords with the micro-economic model of the Marginal Efficiency of Investment, displayed in Figure 4.1.

The MEI shows all available projects arranged in declining order of attractiveness. The wealth-maximizing enterprise will invest until the return on the last £1 invested is equal to k_e, i.e. where the marginal project offers zero NPV. Since investment is assumed to be financed from retentions, more investment requires higher retentions and thus the retention ratio rises as we move along the MEI until R equals k_e at investment level I^*. The optimal retention ratio, b^*, is the fraction of earnings sufficient to finance the optimal investment programme I^*. However, although the declining MEI determines the optimal value for b, the difficulty remains of having access to a series of investments over time requiring the *same* retention ratio.

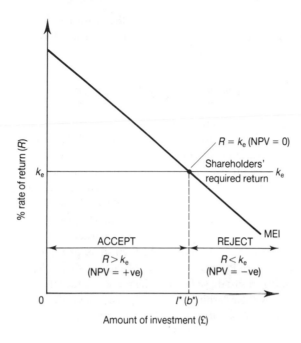

Figure 4.1 The marginal efficiency of investment

The DGM may be used as a vehicle for examining the impact of changes in dividend policy, i.e. changes in b. Detailed analysis of this issue is deferred to Chapter 13. However, we may note here that valuation of the dividend stream implies a known dividend policy, presumably subject to votive control. As a result, the DGM is more applicable to the valuation of investment stakes in companies rather than to the valuation of whole companies as in takeover situations. When company control changes hands, control of dividend policy is also transferred. It seems unrealistic, therefore, to assume an unchanged dividend policy when valuing a company for takeover!

There is one further problem with the DGM. Arguably, it is incomplete, focusing on only the distributed component of company earnings rather than the total earnings figure, all of which shareholders are legally entitled to, and without which dividend payments could not continue. We now examine earnings-based valuation approaches.

4.7 Valuing the earnings stream

The DVM values the income stream of a particular financial instrument, ordinary shares. The market value of all the issued shares (or 'capitalization') should equal the value of the company, so that if we value the earnings stream of the company we should obtain the same result. However, the concept of earnings is a tricky one to pin down. Accounting-based measures of earnings are highly suspect for several reasons, including the arbitrariness of depreciation provisions which are usually based on the historic cost of the assets. Yet we find that one of the commonest methods of valuation in practice is based on accounting profit. This method uses the Price–Earnings (P:E) ratio.

The meaning of the P:E ratio

The P:E ratio is simply the market price per share divided by the last reported profit after-tax or earnings per share (EPS), before extraordinary items. P:E ratios are cited daily in the financial press and vary with market prices. A P:E ratio measures the price which the market attaches to each £1 of company earnings, and thus resembles a pay-back period. For example, for the year ending 30 September 1989, Rolls-Royce plc reported EPS of 21.3p. Its share price in early April 1990 varied around the £1.90 mark, producing a P:E ratio of 8.9. A share price of £1.80 would produce a P:E ratio of 8.4 and at a price per share of £2.00, the P:E ratio becomes 9.4. Allowing for daily variations, the market seemed to indicate that it was prepared to wait about nine years to recover the then share price, on the basis of the current earnings level. So does a high P:E ratio signify a willingness to wait longer? Companies which sell at relatively high P:E ratios do so because the market values their growth potential, their perceived ability to grow their earnings from the present level. The market is impounding a growth premium into the P:E ratios of such firms. In other words, market price reflects growth prospects.

The P:E ratio varies directly with share price, but it also derives from the share price – i.e. from market valuation – so how does this help with valuation? It appears that investment analysts typically have in mind what an 'appropriate' P:E ratio should be for particular share categories and individual companies, and look for disparities between sectors and companies. If, for example, BP is selling at a P:E ratio of 7.5 with EPS of 40p and Shell with EPS of 25p has a P:E ratio of 9.0, then their share values may look out of line. Assuming Shell's shares are correctly valued at $(9.0 \times 25p) = 225p$, then BP's shares, priced at $(7.5 \times 40p) = 300p$, might appear undervalued.

The reader will have spotted the circularity here – this conclusion relies on the assumption that Shell rather than BP is correctly valued! Moreover, despite the apparent similarity of these two oil majors, there may be very good reasons why they should be valued differently. BP's earnings may be subject to a greater degree of variability – it operates further 'upstream' (away from the final consumer) than Shell, and hence, turbulence in the primary oil markets hits its profits harder. Using P:E ratios to detect under- or over-valuation, by definition, implies that markets are slow or inefficient processors of information.

The P:E ratio and the dividend valuation model

If we examine the P:E ratio more closely, we find it has close affinity with the growth version of the DVM. The P:E ratio is defined as price per share (PPS) divided by earnings per share (EPS). In its reciprocal form, it measures the earnings yield of the firm's shares:

$$\frac{1}{P:E} = \frac{EPS}{PPS} = \frac{Earnings}{Company\ value} = \frac{E}{V}$$

This equals the dividend yield plus retained earnings (RE) per share. If, as in the growth version of the DVM, we define the fraction of earnings retained as b, we can write:

$$\frac{E}{V} = \frac{D}{V} + \frac{RE}{V} = \frac{D}{V} + \frac{bE}{V}$$

The ratio E/V is the overall rate of return currently achieved. If this equals R, then bE/V is equivalent to the growth rate g in the DVM. In other words, the earnings yield, E/V, is comprised of the dividend yield plus the growth rate or 'capital gains yield' for a company retaining a constant b and investing at the rate R. The two approaches thus look very similar. However, this apparent similarity should not be over-emphasized for three important reasons:

1. The earnings yield is expressed in terms of the *current* earnings, whereas the DGM deals with the *prospective* dividend yield and growth rate, i.e. the former is historic in its focus, while the latter is forward-looking.
2. The DGM is a discounted cash flow model, while the earnings figure is based on accounting concepts. It by no means follows that cash flows will coincide with accounting profit.
3. For the equivalence to hold, the current rate of return, E/V, would have to equal the rate of return *expected* on future investments.

Despite these qualifications, it is still common to find the earnings yield presented as the rate of return required by shareholders, and hence the cut-off rate for new investment projects. This unfortunately confuses an accounting concept with a DCF model.

4.8   Using a DCF approach

Perhaps then we should revert to a DCF approach. After all, it is rational to attach value to future *cash* proceeds rather than to accounting earnings, which are based on numerous accounting conventions, including the deduction of a notional charge for depreciation. A discounted cash flow approach in theory seems a simple enough exercise. Surely all we need to do is to take the reported profit after tax (PAT) figure and add back depreciation provisions to yield cash flow and then discount accordingly, since depreciation supposedly reflects the expenditure required to make good capital depletion?

We could value a company by valuing the stream of annual cash flows as measured by:

$$\text{Cash Flow} = (\text{Revenues} - \text{Operating Costs} + \text{Depreciation})$$

The depreciation charge is added back because it is merely an accounting adjustment to reflect the diminution in value of assets. However, most firms do replace capacity as it expires, and in principle, this investment should equate to depreciation. In practice, however, only by coincidence does the depreciation charge accurately measure the capital expenditure required to maintain production and thus earnings capacity. Moreover, most companies need investment funds for growth purposes as well as for replacement. The value of growing companies depends not simply on the earning power of their existing assets, but also on their growth potential, in other words, the NPV of the cash flows from all future non-replacement investment opportunities.

This suggests a revised concept of cash flow. To obtain an accurate assessment of the value of a company, we ought to assess its total ongoing investment needs, and set these against its anticipated revenue and operating cost flows, otherwise we might over-value the company.

FREE CASH FLOW

The income remaining net of all investment outlays is referred to as *free cash flow*:
Free Cash Flow = (Revenues − Operating Costs − Investment Expenditure)

Using this measure, the value of a company is:

$$V_0 = \sum_{t=1}^{N} \frac{\mathrm{FCF}_t}{(1+k_e)^t}$$

This approach removes the problem of confining investment financing to retentions, as in the DGM. However, we encounter significant forecasting problems in having to assess the growth opportunities and their financing needs in all future years.

Unfortunately, the accounting data for Revenues and Operating Costs upon which this approach is based may fail to reflect cash flows due to movements in the various items of working capital. For example, a sales increase may raise reported profits, but if made on lengthy credit terms, it will have only a delayed effect on cash flow. Indeed, the net effect may be negative, if suppliers of additional raw materials insist on payment before debtors settle.

It is important to mention two further distortions. First, stock-building, either in advance of an expected sales increase or simply through poor inventory control, will have no effect on profits but can seriously impair cash flow. Second, the timing of tax payments in any one year will reflect profits earned in previous time periods. Hence, this year's FCF less this year's tax *liability does not equal this year's* cash flow.

For these and similar reasons, the estimation of cash flow involves forecasting not merely all future years' sales, relevant costs and profits, but also all movement in working capital and taxation payments. Alternatively, one may assume that these factors will have a net cancelling effect which may be reasonable for longer-term valuations but much less appropriate for short time-horizon valuations as in the case of high-risk activities.

4.9 Shareholder value analysis

During the 1980s, an allegedly new approach to valuation emerged called Shareholder Value Analysis (SVA). In fact, it is not new at all, but a rather different way of looking at value, based on the NPV approach.

The key assumption of SVA is that a business is worth the net present value of its future

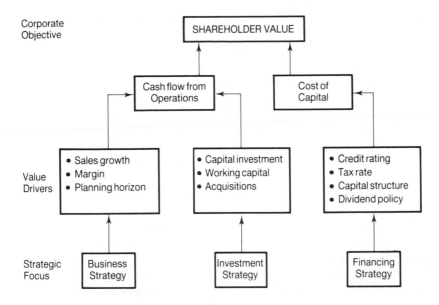

Figure 4.2   Shareholder value analysis framework

cash flows, discounted at the appropriate cost of capital. The reason why so many leading US corporations (like Westinghouse, Pepsi, Quaker and Disney) and a growing number of European companies have embraced SVA is that it provides a framework for linking management decisions and strategies to value-creation. The focus of attention is on how a business can plan and manage its activities to increase value for shareholders and, at the same time, benefit other stakeholders.

How is this achieved? Figure 4.2 shows the relationship between decision-making and shareholder value. Key decisions – whether strategic, operational, investment or financial – with important cash flow and risk implications are specified. Managers should focus on decisions influencing the *value drivers*, the factors which have greatest impact on shareholder value. Typically, these include:

- *Sales growth and margin.* Chapter 1 showed how sales growth and margins are influenced by competitive forces (e.g. threat of new entrants, power of buyers and suppliers, threat of substitutes and competition in the industry). The balance between sales, growth and profits should not be based purely on profit impact but on value impact.
- *Working capital and fixed capital investment.* Over-emphasis on profit, particularly at the operating level, may result in neglect of working capital and fixed asset management. Earlier in this chapter, the free cash flow approach advocated using cashflows after meeting fixed (and working) capital requirements.
- *The cost of capital* is a key value driver. In later chapters, we discuss how it can be estimated, but for the present, it can be said that a firm should seek to make financial decisions which minimize the cost of capital given the nature of the business and its

strategies. As will be seen later, this does not simply mean taking that source of finance which is nominally the cheapest.

- *The tax rate* affects most aspects of business life particularly cash flows and the discount rate. Managers need to be aware of the main tax impact on both investment and financial decisions (discussed in subsequent chapters).

SVA requires the specification of a planning horizon of, say, five or ten years, and forecasting the cash flows and discount rates based on the underlying plans and strategies. Various strategies can then be considered to assess the implications for shareholder value.

A particular problem with SVA is specifying the terminal value at the end of the planning horizon. Various methods have been suggested, none of which is wholly satisfactory. It could be argued, however, that SVA does not have to be used to obtain the value of the business – rather, it can estimate the *additional* value created from implementing certain strategies. Assuming these strategies deliver competitive advantage, and therefore returns in excess of the cost of capital, over the planning horizon, there is no need to wrestle with the terminal value problem.

What, then, are the real benefits of SVA? Simply, that it helps managers focus on value-creating activities. Acquisition and divestment strategies, capital structure and dividend policies, performance measures, transfer pricing and executive compensation are seen in a new light. Short-term profit-related activities may actually be counter-productive in value-creation terms.

4.10   The valuation of unquoted companies

The valuation of a company or of its shares is an inexact science but is made considerably simpler if the shares are traded on a stock market. If trading is regular and frequent, and the market has a high degree of information efficiency, then we may feel able to trust market values. If so, the models of valuation merely provide a check or enable us to assess the likely impact of altering key parameters such as dividend policy or introducing more efficient management.

With unquoted companies, the various models have a leading rather than a supporting role, but give by no means definitive answers. Attempts to use the models inevitably suffer from informational deficiencies, which may only be partially overcome. For example, in using a P:E multiple, a question arises concerning the appropriate P:E ratio to apply. Many experts advocate using the P:E ratio of a surrogate quoted company, one which is similar in all or most respects to the unquoted one we are trying to value. One possible approach is to take a sample of 'similar' quoted companies, and find a weighted average P:E ratio based upon the individual P:E figures using market capitalizations as weights.

However, the shares of a quoted company are, by definition, more marketable than those of unquoted firms, and marketability usually attracts a premium, suggesting a lower P:E ratio for the unquoted company. If the chosen surrogate has a P:E ratio of 10, then we may decide to adjust this to allow for the lack of marketability of the shares of the unquoted company, perhaps by reducing it to, say, 8:1. Any such adjustment is bound to be arbitrary, and different valuation experts might well apply quite different adjustment factors.

Furthermore, a major problem in valuing and acquiring private companies is the need to tie in the key managers for a sufficient number of years to ensure the recovery of the investment. The cost of such 'earn-outs', or 'golden handcuffs', could be a major component of the purchase consideration.

In principle, all the valuation approaches explained in this chapter are applicable to valuing unquoted companies, so long as suitable surrogates can be found, or if reliable industry averages are available. If surrogate data cannot be used, then valuation becomes even more of a subjective exercise. In these circumstances, it is not unusual to find valuers convincing themselves that company accounts are objective and reliable indicators of value. While black-and-white printed figures may offer a veneer of objectivity, we need hardly repeat the pitfalls in interpretation of accounts discussed earlier.

4.11 Summary

This chapter has discussed the reasons why financial managers may wish to value their own and other enterprises, and the problems likely to be encountered and explained the main valuation techniques available.

Given the uncertainties involved in valuation, it seems sensible to compare the implications of a number of valuation models and also to obtain valuations from a number of sources. A 'pooled' valuation is unlikely to be 'correct', but armed with a range of valuations, managers should be able to develop a feel for a likely 'consensus valuation'. This is, after all, what a market value represents, but based upon the views of many times more market participants. There should be no stigma attached to obtaining more than one opinion – experts from another inexact science, medicine, do not hesitate to call for second opinions when unsure about diagnoses!

Key points

- An understanding of valuation is required to appreciate the likely effect of investment and financial decisions, to value other firms for acquisition, and to organize defences against takeover raiders.
- Valuation is easy if the company's shares are quoted! The market value is 'correct' if the EMH applies, but managers may have withheld important information.
- Using published accounts is fraught with dangers, e.g. under-valuation of fixed assets.
- Some companies attempt to value the brands they control. An efficient capital market will already have valued these, but not necessarily in a fully informed manner.
- The economic theory of value tells us that the value of any asset is the sum of the discounted benefits expected to accrue from owning it.
- The value of a share can be found by discounting all future expected dividend payments.
- The retention of earnings for worthwhile investment purposes enhances future earnings, dividends and therefore share price now.

- The dividend valuation model must be treated with caution. It embodies many critical assumptions.
- A company's earnings stream can be valued by applying a P:E multiple, based upon a comparable quoted surrogate company.
- Valuing a company on a DCF basis requires us to forecast all future investment capital needs, tax payments and working capital movements.
- Valuation of unquoted companies is highly subjective. It requires examination of similar quoted companies and applying discounts for lack of marketability.
- The two main lessons of valuation are first, that you should use a variety of methods (or consult a variety of experts) and second, don't expect to get it exactly right!

Further reading

Comprehensive treatments of share and company valuation are quite rare. T. Copeland, T. Koller and J. Murrin, *Measuring and Managing the Value of Companies* (John Wiley and Sons) is probably the best available.

A good overview can be found in Chapter 15 (the contribution by Davies) in M. Firth and S. Keane (eds), (1986).

Questions

Self-test questions

1. Why do even the financial managers of quoted companies need to be able to value shares and companies?
2. What are the dangers in accepting too uncritically the NAV shown in a company's accounts?
3. What are the difficulties with the Dividend Growth Model?
4. Why is it so difficult to measure the actual cash flows of a company?
5. What is 'free cash flow'?

Exercises

1. Cogburn plc, an ungeared company operating in the processed food industry, is contemplating the takeover of Pepper plc, but is unsure how to value its target. Cogburn's analysts have assembled the following information:

   (i) Pepper's Balance Sheet as at 31 December 1992

		£m
Fixed assets (net)		14
Current assets:		
Stocks	4	
Debtors	8	
Cash	—	

Current liabilities:
  Trade creditors   10
  Bank overdraft   3
Net current assets   (1)
              ——
        Net Assets 13
              ——

Financed by:
Issued share capital (50p units)   10
Profit and Loss Account   3
              ——
              13
              ——

(ii) In its most recent trading period, ending December 1992, Pepper's sales were £50m, but after operating costs and other expenses, including a depreciation charge of £2m, its profit after tax was £2m. This figure includes an extraordinary item (sale of property) of £0.5m. The full year dividend was £0.5m in total, paid about a year ago.

(iii) Pepper has recently followed a policy of increasing dividends by 12 per cent p.a. Its shareholders require a return of 17 per cent.

(iv) Cogburn's P:E ratio is 14:1. Pepper's is 8:1.

(v) More efficient utilization of Pepper's assets could generate annual operating savings of £0.5m p.a. after tax.

Required

(a) What is Pepper's current market value?

(b) Why might the market value differ from book value?

(c) What rate of return does Pepper currently achieve for its shareholders?

(d) As financial director of Cogburn, you are required to assess the value of Pepper using a discounted cash flow approach. (Carefully specify any assumptions which you make.)

(e) Explain how you would value Pepper if it were *not* quoted on the Stock Exchange. (Answer in Appendix A)

2. Stainburn plc is an all-equity financed company, whose shareholders require a return of 27% and which currently pays out all its earnings after tax as dividend. Depreciation provisions are sufficient to finance the replacement investment required to maintain earnings at the current level of £6m p.a. before Corporation Tax, which is payable at 33% per cent. Stainburn's (much simplified) Balance Sheet as at 30 June 1992 is as follows:

Asset Employed:	£m
Fixed Assets (net)	12
Net Current Assets	3
	——
Net Assets	15

Financed by:

Issued Share Capital	
(par value 25p)	10
Reserves	5
	—
Shareholders' Funds	15

Required

(a) What rate of return does Stainburn yield on the book value of assets?

(b) How would you account for any discrepancy between asset value and market value?

(c) Stainburn's managers now propose the halving of next year's dividend to finance investment expected to yield a return of 25% p.a. after tax on average. This will be an ongoing programme requiring this retention ratio for the indefinite future.

  (i) Is the programme worthwhile?

  (ii) What effect should it have on Stainburn's value?

3. Zed plc is considering the immediate purchase of some, or all, of the share capital of one of two firms – Red Ltd and Yellow Ltd. Both Red and Yellow have 1 million ordinary shares issued and neither company has any debt capital outstanding.

   Both firms are expected to pay a dividend in one year's time – Red's expected dividend amounts to 30p per share and Yellow's being 27p per share. Dividends will be paid annually and are expected to increase over time. Red's dividends are expected to display perpetual growth at a compound rate of 6 per cent p.a. Yellow's dividend will grow at the high annual compound rate of $33\frac{1}{3}$ per cent until a dividend of 64p per share is reached in Year 4. Thereafter Yellow's dividend will remain constant.

   If Zed is able to purchase all the equity capital of either firm then the reduced competition would enable Zed to save some advertising and administrative costs which would amount to £225,000 p.a. indefinitely and, in Year 2, to sell some office space for £800,000. These benefits and savings will only occur if a complete take-over were to be carried out. Zed would change some operations of any company completely taken over. The details are:

1. Red – No dividend would be paid until Year 3. Year 3 dividend would be 25p per share and dividends would then grow at 10 per cent p.a. indefinitely.

2. Yellow – No change in total dividends in Years 1 to 4, but after Year 4 dividend growth would be 25 per cent p.a. compound until Year 7. Thereafter annual dividends would remain constant at the Year 7 amount per share.

An appropriate discount rate for the risk inherent in all the cash flows mentioned is 15 per cent.

Required

(a) *Ignoring taxation* calculate:

  (i) The valuation per share for a minority investment in each of the firms Red and Yellow which would provide the investor with a 15 per cent rate of return.

    (ii) The maximum amount per share which Zed should consider paying for each company in the event of a complete takeover.

  (b) Comment on any limitations of the approach used in part (a) and specify the other major factors which would be important to consider if the proposed valuations were being undertaken as a practical exercise.

(ACCA Level 3, June 1983)

4. CDC Ltd owns a chain of tyre and exhaust fitting garages in the West of England. The company has been approached by ATD plc, which owns a large chain of petrol stations, with a view to a takeover of CDC Ltd. ATD plc is prepared to make an offer in cash or a share-for-share exchange.

The most recent accounts of CDC Ltd are summarized below:

Profit-and-Loss Account for the year ended 30 November 1991

	£m
Turnover	18.7
Profit before interest and tax	6.4
Interest	1.6
Profit before taxation	4.8
Corporation tax	1.2
Net profit after taxation	3.6
Dividend	1.0
Retained profit	2.6

Balance Sheet as at 30 November 1991

	£m	£m	£m
Fixed assets			
Freehold land and premises at cost		4.6	
Less accumulated depreciation		0.6	
			4.0
Plant and machinery at cost		9.5	
Less accumulated depreciation		3.6	
			5.9
			9.9
Current assets			
Stock at cost		2.8	
Debtors		0.4	
Bank		2.6	
		5.8	

Less: creditors amounts due within			
one year			
Trade creditors	4.3		
Dividends	1.0		
Corporation tax	1.2	6.5	(0.7)

Total assets less current liabilities	9.2
Less: creditors due beyond one year	
Loans	3.6
	5.6

Share capital and reserves	
Ordinary £1 shares	2.0
Profit and loss account	3.6
	5.6

The accountant for CDC Ltd has estimated the future free cash flows of the company to be as follows:

	1992	1993	1994	1995	1996–2008
£m	4.4	4.6	4.9	5.0	5.4 p.a.

Shareholders require a return of 10 per cent.

CDC Ltd has recently had a professional valuer establish the current re-sale value of its assets. The current re-sale value of each asset was as follows:

	£m
Freehold land and premises	18.2
Plant and machinery	4.2
Stock	3.4

The current re-sale values of the remaining assets are considered to be in line with their book values.

A company which is listed on the Stock Exchange and which is in the same business as CDC Ltd has a gross dividend yield of 5 per cent and a price earnings ratio of 11 times.

Assume a standard rate of income tax of 25 per cent.

Required

(a) Calculate the value of a share in CDC Ltd using the following methods:
   (i) Net assets basis
   (ii) Dividend valuation model
   (iii) Price earnings ratio
   (iv) Free cash flows

(b) Briefly evaluate each of the share valuation methods above.

(ACCA Certified Diploma, June 1991)

Practical assignment

Obtain the latest Annual Report and Accounts of a company of your choice. Consult the Balance Sheet and determine the company's Net Asset Value. What is the composition of the fixed assets, i.e. the relative size of fixed and current assets, the relative size of fixed tangible and fixed intangible assets, and the relative importance of stocks and debtors? What is the company's policy towards asset revaluation? What is its depreciation policy? How does it handle 'goodwill' when acquiring other companies?

Now consult the financial press to assess the market value of the company. This is the current share price times the *number* of ordinary shares issued. (The notes to the accounts will indicate the latter.) What discrepancy do you find between the NAV and the market value? How can you explain this? What is the P:E ratio of your selected company? How does this compare with other companies in the same sector? How can you explain any discrepancies? Do you think your selected company's shares are under-or over-valued?

PART II

Investment Decisions and Strategies

Chapters 5–11 apply the underlying concepts laid down in Part I to an investment setting. The appraisal methods (using discounted cash flow and more traditional techniques) are described in Chapter 5, assuming capital is both freely available and rationed. Investment analysis is then applied to practical situations, including the impact of taxation and inflation, in Chapters 6 and 7.

Greater realism is introduced in Chapters 8–10 through the examination of investment decision-making in the face of uncertainty. Portfolio theory and the Capital Asset Pricing model offer managers an approach for estimating the required return on risky projects and securities.

Chapter 11 focuses on the whole process of investment decisions, from the initial idea to the post-completion audit, within a strategic framework.

CHAPTER 5
Investment appraisal methods

THE APPLE TURNS SOUR

The story of the rise and fall of Apple Computer is well known. IBM was the main rival that Apple wanted to beat in personal computers. From the top downwards every Apple manager was young and full of enthusiasm. The result of their amazing creativity and drive was performance levels that made more than 300 of its employees millionaires.

But in 1985 sales fell and profits turned into losses. The co-founders, Jobs and Wozniak, departed and so did much of the managerial enthusiasm and innovativeness. The new chairman replaced the whizz-kids with new structures and controls, installing 'bean counters' (accountants) to supplant visionaries.

5.1 Introduction

We introduce this chapter with the Apple story because it provides a timely reminder that successful business is not all about imposing financial disciplines and employing financial wizards. They have their place, but while the finance function can contribute to the quality of business decisions and take steps to reduce exposure to financial risks, it should only dominate business activity when the firm is on the verge of collapse.

We saw in Chapters 3 and 4 how investing in capital projects which offer positive net present values creates additional wealth for the business and its owners. The NPV method is commonly employed, particularly within larger firms. Once again, Quaker Oats give us a clear statement of policy:

> We measure all potential projects by their cash flow merit. We then discount projected cash flows back to present value in order to compare the initial investment cost with a project's future returns to determine if it will add incremental value after compensating for a given level of risk. (Quaker Oats Annual Report and Accounts 1989)

There are, however, a number of alternative techniques to the NPV method. The aim of this chapter is to present the main methods of investment appraisal and to consider their strengths and limitations. In a later chapter we consider their practical application in business, large and small.

LEARNING OBJECTIVES

Having read this chapter the reader should have a good grasp of the investment appraisal techniques commonly employed in business, and have developed skills in applying them to problems.

Particular attention should be devoted to:

- The three discounted cash flow approaches – net present value, internal rate of return and profitability index.
- The underlying strengths and limitations of the above methods.
- How net present value and internal rate of return methods can be reconciled when they conflict.
- Analysing investments when capital is an important constraint.

5.2   Investment techniques

Discounted cash flow (DCF) analysis is really a family of techniques of which the NPV method is just one variant on a theme. Two other DCF methods are: the internal rate of return (IRR), and the profitability index (PI) approaches. Many managers prefer to use non-discounting approaches such as the payback and return on capital methods; others use both approaches. The following example illustrates the various approaches to investment appraisal.

Example: Appraising the Gooch and Gower projects

Lamb is a manufacturer of sports equipment. He is considering whether to invest in one of two automated processes, the Gooch or the Gower, both of which give rise to manpower and other cost savings over the existing process. The relevant data relating to each are given below:

	Gooch £	Gower £
Investment Outlay (payable immediately)	(40,000)	(50,000)
Year 1 Annual cost savings	16,000	17,000
2 ,, ,, ,,	16,000	17,000
3 ,, ,, ,,	16,000	17,000
4 ,, ,, ,,	12,000	17,000
The cost of finance is 14 per cent p.a.		

The investment outlays are obviously additional cash outflows, while the annual cost savings are cash flow benefits in the sense that total annual expenditures are reduced as a result of the investment.

Should Lamb invest in either of the two proposals and if so, which is preferable?

The NPV solution

The net present value for the Gooch machine is found by multiplying the annual cash flows by the present value interest factor (PVIF) at 14 per cent (using the tables) and finding the total, as shown in Table 5.1. An immediate cash outlay (termed Year 0) is not discounted as it is already expressed in present value terms. The same factors could be applied to evaluate the Gower proposal. However, as the annual savings are constant, it is far simpler to use the present value interest factor for an annuity (PVIFA) of £16,000 p.a. at 14 per cent for four years.

Comparison of the two proposals reveals:

1. The Gooch machine offers a positive NPV of £4,252, and would *increase* shareholder wealth.
2. The Gower machine offers a negative NPV of £467 and would *reduce* value.
3. Given that the proposals are mutually exclusive (i.e. only one is required) it is clear that the Gooch proposal should be accepted.

What does an expected NPV of £4,252 from the Gooch proposal really mean? From the shareholders' viewpoint, it means that Lamb could borrow £44,252 to purchase the machine and pay out a dividend today of £4,252 and still have sufficient funds from the project to pay off the interest at 14 per cent p.a., and annual repayments. This is demonstrated in Table 5.2.

Table 5.1 Net present value calculations

Gooch Proposal

Year		Cash Flow (£)	PVIF Factor 14%	Present Value (£)
0	Outlay	(40,000)	1	(40,000)
1	Cost Savings	16,000	.87719	14,035
2	,,	16,000	.76947	12,312
3	,,	16,000	.67497	10,800
4	,,	12,000	.59208	7,105
		Net Present Value at 14%		4,252

Gower Proposal

		£17,000 × PVIFA$_{(14,4)}$ = £17,000 × 2.9137		49,533
	Outlay			(50,000)
		Net Present Value at 14%		(467)

Table 5.2 Why NPV makes sense to shareholders

Year 0	Borrow: machine £40,000	£
	dividend £4,252	44,252
1	Interest: £44,252 at 14%	6,195
		50,447
	Less: repayment (through annual savings)	16,000
		34,447
2	Interest: £34,447 at 14%	4,822
		39,269
	Less: repayment	16,000
		23,269
3	Interest: £23,269 at 14%	3,257
		26,526
	Less: repayment	16,000
		10,526
4	Interest: £10,526	1,474
		12,000
	Less: repayment	12,000

In practice, it is unlikely that the lender will agree to a repayment schedule which exactly matches the expected annual cash flows of the project. It is also somewhat injudicious to pay as a dividend the whole of the expected NPV before the project commences! However, in theory at least, the proposal creates wealth of £4,252 and the shareholders are that much better off than they were prior to the decision. Note that in our example we assume that borrowing and lending rates of interest are the same.

5.3 Internal rate of return (IRR)

Businessmen frequently ask: 'What is the rate of return I am getting on my investment?' To calculate the correct return, or yield, requires us to find the rate which equates the present value of future benefits with the initial cash outlay. This we term the internal rate of return (IRR), or DCF Yield.

> The IRR is that discount rate, r, which, when applied to project cash flows, produces a net present value of zero.

Suppose a savings scheme offers a plan whereby for an initial investment of £100 you would receive £112 at the year end. The IRR is thus:

$$\left(\frac{£112 - £100}{£100}\right) \times 100 = 12\%$$

If the plan offered a single payment of £148 in three years' time, the rate is found by solving:

$$£100\,(1 + r)^3 = £148$$

or

$$\frac{1}{(1 + r)^3} = \frac{£100}{£148} = 0.6757$$

Turning to the PVIF table (Appendix B) for three years and looking for the rate which comes closest to 0.6757, we find that the rate is approximately 14 per cent, which is the IRR for the investment. The same approach is used for finding the IRR for capital investment, but here the annual cash flows may differ. We find the IRR by solving for the rate of return at which the present value of the cash inflows equals the present value of the cash outflows. That is, we have to solve for

$$I_0 = \frac{X_1}{1 + r} + \frac{X_2}{(1 + r)^2} + \ldots + \frac{X_n}{(1 + r)^n}$$

This is effectively the same as finding the rate of return that produces an NPV of zero.

Return now to our earlier example. The Gooch produced an NPV of £4,252 at 14 per cent. What rate of return reduces the NPV to zero? Given a 'normal' pattern of cash flows, i.e. an outlay followed by cash inflows, we can see that as the discount rate *increases*, the NPV falls. Trial and error (plus a little thought) will give us the discount rate that yields a zero NPV.

Trying 18 per cent, as shown in Table 5.3, gives a positive NPV of £976. Trying 20 per cent gives a negative NPV of £510. Clearly the IRR giving a zero NPV falls between 18 and

Table 5.3 IRR calculations for Gooch proposal

Year	Cash Flow (£)	PVIF 18%	PV(£)	PVIF 20%	PV(£)
0	(40,000)	1	(40,000)	1	(40,000)
1	16,000	0.84746	13,559	0.83333	13,333
2	16,000	0.71818	11,490	0.69444	11,111
3	16,000	0.60863	9,738	0.57870	9,259
4	12,000	0.51579	6,189	0.48225	5,787
NPV			976		(510)

$$\text{IRR} = 18\% + \left(\frac{976}{976 + 510} \times 2\%\right) = 19.31\%$$

20 per cent, probably closer to 20 per cent. Using linear interpolation, we estimate the IRR by applying the formula:

$$IRR = r_1 + \left(\frac{N_1}{N_1 + N_2} \times (r_2 - r_1) \right)$$

where r_1 is the rate of interest and N_1 the NPV for the first guess and r_2 is the rate of interest and N_2 the NPV for the second guess. Applying the formula:

$$IRR = 18\% + \left(\frac{£976}{£976 + £510} \times 2\% \right) = 19.31\%$$

Note that the calculation includes the class interval, in this case $(20\% - 18\%) = 2\%$.

If we had chosen two discount rates further apart, such as 10 and 25 per cent, the linear approximation would be less accurate:

at 10%, NPV = +£7,972
at 25%, NPV = −£3,860

$$IRR = 10\% + \left(\left(\frac{7,972}{7,972 + 3,860} \right) \times 15\% \right) = 20.1\%$$

Even with a range of 15 per cent the accuracy is to within 1 per cent of the true IRR.

In the Gooch example, the NPV at various rates of interest is as follows.

Plotting on a graph the four calculated NPVs against their respective discount rates for the Gooch in Figure 5.1, we can see a clearer relationship between IRR and NPV. We also have an idea of the break-even rate of interest – or IRR – at around 19–20 per cent as calculated earlier. The IRR of 19.31 per cent is well above the required rate of 14 per cent and the project is, therefore, wealth-creating.

Most managers and students these days have access to computer spreadsheets which

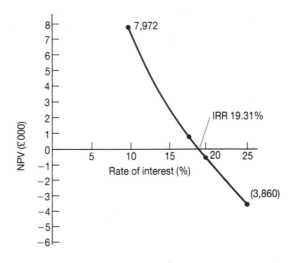

Figure 5.1 Gooch proposal: NPV–IRR graph

solve the equation in a fraction of a second and avoid tedious manual effort. However, our analysis explains the logic behind the computer calculation.

For the Gower proposal, the IRR calculation is much more straightforward as the annual cash flows are constant.

$$£17,000 \times \text{PVIFA}_{(r,4)} = £50,000$$
$$\text{PVIFA}_{(r,4)} = \frac{£50,000}{£17,000} = 2.9411$$

Referring to annuity tables, we find that for four years at 13 per cent the factor is 2.9745 and at 14 per cent it is 2.9137. The IRR is therefore between 13 and 14 per cent. This return falls just below the 14 per cent requirement, making it an uneconomic proposal.

Profitability index

Another method used to evaluate capital projects is the profitability index (PI), sometimes called the benefit–cost ratio.

> The Profitability Index is the ratio of the present value of project benefits to the present value of initial costs.

The PI therefore gives the present value of benefits per £1 of initial outlay. As such, it indicates the 'profitability' per £1 invested, and is thus a measure of the productivity or financial efficiency of the project.

Referring back to the present values calculated in Table 5.1 we can find for the Gooch proposal:

$$\text{PI} = \frac{\text{PV benefits}}{\text{PV outlay}} = \frac{£44,252}{£40,000} = 1.1063,$$

while for the Gower proposal:

$$\text{PI} = \frac{£49,533}{£50,000} = 0.9906$$

The decision rule is: accept projects with a PI greater than 1.0, which means that only the Gooch is acceptable on financial grounds. The higher the PI, the more attractive the project. For *independent* projects, the PI gives the same advice as NPV and IRR methods, although there are important reservations when projects are 'mutually exclusive' (see section 5.5).

The PI can also be expressed as the net present value per £1 invested, i.e.

$$\text{PI} = \frac{\text{NPV}}{\text{PV of outlays}}$$

A moment's thought should convince the reader that this version is entirely consistent with the one above. It differs only in the value derived for the index, and the associated decision rule, namely accept if NPV per £1 invested exceeds zero. If NPV per £1 is greater than zero, it follows that PV per £1 exceeds one. It is a matter of personal preference which version is used.

5.4 Non-discounting approaches

Over the years, managers have come to rely upon a number of simple rule-of-thumb approaches to analyse investments. Two of the most popular of these traditional methods are the payback period and the accounting rate of return.

Payback period (PB)

The payback period is the period of time taken for the future net cash inflows to match the initial cash outlay. Recall that the Gooch proposal, costing £40,000, offered £16,000 in the first three years and £12,000 in the fourth. The payback period in this case is at least two years, the remaining £8,000 of the original investment being recovered in the third year:

$$2 + \frac{8,000}{16,000} = 2.5 \quad \begin{array}{l} \text{years assuming the cash flows} \\ \text{arrive evenly throughout the year} \end{array}$$

For the Gower, the payback period is 2.9 years (i.e. £50,000/£17,000). Many companies set payback requirements for capital projects. For example, if all projects are required to payback within three years, both the Gooch and Gower are acceptable.

> The payback period is the length of time taken to recoup the original investment.

A number of modifications to simple payback are possible. *Discounted payback* addresses the problem of comparing cashflows in different time periods. It calculates how quickly *discounted* cash flows recoup the initial investment. Referring back to the NPV calculation for the Gooch, the discounted payback at 14 per cent period is approximately three and a half years; only in the final year do the cumulative present values recoup the initial outlay.

Bail-out payback period recognizes that there is usually a residual value at the end of each year for which the asset could be sold if necessary. Suppose in the Gooch proposal the residual values for each year were as below:

Year-end	Net Cash Flow (£)	Residual Value (£)
1	16,000	15,000
2	16,000	10,000
3	16,000	5,000
4	12,000	—

If we sold the equipment after one year, the total cash flow would be £16,000 + £15,000 = £31,000. This is not sufficient to cover the initial outlay of £40,000. However, after the second year the cash flow would be £32,000 in operating cash flows plus £10,000 residual value which would recover the initial cost. The bail-out payback period is, therefore, within two years, which is slightly quicker than the payback period calculated earlier. This method is only really feasible where there is an active second-hand market for the assets.

A fuller discussion on the popularity of the Payback Period will be given in Chapter 7. For the present, we should recognize that this approach has some serious problems as a measure of investment worth, such as:

1. The time value of money is ignored (except in the case of discounted payback).
2. Cash flows arising after the payback period are ignored.
3. The payback period which many firms stipulate for assessing projects has little theoretical basis.

Accounting rate of return (ARR)

The accounting rate of return, also known as return on capital employed (ROCE) or return on investment (ROI), compares the average profit of the project with the book value of the asset acquired. The ARR can be calculated on the *original* capital invested or on the *average* amount invested over the life of the asset.

$$\text{ARR (total investment)} = \frac{\text{Average annual profit}}{\text{Initial capital invested}} \times 100$$

$$\text{ARR (average investment)} = \frac{\text{Average annual profit}}{\text{Average capital invested}} \times 100$$

Returning to our example, suppose Lamb's depreciation policy is to depreciate assets over their useful lives on a straight-line basis. The annual depreciation for the Gooch will be £10,000 (i.e. £40,000 over four years) and for the Gower, £12,500. The annual profit from the proposals will be the annual cash saving less the annual depreciation. The ARRs based on initial capital invested for the two proposals are shown in Table 5.4.

Alternatively, we could base the calculation of ARR on the *average* investment, found by summing the opening and closing asset values and dividing by 2. This would yield answers for the Gooch and Gower of 25 per cent and 18 per cent, respectively, double the returns based on the initial capital. (In our case the residual values are zero.)

A particular merit of this approach is that businessmen feel they understand such a profitability measure. Return on capital employed is the primary business ratio and it may appear to make sense to use an investment evaluation measure which is broadly consistent with this ratio. However, the ARR has some definite drawbacks. Suppose the Gooch proposal is expected to continue into Year 5, yielding a profit of £1,000 in that year. Common

Table 5.4   Calculation of the ARR on total assets

	Year					
	1	2	3	4	Average	ARR
Project						
Gooch						
Cash flow (£)	16,000	16,000	16,000	12,000	—	
Depreciation* (£)	10,000	10,000	10,000	10,000	—	
Accounting profit (£)	6,000	6,000	6,000	2,000	5,000	5,000/40,000 $=12\frac{1}{2}\%$
Gower						
Cash flow (£)	17,000	17,000	17,000	17,000	—	
Depreciation* (£)	12,500	12,500	12,500	12,500	—	
Accounting profit (£)	4,500	4,500	4,500	4,500	4,500	4,500/50,000 $=9\%$

*Straight-line depreciation is used in each case.

sense suggests that this would make the proposal more attractive. However, the new ARR actually declines from 25 to 21 per cent as a result of the averaging process being over five rather than four years.

$$ARR = \frac{(£6000 + £6000 + £6000 + £2000 + £1000)/5}{(£40000 + 0)/2} \times 100 = 21\%$$

Furthermore, it takes no account of the size and life of the investment, nor does it consider the timing of cash flows. Moreover, this approach is based on profits rather than cash flows, the significance of which we discuss in the next chapter. Such important weaknesses make this approach inappropriate as a main investment appraisal method, particularly when comparing projects.

5.5   Ranking mutually exclusive projects

Suppose the manufacturers of the Gooch also make the Botham – a larger, more powerful but more erratic model – offering a further 50 per cent in cost savings each year but costing a further 50 per cent to purchase. The NPV will be 50 per cent greater than the Gooch, but the other measures of performance – based on ratios or percentages – will be the same, as shown in Table 5.5.

In ranking mutually exclusive capital projects, we can reject the Gower in the first place for having a negative NPV and, second, for having consistently inferior performance indicators to the other alternatives. While the Botham and Gooch are, pound-for-pound, identical, the Botham creates £2,126 additional wealth and is preferred.

The question frequently raised is: which is the 'best' method? In fact, under the conditions typically found in business, no single method is ideal which is one reason why it is common to find three or four different measures are calculated. The ready availability of spreadsheet packages with graphics facilities makes this a straightforward and inexpensive procedure. Investment appraisal techniques are tools to assist managers in assessing the worth of a given project.

Table 5.5 Comparison of various appraisal methods

	Gooch	*Botham*	*Gower*
Net present value (£)	4252	6378	(467)
Internal rate of return (%)	19.3	19.3	13.5
Profitability Index	1.1	1.1	0.99
Payback period (years)	2.5	2.5	2.9
Accounting rate of return (%)	25.0	25.0	18.0

NPV or IRR?

In many cases the choice of DCF method has no effect on the investment advice, and it is simply a matter of personal preference. In certain circumstances, however, the choice does matter. We shall consider three such situations:

1. Mutually exclusive projects.
2. Variable discount rates.
3. Unconventional cash flows.

Mutually exclusive projects

Our previous examples have assumed that investment projects are *independent*, i.e. the decision to accept or reject can be separated from other investment projects. However, this is not always the case. For example, a company may have a spare plot of land which could be used to build a warehouse or a sports centre. In such cases, we find that only one option can be accepted and the problem is that of evaluating mutually exclusive alternatives.

A FIRST-GLASS INVESTMENT DECISION

In 1988, Pilkington, the St Helens-based glass manufacturer, was evaluating sites for a new £100m float glass plant. Four sites, three in southern England, were considered. The South-East was considered particularly attractive as it was the fastest growing market at that particular time in Europe. Pilkington was also anxious to increase its market share in the area from half to the 65 per cent it enjoyed in the United Kingdom overall. Expecting stronger rivalry from 1992, it wanted a southern presence to counteract European competitors. It already had three plants in Germany and one in Sweden.

In the event, despite the strategic attractions of the south-east site at Thanet in Kent, the vote went to a site at the St Helens headquarters. Two key factors were the anticipated additional cost of some £20m for the Thanet location over the St Helens site, and the support which the local St Helens labour force and township had displayed for Pilkington when it was subject to a takeover bid from BTR in 1986.

Not only is this an excellent example of mutual exclusivity, it also demonstrates that a subtle blend of economic and socio-political issues often determine strategic investment decisions.

In fact, the earlier worked examples comparing the Gooch, Gower and Botham proposals are mutually exclusive. Recall that while the Gooch and Botham offered the same IRR, the latter offered a much higher NPV because it was on a larger scale. *The weakness of IRR is that it ignores the scale of the project.* It assumes that firms would prefer to make a 60 per cent IRR on an investment of £1,000 than a 30 per cent return on a £1 million project. Clearly, project scale should be taken into consideration, which is why we recommend the NPV method when assessing mutually exclusive projects of different size or duration.

Variable discount rates

It is common practice to discount cash flows at a constant rate of return throughout a project's life. This may not always be preferable. The required rate of return is linked to underlying interest rates and cash flow uncertainties, both of which can change over time.

This presents little difficulty in the case of NPV: different discount rates can be set for any particular period. The IRR method, however, is compared against a single required rate of return and cannot handle variable rates.

Unconventional cash flows

There are three basic cash flow profiles:

Type	*Cash Flow Pattern*	*Example*
Conventional	Outlay followed by inflows $(-++)$	Capital project
Reverse	Inflow followed by outflow $(+--)$	Loan
Unconventional	More than one change of sign $(-+-+)$	Two-stage development project

For a reverse cash flow pattern, such as a loan where cash is received and interest paid in subsequent periods, the IRR can be usefully applied. But in interpreting the result, remember that the *lower* the rate of return the better, so the decision rule is accept the loan proposal if the IRR is *below* the required rate of return.

Unconventional cash flow patterns create particular difficulty for the IRR approach. Consider the following project cash flows:

		£
Initial outlay	0	−100,000
Year	1	+360,000
	2	−431,000
	3	+171,600

Rates of return of 10 per cent, 20 per cent and 30 per cent each produce a zero NPV.

Multiple solutions may occur where there are multiple changes of sign. In our example there are three changes in sign – from negative cash flow at the start to positive in Year 1, negative in Year 2 and positive in Year 3. While a conventional project has only one IRR, unconventional projects may have as many IRRs as there are changes in the cash flow sign.

Reinvestment assumptions

To summarize, the use of NPV and IRR is a matter of personal preference in most instances. Where, however, the evaluation is for mutually exclusive projects, or where the discount rate is not constant throughout the project's life, or where an unconventional cash flow pattern is suspected, we recommend use of the net present value approach. To underline the superiority of NPV we need to examine the respective reinvestment assumptions of the two methods.

The NPV method assumes that all cash flows can be reinvested at the firm's cost of capital. This is entirely sensible since the discount rate is an opportunity cost of capital which should reflect the alternative use of funds. The IRR method implicitly assumes that a project's annual cash flows can be reinvested at the project's internal rate of return. Thus, a project offering a 30 per cent IRR, given a 12 per cent cost of capital, assumes that interim cash flows are compounded forward at the project's rate of return (30 per cent) rather than at the cost of capital (12 per cent). In effect, therefore, the IRR method includes a bonus of the assumed benefits accruing from the reinvestment of interim cash flows at rates of interest in excess of the cost of capital. Particularly for projects with IRRs well above the cost of capital, this is a serious error.

Consider the mutually exclusive investment proposals, X and Y, given in Table 5.6. Project rankings reveal that X has the *higher* internal rate of return, but the *lower* net present value. Figure 5.2 shows how this apparent anomaly occurs. (Strictly speaking, the graphs should be curvilinear.)

Table 5.6 Comparison of mutually exclusive projects

| Proposal | Cash Flows (£) | | | | | IRR | NPV at 10% |
	Year 0	Year 1	Year 2	Year 3	Year 4		
X	− 18,896	8,000	8,000	8,000	8,000	25%	6,463
Y	− 18,896	0	4,000	8,000	26,164	22%	8,290

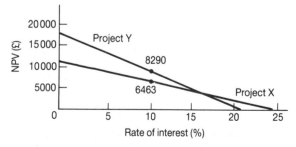

Figure 5.2 NPV and IRR compared

While Project Y has the *higher* NPV when discounted at 10 per cent, it has the *lower* IRR, the two projects intersecting at around 17 per cent. Wherever there is a sizeable difference between the project IRR and the discount rate, this problem becomes a distinct possibility.

5.6 Modified IRR

As will be seen later, most managers prefer the IRR to the NPV method. Is there a way in which the IRR can be adjusted so that it has the same reinvestment assumption as the NPV approach? The modified IRR seeks to do just that.

THE MODIFIED INTERNAL RATE OF RETURN (MIRR)

MIRR is that rate of return which, when the initial outlay is compared with the terminal value of the project's net cash flows reinvested at the cost of capital, gives an NPV of zero.

This involves a two-stage process:

1. Calculate the terminal value of the project by compounding forward all interim cash flows at the cost of capital to the end of the project.
2. Find that rate of interest which equates the terminal value with the initial cost.

Let us return to the Gooch proposal. We established earlier that it offered an NPV of £4,252 (Table 5.1) and an IRR of approximately 19 per cent (Table 5.3). Table 5.7 shows

Table 5.7 Modified IRR for Gooch

Year	Cash flow (£)	Future Value Factor @ 14%	Terminal value (£)
(a) Find the terminal value			
1	16,000	$(1.14)^3$	23,704
2	16,000	$(1.14)^2$	20,794
3	16,000	1.14	18,240
4	12,000	1.00	12,000
			74,738

(b) Find the rate of interest which equates the terminal value with initial cost
$PVIF_{(x\%, 4 \text{ yrs})} = £40,000/£74,738 = 0.535$
Using tables (Appendix B) for 4 years we find that 17 per cent gives a PVIF of 0.534.

	£
To check: £74,738 × 0.534 =	39,910
less initial investment	40,000
NPV	(90) i.e. close to zero

The Modified IRR is approximately 17 per cent compared with the IRR of 19.3 per cent.

that by compounding the interim cash flows at 14 per cent to the end of Year 4, the project offers a terminal value of £74,738. It is a relatively simple operation to find the Year 4 present value factor which comes closest to equating the terminal value with the initial outlay. Simply divide the initial outlay by the terminal value and look up the interest rate which gives this factor in Year 4 (Appendix B). For the Gooch, the MIRR is approximately 17 per cent, a good 2 per cent below the IRR figure. For more profitable projects, the deviation would be greater.

5.7   Investment evaluation and capital rationing

To date we have seen that, under the somewhat limiting assumptions specified, the wealth of a firm's shareholders is maximized if the firm accepts all investment proposals that have positive net present values. Alternatively, the NPV decision rule may be restated as: Accept investments which offer rates of return in excess of their opportunity cost of capital. The opportunity cost of capital is the return shareholders could obtain for the same level of risk by investing their capital elsewhere. *Implicit in the NPV decision rule is the notion that capital is always available at some cost to finance investment opportunities.*

In this section, we relax another assumption of perfect capital markets by considering the practical issue where, for a variety of reasons, firms are restricted from undertaking all the investments offering positive net present values. Although individual projects cannot be accepted/rejected on the basis of the NPV rule, the essential problem remains, namely, to determine the package of investment projects which offers the highest total net present value to the shareholders.

The nature of constraints on investment

In imperfect markets, the capital budgeting problem may involve the allocation of scarce resources among competing, economically desirable projects, not all of which can be undertaken. *Capital rationing*, as this is commonly termed, therefore applies equally to non-capital, as well as capital, constraints. For example, the resource constraint may be the availability of skilled labour, management time or working capital requirements. Investment constraints may even arise from the insistence that top management appraise and approve all capital projects, thus creating a backlog of investment proposals.

Hard and soft rationing

Capital rationing may arise (1) because a firm cannot obtain funds at market rates of return, or (2) because of internally-imposed financial constraints by management. Externally-imposed constraints are referred to as *hard* rationing, and internally-imposed constraints as *soft* rationing. To what extent do these constraints exist among firms? One of the findings of the Wilson Report (1980) was that there was no evidence of any general shortage of finance for industry at prevailing rates of interest and levels of demand.

Table 5.8   Constraints on a company's investment programme that are 'very
important' (100 large UK firms)

	% 1980	% 1986	% 1992
Lack of profitable investment opportunities	21.8	16.0	6.0
General economic uncertainty	15.3	8.2	9.0
Unwillingness to increase level of borrowings	19.5	11.2	19.2
Lack of capital available	10.7	1.0	4.0
Lack of trained managers to implement investment opportunities	9.5	13.3	1.0

Sources: Pike (1988, 1992).

A survey conducted by Pike (1983) found:

1.   The problem of low investment derives essentially not from a shortage of finance but
     from an inadequate demand for funds.
2.   Capital constraints, where they exist, tend to be internally imposed rather than
     externally imposed by the capital market.
3.   Capital constraints are more acutely experienced by smaller, less profitable and
     higher-risk firms.

The first two findings will be observed in Table 5.8.

The lack of profitable investment opportunities and suitably trained managers were
major factors for the low level of investment in the early 1980s. Soft rationing (partly
indicated by the unwillingness to increase borrowings) is also an important constraint; but
hard rationing (shortage of capital) is not seen as a particularly important constraint for larger
companies at least. As it is by no means certain that, for the few firms experiencing difficulty
in gaining access to financial markets, the capital constraint was *binding*, the empirical
existence of the hard form of capital rationing must be questioned.

Soft rationing

We now turn our attention to why the internal management of a company should wish to
impose a capital expenditure constraint which may actually result in the sacrifice of
wealth-creating projects. Soft rationing may arise because:

1.   Management sets maximum limits on borrowing and is unable or unwilling to raise
     additional equity capital in the short term. In effect, therefore, investment is restricted to
     internally-generated funds.
2.   Management pursues a policy of stable growth rather than a fluctuating growth pattern
     with its attendant problems.
3.   Management imposes divisional ceilings by way of annual capital budgets.

The capital budget forms an essential element of the company's complex planning and control process. It may sometimes be expedient for projects to be restricted – in the short term – to permit the proper planning and control of the organization. Institution of divisional investment ceilings also provides a simple, if somewhat crude, method of dealing with biased cash flow forecasts. Where, for example, a division is in the habit of creating numbers to justify the projects it wishes to implement, the institution of capital budget ceilings forces divisional management to set its own priorities and to select those offering highest returns.

One-period capital rationing in Mervtech plc

The simplest form of capital rationing arises when financial limits are imposed for only a single period. This is illustrated in the example below. The manufacturing division of Mervtech plc has been set an upper limit on capital spending for the coming year of £20m. It is not normal practice for the group to set investment ceilings, and it is anticipated that the capital constraint will not extend into future years. Assuming a cost of capital of 10 per cent, which of the following investment opportunities set out in Table 5.9 should divisional management select?

In the absence of any financial constraint, projects A–D, each with positive net present values, would be selected. Once this information has been communicated to investors, the total stock market value would, in theory at least, increase by £44 million – the sum of their net present values.

However, a financial constraint may prevent the selection of all profitable projects. If so, it becomes necessary to select the investment package which offers the highest net present value within the £20 million expenditure limit. A simple method of selecting projects under these circumstances is found in the profitability index, discussed earlier in this chapter. Recall that this measure is defined as:

$$\text{Profitability index} = \frac{\text{Present value}}{\text{Investment outlay}}$$

Project selection is made on the basis of the highest ratio of present value to investment outlay. This method is valuable under conditions of capital rationing because it focuses attention on the net present value of each project *relative* to the scarce resource required to undertake it. Appraising projects according to the NPV per £1 of investment outlay can give

Table 5.9 Investment opportunities for Mervtech plc

Project	Initial cost (£m)	Cash Flows (£m) Year 1	Year 2	Present value at 10%	NPV at 10%
A	− 15	+ 17	+ 17	30	15
B	− 5	+ 5	+ 10	13	8
C	− 12	+ 12	+ 12	21	9
D	− 8	+ 12	+ 11	20	12
E	− 20	+ 10	+ 10	17	− 3

Table 5.10   NPV vs. PI

Project	Profitability index	Outlay (£m)		Outlay (£m)	NPV (£m)
B	2.6	5	accept	5	8
D	2.5	8	accept	8	12
A	2.0	15	accept 7/15	7	7
C	1.7	12	reject	—	—
E	0.8	20	reject	—	—
		60		20	27

different rankings to those obtained from application of the NPV rule. For example, while in the absence of capital rationing, project A ranks highest (using the NPV rule), project B ranks highest when funds are limited, as shown in Table 5.10. Assuming project independence and infinite divisibility, divisional management will obtain the maximum net present value from its £20 million investment expenditure permitted by accepting projects B and D in total and £7,000 or 7/15 of project A.

However, the profitability index rarely offers optimal solutions in practice. In the first place, few investment projects possess the attribute of divisibility. Where it is possible for projects to be scaled down to meet expenditure limits, this is frequently at the expense of profitability. Let us suppose that projects are *not* capable of division. How would this affect the selection problem? The best combination of projects now becomes A and B, giving a total net present value of £23 million. Project D, which, ranked above A using the profitability index, is now excluded. Even more fundamental than this, however, is the limitation that the *profitability index is only appropriate when capital rationing is restricted to a single period.* This is not usually the case. Firms experiencing either form of capital rationing (hard or soft) tend to experience them over a number of periods.

In summary, the profitability index provides a convenient method of selecting projects under conditions of capital rationing when investment projects are divisible and independent, and when only one period is subject to a resource constraint. Where, as is more commonly the case, these assumptions do not hold, investment selections should be made after examining the total net present values of all the feasible alternative combinations of investment opportunities falling within the capital outlay constraints.

Multi-period capital rationing

Many business problems have similar characteristics to those exhibited in the capital rationing problem, namely:

1.   Scarce resources required to be allocated between competing alternatives.
2.   An overriding objective which the decision-maker is seeking to attain.
3.   Constraints, in one form or another, imposed on the decision-maker.

As the number of alternatives and constraints increases, so the decision-making process becomes more complex. In such cases *mathematical programming models* are particularly valuable in the evaluation of decision alternatives for two reasons:

1. They provide descriptive representations of real problems using mathematical equations. Because they capture the critical elements and relationships existing in the real system, they provide insights about a problem without having to experiment directly on the actual system.
2. They provide optimal solutions, that is, the best solution for a given problem representation.

A mathematical programming approach to solving more complex capital rationing problems is provided in the appendix to this chapter.

5.8 Summary

We have examined in this chapter a number of commonly employed investment appraisal techniques and asked the question: to what extent do they assist managers in making wealth-creating decisions?

Key points

- The net present value (NPV) method discounts project cash flows at the corporate cost of capital and then sums the cash flows. The decision rule is: accept all projects whose NPV is positive.
- The internal rate of return (IRR) is that discount rate which, when applied to project cash flows, produces a zero NPV. Projects with IRRs above the cost of capital are acceptable.
- The profitability index (PI) is a ratio of the present value of project benefits to the present value of investment costs. The decision rule is: accept projects with a PI greater than 1.
- The NPV, IRR and PI methods give the same investment advice for independent projects. But where projects are mutually exclusive, differences can arise in rankings.
- The NPV approach is viewed as more sound than the IRR method because it assumes reinvestment at the cost of capital rather than the project's IRR.
- The Modified IRR (MIRR) is that rate of return which, when the initial outlay is compared with the terminal value of the project's cash flows re-invested at the cost of capital, gives an NPV of zero. This method provides a rate of return consistent with the NPV approach.
- Payback in its various forms (simple, discounted and bail-out) is a useful method, but ignores cash flows beyond the payback period. Simple payback also ignores the time-value of money.

- Accounting rate of return (ARR) compares the average profit of the project against the book value of the asset acquired. Its main merit is that as a measure of profitability it can be related to the accounts of the business. However, it takes no account of the timing of cash flows or of the size and life of the investment.
- Capital rationing, where it exists, tends to be of the 'softer' form where management voluntarily imposes investment ceilings in the short term.
- Single-period capital rationing is resolved by ranking projects according to their profitability index. More complex multi-period capital rationing problems demand a mathematical programming approach.

Appendix

Multi-period capital rationing and mathematical programming

Where there exists an overriding financial objective (such as maximizing shareholder wealth) and financial constraints are expected to operate over a number of years, the allocation of capital resources to investment projects is best solved by the mathematical programming approach.

Many programming techniques have been developed. We shall concentrate our discussion on the most commonly found technique of linear programming. The assumptions and limitations underlying the LP approach will be discussed in a subsequent section. Problem-solving using the LP approach involves four basic steps.

1.   Formulate the problem

This requires specification of the objective function, input parameters, decision variables and all relevant constraints. Take, for example, a firm which produces two products, A and B, with contributions of £5 and £10, respectively. The firm wishes to determine the product mix which will maximize its total contribution. The *objective function* may be expressed as follows:

$$\text{maximize contribution: } £5A + £10B$$

A and B are the *decision variables* representing the number of units of products A and B that should be produced. The *input values* £5 and £10 specify the unit profit values for products A and B respectively. Constraint equations may also be determined to describe any limitations on resources whether imposed by managerial policies or the external environment.

2.   Solve the LP problem

Simple problems can be solved using either a graphical approach or the simplex method. More complex problems require a computer-based solution algorithm.

3.   *Interpret the optimal solution*

Examine the effect on the total value of the objective function if a binding constraint were marginally slackened or tightened.

4.   *Conduct sensitivity analysis*

Assess for each input parameter the range of values for which the optimal solution remains valid.

These four stages in the LP process are illustrated in the following example:

Example: Atherton plc

A particularly awkward problem has emerged for Atherton plc following the five-year planning exercise: the cost of its six major projects forming the basis of the firm's investment programme exceeds the planned finance available. Atherton plc is already highly geared and control is in the hands of a few shareholders who are reluctant to introduce more equity funds. Accordingly, the main source of funds is through cash generated from existing operations, estimated to be £300,000 p.a. over the next five years. The six projects are independent and cannot be delayed or brought forward. Each project has a similar risk complexion to that of the existing business. If necessary, projects are capable of division. The planned investment schedule and associated cash flows are given in Table 5.11.

The six projects, if implemented, are forecast to produce a total NPV of £857,000. However, the annual capital constraint of £300,000 means that for the next three years the required investment expenditure exceeds available investment finance, i.e. there is a capital rationing problem.

Solution

1.   *Specify the problem*

$$\text{Max: } 130A + 184B + 35C + 42D + 186E + 280F$$

Table 5.11   Atherton plc: Planned investment schedule (£000)

Year	A	B	Project outlays C	D	E	F	Total Outlay	Available capital
0	−200	—	−220	−110	−24	—	−554	300
1	−220	−220	−100	−150	−48	—	−738	300
2		−66	−50			−500	−616	300
3					−200		−200	300
NPV	130	184	35	42	186	280		
Total NPV = £857,000								

Subject to constraints:

$$\text{Year 0 } 200A + 220C + 110D + 24E \leqslant 300$$
$$\text{Year 1 } 220A + 220B + 100C + 150D + 48E \leqslant 300$$
$$\text{Year 2 } 66B + 50C + 500F \leqslant 300$$
$$\text{Year 3 } 200E \leqslant 300$$
$$A, B, C, D, E, F \geqslant 0 \leqslant 1$$

This LP formulation tells us to find the mix of projects producing the highest total net present value, given the constraint that only £300,000 can be spent in any year and that not more than one of each project is permitted.

2. Solve the problem

Using a linear programme on the computer gives the solution in Table 5.12. Atherton plc should accept investment proposals B and E in full plus 14.5 per cent of project A and 46.8 per cent of project F. This will produce the highest possible total net present value available of £520,000. Notice that this is significantly less than the £857,000 total NPV if no constraints are imposed.

3. Interpret the optimal solution

It will be seen from Table 5.12 that only in Years 1 and 2 is the full £300,000 utilized. These years then are *binding* constraints – their existence limits the company's freedom to pursue its objective of NPV maximization because it restricts the investment finance available to the firm in those years. Conversely, Years 0 and 3 are *non-binding*: they do not constrain the firm in its efforts to achieve its objective. Hence while there is no *additional* opportunity cost (in addition to that already incorporated in the discount rate) for non-binding periods, there is an additional opportunity cost attached to the use of investment finance in the two years where constraints are binding. These additional opportunity costs are termed *shadow prices* (or dual values). Shadow prices show how much the decision maker would be willing to pay to acquire

Table 5.12 Projects accepted based on LP solution

Project	Proportion accepted	NPV (£000)	Capital Outlay (£000)			
			Year 0	Year 1	Year 2	Year 3
A	0.145	19	−29	32	—	—
B	1	184		220	66	
C	0	—				
D	0	—				
E	1	186	−24	−48	—	−200
F	0.468	131	—	—	−234	—
		520	−53	−300	−300	−200

one additional unit of each resource that is constrained in the problem. In our particular problem, the computer analysis reveals that the shadow prices are:

Year	Shadow price	Constraint
0	0	non-binding
1	0.59	binding
2	0.56	binding
3	0	non-binding

This may be interpreted as follows: A £1 increase (reduction) in capital spending in Year 1 would produce an increase (reduction) in total NPV of £0.59. Similarly for Year 2, a £1 change investment expenditure would result in a £0.56 change in total NPV. Because the capital constraints in Years 0 and 3 are non-binding, their shadow prices are zero and a marginal change in capital spending in those years will have no impact on the NPV objective function. Shadow prices, while of value in indicating the additional opportunity cost, can only be used within a specific range. In addition, it is desirable to ascertain the effect of changes in input parameters on the optimal solution. These issues require some form of sensitivity analysis.

4. *Perform sensitivity analysis*

The computer output provides two additional pieces of information. First, it tells the decision-maker the maximum variation for each binding constraint. In our example, the shadow price for the Year 1 constraint has a range of −36 to +188. In other words, the shadow price of £0.59 would hold up to an increase in capital expenditure for that year of £188,000, or a reduction of £36,000.

The programme also indicates the margin of error permitted for input parameters before the optimal solution differs. Thus, in our example, the actual NPV for the optimal investment mix could fall as indicated below and still not change the optimal solution:

Project	Maximum permitted fall in NPV (£000)
A	−68
B	−17
E	−158
F	−280

This facility is particularly appropriate as a means of assessing the margin of error permitted for risky projects under conditions of capital rationing.

LP assumptions

In order to assess the value of the basic linear programming approach for solving the problem of project selection under conditions of capital rationing we must consider the assumptions underlying its application. The main assumptions are:

(i) All input parameters to the LP model are certain.
(ii) There is a single objective to be optimized.
(iii) The objective function and all constraint equations are linear.
(iv) Decision variables are continuous (i.e. divisible).
(v) There is independence among decision variables and resources available.

Most, if not all, of these limiting assumptions can be relaxed by utilizing the more complex mathematical programming models summarized below:

Requirement	Technique
Uncertainty	Stochastic LP
	Chance constrained programming
	LP under uncertainty
Multiple goals	Goal programming
Non-linearity	Non-linear programming
	Quadratic programming
Non-divisibility	Integer programming

Discussion of these developments is beyond the scope of this book.

Further reading

Most good finance texts cover the topic of investment appraisal well, including Lumby (1991), Brealey and Myers (1991) and Levy and Sarnat (1990). These texts also address the capital rationing problem. More detailed treatment of capital rationing is found in Pike (1983), Elton (1970), Lorie and Savage (1955) and Weingartner (1977). For a fuller discussion on the Modified IRR see McDaniel *et al.* (1988).

Questions

Self-test questions

1. List four capital budgeting methods for evaluating project proposals. Identify the main strengths and drawbacks of each.
2. Why do problems arise in evaluating mutually exclusive projects? What approach would you recommend in such circumstances?
3. Describe how the Modified IRR is calculated. What advantages does the MIRR have over the IRR in assessing capital investment decisions?
4. What do you understand by 'soft' and 'hard' forms of capital rationing? Give two approaches available to resolve capital rationing problems.

Exercises

1. Microtic Ltd, a manufacturer of watches, is considering the selection of one from two mutually exclusive investment projects, each with an estimated five-year life. Project A costs £1,616,000 and is forecast to generate annual cash flows of £500,000. Its estimated residual value after five years is £301,000. Project B, costing £556,000 and with a scrap value of £56,000, should generate annual cash flows of £200,000. The company operates a straight-line depreciation policy and discounts cash flows at 15 per cent p.a.

   Microtic Ltd uses four investment appraisal techniques: payback period, net present value, internal rate of return and accounting rate of return (i.e. average accounting profit to initial book value of investment).

   Make the appropriate calculations and give reasons for your investment advice.

   (Solution in Appendix A)

2. Mace Ltd is planning its capital budget for 19_7 and 19_8. The company's directors have reduced their initial list of projects to five, the expected cash flows of which are set out below:

Project	19_7	19_8	19_9	19_0	NPV
1	− 60,000	+ 30,000	+ 25,000	+ 25,000	+ 1,600
2	− 30,000	− 20,000	+ 25,000	+ 45,000	+ 1,300
3	− 40,000	− 50,000	+ 60,000	+ 70,000	+ 8,300
4	0	− 80,000	+ 45,000	+ 55,000	+ 900
5	− 50,000	+ 10,000	+ 30,000	+ 40,000	+ 7,900

   None of the five projects can be delayed and all are divisible. Cash flows arise on the first day of the year. The minimum return required by shareholders of Mace Ltd is 10 per cent p.a. Which projects should Mace Ltd accept if the capital available for investment is limited to £100,000 on 1 January 19_7, but readily available at 10 per cent p.a. on 1 January 19_8 and subsequently?

   (Solution in Appendix A)

3. The directors of Mylo Ltd are currently considering two mutually exclusive investment projects. Both projects are concerned with the purchase of new plant. The following data is available for each project.

	Project	
	1	*2*
	£	£
Cost (immediate outlay)	100,000	60,000
Expected annual net profit (loss)		
Year 1	29,000	18,000
2	(1,000)	(2,000)
3	2,000	4,000
Estimated residual value	7,000	6,000

The company has an estimated cost of capital of 10 per cent and employs the straight-line method of depreciation for all fixed assets when calculating net profit. Neither project would increase the working capital of the company. The company has sufficient funds to meet all capital expenditure requirements.

Required

(a) Calculate for each project:
    (i) the net present value,
   (ii) the approximate internal rate of return,
  (iii) the profitability index,
  (iv) the payback period.
(b) State which, if any, of the two investment projects the directors of Mylo Ltd should accept, and why.
(c) State, in general terms, which method of investment appraisal you consider to be most appropriate for evaluating investment projects and why.

(Certified Diploma, Dec. 1990)

4.   Mr Cowdrey runs a manufacturing business. He is considering whether to accept one of two mutually exclusive investment projects and, if so, which one to accept. Each project involves an immediate cash outlay of £100,000. Mr Cowdrey estimates that the net cash inflows from each project will be as follows:

Net cash inflow at end of:	Project A £	Project B £
Year 1	60,000	10,000
Year 2	40,000	20,000
Year 3	30,000	110,000

Mr Cowdrey does not expect capital or any other resource to be in short supply during the next three years.

Required

(a) Prepare a graph to show the functional relationship between net present value and the discount rate for the two projects (label the vertical axis 'net present value' and the horizontal axis 'discount rate').
(b) Use the graph to estimate the internal rate of return of each project.
(c) On the basis of the information given, advise Mr Cowdrey which project to accept if his cost of capital is (1) 6 per cent; (2) 12 per cent.
(d) Describe briefly any additional information you think would be useful to Mr Cowdrey in choosing between the two projects.
(e) Discuss the relative merits of net present value and internal rate of return as methods of investment appraisal.

Ignore taxation.

(ICA, PE II, July 1981)

5. Raiders Ltd is a private limited company which is financed entirely by ordinary shares. Its effective cost of capital, net of tax, is 10 per cent p.a. The directors of Raiders Ltd are considering the company's capital investment programme for the next two years, and have reduced their initial list of projects to four. Details of the projects' cash flows (net of tax) are as follows (in £000):

Project	Immediately	After 1 year	After 2 years	After 3 years	Net present value (at 10%)	Internal rate of return (to nearest 1%)
A	−400	+50	+300	+350	+157.0	26%
B	−300	−200	+400	+400	+150.0	25%
C	−300	+150	+150	+150	+73.5	23%
D	0	−300	+250	+300	+159.5	50%

None of the projects can be delayed. All projects are divisible; outlays may be reduced by any proportion and net inflows will then be reduced in the same proportion. No project can be undertaken more than once. Raiders Ltd is able to invest surplus funds in a bank deposit account yielding a return of 7 per cent p.a., net of tax.

Required

(a) Prepare calculations showing which projects Raiders Ltd should undertake if capital for immediate investment is limited to £500,000, but is expected to be available without limit at a cost of 10 per cent p.a. thereafter.

(b) Provide a mathematical programming formulation to assist the directors of Raiders Ltd in choosing investment projects if capital available immediately is limited to £500,000, capital available after one year is limited to £300,000, and capital is available thereafter without limit at a cost of 10 per cent p.a.

(c) Outline the limitations of the formulation you have provided in (b).

(d) Comment briefly on the view that in practice capital is rarely limited absolutely, provided that the borrower is willing to pay a sufficiently high price, and in consequence a technique for selecting investment projects which assumes that capital is limited absolutely is of no use.

(ICA, PE II, July 1983)

Practical assignment

6. What are the primary investment appraisal techniques employed in your organization? How well does your organization handle the problems of evaluating mutually exclusive projects and capital rationing?

CHAPTER 6
Project appraisal –
applications

Rick Faldo – the marketing manager of a manufacturer of golf equipment – has recently submitted a proposal for the production of a range of clubs for the beginner. He has just received the following response from the managing director.

MEMORANDUM

To: Rick Faldo

From: Sid Torrance   8 March 1993

Proposal C463

I have examined your proposal for the new 'Clubs for Beginners' range which you say promises a three-year payback and a 30 per cent DCF return. Some hope! You seem to have forgotten the following relevant points.

1. We have a policy that all investment is subject to a depreciation charge of 25 per cent on the reducing balance.

2. The accounting department will need to recover factory fixed overheads on the new machine.

3. We need to charge against the project the £8,000 marketing research conducted to assess the size of the market for the new range.

4. What about the financing costs? I'd have to pay 18 per cent to finance the project.

   I suggest that your 30 per cent return is more like 5 per cent after the above – projects with that level of return I can do without!

6.1   Introduction

Investment decisions, particularly larger ones with strategic implications, are not usually 'spur of the moment' decisions. The whole process, from the initial idea through to project authorization, usually takes many months, even years. We will be examining the investment decision process in Chapter 11, but a vital part of this process involves the gathering of relevant information to identify the *incremental cash flows* pertaining to the investment decision. In this chapter we consider the principles underlying economic feasibility analysis and apply them to particular situations. Particular attention is paid to the treatment of inflation and taxation in project evaluation.

LEARNING OBJECTIVES

Having read this chapter the reader should be well equipped to handle most capital investment decisions found either on an examination paper or in business.
Skills should develop in:

- Identifying the relevant information in investment analysis.
- Evaluating replacement and other decisions.
- Handling inflation.
- Assessing the effects of taxation on investment decisions.

Need for relevant information

In financial management, as with all areas of management, an effective manager needs to identify the right information for decision-making. In the case of capital investment decisions, committing a substantial proportion of the firm's funds to non-routine actions that are largely irreversible can be a risky business and demands a careful examination of all the relevant information available.

Relevant information for investment decision-making has the effect of reducing the uncertainty about a project. Thus, information on the likely costs and benefits of an investment proposal, its expected economic life, appropriate inflation rates and discount rates are gathered to provide a clearer picture of the project's economic feasibility. Frequently, we find that the reliability of the information source varies. Indeed, the origin of the data is information in itself. For example, a demand forecast from a marketing executive with a known track record of being wildly inaccurate in forecasting will be viewed differently to an official quote for the cost of a machine. The accounting system and formal reports provide a part of the relevant information, the remainder coming through informal channels, frequently more qualitative than quantitative in nature.

In identifying and analysing information, managers should remember that effective information should, wherever possible, be relevant, reliable, timely, accurate and cost-efficient.

6.2 Capital investment analysis

The investment decision is the decision to commit the firm's financial and other resources to a particular course of action. Confusingly, the same term is often applied to both *real* investment, such as buildings and equipment, and to *financial* investment, such as investment in shares and other securities. While the principles underlying investment analysis are basically unchanged, it is helpful for us to concentrate on the former category at this stage, usually referred to as capital investment projects. Our particular emphasis on strategic capital projects concentrates on the allocation of a firm's long-term capital resources.

Capital projects include not only investment in plant and equipment or buildings. Other examples of capital projects include:

- costs of developing a new product,
- a marketing campaign designed to increase long-term brand awareness,
- investment in training and management development,
- acquisition of other businesses,
- reorganization and rationalization costs (frequently in the form of redundancy payments), and
- research costs incurred in developing a strategic advantage.

Readers who have some knowledge of accounting will recognize that general accounting practice would recommend that many of the above expenditures are not 'capitalized' but 'expensed' (i.e. charged against profits rather than viewed as assets). This may well be the prudent treatment for accounting purposes, but we are primarily concerned with the analysis of decisions rather than their accounting treatment. Wherever a course of action is considered which has longer-term implications, it makes sense to treat it as a 'capital' project regardless of the accounting treatment.

Cash flow not profit

Managers in business usually view profit as the best measure of performance. It might, therefore, be assumed that capital project appraisal should seek to assess whether the investment is expected to be 'profitable'. Indeed, as we saw in the previous chapter, many firms do use such an approach.

There are, however, many problems with the profit measure for assessing future investment performance. Profit is based on accounting concepts of income and expenses relating to a particular accounting period, based on the *matching* principle. This means that income receivable and expenses payable, but not yet received or paid, along with depreciation charges, form part of the profit calculation. Consider the case of the Antwerp Furniture Company with expected annual sales from its new factory of FL400,000 and profits of FL60,000. In order to stimulate demand, customers are offered two years' credit. While this decision has no impact on the reported profit, it certainly affects the cash position – no cash flow being received for two years! Cash flow analysis considers all the cash inflows and outflows resulting from the investment decision. Non-cash flows, such as depreciation charges and other accounting policy adjustments, are not relevant to the decision. We seek to estimate the stream of cash flows arising from a particular course of action and the period in which they occur.

Timing of cash flows

Project cash flows will usually arrive throughout the year. For example, if we acquire a machine with a four-year life on 1 March 1994 the subsequent cash flows related to it may involve the monthly payment of creditors for purchases and expenses and daily receipt of cash from customers throughout each year. Strictly speaking, these cash flows should be identified on a monthly, even daily, basis and discounted using appropriate discount factors.

In practice, to facilitate the use of annual discount tables, the common convention is to assume that cash flows arising during the year are treated as occurring at the year end. Thus, while the initial outlay is assumed to occur at the start (frequently termed Year 0) subsequent cash flows are deemed to arrive somewhat later than they actually arise. This introduces an element of bias into the analysis which has the effect of producing an NPV slightly lower than the true NPV given that subsequent cash flows are positive.

6.3 Incremental cash flow analysis

Decision-making can be viewed as an *incremental* activity. Businesses generally operate as going concerns with fairly clear strategies and well-established management processes. Decisions are not so much seen in isolation but as part of a sequence of actions seeking to move the organization from its current to its intended position. The same idea is apparent in analysing projects – the decision-maker must assess how the business changes as a direct result of selecting the project. Every project can be either accepted or rejected, and it is the difference between these two alternatives in any time period, t, expressed in cash flow terms (CF_t) that is taken into the appraisal.

INCREMENTAL ANALYSIS

Project $CF_t = CF_t$ for firm with project $- CF_t$ for firm without project

---

This is not always as easy as at first appears. To illustrate this point, we consider how investment analysis handles opportunity cash flows, sunk costs, associated cash flows, working capital changes, interest costs and fixed overheads.

Opportunity cash flows

Capital projects frequently give rise to opportunity cash flows. For example, a company owns a plot of land which is not currently in use and is considering building a warehouse on it offering an NPV of £70,000. If the market value of the land is £90,000, this new use imposes an opportunity cost – the cost of denying its sale by building the warehouse. This opportunity cash flow is a fundamental element in the investment decision and should be deducted from the £70,000 giving a negative NPV of £20,000. The warehouse option is not wealth-creating – other alternatives should be explored, including that of selling the land.

We often see opportunity cash flows in replacement decisions. For example, an existing injection moulding machine can be replaced by an improved model costing £50,000, which generates cash savings of £20,000 each year for five years when it will have a £5,000 scrap value. The equipment manufacturers are prepared to give an allowance on the existing machine of £15,000, making a net initial cash outlay of £35,000. But in pursuing this course of action, we prevent the existing machine continuing its intended life when in three years' time it would yield a £3,000 scrap value. The scrap value denied three years' hence is the opportunity cost of replacing the existing machine. The cash flows associated with the replacement decision are therefore:

Year 0	Net Cost	(£35,000)
„ 1–5	Annual Cash Savings	£20,000
„ 3	Opportunity Cash Flow	(£3,000)
„ 5	Scrap Value on New Machine	£5,000

Sunk costs

By definition, any costs incurred or revenues received prior to a decision are not relevant cash flows; they are *sunk* costs. This does not necessarily imply that previously incurred costs did not produce relevant information. For example, externally conducted feasibility studies are often undertaken to provide important, technical marketing and cost data prior to a major new investment. While there is a clear link between this study and the investment project, it is a *prior* investment decision. The costs of the study should have been measured against the potential benefits in terms of better quality estimates. Sunk costs are excluded from project analysis. We are only concerned with future cash flows arising as a particular consequence of the course of action.

Associated cash flows

Investment in capital projects may have company-wide cash flow implications. There is always a danger that those involved in forecasting cash flows may not realize how the project affects other parts of the business – senior management should therefore carefully consider whether there are any additional cash flows associated with the investment decision. The decision to produce and launch a new product may influence the demand for other products within the product range. Similarly, the decision to invest in a new manufacturing plant in Eastern Europe, or to take over existing facilities may have an adverse effect on the company's exports to such countries. For example, the acquisition by Electrolux of Sweden of 100 per cent of Lehel, Hungary's main manufacturer of refrigerators, may impact on existing sales to the former Eastern bloc countries.

Working capital

It is easy to forget that the total investment for capital projects can be considerably more than the fixed asset outlay. Normally, a capital project gives rise to increased stocks and debtors to support the increase in sales. The increase in working capital (i.e. stocks plus debtors less creditors) brought about by the capital project forms part of the investment outlay, but it is a common error in project appraisal to neglect this often crucial aspect. If the project takes a number of years to reach its full capacity, it is likely that there will be additional working capital requirements in the early years, especially for new products where the seller may have to tempt purchasers by offering more than usually generous credit terms. The investment decision implies that the firm ties up fixed and working capital for the life of the project. At the end of the project, whatever is realized is returned to the firm. For fixed assets, this will be scrap or residual value – usually considerably less than the original cost, except in the case of land and some premises. For working capital, the whole figure – less the value of damaged stock and bad debts – is treated as a cash inflow in the final year.

Occasionally, the introduction of new equipment or technology reduces stock requirements. Here the stock reduction is a positive cash flow in the start year; but one should only include an equivalent negative outflow at the end of the project if it is assumed that the firm will revert to the previous stock levels. A more realistic assumption may be to assume that any replacement would at least maintain existing stock levels, in which case no cash flow for stock in the final year is necessary.

Interest

Capital projects must be financed in some way or another. Commonly, this involves borrowing which requires a series of cash outflows in the form of interest payments. Should these interest charges be included in the cash flows, since they are clearly related to the decision? The answer is a resounding 'No!' Interest charges should *not* be included because they relate to the *financing* rather than the *investment* decision. Were interest payments to be deducted from the cash flows, it would amount to double counting since the discounting process already considers the cost of capital in the form of the discount rate. To include interest charges as a cash outflow could therefore seriously understate the true NPV. Some companies have a policy of including interest on short-term loans (such as for financing seasonal fluctuations in working capital) in the cash flows. If this is the case, it is important that both the timing of the receipt and the repayment of the loan are also included. For example, the NPV on a 15 per cent one-year loan of £100,000, assuming a 15 per cent discount rate must be zero: £100,000 cash received today less the present value of interest and loan repaid after a year (i.e. £115,000/1.15).

Fixed overheads

Only *additional* fixed overheads incurred as a result of the capital project should be included in the analysis. In the short term, there will often be sufficient factory space to house new equipment without incurring additional overheads, but ultimately some additional fixed costs (for rent, heating and lighting, etc.) will be incurred. Most factories operate an accounting system whereby all costs, including fixed overheads, are charged on some agreed basis to cost centres. Investment in a new process or machine frequently attracts a share of these overheads. While this may be appropriate for accounting purposes, only *incremental* fixed overheads incurred by the decision should be included in the project analysis.

Let us return to the memo sent to Rick Faldo at the start of the chapter. The following reply might be appropriate:

MEMORANDUM

To: Sid Torrance
From: Rick Faldo   10 March 1993

Proposal C463

I have re-examined the points raised in your memo dated 8 March and discussed them with our accountant.

In analysing capital projects, only future investment cash flows incremental to the business are relevant to the decision.

1. Depreciation is not a cash flow – it is a charge against profits. By comparing operating cash flows against initial outlay, the need for depreciation becomes unnecessary.

2. Only additional fixed costs resulting from the introduction of the new project should be charged. I have checked that no extra overheads are incurred.

3. The marketing research is a past cost. Its existence is not dependent upon the outcome of the decision so should not be included.

4. I agree that finance costs are important, but the cost of finance has already been accounted for within the discount rate.

My 'Clubs for Beginners' proposal is, I suggest, an attractive one which the business could well benefit from.

6.4 Replacement decisions

The decision to replace an existing machine which has yet to reach the end of its useful life is often necessary because of developments in technology and generous trade-in values offered by manufacturers. In analysing replacement decisions, it is important to recognize that we assess the additional costs and benefits arising from the replacement, rather than the attractiveness of the new machine in isolation.

Table 6.1   Profitability of Sevvie's project

	Old Line (per unit) (p)	New Line (per unit) (p)
Materials	40	36
Labour	22	15
Variable overheads	14	14
Fixed overheads	34	40
	110	105
Selling price	150	155
Profit per unit	40	50

Example of replacement analysis: Sevvie plc

Sevvie plc manufactures components for the car industry. It is considering automating its line for producing crankshaft bearings. The automated equipment will cost £750,000. It will replace equipment with a residual value of £80,000 and a book written-down value of £200,000. It is anticipated that the existing machine has a further five years to run, when its scrap value would be £5,000.

At present, the line has a capacity of 1.25 million units per annum but, typically, it has only been run at 80 per cent of capacity because of the lack of demand for its output. The new line has a capacity of 1.4 million units per annum. Its life is expected to be five years and its scrap value at that time £105,000. The main benefits of the new proposal are the reduction in manpower and the slight improvement in price due to its superior quality.

The accountant has prepared the cost estimates shown in Table 6.1 based on output of 1,000,000 units p.a. Fixed overheads include depreciation on the old machine of £40,000 p.a. and £130,000 for the new machine. It is considered that for the company overall, other fixed overheads are unlikely to change.

The introduction of the new machine will enable the average level of stocks held to be reduced by £160,000. After five years the machine will probably be replaced by a similar machine.

The company uses 10 per cent as its cost of capital. We shall ignore taxation.

The solution is given in Table 6.2. Several comments are worthy of note.

1. It has been assumed that no benefits can be obtained from the additional capacity due to the sales constraints. In reality it would be useful to explore whether, for example, by investing in advertising, demand could be increased.
2. Fixed costs are not relevant. Depreciation is not a cash flow, and we are told that other fixed costs will not alter with the decision. The incremental cash flow per unit is therefore 16p, giving £160,000 (i.e. 1 million units at 16p) additional cash each year on the expected sales.
3. In addition to the scrap values of £80,000 in Year 0 and £105,000 in Year 5 on the old and new machines respectively, there is a £5,000 opportunity cost in Year 5. This is the scrap value no longer available as a consequence of the replacement decision.

Table 6.2 Sevvie plc solution

	Old Line (per unit) (p)	New Line (per unit) (p)
Materials	40	36
Labour	22	15
Variable overheads	14	14
	76	65
Selling price	150	155
Cash contribution	74	90
Incremental cash flow per unit		16p
Total incremental cash flow on 1 million unit sales		£160,000

Year (£000)	0	1	2	3	4	5
Cost savings		160	160	160	160	160
New machine	(750)					105
Scrap old machine	80					(5)
Working capital	160					
Net cash flow	(510)	160	160	160	160	260
Net present value						
Factor at 10%	1.000	0.909	0.826	0.751	0.683	0.621
Present value	(510)	145	132	120	109	161
Cumulative present value	(510)	(365)	(233)	(113)	(4)	157
NPV	157					

4. Working capital will be reduced by £160,000 for the period of the project and it therefore appears as a benefit in Year 0. Because the project will be replaced after five years with a similar machine, this benefit will continue indefinitely.
5. The book value of the existing machine represents the undepreciated element of the original cost, a sunk cost which is not relevant to the decision. Book value of assets, however, may be important in practice, as it can sometimes mean a heavy accounting loss in the year of acquisition. In this case the loss would be £120,000 (i.e. book value of £200,000 less £80,000 residual value). This is not a cash flow, but in practice, it may still be regarded as undesirable to depress reported profit figures in this way although the loss would probably be treated as an extraordinary item. This, of course, raises issues of market efficiency.

The replacement decision is a wealth-creating opportunity offering an NPV of £157,000, although the cumulative present value calculation in Table 6.2 shows that the project does not come into surplus, in net present value terms, until the final year.

Table 6.3 Allis plc cash flows on two projects

Year	Forklift Trucks (£)	Conveyor System (£)
0	(30,000)	(66,000)
1	10,000	12,000
2	15,000	20,000
3	18,000	20,000
4		18,000
5		15,000
6		15,000
NPV at 10%	5,010	6,538

6.5   The problem of unequal lives: Allis plc

In the Sevvie example both the existing and new machine had five-year project lives. Comparing mutually exclusive projects – such as retaining the old asset or replacing it with a new one – frequently involves the problem of assessing projects with different economic lives.

Allis plc is seeking to modernize and speed up its production process. Two proposals have been suggested to achieve this: the purchase of a number of forklift trucks and the acquisition of a conveyor system. The accountant has produced figures for the two proposals using a 10 per cent discount rate, shown in Table 6.3.

At first sight it would seem that the more expensive conveyor system is also more wealth-creating. A moment's reflection, however, will lead the reader to ask whether it is appropriate to compare projects with different lives without some adjustment. Two approaches can be employed to make the necessary adjustment: the *replacement chain* approach and the *equivalent annual annuity* approach.

The replacement chain approach recognizes that while for convenience we usually consider only the time-horizon of the proposal, most investments form part of a replacement chain over a much longer time-period. We therefore need to compare mutually exclusive projects over a *common* period. In the example, this period is six years, two forklift truck proposals (one following the other) being equivalent to one conveyor system proposal. Assuming the cash flows for the original forklift trucks also apply to their replacements in Year 4 (a pretty big assumption given inflation, improvements in technology, etc.), the replacement will produce a further NPV of £5,010 at the start of Year 4. To convert this to the present value (i.e. Year 0) we must discount this figure to the present using the discount factor for 10 per cent for a cash flow three years hence:

$$PV = £5,010 \times PVIF_{(10,3)} = £5,010 \times 0.7513 = £3,764$$

The NPV for the forklift truck proposal, assuming like-for-like replacement after three years, is therefore £5,010 + £3,764 = £8,774. This is well in excess of the NPV of the conveyor system proposal (£6,538) compared over the same time-period.

ALLIS PLC NPV COMPARISON

Years	Forklift Trucks £	Conveyor System £
1–3	5,010	
4–6 £5,010 × 0.7513	3,764	
	——	
1–6	8,774	6,538

A second approach, the equivalent annual annuity approach (EAA) is easier than its name suggests. Using the present value of an annuity table we can establish the constant annual cash flow that offers the same present value as the project's NPV.

$$NPV = PVIFA_{(10,3)} \times EAA$$

Alternatively,

$$EAA = \frac{NPV}{PVIFA_{(10,3)}}$$

For the forklift proposal:

$$EAA = \frac{£5,010}{2.4869} = £2,015$$

For the conveyor system proposal:

$$EAA = \frac{NPV}{PVIFA_{(10,6)}} = \frac{£6,538}{4.3553} = £1,501$$

The forklift proposal offers the higher equivalent annual annuity and is to be preferred. Assuming continuous replacement at the end of their project lives, the NPV for the projects over an infinite time-horizon is found by dividing the EAA by the discount rate.

$$NPV \text{ forklift truck} = £2,014/0.10 = £20,140$$
$$NPV \text{ conveyor} = £1,501/0.10 = £15,010$$

6.6 Inflation

Inflation can have a major impact on the ultimate success or failure of capital projects and we now consider how it should be treated in discounted cash flow analysis. Two problems arise in this regard: first, how does inflation affect the estimated cash flows from the project; and second, how does it affect the discount rate?

Let us consider the following:

A machine costs £18,000 and is projected to produce, in current prices, cash flows over

Table 6.4 The money terms approach

Year	Cash Flow Current prices (£)	Actual Money Prices (£)	Discount Factor @16.6%	Present Value (£)
0	(18,000) × 1.0	(18,000)	1	(18,000)
1	6,000 × 1.06	6,360	$\dfrac{1}{1.166}$	5,454
2	10,000 × (1.06)²	11,236	$\dfrac{1}{(1.166)^2}$	8,264
3	7,000 × (1.06)³	8,337	$\dfrac{1}{(1.166)^3}$	5,259
			NPV	977

the next three years of £6,000, £10,000 and £7,000, respectively. The rate of inflation is expected to run at 6 per cent and the firm's cost of capital is 16.6 per cent.

We can adopt one of two approaches:

1. Forecast cash flows in money terms and discount at the money cost of capital (i.e. 16.6 per cent), or
2. Forecast cash flows in current terms and discount at the real cost of capital.

Money terms here means the actual price levels which are forecast to obtain at the date of each cash flow; current terms means the price level prevailing today and real cost of capital means the net of inflation cost.

The approach displayed in Table 6.4 converts cash flows expressed at current prices to actual money cash flows by compounding at $(1+I)$ where I is the inflation rate. This is then discounted in the normal manner at the money discount factor (the reason for such an awkward rate will become apparent later) to give a positive NPV of £977. Had we not adjusted cash flows for inflation, the NPV would have been incorrectly expressed as a negative value.

In this example we undertook both compounding and discounting. The process could be simplified by multiplying the two elements. For example in Year 2 we could multiply $(1.06)^2$ by $1/(1.166)^2$ to obtain a net inflation discount factor of 0.8264 which, when multiplied by the cash flow in current prices gives a present value of £8,264 as stated above. This gives rise to the formula for the real cost of capital, denoted by P.

CALCULATING THE REAL COST OF CAPITAL

$$(1+P) = \frac{1+M}{1+I}$$

Where: M is the money cost of capital and I the inflation rate, and P is the real cost of capital.

Table 6.5   The real terms approach

Year	Cash Flow Current Prices (£)	Real Discount Rate @10%	PV (£)
0	(18,000)	1	(18,000)
1	6,000	$\dfrac{1}{1.1}$	5,454
2	10,000	$\dfrac{1}{(1.1)^2}$	8,264
3	7,000	$\dfrac{1}{(1.1)^3}$	5,259
			977

In our example, this gives us a real cost of capital of:

$$(1+P) = \frac{1.166}{1.06} - 1 = 0.10, \text{ i.e. a rate of 10 per cent.}$$

Applying the real cost of capital gives the same NPV as before as shown in Table 6.5.

Which is the better method? While the latter approach may be simpler, it is not without its difficulties. In business, the use of a single indicator of the rate of inflation, such as the Retail Price Index, may be inappropriate. Selling prices, wage rates, material costs and overheads rarely change at exactly the same rate each year. Rent, for example, may be fixed for a five-year period; selling prices may be held for more than a year. Furthermore, when taxation is introduced into the analysis, we find that tax relief on capital investment is not subject to inflation. Such complexities, while not unsurmountable, lead us to recommend that both cash flows and discount rates should include inflation.

6.7   Taxation

In Chapter 2, we introduced the subject of taxation and its broad implications for financial management. In this section, we examine in greater depth the taxation considerations for capital investment projects.

Recall that in the United Kingdom Corporation Tax is assessed by the Inland Revenue on the profits of the company after certain adjustments. While it is not calculated on a project basis by the Inland Revenue, the actual tax bill will increase with every new project offering additional profits in the year and reduce with every project offering losses. Corporation Tax is charged on the profits, gains and income of an accounting period, usually the period for which accounts are made up annually. In arriving at assessible profits a deduction is made for capital allowances on certain types of capital investment. Following the principle outlined earlier of identifying the incremental cash flow, we need to ask: By how much will the Corporation Tax bill for the company change each year as a result of the decision? To do this, we must consider the tax charged on project operating profits and the tax relief obtained on the capital investment outlay.

Taxation implications for Woosnam plc

Woosnam plc introduces a new piece of equipment costing £40,000 on 1 January 1993 for which *no* capital allowances can be claimed. It intends to operate the equipment for four years when its scrap value will be zero. Expected project net cash flows are £10,000 in the first year and £20,000 for the next three years. The discount rate is 15 per cent and Corporation Tax is payable at 33 per cent. Depreciation is calculated on a straight-line basis.

The usual assumption made is that tax is paid one year following the cashflow to which it gave rise occurred. Thus, as Table 6.6 demonstrates, the £10,000 in Year 1 will be taxed at 33 per cent and paid in Year 2. Note that this means that a tax charge will be incurred in Year 5, the year after the asset is scrapped. With an after-tax negative NPV of £5,496 the project should be rejected.

A quicker approach to the problem is possible:

1. Evaluate the project without tax.
2. Find the net present value of the taxable cash flows.
3. Assess the present value of the taxation implications, recalling that these occur one year later.

To demonstrate the above using the previous example, Woosnam plc has a positive NPV of £8,390 ignoring tax (see Table 6.7).

The present value of the taxable cash flows (i.e. Years 1–4) total £48,390. Tax on these at 33 per cent lagged one year at a 15 per cent discount rate (i.e. a discount factor of 0.8696) gives a negative present value for tax of:

$$33\% \times 0.8696 \times £48,390 = £13,886$$

The after-tax NPV is therefore £8,390 − £13,886 = (£5,496) which accords with the first method of calculation.

Table 6.6 Woosnam's project (assuming no capital allowances)

Year	Pre-tax Cash Flows (£)	Tax 33%	Net Cash Flows (£)	Discount Factor @15%	PV
0	(40,000)	—	(40,000)	1	(40,000)
1	10,000	—	10,000	0.869	8,690
2	20,000	(3,300)	16,700	0.756	12,625
3	20,000	(6,600)	13,400	0.657	8,804
4	20,000	(6,600)	13,400	0.572	7,665
5	—	(6,600)	(6,600)	0.497	(3,280)
				NPV @15%	(5,496)

Table 6.7　Pre-tax profitability

Year	Pre-tax Cash Flow (£)	Discount Factor @15%	PV (£)
0	(40,000)	1	(40,000)
1	10,000	0.869	8,690
2	20,000	0.756	15,120
3	20,000	0.657	13,140
4	20,000	0.572	11,440
		Pre-tax NPV	8,390

One particular advantage of this approach is that tax can be assessed at a later stage using a single calculation. The impact of taxation can also be more clearly seen; for Woosnam plc what appears to be a wealth–creating project before tax becomes distinctly uneconomic after tax. It should, however, be pointed out that the discount rate itself may be reduced as a result of tax relief. This point is taken up in a later chapter dealing with the cost of capital.

Capital allowances

For many types of capital investment, tax relief is obtainable on the capital expenditure incurred. Prior to 1984, a First-Year Allowance of 100 per cent was generally available in the United Kingdom for capital spending on plant and machinery as an incentive for firms to

Table 6.8　Woosnam's tax reliefs

End of Accounting Year	Tax Written-down value (£)	Writing-Down Allowance (£)	33% Tax Benefit (£)	Cash flow Year
1　Initial outlay	40,000			
Writing-Down Allowance				
(WDA at 25%)	10,000	10,000	3,300	
	30,000			
2　WDA at 25%	7,500	7,500	2,475	3
	22,500			
3　WDA at 25%	5,625	5,625	1,856	4
	16,875			
4　Sale proceeds	—			
Balancing allowance	16,875	16,875	5,569	5
		40,000	13,200	

Table 6.9   Woosnam with tax relief

Year	Pre-tax Cash Flows (£)	Tax @33%	Tax Benefit on WDA	Net Cash Flow (£)	PVIF @15%	PV (£)
0	(40,000)	—		(40,000)	1	(40,000)
1	10,000	—		10,000	0.869	8,690
2	20,000	(3,300)	3,300	20,000	0.756	15,120
3	20,000	(6,600)	2,475	15,875	0.657	10,430
4	20,000	(6,600)	1,856	15,256	0.572	8,726
5		(6,600)	5,569	(1,031)	0.497	(512)
					NPV	2,454

Discounting these at 15 per cent we obtain a positive NPV of £2,454, suggesting that after-tax the project is worthwhile.

invest. UK allowances were then fundamentally changed. In 1992 the main Annual Writing-Down Allowances available in the United Kingdom were as follows:

Plant and machinery   25 per cent on the reducing balance
Industrial buildings   4 per cent on the initial cost

Let us return to the Woosnam plc example, this time assuming that the capital expenditure of £40,000 attracts a 25 per cent Writing-Down Allowance. Tax is payable at 33 per cent one year following the end of the accounting period.

Note that in Table 6.8 the difference between what the investment finally sold for (in this case zero) and the balance at the start of the year is termed a *Balancing Allowance* which is regarded in the same manner as the Writing-Down Allowance. (We will not introduce further complications such as the election to pool plant and machinery in this book. Managers should consult their accountant on such matters.) A useful check is to see that the total WDA equals the initial investment and the tax benefit on this total is correct, in our example, £40,000 @ 33% = £13,200.

These cash flows can then be added to the earlier example, as in Table 6.9, showing that the investment offers a positive NPV of £2,454 after tax.

The date on which an asset is acquired can have a significant effect on the net present value. Suppose in our example Woosnam plc purchased the asset one day earlier – on 31 December 1992 rather than 1 January 1993. By bringing the purchase into the previous accounting year the WDAs would all come one year earlier, thereby improving the project's NPV.

6.8   Strategic investment options

Investment of a more strategic nature frequently offers hidden benefits beyond that found in their underlying cash flows. These hidden benefits may arise during the life of a project, but not be quantifiable, such as the greater production flexibility from the introduction of advanced manufacturing technology. Alternatively, the actual investment could open up the possibility of further wealth-creating opportunities. These we term *strategic options*.

Examples of strategic options include opportunities to:

1. Enter new markets.
2. Develop follow-up products.
3. Improve existing practices.
4. Develop brand extension.

For example, the introduction of new manufacturing technology may provide the right opportunity to introduce new management practices such as Just-in-Time procedures. Again, investment in brands by the confectioners Mars gave rise, through brand extension, to entry into the ice-cream market.

The true NPV is therefore the sum of the project NPV normally calculated and the value of strategic options.

DON'T FORGET STRATEGIC OPTIONS

True NPV = Project NPV + Value of strategic options

There is usually considerable uncertainty attached to the value of such options. An expected value approach can be useful in this regard.

Trevino has developed a new product based on state-of-the-art technology. Traditional appraisal indicates that it is not wealth-creating, offering a negative NPV of £300,000. However, it gives rise to the possibility of profitable follow-up products, yet to be tested, being sold world wide. Such a strategic option has the following possible pay-offs and associated probabilities:

Trevino – Option Value

Option NPV	Probability	£000
£2 million	0.3	600
£1 million	0.2	200
£nil	0.5	—
		___
Expected NPV on follow-up option		800
NPV on original product		(300)
		___
Expected true NPV		500

The true NPV is therefore £500,000, the value of the first investment plus the expected value of strategic option it gives rise to. Chapter 21 will introduce a further element in the decision based on option pricing theory.

6.9 Summary

One of the most difficult aspects of capital budgeting is identifying and gathering the relevant information for analysis. This chapter has examined the incremental cash flow approach to project analysis.

Key points

- Include only future, incremental cashflows relating to the investment decision and its consequences. This implies that:
  1. Only additional fixed overheads incurred are included.
  2. Depreciation (a non-cash item) is excluded.
  3. Sunk (or past) costs are not relevant.
  4. Interest charges are financing (not investment) cash flows and therefore excluded.
  5. Opportunity costs (e.g. the opportunity to rent or sell premises if the proposal is not acceptable) are included.
- Profit is not so relevant as cash flow in decision analysis.
- Replacement decision analysis examines the change in cash flows resulting from the decision to replace an existing asset with a new asset.
- Inflation can have important effects on project analysis. Two approaches are possible: (1) specify all cash flows at 'money-of-the-day' (i.e. including inflation) prices and discount at the money cost of capital, (2) specify cash flows at today's prices and discount at the real (i.e. net of inflation) cost of capital. We recommend the former in most cases.
- Taxation is for most organizations a cash flow. It includes any cash benefits from tax relief on the initial capital expenditure and tax payable on additional cash flows. Care should be taken in estimating the timing of tax cash flows. Generally, tax is assumed to be paid one year following the cash flow upon which it is based, while the tax benefit on capital expenditure occurs one year after the year-end following the end of the accounting period. Strategic options sometimes arise from certain investments. The value of such options should not be ignored.

Further reading

Most finance texts are not particularly strong on the applied aspects of capital budgeting. Levy and Sarnat (1990) and Brigham and Gapenski (1991) have useful chapters, but the US tax system is employed.

Questions

Self-test questions

1. Define the term 'incremental cash flow'.
2. Give an example of an opportunity cash flow and a sunk cost for an investment decision.

3. State two ways in which inflation can be handled in investment analysis. Which would you recommend and why?

4. Your boss says: 'We always evaluate proposals before tax. Every firm has to pay tax so we can ignore it.' Do you agree?

Exercises

1. Bramhope Manufacturing Co. Ltd has found that, after only two years of using a machine for a semi-automatic process, a more advanced model has arrived on the market. This advanced model will not only produce the current volume of the company's product more efficiently, but it will allow an increased output of the product. The existing machine had cost £32,000 and was being depreciated straight-line over a ten-year period, at the end of which it would be scrapped. The market value of this machine is currently £15,000 and there is a prospective purchaser interested in acquiring it.

The advanced model now available costs £123,500 fully installed. Because of its more complex mechanism, the advanced model is expected to have a useful life of only eight years. A scrap value of £20,500 is considered reasonable.

A comparison of the existing and advanced model now available shows the following:

	Existing machine	Advanced model
Capacity p.a.	200,000 units	230,000 units
	£	£
Selling price per unit	0.95	0.95
Production costs per unit		
Labour	0.12	0.08
Materials	0.48	0.46
Fixed overheads (allocation of portion of company's fixed overheads)	0.25	0.16

The sales director is of the opinion that the additional output could be sold at 95p per unit.

If the advanced model were to be run at the old production level of 200,000 units per annum, the operators would be freed for a proportionate period of time for reassignment to the other operations of the company.

The sales director has suggested that the advanced model should be purchased by the company to replace the existing machine.

The cost of capital is 15 per cent.

(i) You are required to calculate:
   (a) payback period,
   (b) the net present value,
   (c) the internal rate of return (to nearest per cent).

(ii) What recommendation would you make to the Sales Director and what other considerations are relevant?   (Solution in Appendix A)

2. Consolidated Oilfields plc is interested in exploring for oil near the west coast of Australia. The Australian government is prepared to grant an exploration licence to the company for a five-year period for a fee of £300,000 p.a. The option to acquire the rights must be taken immediately otherwise another oil company will be granted the rights. However, Consolidated Oilfields is not in a position to commence operations immediately, and exploration of the oilfield will not start until the beginning of the second year. In order to carry out the exploration work the company will require equipment costing £10,400,000 which will be made by a specialist engineering company. Half of the equipment cost will be payable immediately and half will be paid when the equipment has been built and tested to the satisfaction of Consolidated Oilfields. It is estimated that the second instalment will be paid at the end of the first year. The company commissioned a geological survey of the area and the results suggest that the oilfield will produce relatively small amounts of high quality crude oil. The survey cost £250,000 and is now due for payment.

The assistant to the project accountant has produced the following projected profit and loss accounts for the project for Years 2–5 when the oilfield is operational.

Projected profit and loss accounts

		Year						
		2		3		4		5
	£000	£000	£000	£000	£000	£000	£000	£000
Sales		7,400		8,300		9,800		5,800
Less expenses								
Wages and salaries	550		580		620		520	
Materials and consumables	340		360		410		370	
Licence fee	600		300		300		300	
Overheads	220		220		220		220	
Depreciation	2,100		2,100		2,100		2,100	
Survey cost written off	250		—		—		—	
Interest charges	650		650		650		650	
		4,710		4,210		4,300		4,160
Profit		2,690		4,090		5,500		1,640

The following additional information is available:

1. The licence fee charge appearing in the accounts in Year 2 includes a write off for all the annual fee payable in Year 1. The licence fee is paid to the Australian government at the end of each year.
2. The overheads contain an annual charge of £120,000 which represents an apportionment of head office costs. This is based on a standard calculation to ensure

that all projects bear a fair share of the central administrative costs of the business. The remainder of the overheads relate directly to the project.

3. The survey costs written off relate to the geological survey already undertaken and due for payment immediately.

4. The new equipment costing £10,400,000 will be sold at the end of the licence period for £2,000,000.

5. The project will require a specialized cutting tool for a brief period at the end of Year 2, which is currently being used by the company in another project. The manager of the other project has estimated that he will have to hire machinery at a cost of £150,000 for the period the cutting tool is on loan.

6. The project will require an investment of £650,000 working capital from the end of the first year to the end of the licence period.

The company has a cost of capital of 10 per cent.

Ignore taxation.

Required

(a) Prepare calculations which will help the company to evaluate further the profitability of the proposed project.

(b) State, with reasons, whether you would recommend that the project be undertaken.

(c) Explain how inflation can pose problems when appraising capital expenditure proposals, and how these problems may be dealt with.

(Certified Diploma, June 1991)

Practical Assignment: Engineering Products case study

Roger Davis, the newly appointed financial analyst of the steel tube division of Engineering Products plc, shut his office door and walked over to his desk. He had just 24 hours to re-examine the accountant's profit projections and come up with a recommendation on the proposed new computer-numerically-controlled milling machine.

At the meeting he had just left the managing director made it quite clear: 'If the project can't pay for itself in the first three years it's not worth bothering with.' Davis was unhappy with the accountant's analysis and said so at the meeting. He was then given until this time tomorrow to come up with a 'more realistic estimate, otherwise the £240,000 capital project is a non-starter'.

His first task was to re-examine the accountant's profitability forecast (Table 6.10) in the light of the following facts that emerged from the meeting:

1. Given the rapid developments in the arket it was unrealistic to assume that the product had more than a four-year life. The machinery would have no other use and could not raise more than £20,000 in scrap metal at the end of the project.

2. The opening stock in Year 1 would be acquired at the same time as the machine. All other stock movement would occur at the year ends.

3. This type of machine was depreciated over six years on a straight-line basis.

Table 6.10 Profit projection for CNC milling machine (£000)

| | Year | | | |
	1	2	3	4
Sales	400	600	800	600
Less Costs				
Materials				
Opening stock	40	80	80	60
Purchases	260	300	360	240
Closing stock	(80)	(80)	(60)	—
Cost of Sales	220	300	380	300
Labour	80	120	120	80
Other production expenses	80	90	92	100
Depreciation	40	40	40	40
Administrative overhead	54	76	74	74
Interest on loans to				
finance the project	22	22	22	22
Total Cost	496	648	728	616
Profit (Loss)	(96)	(48)	72	(16)

4. Within the 'other production expenses' were apportioned fixed overheads equal to 20 per cent of labour costs.
5. The administration charge was an apportionment of central fixed overheads.

Later that day Davis met the production manager, who explained that if the new machine was installed, it would have sufficient capacity to enable an existing machine to be sold immediately for £20,000 and to create annual operating savings of £18,000. However, the accountant had told him that with the machine currently standing in the books at £50,000 the company simply could not afford to write off the asset against this year's slender profits. 'We'd do better to keep it operating for another four years, when its scrap value will produce about £8,000,' he said.

Davis then raised the proposal with the marketing director. It was not long before two new pieces of information emerged:

1. To stand a realistic chance of hitting the sales forecast for the proposal marketing would require £40,000 for additional advertising and sales promotion at the start of the project and a further £8,000 a year for the remainder of the project's life. The sales forecast and advertising effort had been devised in consultation with marketing consultants whose bill for £18,000 had just arrived that morning.
2. The marketing director was very concerned about the impact on other products within the product range. If the investment went ahead, it would lead to a reduction in sales value of a competing product of around £60,000 a year. 'With net profit margins of around 10 per cent and gross margins (after direct costs) of 25 per cent on these sales, this is probably the "kiss of death" for the CNC proposal,' Davis reflected.

He went home that evening with a very full briefcase and a number of unresolved questions. Even if the proposal were profitable, what was an acceptable return? The latest accounts for the division showed a 16 per cent return on assets, but the MD talked about a three-year payback requirement. His phone call to the finance director at Head Office, to whom this proposal would eventually be sent, was distinctly unhelpful: 'We have, in the past, found that whenever we lay down a hurdle rate for divisional capital projects, it merely encourages unduly optimistic estimates from divisional executives eager to promote their pet proposals. So now we give no guidelines on this matter.'

Davis figured that as an absolute minimum the shareholders would be looking for a return of 10 per cent, the current yield obtainable from risk-free government securities. Any risk associated with the project would be discussed separately. Engineering Products plc pays Corporation Tax at 30 per cent and annual Writing-Down Allowances of 25 per cent on the reducing balance may be claimed. The existing machine has a nil value for tax purposes.

Required

Prepare the case to be presented by Davis at tomorrow's meeting:

1. Ignoring taxation.
2. With taxation.

CHAPTER 7
Investment evaluation in practice

CAN FIRMS AFFORD NOT TO INVEST?

Henry Ford once claimed: 'If you need a new machine and don't buy it, you pay for it without getting it.' The price paid is the loss in competitiveness from not taking advantage of new technology.

In evaluating proposed investments, managers have turned increasingly to sophisticated techniques. Their goal has been greater rationality in making investment decisions, yet their accomplishment has often been quite different – a serious under-investment in the capital stock (the productive capacity, technology and worker skills) on which their companies rest. As a result they have unintentionally jeopardized their companies' futures.

Ingersoll Milling Machine Company took a strategic view that it needed to invest in the latest technology. Therefore, each production department manager must annually write a justification to *keep* any machine that is over seven years old. The only generally accepted reason for not replacing equipment is that a new machine does not offer any significant improvements over older models.

(based on Hayes and Garvin (1982) and Kaplan (1986))

7.1 Introduction

A company's ability to succeed in the hostile environment within which it frequently operates depends to a great extent on its ability to regenerate itself through wealth-creating capital investment decisions compatible with business strategy. In recent years, most of the combined internal and external funds generated by UK firms has been committed to fixed capital investment. Applying such resources to long-term capital projects in anticipation of an adequate return – although a hazardous step – is essential for the vitality and well-being of the organization.

In earlier chapters, we discussed the mechanics of appraising investment projects. We now turn to consider the historical development of capital budgeting, and the extent to which the principles of project appraisal have been *applied* in practice. Attention will focus on the disparities arising between investment theory and practice and the role of traditional measures of investment worth in the modern capital budgeting system.

LEARNING OBJECTIVES

The key learning objectives in this chapter are related to deepening the reader's awareness of why investment in practice often deviates from that prescribed in most finance texts. This appreciation includes:

- The continued popularity of traditional investment appraisal methods.
- The dangers of discounted cash flow techniques.
- The preference for IRR rather than NPV.
- Differences between European and Japanese investment practices.

7.2   Use of DCF techniques

It is a common misconception that the discounted cash flow approach is a relatively recent phenomenon. Historical records, however, reveal an understanding of compound interest (upon which discounted cash flow techniques are based) as far back as the Old Babylonian period (*c.*1800–1600 BC) in Mesopotamia. The earliest manuscripts setting out compound interest tables date back to the fourteenth century, while the first recorded reference to the net present value rule is found in a book by Stevin published in 1582.

In these early days, the application of discounted cash flow methods was restricted to financial investments such as loans and life assurance, where the cash flows were either known or their probabilities could be determined based on actuarial evidence. Only in the nineteenth century, with the industrial revolution well established, did the scale of capital investments lead some engineering economists to begin to apply discounted cash flow concepts to capital assets. However, in practice, discounted cash flow concepts were largely ignored until the early 1950s in America and the early 1960s in the United Kingdom.

Surveys conducted by Pike on the same companies between 1975 and 1992 provide a clearer picture of the changing trends in the practices of larger firms within the United Kingdom. Table 7.1 shows that while all firms surveyed conduct financial appraisals on capital projects, the choice of method varies considerably, and most firms employ a combination of appraisal techniques.

DCF methods have greatly increased in usage from 58 per cent in 1975 to 88 per cent by 1992. Hitherto, the IRR method enjoyed much greater popularity than the theoretically preferred NPV approach. However, in recent years, there has been a marked acceleration in the adoption of the NPV method.

Table 7.1 Capital investment evaluation methods in 100 large UK firms

Firms Using:	1992 (%)	1986 (%)	1981 (%)	1975 (%)
Payback	94	92	81	73
Average accounting rate of return	50	56	49	51
DCF methods (IRR or NPV)	88	84	68	58
Internal rate of return	81	75	57	44
Net Present Value	74	68	39	32

Source: Pike (1988 and 1992).

Table 7.2 Capital investment evaluation methods in 100 large UK firms: frequency of use in 1992

Firms Using:	Total (%)	Rarely (%)	Often (%)	Mostly (%)	Always (%)
Payback	94	6	12	14	62
Average accounting rate of return	50	17	13	5	21
Internal rate of return	81	7	13	7	54
Net present value	74	11	16	14	33

Source: Pike (1992).

The observed increase in DCF approaches has not come at the expense of traditional methods such as payback and return on capital. The payback method is almost universally employed and we will consider why it enjoys such popularity later in this chapter. It is clear that firms do not normally rely on any single appraisal measure but prefer to employ a combination of simple and more sophisticated techniques. Almost two-thirds of the firms surveyed used three or more appraisal techniques. DCF methods therefore complement, rather than substitute for, traditional approaches.

At least two interpretations can be given for this. First, it may indicate that no single appraisal technique is sufficiently simple for managers to understand, yet sufficiently complicated to embody the important relationships holding in the real world. Second, if the formal evaluation stages seek to develop a case to justify the form of project chosen, managements will utilize that technique which reflects the project in the best possible light.

In the remainder of this chapter, we shall examine the disparity existing between investment theory and practice and assess how the two may be reconciled.

7.3 Traditional appraisal methods

Over the years, managers have developed and come to rely upon a number of simple rule-of-thumb approaches to analyse investment worth. Two of the most popular of these traditional methods are the *payback period* and the *accounting rate of return*, both of which were described in earlier chapters. Our present interest is to ask whether they have a valuable role to play in the modern capital budgeting process. Do they in fact offer anything to the decision maker that cannot be found in the DCF approaches?

Accounting rate of return (ARR)

The use of the rate of return on capital employed as a tool for evaluating an organization's past performance and as a criterion for assessing the acceptability of planned operating activities is well established. As Table 7.1 reports, a little over half the companies surveyed employ the accounting rate of return approach in assessing investment decisions. This is not altogether surprising, given that the rate of return on capital remains the single most important financial goal in practice (see Chapter 1, Table 1.1).

The ARR can be criticized on at least two counts: it uses accounting profits rather than cash flows, and it ignores the time-value of money. Despite the theoretical shortcomings, there has been a certain amount of support for the ARR in the literature. Part of the case in favour of retaining the ARR lies in the fact that its absence leads to an inconsistency between methods commonly used to *report* a firm's results and the techniques most frequently employed to *appraise* investment decisions. This inconsistency is most acutely experienced where the divisional manager of an investment centre is expected to use a DCF approach in reaching investment decisions while his short-term performance is being judged on a return on investment basis. Little wonder, then, that the divisional manager generally shows a marked reluctance to enter into any profitable long-term investment decisions which produce low returns in the early years.

An assumption commonly held by managers is that the accounting rate of return and the internal rate of return produce much the same solutions. While there is a relationship between a project's discounted return and the ARR, the relationship is not a simple one. Consider an investment costing £10,000 and generating an annual stream of net cash flows of £3,000. Assuming straight-line depreciation, the relationship between the internal rate of return and the accounting rate of return calculated on both the total investment and the average investment is as shown in Table 7.3.

From this example, the following general observations may be drawn: the accounting rate of return on total investment consistently *understates*, and the accounting rate of return on average investment *overstates*, the internal rate of return. The case for retaining the accounting rate of return is, therefore, only valid when applied as a secondary criterion to highlight the likely impact on the organization's profitability upon which the divisional manager is judged.

Table 7.3 Relationship between ARR and IRR

Project Duration (years)	5	10	20	25
IRR (%)	15.2	27.3	29.8	30
ARR on total investment (%)	10	20	25	27.5
Deviation from IRR	−5.2	−7.3	−4.8	−2.5
ARR on average investment (%)	20	40	50	55
Deviation from IRR	+4.8	+12.7	+20.2	+25

Payback period

While most finance texts have condemned the use of the payback period as potentially misleading in reaching investment decisions, Table 7.1 shows that it continues to flourish as the most widely applied formal technique, being employed within 94 per cent of firms surveyed. Why is payback so popular? Does it possess certain qualities not so apparent in more sophisticated approaches?

The two main objections to payback are well known:

1. It ignores all cash flows beyond the payback period.
2. It does not consider the profile of the project's cash flows within the payback period.

Although such theoretical shortcomings could fundamentally alter a project's ranking and selection, it would seem that the payback criterion possesses more internal theoretical strength than it is sometimes credited with; for a good many investment proposals it provides a reasonable approximation to that obtained from applying the net present value approach. One reason for this is that the two fundamental objections referred to above counteract each other to some extent. Consider the following example, summarized in Table 7.4.

Two mutually exclusive projects both have an investment outlay of £20,000 and an estimated life of eight years. Only the annual net cash flows differ: over the first four years, project A has a uniform annual series of £5,000, while project B has first-year cash flows of £8,100 declining thereafter at the rate of one-third of the previous year's cash flow.

Ranking these proposals according to their payback would lead to project A (with a four-year payback) being accepted; but applying a discounted payback approach which considers the profile of cash flows within the payback period, project B is preferred because it offers a higher present value over the first four years.

In many cases, however, the profile of cash flows in the early years has an information content with regard to the later years. Data collection for the later years is a difficult and costly business, and the estimates so obtained are often subject to a considerable degree of uncertainty. In the absence of specific information to the contrary, it is not unreasonable to assume that for most projects, the profile of the cash flows within the payback calculation is a fair predictor of post-payback cash flows. Consider the figures in Table 7.5.

When all cash flows are included in the computation, project A is seen to be the better option and the only project with a positive net present value, after deducting the £20,000 investment outlay. It will be recalled that this accords with the payback ranking. This example illustrates that in ranking projects using a simple payback method, the error from ignoring post-payback cash flows is, to some extent, compensated by the error arising from failure to consider the time value of money in the payback calculation. It should be noted that

Table 7.4 Project data for A and B, Years 1–4 (£)

Project	Year 1	2	3	4	Total	Present Value (@15%
A	5,000	5,000	5,000	5,000	20,000	14,275
B	8,100	5,400	3,600	2,400	19,500	14,867

Table 7.5 Project data for A and B, Years 5–8 (£)

Project	Year 5	6	7	8	Years 1–4 Present Value @15%	Years 1–8 Present Value @15%	NPV
A	5,000	5,000	5,000	5,000	14,275	22,436	2,436
B	1,600	1,067	711	474	14,867	16,555	(3,445)

these 'compensating errors' only arise where the early cash flows are reasonable predictors of later cash flows.

Payback period does offer a number of benefits.

1. Estimates DCF return

The payback period provides a crude measure of investment profitability. When the annual cash receipts from a project are uniform, the payback reciprocal is the internal rate of return for a project of infinite life, or a good approximation to this rate for long-lived projects. The following mathematical relationship between the IRR and payback reciprocal is derived in the appendix to this chapter.

RELATIONSHIP BETWEEN IRR AND PAYBACK

IRR for projects with long lives and constant cash flow:

$$IRR = \frac{1}{payback\ period}$$

In the case of *very* long-lived projects where the cash inflows are, on average, spread evenly over the life of the project, the payback reciprocal is a reasonable proxy for the internal rate of return. For example, a project offering permanent cash savings and giving a four-year payback period with relatively stable annual cash returns will have approximately a 25 per cent internal rate of return (i.e. the reciprocal of payback period). However, if the project life is only ten years, the IRR would fall to 21 per cent – some four percentage points below the payback reciprocal. In fact, the payback reciprocal consistently overstates the true rate of return for finite project lives. Here, perhaps, is the key: whereas (as will be seen later) the application of discounting approaches tends to be biased *against* investment, payback period – when used as a profitability criterion – is biased in *favour* of investment. The one tends to counteract the other, leaving the decision maker to exercise judgement and consider the non-quantitative aspects.

2. Considers uncertainty

Payback is seen as a useful tool in times of high levels of uncertainty and inflation. Whereas more sophisticated techniques attempt to model the uncertainty surrounding project returns, payback assumes that risk is time related; the longer the period, the greater the chance of failure. The high levels of inflation and worldwide recession experienced in recent years have rendered the task of forecasting cash flows highly speculative; but for the most part, cash flows are correlated over time. If the operating returns are below the expected level in the early years they will probably also be below plan in the later years.

Discounted cash flow, as practised in most firms, ignores this increase in uncertainty over time. Early cash flows, therefore, have an important information content on the degree of accuracy of subsequent cash flows. By concentrating on the early cash flows, the payback approach analyses the data where managers have greater confidence. Should such evaluation provide a different signal from DCF methods, it highlights the need for a more careful consideration of the project's risk characteristics.

3. Screening device

Payback provides a simple and reasonably efficient measure for ranking projects when constraints prevail. The most obvious constraint is the time managers can devote to initial project screening. Only a handful of the investment ideas originally generated may stand up to serious and thorough financial investigation. Payback period serves as a simple, first-level screening device which, in the case of marginal projects, tends to operate in their favour and permits them to go forward for more thorough investigation.

Ranking projects according to their ability to repay quickly, although possessing certain intuitive logic, does not necessarily lead to optimal solutions. Many firms resort to payback period when experiencing liquidity constraints. Such a policy may make sense when funds are constrained and better investment ideas are in the pipeline. The attractiveness of investment proposals considered during the interim period will be more a function of their ability to pay back rapidly than their overall profitability.

4. Assists communication

A good investment appraisal method should be acceptable at all management levels. Why do managers feel more comfortable with payback period than with DCF? In the first place, its acceptability is a function of its simplicity. The non-quantitative manager is reluctant to rely on the recommendations of 'sophisticated' models when he lacks both the time and expertise to verify such outcomes. Confidence in and commitment to a proposal depend to some degree on how thoroughly the evaluation model is comprehended. Another useful role for payback period is as a communication device. It offers convenient shorthand for the desirability of each investment that is understandable at all levels of the organization; namely, how quickly will the project recover its initial outlay? Some firms use a project classification system in which the payback period indicates how rapidly proposals should be processed and put into operation.

Ultimately, it is the manager – not the method – who makes investment decisions and is appraised on their outcome. Payback period is particularly attractive to managers not only because it is convenient to calculate and communicate, but also because it signals good investment decisions at the earliest opportunity.

While the payback concept may lack the refinements of its more sophisticated evaluation counterparts, it possesses many endearing qualities which make it irresistible to most managers. Herein lies the secret of its resilience.

7.4   Why managers prefer IRR to NPV

Table 7.2 shows that, in 54 per cent of the firms surveyed, the internal rate of return is always conducted in project appraisals. This is in contrast to the theoretically more acceptable net present value approach where the comparable usage is only 33 per cent. Why do managers have such a clear preference for the IRR method? It is surely not on theoretical grounds for, as discussed in an earlier chapter, the IRR has a number of technical shortcomings compared with the NPV method. Nor is the preference based on ease of computation – it is actually more complicated to compute, if only because it involves repeated application of the same calculation. Discussions with financial managers suggest that there are three main reasons for their preference for the internal rate of return.

1. *Project Ranking*   The IRR is a convenient method for choosing from mutually exclusive projects or in selecting projects when capital rationing prevails. Comparison between alternatives, it is argued, is simplified by ranking projects according to their rate of return. Although such an approach possesses a certain intuitive appeal, we saw in Chapter 5 that it is exactly in this area that the IRR is most suspect. We noted also that most cases of capital rationing are 'soft', i.e. self-imposed.

2. *Preference for a Rate of Return*   The popularity of the IRR is in part psychological: managers simply prefer a measure of investment worth which is expressed in percentage terms. Managers may feel more comfortable with a rate of return because they wish to relate it to the firm's return on capital. This can be dangerous, as we shall see later.

3. *Timing*   The IRR method permits separation of the *calculation* from its *application* as a decision rule. The analyst can concentrate on the data collection and cash flow estimates which combine to produce a proposal's internal rate of return estimate. Management then receives the proposal and decides what the cut-off rate should be.
    This approach has obvious practical advantages, particularly in large divisionalized firms where project preparation, evaluation and approval are conducted at different stages and at different levels in the organizational hierarchy. It permits the decision-maker to apply the most recent cost of capital estimate without necessitating further computation, as in the case of net present value. Given that risk is generally difficult to quantify and may alter during the decision process, such changes are far easier to accommodate using the IRR method.
    A further practical advantage of distancing the DCF calculation from the cut-off rate concerns the 'numbers game' commonly played within divisionalized organizations, particularly when top management imposes annual capital budget ceilings. Under such competition for a limited available amount of finance, divisional management may feel obliged to submit proposals based on somewhat over-optimistic forecasts to ensure that

the 'essential' elements of its investment programme are approved. (It must be said that this is sometimes encouraged by top management setting unrealistically high target cut-off rates.) A cut-off rate is, therefore, seen as a number to beat rather than the criterion for assessment. When such behaviour is prevalent, it may not be appropriate to communicate the cut-off level to divisional management. Central management would then adjust the required rate of return, not simply for the degree of underlying project risk, but also for the perceived degree of optimism in the underlying forecasts.

In the final analysis, it seems that managers much prefer the internal rate of return to the net present value method. If so, we suggest that the modified IRR, described in Chapter 5, is applied. However, the simple rule we recommend is: When in doubt, use net present value.

7.5 Dangers with DCF: the illusion of accuracy

While we have argued that DCF analysis offers a conceptually sound approach for appraising capital projects, a word of caution is appropriate at this point.

From the emphasis devoted by most textbooks to advanced capital budgeting methods, one might be forgiven for assuming that successful investment is exclusively attributable to the correct evaluation method. Only a handful of businessmen and academics have suggested that the emphasis on sophistication is misplaced. The art of capital investment involves asking the appropriate strategic questions, operating thorough search and screening procedures, and generally providing a framework which permits managers to make better decisions. DCF methods often create an illusion of exactness which the underlying assumptions do not warrant. Experience in many firms has been that greater reliance on such methods has come at the expense of the human element in decision-making. As top management places more weight on the quantifiable element, there is a danger that the unquantifiable aspects of the decision, which frequently have a critical bearing on a project's success or failure, will be devalued. The human element is particularly important with regard to project sponsoring. It is not uncommon to find that the margin between a project's success or failure hinges on the enthusiasm and commitment of the person sponsoring and implementing it.

The survey reported in Table 7.6 supports the importance of unquantified aspects in capital budgeting. Sixty-three per cent of respondents ranked 'qualitative' factors as 'important' or 'very important' in investment decisions, while only 55 per cent gave such ratings to sophisticated investment methods and systematic procedures. The message is clear: formal evaluation such as DCF is just one of many factors in the investment decision process.

The relevance of the DCF methods may be questioned on pragmatic grounds. Executives remain sceptical that adoption of such techniques actually results in a discernible improvement in performance. Indeed, a major reason for the slow acceptance of DCF methods may be the apparent lack of evidence that DCF adoption improves performance.

Empirical studies examining the association between investment sophistication and performance offer little support either. The associations found between the use/non-use of

Table 7.6 Importance of systematic procedures and qualitative factors

Importance Scale	Sophisticated and Systematic Procedures	Qualitative Factors
	%	%
Very important	23	22
Important	32	41
Average importance	29	32
Below average importance	11	3
Relatively unimportant	5	2
	100	100

Source: Pike (1983).

various techniques and corporate performance offers little support for the view that the *more* profitable firms tend to operate sophisticated investment techniques. Given this, managers have every right to be sceptical of advanced techniques which neither they nor academics have been able to demonstrate to be cost-effective in practice.

Discounting approaches may also be questioned in terms of relevance. Managers cannot afford to treat investment decisions in a vacuum, ignoring the complexities of the business environment. Any attempt to incorporate such complexities, however, will, at best, consist of abstractions from reality predicated on generalized and simplified assumptions concerning business relationships and environments. A fundamental assumption underlying DCF methods is that decision-makers pursue the primary goal of maximizing shareholders' wealth. Empirically, this assumption must be questioned. As reported in Chapter 1, a return-on-capital financial goal is the most commonly used objective; more explicit shareholder goals are given a lower priority.

The literature generally assumes that DCF methods are appropriate for all organizations, regardless of context. Such distancing of the technical from the organizational is increasingly coming into question. Employment of sophisticated tools and formal approaches to decision making does not suit all organizations – the investment appraisal process will vary with a firm's external environment (such as intensity of the competition it faces, rate of technological change, etc.) and internal characteristics (such as its systems of control and rewards). A number of studies have developed contingency frameworks which highlight the significance of such characteristics in the design of accounting systems. Extending this notion to capital budgeting, effective and efficient allocation of resources depends to a great extent on how well the investment process fits the corporate context. For example, DCF methods and formal risk analysis may well be appropriate in larger, capital-intensive, decentralized organizations operating in high-technology industries and with a management which feels comfortable with analytical decision methods. But smaller organizations, preferring a more interpersonal managerial approach, may find sophisticated techniques distinctly unhelpful; the price of investment sophistication may be too high if it stifles the intuitively-minded manager.

The final danger with DCF methods arises more from *errors in application* than from the model itself. Time and again, one observes critical errors in the way theory is applied by managers. Usually these errors are biased against investment.

COMMON ERRORS IN APPLYING DCF

- Discount rates are calculated on a pre-tax basis while operating cash flows are calculated after tax.
- Discount rates are increased to compensate for non-economic statutory and welfare investments.
- Reducing cash flows 'to allow for depreciation'.
- Cash flows are specified in today's money (excluding inflation), while hurdle rates are based on the money cost of capital, including inflation.
- Managerial aversion to uncertainty frequently results in conservative project life and terminal value assumptions.
- Use of a single cut-off rate instead of a 'tailor-made' rate: this often leads to deferral of low-risk/low-return replacement projects, sometimes indefinitely.
- Failure to include scrap values.
- Neglect of working capital movements.

7.6 Japanese practices

While British and European companies are often charged with short-termist behaviour when it comes to investment decisions, Japanese manufacturers appear to be more willing to undertake long-term investments. The observation that Japanese managers make little use of DCF methods raises the question of whether adoption of Japanese investment appraisal methods might discourage short-termist behaviour.

What methods, then, do Japanese managers employ in appraising investment projects? The vast majority appear to assess a project's return based on cash flow projections that include imputed interest charges on the project (Hodder 1986). Other Japanese firms adopt a practice analogous to the average rate of return and discounted payback methods.

When it comes to assessing project risk, Japanese managers do not normally increase the imputed interest charge. In other words, higher-risk projects do not usually have a harder passage through the financial evaluation stage, as typically happens in Europe, where a higher discount rate is often employed.

The apparent naivety of Japanese managers in financial analysis of projects is, however, more than compensated for on the non-financial side. Japanese firms generally are much less 'numbers-driven' than European firms. They place great store on involving all managers involved with the project, however remotely, and emphasizing 'consensus' decision-making. In analysing an investment proposal, managers *discuss* the implications of different input prices, competitors' response, government interference, future scenarios, but do not resort to complex quantitative analysis. During this discussion process, every aspect of the proposal is scrutinized. Project risks are identified and, where possible, reduced through project redesign. Their consensus approach and refusal to be driven by numbers makes it easier to accept projects with dubious expected financial returns than might be the case in a European-based company.

7.7   Advanced manufacturing technology (AMT) investment

The 1980s and 1990s saw the growth in new technology capital projects, creating somewhat different problems for the decision-maker. Tomkins (1991) provides the following helpful classification for advanced manufacturing techniques.

Just-in-time methods (JIT)

This approach originated from the Japanese philosophy of continual improvement. Huge reductions in stock levels and wastage have been experienced by many firms following JIT introduction. This is achieved by ensuring that the time between receipt of a sales order and delivery of the product is minimized; and that the flow of deliveries so match the production required that the traditional requirement to purchase materials and produce finished goods for stock is no longer necessary. The key to JIT is found in devising efficient delivery systems, both within the organization and with outside suppliers and customers. With stock levels often one of the major elements of capital investment projects, the effect of JIT on investment performance can be considerable.

'Islands of automation'

Advanced Manufacturing Technology (AMT) projects offer a range of less tangible benefits, for example, greater flexibility with reduced 'downtime' on production changeover. Greater flexibility enables businesses to meet the challenge of increasing competition, shorter product life-cycles and meeting customers' specific requirements. AMT offers a flexible manufacturing system (FMS) in which a sequence of production operations are computer-controlled to respond to ever-changing production and design requirements.

AMT TERMINOLOGY

AMT investment helps companies achieve such competitive advantage through a number of technologies:

- Computer-aided design (CAD) helps the engineer test and modify a design from any viewpoint.
- Computer-integrated manufacture (CIM) brings together the manufacturing process and the computer.
- Computer-numerically-controlled (CNC) machines can be easily reprogrammed to perform different tasks.
- Flexible Manufacturing Systems (FMS) enable the firm to produce a far greater variety of components quickly.
- Direct numerical control (DNC) systems connect a number of numerically controlled machines by computer.

Computer-integrated manufacturing (CIM)

This involves the computerization of functions and their integration into a system that regulates the manufacturing process. It brings together the individual manufacturing techniques referred to earlier under unified computer control.

AMT example: Foster Engineering

Foster Engineering Ltd is considering introducing a flexible manufacturing system (FMS) to modernize the methods of production in one of its departments currently using conventional metal-working machinery. The declining market and the awareness that its main competitors have recently introduced new technology made the need to modernize plant facilities an urgent priority.

An AMT proposal has been put forward offering an FMS capable of producing the present output. It involves two machining centres with CNC lathes, a conveyor system for transferring components and a computer for scheduling, tooling and overall control. The total investment would cost £2.4m, half being incurred at the start and the other half after one year at which point the existing machinery could be sold for £50,000. Any benefit would arise from Year 2 onwards for five years. The two quantified benefits are:

1. A reduction in the number of skilled workers from 50 to 15. The annual cost of a skilled worker is £20,000 (savings of 35 × £20,000 = £700,000 p.a.).
2. Savings in scrap and re-work of £50,000 p.a.

The company requires all projects to offer a positive net present value discounted at 15 per cent.

The accountant produces the following evaluation showing the FMS proposal has a negative NPV of £159,000 and fails to meet corporate investment criteria.

FMS PROPOSAL

		£000
Annual benefit		
PV at Year $1 = £700,000 \times PVIFA_{(15.5)}$		
$= £700,000 \times 3.352$		2,346
PV at Year $0 = £2,346 \quad \times PVIF_{(15.1)}$		
$= £2,346 \quad \times 0.87$		2,041
Initial investment		
Year 0	£1,200	
Year 1 $(£1,200 - 50) \times 0.87$	£1,000	2,200
		————
NPV		(159)

An incensed production engineer in Foster Engineering, on hearing that the proposal is unacceptable, points to the 'intangible' benefits which the FMS will offer:

- Improved quality leading to a significant, but unknown, reduction in sales returns through faulty workmanship.
- Reduced stock and work-in-progress, enabling improved shopfloor layout, greater space and a lower working capital requirement.
- Lower total manufacturing time, enabling the company to respond quicker to customer orders and to further reduce work-in-progress.
- Significantly improved machine utilization rates are expected but the actual degree of improvement is difficult to quantify.
- Increased capacity with the option to operate unmanned night workings.
- Greater flexibility, enabling shorter production runs and faster retooling and rescheduling.

Of course, many of the above could be quantified, at least in part (for example, the savings in working capital), although the degree of confidence in the underlying assumptions may not be high. But even so, there will still be a large element of intangibles which cannot be quantified. This has led to the charge that conventional methods of investment appraisal are biased against AMT investments.

Kaplan (1986) raises the question whether AMT projects must be 'justified by faith alone'. Should managers in the Foster Engineering example turn their back on the DCF approach, which clearly does not capture the total picture, and replace such evaluation with a belief that AMT is the key to the future and that strategic positioning must override economic analysis?

The answer is not to dismiss DCF analysis but to see it within a wider strategic context. A three-stage approach is advocated in analysing AMT capital projects:

1. Does the project fit well within the company's overall corporate strategy?
2. Does the DCF analysis, based on the quantifiable elements of the decision, justify the investment outlay?
3. Where the net present value calculated in stage 2 is negative, examine the shortfall. Does management believe that the 'value' of the intangible benefits exceeds the shortfall. This last stage is a somewhat subjective process whereby managers consider the strategic and operational benefits. No one can put an accurate value on flexibility, for example, but it would be wrong to exclude such a major benefit from the decision process.

7.8   Summary

We have seen in this chapter that over the past thirty or so years there has been an unmistakeable growth in the application of discounted cash flow methods. The financial manager should identify those appraisal techniques which are most useful for the particular organization. But it must be borne in mind that most investment projects are complex; appraisal techniques can be no more than a guide: ultimately the manager must decide.

Key points

- Investment appraisal methods employed in firms are frequently simpler and less sophisticated than those recommended in earlier chapters.
- Accounting rate of return based on total investment consistently understates the internal rate of return for projects.
- Payback, which ignores the time value of money and later cash flows, does offer certain benefits.
- Managers seem to prefer IRR to NPV.
- Most firms employ a combination of methods rather than relying on any single technique.
- Japanese firms tend to be less 'numbers-driven' and to adopt a 'consensus' decision-making approach.
- AMT investment is often difficult to justify using DCF analysis and requires fuller consideration of intangible benefits.

Further reading

Studies on the investment practices of UK firms are well worth reading. For example, Pike (1982 and 1988), McIntyre and Coulthurst (1985), Pike and Wolfe (1988), Mills (1988). Kaplan (1986) and Bromwich and Bhimani (1991) discuss capital budgeting for AMT projects.

Questions

Self-test questions

1. Your boss tells you, 'All this *new* stuff they teach at business schools on capital budgeting may be OK in theory – but it's of no use to me!' Try to explain to him that DCF is not as new as he thinks. Also explain its relevance.
2. Discuss the validity of the following comments made by finance executives:

   'We use payback in support of other methods. It is not sufficiently reliable a tool to be used in isolation.' 'When liquidity is under pressure payback is particularly relevant.'

   'It helps to give some idea of the riskiness of the project – a long time to get one's money back is obviously more risky than a short time.'

3. State whether the following rule-of-thumb approaches under or over-state the internal rate of return.
   (a) Payback period.
   (b) Accounting rate of return on total investment.
   (c) Accounting rate of return on average investment.

4. Payback is a much maligned method which is useful in both project ranking and selection. Discuss.

5. 'At present the methods which are most commonly used to report a firm's operating results are inconsistent with those appraisal techniques which are most frequently advocated as being necessary for sound investment decisions.' Discuss.

Exercises

1. A project costing £20,000 offers an annual cash flow of £5,000 over its life.
   (a) Calculate the internal rate of return using the payback reciprocal assuming an infinite life.
   (b) Use tables to test your answer assuming the project life is (i) twenty years, (ii) eight years.
   (c) What conclusions can be drawn as to the suitability of payback reciprocal in measuring investment profitability?

                                                          (Answer in Appendix A)

2. Most capital budgeting textbooks strongly recommend NPV, but most firms prefer IRR. Explain.

                                                          (Answer in Appendix A)

3. Your firm uses the IRR method and asks you to evaluate the following mutually exclusive projects:

Cash flows (£)			Year		
	0	*1*	*2*	*3*	*4*
Proposal *L*	−47,232	20,000	20,000	20,000	20,000
Proposal *M*	−47,232	0	10,000	20,000	65,350

Using the appropriate IRR method, evaluate these proposals assuming a required rate of return of 10 per cent. Compare your answer with the net present value method.

4. The evidence of many recent studies suggests that there are major differences between current theories of investment appraisal and the methods by which firms actually evaluate long-term investments. For example, the Wilson Committee on the Financing of Industry and Trade reported in 1980 that 'high inflation has greatly increased the uncertainty of business forecasts and has led some companies to abandon the orthodox DCF technique and place more emphasis on payback period and cash flow.'

Required

(a) Present the theoretical arguments for the choice of net present value as the best method of investment appraisal.
(b) Explain why, in practice, the Internal Rate of Return method has proved to be consistently more popular with decision makers than the net present value method.
(c) Explain the continued popularity among decision-makers of non-discounting methods of investment appraisal.

Practical assignment

A. As a management consultant, you have been asked to recommend the investment evaluation methods suitable for a medium-sized engineering company which incurs capital expenditures of between £2,000 and £500,000. What advice would you give?

B. Ask three managers at different levels in your organization how they make investment decisions. How do their approaches differ? How important are financial measures?

Note: Derivation of the payback reciprocal

The internal rate of return is that rate which equates the present value of cash receipts with the initial investment outlay:

$$\frac{A_1}{(1+r)} + \frac{A_2}{(1+r)^2} + \ldots + \frac{A_n}{(1+r)^n} - C = 0$$

Where:

A = the net cash flow receipts
r = the internal rate of return
C = the present value of the investment outlay

Applying the simplifying assumptions that the net cash flow receipts, A, are constant, this formula can be rewritten as:

$$\frac{A}{1+r}\left(1 + \frac{1}{(1+r)} + \frac{1}{(1+r)^2} + \ldots + \frac{1}{(1+r)^{n-1}}\right) - C = 0$$

After summing the geometric progression within the brackets and rearranging we obtain:

$$r = \frac{A}{C} - \frac{A}{C}\left(\frac{1}{1+r}\right)^n$$

As the investment life approaches infinity the last term tends towards zero, leaving

$$r = \frac{A}{C}$$

This last expression is the payback reciprocal.

CHAPTER 8
Analyzing investment risk

THE CANARY THAT FELL OFF ITS PERCH

In July 1987, at the height of the property boom, Olympia and York obtained the rights to develop the Canary Wharf site in London's Dockland. The project involved the construction of 5.4 million square feet of luxury office accommodation within the next five years, the government providing a link road and the Docklands Light Railway at a cost of £700 million.

The Canary Wharf development was successfully implemented, being completed ahead of schedule and within the budget. Yet in May 1992 Canary Wharf filed for insolvency having failed to raise a required £500 million new loan facility. In many ways it was a victim of largely uncontrollable circumstances: a prolonged economic recession, a down spiral in office rents, government abolition of generous tax allowances to the Docklands, and inadequate road and rail infrastructure.

8.1   Introduction

The Canary Wharf example is one of many cases where investment decisions turn out to be far riskier than originally envisaged. Another example is the Channel Tunnel. The *Economist* summed up Eurotunnel's investment potential in October 1987 as 'A hole in the ground that will either make or lose a fortune'.

The finance director of a major UK manufacturer for the motor industry remarked, 'We know that, on average, one in five large capital projects flop, the problem is: we have no idea beforehand which one!'.

Stepping into the unknown – which is what investment decision making effectively is – means that mistakes will surely occur. Entrepreneurs, on average, have nine failures for each major success. Similarly, on average, nine empty oil wells are drilled before the successful oil strikes. In other words, getting it wrong is part of getting it right!

174

This does not, however, mean that managers can do nothing about project failures. In this and subsequent chapters we examine how project risk is assessed and controlled. The various forms of risk are defined and the main statistical methods for measuring project risk within single-period and multi-period frameworks are described. A variety of risk analysis techniques will then be discussed. These fall conveniently into methods intended to *describe* risk and methods *incorporating* project riskiness within the net present value formula. The chapter concludes by examining the extent to which the methods discussed are used in business organizations.

LEARNING OBJECTIVES

For some readers this and the subsequent two chapters on risk will be somewhat more difficult to grasp. The main learning objectives are to:

- Understand how uncertainty affects investment decisions and that most managers are risk-averse.
- Appreciate the levels at which risk can be viewed (project, business or investor's portfolio).
- Be able to measure the expected NPV and its variability.
- Appreciate and apply the main risk-handling techniques to capital budgeting problems.

Defining terms

At the outset we need to clarify our terms:

- *Certainty*   Perfect certainty arises when expectations are single-valued, that is, a particular outcome will arise rather than a range of outcomes. Is there such a thing as an investment with certain pay-offs? Probably not, but some investments come fairly close to it. For example, an investment in three-month Treasury Bills will, subject to the Bank of England keeping its promise, provide a precise return on redemption.

- *Risk and uncertainty*   The terms risk and uncertainty, although used interchangeably in everyday parlance, are not synonymous. *Risk* refers to the set of unique consequences for a given decision which can be assigned probabilities, while *uncertainty* implies that it is not possible to assign probabilities.

The most obvious example of risk is the one in six chance of obtaining a six from a single die. For most investment decisions, however, empirical experience is hard to find. Managers are then forced to estimate probabilities where objective statistical evidence is not available. A manager with little prior experience of launching a particular product in a new market can still subjectively assess the risks involved based on the information available to him. Because subjective probabilities may be applied to investment decisions in a manner similar to

Table 8.1 Betterway plc: expected net present values

Investment	NPV Outcomes (£)		Probability		Weighted Outcomes (£)
A	9,000	×	1	=	9,000
B	− 10,000	×	0.2	=	− 2,000
	10,000	×	0.5	=	5,000
	20,000	×	0.3	=	6,000
			1.0	ENPV =	9,000
C	− 55,000	×	0.2	=	− 11,000
	10,000	×	0.5	=	5,000
	50,000	×	0.3	=	15,000
			1.0	ENPV =	9,000

objective probabilities, the distinction between risk and uncertainty is not critical in practice, and the two terms are often used interchangeably.

Investment decisions are only as good as the information upon which they rest. Relevant and useful information is central in projecting the degree of risk surrounding future economic events and in selecting the best investment option.

8.2   Expected net present value

To what extent is the net present value criterion relevant in the selection of risky investments? Consider the case of Betterway plc contemplating three options with very different degrees of risk. The distribution of possible outcomes for these options is given in Table 8.1.

Clearly, while the NPV criterion is appropriate for investment option A, where the cash flows are certain, it is no longer appropriate for the risky investment options B and C, each with three possible outcomes, at least without adaptation. The whole range of possible outcomes may be considered by obtaining the expected net present value, which is the mean of the NPV distribution weighted by the probabilities of occurrence. The NPV rule may then be applied by selecting projects offering the highest *expected* net present value. In our example, all three options offer the same expected NPV of £9,000. Should the management of Betterway view all three as equally attractive? The answer to this question lies in their attitudes towards risk, for while the *expected* outcomes are the same, the *possible* outcomes vary considerably. Thus, although the expected NPV criterion provides a single measure of profitability, which may be applied to risky investments, it does not, by itself, provide an acceptable decision criterion.

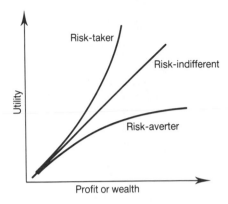

Figure 8.1 Risk profiles

8.3 Attitudes to risk

Business managers prefer less risk to more risk for a given return. In other words, they are *risk-averse*. This is best grasped by introducing the important concept of *utility*, or subjective satisfaction. In general, a businessman derives less utility from gaining an additional £1,000 than he forgoes in losing £1,000. This is based on the concept of diminishing marginal utility, which holds that as wealth increases, marginal utility declines at an increasing rate. Thus the utility function for risk averters is concave as shown on the graph of Figure 8.1. As long as the utility function of the decision maker can be specified, this approach may be applied in reaching investment decisions.

Example: Carefree plc's utility function

The managing director of Carefree plc, a business with a current market value of £30m, has an opportunity to relocate its premises. It is estimated that there is a 50 per cent probability of increasing its value by £12m and a similar probability that value will fall by £10m. The owner's utility function is outlined in Figure 8.2. The concave slope shows that the owner is risk averse. The gain in utility (ΔU_F) as a result of the favourable outcome of £42m, is less than the fall in utility (ΔU_A) resulting from the adverse outcome of only £20m.

The conclusion to be drawn, therefore, is that although the investment proposal offers £1m expected additional wealth (i.e. $0.5 \times £12m + 0.5 \times -£10m$) the project should not be undertaken because total expected utility would fall if the factory were relocated.

While decision-making based upon the expected utility criterion is a conceptually sound approach, it has serious practical drawbacks. A decision-maker may recognize that he is risk-averse, but is unable to define, with any degree of accuracy, the shape of his utility function. This becomes even more complicated in organizations where ownership and management are separated, as is the case for most companies. Here, the agency problem

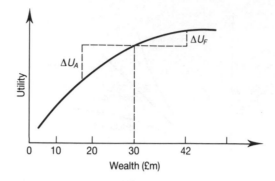

Figure 8.2 Investor's risk-averse utility function

discussed in Chapter 1 arises. Thus we are forced to recognize that while utility analysis provides a useful insight into the problem of risk, it does not provide us with operational decision rules.

8.4 Types of project risk

Risk may be classified into a number of types. A clear understanding of the different forms of risk is useful in the evaluation and monitoring of capital projects.

1. *Business risk* – the variability in operating cash flows or operating earnings before interest and tax are deducted. A firm's business risk depends, in large measure, on its *operating gearing* (the proportion of fixed costs to total costs). The decision to become more capital-intensive generally leads to an increase in the proportion of fixed costs within the cost structure. In turn, this increase in operating gearing leads to greater variability in operating earnings.

2. *Financial risk* – this is the risk, over and above business risk, which results from the use of debt capital. Financial gearing is increased by issuing more debt, thereby incurring more fixed-interest charges and increasing the variability in net earnings. Financial risk is considered more fully in Chapters 14 and 15.

3. *Corporate risk* – is the combination of business and financial risk.

4. *Portfolio or market risk* – the variability in shareholders' returns. Investors can significantly reduce their variability in earnings by holding carefully selected investment portfolios. This is sometimes called 'relevant' risk, because only this element of risk should be considered by a well-diversified shareholder. Chapters 9 and 10 examine such risk in greater depth.

Project risk can be viewed and defined in three different ways: (1) in isolation, (2) in terms of its impact on corporate risk, and (3) in terms of its impact on shareholders'

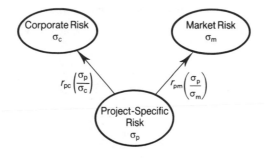

Key:

    r = correlation coefficient

    σ = standard deviation of NPVs or IRRs

p, c and m = the project, company and stock market respectively

Figure 8.3 Project risk type

investment portfolios. These three forms are shown in Figure 8.3. A recent survey (Pike and Ho 1991) found that 79 per cent of managers in larger UK firms use project-specific risk, 61 per cent consider the impact of corporation risk, but only 26 per cent consider the impact on shareholder portfolios.

Figure 8.3 reveals that the risk of the project in isolation, the company and the market portfolio are measured in terms of standard deviations. We need not concern ourselves at this point as to just how these measures are derived, but companies should establish their degree of corporate risk by examining the variability over recent years in the firm's return on capital and other relevant measures. In examining project risk in isolation, it is only the variability in the project returns, or standard deviation, that needs to be considered. However, when assessing the impact of the project's possible cash flows on corporate risk, we must also consider the correlation between the project and company (r_{pc}). Most projects are positively correlated with the rest of the company – some factors, such as economic recession, affect both the project and the company's other assets in much the same way, although not necessarily to the same extent. In most cases, however, the correlation coefficient will be less than $+1$, which means that an element of project risk will be diversified away within overall company operations. As we shall see in the following chapter, the project's degree of market risk is found in much the same way. We first turn our attention to assessing project risk in isolation before moving on to estimating its impact on investors' portfolios (i.e. market risk).

8.5 Measurement of risk

Estimation of the probabilities of future uncertain outcomes, although difficult, is usually possible. With the little knowledge the manager may have concerning the future, and by applying past experience backed by historical analysis relevant to a project and its setting, the experienced manager can construct a probability distribution of a project's cash outcomes.

Table 8.2 Snowglo plc project data

State of Economy	Probability of Outcome	Cash Flow (£) A	Cash Flow (£) B
Strong	0.2	700	550
Normal	0.5	400	400
Weak	0.3	200	300

Once specified, the probability distribution can then measure the risks surrounding project cash flows in a variety of different ways. If we assume that the range of possible outcomes from a decision is distributed normally around the expected value, then the standard deviation and expected value is all that risk-averse investors require to assess project risk. We shall restrict our attention to three statistical measures: the standard deviation, semi-variance and coefficient of variation for single-period cash flows.

Single-period cash flows

To illustrate the measures of risk for single-period cash flows we shall employ the information on two projects for Snowglo plc (Table 8.2).

Standard deviation

We have already seen that expected value is not by itself an acceptable criterion because it overlooks important information on the dispersion (risk) of the outcomes. We know that different people behave differently in risky situations. Consider projects A and B and their NPV distributions in Figure 8.4. Both projects have the same NPV, indicated by M, but project B has greater dispersion. The risk-averter in Snowglo will choose A since he wants to minimize risk. The risk-taker will choose B because the NPV of project B has a chance (W) of being higher than X (which project A cannot offer) but also a chance (L) of being lower than Y.

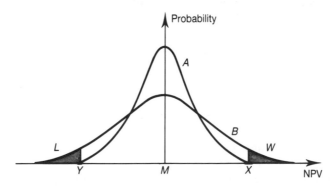

Figure 8.4 Variability of project returns

It is impossible to predict people's choice without knowing their attitudes to risk. In general, people don't like risk. Hereafter we make a reasonable assumption: *most people are risk-averters.* The standard deviation is a measure of the dispersion; the wider the dispersion, the higher the standard deviation. The expected value of cash flows is given by the equation:

$$\bar{X} = \sum_{i=1}^{N} P_i \, X_i$$

and the standard deviation of the cash flows:

$$\sigma = \sqrt{\sum_{i=1}^{N} P_i \, (X_i - \bar{X})^2}$$

Where:

$\bar{X}$ = the expected value of event X
X_i = the possible outcome i from event X
P_i = the probability of outcome i occurring
N = the number of possible outcomes

Table 8.3 provides the workings for Projects A and B.

Applying the formulae, we obtain an expected cash flow of £400 for both project A and project B. If the decision-maker had a neutral risk attitude he would view the two projects

Table 8.3 Project risk for Snowglo plc

Economic State	Probability	Outcome	Expected Value	Deviation	Squared Deviation	Variance
Project A						
Strong	0.2	700	140	300	90,000	18,000
Normal	0.5	400	200	0	0	0
Weak	0.3	200	60	−200	40,000	12,000
		$\bar{X}_A$ =	400	Variance = σ^2_A =		30,000
				Standard deviation = σ_A =		173.2
Project B						
Strong	0.2	550	110	150	22,500	4,500
Normal	0.5	400	200	0	0	0
Weak	0.3	300	90	−100	10,000	3,000
		$\bar{X}_B$ =	400	Variance = σ^2_B =		7,500
				Standard deviation = σ_B =		86.6

Alternatively

$\bar{X}_A = 700 \ (0.2) + 400 \ (0.5) + 200 \ (0.3) = 400$
$\sigma_A = \sqrt{0.2 \ (700 - 400)^2 + 0.5 \ (400 - 400)^2 + 0.3 \ (200 - 400)^2}$
$\quad = 173.2$
$\bar{X}_B = 550 \ (0.2) + 400 \ (0.5) + 300 \ (0.3) = 400$
$\sigma_B = \sqrt{0.2 \ (550 - 400)^2 + 0.5 \ (440 - 400)^2 + 0.3 \ (200 - 300)^2}$
$\quad = 86.6$

equally favourably. As, however, he is likely to be risk-averse, it is appropriate to examine the standard deviations of the two probability distributions. Here we see that project A, with a standard deviation twice that of project B, is more risky and hence less attractive. No doubt the reader could have deduced this fact simply by observing the distribution of outcomes and noting that the same probabilities apply to both projects. Observation cannot, however, tell us by how much one project is riskier than another.

Semi-variance

While deviation above the mean may be viewed favourably by managers, it is only 'downside risk' (i.e. deviations below expected outcomes) that is really considered in the decision process. Downside risk is best measured by the semi-variance, a special case of the variance, given by the formula:

$$SV = \sum_{j=1}^{K} P_j \, (X_j - \bar{X})^2$$

Where:

SV = semi-variance
j = all outcome values which are less than the expected value
K = number of outcomes which are less than the expected value

Applying the semi-variance to the previous example in Table 8.3, the downside risk relates exclusively to the 'weak' state of the economy:

$$SV_A = 0.3 \, (200 - 400)^2 = £12,000$$
$$SV_B = 0.3 \, (300 - 400)^2 = £3,000$$

Once again project B is seen to have a much lower degree of risk. In both cases the semi-variance accounts for 40 per cent of the project variance.

Coefficient of variation

It is not altogether satisfactory to make direct comparison between projects on the basis of *absolute* risk measures such as those previously defined. Where projects differ in scale, a more valid comparison is found by applying a *relative* risk measure such as the coefficient of variation. This is calculated by dividing the standard deviation by the expected value of net cash flows as in the expression:

$$CV = \frac{\sigma}{\bar{X}}$$

In the Snowglo example (Table 8.3) this gives the following coefficients:

	Standard Deviation (1)	Expected Value (2)	Coefficient of Variation (1/2)
Project A	£173.2	£400	0.43
Project B	£86.6	£400	0.22

Both projects have the same expected value but project B has a significantly lower degree of risk. Next we consider the situation where the two projects under review are different in scale:

	Standard Deviation	Expected Value	Coefficient of Variation
Project F	£1,000 ÷	£10,000 =	0.1
Project G	£2,000 ÷	£40,000 =	0.05

Although the absolute measure of dispersion (the standard deviation) is greater for project G, few people in business would regard it as more risky than project F because of the significant difference in the expected values of the two investments. The coefficient of variation reveals that G actually offers the lower amount of risk per £1 of expected value.

Mean-variance rule

Given the expected return and the measure of dispersion (variance or standard deviation), we can formulate the mean-variance rule. This rule states that project X will be preferred to project Y if:

1. The expected return of X exceeds that of Y and the variance is equal to or less than that of Y; or
2. The expected return of X exceeds or is equal to the expected return of Y and the variance is less than that of Y.

This is illustrated in Figure 8.5. Projects A and D are preferable to projects C and B respectively because they offer a higher return for the same degree of risk. In addition, A is

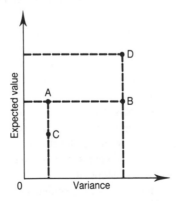

Figure 8.5 Mean–Variance analysis

preferable to B because for the same expected return it incurs lower risk. These choices are applicable to all risk-averters regardless of their particular utility functions. What this rule cannot do, however, is distinguish between projects where both expected returns and risk differ (projects A and D in Figure 8.5). This important issue will be discussed in Chapters 9 and 10. So far our analysis of risk has assumed single-period investments. We have conveniently ignored the fact that, typically, investments are multi-period. The analysis of project risk where there are multi-period cash flows is discussed in the appendix to this chapter.

Risk-handling methods

Two broad approaches may be adopted for handling the risk dimension within the investment decision process. The first approach attempts to *describe* the riskiness of a given project, either using various applications of probability analysis or some simple method. The second approach aims to *incorporate* the investor's perception of project riskiness within the NPV formula.

We now turn our attention to the various techniques available which help describe investment risk.

8.6   Risk description techniques

Sensitivity analysis

In principle, sensitivity analysis is a very simple technique, used to locate and assess the potential impact of risk on a project's profitability. It does not aim to quantify risk, but rather to identify just how sensitive certain factors are to change. Sensitivity analysis merely provides the decision-maker with answers to a whole range of 'what if' questions. For example, what is the NPV if selling price falls by 10 per cent? What is the IRR if the project's life is only three years, not five years as expected? What is the level of sales revenue required to break-even in net present value terms?

Sensitivity graphs permit the plotting of net present values (or IRRs) against the percentage deviation from the expected value of the factor under investigation. This is illustrated by the sensitivity graph in Figure 8.6 depicting the potential impact of deviations from the expected values of a project's variables on NPV. When everything is unchanged, the NPV is £2,000. However, NPV becomes zero when market size decreases by 20 per cent or price decreases by 5 per cent. This shows that profitability is very sensitive to price changes. Similarly, a 10 per cent increase in discount rate will make the NPV equal to zero, while fixed costs must increase to 25 per cent in order to render the project unprofitable. Therefore, the project is more sensitive to discount rate changes than to fixed cost variations. The sensitivity of NPV to each factor is reflected by the slope of the sensitivity line – the flatter the line the greater the impact on NPV of changes in the specified variable.

Sensitivity analysis is widely used because of its simplicity and ability to focus on

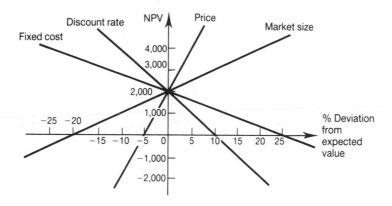

Figure 8.6 Sensitivity graph

particular estimates. It can identify the critical factors which have greatest impact on a project's profitability. It does not however actually *evaluate* risk; the decision-maker must still assess the probability of occurrence for these deviations from expected values.

Break-even sensitivity analysis

An application of sensitivity analysis is illustrated in the following example. The accountant of UMK plc has put together the cash flow forecasts for a new product with a four-year life involving capital investment of £200,000. It produces a net present value, at a 10 per cent discount rate, of £40,920. His basic analysis is given in Table 8.4. Which factors are most

Table 8.4 UMK cost structure

Unit Data	£	£
Selling Price		20
Less: Materials	6	
Labour	5	
Variable Costs	1	
		12
Contribution		8
Annual sales (units)	12,000	
Total Contribution		96,000
Less: Additional fixed costs		20,000
Annual net cash flow		76,000
Present value (4 years at 10%)		
76,000 × 3.17		240,920
Less: Capital outlay		200,000
Net present value		40,920

critical to the decision? The break-even point, in net present value terms, is located where the present value of future benefits equals the investment outlay.

Investment outlay

This can rise by up to £40,920 (assuming all other estimates remain unchanged) before the decision advice alters. A percentage increase of

$$\frac{£40,920}{£200,000} \times 100 = 20.5\%$$

Annual cash receipts

The break-even position is reached when annual cash receipts multiplied by the annuity factor equal the investment outlay. The break-even cashflow is therefore the investment outlay divided by the annuity factor:

$$\frac{£200,000}{3.17} = £63,091$$

This is a percentage fall of $\dfrac{£76,000 - £63,091}{£76,000} = 17.0\%$

Annual fixed costs could increase by the same absolute amount of £12,909 or

$$\frac{£12,909}{£20,000} \times 100 = 64.5\%$$

Annual sales volume

The break-even annual contribution is £63,091 + £20,000 = £83,091.

Sales volume to break-even is $\dfrac{£83,091}{£8} = £10,386$, which is

a percentage decline of $\dfrac{£12,000 - £10,386}{£12,000} \times 100 = 13.5\%$

Selling price can fall by:

$$\frac{96,000 - 83,091}{12,000} = £1.07 \text{ per unit; a decline of}$$

$$\frac{1.07}{20} \times 100 = 5.4\%$$

Variable costs can rise by:

$$\frac{1.07}{12} \times 100 = 8.9\%$$

Discount rate

The break-even annuity factor is $\frac{£200,000}{£76,000} = 2.63$. Reference to the present value annuity tables for four years shows 2.63 corresponds to an IRR of 19 per cent. The error in cost of capital calculation could be as much as 9 percentage points before it affects the decision advice.

Sensitivity analysis, as applied in the above example, discloses that selling price and variable costs are the two most critical variables in the investment decision. The decision-maker must then determine (subjectively or objectively) the probabilities of such changes occurring, and whether he is prepared to accept the risks.

Scenario analysis

Sensitivity analysis, while useful, only considers the effects of changes in key variables one at a time. It does not ask the question: 'How bad could the project look?' Enthusiastic managers can sometimes get carried away with the most likely outcomes and forget just what might happen if critical assumptions – such as the state of the economy or competitors' reactions – are unrealistic.

Scenario analysis seeks to establish 'at worst' and 'at best' scenarios so that the whole range of possible outcomes can be considered.

Simulation approach

Monte Carlo simulation is an operations research technique with a variety of business applications. One of the first writers to apply the simulation approach to risky investments was Hertz (1964) who described the approach adopted by his consultancy firm in evaluating a major expansion of the processing plant of an industrial chemical producer. This approach involved constructing a mathematical model which captured the essential characteristics of the investment proposal throughout its life as it encountered random events. A simulation model considers the following variables which are subject to random variation.

Market-related factors

1. Market size.
2. Market growth rate.
3. Selling price of product.
4. Market share captured by the firm.

Investment-related factors

5. Investment outlay.
6. Useful life of investment.
7. Residual value of the investment.

Cost-related factors

8. Variable operating unit cost.
9. Fixed costs.

Probability distributions are assigned to each of these variables, based upon management's perception of the probability of occurrence, as shown in Figure 8.7.

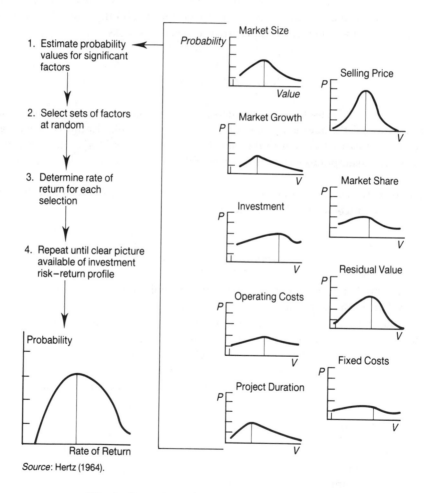

Source: Hertz (1964).

Figure 8.7   Simulation for investment planning

The next step is to determine the net present value that will result from a random combination of the exogenous factors involved. For example, suppose the market share factor has the following distribution:

Market share (%)	Probability
6	0.10
7	0.25
8	0.30
9	0.25
10	0.10

Applying these probabilities we can say that out of a possible total of 100, if a random number is generated between 0 and 10, this simulates a market share of 6 per cent. If a random number is generated between 11 and 35, this simulates a market share of 7 per cent, and so on. This process of simulation is conducted on all variables to produce, after discounting, the net present value of the proposal based on that trial run. The process is repeated many times for each of the nine variables, eventually producing enough outcomes to construct the probability distribution for the proposal's net present value. Comparison is then possible between mutually exclusive projects whose NPV probability distributions have been calculated in this manner (Figure 8.8). It will be observed that Project A, with a higher expected NPV and lower risk is preferable to project B.

In practice, very few companies use this risk analysis approach. Why then is it so rarely employed?

1. The simple model described above assumes the economic factors are independent. Clearly, many of these factors (e.g. market share and selling price) are statistically dependent. To the extent that dependency exists among variables, it must be specified. Such interrelationships are not always clear and are frequently complex to model.
2. Managers are required to specify probability distributions for the exogenous variables. Few managers are able or willing to accept the demands required by the simulation approach.

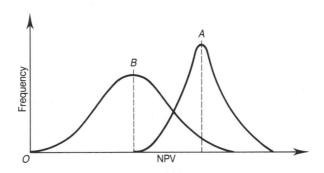

Figure 8.8 Simulated probability distributions

8.7   Adjusting for risk

Two approaches are commonly used to incorporate risk within the NPV formula:

Certainty equivalent method

This conceptually appealing approach permits adjustment for risk by incorporating the decision-maker's risk attitude into the capital investment decision. The certainty equivalent method adjusts the numerator in the net present value calculation by multiplying the expected annual cash flows by a certainty equivalent coefficient. The revised formula becomes:

CERTAINTY EQUIVALENT METHOD

$$\overline{\text{NPV}} = \sum_{t=1}^{N} \frac{\alpha \ \bar{X}_t}{(1+i)^t} - C$$

Where:

$\overline{\text{NPV}}$ = expected net present value
α = certainty equivalent coefficient which reflects management's risk attitude
$\bar{X}_t$ = expected cash flow in period t
i = riskless rate of interest
n = project's life
C = initial cash outlay

The numerator $(\alpha \bar{X}_t)$ represents the figure that management would be willing to receive as a certain sum each year in place of the uncertain annual cash flow offered by the project. The greater is management's aversion to risk, the nearer the certainty equivalent coefficient is to zero. Where projects are of normal risk for the business, and the cost of capital and risk-free rate of interest are known, it is possible to determine the certainty equivalent coefficient.

Example

Calculate the certainty coefficient for a normal risk project with a one-year life and an expected cash flow of £5,000 receivable at the end of the year. Shareholders require a return of 12 per cent for projects of this degree of risk and the risk-free rate of interest is 6 per cent.

The present value of the project, excluding the initial cost and using the 12 per cent discount rate, is:

$$\text{PV} = \frac{£5,000}{1+0.12} = £4,464$$

Using the present value and substituting the risk-free interest rate for the cost of capital, we obtain the certainty equivalent coefficient:

$$\frac{\alpha \cdot £5,000}{1+0.06} = £4,464$$

$$\alpha = \frac{(£4,464)\ (1.06)}{£5,000}$$

$$= 0.9464$$

The management is, therefore, indifferent as to whether it receives an uncertain cash flow one year hence of £5,000 or a certain cash flow of £4,732 (i.e. £5,000 × 0.9464).

Risk-adjusted discount rate

Whereas the certainty equivalent approach adjusted the numerator in the NPV formula, the risk-adjusted discount rate adjusts the denominator:

RISK-ADJUSTED DISCOUNT RATE METHOD

$$\overline{\text{NPV}} = \sum_{t=1}^{N} \frac{\bar{X}_t}{(1+k)^t} - C$$

---

where k is the risk-adjusted discount rate based on the perceived degree of project risk. *The higher the perceived riskiness of a project, the greater the risk premium to be added to the risk-free interest rate.* This results in a higher discount rate and, hence, a lower net present value.

Although this approach has a certain intuitive appeal, its relevance depends very much on how risk is perceived to change over time. The risk-adjusted discount rate involves the risk premium growing over time at an exponential rate, implying that the riskiness of the project's cash flow also increases over time. Consider the case of a manufacturer of confectionery currently appraising a proposal to launch a new product which has had very little pre-launch testing. It is estimated that this proposal will produce annual cash flows in the region of £100,000 for the next five years, after which product profitability declines sharply. As the proposal is seen as a high-risk venture, a 12 per cent risk premium is incorporated in the discount rate. The risk-adjusted cash flow, before discounting at the risk-free discount rate is, therefore, £89,286 in Year 1 (£100,000/1.12) falling to £56,743 in Year 5 (£100,000/(1.12)^5).

To what extent does this method reflect the actual riskiness of the annual cash flows for Years 1 and 5? Arguably, greatest uncertainty surrounds the initial launch period. Once the initial market penetration and subsequent repeat orders are known, the subsequent sales are relatively easy to forecast. Thus, in this example, a single risk-adjusted discount rate is a poor proxy for the impact of risk on value over the project's life, because risk does not increase exponentially with the passage of time, and in some cases actually declines over time. The

Eurotunnel project, discussed below, provides another illustration of this. By far the greatest risks were in the initial tunnelling and development phases.

A deeper understanding of the relationship between the certainty equivalent and risk-adjusted discount rate approaches may be gained by reading the Appendix to this chapter.

8.8   Risk analysis in practice

To what extent do companies employ the techniques discussed in this chapter? Table 8.5 shows just how much progress has been made in recent years in this regard.

Sensitivity analysis and best/worst case (or scenario) analysis are conducted in almost all larger UK companies. Far less common, however, are techniques requiring managers to assign probabilities to possible outcomes; managers prefer to assess the likelihood of outcomes in a more subjective manner. Finally, there is little real evidence that Beta analysis (based on the capital asset pricing model and discussed in Chapter 10) is used extensively in industry.

THE CHANNEL TUNNEL PROJECT

In 1802 Napoleon turned down French mining engineer Matheiu-Favier's proposal for a Channel tunnel, rising in the centre to a man-made island allowing for a change of horses for the stage-coach traffic. Many other such schemes were rejected in subsequent years until, in 1986, the Anglo–French Treaty was signed authorizing the construction, financing and operation of a twin rail tunnel system by Eurotunnel.

The Channel Tunnel is a giant project in every sense. The construction of 150 km of undersea tunnels capable of carrying high speed trains, with an initial cost originally estimated at £5bn, to be financed very largely (80 per cent) by bank borrowings, is both big and risky. Hence, the *Economist's* view of its investment potential as 'a hole in the ground that will either make or lose a fortune'.

The 1986 preliminary prospectus provided financial forecasts upon which expected returns and sensitivities could be prepared. Potential investors and lenders were being asked to invest in a project which would not offer a dividend until at least 1994 and where the expected internal rate of return was around 14 per cent, a rate attainable from far less risky projects. (Subsequent events have shown that the actual capital cost may be double the initial figure.)

It is small wonder, therefore, that the banks and financial institutions were not exactly queuing up to finance the Eurotunnel venture. When the shares first traded on 10 December 1987, the 350p issue price could not be sustained and the shares slithered by 30 percent. Only time will tell whether this venture will turn out to be a disaster or a success for its original investors. But what can be said is that at the time the original investment decision was taken the expected returns looked meagre for the considerable risks involved.

Table 8.5 Risk analysis in 100 large UK firms

	1992 (%)	1986 (%)	1981 (%)	1975 (%)
Sensitivity analysis	86	71	42	28
Best/worst case analysis	95	93	n.a.	n.a.
Reduced payback period	59	61	30	25
Risk adjusted rate	64	61	41	37
Probability analysis	47	40	10	9
Beta analysis	20	16	—	—

Source: Pike (1988 and 1992).

8.9 Summary

Risk is an important element in virtually all investment decisions. Because most people in business are risk-averse, preferring less risk to more, the identification, measurement and, where possible, reduction of risk should be a central feature in the decision-making process. The evidence suggests that firms are increasingly conducting risk analysis. This does not mean that the risk dimension is totally ignored by other firms; rather, they choose to handle project risk by less objective methods such as experience, feel or intuition. In this chapter we have defined what is meant by risk and examined a variety of ways of measuring it. The probability distribution, giving the probability of occurrence of each possible outcome following an investment decision, is the concept underlying most of the methods discussed. Measures of risk, such as the standard deviation, indicate the extent to which actual outcomes are likely to vary from the expected value.

Key points

• The expected NPV, although useful, does not show the whole picture. We need to understand managers' attitude to risk and to estimate the degree of project risk.

• Three types of risk are relevant in capital budgeting: project risk in isolation, the project's impact on corporate risk and its impact on market risk. The last two are addressed more fully in the following two chapters.

• The standard deviation, semi-variance and coefficient of variation each measure, in slightly different ways, project risk.

• Sensitivity analysis and scenario analysis are used to locate and assess the potential impact of risk on project performance. Simulation is a more sophisticated approach, which captures the essential characteristics of the investment which are subject to uncertainty.

• The NPV formula can be adjusted to consider risk. Adjustment of the cash flows is achieved by the certainty equivalent method. The risk-adjusted discount rate increases the risk premium for higher-risk projects.

Appendix

Multi-period cash flows and risk

For the sake of simplicity, our measurement of risk so far has assumed single-period investments. We have conveniently ignored the fact that typically investments are multi-period, and hence our analysis must be based on net present values. As risk is to be specifically evaluated, cash flows should be discounted at the risk-free rate of interest reflecting only the time value of money. To include a risk premium within the discount rate, when risk is already considered separately, amounts to double-counting and typically understates the true net present value. The expected NPV of an investment project is found by summing the present values of the expected net cash flows and deducting the initial investment outlay. Thus, for a two-year investment proposal:

$$\overline{\text{NPV}} = \frac{\bar{X}_1}{1+i} + \frac{\bar{X}_2}{(1+i)^2} - C$$

Where:

$\overline{\text{NPV}}$ = expected NPV
$\bar{X}_1$ = expected value of net cash flow in Year 1
$\bar{X}_2$ = expected value of net cash flow in Year 2
C = cash investment outlay
i = risk-free rate of interest

Independent cash flows

A major problem in the calculation of the standard deviation of a project's NPVs for multi-period projects lies in the fact that the cash flows in one period are typically dependent, to some degree, on the cash flows of earlier periods. Assuming for the present that cash flows for our two-period project are statistically *independent*, the total variance of the NPV is equal to the discounted sum of the annual variances. This is illustrated by the following example: the Bronson project, with a two-year life, has an initial cost of £500 and the possible payoffs and probabilities outlined in Table 8.6. Applying the standard deviation and expected value formulae already discussed, we obtain the results shown in the table.

Perfectly correlated cash flows

At the other extreme to the statistical independence assumption between periods is the assumption that the cash flows in one year are entirely dependent upon the cash flows achieved in previous periods. When this is the case, successive cash flows are said to be perfectly correlated. Any deviation in one year from forecast directly affects the accuracy of subsequent forecasts. The effect of cash flows being correlated over time is that the standard

Table 8.6 Bronson project payoffs

Probability	Year 1 Cash Flow (£)	Year 2 Cash Flow (£)
0.1	100	200
0.2	200	400
0.4	300	600
0.2	400	800
0.1	500	1,000

	Year 1	Year 2
Expected value	£300	£600
Standard deviation	£109	£219

Assuming a risk-free discount rate of 10 per cent, the expected NPV is:

$$\overline{NPV} = \frac{300}{(1.10)} + \frac{600}{(1.10)^2} - 500 = £268$$

The standard deviation of the entire proposal is found by discounting the annual variances to their present values, applying the equation:

$$\sigma = \sqrt{\sum_{t=1}^{N} \frac{\sigma_t^2}{(1+i)^2}}$$

In our simple case this is:

$$\sigma = \sqrt{\frac{\sigma_1^2}{(1+i)^2} + \frac{\sigma_2^2}{(1+i)^4}} = \sqrt{\frac{12,000}{(1.1)^2} + \frac{48,000}{(1.1)^4}} = £206$$

The project therefore offers an expected NPV of £268 and a standard deviation of £206.

deviation of the probability distribution of net present values increases. The standard deviation of a stream of cash flows perfectly correlated over time is:

$$\sigma = \sum_{t=1}^{N} \frac{\sigma}{(1+i)^t}$$

Returning to the example in Table 8.6, but assuming perfect correlation of cash flows over time, the standard deviation for the project is:

$$\sigma = \frac{£109.5}{1.1} + \frac{£219.1}{(1.1)^2}$$
$$= £280.6$$

Thus the risk associated with this period project is £280.60, assuming perfect correlation. Reference back to the calculation assuming independence of cash flows gives a lower standard deviation of £206. Obviously, this difference would be considerably greater for longer-lived projects.

Interpreting results

While decision-makers are interested to know the degree of risk associated with a given project, their fundamental concern is, will this project produce a positive net present value? Risk analysis can go some way to answering this question. If a project's probability distribution of expected NPVs is approximately normal, we can estimate the probability of failing to achieve at least zero NPV. In the previous example the expected NPV was £268. This is then standardized by dividing it by the standard deviation using the formula:

$$S = \frac{X - \overline{NPV}}{\sigma}$$

where X is in this case zero. Thus, we have in the case of the independent cash flow assumption:

$$S = \frac{0 - £268}{£206}$$
$$= -1.30 \text{ standard deviation}$$

Reference to normal distribution tables reveals that there is a 0.0968 probability that the NPV will be zero or less. Accordingly there must be a $(1 - 0.0968)$ or 90.32 per cent probability of the project producing an NPV in excess of zero. The decision-maker can then subjectively relate this risk to his particular utility function before reaching a decision.

In reality, few projects are either independent or perfectly correlated over time. How then should the standard deviation of the net present values be computed? The answer lies somewhere between the two, and will be based on the formula for the independence case but with an additional term for the covariance between annual cash flows.

Further reading

A fuller treatment of risk is found in Levy and Sarnat (1990). Useful research studies on the use of risk analysis are given in Pike (1988) and Pike and Ho (1991), Mao and Helliwell (1969), and Bierman and Hass (1973).

Questions

Self-test questions

1. Explain the importance of risk in capital budgeting.
2. What do you understand by the following?
   (a) risk
   (b) uncertainty
   (c) risk-aversion

(d) expected value

(e) standard deviation

(f) semi-variance

(g) mean-variance rule

3. Explain the distinction between project risk, business risk, financial risk and portfolio risk.

4. Project X has an expected return of £2,000 and a standard deviation of £400. Project Y has an expected return of £1,000 and a standard deviation of £400. Which project is more risky?

5. What do you understand by Monte Carlo simulation? When might it be useful in capital budgeting?

Exercises

1. The 'woodpulp' project has an initial cost of £13,000 and the firm's risk-free interest rate is 10 per cent. If certainty equivalents and net cash flows for the project are as below, should the project be accepted?

Year	Certainty Equivalents	Net Cash Flows (£)
1	0.90	8,000
2	0.85	7,000
3	0.80	7,000
4	0.75	5,000
5	0.70	5,000
6	0.65	5,000
7	0.60	5,000

(Solution in Appendix A)

2. Mystery Enterprises has a proposal costing £800. Using a 10 per cent cost of capital, compute the expected NPV, standard deviation and coefficient of variation assuming independent interperiod cash flows.

Probability	Year 1 Net cash flow (£)	Year 2 Net cash flow (£)
0.2	400	300
0.3	500	400
0.3	600	500
0.2	700	600

(Solution in Appendix A)

3. Mikado plc is considering launching a new product involving capital investment of £180,000. The machine has a four-year life and no residual value. Sales volumes of 6,000 units are forecast for each of the four years. The product has a selling price of £60 and a

variable cost of £36 per unit. Additional fixed overheads of £50,000 will be incurred. The cost of capital is $12\frac{1}{2}$ per cent p.a. Present a report to the directors of Mikado plc giving:

(a) the net present value;
(b) the percentage amount each variable can deteriorate before the project becomes unacceptable;
(c) a sensitivity graph.

4. Devonia (Laboratories) Ltd has recently carried out successful clinical trials on a new type of skin cream, which has been developed to reduce the effects of ageing. Research and development costs incurred by the company in relation to the new product amount to £160,000. In order to gauge the market potential of the new product an independent firm of market research consultants were hired at a cost of £15,000. The market research report submitted by the consultants indicates that the skin cream is likely to have a product life of four years and could be sold to retail chemists and large department stores at a price of £20 per 100 ml container. For each of the four years of the new product's life sales demand has been estimated as follows:

Number of 100 ml containers sold	Probability of occurrence
11,000	0.3
14,000	0.6
16,000	0.1

If the company decides to launch the new product it is possible for production to begin at once. The necessary equipment to produce the product is already owned by the company and originally cost £150,000. At the end of the new product's life it is estimated that the equipment could be sold for £35,000. If the company decides against launching the new product the equipment will be sold immediately for £85,000 as it will be of no further use to the company.

The new skin cream will require two hours labour for each 100 ml container produced. The cost of labour for the new product is £4.00 per hour. Additional workers will have to be recruited to produce the new product. At the end of the product's life the workers are unlikely to be offered further work with the company and redundancy costs of £10,000 are expected. The cost of the ingredients for each 100 ml container is £6.00. Additional overheads arising from production of the product are expected to be £15,000 p.a.

The new skin cream has attracted the interest of the company's competitors. If the company decides not to produce and sell the skin cream it can sell the patent rights to a major competitor immediately for £125,000.

Devonia (Laboratories) Ltd has a cost of capital of 12 per cent.

Ignore taxation.

Required

(a) Calculate the expected net present value (ENPV) of the new product.
(b) State, with reasons, whether or not Devonia (Laboratories) Ltd should launch the new product.
(c) Discuss the strengths and weaknesses of the expected net present value approach for making investment decisions.

(Certified Diploma, June 1990)

5. The managing director of Tigwood Ltd believes that a market exists for 'microbooks'. He has proposed that the company should market 100 best-selling books on microfiche which can be read using a special microfiche reader that is connected to a television screen. A microfiche containing an entire book can be purchased from a photographic company at 40 per cent of the average production cost of best-selling paperback books.

It is estimated that the average cost of producing paperback books is £1.50, and the average selling price of paperbacks is £3.95 each. Copyright fees of 20 per cent of the average selling price of the paperback books would be payable to the publishers of the paperbacks plus an initial lump sum which is still being negotiated, but is expected to be £1.5 million. No tax allowances are available on this lump-sum payment. An agreement with the publishers would be signed for a period of six years. Additional variable costs of staffing, handling and marketing are 20 pence per microfiche, and fixed costs are negligible.

Tigwood Ltd has spent £100,000 on market research, and expects sales to be 1,500,000 units per year at an initial unit price of £2.

The microfiche reader would be produced and marketed by another company.

Tigwood would finance the venture with a bank loan at an interest rate of 16 per cent per year. The company's money (nominal) cost of equity and real cost of equity are estimated to be 23 per cent p.a. and 12.6 per cent p.a., respectively. Tigwood's money weighted average cost of capital and real weighted average cost of capital are 18 per cent p.a. and 8 per cent p.a. respectively. The risk free rate of interest is 11 per cent p.a. and the market return is 17 per cent p.a.

Corporate tax is at the rate of 35 per cent, payable in the year the profit occurs. All cash flows may be assumed to be at the year end, unless otherwise stated.

Required

(a) Calculate the expected net present value of the microbooks project.
(b) Explain the reasons for your choice of discount rate in your answer to part (a). Discuss whether this rate is likely to be the most appropriate rate to use in the analysis of the proposed project.
(c) (i) Using sensitivity analysis, estimate by what percentage each of the following would have to change before the project was no longer expected to be viable:
    – initial outlay
    – annual contribution
    – the life of the agreement
    – the discount rate.

    (ii) What are the limitations of this sensitivity analysis?

(d) What further information would be useful to help the company decide whether to undertake the microbook project?

(ACCA Level 3, June 1991)

6. The general manager of the nationalized postal service of a small country, Zedland, wishes to introduce a new service. This service would offer same-day delivery of letters and parcels posted before 10 am within a distance of 150 km. The service would require 100 new vans costing $8,000 each and 20 trucks costing $18,000 each. 180 new workers would be employed at an average annual wage of $13,000 and five managers at average annual salaries of $20,000 would be moved from their existing duties, where they would not be replaced.

    Two postal rates are proposed. In the first year of operation letters will cost $0.525 and parcels $5.25. Market research undertaken at a cost of $50,000 forecasts that demand will average 15,000 letters per working day and 500 parcels per working day during the first year, and 20,000 letters per day and 750 parcels per day thereafter. There is a five-day working week. Annual running and maintenance costs on similar new vans and trucks are currently estimated in the first year of operation to be $2,000 per van and $4,000 per truck respectively. These costs will increase by 20 per cent p.a. (excluding the effects of inflation). Vehicles are depreciated over a five-year period on a straight-line basis. Depreciation is tax allowable and the vehicles will have negligible scrap value at the end of five years. Advertising in Year 1 will cost $500,000 and in Year 2 $250,000. There will be no advertising after Year 2. Existing premises will be used for the new service but additional costs of $150,000 per year will be incurred.

    All the above cost data are current estimates and exclude any inflation effects. Wage and salary costs and all other costs are expected to rise because of inflation by approximately 5 per cent p.a. during the five year planning horizon of the postal service. The government of Zedland will not permit annual price increases within nationalized industries to exceed the level of inflation.

    Nationalized industries are normally required by the government to earn at least an annual after-tax return of 5 per cent on average investment and to achieve, on average, at least zero net present value on their investments.

    The new service would be financed half with internally generated funds and half by borrowing on the capital market at an interest rate of 12 per cent p.a. The opportunity cost of capital for the postal service is estimated to be 14 per cent p.a. Corporate taxes in Zedland, to which the postal service is subject, are at the rate of 30 per cent for annual profits of up to $500,000 and 40 per cent for the balance in excess of $500,000. Tax is payable one year in arrears. All transactions may be assumed to be on a cash basis and to occur at the end of the year with the exception of the initial investment which would be required almost immediately.

Required

(a) Acting as an independent consultant prepare a report advising whether the new postal service should be introduced. Include in your report a discussion of other factors that might need to be taken into account before a final decision was made with respect to the introduction of the new postal service.

State clearly any assumptions that you make.

(b) Monte Carlo simulation has been suggested as a possible method of estimating the net present value of a project. Briefly assess the advantages and disadvantages of using this technique in investment appraisal.

(ACCA Level 3, December 1989)

Practical Assignment

How is risk formally assessed in your organization? Talk to a manager involved in larger capital projects. Find out how risks are assessed.

CHAPTER 9
Relationships between investments: portfolio theory

PEARSON'S DIVERSIFICATION

The following extract from an article in *The Guardian*, during the recession of the early 1980s, illustrates the experience of Pearson plc, a company which had grown by extensive diversification.

'Even secure diversified groups like Pearson are not immune from the recession. There, the downturn has been particularly marked at the Pearson Longman subsidiary, underlining both the cyclical nature of the publishing business, and the particular pressure on some sections of it, like Penguin. But the more fundamental point must be that diversification of itself is no real protection – in this case, the bits of the business that are doing better are too small a proportion to help the total very much. While some bits – like Midhurst Corporation in the US, and the London merchant bank Lazard – are virtually recession proof, the body of the business has to move in line with the economy as a whole. And recent diversification into things like Madame Tussauds hardly helps as that is affected by just the same strong pound as the publishing trade.'

9.1 Introduction

This chapter deals with the theory underlying *diversification decisions*. Diversification is an additional strategic device in the financial manager's armoury of weapons for dealing with risk. Whereas the previous chapter examined methods of risk analysis which focused on individual projects, here we study how the financial manager can exploit *interrelationships* between projects to adjust the risk-return characteristics of the whole enterprise. In the process, we will shed much more light on why firms like Pearson have developed a wide variety of activities or *portfolios*. The term 'portfolio' is usually applied to combinations of securities, but we will show that the principles underlying security portfolio formation can be applied to combinations of any type of asset, including investment projects.

Most firms, like Pearson, diffuse their efforts across a range of products, market segments and customers in order to spread more thinly the risks of declining trade and profitability. If a firm can reduce its reliance on particular products or markets, then it can withstand more comfortably the impact of a major reverse in any single market. However, firms do not reduce their exposure to the threat of new products or new competitors for entirely negative reasons. Diversification can generate some major strategic advantages, for example, the wider the spread of activities, the greater the potential access to high performing market sectors.

Imagine an economy divided into five sectors, where the identity of the star performer is always random. A company operating in a single sector is likely to miss out in four years out of five. In such a world, it is prudent to have a stake in every sector by building a portfolio of all five activities. The US aircraft manufacturer McDonnell Douglas, already operating in both civil and military aircraft production, utilized the expertise it developed in electronic systems by diversifying into computer system design, which it perceived to be a high-growth sector. Strong trading performance in computer systems could partially compensate for relatively poor trading in a sector such as defence procurement business during more peaceful times.

This sort of diversification is designed to even out the bumps in the time profile of profits and cash flows. The ideal form of diversification is to engage in activities which behave in exactly opposite ways. When sales, and the resulting earnings in one area, are relatively low, the adverse consequences can be offset by participation in a sector where sales and profits are relatively high. With perfect synchronization, the time profile of overall returns will describe the pattern shown in Figure 9.1. The figure shows the returns from two activities: A, which parallels the economy as a whole, and B, which moves in an exactly opposite way. The equal and opposite fluctuations in the returns from these two activities result in a perfectly level profile for an enterprise comprising both activities. In generally adverse economic conditions, the returns from activity A, closely following the economy as a whole, will be depressed, but involvement in activity B has an exactly compensating effect. The reverse applies when the economy is expanding. The returns from B are said to be *contra-cyclical*.

In the case of Pearson, there are two important messages in the report. First, it is not

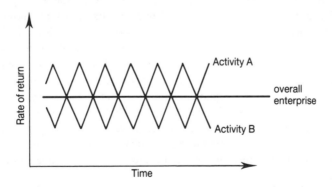

Figure 9.1 Equal and offsetting fluctuations in returns

enough simply to spread your activities. Different activities are subject to different types of risk, which are not always closely related. The factors affecting the profitability of publishing operations, such as the price of newsprint, are rather different from those which determine the returns from major tourist attractions like Madame Taussauds, such as the £/$ exchange rate. If changes in these influences are random and relatively uncorrelated, diversification may significantly reduce the variability of company earnings. Second, to generate an appreciable impact on overall returns, diversification must usually be substantial in relation to the whole enterprise. These are the key principles of portfolio diversification – look for unrelated activities, and engage in significant diversifications.

LEARNING OBJECTIVES

A basic axiom of life is 'don't put all your eggs in one basket'. This chapter is designed to explore the financial equivalent of this maxim. In particular, it aims to:

- Give the reader an understanding of the rationale behind the diversification decisions of both shareholders and of companies.
- Illustrate the mechanics of portfolio *construction* with a user-friendly approach to statistics, using several numerical examples.
- Emphasize that portfolio *selection* is a matter of personal choice.
- Examine the drawbacks of portfolio analysis as an approach to project appraisal.

A good grasp of the principles of portfolio analysis is an essential underpinning to the Capital Asset Pricing Model covered in Chapter 10.

9.2 Portfolio analysis: the basic principles

The theory of diversification can be reduced to the old proverb about not putting all one's eggs in one basket, a simple truth but one that many investors persistently ignore. How often have we read in the financial press heart-rending stories of small investors who have lost their life savings in some shady venture? Why is it that over 50 per cent of private investors persist in holding a single security in their investment portfolios? There are several possible answers to these questions. Such investors may be unaware of the advantages of spreading their risks, they may not have understood the arguments, they may not be risk-averse or, perhaps, they are simply irrational. Rational risk-averters appreciate that not all investments perform well at the same time, that some may never perform well, and that a few may perform spectacularly well. Since no one is gifted with the ability of predicting which investments will fall into each category in any one time period, it is rational to spread one's funds over a wide set of investments.

A simple example will illustrate the remarkable potential benefits of diversification. The key information is displayed below.

Alpha and Beta example

An investor can undertake one or both of the two investments, Alpha and Beta. Alpha has a 50 per cent chance of an 8 per cent return and a 50 per cent chance of returning 12 per cent. Beta has a 50 per cent chance of generating a return of 6 per cent and a 50 per cent chance of yielding 14 per cent. The two investments are in sectors of the economy which move in direct opposition to each other. The investor expects the return on investment Alpha to be relatively high when that on Beta is relatively low, and vice versa. What is the best portfolio to hold?

First of all, note that the expected value (EV) of each investment's return is identical:

$$\text{Investment Alpha: } EV = (0.5 \times 8\%) + (0.5 \times 12\%) = 4\% + 6\% = 10\%$$
$$\text{Investment Beta: } EV = (0.5 \times 6\%) + (0.5 \times 14\%) = 3\% + 7\% = 10\%$$

At first glance, it may appear that the investor would be indifferent between Alpha and Beta or indeed, any combination of them. However, there is a wide variety of possible expected returns according to how the investor allocates his funds, or 'weights' the portfolio. Moreover, a badly weighted portfolio can offer wide variations in returns in different time periods.

For example, when Beta is the star performer, a portfolio comprising 20% of Alpha and 80% of Beta will offer a return of:

$$(0.2 \times 8\%) + (0.8 \times 14\%) = (1.6\% + 11.2\%) = 12.8\%$$

When Alpha is the star, the return is only

$$(0.2 \times 12\%) + (0.8 \times 6\%) = (2.4\% + 4.8\%) = 7.2\%$$

Although, over the long term, there should be as many good years for Alpha as for Beta, resulting in a long-term average return of 10 percent, *in the shorter term*, the investor would be over-exposed to the risk of a series of bad years for Beta. Happily, there is a portfolio which removes this risk entirely.

Consider the portfolio invested two-thirds in Alpha and one-third in Beta. This has some interesting properties. When Alpha is the star, the return on the portfolio, R_p, is given by a weighted average expression:

$$R_p = (2/3 \times 12\%) + (1/3 \times 6\%) = (8\% + 2\%) = 10\%$$

Conversely, when Beta is the star, the portfolio offers a return of:

$$R_p = (2/3 \times 8\%) + (1/3 \times 14\%) = (5.33\% + 4.67\%) = 10\%$$

With this combination, the investor cannot go wrong! The portfolio completely removes variability in returns as there are only two possible states of the economy. Any rational risk-averting investor should select this combination of Alpha and Beta to minimize risk for a guaranteed 10 per cent return. This is called a *perfect portfolio effect*.

This example, admittedly extreme, is given for explanatory purposes. The opportunity to eliminate all risk arises from the *perfect negative correlation* between the two investments, but this fortunate property can only be exploited by weighting the portfolio in a particular way. Thus, there are two requirements for total elimination of risk.

Unfortunately, cases of perfect negative correlation between the returns from securities are few and far between. In practice, most investment returns exhibit varying degrees of positive correlation, largely according to how they depend on overall economic trends. However, this does not rule out risk-reducing diversification benefits, but suggests they may be less pronounced than in our simple example. As we will see, the extent to which portfolio combination can achieve a reduction in risk depends on the degree of correlation between returns. Later in the chapter, we will examine more realistic cases, but first, we need to explore more fully the nature and measurement of portfolio risk.

9.3   How to measure portfolio risk

We have just seen the importance of assessing the degree of correlation between the returns from two investments. In our example, life was made considerably easier by the assumption of perfect negative correlation. We saw also how the return from a portfolio could be expressed as a weighted average of the individual asset returns, the weights being the proportions of the portfolio accounted for by each of the various components. A similar relationship applies *ex ante*, that is, if we consider the *expected value* of the return from the portfolio. The expected return on a portfolio (ER_p) comprising two assets, A and B, whose individual expected returns are ER_A and ER_B respectively, is given by:

$$ER_p = \alpha\ ER_A + (1-\alpha)ER_B$$

where α and $(1-\alpha)$ are the respective weightings of assets A and B, so that $\alpha + (1-\alpha) = 1$.

The riskiness of the portfolio expresses the extent to which the actual return may deviate from the expected return. This may be expressed in terms of the variance of the return, σ_p^2, or in terms of its standard deviation, σ_p.

The expression for the standard deviation of a two-asset portfolio is:
$$\sigma_p = \sqrt{\alpha^2\ \sigma_A^2 + (1-\alpha)^2\sigma_B^2 + 2\ \alpha\ (1-\alpha)\mathrm{cov}_{AB}}$$

This has some significant features. First, it contains the term cov_{AB}, the *covariance* between A and B. This, like the correlation coefficient, is a measure of the interrelationship between random variables, in this case, the returns from the two investments A and B. In other words, it measures *co-movement* or *co-variability*. When the two returns generally move

---

The correlation coefficient between the return on A and the return on B, r_{AB}, is simply the covariance, normalized or standardized, by the product of the two relevant standard deviations:

$$\frac{\text{correlation}}{\text{coefficient}} = r_{AB} = \frac{\text{covariance}_{AB}}{(\text{std. dev. of A}) \times (\text{std. dev. of B})} = \frac{\mathrm{cov}_{AB}}{\sigma_A \times \sigma_B}$$

Table 9.1 Returns under different states of the economy

State of the Economy	Probability	Return from A	Return from B
E_1	0.25	−10%	+60%
E_2	0.25	−10%	−20%
E_3	0.25	+50%	−20%
E_4	0.25	+50%	+60%

together it has a positive value, when they generally move away from each other it has a negative value, and when there is no co-variability at all its value is zero. However, unlike the correlation coefficient whose value is constrained to locate on a scale ranging from −1 to +1, the covariance can assume any value. It measures co-movement in *absolute* terms whereas the correlation coefficient is a *relative* measure.

This relationship may be more easily understood with a numerical example. Table 9.1 shows the possible returns from two assets under four different economic conditions, with associated probabilities. The reader should check that the expected values for both A and B are 20 per cent, and that their respective standard deviations are 30 per cent and 40 per cent.

The expression for the covariance, cov_{AB}, between the returns on two investments, A and B, is:

$$\text{cov}_{AB} = \sigma_{AB} = \sum_{i=1}^{N} [(R_A - ER_A)(R_B - ER_B).p_i]$$

Where:

R_A = realized return from investment A
ER_A = expected value of the return from A
R_B = realized return from investment B
ER_B = expected value of the return from B
p_i = the probability of the *i*th pair of values occurring

This tells us to examine for each pair of simultaneously occurring outcomes, their deviations from their respective expected values, to multiply these deviations together and then to weight the resulting product by the relevant probability for each pair. Finally, the sum of all weighted products of paired outcome/expected divergences defines the covariance. The full calculation is given in Table 9.2.

In this case, there is no covariability at all between the returns from the two assets. If the return from A increases, it is just as likely to be associated with a fall in the return from B as a concurrent increase. If the covariance, measuring the degree of co-movement in absolute terms, is zero, we should expect to find the correlation coefficient, the relative measure of co-movement, is also zero. We may now demonstrate this:

$$\text{Correlation coefficient} = r_{AB} = \frac{\text{cov}_{AB}}{(\sigma_A \times \sigma_B)} = \frac{0}{(30 \times 40)} = 0$$

Table 9.2 Calculating the covariance

R_A	ER_A	R_B	ER_B	$(R_A - ER_A)$	$(R_B - ER_B)$	Product	Prob.	Weighted Product
−10	20	+60	20	−30	+40	−1200	0.25	−300
−10	20	−20	20	−30	−40	+1200	0.25	+300
+50	20	−20	20	+30	−40	−1200	0.25	−300
+50	20	+60	20	+30	+40	+1200	0.25	+300

$$\text{covariance}_{AB} = 0$$

Note: Although these figures are percentages, they have been treated as integers to clarify exposition.

The case of zero covariance is a convenient one as we can see from inspection of the expression for portfolio risk, σ_p. When the covariance is zero, then the whole of the third term is zero-valued, and portfolio risk reduces to:

$$\sigma_p = \sqrt{\alpha^2 \sigma_A^2 + (1-\alpha)^2 \sigma_B^2}$$

Portfolio risk is thus smaller for any portfolio compared to the case where the covariance is positive. Even better, when the covariance is negative, the third term becomes negative and risk is further reduced. In general, the lowest achievable portfolio risk declines as the covariance diminishes, i.e. the more negative the better. There is, however, no limit on the covariance value. If we re-express portfolio risk in terms of the correlation coefficient, we can be more specific about the greatest achievable degree of risk reduction. The formula relating covariance and correlation coefficient can be rewritten as:

$$\text{cov}_{AB} = (r_{AB} \times \sigma_A \times \sigma_B)$$

Substituting into the general expression for portfolio risk, we derive:

$$\sigma_p = \sqrt{\alpha^2 \sigma_A^2 + (1-\alpha)^2 \sigma_B^2 + 2\alpha(1-\alpha)\sigma_A \sigma_B r_{AB}}$$

Clearly, when the correlation coefficient is negative, risk will be reduced, but since the limit to negative correlation is minus one, this places a lower limit on σ_p. As we saw in our first example, this may fall to zero if the portfolio is appropriately weighted. Whether one works in terms of the covariance or the correlation coefficient is generally a matter of preference, but sometimes it is dictated by the information available.

The optimal portfolio

An obvious question to ask is, which is the best portfolio to hold? In this example, the answer is simple. Because the two investments have the same expected values, any portfolio we construct by combining them will have the same expected value. The optimal portfolio is simply the one that offers the lowest level of risk. Although very few decision-makers will always wish to minimize risk, any rational risk-averter would adopt the risk-minimizing action where every alternative offers an equal expected pay-off.

THE MINIMUM RISK PORTFOLIO WITH TWO ASSETS

The expression for finding the weighting required to minimize the risk of a portfolio comprising two assets, A and B, where $\alpha_A{}^*$ = the proportion invested in asset A is:

$$\alpha_A{}^* = \frac{\sigma_B{}^2 - \mathrm{cov}_{AB}}{\sigma_A{}^2 + \sigma_B{}^2 - 2\mathrm{cov}_{AB}}$$

Substituting, we find:

$$\alpha_A{}^* = \frac{£40^2}{£40^2 + £30^2} = \frac{£1,600}{£2,500} = 0.64$$

Using this formula, we find that to minimize risk, we should place 64 per cent of our funds in A and 36 per cent in B. The reader should verify that the standard deviation of this portfolio is 24 per cent.

In the next section, we analyse the more interesting and more likely case where both the risks and returns of the two components differ.

9.4   Portfolio risk-return analysis

Suppose we are offered the two investments, Z and Y, whose characteristics are shown in Table 9.3. Which should we undertake? Or should we undertake some combination? To answer these questions, we need to consider the possible combinations of risk and return.

Let us assume that the two assets can be combined in any proportions, i.e. the two assets are perfectly divisible as with security investments. There is an infinite number of possible combinations of risk and return. However, for simplicity, we confine our attention to the restricted range of portfolios whose risk and return characteristics are shown in Table 9.4.

Aiming to minimize risk, we might initially be inclined to invest solely in asset Z, since this has the lowest standard deviation. However, this would be mistaken because, owing to the negative correlation between Z and Y, a lower risk can be achieved. This may seem contrary to intuition. As we move from the all-Z portfolio to the 75 per cent-of-Z-plus-25 per

Table 9.3   Differing returns and risks

Asset	Expected Return (ER)	Standard deviation
Z	15%	20%
Y	35%	40%
Covariance$_{ZY}$		-2%
Hence,		
correlation coefficient$_{ZY}$	$=$	$\dfrac{-0.02}{(0.2)(0.4)} = -0.25$

Table 9.4 Risk–return combinations

Z Weighting	Y Weighting	Expected return	Standard deviation
100%	0	15%	20%
75%	25%	20%	16%
50%	50%	25%	20%
25%	75%	30%	29%
0	100%	35%	40%

cent-of-Y combination, thus substituting a more risky asset for a relatively low-risk investment, the risk of the whole portfolio actually diminishes! Moreover, the expected return increases! However, this apparently magical effect cannot continue across the board. Eventually, for portfolios more heavily weighted toward Y, the effect of Y's higher risk outweighs the beneficial effect of negative correlation, resulting in rising overall risk.

Figure 9.2 traces the set of available opportunities, or the *risk–return profile*, which is shaped like the nose cone of an aircraft. The profile ranges from point A representing total investment in Y through to point C representing total investment in Z, having described a U-turn at B. (Readers may care to verify that the portfolio at B, involving 75 per cent of Z and 25 per cent of Y is the minimum risk combination.)

However, not all combinations are of interest to the rational risk-averter. Comparing segment AB with the segment BC, we find that combinations lying along the latter are inefficient. For any combination along BC, we can achieve a higher return for the same risk by

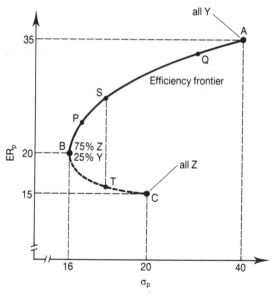

Figure 9.2 Available portfolio risk–return combinations when both component risks and return are different

moving to the combination vertically above it on AB. This relationship is demonstrated by the pair of points S and T. Clearly, S is superior to T, i.e. S is said to *dominate* T. Applying similar logic to the whole of BC, we are left with the segment AB summarizing all efficient portfolios, i.e. those that maximize return for a given risk. AB is thus called the *efficiency frontier*.

However, we cannot specify an *optimal portfolio*, except for an outright risk-minimizer, who would select the portfolio at B. A risk-averter might select any portfolio along AB, depending on his degree of risk-aversion, that is, what additional return he would require to compensate for a specified increase in risk. For example, a highly risk-averse person might locate at point P, while the less demanding risk-averter might locate at point Q.

This is a crucial result. *We have found that the most desirable combination of risky assets depends on the decision-maker's attitude towards risk. If we know the extent of his risk-aversion, that is, how large a premium he requires for a given increase in risk, we can specify his best portfolio.*

9.5 A worked example: Gerrybild plc

Gerrybild plc is a firm of speculative housebuilders, which builds in advance of firm orders from customers. It has a given amount of capital to purchase land and raw materials, and to pay labour for development purposes. It is considering two design types – a small two-bedroomed terraced town house and a large four-bedroomed 'executive' residence. The project could last a number of years and its success depends largely on general economic conditions which will influence the demand for new houses. Some information is available on past sales patterns of similar properties in roughly similar locations – the demand for larger properties being relatively greater in buoyant economic conditions and higher for smaller properties in relatively depressed states of the economy. Since there appears to be a degree of inverse correlation between demand, and therefore, net cash flows, from the two products, it seems sensible to consider diversified development – but to what extent? What advice can we offer? Table 9.5 shows annual net cash flow estimates for various economic conditions.

To analyse this decision problem, we need first to calculate the risk-return parameters of the investment, and second, to assess the degree of correlation that exists. This information may be obtained by performing a number of statistical operations.

Table 9.5 Returns from Gerrybild

State of the Economy	Probability	Estimated Net Cash Flows (£) from:	
		Large Houses	Small Houses
E_1	0.2	2,000	2,000
E_2	0.3	2,000	3,000
E_3	0.4	4,000	2,000
E_4	0.1	4,000	3,000

Calculation of expected values

A shortcut is available since some outcomes may occur under more than one state of the economy. Grouping data where possible, we have:

$$EV_L = \text{Expected value of large project} = (0.5 \times £2,000) + (0.5 \times £4,000)$$
$$= £3,000$$
$$EV_S = \text{Expected value of small project} = (0.6 \times £2,000) + (0.4 \times £3,000)$$
$$= £2,400$$

Calculation of project risks

We now apply the usual expression for the standard deviation. The calculations for each activity are shown in Table 9.6. Clearly, the relative money-spinner, the large house project, is also the more risky activity.

Calculation of covariability

Again, in Table 9.7 we present the calculation of the covariance in tabular form, following the steps itemized in section 9.3.

The covariance of $-£200,000$, suggests a strong element of inverse association (and rather lower than we might expect in reality!). This is confirmed by the value of the correlation coefficient which is:

$$r_{LS} = \frac{\text{cov}_{LS}}{\sigma_L \times \sigma_S} = \frac{-£200,000}{(£1,000)\ (£489)} = -0.41$$

Table 9.6   Calculation of standard deviations

Outcome (£)	Prob	EV (£)	Deviation (£)	Squared Deviation (£)	Weighted Squared Deviation (£)
Large Houses					
2,000	0.5	3,000	−1,000	1m	0.5m
4,000	0.5	3,000	+1,000	1m	0.5m
				$\sigma_L{}^2 =$ Variance =	1m
				hence $\sigma_L = \sqrt{1m}$	
				=	1,000
Small Houses					
2,000	0.6	2,400	−400	160,000	96,000
3,000	0.4	2,400	+600	360,000	144,000
				$\sigma_S{}^2 =$ Variance =	240,000
				hence σ_S = $\sqrt{240,000}$	
				=	489

Table 9.7 Calculation of the covariance

Possible Outcomes (£)		Prob	$(EV_L - R_L)$ (£)	$(EV_S - R_S)$ (£)	Product (£)	Weighted Product (£)
R_L	R_S					
2,000	2,000	0.2	−1,000	−400	+400,000	+80,000
2,000	3,000	0.3	−1,000	+600	−600,000	−180,000
4,000	2,000	0.4	+1,000	−400	−400,000	−160,000
4,000	3,000	0.1	+1,000	+600	+600,000	+60,000
					$cov_{LS} =$	−200,000

There are clearly significant portfolio benefits to exploit. To offer concrete advice to the builder, we would require information on his risk-return preferences, but we can at least specify the available set of portfolio combinations. Rather than compute the full set of opportunities, we will identify the minimum risk portfolio which will then enable us to draw the overall risk-return profile, which will follow the nose cone shape.

The minimum risk portfolio

Using the expression from Section 9.4, and defining α_L as the proportion of the portfolio invested in large houses, we have:

$$\alpha_L^* = \frac{(\sigma_S^2 - cov_{LS})}{(\sigma_S^2 + \sigma_L^2 - 2cov_{LS})} = \frac{£240,000 + £200,000}{£240,000 + £1m + £400,000}$$

$$= \frac{£440,000}{£1,640,000} = 0.27$$

This result indicates that if Gerrybild wanted to minimize risk, it would have to invest 27 per cent of its capital in large houses and the greater part, 73 per cent, in small houses. The reader should verify that the lowest achievable portfolio standard deviation is £349 and the expected return from the minimum risk portfolio is £2561.

The opportunity set

We now have sufficient information to display the full range of opportunities available to Gerrybild. The opportunity set ABC is shown on Figure 9.3 as the familiar nose cone shape. If Gerrybild risk-averts, only segment AB is of interest, but precisely where along this segment it will choose to locate, depends on its attitude towards risk.

9.6 Some reservations

The Gerrybild example allows us to pinpoint some drawbacks with the portfolio approach as a general means of handling project risk.

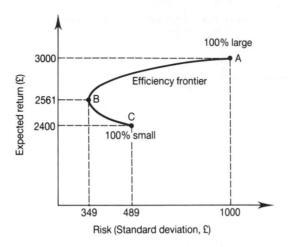

Figure 9.3 Gerrybild's opportunity set

(1) In practice, there are major difficulties in dividing up projects to achieve the precise portfolio weights recommended by our numerical analysis. Rather than having access to a smooth continuous opportunity set as in Figure 9.3, we find that most projects can only be undertaken in a very restricted range of sizes or even on an 'all-or-nothing' basis. This does not entirely undermine the portfolio approach – it simply means that the range of combinations available is much narrower. Besides, enterprises are often undertaken on a joint venture basis, e.g. in large, high-risk activities like Eurotunnel and Airbus, the various parties had some freedom to select the extent of their participation.

(2) A more severe problem is the implication of constant returns to scale. Our analyses imply that if a smaller version of a project is undertaken, the percentage returns or the absolute return per pound invested will remain unchanged. For example, if the return on the whole project is 20 per cent, the return from doing 30 per cent of the same project is still 20 per cent. This may apply for investment in securities, but is unlikely for investment projects where there is often a minimum size below which there are zero or negative returns, and thereafter, increasing returns to scale.

(3) We should be wary of any approach that relies on subjective assessments of probabilities, or at least of the probabilities themselves. In the case of repetitive activities such as replacement of equipment about which a substantial data bank of costs and benefits has been compiled, the probabilities may have some basis in reality. In other cases, such as major new product developments, probabilities are largely based on inspired guesswork. Different decision analysts may well formulate different 'guesstimates' about the chances of particular events occurring. However, the subjective nature of probabilities in practice need not be a deterrent if they are well supported by reasoned argument, and therefore instil confidence.

(4) Even if we trust our probabilistic 'guesstimates', and are able to construct an efficient set of portfolio combinations, we still need a criterion to assist us in selecting from among the available candidates. Since attitudes to risk determine choice, we would want to know the decision-maker's utility function which summarizes his preferences as between different monetary amounts. The difficulties of obtaining information about an individual manager's utility function (let alone for a group) are formidable, as Swalm (1966) has shown. Besides, we should really be seeking to apply the risk-return preferences of the shareholders rather than those of the managers.

(5) Given the problems of utility measurement, and since managers rather than share-holders take the investment decisions, we should not be too surprised to encounter some significant agency problems. The portfolio approach to risk analysis does seem to be unduly management-oriented. Managers formulate the assessments of alternative payoffs, managers assess the relevant probabilities and managers determine what combinations of activities the enterprise should undertake. Managers are considerably less mobile and less well diversified than shareholders who can buy and sell securities more or less at will. Managers can hardly shrug off a poor investment outcome if it jeopardizes the future development of the whole enterprise or, more pertinently, their job security. Most managers are more risk-averse than shareholders, resulting in the likelihood of sub-optimal investment decisions.

These may appear to be highly damaging criticisms of the portfolio approach, and at a practical level, as applied to physical investment decisions, they probably are. However, help is at hand. The portfolio combination model, although having limited operational usefulness for many investment projects, provides the infrastructure of a more sophisticated approach to investment decision-making under risk, the *Capital Asset Pricing Model (CAPM)*. This is based on an examination of the risk-return characteristics and resulting portfolio opportunities of securities, rather than physical investment opportunities.

The CAPM explains how individual securities are valued, or priced, in efficient capital markets. Essentially, this involves discounting the future expected returns from holding a security at a rate which adequately reflects the degree of risk incurred in holding that security. A major contribution of the CAPM is the determination of the premium for risk demanded by the market from different securities. This provides a clue as to the appropriate discount rate to apply when evaluating risky projects. A critical component in the explanation is the portfolio combination model. The CAPM is analysed in the next chapter.

9.7 Summary

In this chapter, we have examined some reasons why firms diversify their activities, and have considered the extent to which the theory of portfolio analysis can provide operational guidelines for diversification decisions.

Key points

- Both firms and individuals diversify investments – firms build portfolios of business activities and individuals build portfolios of securities.
- Diversification is mainly designed to reduce fluctuations in returns.
- Variations in returns can be totally eliminated only if the investments concerned have perfect negative correlation *and* if the portfolio is weighted so as to minimize risk.
- The expected return from a portfolio is a weighted average of the returns expected from its components, the weights determined by the proportion of capital invested in each activity or security. For a portfolio comprising the two assets, A and B:

$$ER_p = \alpha\ ER_A + (1-\alpha)\ ER_B$$

- Portfolio risk, however, is given by a square-root formula:

$$\sigma_p = \sqrt{\alpha^2\sigma_A{}^2 + (1-\alpha)^2\ \sigma_B{}^2 + 2\alpha(1-\alpha)\ cov_{AB}}$$

- The degree of covariability between the returns expected from the components of the portfolios is measured by the covariance, cov_{AB}, or by the correlation coefficient, r_{AB}. The lower the degree of covariability, the lower is the risk of the portfolio (for given weightings).
- The available risk–return combinations for mixing investments is shown by the opportunity set.
- Some combinations can be rejected as inefficient. Rational risk-averting investors choose from only the efficient set.
- The optimal portfolio for any investor depends on his attitude to risk, that is, how risk-averse he is.
- In practice, there are serious difficulties in applying the portfolio techniques to *physical* investment decisions.

Further reading

The classic works on portfolio theory are by Markowitz (1952), Sharpe (1964) and Tobin (1958) (all of whom have won Nobel Prizes for Economics). See also Fama and Miller (1972) and Copeland and Weston (1988) for more developed analyses, and also proofs and derivations of the formulae used in this chapter. Finally, Markowitz's Nobel address (1991) is well worth reading.

Questions

Self-test questions

1. What are the two required conditions for total elimination of risk in a portfolio of investments?
2. Can you explain the concept of an efficiency frontier?

3. Can you distinguish between an available portfolio, an efficient portfolio and an optimal portfolio?
4. Can you distinguish between risk-aversion and risk-minimization?
5. For what reasons are we unlikely to be able to apply the 'pure' portfolio theory to physical investment decisions?

Exercises

1. Nissota, a Japanese-based car manufacturer, is evaluating two overseas locations for a proposed expansion of production facilities, one site in Ireland and the other on Humberside. The likely future return from investment in each site depends to a great extent on future economic conditions. Three scenarios are postulated, and the internal rate of return from each investment is computed under each scenario. The returns with their estimated probabilities are shown below:

| | Internal Rate of Return (IRR) | |
Probability	Eire	Humberside
0.3	20%	10%
0.3	10%	30%
0.4	15%	20%

Required
(a) What is the expected value of the IRR from investment in each location?
(b) What is the standard deviation of the return from investment in each location?
(c) What would be the expected return and the standard deviation of a split investment strategy:
  (i) committing 50 per cent of available funds to the Eire site and 50 per cent to Humberside;
  (ii) committing 75 per cent of funds to the Eire site and 25 per cent to the Humberside site?
  (There is thought to be zero correlation between the returns from the two sites.)
(d) Explain the practical advantages and disadvantages of split investments such as those suggested in part (c).
(e) Briefly assess the contribution of portfolio theory to the evaluation of physical investment decisions.

(Solution in Appendix A)

2. The management of Gawain plc is evaluating two projects whose returns depend on the future state of the economy as shown below:

Probability	$IRR_A\%$	$IRR_B\%$
0.3	27	35
0.4	18	15
0.3	5	20

The project (or projects) accepted would double the size of Gawain. Gawain is debt-free.

Required

(a) Explain how a portfolio should be constructed to produce an expected return of 20 per cent.

(b) Calculate the correlation between A and B, and assess the degree of risk of the portfolio in (a).

(c) Gawain's existing activities have a standard deviation of 10 per cent. How does the addition of the portfolio analysed in (a) and (b) affect risk?

3. Teniers plc is considering investing in a new product line, currently referred to as 'Project X'. The expected value and standard deviation of the probability distribution of possible net present values for the product line are £12,000 and £9,000, respectively.

   The company has two existing lines which may be referred to simply as A and B. The expected values of net present value and standard deviation of these product lines are:

	NPV £	σ £
Product A	16,000	10,000
Product B	10,000	4,000

The correlation coefficients of the returns between each product line are estimated as:

	A	B	X
A	1.00	—	—
B	0.90	1.00	—
X	0.40	0.80	1.00

Capacity constraints dictate that it is possible for the company to operate only two production lines at any one time, and having made the decision it would not be possible to change because of tooling and marketing problems. Available portfolios, including the proportions invested in each production line are:

Proportion invested in: Portfolio	A	B	X
A	1.00	—	—
B	—	1.00	—
X	—	—	1.00
A+B	0.50	0.50	—
A+X	0.50	—	0.50
B+X	—	0.50	0.50

Required

(a) Advise the company on the most suitable combination of product-lines, and state the assumptions made in relation to the company's objectives and attitudes to risk.

You may assume that the proportion invested in each project and the NPV are linearly related.

(b) State what additional information you would need in order to select an 'optimal' portfolio.

(CIMA Stage IV, 1987)

Practical assignment

Select a company with a reasonably wide portfolio of activities. Such companies do not always give segmental earnings figures but they usually divulge sales figures for their component activities. By looking at the Annual Reports for three of four years, or at Extel cards, you can obtain a series of annual sales figures for each activity.

Assess the degree of past volatility of the sales of each sub-unit and their degree of inter-correlation. Also, see whether you can assess the extent of the correlation between each segment and the overall enterprise.

How well diversified does your selected company appear to be? What qualifications should you make in your analysis?

CHAPTER 10
Setting the risk premium: the capital asset pricing model

NOBEL PRIZES FOR ECONOMISTS

Nobel prizes in Economics were awarded in 1990 to Harry Markowitz and William Sharpe for their path-breaking work on portfolio theory, outlined in the previous chapter, and asset pricing, respectively. These awards drew high praise from the financial press. For example, *The New York Times* declared:

> 'To academics, they are top-shelf theoreticians whose quarter-century old insights into the economics of finance still dazzle the brightest graduate students. To nuts-and-bolts types, they are researchers whose ideas have changed Wall Street and the investment habits of millions of people.'

The *Wall Street Journal* made our two heroes sound more like Batman and Robin!

> 'Widows live safer lives because their portfolios are invested according to the diversification principles developed by Markowitz and elaborated by Sharpe.'

The Capital Asset Pricing Model (CAPM) has dominated the finance literature for two decades. Is this because it works, or simply because we have yet to develop a better model of market behaviour and security valuation?

10.1 Introduction

In Chapters 8 and 9, we examined various methods of handling risk and uncertainty in project appraisal, ranging from sensitivity analysis to the analysis of portfolio combinations designed to exploit less than perfect correlation between the returns from risky investments. Most of these approaches aim to identify the sources and extent of project risk and to assess whether the expected returns sufficiently compensate for bearing the risk. Utility theory suggests that as risk increases, rational risk-averters require higher returns, providing the rationale for the common practice among firms of adjusting discount rates for risk. However, none of the approaches studied so far offers an explicit guide to measuring the precise reward investors should seek for incurring a given level of risk.

This chapter examines the Capital Asset Pricing Model (CAPM), a theory originally erected by Sharpe (1964) to explain how the capital market sets share prices. It now provides the infrastructure of much modern financial theory and offers important insights into the measurement of risk and for setting risk premia. In particular, it shows how study of security prices can help in assessing required rates of return on investments.

Security valuation and discount rates

Chapter 4 showed that asset value is governed by two factors – the stream of expected benefits from holding the asset and their 'quality', or likely variability. For example, the value of a single-project company would be assessed by discounting its future cash flow stream at a discount rate suitably reflecting its riskiness. Taking a simple example, the value, V_0, of a company newly formed by issuing one million shares to exploit a one-year project offering a single net cash flow of £10m, at a 25 per cent discount rate, is:

$$V_0 = \frac{£10m}{(1.25)} = £8m$$

This corresponds to a market price per share of £8m/£1m = £8. This would be the value established by an efficient capital market taking account of all known information about the company's future prospects.

Sometimes, however, the 'correct' discount rate is unknown to the firm. A major contribution of the CAPM is to explain how discount rates are established and hence how securities are valued. From the capital market value of a company, we can infer what discount rate underlies the market price. In the example, an observed market price of £8 suggests a required return of 25 per cent.

By implication, if the market, the vast impersonal mass of investors, sets a value on a security which implies a particular discount rate, it is reasonable to conclude that any further activity of similar risk to existing ones should offer at least the same rate. This argument depends critically on market prices being unbiased indicators of the intrinsic worth of companies, thus resting heavily on the validity of the Efficient Markets Hypothesis.

Any discount rate is an amalgam of three components:

1. Allowance for the time value of money – the compensation required by investors for having to wait for their payments.
2. Allowance for price level changes – the additional return required to compensate for the impact of inflation on the real value of capital.
3. Allowance for risk – the promised reward which provides the incentive for exposing capital to risk.

Ignoring expected inflation (or assuming that it is 'correctly' built into the structure of interest rates), *discount rates have two components – the rate of return required on totally risk-free assets, such as government securities, and a risk premium.*

LEARNING OBJECTIVES

This chapter deals with the rate of return required by shareholders in an all-equity financed company by extending the treatment of portfolio theory to the analysis of the Capital Asset Pricing Model. Its specific aims are to:

- Enable the reader to understand what element of the overall risk of a security is relevant to its valuation.
- Explain what a 'Beta coefficient' is.
- Enable the readers to determine the appropriate risk premium to incorporate into a discount rate.
- Question whether corporate diversification is always desirable.

An understanding of the significance of Betas is particularly important in appreciating how a financial manager should view risk. Betas will re-appear in later chapters!

10.2   Concepts of return and risk

In this section, we examine risk and return concepts relevant for security valuation.

The returns from holding shares

Investors hold securities because they hope for positive returns. Purchasers of ordinary shares are attracted by two components of return, first, the anticipated dividend(s) payable during the holding period, and second, the expected capital gain.

THE RETURNS FROM HOLDING ORDINARY SHARES

In general, for any holding period, t, and company, j, the percentage return from holding its shares is:

$$R_{jt} = \frac{D_{jt} + (P_{jt} - P_{jt-1})}{P_{jt-1}} \times 100$$

Where:

D_{jt} = the dividend per share paid by company j in period t
P_{jt} = the share price for company j at the end of period t
P_{jt-1} = the share price for company j at the start of period t

Table 10.1 The annual returns on Pilkington shares, 1980–90

Year	% Return
1980–1	+53.8
1981–2	−8.4
1982–3	+16.3
1983–4	+57.4
1984–5	−8.1
1985–6	+59.5
1986–7	+83.9
1987–8	−16.6
1988–9	+21.1
1989–90	−10.0
Average	26.6%
Standard deviation	34.9%

To illustrate this calculation (and to show that returns are not always positive!), consider the following figures for Pilkington plc:

share price at end of March 1989 = 246p
share price at end of March 1990 = 211p
net dividend paid during 1989–90 = 10.5p per share

The percentage return 'enjoyed' over this period was:

$$\frac{10.5p + (211p - 246p)}{246p} \times 100 = -10\%$$

Pilkington ordinary shares have a high degree of risk, with a high standard deviation of returns relative to the average. This volatility over time is demonstrated in Table 10.1.

If we regard past returns on Pilkington shares as a good guide to likely future returns and also believe that future annual returns will be randomly distributed about the mean, then we might assess the expected value of holding Pilkington shares for a given year as 26.6 per cent. However, the actual return in any one year may diverge considerably from this average, because Pilkington's shares look quite risky. However, to judge the riskiness of a security, we have to assess what risks are relevant for valuation purposes.

The risk of holding ordinary shares

In Chapter 9, we saw the power of portfolio combination in reducing the risk of a collection of investments held as a portfolio. Risk was measured by the variance or standard deviation of the return on the combination. This measure can also be applied to portfolios of securities, with some remarkable results, as shown in Figure 10.1.

As the number of securities held in the portfolio increases, the overall variability of the portfolio's return, measured by its standard deviation, diminishes very sharply for small portfolios, but falls more gradually for larger combinations. This decline in risk is achieved

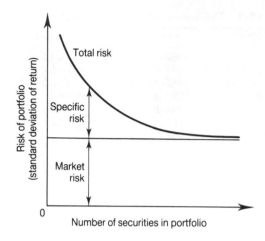

Figure 10.1   Specific vs. market risk of a portfolio

because the exposure to the risk of volatile securities like Pilkington can be offset by the inclusion of low-risk securities or even other high-risk ones, so long as their returns are not closely correlated. As we saw with combinations of physical projects, 'lows' in some areas can be compensated by 'highs' in other areas.

Specific and systematic risk

The key point here is that not all the risk of individual securities is relevant for assessing the risk of a portfolio of risky shares, i.e. risk is not additive. The CAPM separates the total risk of securities (and also of portfolios) into two components. These are:

TWO KEY TYPES OF RISK

1. Specific risk   The variability in return due to factors unique to the individual firm.
2. Systematic risk   The variability in return due to the dependence on factors which influence the return on all securities to varying degrees.

Specific risk refers to the expected impact on sales and earnings of largely random events like industrial relations problems, equipment failure, R&D achievements, etc. In a portfolio of shares, such factors tend to cancel out as the number of component securities increases. *Systematic risk* refers to the impact of movements in the macro-economy, such as fiscal changes, swings in exchange rates and interest rate movements, all of which cause reactions in security markets, represented by some index of securities such as the Financial Times All-Share Index in the United Kingdom or the DAX index in Germany. No firm is entirely insulated from these factors, and even portfolio diversification cannot provide protection against this form of risk. For this reason, it is often called *market risk*.

Returning to Figure 10.1, we see that the reduction in the total risk of a portfolio is achieved by gradual elimination of the risks unique to individual companies, leaving an

Table 10.2 How to remove portfolio risk

Number of Securities (*N*)	Reduction in Specific Risk
1	0%
2	46%
4	72%
8	81%
16	93%
32	96%
64	98%
500	99%

Source: Fosback (1985).

Table 10.3 Gains from diversification

Number of Securities	Specific/Total Risk
1	42%
2	27%
3	19%
4	15%
6	11%
8	8%
10	6%
15	5%
Market Portfolio	0%

Source: Mittra and Gassen (1985).

irreducible, undiversifiable, risk floor. The extent to which unique risk declines for a portfolio comprising N-equally-weighted and randomly selected securities is also shown in Table 10.2.

Substantial reductions in specific risk can be achieved with quite small portfolios, and the main scope for risk reduction is achieved with a portfolio of around thirty securities. To eliminate unique risk totally would involve holding a vast portfolio comprising all the securities traded in the market. This construct, called the 'market portfolio', has a pivotal role in the CAPM, but for the individual investor it is neither practicable nor cost-effective, in view of the likely scale of the dealing fees required to construct and manage it. Since relatively small portfolios can capture the lion's share of diversification benefits, it is only a small simplification to use a well-diversified portfolio as a proxy for the overall market. To illustrate further the power of diversification, Table 10.3 examines the composition of overall risk as the number of securities held in a portfolio increases.

Implications

Three major implications now follow:

(1) *It is clear that risk-averters should diversify*. Yet in reality, over half of UK investors hold just one security (usually British Gas). However, the major players in capital markets,

holding over 60 per cent of all quoted UK ordinary shares, are financial institutions such as pension funds and insurance companies, which do hold *highly* diversified portfolios.

(2) *Investors should not expect rewards for bearing specific risk.* Since risk unique to particular companies can be diversified away, the only relevant consideration in assessing risk premia is risk which cannot be dispersed by portfolio formation. If bearing unique risk was rewarded, astute investors prepared to build portfolios would snap up securities with high levels of unique risk to diversify it away, yet still hoping to enjoy disproportionate returns. As they did this, the value of such securities would rise and the returns on them would fall until only systematic risk were rewarded.

(3) *Securities have varying degrees of systematic risk.* Few securities exhibit patterns of returns rising or falling exactly in line with the market as a whole. This is partly because in the short term, unique random factors affect particular companies in different ways. Yet even in the long term, when such factors tend to even out, very few securities track the market. Some appear to outperform the market by offering superior returns and some appear to underperform it. However, performance relative to the market should not be too hastily judged because the returns on different securities do not always depend on general economic factors in the same way.

For example, in an expanding economy, retail sales tend to increase sharply but sales in less responsive sectors like water and defence equipment are barely altered. Share prices of retailers usually increase quite sharply in an expanding economy, but the share prices of water companies and armaments suppliers respond far less dramatically. Systematic or market risk varies between companies and so we find different companies valued by the market at different discount rates. Quite simply, the premium for relevant risk varies between companies. Already, we begin to see that the CAPM, based on the premise that rational investors can and do hold efficiently diversified portfolios, may show us how these discount rates might be assessed. Clearly, we need to measure systematic risk.

10.3   Systematic risk and the valuation of individual securities

As specific risk can be diversified away by portfolio formation, rational investors expect only to be rewarded for bearing systematic risk. How is systematic risk to be measured? Given that systematic risk indicates the extent to which the return on individual shares varies with that of the overall market, we have to assess the extent of this co-movement. This is given by the slope of a line relating the expected return on the share, ER_j, to the return expected on the market, ER_m.

Walkley Wagons examples

Consider the case of Walkley Wagons, shown in Table 10.4. Investors anticipate four possible states of the economy. For every percentage point increase in the market return, the

Table 10.4   Possible returns from Walkley Wagons

State of the Economy	ER_m	ER_j
E_1	10%	12%
E_2	20%	24%
E_3	5%	6%
E_4	15%	18%

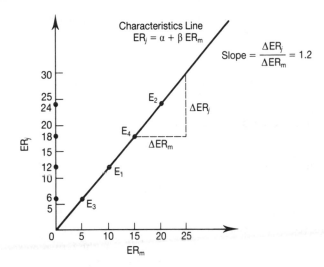

Figure 10.2   The Characteristics Line: no specific risk

return on Walkley shares rises by 1.2 percentage points. Walkley thus outperforms a rising market. The graphical relationship between ER_j and ER_m, shown in Figure 10.2, has a slope of 1.2. This is known as the *Characteristics Line* (CL) and its slope is the *Beta Coefficient*. Beta indicates how the return on Walkley is expected to vary for given variations in the return on the overall stock market, i.e. how ER_j and ER_m are *systematically* related.

The market model

However, in practice, because it is not possible to record people's expectations, the measurement of Beta cannot be done *ex ante*. Of necessity, we have to measure Beta using *past* observations of the actual values of R_j and R_m. So long as the past is accepted as a reliable indication of likely future events (i.e. people's expectations are moulded by examination of the frequency distribution of past recorded outcomes), observed Betas can be taken to indicate the extent to which R_j may vary for specified variations in R_m. A regression line is fitted to a set of recorded relationships, as in Figure 10.3. The hypothesized relationship is:

$$R_j = \alpha_j + \beta_j \, R_m$$

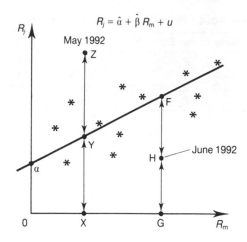

Figure 10.3 The Characteristics Line: with specific risk

And the fitted line is given by:

$$R_j = \hat{\alpha}_j + \hat{\beta}_j \, R_m + u$$

where $\hat{\alpha}_j$ and $\hat{\beta}_j$ are estimates of the 'true' values of α_j and β_j, and u is an (assumed) random error term. This regression model is called the 'Market Model'.

The intercept term, α_j, deserves explanation. This is the return on security j when the return on the market is zero, i.e. the return on j, with the impact of market or systematic risk stripped out. Consequently, it indicates what return the security offers for unsystematic risk. We might expect this to average out at zero over time, given the random character of sources of specific risk. However, it is by no means uncommon in practice to record non-zero values for α.

Systematic and unsystematic returns

Figure 10.3 shows an imaginary set of monthly observations relating to a given year, say 1992, to which has been fitted a regression line. Clearly, unlike the expected values displayed in Figure 10.2, most values actually lie off the line of best fit. These divergences are due to the sort of random, unsystematic factors suggested in section 10.2. For example, consider observation Z, which relates to the returns in May 1992. The overall return on security j in this month, XZ, can be broken down into the market-related return, XY, due to co-movement with the overall market, and the non-market return, YZ, due to unsystematic factors, which in this particular month have operated favourably. The opposite appears to have applied in June 1992, indicated by point H. The market-related return 'should' have been FG, but the actual return of GH was dampened by unfavourable unsystematic factors represented by FH. *This analysis implies that variations in* R_j along *the Characteristics Line stem from market-related factors, which systematically affect all securities, and that variations* around *the line represent the impact of factors specific to company* j.

BETA VALUES: THE KEY RELATIONSHIPS

Beta is the slope of a regression line, and this equals the covariance of the return on security j with the return on the market divided by the variance of the market return:

$$\text{Beta}_j = \frac{\text{cov}_{jm}}{\sigma_m^{\,2}}$$

Since the covariance is equal to $r_{jm}\sigma_j\sigma_m$ (see Chapter 9), Beta is also equivalent to:

$$\text{Beta}_j = \frac{r_{jm}\cdot\sigma_j\cdot\sigma_m}{\sigma_m^{\,2}} = \frac{r_{jm}\cdot\sigma_j}{\sigma_m}$$

Beta is thus the correlation coefficient multiplied by the ratio of individual security risk to market risk. If the security concerned has the same total risk as that of the market, Beta equals the correlation coefficient. For a given correlation, the greater the security's risk in relation to the market's risk, the greater is Beta. Conversely, the lower the degree of correlation, for a given risk ratio, the lower the Beta. *Therefore, while Beta does not directly measure risk, it is a crucial risk indicator, reflecting the extent to which the return on the single asset moves with the return on the market.* To obtain a direct risk measure, we have to examine the total risk of the security in more detail, using a statistical technique called *Analysis of Variance*. This is explained in Appendix I to this chapter.

Systematic risk: Beta measurement in practice

Betas are regularly calculated by several agencies. Of these, the Risk Measurement Service (RMS) operated by the London Business School (LBS) is the best known in the United Kingdom. The RMS is a quarterly updating service, based on monthly observations extending back over five years, which computes the Betas of all constituents of the FT All-Share Index. For each of the preceding 60 months, R_j is calculated for every security and regressed against R_m. An extract from the RMS is given in Table 10.5.

The Beta values of securities fall into three categories: 'defensive', 'neutral' and 'aggressive'. An *aggressive security* has a Beta greater than 1. Its returns move by a greater proportion than the market as a whole. For example, in the case of Courtaulds, with a Beta of 1.29, for every percentage point change in the market's return, the return from holding Courtauld's shares changes by 1.29 points. Such stocks are highly desirable in a rising market, although the excess return is not *guaranteed* due to the possible impact of company-specific factors. A *defensive share* is one like British Telecom, movements in whose returns tend to understate those of the whole market. The returns on *neutral stocks* like Guinness, with its Beta of 1.00, parallel those on the market portfolio.

Table 10.5   Beta values of the constituents of the FT 30 Share Index

Company Name	S.E. Industry Classification	Beta	Vari-ability	Specific Risk	Std Error	R-Sq'rd
Allied Lyons	Brewery	.97	27	15	.09	66
Asda Group	Food ret	.87	44	40	.19	19
BICC	Electrcl	1.07	30	18	.10	64
Blue Circle Industries	Cement	1.14	33	21	.12	58
BOC Group	Gen. chem	1.19	31	16	.09	73
Boots Co.	Str. mult	.90	29	21	.11	49
British Airways	Transpor	1.20	32	16	.09	73
British Gas	Oil & gas	.80	26	19	.10	48
British Petroleum	Oil & gas	.85	25	16	.09	57
British Telecom	Tele. net	.74	24	17	.10	47
BTR	Othindcp	1.11	31	18	.10	65
Cadbury-Schweppes	Food man	.84	32	26	.14	35
Courtaulds	Gen. chem	1.29	34	19	.11	69
Forte	Hotl & cat	1.17	32	19	.10	66
General Electric	Electrnc	.80	26	18	.10	49
GKN	Mtr. comp	1.18	31	17	.10	70
Glaxo Holdings	Hlth & hsh	1.13	32	19	.11	63
Grand Metropolitan	Brewery	1.14	30	17	.09	69
Guinness	Wine & spr	1.00	27	15	.08	69
Hansons	Conglom	.96	25	14	.08	70
Hawker Siddeley Grp	Electrcl	1.12	31	18	.10	65
Imperial Chemical Indust	Gen. chem	1.10	29	16	.09	69
Lucas Industries	Mtr. comp	1.23	34	20	.11	65
Marks & Spencer	Str. mult	.89	27	18	.10	53
Natnl Westminster Bank	Bank	1.04	29	17	.09	65
Peninsular & Orient 'DFD'	Transpor	1.09	28	14	.08	75
Royal Insurance Hldgs pl	Ins. comp	1.13	30	16	.09	71
SmithKline Beecham plc	Hlth & hsh	.80	23	14	.08	61
Tate & Lyle plc	Food man	1.09	30	17	.10	66
Thorn EMI plc	Leisure	1.05	29	18	.10	64

Source: Risk Measurement Service (October 1991).

10.4   Completing the model

We can now specify the required risk premiums for individual securities. We argued that only systematic risk is relevant in assessing these and we have established that Beta values reflect the sensitivity of the returns on securities to movements in the market return. However, the size of the risk premium on individual securities (or on efficient portfolios) will depend on the extent to which the return on the investment concerned is correlated with the return on the market. For a security perfectly correlated with the market, the market risk premium would be suitable, otherwise the required return depends on the Beta.

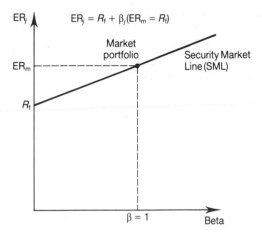

Figure 10.4 The Security Market Line

The CAPM postulates that when the capital market is in equilibrium, i.e. all securities are correctly priced, the relationship between risk and return is given by an expression known as the *Security Market Line* (SML), depicted in Figure 10.4.

THE SECURITY MARKET LINE

The equation of the SML states that the required return on shares is made up of two components, the return on a risk-free asset, plus a premium for risk related to the market's own risk premium, but which varies according to the Beta of the share in question:

$$\mathrm{ER}_j = R_f + \beta_j(\mathrm{ER}_m - R_f)$$

If Beta is 1, then the required return is simply the average return for all securities, i.e. the return on the market portfolio; otherwise, the higher the Beta, the higher the risk premium and the total return required. *A relatively high Beta does not, however, guarantee a relatively high return.* The actual return depends partly on the behaviour of the market, which acts as a proxy for general economic factors. Similarly, *expected* returns for the individual security hinge on the *expected* return for the market. If the market booms, high Beta securities generally do well, and vice versa. In a 'bull', or rising, market, it is worth holding high Beta securities, or aggressive securities. Conversely, defensive securities offer some protection against a 'bear', or falling, market. However, it must be stressed that *holding a single high Beta security is foolhardy even on a rising market. Undiversified investments, whatever their Beta values, are prey to specific risk factors. Portfolio formation is essential to eliminate the risks unique to individual companies.*

10.5   Using the CAPM: assessing the required return

We may now apply the CAPM formula to derive the rate of return required by shareholders. To do this, we require information on three elements: the risk-free rate, the risk premium on the market portfolio and the Beta coefficient.

Specifying the risk-free rate

No asset is totally risk-free. Even governments default on loans and defer interest payments. However, in a stable political and economic environment, government stock is about the nearest we can get to a risk-free asset. Most governments issue an array of stock with varying years to maturity, ranging from very short-dated securities, such as Treasury Bills, maturing in 1–3 months, to long-dated stock, maturing in fifteen years or more, and even exceptionally, irredeemable stock, such as 3.5 per cent War Loan with no redemption date. It is tempting to try to match up the life of the investment project with the corresponding government stock when assessing the risk-free rate. For example, when dealing with a ten-year project, we might look at the yield on ten-year government stock.

    This is unsatisfactory for several reasons. First, although the *nominal* yield to maturity is guaranteed, the *real* yield may well be undermined by inflation over this period and at an unknown rate. Second, there is an element of risk, however small, in holding government stock, and this is reflected in the 'yield curve', which normally rises over time to reflect the increasing risk of longer-dated stock. Third, although the yield to maturity is given, a forced seller of the stock might have to take a capital loss during the intervening period, since bond values fluctuate over time with oscillations in interest rates.

    A better way to specify R_f is to take the shortest-dated government stock available, three-month Treasury Bills, for which these risks are minimized. The current yield appears in the financial press.

Finding the risk-premium on the market portfolio

The risk premium on the market portfolio, $(ER_m - R_f)$, is an *expected* premium. Therefore, having assessed R_f, we need to specify ER_m by finding a way of capturing the market's expectations about future returns. An approximation can be obtained by looking at past returns which, taken over lengthy periods, are quite stable. For example, studies by Dimson and Brealey (1978) and Allen *et al.* (1987), for the periods 1918–77 and 1919–84, respectively, have shown average annual returns above the risk-free rate of 9 per cent and 9.1 per cent (before taxes) for the market index in the United Kingdom. Similar estimates have been obtained in the United States. For example, Ibbotson Associates (1990) estimated a risk premium above the US Treasury Bill return at 8.6 per cent for the period 1926–89.

    However for shorter periods, say five or ten years (more akin to project lifetimes), returns are highly volatile, and sometimes negative. Clearly, people neither *require* nor *expect* negative returns for holding risky assets! It therefore seems more sensible to take the long-term average, and to accept that in the short term markets exhibit variations of an unpredictable nature.

Finding Beta

Now we come to the easy bit! Beta values appear to be fairly stable over time, so we can use Beta values based on past recorded data, such as those provided by the RMS, with a fair degree of confidence. This is acceptable so long as the company is not expected to alter its risk characteristics in the future, by, for example, a take-over of a company in an unrelated field.

The required return

We now demonstrate the calculation of the required return for the engineering concern, GKN, using the equation for the SML:

$$ER_j = R_f + \beta_j (ER_m - R_f)$$

The Beta recorded by the RMS at October 1991 was 1.18. At the same date, the yield on three-month Treasury Bills was about 10 per cent. For GKN, this results in the following required return, assuming the historical average for the market risk premium of about 9%:

$$ER = 10\% + 1.18 \ (9\%) = 10\% + 10.6\% = 20.6\%$$

Application to investment projects

If GKN shareholders appear to require a return of 20.6 per cent, it seems reasonable to use this rate as a cut-off for new investment projects. However, before accepting this conclusion, two warnings are in order.

First, *the discount rate applicable to new projects often depends on the nature of the activity.* For example, if a new project takes GKN away from its present spheres of activity into, say, chemicals, its systematic risk will alter. The relevant premium for risk hinges on the systematic risk of chemicals rather than of engineering. This suggests that we 'tailor' risk premium, and thus discount rates, to particular activities (see Chapter 18).

Second, *the appropriate discount rate may depend upon the method of financing used.* Until now, we have implicitly been dealing with an all-equity financed company whose premium for risk is a reward purely for the business risk inherent in the company's activity. In reality, most firms are partially debt-financed, exposing shareholders to a second type of risk – financial risk. Using debt capital increases the risk to shareholders because of the legally preferred position of creditors. Defaulting on the conditions of the loan, e.g. failure to pay interest, can result in liquidation if creditors apply to have the company placed into receivership. The more volatile the earnings of the firm, the greater the risk of default.

Financial risk raises the Beta of the equity, as shareholders demand additional returns to compensate. The Beta of the equity becomes greater than the Beta of the underlying activity. In Chapter 15, we shall see that observed Betas have two components, the first to reflect business risk and the second to allow for financial risk. The Betas recorded by the RMS are actually equity Betas so the required return computed for GKN is the shareholders' required return part of which is to compensate for financial risk. However, when a company borrows, only the method of financing changes, nothing happens to alter the riskiness of the basic activity. The cut-off rate reflecting the basic risk of physical investment projects could well be lower than the *shareholders'* required return.

In the previous sections, we have concentrated on exposing the 'bare bones' of the CAPM, without explaining the underlying theoretical relationships. The underlying theory is explained in sections 10.6 and 10.7, which the reader may elect to pass at this stage, moving instead to section 10.9 which discusses some issues raised by the CAPM.

10.6   Developing the CAPM: the underlying assumptions

All theories rely on assumptions in order to simplify the analysis and expose more clearly the important relationships between key variables. If these relationships can be expressed concisely to generate testable implications, or predictions, then we may assess the value of the theory by comparing these predictions against observations recorded in the real world. In economic sciences, it is generally accepted that the validity of a theory depends on the empirical accuracy of its predictions rather than on the realism of its assumptions. However, if we find that the predictions fail to correspond with reality, and we are satisfied that this is not due to measurement errors or random influences, then it is appropriate to re-assess the assumptions. The ensuing analysis of an amended set of assumptions may lead to the generation of alternative predictions which accord more closely with reality.

The assumptions of the CAPM

This discussion is intended to warn readers that the assumptions of the CAPM may appear at first blush to be wildly unrealistic, but also to suggest that the proof of the pudding is in the testing. The most important assumptions are:

1. All investors aim to maximize their expected utility of wealth.
2. All investors operate on a common single-period planning horizon.
3. All investors select from alternative investment opportunities by looking at expected return and risk.
4. All investors are rational risk-averters.
5. All investors arrive at similar assessments of the probability distributions of returns expected from traded securities.
6. All such distributions of expected returns are normal.
7. All investors can lend or borrow unlimited amounts at a common rate of interest.
8. There are no transaction costs entailed in trading securities.
9. Dividends and capital gains are taxed at the same rates.
10. All investors are price-takers, that is, no investor can influence the market price by the scale of his own transactions.
11. All securities are highly divisible, i.e. can be traded in small parcels.

Several of these assumptions are patently untrue in the literal sense, but it has been shown that the CAPM is remarkably robust (it stands up well) to relaxation of many of them. Incorporation of apparently more realistic assumptions does not materially affect the implications of the analysis. A full discussion of these adjustments is beyond our scope, but van Horne (1986) offers an excellent analysis.

10.7 Portfolios with many components: the capital market line

It is time to demonstrate the theory behind the CAPM which incorporates the 'risk–return trade-off', first encountered in Chapter 1. This suggested that investors demand progressively higher returns as compensation for undertaking successive increases in risk. The derivation of this relationship, known as the *Capital Market Line (CML)*, relies on portfolio analysis techniques examined in Chapter 9.

However, whereas we previously studied combinations of two securities, we now examine more comprehensive portfolios. To begin with, imagine there are four available securities, A, B, C and D, for each of which we have estimated the expected return and the standard deviation, and also the covariance between each pair. Using a technique called Quadratic Programming (Sharpe 1963), we can specify all available portfolios comprising one, two, three or four securities. Although there are only fifteen possible combinations of whole investments, there are myriads of combinations if we allow for divisibility of assets. The full range of available portfolios, i.e. risk-return combinations, is shown by the opportunity set in Figure 10.5 in envelope or 'batwing' form.

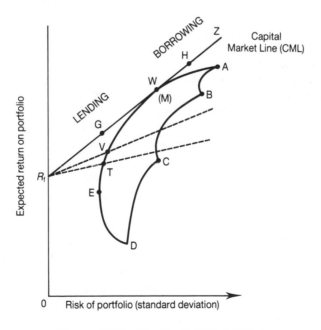

Figure 10.5 The Capital Market Line

Corners such as A and B represent individual securities, points along the lower edge of the envelope represent combinations of two securities, e.g. points along CD refer to combinations of securities C and D, while points within the envelope or along the upper edge represent combinations of three or four securities. The reader should note the obvious similarity in shape with the two-investment opportunity set shown in Figures 9.2 and 9.3. As before, we can apply the concept of dominance to differentiate between efficient and inefficient combinations. Clearly, all points beneath the upper edge and along the segment ED are inefficient. The efficient set is therefore AE, identical in shape to our earlier profile, except that we are dealing with combinations of four securities (enabling us to achieve lower levels of risk for given returns by diversifying away more specific risk). The same principles would apply if we were dealing with 40 or 4,000 securities, although the information requirements would be formidable in the latter case. A further similarity with our previous analysis is that the optimal portfolio would once again depend on the investor's risk–return preferences.

Introducing a risk-free asset

This last conclusion only applies in the absence of a risk-free asset. If we allow for investment in such a security, the range of opportunities widens much further. For example, on Figure 10.5, consider the line drawn from R_f, representing the return available on the risk-free asset, passing through point T on the efficient frontier. This line represents all possible combinations of the risk-free asset and the portfolio of risky securities represented by T. To the left of T, both portfolio return and risk are less than those for T, and conversely for points to the right of T. This implies that between R_f and T the investor is tempering the risk and return on T with investment in the risk-free asset, i.e. he is lending at the rate R_f, while above T he is seeking higher returns even at the expense of greater risk, i.e. he borrows in order to make further investment in T.

However, he can improve portfolio performance by investing along the line R_fV, representing combinations of the risk-free asset and portfolio V. He can do better still by investing along R_fW, the tangent to the efficient set. This schedule describes the best of all available risk-return combinations. No other portfolio of risky assets when combined with the risk-free asset allows the investor to achieve higher returns for a given risk. The line R_fW becomes the new efficiency boundary.

Portfolio W is the most desirable portfolio of risky securities as it allows access to the efficiency frontier R_fW. If the capital market is not already in equilibrium, then investors will compete to buy the components of W and tend to discard other investments. As a result, realignment of security prices will occur, the prices of assets in W will rise, and hence their returns will fall, and conversely, for assets not contained in W. The process of readjustment of security prices will continue until all securities traded in the market appear in a portfolio like W, where the line drawn from R_f touches the efficient set. *This adjusted portfolio is the 'market portfolio' and denoted by M, to signify that it contains all traded securities, weighted according to their respective market capitalizations. For rational risk-averting investors, this is now the only portfolio of risky securities worth holding.*

This is an important result. There is now a definable optimal portfolio of risky securities, portfolio M, which all investors should seek, and which does not depend on risk–return preferences. This proposition is known as the *Separation Theorem* – the most preferred portfolio is separate from individuals' attitudes to risk. The beauty of this result is that we need not know all the expected returns, risks and covariances required to derive the efficient set in Figure 10.5. We need only define the market portfolio in terms of some widely used index.

However, having invested in M, if investors wish to vary their risk–return combination, they only need to move along R_fMZ, lending or borrowing according to their risk–return preferences. For example, a relatively risk-averse investor will locate at point G, combining lending at the risk-free rate with investment in M. A less cautious investor may locate at point H, representing borrowing at the risk-free rate in order to raise his returns by further investment in M, but incurring a higher level of risk. In this respect, we would need information on attitudes to risk to *predict* how specific investors behave.

The line R_fMZ is highly significant. It describes the way in which rational investors – those who wish to maximize returns for a given risk, or minimize risk for a given return – seek compensation for any additional risk they incur. In this sense, R_fMZ describes an optimal risk-return trade-off which all investors and thus the whole market will pursue, hence, it is called the *Capital Market Line (CML)*.

THE CAPITAL MARKET LINE

The CML traces out all optimal risk-return combinations for those investors astute enough to recognize the advantages of constructing a well-diversified portfolio. Its equation is:

$$ER_p = R_f + \left[\frac{(ER_m - R_f)}{\sigma_m} \right] . \sigma_p$$

Its slope signifies the rate at which investors travelling up the line will be compensated for each extra unit of risk, i.e. $(ER_m - R_f)/\sigma_m$ units of additional return.

For example, imagine investors expect the following:

$$R_f = 10\%$$
$$ER_m = 20\%$$
$$\sigma_m = 5\%$$

$$\text{so that} \quad \left[\frac{ER_m - R_f}{\sigma_m} \right] = \left[\frac{20\% - 10\%}{5\%} \right] = 2$$

Every additional unit of risk which investors are prepared to incur, as measured by the portfolio's standard deviation, attracts compensation of two units of extra return. With a standard deviation of 2%, the appropriate return is:

$$ER_p = 10\% + (2 \times 2\%) = 14\%$$

For $\sigma_p = 3\%$, $ER_p = 16\%$, for $\sigma_p = 4\%$, $ER_p = 18\%$, and so on.

Anyone requiring greater compensation will be sorely disappointed.

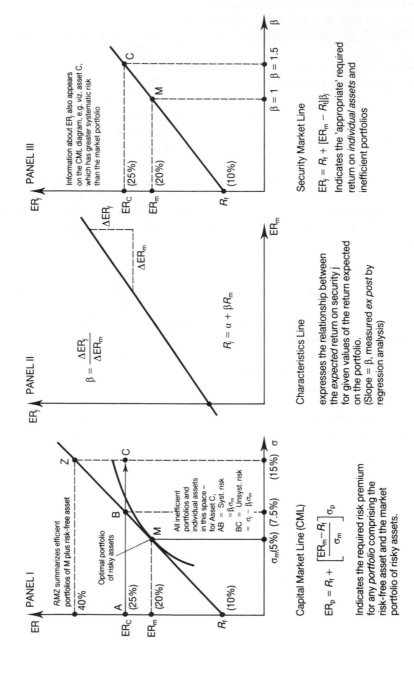

Figure 10.6   CAPM: the three key relationships

To summarize this section, we are now able to assess the appropriate risk premiums for combinations of the risk-free asset and the market portfolio, and therefore the discount rate to be applied when valuing such portfolio holdings. However, the final link in the explanation of risk premiums is an explanation of how the discount rates for individual securities are established and hence how these securities are valued. This was provided by the discussion of the SML in section 10.4.

10.8 How it all fits together: the key relationships

The CAPM on first acquaintance may look complex. However, its essential simplicity can be analysed by reducing it to three key diagrams, as shown by the three panels of Figure 10.6.

Panel I shows the *Capital Market Line (CML)*, derived using the principles of portfolio combination developed in Chapter 9. The CML is a tangent to the envelope of efficient portfolios of risky assets, the point of tangency occurring at the market portfolio, M. Any combination along the CML (except M itself) is superior to any combination of risky assets alone. In other words, investors can obtain more desirable risk–return combinations by mixing the risk-free asset and the market portfolio to suit their preferences, i.e. according to whether they wish to lend or borrow.

The slope of the CML, given by $(ER_m - R_f)/\sigma_m$, defines the best available terms for exchanging risk and return. It is desirable to hold a well-diversified portfolio of securities in order to eliminate the specific risk inherent in individual securities like C. When holding single securities, investors would be mistaken in expecting to be rewarded for their total risk, e.g. 15 per cent for C, because the market rewards investors only for bearing the undiversifiable or systematic risk. The extent to which risk can be eliminated depends on the covariability of the share's return with the return on the overall market. Hence, the degree of correlation with the return on the market influences the reward from holding a security and thus its price.

The *Characteristics Line (CL)* in Panel II shows how the return on an individual security, such as C, is expected to vary with changes in the return on the overall market. The slope of the CL, Beta, indicates the degree of systematic risk of the security.

The *Security Market Line* in Panel III shows the equilibrium relationship between risk and return which holds when all securities are 'correctly' priced. Clearly, the higher the Beta, the higher the required return. Although Beta is not a direct measure of systematic risk, it is an important indicator of relevant risk.

The decomposition of the overall variability, or variance, of the security's return into its systematic and unsystematic components is explained in Appendix I. It can be demonstrated by focusing on security C in Panel III of Figure 10.6. Security C lies above the market portfolio because its Beta of 1.5 exceeds that of the overall market. If the market as a whole is expected to generate a return of 20 per cent, and the risk-free rate is 10 per cent, C's required return is thus:

$$ER_C = 10\% + 1.5(20\% - 10\%) = 25\%$$

This reward compensates only for systematic risk, rather than for the security's total risk.

The risk–return trade-off, given by the slope of the CML, is $(20\% - 10\%)/5\% = 2$, since the risk of the market itself is 5 per cent. For security C, with overall risk of 15 per cent, we would not expect to obtain compensation at this rate, i.e. $2 \times 15\% = 30\%$, (giving an overall return of 40 per cent), because some of the risk can be diversified away. To demonstrate this, recall the equivalent expressions for Beta used in section 10.3, viz.:

$$\text{Beta} = \frac{\text{cov}_{ij}}{\sigma_m^{~2}} = \frac{r_{jm}\sigma_j\sigma_m}{\sigma_m^{~2}} = \frac{r_{jm}\sigma_j}{\sigma_m}$$

Taking the Beta of 1.5 for security C, we find:

$$1.5 = \frac{r_{jm}\sigma_j}{\sigma_m} = \frac{r_{jm}(15)}{5}$$

so that r_{jm} is 0.5.

Knowing the correlation coefficient enables us to analyse the composition of total risk of the security into its systematic, or relevant, and specific risk components. The relevant risk component depends on the correlation between the return of the security and that of the market, i.e. rearranging our expression for Beta

$$\text{Systematic risk} = \beta_j\sigma_m = r_{jm}\sigma_j$$

Hence the lower the correlation, the lower the systematic risk. In the case of security C, 50% of its overall risk can be eliminated by efficient portfolio diversification, namely

$$\text{Systematic risk} = (1.5) \ . \ (5\%) = (0.5) \ . \ (15\%) = 7.5\%$$

Hence, unsystematic, or specific, risk is

$$(\sigma_j - \beta_j\sigma_m) = (15\% - 7.5\%) = 7.5\%$$

If the market rewarded total risk, the return offered on security C would be the risk-free rate of 10 per cent supplemented by the risk–return trade-off ($2 \times$ the total security risk of 15 per cent), yielding a total of 40 per cent. However, because half the total risk is diversifiable, the market offers a return of just 25 per cent for security C. This relationship is indicated on Panel I of Figure 10.6 by the distances AB and BC representing respectively the systematic and specific risk components for security C.

10.9   Reservations in using the CAPM

The CAPM analyses the sources of risk and offers key insights into what rewards investors should expect for bearing these risks. However, like all economic models we should not apply it blindly, however appealing it may appear in the simplicity of its ultimate formula. Several limitations detract from its general applicability.

It relies on a battery of 'unrealistic' assumptions

It is often easy to criticize theories over the lack of realism of their assumptions, and certainly many of those embodied in the CAPM, especially concerning investor behaviour, do not seem to reflect reality. However, Milton Friedman (1953) warned against judging a theory on this basis, unless one aims to provide a descriptively accurate explanation of behaviour. If the aim is to provide predictions which can be tested against real world observations, the realism of the underlying assumptions is secondary. In his famous example concerning the theory of billiards, he explained that although we *know* that expert billiard players do *not* make all the complex mathematical calculations required to assist them in planning their shots, a theory based upon the assumption that they act *as if* they reckon in this way may still be valid. In other words, expert billiard players would not be experts if they did not play *as if* they made these calculations. It is easy to substitute 'investors' for 'billiard players' in this analogy. Obviously, if the predictions themselves do not accord reasonably closely with reality, then the theory is undoubtedly suspect.

Testing difficulties

The fundamental prediction of the CAPM is that an efficient capital market in equilibrium exhibits a linear risk–return relationship. Attempts to test this proposition, using *ex post* data, have often found that such a relationship does exist, but it is considerably flatter than might be expected, i.e. the premium for systematic risk is much lower than intuition would suggest, and the intercept term, R_f, is considerably higher than prevailing yields on government stock during the testing period. However, we should remember that the CAPM deals with *expected* returns so empirical tests have, of necessity, to examine actual returns. Consequently, some writers have cast doubt upon the validity of these tests, even to the extent of arguing that the CAPM is inherently untestable.

Roll (1977), for example, in a famous critique of the CAPM, pointed out that adequate testing of the CAPM requires both the specification of the risk-free asset and a comparison of returns for various securities against the benchmark of an all-security market portfolio. Some capital markets have several share price indices which move very closely together but none of which contains every security. It is possible that tests are flawed if the benchmark portfolio used to compare returns is itself inefficient compared to the whole market. Besides, Roll argued, any such market portfolio only includes traded securities. It excludes a wide range of other capital assets which offer the investor the prospect of uncertain returns. These range from untraded securities to real assets such as coins, postage stamps, paintings and real estate. It would be virtually impossible to construct a portfolio incorporating all such candidates for inclusion in a true market portfolio of capital assets, but unless we can do so, the CAPM as it stands, only constitutes a *security* pricing model. One alternative model to the CAPM is the Arbitrage Pricing theory, which is outlined in Appendix II to this chapter.

It is a one-period model

A key assumption of the CAPM is that investors adopt a one-period time horizon for holding securities. Whatever the length of the period (which may or may not be one year), the rates of return incorporated in investor expectations are rates of return over the whole holding period, assumed to be common for all investors. This provides obvious problems when we come to use a required return derived from a CAPM exercise in evaluating an investment project. Quite simply, we may not compare like with like. If an investor requires a return of, say, 25 per cent, over a five-year period, this is rather different from saying that the returns from an investment project should be discounted at 25 per cent p.a. Attempts have been made, notably by Mossin (1966), to produce a multi-period version of the CAPM, but its mathematical complexity takes it out of the reach of most practising managers, especially those inclined to be sceptical about the CAPM anyway.

10.10   Issues raised by the CAPM: some food for managerial thought

The CAPM raises a number of important issues, which have fundamental implications for the applicability of the model itself and the role of diversification in the armoury of corporate strategic weapons.

Should we trust the market?

Legally, managers are charged with the duty of acting in the best interests of shareholders, i.e. maximizing their wealth (although company law does not express it quite like this!). This requires them to invest in all projects offering returns above the shareholders' opportunity cost of capital. The CAPM provides a way of assessing the rate of return required by shareholders from their investments, albeit based partly on past returns. If the Beta is known and a view is taken on the future return on the market, then the apparently required return follows and becomes the cut-off rate for new investment projects, at least for those of similar systematic risk to existing activities. This implies that managers' expectations coincide with those of shareholders, or more generally, with those of the market. If, however, the market as a whole expects a higher return from the market portfolio, then some projects deemed acceptable to managers, may not be worthwhile from a shareholder perspective.

   The subsequent fall in share price provides the mechanism whereby the market communicates to managers that the rate of return standard was too low. It is essential to grasp that the CAPM relies on efficiently set market prices to reveal to managers the 'correct' hurdle rate in the first instance, and to reveal any mistakes, caused by misreading the market, in the second. The implication that one can trust the market to arrive at correct prices and hence required rates of return is problematic for many practising managers, who are prone to believe that the market persistently undervalues the companies which they operate. Managers who doubt the validity of the EMH are unlikely to accept a CAPM-derived discount rate.

Should companies diversify?

The CAPM is based on the premise that rational shareholders form efficiently diversified portfolios, realizing that the market will reward them only for bearing market-related risk.

The benefits of diversification can easily be obtained by portfolio formation, i.e. buying securities at relatively low dealing fees. The implication of this is that *corporate diversification is perhaps pointless because companies are seeking to achieve what shareholders can do themselves probably more efficiently.* Securities are far more divisible than investment projects and can be traded much quicker when conditions alter. So why do managers diversify company activities?

An obvious explanation is that managers have not understood the message of the EMH/CAPM, or if they have, they doubt its validity, believing instead that shareholders' best interests are enhanced by reduction of the total variability of the firm's earnings (as outlined in Chapter 8). For some shareholders, this may indeed be the case. One of the assumptions of the CAPM is that investors hold well-diversified portfolios. This is undoubtedly true for the major financial institutions, holding over 60 per cent of all UK quoted ordinary shares, but a large proportion of those investing directly on the stock market hold undiversified portfolios.

Many small shareholders have been attracted to equity investment by the recent privatization issues or by Personal Equity Plans (see Chapter 13). Larger shareholders sometimes tie up major portions of their capital in a single company in order to take, or retain, an active part in its management. In such cases, market risk, based on the covariability of the return on a company's shares with that on the market portfolio, is an inadequate measure of risk. The appropriate measure of risk for capital budgeting decisions probably lies somewhere between total risk, based on the variance, or standard deviation, of a project's returns, and market risk, depending on the degree of diversification of shareholders.

A more subtle explanation of why managers diversify is offered by the 'divorce of ownership and control' school of thought. Managers who are relatively free from the threat of shareholder interference in company operations may pursue their own interests above those of shareholders. If an inadequate contract has been written between the manager-agents and the shareholder-principals, managers may be inclined to promote their own job security. This is highly understandable, because whereas shareholders are highly mobile between alternative security holdings, managerial mobility is often low. *To managers, the distinction between systematic risk and specific risk may be relatively insignificant since they have a vested interest in minimizing total risk.* The lower the overall risk, the greater their job security. If the company goes under, it is little comfort for them to know that their personal catastrophe has only a minimal effect on a well-diversified shareholder.

As we will see in Chapter 22, there are many motives for diversification beyond mere risk reduction. However, it is common to justify diversification to shareholders purely for this motive, at least under certain types of market imperfection. In the real world, corporate failure cannot be simply shrugged off because it carries costs. When a company fails, there are liquidation costs to bear as well as the losses entailed in selling assets at 'knock-down' prices in a forced sale. These costs may result in both creditors and shareholders failing to receive full economic value in the asset disposal, and although this will not crucify a well-diversified shareholder, the resulting dent in his portfolio will require filling in order to restore balance. Company diversification may reduce these risks and costs of portfolio disruption and readjustment.

10.11   Summary

In this chapter, we have examined the nature of the risks affecting the holders of securities and discussed whether the return required by shareholders, as implied by market valuations, can be used as a cut-off rate for new investment projects.

Key points

- Security risk can be split into two components: risk specific to the company in question, and the variability in return due to general market movements.
- Rational investors form well-diversified portfolios to eliminate specific risk.
- The most efficient portfolio of risky securities is the market portfolio, although investors may mix this with investment in the risk-free asset in order to achieve more preferred risk–return combinations along the Capital Market Line.
- The risk premium built into the required return on securities reflects a reward for systematic risk only.
- The risk premium depends on the risk premium on the overall market and the extent to which the return on the security moves with that of the whole market, as indicated by the Beta coefficient.
- This premium for risk is the second term in the equation for the Security Market Line: $ER_j = R_f + \beta_j(ER_m - R_f)$.
- Practical problems in using the CAPM centre on measurement of Beta, specification of the risk-free asset and the measurement of the market's risk premium.
- The return required by shareholders can be used as a cut-off rate for new investment if the new project has similar systematic risk as the company's other activities and is to be financed in the same way.
- There is some debate whether managers should diversify company activities merely in order to lower risk.

Appendix I: Analysis of variance

The total risk of a security (σ_T), comprising both unsystematic risk (σ_{USR}), and systematic risk (σ_{SR}), is measured by the variance of returns, which can be separated into the two elements. Imagine an asset with total risk of $\sigma_T{}^2 = 500$, of which 80 per cent (400) is explained by specific risk factors, the remainder resulting from market-related factors:

$$\sigma_T{}^2 = 500 = \sigma_{SR}{}^2 + \sigma_{USR}{}^2 = 100 + 400$$

In terms of standard deviations, $\sigma_{SR} = \sqrt{100} = 10$ and $\sigma_{USR} = \sqrt{400} = 20$. Notice that we cannot express the overall standard deviation by summing the two component standard deviations – variances are additive unlike standard deviations – the square root of the total risk is $500 = 22.4$, rather than the sum of σ_{SR} and σ_{USR}.

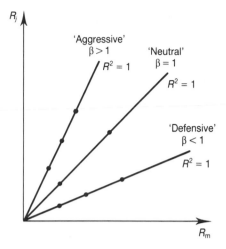

Figure 10.7 Alternative Characteristics Lines

In regression models, the extent to which the overall variability in the dependent variable is explained by the variability in the independent variable is given by the R-squared (R^2) statistic, the square of the correlation coefficient. The R^2 is thus a measure of 'goodness of fit' of the regression line to the recorded observations. If all observations lie on the regression line, R^2 equals 1 and the variations in the market return fully explain the variations in the return on security j. In this case, all risk is market risk. It follows that the lower the R^2, the greater the proportion of specific risk of the security. For investors wishing to diversify away specific risk, such securities are highly attractive. Notice that an R^2 of 1 does not entail a Beta of 1, as Figure 10.7 illustrates. All three securities have R^2 of 1, but they have different degrees of market risk, as indicated by their Betas.

An R^2 of 80 per cent corresponds to a correlation coefficient, r_{jm}, of $\sqrt{0.8} = 0.89$. Looking at the standard deviations, we can infer that 0.89 of the overall risk is market risk, i.e. $0.89 \times 22.4 = 19.94$, while the specific risk $= (1 - r_{jm}) \times 22.4 = 0.11 \times 22.4 = 2.46$. In order to avoid confusion, let us re-emphasize these relationships:

Market, or Systematic Risk is:
$R^2 \times$ the overall variance, σ_T^2 or ($r_{jm} \times$ the overall standard deviation, σ_T)

Specific Risk is:
$(1 - R^2) \times$ overall variance, σ_T^2 or $(1 - r_{jm}) \times$ overall standard deviation, σ_T

Appendix II: Arbitrage pricing theory

An alternative theory to the CAPM is *arbitrage pricing theory (APT)*, developed by Ross (1976). Unlike the CAPM, APT does not assume that shareholders evaluate decisions within a mean-variance framework. Rather, it assumes the return on a share depends partly on macro-economic factors and partly on events specific to the company. Instead of specifying a share's returns as a function of one factor (the return on the market portfolio) it specifies the returns as a function of macro-economic factors upon which the market portfolio depends.

The expected risk premium of a share would be:

$$ER_j - R_f = \beta_1 (ER_{factor\ 1} - R_f) + \beta_2 (ER_{factor\ 2} - R_f) + \ldots + u_j$$

Where:

ER_j = the expected rate of return on security j
$ER_{factor\ 1}$ = the expected return on macro-economic factor 1
β_1 = the sensitivity of security j to factor 1
u_j = the random deviation based on unique events on the security's returns.

Diversification can eliminate the specific risk associated with a security, leaving only the macro-economic risk as the determinant of required security returns.

The APT model does not *specify* what the explanatory factors are; they could be the stock market index, Gross National Product, oil prices, interest rates, and so forth. Different companies will be more sensitive to certain factors than others.

In theory, a riskless portfolio could be constructed (i.e. a 'zero Beta' portfolio) which would offer the risk-free rate of interest. If the portfolio gave a higher return, investors could make a profit without incurring any risk by borrowing at the risk-free rate to buy the portfolio. This process of 'arbitrage' (i.e. taking profits for zero risk) would continue until the portfolio's expected risk premium was zero.

Arbitrage Pricing theory avoids the problem with the capital asset pricing model of having to estimate the market portfolio. But it replaces this problem with, possibly, more onerous tasks. First, there is the requirement to identify the macro-economic variables. Recent American research indicates that the most influential factors in explaining asset returns in the APT framework are changes in industrial production, inflation, personal consumption, money supply and interest rates (McGowan and Francis 1991).

Once the main factors influencing share returns are established, there are still the problems of estimating risk premiums for each factor and measuring the sensitivity of share returns to these factors – no easy task! For this reason, the APT is currently only in the prototype stage.

Further reading

As with basic portfolio theory, Copeland and Weston (1988) offer a rigorous treatment of the derivation of the formulae used in this chapter. Brealey and Myers (1991) also offer an alternative, and less mathematical treatment. Students should also read the famous critique of the CAPM by Roll (1977).

Questions

Self-test questions

1. What is the difference between specific and systematic risk? Give examples of each.
2. What is the Capital Market Line? Can you use this relationship to assess the rate of return required on individual assets?
3. In terms of the market model, explain the significance of movements along the Characteristics Line and variations around the line itself.
4. The Beta of a security does not directly measure systematic risk. What does it signify? How is systematic risk measured? How is Beta used in assessing the required return for individual shares?
5. If you wanted to beat the market return, could you do this with a portfolio of say, ten, aggressive shares?

Exercises

1. Megacorp plc, an all-equity financed multinational, is contemplating an expansion into an overseas market. It is considering whether to invest directly in the country concerned by building a greenfield-site factory. The expected pay-off from the project would depend on the future state of the economy of Erewhon, the host country, as shown in the following table.

State of Erewhon economy	Probability	IRR from project
E_1	0.1	10%
E_2	0.2	20%
E_3	0.5	10%
E_4	0.2	20%

Megacorp's existing activities are expected to generate an overall return of 30 per cent with a standard deviation of 14 per cent. The correlation coefficient of Megacorp's returns with that of the new project is -0.36, Megacorp's returns have $+80$ per cent correlation with the return on the market portfolio, while the new project has a correlation coefficient of -0.10 with the UK market portfolio.

The Beta coefficient for Megacorp is 1.20.
The risk-free rate is 12 per cent.
The risk premium on the UK market portfolio is 15 per cent.
Assume Megacorp's shares are correctly priced by the market.

Required

(a) Determine the expected rate of return and standard deviation of the return from the new project.

(b) If the new project requires capital funding equal to 25 per cent of the value of the existing assets of Megacorp, determine the return required by Megacorp's shareholders after the investment.

(c) What effect will the adoption of the project have on the Beta of Megacorp?

(d) Does acceptance of this project appear desirable from the standpoint of Megacorp's shareholders? Explain your answer.

Ignore all taxes.

(Solution in Appendix A)

2. Five wealthy individuals have each put £200,000 at your disposal to invest for the next two years. The funds can be invested in one or more of four specified projects and in the money market. The projects are not divisible and cannot be postponed. The investors require a minimum return of 24 per cent over the two years.

Details of the possible investments are:

	Initial cost (£000)	Return over two years (%)	Expected standard deviation of returns over two years (%)
Project 1	600	22	7
Project 2	400	26	9
Project 3	600	28	15
Project 4	600	34	13
Money market minimum	100	18	5

Correlation coefficients of returns (over two years)

Between projects	Between projects and the market portfolio	Between projects and the money market
1 and 2 0.70	1 and market 0.68	1 and money market 0.40
1 and 3 0.62	2 and market 0.65	2 and money market 0.45
1 and 4 0.56	3 and market 0.75	3 and money market 0.55
2 and 3 0.65	4 and market 0.88	4 and money market 0.60
2 and 4 0.57		
3 and 4 0.76	*Between the money market and the market portfolio* 0.40	

The risk-free rate is estimated to be 16 per cent, the market return 27 per cent and the variance of returns on the market 100 per cent (all for the two-year period).

Required

(a) Evaluate how the £1m should be invested using:
   (i) Portfolio theory,

(ii) The capital asset pricing model (CAPM).

Portfolio risk may be estimated using the formula

$$\sigma_p = \sqrt{x^2\ \sigma_a^2 + (1-x)^2\ \sigma_b^2 + 2(x)(1-x)\ r_{ab}\sigma_a\sigma_b}$$

(b) Explain why portfolio theory and CAPM might give different solutions as to how the £1m should be invested.

(c) Discuss the main problems of using CAPM in investment appraisal.

(ACCA Level 3, December 1990)

3. Thornton plc has the opportunity to undertake the two projects whose possible returns under different economic conditions are set out below:

State of Economy	Probability	Internal Rate of Return Project A	Project B
5% growth	0.3	12%	13%
2% growth	0.5	11%	15%
0% growth	0.2	10%	20%

Thornton is debt-free and the project would be financed from retentions. Ignore tax.

Required

(a) Calculate the expected IRR and the associated standard deviation for each project.

(b) If only one project can be accepted, which would you recommend? Why?

(c) Further analysis reveals that Thornton's Beta is 0.6, the risk-free rate is 8 per cent, and the risk premium on the market portfolio has averaged 8 per cent in the past. What is the rate of return required by Thornton on new projects?

(d) In view of your answer to (c), is project A worthwhile:

(i) in isolation? Why?

(ii) in conjunction with B? (Find a portfolio of A and B which meets the required return standard.)

(iii) what is the risk of the portfolio which you have constructed in (b)? (the relevant covariance is −1.64).

4. The following table shows the *gross* rate of return achieved by a number of unit trust fund managers during 1991. This includes both dividend and capital appreciation as a proportion of the value of the fund portfolio at the start of the year. Also shown is the 'expense ratio', i.e. the expenses incurred as a proportion of the fund's value at start year, and the Beta for each fund. The return on the FTSE 100 Index in 1991 was 20 per cent and the return on 3-month Treasury Bills was 8 per cent.

Fund	Gross Return	Expense Ratio	Beta
A	21%	3%	1.2
B	20%	2%	1.0
C	18%	2%	0.8
D	19%	2%	0.9
E	24%	4%	1.1

Required

(a) Do any of these fund managers have reason to congratulate themselves?

(b) How useful a guide are these results to an investor seeking an investment strategy for 1992 and beyond?

(c) What light do these figures cast on the Efficient Markets Hypothesis?

(d) Is the management of a portfolio such as a unit trust fund simply a question of 'sticking in a pin'?

Postscript and practical assignment

At the head of Chapter 9 we discussed the diversification policy of Pearson plc. Re-read the earlier discussion and the following postscript, and then consider the questions below.

PEARSON PLC TEN YEARS AFTER

During the 1980s, there was considerable debate in academic and business circles about the relative merits of a business strategy focusing on one or a limited range of activities versus the conglomerate style of organization favoured during the 1970s.

Focusing, according to proponents like Peters and Waterman (1982) and Porter (1985), would generate scale economies and allow companies to capitalize on their distinctive competences. Conversely, the very point of conglomerate diversification was supposed to be that downswings in some businesses are offset by upswings in others, thereby dampening oscillations in sales and earnings.

During the 1980s, Pearson had sold off some activities such as Fairey Engineering and Château Latour, but consolidated its book and newspaper publishing and entertainments businesses by acquiring the French newspaper *Les Echos*, Addison-Wesley publishers and the Alton Towers leisure park, as well as a stake in BSkyB. As the UK economy entered the recession of the early 1990s, the Pearson finance director was quoted as saying: 'There is no such thing as recession-proof, but our business is less cyclical than some.'

However, the effectiveness of Pearson's diversification strategy was called into question as early as 1991, when it reported half-year profits down by over half, considerably worse than some more focused companies, such as ICI, which reported a reduction of about a third over the same period.

Questions

1. Discuss whether Pearson appear to have diversified into the 'right' areas.

2. Given the present structure of Pearson, how would you attempt to assess the rate of return required:

(a) for the whole company

(b) for component activities.

(You will find it useful to refer to the latest Pearson accounts or to the relevant Extel card.)

CHAPTER 11
The capital investment process

THE CASE OF THE DISAPPEARING PROJECTS

Ameritech, a major US company operating in the electronics industry, invests over $2 billion a year, mostly in thousands of relatively small-scale projects. When the company announced that it proposed to monitor and audit capital projects, that year's budgets had already been submitted. But the company told every division to take back their submissions and think about the fact that everyone who worked on the project was going to be 'tracked', and then resubmit the estimates. Seven hundred projects never came back – they just disappeared. Many others had much lower estimates. We will never know just how many of those 700 projects could have been investment 'winners'.

This illustrates just how influential capital budgeting controls can be on managerial investment behaviour!

(based on Weaver *et al.* 1989)

11.1 Introduction

Sir John Harvey-Jones (1989), former chairman of ICI, argues: 'There is an intrinsic impermanence in industry, and indeed the management task is to recreate the company in a new form every year.' Rather like the human body, unless new 'cells' (i.e. ideas, strategies, etc.) are created within a business, sooner or later the whole organization will collapse or fade away. Capital investment is the main means by which the company is 'recreated' year by year, but such decisions require a clearly understood capital budgeting process.

This chapter examines the role of investment analysis within the sort of decision-making process typically found in larger organizations. It considers the main stages within the process, and the strategic context of, capital investment.

251

LEARNING OBJECTIVES

The reader should appreciate how investment decisions are made and monitored. This involves:

- Awareness of the whole investment process rather than merely the appraisal techniques.
- The value of commonly used UK investment control procedures, particularly post-audit reviews.
- Strategic inputs to investment decision-making.

Many capital investment decisions are, by their very nature, non-routine (that is, 'one-offs') which emerge from, or are compatible with, corporate strategic thinking. Indeed, it is primarily through capital investment decisions that the firm's strategy evolves and is implemented. We will discuss the various stages of the investment decision process and the strategic approaches to investment decision-making.

The focus of attention so far in this book has been directed towards the appraisal of investment options. Similar emphasis is found in much of the capital budgeting literature, the assumption being that application of theoretically correct methods leads directly to optimal investment selection and, hence, maximizes shareholders' wealth. The decision-maker is viewed as having a passive role, acting more as a technician than as an entrepreneur. Somehow, investment ideas come to the surface; various assumptions and cash flow estimates are made; and risk is incorporated within the discounting formula to produce the project's net present value. If this is positive, the proposal becomes part of the admissible set of investment possibilities. This set is then further refined by the evaluation of mutually exclusive projects and the appraisal of projects under capital rationing, where appropriate. Inherent in this approach to capital budgeting are the following assumptions, few of which bear much relevance to the world of business:

1. Investment ideas simply emerge and land on the manager's desk.
2. Projects can be viewed in isolation, i.e. projects are not interdependent.
3. Risk can be fully incorporated within the net present value framework.
4. Non-quantifiable or intangible investment considerations are unimportant.
5. Cash flow estimates are free from bias.

Increasingly, it has become apparent that the emphasis on investment appraisal rather than on the whole capital investment process is misplaced and will not necessarily produce the most desirable investment programme. The important question raised in this chapter is: *How can an organization develop a framework within which sound and successful investment programmes can flourish?* This does not necessarily imply the use of sophisticated methods or procedures. Investment decision-making could be improved significantly if the emphasis were placed on asking the appropriate strategic question rather than on increasing the sophistication of measurement techniques. Managers need to re-evaluate the investment procedures within their organizations, not to determine whether they are aesthetically and theoretically correct, but to determine whether they allow managers to make better decisions.

Capital budgeting may best be understood when viewed as a process with a number of distinct stages. Decision-making is an incremental activity, involving many people throughout the organizational hierarchy, over an extended period of time. While senior management may retain final approval, actual decisions are effectively taken much earlier at a lower level, by a process that is still not entirely clear, or the same in all organizations.

Figure 11.1 shows the key stages in the capital budgeting process.

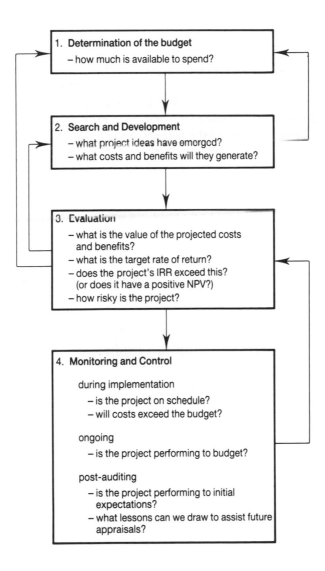

Figure 11.1 A simple budgeting system

Its primary aim is to ensure that the limited capital resources available are distributed to wealth-creating capital projects which make the best contribution to corporate goals. A second goal should be to see that good investment ideas are not held back and that poor or ill-defined proposals are rejected or further refined. The four stages, which we shall explore in some depth in this chapter, are:

1. Determination of the budget.
2. Search for, and development of, projects.
3. Evaluation and authorization.
4. Monitoring and control.

11.2   Determination of the budget

In theory at least, all capital projects could be put to the capital market for funding (individually or collectively as investment programmes), the availability of funds for projects and rate required being a function of the market's perception of the prospective returns and associated risks. In practice, multi-divisional organizations operate an internal capital market in which senior management is better informed than the external capital market to assess capital proposals and allocate scarce resources. There is some evidence (e.g. Pike 1985) that the constraints that prevail within firms are imposed by top management (i.e. the internal capital market) rather than the external capital market.

If the investment decision-making body is a sub-unit of a larger group, then the budget may be more or less rigidly imposed on it from above. However, for quasi-autonomous centres (divisions of larger groups with capital-raising powers) and/or independent units, the amount to be spent on capital projects is largely under their control, subject of course to considerations of corporate control and gearing.

11.3   Search for and development of projects

Economic theory views investment as the interaction of the supply of capital and the flow of investment opportunities. It would be quite wrong, however, to assume that there is a continuous flow of investment ideas. In general, the earlier an investment opportunity is identified, the greater is the scope for reward.

Possibly the most important role which top management can play in the capital investment process is to cultivate a corporate culture which encourages managers to search for, identify and sponsor investment ideas. Questions to be asked at the identification stage include:

1. How are project proposals initiated?
2. At what level are projects typically generated?
3. Is there a formal process for submitting ideas?
4. Is there an incentive scheme for identifying good project ideas?

Generating investment ideas involves considerable effort, time and personal risk on the part of the proposer. Any manager who has experienced the frustration of having an investment proposal dismissed or an accepted proposal fail is likely to develop an inbuilt resistance to creating further proposals unless the organisation culture and rewards are conducive to such activity. There is some evidence (Larcker 1983) that firms adopting long-term incentive plans tend to increase their level of capital investment. It also seems that the best *ideas* emerge from an unstructured *research* process, but that the best *projects* emerge from a more tightly controlled *development* process.

For the identification phase of non-routine capital budgeting decisions, especially those of a more strategic nature, to be productive, managers need to conduct environmental scanning, gathering information which is largely externally oriented. We should not expect the formal information system within most organizations, which are set up to help control short-term performance, to be particularly helpful in identifying non-routine investment ideas.

Development of proposal

At this early stage, a preliminary screening of all investment ideas is usually conducted. It is neither feasible nor desirable to conduct a full-scale evaluation of each investment idea. The screening process is an important means of filtering out projects not thought worthy of further investigation. Ideas may not fit with strategic thinking, or fall outside business units designated for growth or maintenance.

Preliminary screening

Screening proposals address such questions as:

1. Is the investment opportunity compatible with corporate strategy? Does it fall within a section of the business designated for growth, maintenance or divestment?
2. Are the resources required by the project available (e.g. expertise, finance, etc.)?
3. Is the idea technically feasible?
4. What evidence is there to suggest that it is likely to provide an acceptable return?
5. Are the risks involved acceptable?

As the quality of data used at the screening stage is generally poor, it makes little sense to apply sophisticated financial analysis. Accordingly, the simple payback method is frequently used at this stage because it offers a crude assessment of project profitability and risk.

Definition and classification

Any investment proposal is vague and shapeless until it has been properly defined. At the definition stage of the capital investment process, detailed specification of the investment proposal involves the collection of data describing its technical and economic characteristics. For each proposal, a number of alternative options should be generated, defined, and subsequently, appraised in order to create the project offering the most attractive financial characteristics.

Even at this early stage, proposals are gaining commitment. *The very act of collecting information necessitates communicating with managers who may either lend support or seek to undermine the proposal.* The danger is that in this process commitments are accumulated until a situation is created which leads almost inevitably to investment. The amount of information gathered for evaluation is largely determined by:

1. the data perceived as desirable to gain a favourable decision,
2. the ease of its development, and
3. the extent to which the proposer will be held responsible for later performance related to the data.

How does top management seek to ensure that the most suitable projects are submitted by managers in the organization? It should establish mechanisms which induce *behaviour congruence*. The accounting information system, reward system and capital budgeting procedures should all encourage managers to put forward the very proposals that top management is looking for. For many firms, however, the accounting information system and reward mechanism encourages divisional managers to promote their own interests at the expense of those of the organization, and to emphasize short-term profit performance at the expense of the longer-term. Capital budgeting becomes a 'game' with the accounting and reward systems the rules of the game. Cash flow estimates are biased to maximize the gains to individuals within such rules.

The information required and method of analysis will vary according to the nature of the project. A suggested investment proposal classification is given below:

1. Replacement.
2. Cost reduction.
3. Expansion or improvement.
4. New products.
5. Strategic.
6. Statutory and welfare.

Replacement proposals are justified primarily by the need to replace assets that are nearly exhausted or have excessively high maintenance costs. Little or no improvement is expected from the replacement, but the expenditure is essential to maintain the existing level of capacity or service (e.g. replacement of vehicles). Engineering analysis plays an important role in these proposals.

Cost reduction proposals (which may also be replacement proposals) are intended to reduce costs through addition of new equipment or through modification to existing equipment. Line managers and specialists (such as industrial engineers and work study groups) should conduct a continuous review of production operations for profit improvement opportunities.

Expansion or improvement proposals relate to existing products, and are intended to increase production, service and distribution capacity, to improve product quality, or to maintain and improve the firm's competitive position.

New product proposals refer to all capital expenditures pertaining to the development and implementation of new products.

Strategic proposals are generated at senior management level and involve expenditure in new areas, or where benefits extend beyond the investment itself. A project may at first sight appear to offer a negative net present value and yet create further valuable strategic opportunities. Three examples demonstrate this point:

1. Diversification projects may have the effect of bringing the company into a lower risk category (this assumes that specific risk is important, as may be the case for a family-controlled company).
2. A patent may be acquired not for use within the firm, but to prevent its use by competitors.
3. Where information is difficult to obtain, such as in overseas markets, it may make sense to set up a small plant at a loss because it places the firm in a good position to build up information and to be ready for major investment at the appropriate time.

Statutory and welfare proposals do not usually offer an obvious financial return, although they may contribute in other ways, such as enhancing the productivity of a more contented labour force. The main consideration is whether standards are met at minimum cost.

Each proposal should be ranked within each category in terms of its effect on profits, its degree of urgency, and whether or not it can be postponed.

11.4   Evaluation and authorization

The evaluation phase involves appraisal of the project and decision choice (e.g. accept, reject, request further information, etc.). Project evaluation, in turn, involves the assembly of information (usually in terms of cash flows) and the application of specified investment criteria. Each firm must decide whether to apply rigorous, sophisticated evaluation models or simpler models which are easier to grasp yet capture many of the important elements in the decision.

The capital appropriation request forms the basis for the final decision to commit financial and other resources to the project. Typical information included in an appropriation request is given below:

*   *Purpose of project* – why it is proposed and the fit with corporate strategy and goals.

*   *Project classification* – e.g. expansion, replacement, improvement, cost saving, strategic, research and development, safety and health, legal requirement, etc.

- *Finance requested* – amount and timing, including net working capital, etc.

- *Operating cash flows* – amount and timing, together with the main assumptions influencing the accuracy of the cash flow estimates.

- *Attractiveness of the proposal* – expressed by standard appraisal indicators, such as net present value, DCF rate of return and payback period calculated from after-tax cash flows.

- *Sensitivity of the appraisal indicators* – to changes in the main investment inputs. Other approaches to assessing project risk should also be addressed (e.g. best/worst scenarios, estimated range of accuracy of DCF return etc.).

- *Review of alternatives* – why they were rejected and their economical attractiveness.

- *Implications of not accepting the proposal* – some projects which may have little economic merit according to the appraisal indicators may be 'essential' to the continuance of a profitable part of the business or to achieving agreed strategy.

Following evaluation, larger projects may require consideration at a number of levels in the organizational hierarchy until it is finally approved or rejected. The decision outcome is rarely based wholly on the computed signal derived from financial analysis. Considerable judgement is applied in assessing the reliability of data underlying the appraisal, fit with corporate strategy, and track record of the project sponsor. Careful consideration is required regarding the influence on the investment of such key factors as markets, the economy, production, finance and people. In the Appendix to this chapter a checklist of questions outlines the most important questions to be addressed.

Authorization

Following evaluation, the proposal is transmitted through the various authorization levels of the organizational hierarchy until it is finally approved or rejected. The driving motive in the decision process is the willingness of the manager to make a commitment to sponsor a proposal. This is based not so much on the grounds of the proposal itself as on whether or not it will enhance the manager's reputation and career prospects. It is not altogether uncommon for those involved in the preliminary investigation and appraisal of major projects to be promoted into head office decision-making positions in time to support and speed the approval of the same projects!

In larger organizations the authorization of major projects is usually a formal endorsement of commitments already given. Complete rejection of proposals is rare but proposals are, on occasions, referred back. The approval stage would appear to have a two-fold purpose:

1. *A quality control function*   As long as the proposals have satisfied the requirements of all previous stages, there is no reason for their rejection other than on political grounds. Only where the rest of the investment planning process is inadequate will the approval stage take on greater significance in determining the destiny of projects.

2. *A motivational function*   An investment project and its proposer are inseparable. The decision maker, in effect, forms a judgement on the proposal and the person or team submitting the proposal at the same time.

Sometimes the costs associated with rejection of capital projects, in terms of managerial motivation, far exceed the costs associated with accepting a marginally unprofitable project. The degree of commitment, enthusiasm and drive of the management team implementing the project is a major factor in determining the success or failure of marginal projects.

11.5   Monitoring and control

The capital budgeting control process can be classified in terms of *pre-decision* and *post-decision* controls as shown in Table 11.1. Pre-decision controls are mechanisms designed to influence managerial behaviour at an early stage in the investment process. Examples of such controls include the selection and training of subordinates to possess goals and risk attitudes consistent with senior management (selection controls), setting authorization levels and procedures to be followed (intervention controls) and influencing the proposals submitted by setting goals, hurdle rates, cash limits and identifying strategic areas for growth (influencing controls).

Table 11.1   Capital budgeting control procedures within 100 large UK firms

	1992	1986	1981	1975
	(%)	(%)	(%)	(%)
Pre-decision Controls				
Firms with:				
Capital budget looking beyond two years	68	64	64	57
An up-to-date capital budgeting manual	86	84	76	65
A formal screening and reviewing body	85	83	84	78
At least one person fully engaged in capital budgeting	23	26	33	31
A specific search and screening of alternatives	100	98	84	76
A regular review of hurdle rates	69	71	61	43
A formal financial evaluation	100	100	95	93
A formal analysis of risk	92	86	38	26
Post-decision Controls				
Firms which:				
Monitor project performance	84	84	76	69
Reconsider major projects after approval if cost over runs are likely	92	85	82	72
Require post-completion audits on most major projects	72	64	46	33

Source: Pike (1988 and 1992).

We now turn our attention to post-decision controls. The capital appropriation request approved at the decision stage will stipulate the total amount and timing of capital spending, but the real control of expenditure commences with the placing of orders. Ordering involves:

1. Precise specification of requirements in terms of delivery and erection time-scales, etc.
2. Selection of suppliers to submit quotations.
3. Selection of the best quotation.

Major investment projects may justify determining the *critical path* in the delivery and installation schedule. The critical path is defined as the longest path through a network. Control is established by accounting procedures for recording expenditures. Progress reports usually include actual expenditure; amounts authorized to date; amounts committed against authorizations; amounts authorized but not yet spent; and estimate of further cost to completion.

Investment controls in practice

Table 11.1 provides a summary of the capital budgeting control procedures found in 100 large UK firms. Almost two-thirds of the sample prepare a capital budget which looks beyond two years. One way of influencing managerial investment behaviour is by formalizing control procedures in the form of an up-to-date budgeting manual. The table reveals that this is a very common practice.

Increasing attention is devoted to setting and reviewing investment hurdle rates. One effect of a regular review of the required rates of return on investment projects is that it keeps financial considerations high on the decision-making agenda. There is, however, evidence from the survey that unduly high hurdle rates adversely affect the number of proposals put forward for consideration.

The dramatic increase in the extent to which firms formally analyse project risk (from 26 per cent in 1975 to 92 per cent in 1992) is a particularly interesting finding. Risk analysis is not simply conducted on the occasional project: approximately one-half of the respondents conduct risk analysis, in some form, on most projects.

11.6   Post-auditing

The final stage in the capital budgeting decision-making and control sequence is the post-completion audit. UK firms have been considerably more hesitant in appreciating the need to post-audit as compared to their North American counterparts, although there is evidence that this is changing. In a 1985 survey Neale and Holmes showed that 48 per cent of large quoted UK companies had adopted post-audits, while a later survey (1991) showed this proportion to have risen to 77 per cent, with about half of these firms having adopted post-audits between 1986 and 1990. A post-audit aims to compare the actual performance of a project after, say, a year's operation with the forecast made at the time of approval, and ideally also with the revised assessment made at the date of commissioning. *The aims of the exercise are two-fold. First, post-audits may attempt to encourage more thorough and realistic appraisals of future investment projects and secondly, they may aim to facilitate major overhauls of ongoing projects perhaps to alter their strategic focus.* These two aims differ in an important respect. The first concerns the overall capital budgeting system, seeking to improve its quality and cohesion. The second concerns the control of existing projects, but with a broader perspective than is normally possible during the regular monitoring procedure when project adjustments are usually of a fire-fighting nature.

If these objectives are achieved, then post-auditing may confer substantial benefits on the firm. Among these are:

1. the enhanced quality of decision-making and planning which may stem from more carefully and rigorously researched project proposals,
2. tightening of internal control systems,
3. the ability to modify or even abandon projects on the basis of fuller information, and
4. the identification of key variables on whose outcome the viability of the current and similar future projects may depend.

Problems with post-auditing

There are many possible reasons why UK firms have been slow to adopt post-audits. An insight into these can be obtained by listing some of the problems frequently cited by executives responsible for undertaking post-audits.

The disentanglement problem

It may be difficult to separate out the relevant costs and benefits specific to a new project from other company activities, especially where facilities are shared and the new project requires an increase in shared overheads. Newly developed techniques of overhead cost allocation may prove helpful in this respect.

Projects may be unique

If there is no prospect of repeating a project in the future, there may seem to be little point in post-auditing, since the lessons learned may not be applicable to any future activity. Nevertheless, useful insights into the capital budgeting system as a whole may still be obtained.

Prohibitive cost

To introduce post-audits may involve interference with present management information systems in order to generate flows of suitable data. Since post-auditing *every* project may be very resource-intensive, firms tend to be selective in their post-audits.

Biased selection

By definition, only accepted projects can be post-audited, and among these it is often only underperforming ones that are singled out for detailed examination. Because of this biased selection mechanism, the forecasting and evaluation expertise of project analysts may be cast in an unduly bad light – they might have been spot on in evaluating rejected and acceptably performing projects!

Lack of co-operation

If the post-audit is conducted in too inquisitorial a fashion, project sponsors are likely to offer grudging co-operation to the review team and be reluctant to accept and act upon their findings. The impartiality of the review team is paramount in this respect – for example, it would be inviting resentment to draw post-auditors from other parts of the company which may be competitors for scarce capital. Similarly, there are obvious dangers if reviews are undertaken solely by project sponsors. There is thus a need to assemble a balanced team of investigators.

Encourages risk-aversion

If analysts' predictive and analytical abilities are to be thoroughly scrutinized, then they may be inclined to advance only 'safe' projects where little can go awry and where there is less chance of being 'caught out' by events.

Environmental changes

Some projects can be devastated by largely unpredictable swings in market conditions. This can make the post-audit a complex affair as the review team are obliged to adjust analysts' forecasts to allow for the moving of the goalposts.

The conventional wisdom

Studies of investment appraisal, largely undertaken in North America, have generated a conventional wisdom about corporate post-auditing practices. Its main elements are:

1. Larger firms are more likely to post-audit.
2. Few firms post-audit every project, and the selection criterion is usually based on size of outlay.
3. Few projects are post-audited more than once.
4. The commonest time for a first post-audit is about a year after project commissioning.
5. The most effective allocation of post-audit responsibility is to share it between central audit departments and project initiators to avoid conflicts of interest, while utilizing relevant expertise.
6. The 'threat' of post-audit is likely to spur the forecaster to greater accuracy but it can lead to excessive caution, possibly resulting in suppression of potentially worthwhile ventures.

The UK experience

The UK research by Neale and Holmes (1991) broadly confirms these aspects. Among their most important findings are the following:

1. Firms larger by size, whether measured by capital employed or by turnover, are more likely to post-audit. This suggests a 'sophistication factor', or a resource effect.
2. Firms that are subsidiaries of overseas enterprises are more likely to post-audit, suggesting the importation of more developed parent company control procedures.
3. Firms in manufacturing sectors are more likely to post-audit, suggesting either that there are particular difficulties in post-auditing service activities, such as measurement of outputs, or that service sector executives do not regard post-auditing as appropriate for their activities.
4. Despite the differences in adoption rates among different categories of firms, there are no systematic differences in the objectives which they pursue in post-auditing, the benefits they obtain and the problems they encounter.
5. Post-audit benefits can be broadly classified into control benefits and decision-making benefits. The first type are found to be greatest when the firm places greatest emphasis on post-auditing as a control device, while the second type are greatest when the main concern is to improve investment decision-making and planning. In other words, the nature and magnitude of post-audit benefits depend upon having clearly specified objectives but realistic expectations from the operation.
6. One of the major problems cited regarding post-audits is that of environmental turbulence, which many firms use as a reason for not adopting post-audits. However, many of the benefits of post-auditing are most pronounced under precisely these conditions. This suggests that more astute managers use post-audits as a device for exploring the complexity of their operating environments. In this respect, post-auditing may have an important role to play in the strategic planning process.

When does post-auditing work best?

Finally, how do these findings help the practising manager? Specifically, what guidelines can we offer to managers who wish to introduce post-audit from scratch or to overhaul an existing system? Here are some key points:

1. When introducing and operating post-audit, emphasize the learning objectives and minimize the likelihood of its being viewed as a 'search for the guilty'.
2. Clearly specify the aims of a post-audit. Is it to be primarily a project control exercise, or does it aim to derive insights into the overall project appraisal system?
3. When introducing post-audit, start the process with a small project to reveal as economically as possible the difficulties which need to be overcome in a major post-audit.
4. Include a pre-audit in the project proposal. When the project is submitted for approval, the sponsors should be required to indicate what information is required to undertake a subsequent post-audit.

5. Be prepared to alter the information system to ensure that the required data will be available when required.
6. Do not judge project analysts on the basis of a single project. To obtain their willing co-operation, it seems fair to make assessments across a spread of projects.

If all other components of the capital budgeting system operate properly, i.e. if projects are carefully evaluated, planned and controlled during implementation, then major problem areas will be anticipated and acted upon swiftly and their impact minimized. Indeed, thorough post-auditing may hone the system to such a degree of keenness that post-audits become redundant. However, it is doubtful whether a high proportion of UK firms operate such sophisticated capital budgeting systems that they could afford to dispense with post-audits completely. Besides, even firms with highly-tuned systems find it instructive to study successful ventures and to demonstrate 'ideal' procedures to other staff. After smoothing the rough edges off a possibly ramshackle system, it seems dangerous to abandon outright the threat of post-audit, since even well-oiled human machinery can malfunction through complacency and personnel changes.

11.7   Strategic considerations

The investment process usually forms part of a wider strategic process. Capital projects are not normally viewed in isolation, but within the context of the business, its goals and strategic direction, often termed *strategic portfolio analysis.*

The attractiveness of investment proposals coming from different sectors of the firm's business portfolio depends not only on the rate of return offered, but also on the strategic importance of the sector. Business strategies are formulated which involve the allocation of resources (capital, manpower, plant, marketing support, etc.) to these business units. The allocation may be based on analysis of the market's attractiveness and the firm's competitive strengths, such as the McKinsey-GE portfolio matrix outlined in Figure 11.2.

The attractiveness of the market or industry is indicated by such factors as the size and growth of the market, ease of entry, degree of competition and industry profitability for each strategic business unit. Business strength is indicated by a firm's market share and its growth rate, brand loyalty, profitability and technological and other comparative advantages. Such analysis leads to three basic strategies:

1. Invest in and strengthen businesses operating in relatively attractive markets. This may mean heavy expenditures on capital equipment, working capital, research and development, brand development and training.
2. Where the market is somewhat less attractive and the business less competitive (the diagonal unshaded boxes), the business strategy is one of getting the maximum out of existing resources. The financial strategy is therefore one of maximizing or maintaining cash flows whilst incurring capital expenditures mainly of a replacement nature. Tight control over costs and management of working capital lead to higher levels of profitability and cash flow.

Business Strength

	High	Medium	Low
High	INVEST & GROW	INVEST & GROW	IMPROVE & DEFEND (Selective Investment)
Medium	INVEST & GROW	IMPROVE & DEFEND (Selective Investment)	HARVEST OR DIVEST
Low	IMPROVE & DEFEND (Selective Investment)	HARVEST OR DIVEST	HARVEST OR DIVEST

Market Attractiveness

Figure 11.2 McKinsey-GE Portfolio matrix

3. The remaining businesses have little strategic quality and may, in the longer term, be run down or divested unless action can be taken to improve their attractiveness.

An alternative analysis is the Boston Consulting Group approach, which describes the business portfolio in terms of relative market share and rate of growth as shown in Figure 11.3. This 2 × 2 matrix identifies four product markets within which a firm may operate: (1) 'stars' (high market share, high market growth), (2) 'cash cows' (high market share, low market growth), (3) 'question marks' (low market share, high market growth) and (4) 'dogs' (low market share, low market growth). The normal progression of a product over time, as shown in Figure 11.3, starts with the potentially successful product ('question mark') and moves in an anti-clockwise direction, eventually to be withdrawn (divested).

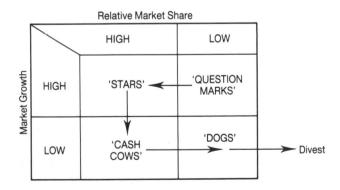

Figure 11.3 Normal Progression of Product Over Time

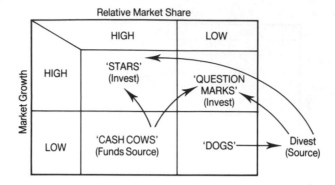

Figure 11.4   Investment strategy

From this strategic analysis of the firm's business portfolio we suggest the pattern of resource allocation outlined in Figure 11.4. The diagram shows how this analysis aids resource allocation strategy. Businesses offering high growth and the possibility of acquiring market dominance are the main areas of investment ('stars' and 'question marks'). Once such dominance is achieved the growth rate declines and investment is necessary only to maintain market share. These 'cash cows' become generators of funds for other growth areas. Business areas which have failed to achieve a sizeable share of the market during their growth phase ('dogs') become candidates for divestment and should be evaluated accordingly. Any cash so generated should be applied to high-growth sectors.

The above method is one of many approaches available to the firm in determining the impact of strategy on resource allocation. For example, Porter's (1985) framework for analyzing industrial structure and attractiveness (outlined in Chapter 1) argues that there are really only three logical strategies for strategic business units:

1.   to be the lowest cost producer,
2.   to focus on a niche or segment within the market, or
3.   to differentiate the product range so that it does not compete directly with lower-cost products.

Having developed its investment strategy, management can then assess individual projects in terms of where they fit into the firm's long-term strategic plan. It will be recognized from this that project appraisal or, in the case of capital shortage, project ranking, is not simply judged according to rates of return. Many companies will reject projects offering high returns because they fall outside strategic thinking. Ultimately, the capital budget must tie up with corporate strategy so that each project contributes to the implementation of some element of that strategy.

WHY M&S ALWAYS DELIVERS THE GOODS

Nothing seems to be able to stop Marks & Spencer from its remorseless progress towards ever-bigger profits. For as long as one can remember, the company has delivered to its shareholders higher earnings (a record few other companies can match) making it Britain's most profitable retailer in 1993.

What is the secret of its success? There is no mystery: it sticks to the same value-for-money approach established by Michael Marks on a Leeds market stall in 1884. It sets a high priority on creating further efficiency gains and greater customer loyalty. It also minimizes risk by taking advantage of its relations with its suppliers, 80 per cent of whom are in the UK. This has led to flexibility in ordering stock and has avoided many of the problems caused by the devaluation of sterling following Britain's departure from the Exchange Rate Mechanism in September 1992.

11.8 Summary

The resource allocation process is the main vehicle by which business strategy can be implemented. We have seen that investment decisions are not simply the result of applying some evaluation criterion. Investment analysis is essentially a search process: search for ideas, search for information, search for alternatives, and search for decision criteria. The prosperity of a firm depends more on its ability to create profitable investment opportunities than on its ability to appraise them.

Key points

- The four main stages in the capital budgeting process are:
  1. Determine the budget.
  2. Search for and develop projects.
  3. Evaluation and authorization.
  4. Monitor and control.
- Once a firm commits itself to a particular project, it must regularly and systematically monitor and control the project through its various stages of implementation.
- Post-audit reviews, if properly designed, fulfil a useful role in improving the quality of existing and future investment analysis and provide a means of initiating corrective action for existing projects.
- The investment process forms part of a wider strategic process. Capital projects should be viewed within this wider context.
- Post-audit benefits fall broadly into control benefits and decision making benefits. The nature and magnitude of post-audit benefits depend upon having clearly specified objectives but realistic expectations from the operation.

Appendix: Checklist of the main considerations for assessing

capital projects

Marketing factors

1.   To which segment of the market does the investment proposal relate?
2.   How critical is the proposal to the marketing strategy?
3.   Does the asset life exceed the economic life of the product?
4.   What market research has been conducted to support the marketing assumptions within the proposal?
5.   In the case of an expansion proposal:
     (a) has the market reached or passed its peak?
     (b) can projected volume increases be sold?
     (c) how will such increases affect market size, prices and margins?
     (d) could a price war result from a reduction in price to achieve higher volumes?
6.   In the case of a new product, has the product been fully tested?

Production factors

1.   What stage has the product specified in the investment proposal reached in its life-cycle (gestation, development, maturity, decline)? How does this relate to the assumptions concerning volume, unit cost and selling price?
2.   Is there any known experience of the use of the proposed investment:
     (a) within the organization?
     (b) outside the organization?
     If so, how can such experience be drawn upon?
3.   Can the production facilities adequately achieve the quality, timing and cost specifications assumed by the proposal?
4.   How will the investment affect capacity utilization in the short and medium term?

Financial factors

1.   How is the discount rate applied to this proposal justified?
2.   Does the project give rise to any special financing opportunities (e.g. low-cost loans linked specifically to the project)?
3.   Have 'at best' and 'at worst' scenarios been quantified in addition to the actual assumptions?
4.   Has sensitivity analysis been conducted? What percentage fall in assumed values of key variables is required for the project to become unacceptable?
5.   To what extent does the riskiness of the project arise from microeconomic factors (i.e. *specific* risk, such as changes in competition) or from macroeconomic factors (i.e. *market* risk, such as government economic policies)?

External economic factors

1. To what extent is the project's success sensitive to fluctuations in the following external economic factors:
    (a) foreign exchange movements?
    (b) commodity prices?
    (c) inflation rates?
    (d) interest rates?
    (e) government economic and fiscal policies?
2. To what extent is the project's viability dependent upon government grants and other inducements? What costs (economic and social) are incurred? (For example, relocation of a factory induced by generous government incentives may result in the transfer of staff who will be dependent on the continuation of the project.)

'People' factors

A major reason why projects do not live up to their original expectations is because 'people problems' are ignored. Major projects create structural changes and affect managerial motivation.

1. Will the proposal require additional manning or further training?
2. Is management able to cope with the proposal?
3. Is the individual/team sponsoring the proposal best suited to implementing it?
4. Are existing management structures and procedures adequate for the new investment?
5. What effect will the new investment have on management and the existing workforce?
6. Have the workforce and trade unions been properly consulted?

Further reading

Useful references on the capital budgeting process are Cooper (1975), King (1975), Pinches (1982), and Neale and Holmes (1991). Tomkins (1991) explores the strategic and organizational aspects in greater depth.

Questions

Self-test questions

1. 'Capital budgeting is simply a matter of selecting the right decision rule.' How true is this statement?
2. Outline the important stages in the capital budgeting process.
3. What are the aims of post-audits?
4. Why is it important to view capital budgeting within a strategic framework?

Exercises

1. Discuss how bias and forecasting errors may creep into the investment process. What steps can be taken to reduce them?

(Answer in Appendix A)

2. Investment evaluation is as much an appraisal of the proposer as the proposal. Do you agree?

(Answer in Appendix A)

3. Discuss the value of post-audits. Who should conduct them? When should they be carried out? What should they entail?

4. Discuss the procedures a business should adopt for approving and reviewing large capital expenditure projects.

(Certified Diploma, June 1990)

Practical assignment

Document the capital budgeting process in your organization (or get hold of such a document if it already exists!). Consider how this process fits into the strategic planning process (formal or otherwise). What issues emerge from this?

PART III

Financing Decisions and Policy

Financial managers face two key decisions: which assets to invest in and how to finance them. Having analysed the selection of wealth-creating investments in Part II, we now turn to the second category of decisions.

We begin in Chapter 12 by outlining the major sources of long-term finance available to firms. Choices between alternative forms of finance essentially reduce to choices between different mixes of borrowing and equity capital in the firm's capital structure. We therefore examine, in Chapter 13, the factors that determine a firm's dividend policy – a decision to distribute higher dividends has implications for the debt–equity mix, but there are important constraints on dividend policy.

In Chapters 14 and 15 we examine how the use of borrowed funds can affect the value of the company and the return required on new investments. Chapter 14 presents the 'traditional' view on these issues, while Chapter 15 presents the 'modern' theory of capital structure, which emphasizes the essential underlying relationships. We will also discover how borrowing affects the Beta coefficient.

An increasingly popular alternative to borrowing, but with many similarities, is lease finance, the subject of Chapter 16. Lease contracts can be written over varying periods, so leasing is effectively a hybrid between long-term and short-term capital. Finally in Chapter 17, we examine working capital policy, in which the use of short-term forms of finance plays an important part.

CHAPTER 12

Sources of finance

THE RICH VARIETY OF FINANCIAL PRODUCTS

The 1990 annual report of The Burton Group, a major high street clothing retailer, lists the following sources of long-term loans in its accounts.

The Burton Group Loan Stock 1990

Debenture loans	£m
$6\frac{1}{2}$% Unsecured Loan Stock 1986/91	5.1
8% Convertible Unsecured Loan Stock 1996/2001	34.4
$7\frac{1}{4}$% Unsecured Loan Stock 2002/07	2.6
$7\frac{3}{4}$% Unsecured Loan Stock 2002//07	0.9
FF $5\frac{3}{4}$% Convertible Guaranteed Loan 1992	0.1
$6\frac{1}{4}$% Second Debenture Stock 1990/95 (Floating charge)	2.6
$7\frac{1}{4}$% Second Debenture Stock 1991/96 (Floating charge)	2.5
US $9\frac{3}{4}$% Guaranteed Notes 1991 (Repayable within one year)	57.0
$4\frac{3}{4}$% Convertible Bonds 2001	110.0
	215.2

In addition, the company's balance sheet lists many other sources of finance, including share capital and reserves, bank loans, overdrafts and leasing obligations.

The question readers may be asking, faced with such a wide variety of financial instruments, is: Why should a fairly straightforward retailing operation require such complex financing arrangements?

12.1 Introduction

Before embarking on the analysis of financing decisions in subsequent chapters, it is necessary to consider in greater depth the main sources of finance available to companies. To the lay person the host of different types of finance and financial instruments is rather daunting. We simplify the choice to three broad categories: equity finance, debt finance and 'other' finance.

LEARNING OBJECTIVES

After reading this chapter, students should have grasped:

- The main sources of finance, their benefits and drawbacks.
- The main factors in considering the appropriate sources of finance.
- The terminology involved.

Main factors in choosing long-term finance

Equity finance is capital paid into or kept in the business by the shareholders – the owners of the business. It is long-term capital and carries the greatest risk and attracts the highest returns. *Debt* finance is money invested in the business by third parties, usually for a shorter period of time than equity and carrying a lower risk and lower return. Other sources of finance include a variety of specifically tailored financing methods such as leasing, export finance, government grants and small business finance.

Financing a business: Mitre Ltd

Mitre Ltd is a relatively young, rapidly growing company operating in the highly competitive computer software market. To date, it has financed its operations through equity capital provided by the five founder members and directors of the company, plus bank borrowings. The business is planning to expand rapidly over the next three years and requires the appropriate finance for such development.

Choosing the financing mix of short- and long-term finance, debt and equity that best meets the investment requirements of a business is a key element of corporate financial management. Four strategic issues need to be addressed in this regard.

Risk

How uncertain is the environment in which the business operates? How sensitive is it to downturns in the economy? Mitre Ltd would probably be viewed by potential investors as relatively high risk, particularly if the existing level of borrowing was high.

Ownership

A major injection of equity capital by financiers would dilute the control currently exercised by the founder members/directors. The desire to retain control of the company's activities may well mean that borrowing is preferred.

Duration

The finance should match the use to which it is put. If, for example, Mitre Ltd required finance for an investment in which no profits were anticipated in the early years, it may be desirable to raise capital which has little, if any, further drain on cash flow in these years. Conversely, it would be unwise for Mitre Ltd to raise long-term finance if the projects to be funded have a relatively short life. This could result in the business being over-capitalized, and unable to generate an adequate return to service and repay the finance.

Debt capacity

If Mitre Ltd has a low level of borrowing at present, it has a greater capacity to raise debt than a similar firm with a higher borrowing level. Debt capacity is not simply a function of current borrowing levels, but also depends on the type of industry, security offered, etc. One important benefit of borrowing is that the interest paid attracts tax relief and, hence, reduces the cost of capital.

12.2 Types of corporate finance

The financial manager (or treasurer) can generate capital *internally*, through the company's net operating cash flows, or *externally*, via the capital market, bond market or the banking system. These markets, in turn, raise funds through financial institutions such as pension funds, insurance companies and banks.

What then are the main types of company finance? Table 12.1 indicates that in the five years 1986–1990 the bulk of the funds (53 per cent) has been internally generated through retained profits. Obviously, the level of retained profits in any year depends on how profitable companies have been and the dividend policies adopted.

Second to retained profits over this period is bank and other short/medium-term borrowing (34 per cent), this proportion having doubled in recent years as business

Table 12.1 Sources of new finance for UK companies

	Retained Profits (%)	Ordinary Shares (%)	Debentures & Preference Shares (%)	Bank and other Borrowings (%)	Total Finance (£bn)
1986	64	10	5	21	51.4
1987	56	18	5	21	75.0
1988	49	5	4	42	90.4
1989	44	2	6	48	86.8
1990	51	4	5	40	68.0
Average 1986–90	53	8	5	34	

Source: Financial Statistics (December 1991).

confidence increased and interest rates became relatively inexpensive. Finally, the new capital raised through the capital markets, in the form of ordinary shares (8 per cent), preference shares and debentures (5 per cent), is relatively small in relation to profit retentions and bank borrowings. Much of these capital market issues were used to finance corporate mergers and acquisitions.

The main types of equity and debt finance are discussed in the following sections.

12.3   Equity finance

Share ownership lies at the heart of modern capitalism. By purchasing a portion or 'share' a person can become a shareholder with some degree of control over a company. A share is therefore a 'piece of the action' in a company. There are three main types of equity capital.

Ordinary Share Capital is the main source of equity finance. Shareholders carry full rights to participate in the business through voting in general meeting. They are entitled to payment of a dividend out of profits and ultimate repayment of capital in the event of liquidation only after all other claims have been satisfied. As owners of the company, the ordinary shareholders bear the greatest risk, but also enjoy the fruits of corporate success in the form of higher dividends and/or capital gains.

When shares are first issued, they are given *nominal* or *par* values. For example, a company could issue £5 million ordinary share capital in a variety of configurations, such as 10 million shares at a nominal value of £0.50 each, or 500,000 shares of £10 each. The main consideration in setting the nominal values is that of *marketability*. Investors tend to view shares with lower nominal values (e.g. 50 pence) as more easily marketable particularly when, after a few years, shares often trade well above their nominal value. The most popular unit nowadays is 25p.

Shares are rarely issued at their nominal value, but at a *premium*. Share premium forms an integral part of the share capital. Most companies are limited liability companies incorporated under the Companies Acts. Limited liability implies that the owners (or shareholders) have obligations limited to the amount they have invested. If the company was ever wound up or liquidated, leaving outstanding debts, the shareholders would not be liable to meet such claims. Limited liability companies in the United Kingdom with a capitalization over £50,000 and shares held by the public are termed public liability companies and denoted by the letters 'plc'. This does not necessarily mean that their shares are quoted on a stock exchange.

Preference Shares are really hybrid securities, falling between equity and debt. They usually carry no voting rights, except in the event of liquidation, and have preferential rights over ordinary shareholders regarding dividends and ultimate repayment of capital. This may suit a risk-averse investor looking for a reliable income, but only limited participation in a company. Preference shares have priority over ordinary shares in dividend payment and in the event of liquidation.

Preference dividends may be termed *cumulative* – carrying forward rights to dividends if profits are insufficient in any year – or *non-cumulative*. When the dividend rate is fixed, the preference shares are simply an alternative to debt finance, particularly when the company pays no tax, because interest – but not dividends – are allowed for tax purposes. When, however, *participating* preference shares are issued, the dividend is linked to corporate performance, more like ordinary shares.

Companies can issue ordinary or preference shares that are *redeemable* at the option of the company or the shareholder within the terms of the Articles of Association (the company's internal regulations) and the Companies Act.

Retained Profits and Reserves. It is a common mistake to assume that the reserves and retained profits figure specified in a company's balance sheet represents cash balances. However, the term simply means that profits, whether realized or unrealized, have been reinvested and not distributed to shareholders in the form of dividends. Almost certainly such reserves have been reinvested in wealth-creating assets such as plant and machinery, stocks and debtors.

We saw in Table 12.1 that retained profits provide the main source of new capital for most businesses. This is because they are cheaper than a new issue of shares, avoiding expensive issuing costs, and also because directors have control over the dividend to be paid each year. To the lay person, it may seem that retained earnings are a free source of finance and far more attractive to management than, say, raising interest-bearing loans. A moment's reflection, however, will show that retained earnings incur an opportunity cost; if returned to shareholders by way of dividend, the cash could be invested to yield a return. The cost of retained earnings is therefore the return that could be achieved by shareholders on investments of comparable risk to the company.

Issuing new shares

Private companies usually rely on the individual owners as the main source of equity finance. Additional equity can be raised by widening the ownership, without going to the general public, by a *private placing*. This is arranged through a stockbroker or Issuing House which, for a fee, buys the shares and then 'places' them with (i.e. sells to) selected clients. Alternatively, a Venture Capital or investment bank may take a minority stake in the company.

'Going public'

Eventually, the private company may require such a large amount of new capital that it needs to go 'public' by raising finance from the general public through the Stock Exchange. The managers of new issues are usually from merchant banks, issuing houses or Stock Exchange member firms. They advise the company on such details as the issue price and launch date. Some of the largest issues in recent years have been government privatization issues, such as British Gas. In such cases, the new company gets no new money; rather the government raises money by selling off its shares to the public. There are over 2,000 British companies with shares listed on the Stock Exchange. This market exists for well-established companies which must comply with stringent regulations. For example, to obtain a listing, a company must demonstrate a five-year trading record.

Companies can raise additional share capital by attracting new shareholders or by giving existing shareholders first opportunity to further invest in the business via a *rights issue*. Various methods are available for offering shares to the general public. The most common way is an *offer for sale*, where shares are first sold to an Issuing House which then offers them for sale to the public. The Issuing House will first underwrite the share issue, for a fee, thus guaranteeing that all the shares are taken up.

Where the company is unsure of the price to issue the shares, an *issue by tender* becomes attractive. A minimum price for the shares is set and investors are invited to bid for shares at or above this level. Shares are then allotted to successful bidders at the highest price (the 'striking price') which ensures that all shares are taken up, even though some subscribers will have offered to buy shares above this price. Alternatively, the company may adopt a lower price and then allow each subscriber at, or above, this price only a proportion of the shares for which they have tendered, thus giving a wider share representation.

From a company's viewpoint, such a method is desirable where there is uncertainty concerning the appropriate price at which to sell the shares. For example, the market may be unsettled or the company coming to the market may have unique characteristics, as with some of the privatization issues. In such cases, a tender issue avoids the problem of underpricing (i.e. raising less capital than might have been the case) or overpricing, in which case the success of the issue may be threatened.

A *Stock Exchange Placing* is a means by which a company can gain a Stock Exchange listing and additional share capital. A merchant bank arranges for a number of its clients (usually institutional investors) to buy shares in the newly quoted company. At least 25 per cent of the shares placed have to go to market dealers for dissemination around the market.

Rights issues

These are new shares offered to existing shareholders and easily the most common method of raising equity capital for existing companies. Shareholders are granted the right to subscribe for shares in proportion to their existing holdings, thus enabling them to retain their current voting control. Apart from the control factor, rights issues have certain other attractions:

1. They are far cheaper than a public share issue. Provided the issue is for less than 10 per cent of the class of capital there is no need for a *prospectus*, although a brochure must still be made available.

2. They may be made at the discretion of the directors without consent of the shareholders or the Stock Exchange. Except for larger issues, the timing of the issue is controlled by the directors, whereas a public issue or larger rights issue requires companies to 'book a place in the queue' operated by the government broker.

3. They rarely fail. Existing shareholders are given an incentive either to take up their rights or to sell their rights. It is not a sensible option to do nothing as this effectively reduces their wealth as shares are typically offered at a discount of about 20 per cent below the current market price.

4. When stock market prices are generally high, companies have been known to raise cash through rights issues and to place it on deposit while seeking suitable candidates for acquisition. Hanson raised over £500 million in this way in 1985 specifically to finance its planned acquisition programme.

Shareholders' options with rights issue: Grow-up plc

Let us consider in greater depth the rights issue choices available to existing shareholders. Grow-up plc decides to make a rights issue of one new share for every three held. The share price prior to the issue is 200p and the new shares are to be offered at 160p. *The* ex-rights *price is the price which all shares are expected to trade at after the rights issue has taken place.* It is calculated below at 190p:

3 old shares prior to rights issue at 200p each	600p
1 new share at 160p	160p
4 shares worth	760p
1 share is therefore worth 760/4	= 190p

The value of the rights is the difference between the pre-rights share price and the ex-rights price. In the case of Grow-up plc this is $(200p - 190p) = 10p$ for every share held, or $(190p - 160p) = 30p$ for every new share. The first option for shareholders is therefore to sell their rights, obtaining 10p per share, less any costs. A shareholder with 3,000 shares in the company would have a market value prior to the rights issue of $(3,000 \times £2) = £6,000$. After the issue, the value will fall to $£3,000 \times £1.90 = £5,700$, a decline of £300, which is the amount he would receive for the rights sold (1,000 new shares $\times$ 30p).

The second option is to subscribe for the new shares by *taking up the rights*. This should only happen if the shareholder has the resources to acquire the additional shares and is of the opinion that this is the best way to invest such money. The fact that no stamp duty or brokers' commission is payable if the original shareholder takes up the rights, and the desire to maintain the existing degree of voting control, are additional reasons for taking up the rights.

A third option is to *sell sufficient of the rights to provide the cash to take up the balance.* This option makes obvious sense for shareholders who want to retain their existing investment in the company in value terms.

The formula for calculating the number of shares is:

$$\frac{\text{Nil paid price}}{\text{ex-rights price}} \times \text{Number of shares allotted}$$

The *nil paid price* is the difference between the ex-rights price and the subscription price, in our case $(190p - 160p) = 30p$. The number of shares retained for our investor with 3000 shares is therefore:

$$\frac{30p}{190p} \times 1000 = 157 \text{ shares}$$

The purchase of 157 shares at 160p will cost	£251.20
Funded from $\frac{843}{1,000}$ rights sold at 30p	£252.90

The total investment is now worth $3,157 \times 190p = £5,998$ which (subject to rounding) is equivalent to the original investment of £6,000.

The final option is to *let the rights lapse* by doing nothing. In this case the company will sell the new shares in the market and, depending on the terms of the issue, may or may not reimburse the shareholder. This last option is not advisable.

The real message from rights issues is that shareholders cannot expect to receive something for nothing. The apparent gain from the invitation to purchase new shares at a discount on the existing price is more illusory than real.

Scrip issues and share splits

Scrip issues – often called bonus or capitalization issues or 'share splits' – are a free issue of shares to existing shareholders. These terms are often used interchangeably, although there are technical differences between a scrip issue and a share split. A scrip issue is usually made as an alternative to a dividend payment (either wholly or partially – sometimes shareholders can choose between cash dividends and new shares), and usually involves a minor increase in shares issued, e.g. 'one for twelve'. However, a share split, e.g. the 'two for one' operation conducted by Bass plc in 1991, reflects a major restructuring of the shareholders' funds in the balance sheet. Bass, for example, doubled its number of issued shares, but halved its reserves, although no cash actually changed hands.

Companies with very high share prices and large reserves on their balance sheet may decide to capitalize these reserves via a share issue. One reason for so doing is that management often regards high unit prices, say over £10 a share, as less marketable. The effect of a share split is generally to lower the share price.

For example, in a 1-for-2 share split, the shareholder receives a 50 per cent increase in shares held (3 after compared with 2 before). If the share price was £2.10 before the issue, it should fall to £1.40 after the issue ($£2.10 \times 2/3$). The value to the holder of two shares before the issue is unchanged:

$$\begin{aligned} \textit{Before} \quad & 2 \times £2.10 = £4.20 \\ \textit{After} \quad & 3 \times £1.40 = £4.20 \end{aligned}$$

In other words, such issues do not offer shareholders something for nothing.

Scrip issues can, however, be used to convey new information to investors. For example, a 1-for-10 scrip issue may signal that the directors are confident that the dividend can be maintained, even though the number of shares will increase. In such a case, the share price may not fall quite so far as the arithmetic would suggest, and may even increase as the market responds to the 'signals' emitted by the company.

Having outlined the main types of equity finance available, let us now consider equity finance as a long-term source of finance.

EVALUATION OF EQUITY CAPITAL

For

- No fixed charges (e.g. interest payments). Dividends are paid if the company generates sufficient cash, the level being decided by the directors.
- No repayment required. It is truly permanent capital.
- In the case of retained profits and rights issues, directors have greater control over the amount and timing, with minimal paperwork or issuing costs.
- Carries a higher return than loan finance and acts as a better hedge against inflation than loan stock.
- Shares in listed companies can be easily disposed of at a fair value.

Against

- Issuing equity finance can be inexpensive (as in the case of retained profits or a rights issue) but expensive in the case of a public issue (anything up to 15 per cent of the finance raised).
- Issuing ordinary shares to new shareholders dilutes the degree of control of existing members.
- Dividends are not tax deductible, which makes equity relatively more expensive than loans.
- A high proportion of equity can increase the overall cost of capital for the company.
- Shares in unlisted companies are difficult to value or dispose of.

12.4 Debt finance

An even greater array of instruments for raising debt finance has developed than for equity finance. To illustrate some of the variety, examine again the loans in issue by The Burton Group in 1990, as shown at the start of the chapter. Notice the variation in interest rates, security, repayment dates, convertibility and currency. We will consider many of these aspects in the following sections.

Debentures

A debenture is the legal term for secured loan stock. Debenture stock is divided up into securities (with a nominal value of £100) and sold via the stock market to a variety of investors. Take, for example, one of The Burton Group's debentures:

7¼% Second Debenture Stock 1991/96 (floating charge)   £2.5 million

This description indicates a total issue of £2.5 million at a fixed rate of 7¼ per cent with a variable redemption date between 1991 and 1996, most likely at the option of the company. The debenture is secured by a *floating charge* attached to all the present and future assets of the company without any particular assets being specified. The company is free to dispose of these assets without referring to the debenture holders or their trustees so long as the company fulfils its contractual obligations. If, however, it defaults (e.g. on the interest payment or loan repayment), or if the company is wound up, the floating charge crystallizes and becomes a *fixed charge*. A fixed charge or mortgage debenture is based on specific secured assets, usually land and buildings. In the event of liquidation, the assets will be sold and the proceeds used first to meet debenture holders' claims.

Unsecured loan stock

This will normally be higher-risk stock than secured debentures. Thus, the interest rate (often termed *coupon rate*, referring to the days when loan stock certificates had detachable coupons for holders to claim interest) is usually higher than for secured loans. It is common for a loan agreement to specify *restrictive covenants*. Such conditions might include:

1. *Dividend restrictions* – limitations on the level of dividends a company is permitted to pay. This is designed to prevent excessive dividend payments which may seriously weaken the company's future cash flows and thereby place the lender at greater risk.
2. *Financial ratios* – specified levels below which certain ratios may not fall, e.g. debt to net assets ratio, current ratio, etc.
3. *Financial reports* – regular accounts and financial reports to be provided to the lender to monitor progress.
4. *Issue of further debt* – the amount and type of debt that can be issued may be restricted. Subordinated loan stock (i.e. stock ranking below the existing unsecured loan stock) can usually still be issued.

EVALUATION OF DEBENTURES AND UNSECURED LOAN STOCK

For
- Most loan stocks give ten or more years before repayment is due. A 'bullet' loan is where there is just one final repayment, and a 'balloon' loan is where the repayment schedule is spread over a number of years following a period when little or no repayment is required. Bullet and balloon loans give tremendous cash flow benefits in the early years where only interest is payable.
- A successful issue will often enable the company eventually to redeem the loan stock through a new issue, without drawing upon the operational cash flows.
- Interest is tax-deductible.

Against
- Restrictions are placed on the company either in terms of the charge over assets, or the restrictive covenants imposed.
- Unsecured loan stock may impose demanding performance requirements.
- Greater monitoring and control takes place over a public issue such as a debenture than with, say, a term loan with a bank.

Convertible unsecured loan stock

A *convertible* is a debt instrument which can, at the option of the holder, be converted into equity capital. This security is the same as ordinary loan stock except that it usually pays a lower rate of interest and the holders have the option to convert their stock into a fixed number of ordinary shares at a predetermined rate. Up to the date of conversion, the holder receives a fixed rate of interest and is a creditor of the company, but also has the possibility of capital gain if the option to convert to equity is exercised. Returning to The Burton Group loans we see:

4¾% Convertible Bonds 2001   £110 million

Holders of this stock have the right, at any time until August 2001, to convert their stock into ordinary shares in the company at a price of 315p per share. The market price of the ordinary shares when the bonds were issued was 259p per share.

It is usual to have a period of several years between the issue date and the first possible conversion date to ensure that interest rather than dividends will be payable in the early years.

EVALUATION OF CONVERTIBLE LOAN STOCK

- Convertible loan stock can be issued more cheaply than a 'straight' loan because it offers an equity incentive.
- Companies perceived as relatively high risk can attract loan finance by offering the possibility of participating in future growth.
- Interest on loans is tax-deductible.
- Where it is believed that the true worth of the company is not adequately reflected in the share price, convertibles provide a means of raising capital which may eventually become equity without diluting the value of existing equity.
- Convertibles offer the benefits of both equity and loan stock, thereby attracting additional investors.
- If all goes as planned, the conversion to equity will occur, enabling more debt to be raised.
- If the conversion price is misjudged, the company is left with unwanted debt. If the equity growth is faster than expected, conversions will take place on over-generous terms at the expense of existing shareholders.

Share warrants

A warrant is an option to buy ordinary shares. We include it in the section on debt finance because it is frequently linked to debt issues. The warrant holder is entitled to buy a stated number of shares at a specific price up to a certain date. Each warrant will state the number of shares the owner may purchase and the time limit (unless a perpetual warrant) within which the option to purchase can be exercised. For example, The Burton Group's issue of US$ 9¾% Guaranteed Notes 1991 also gave holders warrants carrying rights to subscribe for 26 million ordinary shares in the company at a price of 272p each, exercisable at any time before 27 February 1991 or at such later dates as the company may determine.

Companies issue warrants for a number of reasons. They can be attached to loan stock (as in The Burton Group case), thus providing loan stock holders with an opportunity to participate in the future growth and prosperity of the company or, alternatively, used to attract investors by new and expanding companies. They may be part of the purchase consideration in a takeover. In both cases they act as a 'sweetener' to the particular decision. Frequently, such an inducement enables the company to obtain a lower rate of interest or less restrictive conditions in the debenture agreement. Whether or not such warrants eventually give rise to additional finance by holders taking up their option to purchase depends, of course, on the future trading success of the company and the exercise price.

Interest payment

Traditionally, loans have tended to incur fixed interest payable semi-annually with a 'balloon' payment on maturity after benefitting from a number of years when no repayment was required. Recent innovations have introduced ways of reducing the risks surrounding interest rate, inflation and default, such innovations being termed *financial engineering*.

Investors may be reluctant to lend long term at a fixed rate when interest rates are likely to fluctuate greatly. *Floating rate notes* enable a company to issue long-term debt where the rate of interest is linked to short-term interest rates, usually the three- or six-month London Interbank Offered Rate (LIBOR).

The Corporate treasurer is not forced to live with a floating interest rate. Interest rate *swaps* enable firms, in effect, to move from floating to fixed rate (or vice versa) depending on their view of future interest rates and their willingness to speculate or hedge borrowings. One borrower issues a fixed rate loan while the other issues floating rate notes and they then exchange (swap) their interest rate payments.

Floating-rate bonds can stipulate limits to protect interest payments from rises in interest rates, in which case interest rates will not exceed a pre-set maximum ('cap'), fall below a pre-set minimum ('floor') or stay within both ('collar').

Caps and *collars* are really interest rate options offering the borrower protection against adverse movements in interest rates whilst offering some scope for profit from favourable interest rate movements. Interest rate caps (or ceilings) offer protection from interest rate rises. Periodically, the actual interest rate (LIBOR) is compared with the agreed cap rate. If the LIBOR is above the cap rate the buyer of the cap (i.e. borrower) would be compensated for the difference. This effectively means that, no matter how high interest rates go, the borrower pays no more than the agreed interest rate.

Collars would be arranged when it cannot be predicted which way interest rates will move. The borrowing company simultaneously buys a cap and sells a *floor*, thus setting defined upper and lower limits for the interest rate payable. As a collar offers even less scope for possible gains, its cost is lower than the equivalent cap.

Mezzanine finance, as the name suggests, is part-way between debt and equity finance. It is a high-yield loan and normally has equity warrants attached. Mezzanine finance ranks below all other forms of debt in liquidation and therefore carries greater risk. The expected returns are therefore commensurately higher. This form of finance is frequently used in corporate restructuring and in funding management buy-outs or leveraged takeovers.

Investment yields

Investors who buy debentures and loan stock will want to know the yield on their investment. Two ratios are commonly given in this regard. The *flat yield* or *interest yield* is the gross interest receivable expressed as a percentage of the current market value of the loan. Thus a 7 per cent loan issued at £85 with a nominal value of £100 has a flat yield of:

$$\frac{£7}{£85} \times 100 = 8.2\%$$

This represents the gross yield. The net-of-tax yield will be affected by the investors' tax position:

$$\text{Net Interest Yield} = \text{Gross Yield} \times (1 - t)$$

Where: t = the rate of personal tax.

The *redemption yield* combines the income accruing from interest payments plus the capital gain or loss on maturity. It will be greater than the flat yield where the current value is below the redemption value because the investor will also receive a capital gain.

Deep discount loans arise when bonds are issued with very low interest rates (even 0 per cent!) at well below nominal value. Investors therefore receive a large capital gain on redemption which means that the tax charge on income is deferred until the gain is realized.

Long-term financing packages

Start-up capital is the capital for funding new businesses or management buy-outs (MBOs). Clearing banks and venture capitalists such as 3i offer tailor-made financing packages for new businesses, taking advantage of available government incentives. Specialist institutions may also be able to arrange start-up capital for certain types of business such as high-technology ventures. Capital for MBOs – where the existing managers acquire all or part of the business – would come from much the same sources of finance.

A leveraged buy-out (LBO) occurs where the management of a company undertakes to purchase the shares of that company from the other shareholders, with most of the finance for the purchase being raised through borrowing. In the case of an LBO of a quoted company, the status of the company may well change from public to private limited company. A conflict can occur between purchasers and sellers. Managers wishing to buy out the company may be tempted to run down the company or depress the share price immediately prior to the offer in order to gain control as cheaply as possible. However, managers have a duty to act in the shareholders' best interests and to offer a price which is 'fair' and to provide investors with all relevant information on which to form a decision.

Venture capital is the term often used to cover both start-up equity capital and high-risk loans. Venture capital companies select investment in relatively high-risk businesses requiring capital where the pay-offs for successful ventures are expected to more than recoup the losses sustained on unsuccessful ventures. They are not usually permanent investors, but look to liquidate their investment once the business is well established. This could be achieved through the company going public (for example, on the Unlisted Securities Market) or being taken over. Most venture capitalists require active involvement in the running of the company, such as representation on the board of directors.

Development capital refers to the long-term financial requirements of existing businesses looking to expand their operations. The sources of finance available are far greater, ranging from a rights issue to a full listing on the Stock Exchange.

12.5   Other sources of finance

Various other methods of raising medium-to-long-term finance are available to the corporate treasurer.

Sale and leaseback arrangements permit the sale of property and large items of plant to an investment institution, such as an insurance company, with immediate renting back. The ownership is sold, but the use is retained.

EVALUATION OF SALE AND LEASEBACK

- Usually raises more cash than a mortgage debenture.
- Does not involve restrictive covenants.
- Ownership is lost, including any possible capital appreciation and any opportunity to offer security for loans.
- Rent reviews can make it very expensive.
- Difficult to move to other premises.

Leasing

Leasing is a form of rental. Unlike most other methods of finance where money is raised to purchase assets, leasing is a method of financing the *use* rather than the ownership. Chapter 16 is devoted to leasing, while Chapter 17 covers other short-term sources of finance.

Eurobonds

Eurobonds are international bonds (loans) denominated in a currency other than the currency of the issuer. The Eurobond market is an international capital market trading in unsecured loans outside the country of residence of the borrower. For example, a Eurobond might be a sterling loan issued in Germany, a Swiss franc loan issued in Britain, or a US dollar-denominated bond issued in several European countries. They are only available to large companies and state-owned businesses, and are generally unsecured. Unlike domestic capital markets, the Eurobond market is not subject to a regulatory framework. This has enabled it to be more innovative in terms of bond features ('bells and whistles') tailored to meet corporate requirements. Apart from the conventional (so-called 'straight' or 'vanilla' bonds), there are Floating Rate Notes (previously discussed), Drop Lock bonds (floating rate notes with a fixed floor below which the rate will not fall), Zero Coupon bonds (i.e. deep discounting), Convertible bonds, and Multi-Currency bonds (a means of hedging against currency movements, e.g. ECU bonds).

EVALUATION OF EUROBONDS

Benefits
- Usually cheaper than equivalent domestic bonds.
- Interest is paid gross, i.e. without deduction of tax
- The market is more flexible and less restrictive, giving rise to more innovative, tailor-made financial instruments.
- They are issued as bearer securities which means the investors need not disclose their identity.
- Very large loans can be raised for long time periods more easily than in domestic markets.
- Eurobonds are a particularly good hedge against interest rate or currency movements.

Drawbacks
- The market is restricted to major bond issues for large internationally recognized organizations.
- Bearer securities require safe storage.
- The secondary market for Eurobonds is limited.

Small business finance

Small companies frequently experience difficulties in raising finance. Various government committees have looked into what has been termed the 'equity' gap, the most recent being the Committee to Review the Functioning of Financial Institutions in 1980 (the Wilson Committee). Each of these Committees discovered that small firms experience greater difficulty in raising finance than do larger firms. However, it seems that this difficulty is due not so much to the lack of financial sources available as to an 'information' gap, the managers of small businesses being unaware of such sources.

Financial institutions obviously prefer to invest in larger companies where the administrative costs in relation to the sum invested are lower and the information available greater. There is also a general belief that smaller firms are more risky than larger firms.

Banks and other financial institutions require a considerable amount of documentation (cash flow forecasts, etc.) and a track record which for recently formed smaller firms may be difficult and expensive to provide.

Long-term borrowing is often difficult to obtain, although funded largely by the clearing banks, is active in providing both share and loan capital to smaller firms. The main source of borrowing tends to be bank overdraft which is very short-term finance, yet many small businesses use it as medium-term finance, which can lead to financial difficulties. The development of the Unlisted Securities Market has made it easier for small companies to raise public issues.

Government grants

The United Kingdom and European Community provide various financial incentives and grants to the business community in such areas as research and development, training, investment and energy conservation.

Development grants provide financial assistance to industry investing in selected regions. The grant can be as much as 20 per cent of the cost of buildings and plant and machinery. *Selective assistance* for companies in certain areas is available to fund expansion that would not otherwise be undertaken.

The introduction of the *Business Expansion Scheme (BES)* has stimulated the provision of equity finance to smaller businesses either directly by individuals, or through an approved investment fund. Investors obtain relief from both income tax and capital gains tax, provided they hold the shares for at least five years, and the company does not obtain a public quotation for at least three years.

The *Government Loan Guarantee Scheme* was introduced in 1981 to stimulate banks to lend finance to smaller companies. The government guarantees 70 per cent of the loan in return for a small premium. Loans can be guaranteed for up to seven years.

Small to medium size companies may be able to obtain finance from the *European Investment Bank*. Loans are usually for up to eight years with no capital repayment requirement in the early years.

12.6 Short-term finance

So far we have only considered longer-term finance. Brief mention is given in this section of the main types of short-term finance used to fund seasonal business fluctuations and other non-permanent financing requirements.

Overdrafts are perhaps most commonly employed. They are relatively easy to negotiate, flexible and linked to a current account. The interest rate is fluctuating, linked to the bank base rate, and payable only on the amount outstanding each day. However, the great drawback is that an overdraft is repayable on demand, making it a highly risky source of finance, although banks rarely exercise this option.

Short-term loans are usually granted for specific purposes and for a fixed period of time of up to one year (or occasionally two years). A short-term loan might be granted to finance the build up of stock by a retailer prior to the pre-Christmas busy season.

Short-term loans are preferable to overdrafts where the purpose can be clearly identified, and the interest rate is usually lower. However, they are less flexible than overdrafts; often finance must be drawn and subsequently repaid in predetermined amounts.

Acceptance credits (bank bills)

Acceptances are bills of exchange drawn on and accepted by a bank (or acceptance house) and then sold to realize the full amount less a discount. When the bill eventually falls due for payment the bank must pay it, having first been reimbursed by the company originally drawing the bill. Even after payment for accepting and discounting the bill, it often works out cheaper than other forms of short-term finance. The rate of interest is known in advance, which eliminates the problem of interest rate fluctuations. Use of acceptance credits means that overdraft facilities need not be so heavily relied upon, and can be seen as a valuable stand-by facility.

Export finance

Various forms of finance can be used to finance exports, but the principal ones are overdrafts, acceptance credits and bill finance. The overdraft, whether in sterling or foreign currency, is the most common form of export financing in the United Kingdom. An overdraft facility is arranged with a bank, and floating rate interest is payable on the amount outstanding. Overdrafts may be secured by the shippping documents and related goods. Many export contracts require a Letter of Credit from the importer's bank guaranteeing immediate payment in cash or through a discounted bill of exchange. Governments usually encourage exports by providing credit insurance covering the risk of non-payment by an overseas customer.

HOW ICI RAISES FINANCE

The treasury function in ICI is centralized, co-ordinating cash flows arising throughout the world, foreign exchange exposures and funding activities.

Each year the Controller's Department – which encompasses the treasury function – prepares the annual operating budget, capital expenditure programme and financing plan which are then presented to the board for approval. A key decision is when to go to the market to raise the finance. For example, in May 1991, having witnessed a fall in interest rates in the United States, ICI felt it was the right time to raise longer-term funding through a $250 million ten-year loan issue.

Broad policies and guidelines are laid down as to the balance of long- and short-term financing, and how much should be variable- or fixed-rate. ICI views its marketplace for raising capital on a world-wide basis. However, it does seek to maintain levels of borrowing within its main locations (e.g. North America, Europe, etc.) broadly in line with the group's borrowing level.

(Based on *Accountancy*, July 1991)

12.7 Summary

Key revision points

- The main factors in considering the appropriate source of finance are risk, ownership, duration and debt capacity.
- Over half of the new finance raised for UK companies is through retained profits. This is not a free source of finance as it involves an opportunity cost in terms of the return shareholders would have obtained had they received the profit as dividends and reinvested it elsewhere.
- New shares are issued through a private placing, stock exchange placing, public issue (prospectus issue, offer for sale or issue by tender), or rights issue.
- Rights issues to existing shareholders are the cheapest and most common form of new issue.
- Equity capital is an attractive form of finance to companies in that there are no interest charges or capital repayments; to investors they offer a hedge against inflation, and a higher yield than loan stock. On the other hand, it can be expensive to raise and new issues to the public dilute the control of existing members.
- Debt finance (debentures, loan stock, etc.) is flexible, offering a wide range of financial products to the corporate treasurer. Interest payments are tax deductible, but restrictions (e.g. charges over assets and monitoring of activities) are common practice.
- Convertible loan stock is a debt instrument which can, at the option of the holder, be converted into equity. It offers investors and firms the benefit of loan stock in the early years and, if all goes to plan, will enable the benefits of equity to be captured when the business is better established.
- Small businesses have particular financing needs (e.g. start-up or venture capital) and experience greater difficulty in raising finance than do larger firms. The problem appears to be more that of an 'information' gap than an 'equity' gap.

Further reading

Weston and Copeland (1988) devotes considerably more space to this area than we have been able to. A practitioner's guide is found in Rutterford and Carter (1988).

Questions

Self-test questions

1. Describe the main sources of finance for companies. Give reasons for their popularity.
2. The Stock Exchange has estimated that the average cost of rights issues is 4 per cent of the new capital raised, compared with 7.6 per cent for offers for sale. Discuss the benefits

of the two methods of finance. Under what circumstances might the second, more expensive, option be advisable?

3. Explain what is meant by the 'flat yield' and 'yield to maturity' for a loan.

4. What is an 'issue of shares by tender'? Why might a company decide to issue shares by this method?

5. Explain the term 'leveraged buy-out'. How is it possible for a leveraged buy-out to create conflict between the managers of a company and its existing shareholders?

6. Explain what is meant by the term 'share warrant'. What are the advantages of issuing share warrants from the company's viewpoint?

7. You are the treasurer of Bravado plc and wish to raise funds through a debenture issue. In discussion with the advising merchant bank, what features would you wish to include and what would you expect the trustees for the debenture holders to demand? Bravado plc has good growth prospects but the economy is currently in recession and your liquidity is not particularly healthy at present.

Exercises

1. The ordinary shares of Anglia Paper Company are currently trading at £3.20. Existing shareholders are offered one new share at £2 for every three held. What is the value of each right?

   (Solution in Appendix A)

2. Cambridge Castings Ltd is planning to undertake a major expansion and modernize its manufacturing plant, thereby improving productivity and reducing unit costs. The company's existing capital base is fairly evenly divided between equity and debt and it is clear that the capital investment programme can only partly be funded through profit retention.

   The suggestion has been made that the additional finance could be raised through a preference share issue. You are required to evaluate this source of finance for the company, compared with equity or debt:

   (a) from the company's point of view.

   (b) from the viewpoint of investors.

   (Solution in Appendix A)

3. Shaw Holdings plc has 20 million ordinary shares of 50p in issue. These shares are currently valued on the Stock Exchange at £1.60 per share. The directors of Shaw Holdings believe the company requires additional long-term capital and have decided to make a one-for-four rights issue at £1.30 per share.

   An investor with 2,000 shares in Shaw Holdings has contacted you for investment advice. She is undecided whether to take up the rights issue, sell the rights, or allow the rights offer to lapse.

Required

(a) Calculate the theoretical ex-rights price of an ordinary share.

(b) Calculate the value at which the rights are likely to be traded.

(c) Evaluate each of the options being considered by the owner of 2,000 shares.

(d) Explain why rights issues are usually made at a discount.

(e) From the company's viewpoint, how critical is the pricing of a rights issue likely to be?

(Certified Diploma)

4. The senior management of Allodge is reviewing the company's capital structure.

Allodge plc
Balance Sheet as at 31 December 1988

	£m
Tangible assets	318
Investments	3
	———
Total fixed assets	321
Current assets	
Stocks	20
Debtors	280
Investments	10
Cash at the bank and in hand	1
	———
	311
Creditors: amounts falling due within one year	
Bank loans and overdrafts	43
Unsecured loan stock	5
Taxes	56
Trade creditors	254
Accrued expenses	1
Other creditors	24
Dividends	13
	———
	396
Net current liabilities	(85)
	———
Total assets less current liabilities	236
Financed by:	
Creditors: amounts falling due after more than one year	
13.5% Debenture 1995	30
US dollar 8% bonds 1996[1]	25
7.5% Convertible debenture 1998	15

[1] The principal of the fixed interest rate US dollar bond has been swapped into floating rate sterling.

Capital and reserves
Called up share capital

Preference shares (£1 par value)	20
Ordinary shares (50 pence par value)	35
Share premium account	4
Profit and loss account	107
	236

The company requires £30 million in usable new finance to expand its existing operations. The suggested sources of this finance are:

(i) An underwritten rights issue at a price of 348 pence per share.
(ii) A rights issue which is not underwritten at a price of 302 pence per share.
(iii) A placing at the current market price with the company receiving a price of 368 pence per share.
(iv) Early redemption of the 13.5 per cent debenture which is to be replaced by a new £60 million debenture at an interest rate of 12 per cent p.a. maturing at the same date as the existing debenture. Corporate tax is at the rate of 35 per cent.

The market price of the company's ordinary shares is 375 pence, of the preference shares 305 pence, of the 13.5 per cent debenture £104, the convertible debenture £97, and the total market value of the US bond is $41.25 million. The current spot rate is $1.7106–$1.7140/£. Issue costs are expected to be 1.5 per cent of gross proceeds for the underwritten rights issue, and 0.5 per cent for the non-underwritten rights issue. Redemption of the debenture would incur administrative costs of £50,000 and issue of a new debenture a further £25,000.

Required

(a) One manager states that suggestion (ii) will be unfair to existing shareholders as it will lead to a fall in share price approximately six pence greater than suggestion (i).
   If the ex-rights market price moves to its theoretical value demonstrate numerically whether a shareholder with 5,000 shares who purchased 60 per cent of his allocated new shares would suffer with suggestion (ii) relative to suggestion (i).
(b) Briefly discuss the relative advantages and disadvantages of each of these suggested forms of equity finance.
(c) If suggestion (iv) is adopted there would be a premium of £1,500,000 payable for early redemption of the existing 13.5 per cent debenture.
   The existing debenture may be assumed to have six years to maturity.
   Calculate whether early redemption of the debenture would be beneficial to Allodge.
   Recommend whether the company should make a new £60 million debenture issue.
(d) Suggest why the company has swapped the principal of the US fixed interest rate dollar bond into floating rate sterling.

(ACCA Level 3, December 1989)

5. Willoughby's last set of accounts show the following:

Assets employed:	£m
Fixed Assets	40
Net Current Assets	20
	60

Financed by:	
Issued Share Capital	5 (25p units)
Reserves	55
	60

Earnings after tax and before extraordinary items are currently £4m, and the dividend cover is two. Willoughby's shareholders *require* a return of 16 per cent.

Required

(a) Explain what is meant by a semi-strong efficient capital market. How could you test for semi-strong efficiency?

(b) Assuming Willoughby's shares are still quoted cum-dividend, what is the share price if the P:E ratio is 11:1? What will be the ex-dividend share price?

(c) Willoughby plans to make a share-split in order to write down reserves to £10m. What will be the effect on both the balance sheet and the share price?

(d) What will be the effect on both the balance sheet and the share price of a one-for-three rights issue offered at 75p per share?

Practical Assignment

Consider the long-term financing of a company with which you are familiar. Evaluate each of the main sources of finance and suggest, with reasons, two methods of finance which are not currently used but which may prove attractive to the company.

CHAPTER 13

The dividend decision

HOW LONRHO WOOED ITS SHAREHOLDERS

In early 1989, Lonrho plc faced a possible bid from the Australian Bond Corporation which held over 20 per cent of Lonrho's equity. On 26 January, the Lonrho chairman, Sir 'Tiny' Rowland, delivered 'an impassioned rallying cry' to the company's hitherto loyal band of small shareholders, holders of some 20 per cent of Lonrho's equity. (Rowland himself held 15 per cent.) Part of this plea for loyalty comprised a declaration of a tripled interim dividend and the issue of one free share for every six already held by investors. At the same time, Lonrho revealed that pre-tax profit had risen by 12 per cent for the previous financial year. A leading analyst remarked: 'with a big dividend increase and the scrip issue, Lonrho should have secured the loyalty of its private shareholders in a year when their loyalty could be badly needed.' The news of the profits increase, higher dividend and the bonus issue helped Lonrho's share price rise by 11p. The feared takeover bid never materialized, although this was due also to the well-known problems of the Bond Corporation.

13.1 Introduction

Most quoted companies pay two dividends to shareholders each year: first, an *interim*, a 'taster', based on half-year results, followed by the main, or *final*, dividend, based on the full year reported profits. The amount of dividend is determined by the Board of Directors, with the advice of financial managers, and presented to the Annual General Meeting of shareholders for approval.

Until a specified *Record Day*, the shares are traded *cum-dividend*, that is, purchasers will be entitled to receive the dividend. The approved dividends are paid to all shareholders appearing on the share register on the Record Day, after which the shares are quoted *ex-dividend*, i.e. without entitlement to the dividend. As subsequent purchasers do not qualify for the dividend, the share price will fall by the amount of the dividend. The board and their advisers thus face a twice-yearly decision as to what percentage of post-tax profits to distribute to shareholders and hence what percentage to retain.

How should top management approach the dividend decision? Should it be generous and follow a high pay-out policy, or more circumspectly, retain the bulk of earnings? The pure theory of dividend policy shows that under certain conditions, it makes no difference what they do, i.e. dividend policy is irrelevant! One authority argues: 'to the management of a company acting in the best interests of its shareholders, dividend policy is a mere detail' (Miller and Modigliani 1961). However, the conditions required to support this conclusion are highly restrictive and unlikely to apply in real-world capital markets. Indeed, many financial managers and investment analysts take the opposite view, appearing to believe that the dividend pay-out decision is critical to company valuation and hence a central element of corporate financial strategy. These are the extreme views – an evaluation of the case for-and-against dividend generosity leads to more pragmatic conclusions.

In this chapter, we consider the strategic, theoretical and practical issues surrounding dividend policy, with discussion of some of the alternatives to dividend payment. *The basic message for management is: Define the dividend policy, make a smooth transition towards it and think very carefully before changing it.*

Few people doubt that dividends influence share prices. Indeed, a primary method of valuation, the dividend valuation model, relies on discounting the future dividend stream. However, debate turns on the issue of the most attractive *pattern* of dividend payments.

Shareholders can receive returns in the form of dividends and/or capital appreciation, which is the market's valuation of future expected dividends. But are shareholders more impressed by near-in-time dividends as implied by a high pay-out policy, than by capital gain generated by a policy of low current payments, with retentions used to finance investment designed to grow earnings? Graham, Dodd and Cottle (1962) claimed that $1 of dividend was worth four times as much to shareholders as $1 of retained earnings. This, of course, argues for very high pay-outs, yet a glance at the financial press reveals some almost parsimonious pay-out ratios, with very few companies applying a dividend cover (profit after tax divided by dividend payments) below 2.0, that is, most companies distribute well under half of their earnings to owners.

Table 13.1 shows the dividend cover for selected firms from the *Financial Times* listing categories 'Beers, Wine and Spirits', and 'Engineering'. The figures suggest that larger drinks firms tend to be less generous dividend payers than smaller brewers. However, we cannot attribute differences in pay-outs to size alone. When we compare industrial sectors, we see that engineering firms are more restrictive in their dividend policy than drinks companies. This is partly due to the greater volatility of profits in engineering, and the reluctance of managers to pay out high, and possibly unsustainable, dividends.

What is the significance of a low pay-out policy? Does it mean that many managers are failing to pursue wealth-maximization? What does the Lonrho episode, with which we opened this chapter, reveal about dividend policy? Does failure to pay 'adequate' dividends lead to share price undervaluation and the threat of takeover? Can unwelcome bids be fended off by promising higher dividends? Most bidders promise higher pay-outs anyway, usually on the back of higher promised profits. To what extent can share price be manipulated by

Table 13.1   Dividend covers of selected companies

Company	Cover	Capitalization
Beers, Wines and Spirits:		(£m)
Scottish & Newcastle	4.3	1.314
Whitbread	4.1	1,695
Allied Lyons	4.0	3,831
Guinness	2.3	5,912
Highland Distilleries	2.1	308
Marston Thompson	2.1	188
Engineering:		
Babcock Interntl.	8.1	233
GKN	5.3	1,093
Glynwed	5.2	505
Hall Engineering	5.1	55
Simon Engineering	4.7	256

Source: *Financial Times* (January 1990).

variations in dividend payouts? Would it ever make sense to cut dividends? In short, what precisely is the relationship between dividend pay-outs and share values? This is the primary focus of this chapter.

LEARNING OBJECTIVES

There is some dispute whether companies should pay dividends at all. Some observers say it makes no difference whether a company pays dividends or not! After reading this chapter, you should:

- Understand the competing views about the role of dividend policy.
- Understand what factors a financial manager should consider when deciding to recommend a change in dividend pay-outs.
- Understand what is meant by the 'information content' of dividends.
- Appreciate the impact of taxation on dividend decisions.
- Understand why changes in dividend payments usually lag behind changes in company earnings.

In the next sections, we consider strategic and legal issues before examining the theory of dividend policy, and in particular, the 'irrelevance' hypothesis. We then consider the major qualifications to the theory suggesting reasons why some shareholders may in practice prefer dividend income. In this discussion, readers will find that dividend policy is something of an enigma with no obvious optimal strategy. Perhaps a case-by-case analysis is required in the absence of a universally applicable prescription for decision-making. However, some broad recommendations to guide the financial manager are possible. We must stress that *dividend decisions are really financing decisions*, that is, they are about how the firm should raise capital to finance desired investment projects. This will be made clearer by considering the strategic implications of the dividend decision.

13.2 The strategic dimension

Formulating corporate strategy requires specification of clear objectives and delineation of the strategic options contributing to the achievement of these objectives. Although maximization of shareholder wealth may be the paramount aim, there may be various routes to this goal. For example, diversifying into new industrial sectors involves a choice between internal growth and growth by acquisition. Whichever alternative is selected, the enterprise will need to consider both the level of required financing and the possible sources. The main alternatives for the listed company are short- and long-term debt capital, new share issues (normally rights issues) and internal financing (via retention of profits and depreciation provisions).

This is where we encounter the role of dividend policy. The amount of capital required to support the selected strategic option may exceed the borrowing capacity of the company, necessitating the use of additional equity funding. A capital-hungry firm therefore faces the choice between retention of earnings, i.e. restricting the dividend payout, or paying out high dividends but clawing back capital via a rights issue. Neither policy is risk-free as both may have undesirable repercussions on the ability to exploit strategic options. Retention may offend investors reliant on dividend income, resulting in share sales and lower share price, conflicting with the avowed aim of wealth-maximization, as well as exposing the company to the threat of takeover. Alternatively, there are costs involved in the dividend payment-plus-rights issue option, for example, administrative expenses and the risk of seeking more money from shareholders on a flat or falling market (as well as possible adverse tax implications, examined later in the chapter). To this extent, the dividend decision is a strategic one since an ill-judged financial decision could subvert the overall strategic aim. As a result, financial managers must carefully consider the likely reaction of shareholders and of the market as a whole to dividend proposals.

13.3 The legal dimension

Further constraints on managers' freedom of action in deciding dividends are imposed by the legal system. Although shareholders are the main risk-bearers in a company, other stakeholders, such as creditors and employees, carry a measure of risk. Accordingly, shareholders can only be paid a dividend if the company has accumulated sufficient profits. They cannot be paid out of capital, except in a liquidation, as to do so would mean they would be paid ahead of preferential claims on the business.

Section 264 of the Companies Act 1985 states that, for public companies, the maximum distribution is the net total of accumulated profits whether *realized* or *unrealized*. Private companies are restricted to accumulated *realized* profits. Furthermore, bondholders may insist on restrictive covenants being written into loan agreements to prevent large dividends being declared.

Of course, paying the maximum legally permitted dividend is rarely likely to make much strategic sense. For example, it would be highly risky for a listed company to increase its dividend based on the unrealized profit resulting from a recent property revaluation (although this is quite common in takeover battles). It must be remembered that dividends are not, except in law, paid out of profits, but out of cash or borrowings. It was common in the early 1990s for companies to report low or negative profits yet to maintain the previous year's dividend. If the company had retained sufficient profits in earlier years and its cash position was reasonably healthy, this was fairly acceptable. Indeed, the share prices of some companies actually rose when they paid a maintained dividend out of reserves!

13.4   The theory of dividend policy

We show in this section that *dividends are relevant in the absence of external financing if the company has better investment opportunities than its shareholders and payment of dividends prevents worthwhile investment being made.* With external financing, however, at least in a perfect market, dividends become totally irrelevant since payment no longer precludes worthwhile investment simply because the firm can recoup the required finance via a rights issue.

In Chapter 4, we saw that the value of a company ultimately depends on its dividend-paying capacity. For a company with free cash flows[1] of E_t in any year t, paid *wholly* as dividend, D_t, and with E_t constant and perpetual, the market will discount this stream at the rate of return required by shareholders, k_e, so that:

$$V_0 = \sum_{t=1}^{N} \frac{E_t}{(1+k_e)^t} = \frac{E_t}{k_e} \ \left(\text{or } V_0 = \frac{D_t}{k_e} \text{ since } E_t = D_t\right)$$

If a proportion, b, of earnings is retained each year, beginning in the next period, thus reducing the next dividend payable to $E(1-b)$, company value is given by the forthcoming dividend divided by the cost of equity less the growth rate. The growth rate, g, is given by the retention ratio, b, times the return on reinvested funds, R (as explained in Chapter 4):

$$\text{Company Value} = V_0 = \frac{E_1(1-b)}{(k_e - g)} = \frac{D_1}{(k_e - g)} = \frac{D_1}{(k_e - bR)}$$

These expressions can cause confusion. In the first case, the market appears to value the stream of earnings, while in the second, the valuation is based upon the stream of dividends. Indeed, in the early stages of the debate about the importance and role of dividend policy, much attention was paid to the issue of whether the market values earnings or dividends.

---

1. In this and subsequent chapters, the letter E is used to denote the free cash flow concept of earnings as explained in Chapter 4. Because free cash flow is likely to deviate from accounting earnings, when the latter accounting concept is intended, the phrases 'accounting profit' or 'reported earnings' are utilized.

This apparent dichotomy can be easily resolved if we focus on the reasons for earnings retention. Retention may occur for two main reasons.

First, the company may wish to *bolster its holdings of liquid resources*. For example, dividend distribution may run down current assets or perhaps increase borrowings. Many profitable companies borrow to avoid having to reduce or pass a dividend for reasons explained later.

However, the primary reason for retention is to *finance investment in fixed and other assets* to generate higher future earnings and hence, enhanced dividend-paying capacity. The growth rate of earnings depends on the retention ratio b, and also the rate of return achieved on ploughed-back funds, R, i.e. $g = (b \times R)$.

It is important to remember that the DGM assumes a constant retention ratio and a constant return on new investment projects. If these assumptions hold, both earnings and dividends grow at the same rate. Whether this rate is acceptable to shareholders depends on the return they require from their investments, k_e. The relationship between k_e and R, the return on reinvested earnings, provides the key to resolving the valuation dispute mentioned above.

Dividend irrelevance in perfect capital markets

Miller and Modigliani (MM) pointed out in a famous paper in 1961 that earnings retention was simply one way of financing investment. If the company has access to better investment opportunities than its shareholders, under perfect capital market conditions, investors may benefit from retention. Retention may only temporarily lower the dividend payment, resulting in a rate of growth yielding higher dividends discounted through time. This is shown in Figure 13.1. At point-in-time t_1, the company, which currently pays out all its earnings, E_0, plans to cut dividends from D_0 to $(1-b)D_1$, where b is the retention ratio.

Dividends do not regain their former level until point-in-time period t_N, involving a cumulative loss in dividend payments equal to area XYZ. Beyond time t_N, dividends exceed their original level as a result of continued reinvestment of earnings. Clearly, shareholders will be better off if the area of subsequently higher dividends, ZVW, exceeds XYZ (allowing for the discounting process). This holds if R, the return on retained funds, exceeds k_e. This contention can be illustrated using an example.

Divicut plc

Divicut currently generates a free cash flow of £1,000 p.a. Its shareholders require a return of 10 per cent. The market will value Divicut at £1,000/10% = £10,000 on unchanged policies. If the company announces its intention to retain 50 per cent of earnings in *all* future years to finance projects offering a perpetual yield of 15 per cent, market value according to the dividend growth model is, recalling that growth $= bR$:

$$V = \frac{E_1(1-b)}{(k_e - g)} = \frac{E_1(1-b)}{(k_e - bR)} = \frac{£1,000(1-0.5)}{0.1 - (0.5 \times 0.15)} = \frac{£500}{0.025} = £20,000$$

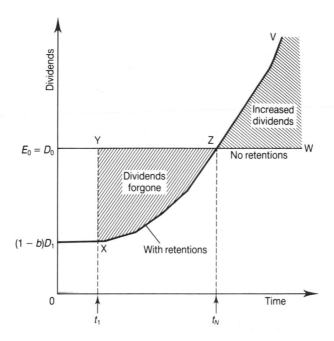

Figure 13.1 The impact of a dividend cut

This may seem a remarkable result. The decision to retain and reinvest doubles company value! Does this mean that dividend payments make shareholders worse off? The answer is simple.

Payment of dividends may make shareholders worse off than they otherwise might be if distribution results in failure to exploit a worthwhile investment opportunity. In other words, the beneficial impact on Divicut's value is achieved because of the inherent attractions of the projected investments. Conversely, if the funds had been invested to yield only 5 per cent, market value would fall to £6,666.

The in-between case, where the return on reinvested funds, $R = k_e = 10$ percent, leaves company value unchanged. This suggests that if we strip out the effects of the investment decision, the dividend decision itself has a *neutral* effect. This can be done by assuming retained earnings are used to finance projects which yield an aggregate NPV of zero, i.e. yielding a return of k_e. With this assumption, we find that dividend decisions are irrelevant to shareholder wealth. If Divicut achieves a return on reinvested funds of 10 per cent, the company's value is:

$$V_0 = \frac{E(1-b)}{(k_e - g)} = \frac{£1,000(1-0.5)}{0.1 - (0.5 \times 0.1)} = \frac{£500}{0.05} = £10,000$$

Here, we have valued the dividend stream, and the result is equivalent to valuing the steady stream of earnings with no retentions. This equivalence may perhaps be more readily seen by manipulating the expressions for value. If we neutralize the effect of the investment decision so that $k_e = R$, we may write:

$$V_0 = \frac{E(1-b)}{(k_e - g)} = \frac{E(1-b)}{(k_e - bR)} = \frac{E(1-b)}{(k_e - bk_e)} = \frac{E(1-b)}{k_e(1-b)} = \frac{E}{k_e}$$

There are clear conclusions from this analysis:

1. *If the expected return on reinvested funds exceeds k_e*, it is beneficial to retain (in the absence of alternative financing). A dividend cut will lead to higher value but only because funds are used to finance worthwhile projects.
2. *If the return on reinvested funds is less than k_e*, retention damages shareholder interests. A dividend cut would lower company value because shareholders have more profitable uses for capital.
3. *If the return on reinvested funds equals k_e*, the impact of a dividend cut to finance investment is neutral.

Dividends as a residual

The dividend decision is simply the obverse of the investment decision. As we observed earlier, we are examining the impact of one of the various ways in which proposed investment may be financed. By implication, we have been looking at a case where the company feels obliged to retain funds through lack of alternative financing options. If we make this assumption more explicit, i.e. that the firm is capital-rationed with access only to internal sources of finance, we can illustrate the *residual theory of dividends*.

This argues that dividends should only be paid when there are no further worthwhile investment opportunities. Having decided the optimal set of investment projects, and determined the required amount of financing, the firm should distribute to shareholders only those monies not required for investment financing. It follows that dividends are merely a residual after meeting the financing needs of acceptable new investments. This idea is shown graphically in Figure 13.2, using the *Marginal Efficiency of Investment (MEI) model*.

With current year free cash flow of OE_0, there is scope for dividend payments. The limit of worthwhile investment is at X where the return on the last unit of investment is equal to the minimum required return k_e. The company can now make residual dividend payments of XE_0. However, if the free cash flow is OE_1, distribution would impose an opportunity cost on shareholders. The whole cash flow should be reinvested, but it falls short of the finance required to support the optimal programme. The shortfall is E_1X, which could be plugged by external sources of funds if we relax the assumption of capital rationing. External financing is considered later in this section.

One-off dividend cuts

The original MM analysis contains a proof of dividend irrelevance in terms of a single dividend cut rather than the switch from a policy of no retentions to one of permanent

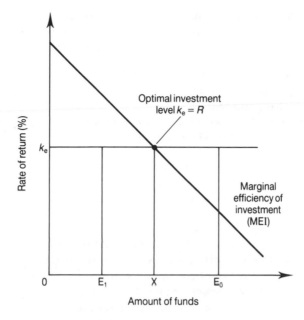

Figure 13.2 Dividends as a residual

internal financing. MM envisaged an all-equity-financed company which has previously paid out its entire annual net cash flow as dividend. To illustrate their analysis, let us return to Divicut. Recall that prior to any alteration in dividend policy, the value of Divicut was £10,000, derived by discounting the earnings stream to infinity. If the management now decide to retain the whole of next year's dividend in order to invest in a project offering a single cash flow of £1,200 in the following year, the new market value of Divicut equals the present value of the revised dividend flow, assuming a reversion to 100 per cent payouts:

Year	1	2	3	4	etc.
Dividend (£)	0	1,200	1,000	1,000	

This revised dividend flow is only acceptable if the resulting market value is at least equal to the pre-decision value, i.e. if the NPV of the project exceeds zero. Clearly, this is the case as:

PV of £1,200 in two years > P.V. of £1,000 in one year, i.e.:

$$\frac{£1,200}{(1.1)^2} > \frac{£1,000}{(1.1)}$$
$$£992 > £909.$$

Divicut's shareholders are better off by £83. As in the continuous reinvestment case, shareholder wealth is enhanced since Divicut has utilized the funds released by the dividend cut to finance a worthwhile project. Parallel conclusions apply to the cases where $R < k_e$ and where $R = k_e$. In every case, any impact on company value is attributable to the investment, rather than the dividend, decision.

MM's dividend irrelevance conclusion was obtained in a world of certainty, then extended to the case of risk/uncertainty where the same conclusions emerge so long as investor behaviour and attitudes conform to 'symmetric market rationality'. This requires:

1. All investors are maximizers of expected wealth.
2. All investors have similar expectations.
3. All investors behave rationally.
4. All investors believe that other market participants will behave rationally and that other investors expect rational behaviour from them.

These assumptions were spelled out by Brennan (1971) and form part of the battery of conditions required for a perfect capital market. The additional assumptions required to support the 'irrelevance' hypothesis are:

1. No transaction costs or brokerage fees.
2. All investors have equal and costless access to information.
3. All investors can lend or borrow at the same rate of interest.
4. No buyer or seller of securities can influence prices.
5. No personal or corporate income or capital gains taxes.
6. Dividend decisions are not used to convey information.

The full significance of some of these assumptions will be highlighted when we examine some of the reasons why, in practice, shareholders may have a definite preference for either dividends or retentions. First, however, we need to consider the case where the firm has access to external financing. Rather than use earnings retention to finance investment, the firm may make a rights issue of shares, i.e. offer existing shareholders the right to buy new shares in proportion to their present holdings. If they all exercise their rights, then the existing balance of control is unchanged. To sustain the irrelevance conclusion, we need to show that shareholder wealth is unaffected by choice of financing medium.

External equity financing: yet more Divicut

To illustrate the effect of using external equity funding, consider the case where Divicut contemplates a one-off dividend cut to finance a project requiring an outlay of £1,000, and offering perpetual annual earnings of £200. It is not yet quoted ex-dividend. Its options are to retain or to pay the dividend out of current earnings and then recoup the required finance via a rights issue. The project itself is worthwhile since its NPV is:

$$\text{NPV} = -£1,000 + \frac{£200}{0.1} = -£1,000 + £2,000 = +£1,000$$

The implications for shareholder wealth of each of the two financing alternatives are:

1. If the dividend is passed, the value of shareholder wealth (W) is:

$W =$ (dividend in year 0) + (P.V. of dividends from existing projects) + (P.V. of dividends from new projects)

$$=0+\frac{£1,000}{0.1}+\frac{£200}{0.1}=£10,000+£2,000=£12,000$$

Retention therefore benefits Divicut's shareholders since £1,000 now is exchanged for a dividend stream with present value of £2,000.

2. If a rights issue is used to recoup the required capital, the wealth of shareholders is:

$W=$(dividend in year 0)$+$(P.V. of dividends from existing projects)
$+$(P.V. of dividends from new projects)
$-$(amount subscribed for new shares)

$$=£1,000+\frac{£1,000}{0.1}+\frac{£200}{0.1}-£1,000$$
$$=£1,000+£10,000+£2,000-£1,000=£12,000$$

Shareholders' wealth is unaffected if they elect to subscribe for the new shares, anticipating the higher future stream of dividends implied by the new venture. The attraction of the rights issue alternative to some people is that it offers a choice between further investment in the company and an alternative use of capital (although this second option may be irrational if k_e accurately measures the opportunity cost of capital). Either way, companies ensure they obtain the required funds by employing specialist financial institutions to underwrite such issues.

Summary

This section has demonstrated that *dividends are only relevant to company valuation in the absence of external financing* in the sense that, if the company has better investment opportunities than its shareholders, payment of dividends prevents worthwhile investment being undertaken. *With external financing, however, in a perfect market, dividends become totally irrelevant since dividend payment no longer precludes worthwhile investment.* The firm can simply recoup the required finance via a rights issue.

In the next section, we begin to unpick some of the assumptions underpinning the irrelevance theory and consider the implications.

13.5 Objections to dividend irrelevance

This section examines some of the arguments advanced against the irrelevance theory. We will discover that there are several important considerations which the practising financial manager should weigh up before deciding the appropriate dividend payout policy. These are:

1. To what extent do shareholders rely on dividend income?
2. Are nearer-in-time dividends less risky than future dividends?
3. Do market imperfections lead companies to adopt policies which attract a certain clientele of investors?

4. How does taxation affect dividend policy?
5. Are dividend announcements used to convey information about company prospects?

Let us deal with these questions in turn.

Do shareholders rely on dividend income to support expenditures?

Shareholders who require a steady and reliable stream of income from dividends may be concerned by a sudden change in dividend policy, especially a dividend cut, albeit to finance worthwhile projects. Some groups of shareholders may well exhibit a marked preference for current income, for example, the elderly and institutions such as pension funds, which depend on a stable flow of income to meet their largely predictable liabilities. However, in an efficient capital market, such shareholders should be no worse off after a dividend cut since they will find that the value of their holdings will rise on the news of the new investment. They can realize some or all of their gains, thus converting capital into income. The capital released is called a 'home-made dividend'. An example to show how this works is given in the Appendix.

There are several criticisms of the validity of the home-made dividends mechanism for supporting the irrelevance thesis. Even in the absence of market imperfections, the investor is forced to incur the inconvenience of making the required portfolio adjustments. Allowing for brokerage and other transactions costs, the net benefits of the project for the income-seeking investor are reduced. Also, if the fiscal regime includes taxation of capital gains, the enforced share sale may trigger a tax liability. In the case of only marginally attractive projects, these effects may be sufficient to more than offset the benefits of the project, at least for some groups of investors. (Conversely, it can be argued that payment of a dividend to investors who then incur brokerage fees in reinvesting their income is equally disadvantageous.)

Are future dividends seen as more risky by shareholders?

The practical limitations on the unfettered ability to home-make dividends were spelt out by Myron Gordon (1963) in a ringing attack on MM's irrelevance conclusion. However, Gordon extended his critique of MM to argue that $1 of dividend now is valued more highly than $1 of retained earnings because investors regard the albeit higher future stream of dividends stemming from a new project as carrying a higher level of risk. In other words, investors prefer what Gordon called an *early resolution of uncertainty*. Gordon was, in effect, arguing that shareholders evaluate future expected dividends using a set of rising discount rates. If present dividends are reduced to allow greater investment, thus shifting the dividend pattern into the future, company value will fall. Keane (1974) refined Gordon's position by suggesting that it is secondary whether, in fact, future dividends *are* more risky than near ones. If investors *perceive* them to be riskier, a policy of higher retentions, while not actually increasing risk, may unfavourably alter investor attitudes. In capital markets where full information is not released about investment projects, investors' subjective risk assessments may result in low pay-out companies being valued at a discount compared to high pay-out companies; that is, investors' imperfect perception of risk may lead them to undervalue the future dividend stream generated by retentions.

The 'bird-in-the-hand fallacy'

If the firm's dividend policy does alter the perceived riskiness of the expected dividend flow, there may be an optimal dividend policy which trades off the beneficial effects of an enhanced growth rate against the adverse impact of increased perceived risk, so as to maximize the market value. However, advocates of dividend irrelevance argue that the Gordon analysis is inherently fallacious. More distant dividends are only more risky if they stem from riskier investment projects. Risk will already have been catered for by discounting cash flows at a suitably risk-adjusted rate, using the CAPM. To deflate future dividends for risk further would involve double-counting. There is no reason why risk *necessarily* increases with time – a model based on this supposition incorporates the 'bird-in-the-hand fallacy'. According to MM, dividend policy remains a mere detail once a firm's investment policy, and its inherent business risks, is made known.

Market imperfections and the clientele effect

The extent to which investors are willing and able to home-make dividends, and thus adjust the company's actual dividend pattern to suit their own personal desired consumption plans, depends on the degree of imperfection within the capital market. In practice, there are numerous impediments hindering this process which, although taken in isolation may appear relatively trivial, when aggregated, may significantly offset the benefits endowed on shareholders by the exploitation of a profitable project. Some of these have already been mentioned, but the main ones are:

1. Brokerage costs incurred when shares are sold.
2. Other transaction costs incurred, e.g. the costs of searching around for the cheapest brokerage facilities.
3. The loss in interest incurred in waiting for settlement.
4. The problem of indivisibilities whereby investors may be unable to sell precisely the number of shares required, forcing them to deal in sub-optimal batch sizes.
5. The sheer inconvenience of being forced to alter one's portfolio.
6. Share sales may trigger a capital gains tax liability.
7. If the company is relatively small, its shares may lack marketability, requiring a significant dealing spread and hence a leakage of shareholder capital.
8. If the company is unquoted, it may be extremely difficult to find a buyer for the shares at all.

Under such imperfections, maximization of the firm's market value may not be the unique desire of all shareholders, i.e. the pattern of receipt of wealth may become equally or more important. Some shareholders may actively prefer companies that offer dividend flows which correspond to their desired consumption, perhaps being prepared to pay a premium to hold these shares. In this way, they avoid having to make their own adjustments. The vehicle for aiding such investors is to provide a stable and known dividend stream. Shareholders can perceive the nature of the likely future dividend pattern and decide whether or not the company's policy meets their requirements. In other words, the company attracts and attempts to cater for a clientele of shareholders.

However, there are costs of pursuing such a policy, even though shareholders may be spared the adjustment costs of a fluid dividend policy. Among these are the forgone benefits from projects which have to be passed over, the costs of borrowing if debt finance is used, and/or the issue expenses of a rights issue if external financing is employed. The possible implications for control if rights are not fully exercised by the shareholders themselves may be another issue.

The difficulty facing the financial manager stems from lack of knowledge of shareholder preferences, without which he has little to guide him in attempting to balance the two sets of costs. *A consistent, stable dividend policy may seem the best way of attracting and retaining a clientele of shareholders whose needs are matched to company pay-out policy.* In this respect, stability means a roughly constant and predictable rate of dividend growth, rather than erratic increases, however large.

Problems with rights issues: Rawdon plc

The costs of making rights issues can be substantial, and will affect the required return on new investment. Among the costs are the administrative expenses, the costs of printing and circularizing shareholders, and also the underwriters' fees. The impact of these costs is examined using the case of Rawdon plc, whose details are shown in Table 13.2.

Although Rawdon's shareholders require a return of 20%, the new project has to offer a return of *over* 20 per cent. This is because some of the finance raised by the share issue is required to meet the costs of the issue but the holders of those shares will nevertheless demand a return. Total share capital is now £6m, and earnings of £1.2m are now required to generate a 20 per cent return overall. However, the required increase in earnings of £0.2m must be generated by an investment of £950,000, necessitating a return of (£0.2m/ £0.95m) = 21.1 per cent. Rawdon's required return on this project is also given by:

$$\frac{\text{Normally required return}}{(1-\% \text{ issue costs})} = \frac{k_e}{(1-c)} = \frac{0.2}{1-0.05} = 0.211, \text{ i.e. } 21.1\%$$

The problem of transactions costs may operate in another direction, however. There may be some shareholders who, when paid a dividend, incur personal reinvestment costs.

Table 13.2 Rawdon plc

1m shares have been issued in the past,	$k_e = 20\%$
Market price per share is £5	Rawdon's value = £5m
Current company earnings =	£1m i.e. EPS = £1
Proposed investment outlay =	£950,000.
The project has a perpetual life.	

Terms of rights issue: One share for every five held, i.e. 200,000 new shares
Purchase price £5: Gross Proceeds = £1m
Issue costs 5% of gross receipts = 0.05 × £1m = £50,000.
Net Proceeds = £950,000

The higher the proportion of investors who wish to reinvest, either in the same or in another company, the greater the total saving of brokerage and other fees enjoyed by shareholders, which the company retains. Hence, the greater is the attraction of retained earnings to finance investment.

The Rawdon example assumes that the rights issue is made at the current share price. In practice, rights issues are made at a discount, partly to make them look attractive and thus encourage shareholders to subscribe, and partly to safeguard against the risk that prices will fall during the offer period (i.e. between the announcement of the issue and the first day of dealing, when the shares go 'ex-rights'). For example, instead of Rawdon offering a one-for-five rights at the market price of £5, it may offer two-for-five at the discount price of £2.5 per share. This looks a bargain until it is realized that the same amount of earnings will now be distributed among a larger number of shares (although to the same number of shareholders if the issue is fully subscribed). Post-issue, there will be 7m shares resulting in EPS of £1m divided by 7m shares, that is, 14p per share, and earnings are said to have been 'diluted'. This is likely to reduce share price simply because fewer earnings are now attributable to each share. The ex-rights share price can be predicted. Consider the holder of each five-share 'package':

Before issue	After issue
5 shares at £5 = £25	5 shares at £5 = £25
Cash = £5	2 shares at £2.5 = £5
Total £30	Total £30
	Price per share = £30/7 = £4.29

Clearly, the proffered discount looks much less attractive (although the likely impact on share price will be less pronounced if the market regards the project as a positive NPV proposition). Anyone who fails to take up the offer thus loses 71p per share. To compensate, the right to subscribe at the discount price can be sold on the market for:

$$\text{(Expected post-issue price} - \text{discount price)} \times \text{Number of shares}$$
$$= \quad £4.29 \quad - \quad £2.50) \quad \times \quad 2 \quad = £3.58$$

Allowing for rounding, this corresponds to the loss in wealth incurred by someone who failed to take up the issue, i.e. $5 \times (£5.00 - £4.29)$.

It can be appreciated that the announcement of a rights issue is not always greeted with delight. The shareholder is forced either to take up or sell the rights if he or she wishes to avoid losing money (even sale of rights will result in brokerage fees), and thus incur the inconvenience involved simply to stand still! If the market takes a dim view of the proposed use of the capital thus raised (for example, if the funds to be raised are required to finance a takeover whose benefits look distinctly speculative), there could also be a downward adjustment of share price prior to their going ex-rights. *It is important to recognize that this would be a consequence of a faulty investment decision rather than the financing decision itself.*

The impact of taxation

In many economies, the tax treatment of dividend income and realized capital gains differs, either via differential tax rates or via different levels of exemption allowed, or both. In such regimes, the theoretical equivalence between dividends and retention becomes further distorted. Some shareholders might prefer 'home-made dividends' as the Capital Gains Tax (CGT) may be lower than the marginal rate of income tax applied to dividends. Others may prefer dividend payments because their income tax liability plus any reinvestment costs are lower than CGT payments.

Elton and Gruber (1970) noted the importance of marginal tax brackets in determining the return required by shareholders. They defined the cost of using retained earnings as 'that rate which makes a firm's marginal shareholders indifferent between earnings being retained or paid out in the form of dividends'. Under differential tax treatments of dividend income and capital gains, the cost of using retained earnings is a function of the shareholder's marginal tax bracket. We might also expect companies whose shareholders incur high rates of income tax to exhibit low pay-out rates. Such a relationship between corporate dividend policy and shareholder tax brackets would support the notion of the 'clienteles' whereby companies seek to tailor their pay-out policies to the needs of particular shareholders. Elton and Gruber's empirical work seemed to indicate that firms attract rational clienteles – *shareholders gravitate to companies whose distribution policy is compatible with their personal tax situations.*

In addition to considerations of personal taxation, where the financial manager has little way of knowing the particular tax positions of shareholders (a major exception to this is the case of institutional investors), there may also be complications imposed by the nature of the corporate tax system. In an imputation tax system, shareholders receive dividend income net of basic rate tax, while the rate of tax applied to corporate profits is designed to include an element of personal tax, thus making the distribution of dividends tax-neutral. However, in the United Kingdom, the payment of a dividend triggers off liability to pay Advance Corporation Tax (ACT), although this can be 'relieved', that is, offset, against Mainstream Corporation Tax (MCT) liability. The dividend-paying company effectively makes an interest-free loan to the tax authorities, the costs of which depend on how soon the company can relieve the ACT. In the extreme case of a company never expected to have any taxable capacity, dividend payment offers the tax authorities a permanent loan!

Further tax complications may apply when firms earn a substantial portion of their total profits overseas. For example, a UK-based company which pays dividends in the United Kingdom, will incur an ACT liability which it may be unable to relieve against its MCT liability because its UK profits (and hence MCT liability) are too low. The United Kingdom has a Double Tax Agreement with many other nations so that profits already taxed abroad are not taxed again when repatriated. However, ACT paid to the Inland Revenue in the United Kingdom cannot be offset against tax payable to foreign tax authorities. Yeadon plc illustrates this point (Table 13.3).

An ACT problem may constrain company dividend policy and also influence corporate strategy. In the early 1980s, a major motive for Rio Tinto Zinc's takeover of T. W. Ward, an engineering and building materials group, was to establish a larger UK profits base to afford a faster rate of recovery of ACT.

Table 13.3 Yeadon plc

UK Profits	Profits Earned Overseas	Total
£10.0m	£100.0m (overseas tax paid)	£110.0m

UK Corporation Tax liability at 33%	= £3.3m
Dividend payout from total profits	= £30.0m
ACT = 25/75 × £30.0m	= £10.0m
MCT = 0 since ACT exceeds UK tax liability	
Unrelieved ACT = (£10.0m − £3.3m)	= £6.7m

Two more recent manifestations of the ACT phenomenon are equally interesting. First, consider the difficulty faced by BP, when ordered by the Monopolies and Mergers Commission to repurchase 12 per cent of its own shares, involving an outlay of some £2,400m, from the Kuwaiti Investment Office, which had built up a 22 per cent holding, deemed by the MMC as likely to operate against the public interest. Share repurchase is treated as a dividend for tax purposes and thus triggers an ACT liability. Over the required repurchase period of two years, BP was barely able to earn sufficient UK profits to offset the ACT payable via its MCT liability, producing a less generous distribution policy than it might otherwise have followed.

Second, consider the purchase in 1989 by Fisons, the scientific instrument maker, of VG Instruments from BAT Industries. The outlay was £270m, some 21 times current VGI's reported profit. This reduced the net cost by £25m due to Fisons' ability to recover from the Inland Revenue ACT relating to previously paid dividends. This was possible because most of VGI's profits were generated in Britain while Fisons' earnings mainly arose overseas.

The information content of dividends

Possibly the most important consideration which corporate decision-makers should recognize is the information-processing capacity of the market. Any dividend declaration, whether an increase, a decrease or even no change, can be interpreted by the market in a variety of ways. In an uncertain world, information regarding a company's prospects is neither generally available nor costless to acquire. Managers possess more information about the company's trading position than is available to investors as a whole. This so-called *information asymmetry* may mean that the announcement of a new or changed company policy may be interpreted by the market as a signal conveying particular information about a company's prospects.

For example, the decision to pay an unexpectedly high dividend may be seized upon by a market avid for new information as evidence of a greater expected dividend-paying capacity in both near and future time periods. It may be taken as guaranteeing an ability to sustain at least the higher declared dividend and probably more in the future. The dividend decision as an imparter of hitherto unavailable information thus becomes an important indicator of future prospects (or manager's assessment of them). As a result, *the financial manager should consider carefully how the market is likely to decode the signals contained in the dividend decision, and the likely consequences for share price.*

The dividend puzzle

Let us briefly review the 'dividend puzzle'. In theory, dividend policy is irrelevant in terms of its impact on shareholder wealth once we strip out the impact of the investment decision (unless shareholders suffer from the 'bird-in-the-hand fallacy'). This suggests companies might, with impunity, impose dividend cuts in order to finance worthwhile investment projects, leaving income-seeking shareholders to home-make their required level of dividends.

Yet, as the case of Lonrho indicates, the City views dividend increases with enthusiasm, especially unexpectedly high ones, and regards dividend cuts with horror. Moreover, empirical work by Ghosh and Woolridge (1989) suggests only a small minority of dividend cuts was in practice motivated by the need to conserve investment funds but, in these cases, shareholders suffered significant capital losses despite the merits claimed for the proposed investments.

Few financial managers are prepared to post higher dividends when the firm's ability to maintain these higher payments is in doubt, and then have to suffer the indignity of subsequently having to rescind the increase. This appears to be because dividend decisions are widely considered to signal information to the market about future company prospects. Certainly, when we examine the time profile of dividend payments over time, as shown in Figure 13.3 relating to all quoted UK companies, we see that dividends are far less volatile than earnings.

At a practical level, we thus encounter a dilemma. Dividend cuts are undesirable yet dividend payments are not always in the best interests of shareholders! For example, under many tax regimes, dividends are immediately taxed, while the tax on capital gains can be deferred indefinitely. Also, dividend distribution may force a firm subsequently to issue equity or debt instruments which incur issue costs and interfere with gearing ratios (examined in the next chapter). Furthermore, UK firms face the extra tax penalty of ACT. However, markets *do* react favourably to news of unexpectedly high dividend increases

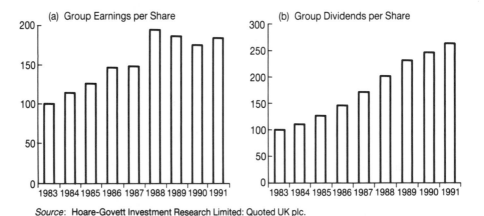

Source: Hoare-Govett Investment Research Limited: Quoted UK plc.

Figure 13.3 EPS and DPS for Quoted UK companies

despite the acknowledged costs of dividends. The message conveyed by firms when raising dividends seems to be:

> 'Despite the costs of dividend payments, we are prepared to pay higher dividends because we are confident of our ability to withstand these costs and to at least maintain these higher disbursements.'

13.6 The case for a stable dividend policy

Astute financial managers appreciate that different shareholders have different needs. A financial institution reliant on a stream of income to match its stream of liabilities will prefer *stable* dividends, while a 'gross fund', i.e. one exempt from tax on its income, will prefer shares which offer a *high* level of dividends. The private individual in the 40 per cent tax bracket will prefer capital gains, at least up to the £5,800 exemption limit (1992/3), while the old-age pensioner with a relatively short time horizon is likely to seek income rather than capital appreciation. Given the wide diffusion of shareholdings, it is nigh impossible for most financial managers to begin to assess the needs of all their shareholders, especially if their identity alters as holdings are bought and sold. This is an argument for a stable dividend policy, e.g. the application of a fairly constant dividend cover, implying that dividends rise at the same rate as corporate post-tax earnings, subject perhaps to the proviso that dividends should not be allowed to fall, unless earnings suffer a serious reverse. This will enable *shareholders to gravitate towards companies whose pay-out policies suit their particular income needs and tax positions.* In this way, companies can expect to build up a clientele of shareholders attracted by a particular dividend pattern.

A new development: Personal Equity Plans

As an inducement to wider share ownership, the British government announced in its 1986 Budget the introduction of Personal Equity Plans (PEPs), which first became available on 1 January 1987. These plans provide a vehicle for equity investment and are operated by professional managers, usually financial institutions, approved by the Inland Revenue. The main attractions of PEPs are the exemption from tax of any dividend income and capital gains relating to all the component equities held in the plan portfolio. Initially, the main appeal was for high rate tax payers for whom the income tax relief enjoyed would outweigh the often substantial management charges levied by the plan operators. A drawback of the initial scheme was the requirement that a plan be held for at least a calendar year, a restriction since removed. But the appeal of PEPs was diminished by tax reforms in 1988, cutting the top rate of income tax from 60 per cent to 40 per cent, and making capital gains above the exemption taxable as income.

Despite the lower income tax benefits, the popularity of PEPs has steadily increased, partly due to wider publicity, and partly due to greater competition among plan managers resulting in lower management charges. Investors may select high-yielding shares to incorporate into PEPs to maximize tax benefits. For example, an investment of £6,000 (the limit for 1992/3) in shares with a 7 per cent gross-of-tax dividend yield generates net income of £252 for a 40 per cent rate taxpayer, but invested in a PEP, the tax credit of £168 can be reclaimed. An alert financial manager is likely to consider the tax attractions of PEPs when formulating dividend policy since high payouts may attract a clientele of PEP investors seeking tax shelters.

13.7   Conclusions

What advice can be offered to the practising financial manager? We suggest the following guidelines.

(1)   Remember the capacity of ill-advised dividend decisions to inflict damage. In view of the market's often savage reaction to dividend cuts, the financial manager should operate a safe dividend cover, allowing sufficient pay-out flexibility should earnings decline. This suggests a commitment to a clientele of shareholders who have come to expect a particular dividend policy from their company. This in turn suggests a long-term pay-out ratio sufficient to satisfy shareholder needs, but also generating sufficient internal funds to finance 'normal' investment requirements. Any 'abnormal' financing needs can be met by selling securities, rather than by dividend cuts. However, as a long-term aim, it seems sensible to minimize reliance on external finance, but not to the extent of building up the sort of 'cash mountains' which some companies have erected. While the company may regard these as funds for financing future investment, they merely signal to the financial world that the company has run out of acceptable investment projects. If there is no worthwhile alternative use of capital, then dividends should be paid, certainly now that tax penalties on distribution have been lowered.

(2)   If an alteration in dividend policy is proposed, the firm should carefully prepare the way to minimize the shock effect of an unanticipated dividend cut, e.g. by explaining in advance the firm's investment programme and its financing needs.

(3)   Managers should realize why the market reacts so strongly to unexpected dividend changes. In an efficient capital market, the dividend announcement, 'good' or 'bad', will be immediately impounded into share price in an unbiased fashion. News of higher dividends will lead to a higher share price because it conveys the information that management believe there is a strong likelihood of higher future earnings and dividends. In view of this, many observers argue that the primary role of dividend policy should be to *communicate information* to a security market otherwise starved of hard financial data about future company prospects and intrinsic value, while pursuing a year-by-year distribution rate which does not violate the interests of the existing clientele of shareholders.

Table 13.4 Dividends are preferable

- The greater the shareholders' reliance on current income.
- The more difficult it is to generate home-made dividends.
- The greater the impact of imperfections, e.g. brokerage fees.
- The lower are income taxes compared to capital gains taxes.
- The lower the costs of a rights issue.
- The greater the ease of re-investment by shareholders.
- The greater the ability of the company to relieve ACT.
- The more often past dividend increases have heralded subsequent earnings and dividend increases.

(4) While it is impossible to be definitive in this area, it is possible to offer a checklist of circumstances in which shareholders are more likely to prefer dividends to retention and potential capital appreciation. These circumstances are indicated in Table 13.4.

(5) Finally, consider whether the dividend decision is as important as it appears! It is 'only' a financing decision, in so far as paying a dividend may necessitate alternative arrangements for financing investment projects. There can be few companies (at least, quoted ones) for whom dividends have constrained worthwhile investment. For most companies, it is often sensible to adopt a modest target pay-out ratio. It is not too clever to pay large dividends and then have to incur the costs of raising equity from the very same shareholders.

13.8 Summary

In this chapter, we have reviewed the competing arguments regarding the relative desirability of paying out dividends to shareholders and retaining funds to finance investment, resulting in capital gains.

Key points

- The market value of a company ultimately depends on its dividend-paying capacity.
- The irrelevance or residual theory of dividends argues that, under perfect capital market conditions, an alteration in the pattern of dividend payouts has no impact on company values, once the effect of the investment decision is removed.
- If retentions are used to finance worthwhile investment, company value increases, and vice versa, both for one-off retentions and for sustained retention to finance an ongoing investment programme.
- Failure to retain can damage shareholder interests if the company has better investment opportunities than shareholders, unless outside capital sources are available and utilized.
- The examination of ongoing retention is problematic, due to the assumptions of the DGM.

- Dividend irrelevance implies that shareholders are indifferent between dividends and capital gains, because the latter can be converted into income.
- In practice, various market imperfections, especially transactions costs and taxes, interfere with this conclusion, although it is difficult to be categoric about the net directional impact.
- Companies are generally unable to detect shareholder preferences, so they should follow a stable dividend policy, designed to suit a particular category, or 'clientele', of shareholders.
- In practice, companies are reluctant to cut dividends for fear of adverse interpretation by the market of the information conveyed in the announcement.
- Similarly, companies are reluctant to increase dividends too sharply for fear of encouraging over-optimistic expectations about future performance.
- This 'information content' in dividend decisions provides a further argument for dividend stability.

Appendix Home-made dividends

Kirkstall plc is financed solely by equity. Its cash flow from existing operations is expected to be £24m p.a. in perpetuity, all of which has hitherto been paid as dividend. Shareholders require a return of 12 per cent. Kirkstall has previously issued 50m shares. The value of the dividend stream is:

$$V = \frac{£24m}{0.12} = £200m, \text{ yielding share price of } \frac{£200m}{50m} = £4 \text{ (ex-div)}$$

Imagine you hold 1 per cent of Kirkstall's equity, worth £2m. This yields an annual dividend income of £240,000, all of which you require to support your lavish lifestyle. Kirkstall proposes to pass the dividend payable in one year's time in order to invest in a project offering a single net cash flow after a further year of £40m, when the previous 100 per cent payout policy will be resumed. Your new expected dividend flow is:

Year 1	Year 2	Year 3
0	£240,000 + (1% × £40m) = £640,000	£240,000

The market value of Kirkstall rises to:

$$\begin{aligned} V &= 0 + \frac{£64m}{(1.12)^2} + \left[\frac{£24m}{(0.12)} \times \frac{1}{(1.12)^2} \right] \\ &= £51.02m + £159.39m = £210.41m. \end{aligned}$$

The increase in value reflects the NPV of the project. Share price rises from £4 to £4.21, thus raising the value of your holding from £2m to £2.104m. To support your living standards, you could either borrow on the strength of the higher expected dividend in Year 2 or sell part of your share stake in Year 1 when there is no dividend proposed.

In Year 1, the value of your holding will be £2.356m, and each share will be priced at

£4.71. To provide sufficient capital to finance expenditure of £240,000 you need to sell £240,000/£4.71 = 50,955 shares, reducing your holding to (500,000 − 50,955) = 449,045 shares. In Year 2, Kirkstall will distribute a dividend of £64m (£1.28 per share) of which your share will be £574,778. Out of this, you will require £240,000 for immediate consumption, leaving you better off by £334,778. This may be used to restore your previous shareholding, and thus your previous flow of dividends. The ex-dividend share price in Year 2 will settle back to £4, at which price the repurchase of 50,955 shares will require an outlay of £203,820, leaving you a surplus of (£334,778 − £203,820) = £130,958. The net effect of your transactions is to yield an income flow of:

Year	1	2	3 etc.
Dividend paid by company	0	£574,778	£240,000
Market transaction	£240,000	− £203,820	
Net income	£240,000	£370,958	£240,000

Overall, your shareholding remains the same, and you earn extra income in Year 2 of £130,958. This has a present value of £104,000, the amount of your wealth increase when Kirkstall first announced details of the project:

i.e. 1% × change in market value
= 1% × (£210.41m − £200m)

(note that rounding errors account for minor deviations).

Further reading

A good feel for the dividend policy debate can be obtained from the early articles by Gordon (1959) and Miller and Modigliani (1961), and Gordon's rejoinder to MM (1963). Bhattacharya (1979) gives a vigorous treatment of the bird-in-the-hand fallacy, while Miller (1986) provides an overview of the debate so far. Copeland and Weston (1988) offer chapters on both the theory of dividend policy and also the empirical evidence.

Questions

Self-test questions

1. Explain the conditions under which sustained retention can raise company value and shareholder wealth.
2. What is suspect about Gordon's argument regarding the impact of retention on company value?
3. What conditions are required to make shareholders indifferent between dividend income and capital gain?

4. Why may Advance Corporation Tax present a problem regarding dividend policy in the United Kingdom?

5. What are the arguments in favour of a stable dividend policy?

6. What is meant by a shareholder 'clientele'?

Exercises

1. Galahad plc, a quoted manufacturer of textiles, has followed a policy in recent years of paying out a steadily increasing dividend per share as shown below:

Year	EPS	Dividend (net)	Cover
1986	11.8p	5.0p	2.4
1987	12.5p	5.5p	2.3
1988	14.6p	6.0p	2.4
1989	13.5p	6.5p	2.1
1990	16.0p	7.3p	2.2

Galahad has only just made the 1990 dividend payment, and so the shares are quoted ex-dividend. The main board, which is responsible for strategic planning decisions, is considering a major change in strategy whereby greater financing will be provided by internal funds, involving a cut in the 1991 dividend to 5p (net) per share. The investment projects thus funded will increase the growth rate of Galahad's earnings and dividends to 14 per cent. Some operating managers, however, feel that the new growth rate is unlikely to exceed 12 per cent. Galahad's shareholders seek an overall return of 16 per cent.

Required

(a) Calculate the market price per share for Galahad, prior to the change in policy, using the dividend growth model.

(b) Assess the likely impact on Galahad's share price of the proposed policy change.

(c) Determine the break-even growth rate.

(d) Discuss the possible reaction of Galahad's shareholders and of the capital market in general to this proposed dividend cut in the light of Galahad's past dividend policy.

(Solution in Appendix A)

2. Laceby manufactures agricultural equipment and is currently all-equity financed. In previous years, it has paid out a steady 50 per cent of available earnings as dividend and used retentions to finance investment in new projects, which have returned 16 per cent on average.

Its Beta is 0.83, the return on the market portfolio is expected to be 17 per cent in the future, offering a risk premium of 6 per cent.

Laceby has just made earnings of £8m before tax and the dividend will be paid in a few weeks' time. Some managers argue in favour of retaining an extra £2m this year in order to finance the development of a new CAP surplus crop disposal machine. This may offer the following returns under the listed possible scenarios:

	Prob	(£mpa) Cash Flow (pre-tax)
GATT talks succeed	0.2	0.5
No reform of CAP	0.6	1.5
CAP extended to Eastern Europe	0.2	4.0

The project may be assumed to have an infinite life, and to attract an EC agricultural efficiency grant of £1m. Corporation Tax is paid at 33 per cent (assume no tax delay).

Required

(a) What is the NPV of the proposed project?
(b) Value the equity of Laceby:
   (i) before undertaking the project,
   (ii) after announcing the acceptance of the project.
(c) Assuming you have found an increase in value in (b) (ii), explain what conditions would be required to support such a conclusion.

3. (a) Pavlon plc has recently obtained a listing on the Stock Exchange. Ninety per cent of the company's shares were previously owned by members of one family but, since the listing, approximately 60 per cent of the issued shares have been owned by other investors.

Pavlon's earnings and dividends for the five years prior to the listing are detailed below:

Years Prior to Listing	Profit after Tax (£)	Dividend per Share (pence)
5	1,800,000	3.60
4	2,400,000	4.80
3	3,850,000	6.16
2	4,100,000	6.56
1	4,450,000	7.12
Current Year	5,500,000 (estimate)	

The number of issued ordinary shares was increased by 25 per cent three years prior to the listing and by 50 per cent at the time of the listing. The company's authorized capital is currently £25,000,000 in 25p ordinary shares, of which 40,000,000 shares have been issued. The market value of the company's equity is £78,000,000.

The board of directors is discussing future dividend policy. An interim dividend of 3.16p per share was paid immediately prior to the listing and the finance director has suggested a final dividend of 2.34p per share.

The company's declared objective is to maximize shareholder wealth.

Required

(i) Comment upon the nature of the company's dividend policy prior to the listing and discuss whether such a policy is likely to be suitable for a company listed on the Stock Exchange.

(ii) Discuss whether the proposed final dividend of 2.34 pence is likely to be an appropriate dividend:

(1) If the majority of shares are owned by wealthy private individuals;

(2) If the majority of shares are owned by institutional investors.

(b) The company's profit after tax is generally expected to increase by 15 per cent p.a. for three years, and 8 per cent per year after that. Pavlon's cost of equity capital is estimated to be 12 per cent per year. Dividends may be assumed to grow at the same rate as profits.

Required

(i) Using the dividend valuation model give calculations to indicate whether Pavlon's shares are currently undervalued or overvalued.

(ii) Briefly outline the weaknesses of the dividend valuation model.

(ACCA level 3, June 1986)

4. The board of directors of Deerwood plc are arguing about the company's dividend policy.

Director A is in favour of financing all investment by retained earnings and other internally generated funds. He argues that a high level of retentions will save issue costs, and that declaring dividends always results in a fall in share price when the shares are traded ex div.

Director B believes that the dividend policy depends upon the type of shareholders that the company has, and that dividends should be paid according to shareholders' needs. She presents data to the board relating to studies of dividend policy in the United States in 1983, and a breakdown of the company's current shareholders.

USA Dividend Research

Company Group (10 companies per group)	Mean Dividend Yield (%)	Average Marginal Tax Rate of Shareholders (%)
1	7.02	16
2	5.18	22
3	4.17	25
4	3.52	33
5	1.26	45

Deerwood plc: analysis of shareholding

	Number of shareholders	Shares held (million)	% of total shares held
Pension funds	203	38.4	25.1
Insurance companies	41	7.8	5.1
Unit and investment trusts	53	18.6	12.1
Nominees	490	32.4	21.2
Individuals	44,620	55.9	36.5
	45,407	153.1	100.0

She argues that the company's shareholder 'clientele' must be identified, and dividends fixed according to their marginal tax brackets.

Director C agrees that shareholders are important, but points out that many institutional shareholders and private individuals rely on dividends to satisfy their current income requirements, and prefer a known dividend now to an uncertain capital gain in the future.

Director D considers the discussion to be a waste of time. He believes that one dividend policy is as good as any other, and that dividend policy has no effect on the company's share price. In support of his case he cites Miller and Modigliani.

Required

Critically discuss the arguments of each of the four directors using the information provided.

(ACCA Level 3, December 1989)

Practical assignment

Boots plc

Boots plc provides an excellent example of a company which apparently follows a stable dividend policy. Its earnings and dividends over a decade are shown in Table 13.5. There are some very clear features in this record. Your task is to uncover them!

Required

(a) What is the minimum annual percentage dividend increase which Boots seems to want to award its shareholders?
(b) What is the apparent relationship between the earnings increase and the rise in dividends in (i) 'good' years, and (ii) 'bad' years?
(c) Does Boots appear to have a long-term target pay-out ratio?
(d) What sort of clientele do you think Boots is attempting to serve?
(e) Obtain data for subsequent years and consider whether the policy criteria which you have identified have been adhered to.

Table 13.5   Dividend payment record of Boots plc, 1980–90

Year	Reported Earnings per share (p) (1)	% Increase (2)	Dividend per Share (p) (3)	% Increase (4)	Payout (%) (3)/(1)
1980	11.4	—	3.40	—	29.8
1981	10.7	(6.1)	3.75	10.3	35.0
1982	12.3	15.0	4.25	13.3	34.6
1983	12.7	3.3	4.75	11.8	37.4
1984	14.4	13.4	5.50	15.8	38.2
1985	15.5	7.6	6.20	12.7	40.0
1986	18.6	20.0	7.10	14.5	38.2
1987	19.5	4.8	8.00	12.7	41.0
1988	20.4	4.6	8.80	10.0	43.1
1989	22.6	8.8	10.00	13.6	44.2
1990	25.5	12.8	11.00	10.0	43.1

CHAPTER 14

Gearing and the required return

SKETCHLEY CLEANED OUT

The experiences of the dry cleaning and vending machine company Sketchley, in 1989/90, read like a corporate horror story. It made a pre-tax loss of £2m, reporting an overall loss of £8m – this in a year during which it had to stave off two hostile takeover bids incurring defence costs of £1.7m. Both bids were abandoned when the predators realized the full extent of Sketchley's trading problems, especially mounting losses in its vending division, which swung from an operating profit of £6.5m in 1988/9 to an operating loss of £1.3m in 1989/90. Increased borrowings, together with 'a more prudent accounting policy', resulting in a write-off of various bad debts, stocks and fixed assets, led to a gearing ratio of 198 per cent, breaching the borrowing levels agreed with creditors. This necessitated a £20.6m rights issue of ordinary shares, designed to lower gearing to 85 per cent. News of the issue, deeply discounted by 83p, resulted in a fall in share price of 20p. In addition, Sketchley paid no final dividend. These events reduced its capitalization to £66m, well below both the £96.5m offered by the catering services group Compass in March 1990, and the bid of £133m made by Godfrey Davis, the car-hire firm, in February 1990. Ironically, Godfrey Davis was scared off by a profits forecast of £6m, made in March 1990, which appeared disastrous compared to the profit of £17m achieved in the previous year. As the Lex column in *The Financial Times* put it: 'Shareholders in Sketchley have been kicked in the teeth so many times, they must be sending out for dentures.'

14.1 Introduction

Among the array of financing instruments available in modern capital markets, the essential choice is between debt and equity. The finance manager wishing to fund a new project, but who is reluctant to cut dividends or to make a rights issue, has to consider the borrowing option. In this chapter, we examine the arguments for and against the use of borrowed capital to finance company activities, and in particular, consider the impact which gearing may have on the overall rate of return which the company must achieve on its activities.

The main advantages of debt capital centre on its relative cost. Debt capital is usually cheaper than equity because:

1. The administrative and issuing costs are normally lower, e.g. underwriters are not usually required.
2. Debt interest is allowable against profits for tax purposes.
3. Perhaps most importantly, the pre-tax rate of interest is invariably lower than k_e, the return required by shareholders. This is due to the legally preferred position of lenders who have a prior claim on the distribution of the company's income and, in the event of liquidation, precede ordinary shareholders in the queue for the settlement of claims. Debt is usually secured on the assets of the company which can then be sold to pay off lenders in the event of default, e.g. failure to pay interest and capital according to the pre-agreed schedule.

Hence, the downside is that debt introduces *default risk*, the risk of financial failure – excessively high borrowing levels can lead to inability to meet debt interest payments in years of poor trading conditions. Shareholders are thus exposed to a second tier of risk above the inherent business risk of the trading activity. As a result, rational shareholders seek additional compensation for this extra exposure. In brief, debt is desirable because it is relatively cheap, but there may be limits to the prudent use of debt financing because, although of relatively low risk to the lender, it can be highly risky for the borrower.

In general, larger, well-established companies are likely to have a greater ability to borrow because they generate a more reliable stream of income, enhancing their ability to service (make interest payments on) debt capital. Ironically, in practice we often find that small developing companies who should not over-rely on debt capital are forced to do so through sheer inability to raise equity, while larger enterprises often operate with what appear to be very conservative gearing ratios compared with their borrowing capacities. Against this, we often encounter cases of over-geared enterprises who thought their borrowing levels were safe until they were caught out by adverse trading conditions. As Sketchley's tale of woe illustrates, *corporate problems rarely come singly and they are often associated with, and are compounded by, high borrowings.*

Clearly, Sketchley's borrowing was excessive in their particular circumstances, but is there a 'correct' level of debt? Quite how much companies should borrow is another puzzle in the theory of business finance. There are cogent arguments for and against the extensive use of debt capital and many academics have developed sophisticated models, which attempt to expose and analyse the key theoretical relationships.

For many years, the conventional wisdom was that it was advantageous to borrow so long as the company's capacity to service the debt was unquestioned. The result would be higher earnings per share and higher share value provided that the finance raised was invested sensibly. The dangers of excessive levels of borrowing would be forcibly articulated by the stock market by a downrating of the shares of a highly geared company. This prompted the concept of an 'optimal' capital structure where company value was maximized and which, therefore, companies should attempt to achieve. While the critical gearing ratio is thought to depend on factors such as the steadiness of the company's cash flow and the saleability of its assets, it has proved to be something of a Holy Grail, highly desirable but illusory and difficult to grasp. To some academics, there seemed to be a need for a firmer theoretical underpinning to facilitate the analysis of capital structure decisions and to offer more helpful guidelines to practising managers.

LEARNING OBJECTIVES

Some companies avoid debt finance like the plague. Perhaps you will sympathize after reading this chapter! It aims to:

- Explain some of the ways of measuring gearing.
- Enable you to understand more fully the advantages of debt capital.
- Enable you to understand the likely limits on the extent to which debt can be used, and the nature of 'financial distress' costs.
- Enable you to understand, as a result, the factors which a finance manager should consider when designing a capital structure policy.

The Modigliani and Miller contribution

When Nobel laureates Modigliani and Miller (MM) published their seminal paper in 1958, finance academics began to examine in depth the relationship between borrowing and company value. MM's work on the pure theory of capital structure initially suggested that company value was invariant to gearing. This conclusion prompted a furore of critical opposition largely of the 'You cannot be serious!' variety, leading to a coherent theory of capital structure, the current version of which looks remarkably like the traditional view itself! However, this is the essence of progress, however tortuous, in economic science. It involves the processes of model-building, testing and refinement until there emerges a generally accepted and coherent body of analysis not demonstrably at odds with observed practice and which can also provide operational guidelines for practising managers.

Because this is a complex topic, we have organized our treatment of the impact of gearing into two chapters. This chapter is mainly devoted to the analysis of the 'traditional' theory of capital structure and the issue of how much a company should borrow. In the following chapter, we deepen the analysis by discussing the 'modern' theory. However, although it is important to view the two chapters as a package, the main flavour of the issues involved can be obtained from the present chapter.

The package is designed to examine the following issues:

1. Why do companies use debt capital at all?
2. How is the cost of debt capital measured?
3. What are the dangers of debt capital? How do shareholders react to 'high' levels of gearing?

4. What do the competing theories of capital structure tell us about optimal financing decisions?
5. How does taxation affect the analysis?
6. What overall return should be achieved by a company using debt?
7. What guidelines can we offer to practising financial managers?

These, then, are the issues. However, it is useful to set the scene by looking at how indebtedness, or 'gearing', may be measured.

14.2   Measures of gearing

There are two basic ways to express the indebtedness of a company. We may either look at *capital gearing*, which indicates the proportion of debt capital in the firm's overall capital structure, or at *income gearing*, which indicates the extent to which the company's income is pre-empted by prior interest charges.

Capital gearing: alternative measures

The most widely used measure of capital gearing is simply the ratio of long-term debt (LTD) to shareholder funds. This purports to indicate how easily the firm can repay debts from selling assets, since shareholder capital measures net assets:

$$\text{capital gearing} = \frac{\text{LTD}}{\text{Shareholders' Funds}}$$

There are a few drawbacks to this approach.

First, market values may be considerably higher than the book value of the assets concerned. However, the notion of the market value itself needs to be clarified. When a company is forced to sell assets hurriedly in order to repay debts, it is by no means certain that a buyer can be found to pay an acceptable price. The break-up values of assets are often lower than those expressed in the accounts, which assume that the enterprise is a going concern. In other words, in a distress sale, the net realizable value may be less than both the 'market' and book values. Using book values to measure gearing does at least have an element of prudence. In addition, the oscillating nature of market values may emphasize the case for conservatism, even for companies with 'safe' gearing ratios.

A second problem, the lack of an upper limit to the ratio, hindering inter-company comparisons, is easily remedied by expressing long-term debt as a fraction of all forms of long-term capital, thus constraining the upper limit to 100 per cent. The gearing measure becomes:

$$\frac{\text{LTD}}{\text{LTD} + \text{Shareholders' Funds}}$$

A third problem is the treatment of provisions made out of previous years' income.

Technically, provisions represent expected future liabilities. Companies provide for contingencies such as warranty claims as a matter of prudence. Provisions thus result from a charge against profits and result in lower equity. Therefore to treat provisions as debt may involve an element of double counting which increases the measured gearing ratio. Provisions could be treated as either equity or debt according to the degree of certainty of the anticipated contingency. If the liability is 'highly certain', then it is reasonable to treat it as debt but if the provision is the result of ultra-prudence, it may be treated as equity. For example, deferred taxation is a provision against the possibility of incurring a Corporation Tax charge if assets are sold above their written-down value for tax purposes. For most firms, this risk will diminish over time and the provision can safely be treated as equity. In practice, however, company accounts carry a mixture of provisions of varying degrees of certainty, and it is tempting to ignore the item completely in expressing the gearing ratio. However, the nature of provisions should be questioned when the item appears substantial. Adjusted to exclude provisions, the capital gearing ratio becomes:

$$\frac{\text{LT Borrowing}}{\text{All LT Funds}}$$

Arguably, any borrowing figure should take into account both long-term debts and also short-term borrowing. Many companies depend heavily on short-term borrowing, especially bank overdrafts, and having to repay these debts quickly would place a significant burden on the cash flow and liquidity of such companies. For this reason, some firms, e.g. British Petroleum, present their gearing ratios inclusive of such liabilities. BP's own measure of gearing is:

$$\frac{\text{Market Debt}}{\text{Market Debt} + \text{Shareholder Funds}}$$

BP's measure focuses on the book value of borrowings from capital market institutions rather than market values, which may not coincide. There are two objections to this approach. First, cash holdings could be allowed for as an offset to short-term debt, to leave a 'net debt' measure; and second, since short-term borrowing is highly volatile, the year-end figure in the Balance Sheet is not always a reliable guide to short-term debts. However, many companies effectively use their bank overdraft as a long-term form of finance. In other words, the actual bank overdraft figure may include a hard core element of long-term capital and a fluctuating component, although it is not easy to separate these two items from external examination of the accounts.

Income gearing

All the above measures attempt to express the ability of the company to repay loans out of capital. However, they are only really helpful if book values and market values of the assets which would have to be sold to repay creditors approximate to each other but, as we have noted, the market value of assets is difficult to assess and is volatile. Moreover, capital gearing only indicates the security of creditors' funds *in extremis* and may be an unduly cautious way of viewing debt exposure.

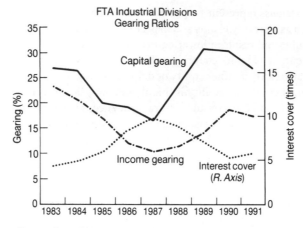

Source: Hoare-Govett Investment Research Limited: Quoted UK plc.

Figure 14.1 Gearing ratios for UK companies

The trigger for a debt crisis is usually the inability to make interest payments, and the 'front line' is therefore the size and reliability of the company's income in relation to its debt interest commitments. Although, in reality, cash flow is the more important consideration, income gearing is usually measured by the ratio of *profit* before tax and interest, to interest charges, or *interest cover*, i.e.:

$$\text{Interest Cover} = \frac{\text{Profit before Interest and Tax}}{\text{Interest Charges}}$$

To adjust the formula to allow for interest income, the numerator should include interest received, and the denominator should become interest outgoings. This adjustment is rarely made in practice; it is common to find *net* interest charges used as the denominator.

The inverse of interest cover is called 'income gearing', indicating the proportion of pre-tax earnings committed to prior interest charges. Figure 14.1 shows movements in income gearing for all UK industrial and commercial companies during the period 1983–91. It clearly reveals the deterioration of the financial security of firms in general during the late 1980s as borrowings rose, interest rates increased and company earnings faltered.

Illustration: Rolls-Royce's borrowings

The figures in Table 14.1 are taken from the Annual Report for Rolls-Royce (RR) plc for the year ended 31 December 1989.

Table 14.1 Financial data for Rolls-Royce plc

Shareholders' Funds	£1199m (including minorities of £73m)
Creditors:	
Amounts falling due after one year	
Borrowings	£162m
Other Creditors	£68m
Provisions:	£173m (to be treated as debt)
Short-term borrowing	£52m
Profit before interest and tax	£222m
Net interest receivable	£15m
(Received £50m,	
Paid £35m)	

These figures allow us to compute the following measures of gearing:

$$\frac{\text{LTD}}{\text{Shareholders' Funds}} = \frac{£162m + £68m + £173m}{£1199m} = 34\%$$

$$\frac{\text{LTD}}{\text{All LT Capital}} = \frac{£403m}{£1199m + £403m} = 25\%$$

$$\frac{\text{LT Borrowing}}{\text{Shareholders' Funds}} = \frac{£162m}{£1199m} = 14\%$$

$$\frac{\text{LT Borrowing}}{\text{All LT Funds}} = \frac{£162m}{£1199m + £403m} = 10\%$$

$$\frac{\text{All Borrowing}}{\text{Shareholders' Funds}} = \frac{£162m + £52m}{£1199m} = 18\%$$

$$\text{Interest Cover} = \frac{£222m + £50m}{£35m} = 7.8, \text{ Income gearing} = 1/7.8 = 12.8\%$$

Which measure is most useful? This depends on why we need to measure gearing. Remembering that capital gearing purports to indicate ability to *repay* debts and income gearing to measure ability to *service* debts, all RR's measures, on face value, look eminently 'safe'. However, the figures should be assessed in relation to the nature of the industry. For example, the manufacture and sale of aero-engines is a high-risk activity with a long lead-time between beginning a project and hitting the market. Besides, RR has already been declared insolvent once before, in 1971, when it was nationalized. To assess RR's degree of safety, we might compare it with firms in industries with similar risk profiles. Also, examining the *movements* in gearing over time may identify any adverse trends.

14.3 The 'magic' of gearing

A major reason for using debt is to enhance or 'gear up' shareholder earnings, an effect similar to when an activity, or whole company, exhibits *operating gearing*. For a project with a high proportion of fixed costs in its cost structure, once it is operating beyond break-even, any increase in sales feeds through directly into profit. This effect is particularly pronounced in activities like steel-making, where most factors of production, and hence operating costs, are effectively fixed. When a company uses financial gearing, variations in the level of Earnings Before Interest and Tax (EBIT) caused by variations in trading conditions, generate a more than proportional variation in shareholder earnings because long term debt interest commitments are fixed. In other words, if EBIT rises by X per cent, the residual earnings available for shareholders after paying a fixed interest charge rise by more than X per cent. This contention is best illustrated numerically.

Lindley plc

Lindley plc retains no earnings and its shareholders require a 20 per cent return. Issued share capital is £100m, denominated in £1 units. Lindley's income can vary as shown in Table 14.2, according to trading conditions characterized as bad, indifferent and good, denoted by scenarios A, B and C, which have probabilities of 0.25, 0.50 and 0.25, respectively.

After all costs, but before deducting debt interest, earnings are £5m, £20m and £35m under scenarios A, B and C, respectively. This measure of earnings is termed *Net Operating Income (NOI)*. (For simplicity, taxation is ignored.) Let us examine shareholder returns under gearing ratios of zero, 25 per cent and 50 per cent, measured by long-term debt (coupon rate 10 per cent) to total long-term capital, which remains constant at £100m.

Table 14.2　How gearing affects shareholder returns in Lindley plc

	Trading Conditions		
	Scenario A ($p=0.25$)	Scenario B ($p=0.50$)	Scenario C ($p=0.25$)
Earnings before interest* (Net operating income)	£5m	£20m	£35m
Zero gearing (£100m equity, £0m debt)			
Debt interest at 10%	—	—	—
Shareholder earnings	£5m	£20m	£35m
Return on equity (ROE)	5%	20%	35%
25% gearing (£75m equity, £25m debt interest 10%)			
Debt interest at 10%	£2.5m	£2.5m	£2.5m
Shareholder earnings	£2.5m	£17.5m	£32.5m
Return on equity (ROE)	3.3%	23.3%	43.3%
50% gearing (£50m equity, £50m debt, interest rate 10%)			
Debt interest at 10%	£5m	£5m	£5m
Shareholder earnings	0	£15m	£30m
Return on equity (ROE)	0	30%	60%

*Taxes are ignored.

For a given increase in income, shareholder earnings rise by a greater proportion; e.g. with gearing of 25 per cent, if EBIT rises by 300 per cent from £5m to £20m, shareholder earnings increase by 500 per cent from £2.5m to £17.5m. It is easy to see why adding debt to the capital structure is called gearing – the change in earnings is magnified by a factor of 1.6 in shareholders' favour. Unfortunately, this effect also applies in a downward direction – a given proportionate fall in earnings generates a more pronounced decrease in shareholder earnings. Indeed, with 50 per cent gearing, under scenario A, shareholder earnings are entirely wiped out by prior interest charges. The return on equity would be negative at any higher gearing level.

Negative returns are not necessarily fatal – companies often survive losses in especially poor trading years, but the likelihood of survival when continued trading losses combine with high fixed interest charges is lowered if the company cannot pay interest charges. In these cases, the enterprise is technically insolvent although it is not unknown for creditors to agree to restructure the company's capital, for example, by converting debt into preference shares. There is, however, an effective upper limit of gearing for Lindley. Beyond 50 per cent gearing, it may be unable to meet interest charges out of earnings. For practical purposes, the lower limit of earnings will dictate maximum borrowing capacity, although, in reality, this lower limit is uncertain (and not necessarily positive). This is why it is usually argued that the more reliable the company's expected cash flow stream, the greater its borrowing capacity.

The Lindley example also demonstrates that, under debt financing, although share-holders may achieve enhanced returns in good years, they stand to achieve much lower returns in bad years. In other words, the residual stream of shareholder earnings exhibits greater variability – it has become more risky. *Financial risk, therefore, has two dimensions: as well as a higher probability of bankruptcy, there is greater variability of shareholder earnings.* This second dimension can be examined by computing the expected value and the range, or dispersion, of the return on equity (ROE) with each of the three gearing ratios, as shown in Table 14.3.

Table 14.3 shows that although the expected value of the return on equity is greater at higher levels of gearing, the dispersion of possible returns is also wider, a phenomenon which may concern risk-averting shareholders. Notice also that we can decompose the overall risk incurred by shareholders into its underlying business and financial elements. Regardless of the gearing ratio, the dispersion of returns due to underlying business risk is unchanged – nothing has happened to its product range, its customer base or any other aspect of its trading activities. Lindley would simply share out the proceeds of its operations in different ways at different gearing ratios.

This discussion of the impact of gearing is still incomplete in one important respect. The analysis has been based on book values, despite earlier remarks that gearing ratios may often

Table 14.3 How gearing affects the risk of ordinary shares

Gearing	Expected ROE	Dispersion	Due to: Business Risk	Financial Risk
0%	20%	15%	15%	0
25%	23.3%	20%	15%	5%
50%	30%	30%	15%	15%

Table 14.4   How gearing can affect share price

Gearing	Number of Shares	Expected Shareholder Earnings	EPS	Share Price*
0%	100m	£20m	20.0p	20.0p/0.2 = £1.00
25%	75m	£17.5m	23.3p	23.3p/0.2 = £1.17
50%	50m	£15m	30.0p	30.0p/0.2 = £1.50

*Share price is found by discounting the perpetual and constant EPS at 20 per cent.

be better measured in terms of market values. In particular, we need to ask whether these alterations in the respective entitlements to share in company earnings are beneficial – do they actually make shareholders better off? To examine the effect on share price, we need to focus on the expected earnings figure and recall that the value of a share can be found by discounting its stream of earnings as a perpetuity. (No distinction is needed between earnings and dividends as Lindley has no retentions.) The expected values of shareholder earnings for each of the three gearing ratios are shown in Table 14.4. Recalling that Lindley's shares have a nominal value of £1, we can specify the number of shares corresponding to each gearing ratio and hence the expected value of the EPS. Share prices are found by applying the valuation formula, discounting the perpetual EPS at 20 per cent, the return required by Lindley's shareholders.

It appears that by using debt capital, financial managers can achieve significant increases in shareholder wealth. However, we ought to be suspicious of this somewhat magical effect. Why should shareholder wealth increase when there have been no changes in trading activity or in expected aggregate income – the wealth-creating characteristics of the project? To achieve this effect surely someone, somewhere must be worse off! Or is the analysis wrong?

Readers may have spotted one possible flaw in the argument. It assumes that shareholders are prepared to accept a return of 20 per cent at all permissible gearing levels – they seem to be unconcerned by financial risk. In the Lindley example, even while there is no risk of bankruptcy, gearing exposes shareholder earnings to greater variability. With greater uncertainty regarding earnings levels, we might expect to find that shareholders react to gearing by demanding higher returns on their capital. If they think gearing is too risky, they may sell their holdings, thus driving down share price. We need to examine in rather more detail the likely reaction of shareholders to increased gearing; indeed, we will find that this is a key element in the debate about optimal capital structure. In the next section, we examine the so-called 'traditional' view of gearing, probably still the most widely supported explanation, at least by 'practical people'.

14.4   The 'traditional' view

The traditional viewpoint emphasizes the benefits of utilizing relatively cheap debt capital rather than more expensive equity finance. To analyse this approach, we first need to make some definitions.

In the case of the ungeared company, market value would be found by discounting (or capitalizing) its stream of annual earnings, E, at the rate of return required by shareholders, k_e.

The value of an ungeared company, V_0, is simply the value of the shares, V_S. For a constant and perpetual stream of annual earnings, E:

$$V_0 = V_S = \frac{E}{k_e}$$

so that $k_e = \dfrac{E}{V_S}$

Much of the argument about capital structure centres on what happens to the discount rate (or capitalization rate) as gearing increases. If the analysis is conducted in terms of substituting debt for equity, as we did in the Lindley example, the effect of gearing can be examined while holding E constant. In this case, gearing simply re-arranges the shareout of E among the company's stakeholders. We denote the book value of borrowings as B and the interest rate as i, involving a prior interest charge of $(i \times B)$. Gearing requires that the *Earnings Before Interest and Tax (EBIT) or Net Operating Income (NOI)* of the company be split into two components, the prior interest charge and the portion attributable to shareholders, the Net Income of $(E - iB)$. The overall value of the company is the value of the share capital plus the value of the debt capital, each capitalized at its respective rate of discount. For debt capital, where there is no discrepancy between book values (B) and market values (V_B), the capitalization rate is simply the nominal interest rate (see below). Therefore, the overall value of the company is the combined value of its shares, and its debt:

$$V_0 = V_S + V_B = \frac{(E - iB)}{k_e} + \frac{iB}{i} = \frac{(E - iB)}{k_e} + V_B$$

The *overall* capitalization rate (denoted by k_0) for a company using a mixed capital structure is a weighted average, whose weights depend on the relative importance of each type of finance in the capital structure, i.e. V_S/V_0 and V_B/V_0 for equity and debt, respectively:

$$k_0 = \left(k_e \times \frac{V_S}{V_0} \right) + \left(i \times \frac{V_B}{V_0} \right)$$

This weighted average expression simplifies to:

$$k_0 = \frac{k_e V_S + iB}{V_0} = \frac{E}{V_0}$$

It is important to recognize that for both ungeared and geared firms alike, k_0 is found by dividing the EBIT by the value of the whole firm. k_0 is also known as the *Weighted Average Cost of Capital (WACC)* since it expresses the overall return required on existing operations in order to satisfy the demands of both groups of stakeholders. The WACC may thus be interpreted as an average discount rate applied by the market to the company's future operating cash flows to derive the capitalized value of this stream.

It thus appears that a company could lower the WACC by adding 'cheap' debt to an equity base. For instance, in the Lindley example, while the required return in the all-equity case is 20 per cent, the cost of equity, with gearing at 25 per cent, the WACC becomes:

$$k_0 = (0.75 \times 20\%) + (0.25 \times 10\%) = 17.5\%$$

Apparently, gearing can lower the overall cost of capital if both k_e and i remain constant. The effect of this is highly significant. In the traditional view of gearing, shareholders are deemed unlikely to respond adversely (if at all) to low levels of gearing so long as the prospect of default looks remote. If the cost of equity remains static, substitution of debt for equity will lower the overall cost of capital applied by the market in valuing the company's stream of earnings. This is shown in Figure 14.2 by the decline in the k_0 schedule between A and B. Corresponding to this fall in k_0 is an increase in the value of the whole geared company, V_g, in relation to that of an equivalent ungeared company, V_u.

This benign impact of gearing has already been shown in the Lindley example. Looking back to Tables 14.3 and 14.4, consider the movement from zero to 25 per cent gearing. Assuming shareholders continue to seek a return of 20 per cent, the EPS discounted to

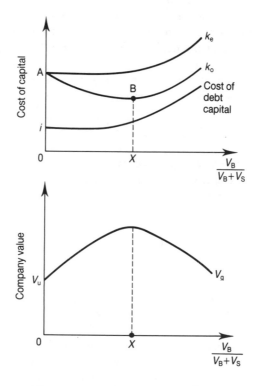

Figure 14.2 The 'traditional' view

infinity yields a share price of £1.17. The value of the equity becomes (£1.17 × 75m) = £88m, and the overall company value is:

$$V_o = V_S + V_B = £88m + £25m = £113m.$$

Gearing up to 25 per cent raises market value by £13m above book value, thus demonstrating the benefits of gearing to shareholders. The market value of the whole company rises because the value per unit of the residual equity increases due to the increase in EPS. Without gearing, each share would sell at £1.

However, these delights cannot extend indefinitely. Sooner or later shareholders will become concerned by the greater financial risk to which their earnings are exposed and begin to seek higher returns. In addition, providers of additional debt are likely to raise their requirements as they perceive the probability of default increasing. The k_e schedule will probably turn upwards before any upturn in i, given the legally preferred position of debt-holders, although the phasing of these movements is not clear in this model. Whatever the sequence of the upward revisions in required returns, the WACC profile will eventually be forced to rise, and the value of the company will fall. The NI model in this form clearly involves an optimal debt/equity mix, where company value is maximized and the WACC is minimized. This is gearing ratio X in Figure 14.2.

To financial managers, a major disappointment of this approach is its failure to pinpoint a specific optimal gearing ratio for all firms in all circumstances. The optimal ratio is likely to depend on the nature of the industry, e.g. whether the activity generates rapid cash flow, on the general marketability of the company's assets, on expectations about the prospects for the industry, and on the general level of interest rates. Clearly, many of these factors vary over time as well as between industries. However, a few pointers are possible.

We might expect, for example, a supermarket chain, characterized by strong cash flow, to sustain a higher level of gearing than a heavy engineering enterprise, where the working capital cycle is lengthy; while we might expect an airline, for whose assets there is a ready and active second-hand market, to withstand a higher gearing level (especially as flights are often paid for well in advance) than a steel company with both a high level of operational gearing and also highly specific and difficult-to-sell assets.

14.5 The cost of debt capital

Our analysis has so far assumed that market and book values of debt coincide. This is by no means always the case in practice. Corporate debt values behave in the same way as the market prices of government stock, or gilt-edged securities. When general market interest rates increase, the returns on previously issued 'gilts' may look unattractive compared to the returns available on newly issued stock. As a result, bond dealers mark down the value of existing stocks until they offer the same yield as investors can obtain by purchasing new stocks. In other words, equilibrium in the gilts market is achieved when all stocks subject to the same degree of risk and with the same period to redemption offer the same yield. The simplest case to illustrate is that of perpetual (irredeemable) stock such as 3.5% War Loan. These were issued, never to be repaid, to support the British war effort between 1939 and

1945. They offer the holder a return of 3.5 per cent (the nominal rate of interest, or 'coupon rate') on the par value of the stock, i.e. £3.50 per £100 of stock. With higher market rates, say, 7 per cent, War Loan would look unattractive, and its value would fall, e.g. a £100 unit would have to sell at £50 to generate a yield of 7 per cent. An inverse relationship applies between fixed-interest bond prices and interest rates:

The market value of an irredeemable bond is:

$$\text{nominal value} \times \frac{\text{coupon rate}}{\text{market rate}}$$

In practice, the calculation is made more complex when we consider the far more common case of bonds with limited lifetimes until maturity. In assessing the value of such bonds, the market will also anticipate the value of the eventual capital repayment. For example, if the market rate is 10 per cent, a ten-year bond with a coupon rate of 10 per cent, denominated in £100 units would have the following (present) value:

$$
\begin{aligned}
PV = {}&\text{discounted interest} &&+\text{discounted capital}\\
&\text{payments over 10 years} &&\text{repayment in year 10}
\end{aligned}
$$

$$
\begin{aligned}
&= (10\% \times £100).(\text{PVIFA}_{(10,10)}) &&+ (£100).(\text{PVIF}_{(10,10)})\\
&= (£10 \times 6.1446) &&+ (£100 \times 0.3855)\\
&= £61.45 &&+ £38.55 = £100
\end{aligned}
$$

The market value coincides with the par value because the coupon rate equals the going market rate. If however, the market rate were to rise to 12 per cent, all future payments to the bond holder, both capital and interest, would be more heavily discounted, i.e. at 12 per cent, reducing the market value to £76.55.

Values of corporate debt instruments behave in essentially the same way although, since companies are more risky than governments, they have to offer investors a rather higher rate of interest. This finding allows us to identify the cost of debt capital. A company can discern the appropriate rate of interest at which it could raise debt capital by looking at the market value of its own existing debt or that of a similar company. For example, if the market value of each £100 unit of Lindley's debenture stock was £95 and it was expected to be repaid in full in two years' time, the cost of Lindley's debt can be found by solving a simple IRR expression. Someone who decided to purchase the stock in the market would anticipate two interest payments of £10 and a capital repayment of £100. The return expected is denoted by k_d in the following expression:

$$£95 = \frac{£10}{(1+k_d)} + \frac{£10 + £100}{(1+k_d)^2}$$

The solution for k_d is 13 per cent. The market signals this rate as the cost of raising further debt.

There is one further adjustment to make. Thus far, we have ignored the tax relief enjoyed on debt interest payments. To allow for tax, we have to look at the cost of debt from the company's perspective since it is the company which enjoys the tax break. With a Corporation Tax rate of 33 per cent, each £10 interest payment will generate a tax saving of £3.30 for the company, reducing the effective interest cost to £10$(1-33\%)=$£6.70. The IRR equation becomes:

$$£95 = \frac{£6.70}{(1+k_d)} + \frac{£6.70 + £100}{(1+k_d)^2}$$

The reader should verify that the solution rate is 9.6 per cent. The tax benefits from using debt can be substantial. Take the case of a 10-year bond, issued and redeemable at a price of £100, with a coupon rate of 10%. The value of the tax savings, or the '*Tax Shield*', is:

$$\begin{aligned} \text{Tax Shield} &= \text{interest charge} \times (\text{tax rate}) \times \text{PVIFA}_{(10.10)} \\ &= (10\% \times £100) \times (33\%) \times 6.1446 \\ &= £20.28 \end{aligned}$$

In practice, this value is reduced by delay in tax payments, which in turn delays the receipt of tax benefits. Also, the discount rate itself may require adjustment for the tax effect (see Chapter 16).

14.6 The overall cost of capital

In section 14.4, we encountered the Weighted Average Cost of Capital (WACC) concept. This was interpreted as the overall rate of return required in order to satisfy all stakeholders in the company. We saw that it described a U-shaped profile as the firm's level of gearing increased. Initially, it fell as cheap debt was added to the capital structure, reached a minimum at the optimal gearing ratio, then rose as gearing came to be regarded as 'excessive'. The behaviour of this schedule provides a clue to the appropriate rate of return required on the company's activities, and, by implication, on new investment projects, an issue we examine using the Lindley example.

Lindley again

Lindley's shareholders require a 20 per cent return and its pre-tax cost of debt is 10 per cent. Let us make the simplifying assumptions that Lindley's debt is perpetual and sells at par. Adjusting for tax, as explained above, this corresponds to an after-tax cost of 6.7 per cent. What return on investment should Lindley achieve when raising debt finance of £10m to finance a new project? It is tempting to argue that the cut-off rate on this new project should be the cost of servicing the finance raised specifically to undertake the project – tempting but probably erroneous.

This is because using debt has an opportunity cost. The use of 'cheap' debt *now* may erode the company's ability to undertake worthwhile projects in the future by the depletion of credit lines. For example, assume that in 1992 Lindley used debt costing 6.7 per cent after tax to finance a project offering a return of 12 per cent, but this exhausted its credit-raising capacity. As a result it was unable to exploit a project available in 1993 which offered 14 per cent. This suggests that the 'true' cost of the finance used in 1992 exceeds 6.7 per cent. This creates a significant problem. To assess the 'correct' cost of capital really requires the forecasting of all future investment opportunities and capital supplies. In addition, our previous analysis leads us to expect, at some level of gearing, an adverse reaction by shareholders who may demand higher returns to compensate for higher financial risk. To resolve this issue we must again inspect the U-shaped WACC profile.

If the company is at such a 'low' level of gearing that no adverse consequences may be expected from the issue of further debt, it may be reasonable to use the cost of debt as a cut-off rate for new investment. However, at higher levels of gearing, we must allow for shareholders' reactions. Continuing with the Lindley example, consider two possible cases, denoted by points A and B, respectively on the WACC profile on Figure 14.2. Note that A corresponds to zero gearing and B to the critical ratio.

Case A

Lindley has no debt at present and shareholder capital is £100m. A new project is to be financed by the issue of £10m debt at an after-tax cost of 6.7 per cent. No impact on the cost of equity is expected. In this case, the company will have to generate additional annual returns of £0.67m in order to meet the extra financing costs associated with the new project, so that the hurdle rate for the new project is 6.7 per cent. Here, with the explicit assumption that shareholders will not react adversely, it may be reasonable to use the cost of debt as the cut-off rate. In this case, the required return would be simply the interest cost divided by the debt financing provided, i.e. the interest rate:

$$\text{required return} = iB/B = i$$

However, the reader should appreciate that this position is unlikely to be tenable, except for relatively small projects, and hence small borrowings, as it ignores the opportunity cost of debt.

Case B

We will assume that the optimal gearing ratio involves a capital structure with £50m of each type of capital. Any further debt financing, even at a constant debt cost, will cause the cost of equity to increase. Assume that the extra £10m debt financing will provoke shareholders to demand a return of 24 per cent. This would be expressed by downward pressure on share price until the return on holding Lindley's shares became 24 per cent. Now, the project has to meet not only the debt financing costs, but also the additional returns required by shareholders. The total additional required income is:

Required extra income	= debt financing costs	+ extra return on equity
	= (6.7% × £10m)	+ (4% × £50m)
	= £0.67m + £2m	
	= £2.67m	

Instead of an apparent cost of just 6.7 per cent, the true cost of using debt to finance this project is actually $£2.67m/£10m = 26.7$ per cent!

This discussion suggests that the Marginal Cost of Capital (MCC) should be used as the cut-off rate for new investment rather than either the cost of debt or the WACC itself. However, the MCC does have operational limitations. In particular, we are required to anticipate how the capital market is likely to react to the issue of additional debt capital. Given that we seem unable to define the WACC profile or pinpoint the optimal gearing ratio at any one time, this presents a problem. We could assume that the present gearing ratio is optimal, but this prompts the question why different firms in the same industry have different gearing ratios – they cannot all be correct!

The target capital structure

A solution commonly adopted in practice is to specify a target capital structure. The firm defines what it regards as the optimal long-term gearing ratio, and then attempts to adhere to this ratio in financing future operations. For example, if the optimal ratio for Lindley is deemed to involve 50 per cent debt and 50 per cent equity, i.e. a debt-to-equity ratio of 100 per cent, then any future activities should be financed in these proportions so as not to disturb the ratio. For example, the £10m project would be financed by £5m debt and £5m equity, perhaps via retained earnings or a rights issue. The corollary is the use of the WACC as the cut-off rate for new investment. Here, the WACC is:

$$\text{(cost of equity} \times \text{equity weighting)} + \text{(cost of debt} \times \text{debt weighting)}$$
$$= (20\% \times 50\%) + (6.7\% \times 50\%) = (10\% + 3.35\%) = 13.35\%$$

It is important to appreciate why the WACC is recommended here. Generally, the MCC is the correct cut-off rate for new investment, but in practice, it is difficult to anticipate with any precision how shareholders are likely to react to a change in gearing. The solution proposed here is a somewhat pragmatic one, which assumes that the new project will have no appreciable impact on gearing. *In other words, using the WACC implies that the company is already at the optimal gearing ratio and does not deviate from it.* Obviously, the WACC and the MCC will coincide in this case.

14.7 Financial distress

This is an appropriate stage to clarify our terminology. Up to this point, we have implied that the reason for the upturn in the WACC profile is the threat of 'bankruptcy' resulting in 'liquidation', i.e. a company that fails to meet its debts will be forced to liquidate by its creditors. The term 'bankruptcy' in the United Kingdom strictly applies to *personal* insolvency, whereas for *companies* in financial distress, a variety of procedures can be adopted.

If a creditor, such as a bank, has made a loan secured on the company's assets, then it can appoint a receiver to recover the debt if the company defaults on interest or capital repayments. This procedure was adopted by the Norwegian Christiana Bank, which, in June 1990, called in receivers, for Brown Group International (BGI), makers of construction equipment and operators of Capital Airlines, rather than offer continued support in the face of a slump in the construction industry. At the time of its receivership, when interest rates were exceptionally high, BGI had a debt/equity ratio of around 5 to 1 (based on book value).

The receiver may sell the business, or parts of it, as a going concern, which continues to trade in a different guise, often involving a reduced scale of operations, as in the case of Capital Airlines. However, the receiver's primary duty is to the appointing bank, and once sufficient funds have been realized to repay the loan, he is under no obligation to maximize the proceeds of the sale of the remaining assets, or even to keep them operating. He may choose to liquidate them *in toto* and disburse the net proceeds to remaining creditors and then any residue to shareholders.

The Insolvency Act 1986 introduced a new procedure, *administration*, as an attempt to rescue ailing companies and to protect employment. The company is allowed to continue trading under the overall control of an Administrator, who will attempt to reorganize the company's finances and its operating structure. The Administrator is appointed by a court at the request of the directors and has an equal duty to all creditors. In effect, administration, rather like Chapter 11 bankruptcy in the United States, is an attempt to protect the company from its creditors thus giving the Administrator a breathing space, during which he can attempt to secure the company's survival as a reorganized going concern. The main difference compared to the US equivalent is that Chapter 11 bankruptcy allows the incumbent managers and owners to retain control.

An Administrator was appointed in 1990 for the niche retailer Sock Shop, resulting in closure of half of its outlets, but allowing its continued survival as a going concern. The Administrator of Sock Shop was reported as saying that the procedure was 'a fantastic piece of assistance against creditors chucking writs at us'. He did not mention its often substantial costs, which may render it uneconomic for the creditors of smaller companies.

Any visitor to an auction of bankrupt stock will have no difficulty in appreciating the importance of postponing the break-up decision. Similarly, when repossessed assets, such as consumer durables and houses, are sold by hire-purchase companies and Building Societies respectively, they rarely fetch 'market values'. This is partly because the vendor often only needs, and expects, to recover an amount less than the market value, having deliberately set the loan itself at less than the market value of the asset upon which it is secured. The vendor is interested in a quick sale to minimize depreciation, interest and other carrying costs, and it is generally known that the goods are offered under distressed conditions. In 1990, the Bond Corporation, an Australian media group, was seeking to realize assets to repay huge debts, estimated at A$8 billion. The chairman, Alan Bond, was enraged when obliged to sell Australia's Channel Nine TV network for only £88m to Kerry Packer, who had sold it to the Bond Corporation for £490m only two years earlier! Prices usually head south in a distress sale!

While the Bond example is possibly an extreme one (for instance, Bond may have originally paid an inflated price), empirical studies (e.g. van Horne 1975; Sharpe 1981) have suggested that liquidation costs, including legal and administrative charges, may lower the resale value of distressed companies by 50 per cent or more. However, there is a more insidious form of financial distress. This is the impact of increasing gearing on profitability where it distracts managerial decision-making. As a firm's indebtedness begins to look excessive, it may develop an overriding concern for short-term liquidity. This may be manifested in reduced investment in training and R & D, which damages long-term growth capability, and a reduction in credit periods and stock levels, which may hamper marketing efforts. More obviously, it may sell established operations at bargain prices, sell or abandon promising new product developments, and, to the extent that it does continue to invest, it may exhibit a preference for short-payback, cash-generating projects, rather than strategic activities. Troubled companies often cut their dividends to preserve liquidity but this often signals to the market the extent of their difficulties via the information content. Finally, there may be a pervasive 'corporate gloom effect', which saps morale internally and damages public image externally.

Such costs are likely to be encountered well before the trigger point of cash flow crisis, and, of course, many firms have successfully surmounted them in a 'corporate turnround', but not without an often prolonged dip in the value of the company. In other words, both actual and anticipated liquidation costs detract from company value, effectively lowering the practical limit to debt capacity.

Returning to our discussion of UK insolvency procedures, the practical importance of the facility to appoint an Administrator before creditors can appoint receivers may now be seen. Administration enhances the probability of survival of a company unable to meet its immediate liabilities and may thus lead to lower costs of financial distress and the optimal capital structure may be achieved at a higher gearing ratio. There may, of course, be an element of 'moral hazard' here to the extent that financial managers might undertake more dangerous levels of debt knowing that there is a more relaxed legal procedure in the event of insolvency. Gearing levels have increased in the United Kingdom since 1986, but the extent to which this can be attributed to the 1986 Act is unclear.

14.8 Predicting corporate failure

Excessive levels of gearing are often responsible for corporate failure. However, very highly geared companies do survive and conversely, some low-geared companies fail. This suggests that there are many other clues to assessing the viability of a company, and it is not enough simply to examine a single Balance Sheet ratio when attempting to predict financial failure.

An approach which attempts to balance out the relative importance of different financial indicators is the 'Z-score' method developed by Altman (1968). This was based on examining the financial characteristics of two samples of failed and surviving US companies to detect which ratios were most important in discriminating between the two groups. For example, were past failures characterized by low liquidity ratios? What other ratios were important discriminators, and what was their relative importance?

Using a technique called *discriminant analysis*, the relative significance of each critical ratio can be expressed in an equation which generates a 'Z-score', a critical value below which failed firms typically fall and above which, survivors locate. In general terms, the equation is:

$$Z = a + bR_1 + cR_2$$

In this equation, a, b and c are constants derived from past observations and R_1 and R_2 are identified key discriminatory ratios.

A Z-score model using data for UK firms was developed by Marais (1982), an extension of which is currently used by the Datastream database. For Datastream, Marais examined over forty ratios before settling on four critical ones in his final model:

$$\text{Profitability} = \frac{\text{Pre-tax Profit} + \text{Depreciation}}{\text{Current Liabilities}}$$

$$\text{Liquidity} = \frac{\text{Current Assets less Stocks}}{\text{Current Liabilities}}$$

$$\text{Gearing} = \frac{\text{All Borrowing}}{\text{Total Capital Employed less Intangibles}}$$

$$\text{Stock Turnover} = \frac{\text{Stock}}{\text{Sales}}$$

Other analysts (e.g. Taffler 1991), using different samples of firms, employ different ratios and weightings in the equation for Z. In Marais' model, the critical Z-value based on the examination of failures and comparable survivors over the period 1974–80, is zero. This does not necessarily imply that an existing company displaying a Z-score of around zero is on the brink of insolvency, merely that the firm is displaying characteristics similar to previous failures. A steadily declining Z-score suggests a worsening financial condition, while an improving Z-score indicates strong corporate financial management.

Z-scoring is used primarily for credit risk assessment by banks and other financial institutions, industrial companies and credit insurers. While it does not tell the whole story behind the company's prospects (for example, it is based on past accounting data), it is still widely regarded as an important indicator of a company's financial health and hence its credit status.

14.9   Two more issues: signalling and agency costs

Of course, managers have a vested interest in not breaking the company, and so an increase in gearing might be construed by the market as signalling a greater degree of managerial confidence in the ability of the company to service a higher level of debt. This argument, propounded by Ross (1977), relies on asymmetry of information as between managers and shareholders. If we assume that managers are rational job protectors, then an increase in gearing may be taken as an attempt to convey more information to the market about future prospects. It is not clear whether the market should attach the same information content to a reduction in gearing. Irrational though it may seem, while a debt increase can be regarded in a favourable or unfavourable light depending on the accompanying arguments, an unexpected reduction in indebtedness is usually greeted by the market with pleasure.

The previous paragraph reflects the pervasive principal/agent problem. Financial managers, as appointees of the shareholders, are expected to maximize the value of the enterprise, but it is difficult for the owners to devise an effective, but not excessively costly, service contract to constrain managerial behaviour to this goal. In the context of capital structure theory, the financial manager acts as an agent for both shareholders and debt-holders. Although the latter do not offer remuneration, they do attempt to limit managers' freedom of action by including restrictive covenants in the debt contract, such as restrictions on dividend payouts, to protect the asset base of the company.

Such restraints on managerial decision-making may adversely affect the development of the firm, and together with the monitoring costs incurred by the shareholders themselves, may detract from company value. Conversely, it is not inconceivable that the close monitoring by a small group of creditors, aiming to protect their capital, may induce managers to pursue more responsible policies likely to enhance the wealth of a widely diffused group of shareholders. A company which has experienced very close monitoring is Eurotunnel plc, whose activities and plans have been finely scrutinized both in public (e.g. Wearing 1989) and in private, prior to creditors agreeing to release further capital, and the depth of scrutiny has increased with the level of gearing. However, it is by no means obvious that shareholders' interests have suffered as a result.

14.10   Conclusions

Where does this leave us? What recommendations can we make to the financial manager?

(1)   Gearing can lower the overall or Weighted Average Cost of Capital which the company is required to achieve on its operations, and up to a point, raise the market value of the enterprise. However, this benign effect can only be relied upon at relatively safe gearing levels. Companies can expect the market to react adversely to 'excessive' gearing ratios. The implications for project appraisal are reasonably clear. Strictly, the appropriate cut-off rate for new investment is the Marginal Cost of Capital, but if no change in gearing is caused by the new activity, the WACC can be used.

(2)   Although debt has its attractions, it is potentially lethal. Considerable care should be taken when prescribing the appropriate use of debt that will enhance shareholder wealth without ever threatening corporate collapse. Levels of gearing that look quite innocuous in calm trading conditions may suddenly appear ominous when conditions worsen. Corporate difficulties do not usually occur in ones, and highly geared companies are relatively less well placed to surmount them.

(3)   The capital structure decision, like the dividend decision, is a secondary decision – secondary, that is, to the company's primary concern of finding and developing wealth-creating projects. Many people argue that the beneficial impact of debt examined in this chapter is largely an illusion. Clever financing cannot create wealth (except to the extent that it enables the exploitation of projects which would not otherwise have proceeded). It may, however, *transfer* wealth if some stakeholders are prepared, perhaps due to information asymmetry, to accept too low a return for the risks they incur, or if the government offers a tax subsidy on debt interest.

(4) The decision to borrow should not be over-influenced by tax considerations. There are other ways of obtaining tax subsidies, for example, investing in fixed assets which qualify in the United Kingdom for the 25 per cent Writing Down Allowance. A highly geared company could perhaps find itself unable to exploit the other tax-breaks offered by governments when a favourable opportunity is uncovered. (We will find, in Chapter 16, that there is a device, leasing, whereby a tax-exhausted company can still enjoy tax breaks.)

(5) The finance manager should question whether debt is the most suitable form of funding in the particular circumstances. For example, there should be a clear rationale to support the case for debt rather than retentions (i.e. lower dividends) or a rights issue. He should especially recognize the value of retaining reserve borrowing capacity to draw upon under adverse circumstances or when favourable opportunities, like falling interest rates, arise.

(6) Remember that interest rates fluctuate over time. If interest rates move from what seems a 'high' level, take advantage of the reduction. For example, if 10 per cent seems like the 'normal' long-term level of interest rates, when rates next fall below 10 per cent, and bankers are offering variable rate loans at say 9 per cent, he should not be afraid to take a fixed rate loan at, say, 9.5 per cent. Readiness to work with a slightly higher than minimum rate in the short term could have significant pay-offs in the longer term. Anyone who thinks that rates will continue to fall should reserve some borrowing capacity to retain flexibility.

(7) Firms should avoid relying on too many bankers, as with syndicated loans, despite the benefits from having access to a variety of banking facilities. If the company hits trading and liquidity problems, it is hard enough to convince one banker that the company should be saved. But if it has to persuade ten or twenty, and their decision has to be unanimous, it is virtually impossible to reach a satisfactory conclusion about capital restructuring. The UK entertainments group Brent-Walker had to negotiate with forty-seven banks in its efforts to rebuild its capital structure during 1991, while the liquidators of Polly Peck had to deal with seventy.

In the next chapter, we examine the modern treatment of gearing, which attempts to isolate the fundamental relationships between company value, the required rate of return, and capital structure.

14.11 Summary

This chapter has explained the meaning of gearing, its likely benefits to shareholders, its dangers and its possible impact on the required return on investment projects.

Key points

- Using debt finance, or gearing, often looks more attractive than equity due to its lower cost of servicing, tax deductibility of interest and low issue costs.

- The sum of discounted tax savings conferred by the tax deductibility of debt interest is called the Tax Shield.
- In a geared company, variations in earnings before interest and tax generate a magnified impact on shareholder earnings.
- The downside of gearing is the creation of a prior charge against profits, which results in the risk of possible default as well as greater variability of shareholder earnings.
- Default risk is likely to impose further costs on the geared company's shareholders, the 'costs of financial distress'.
- An insolvent company, i.e. one unable to meet its immediate commitments, is unlikely to achieve full market value in a sale of assets.
- A company's indebtedness can be expressed in terms of its capital gearing or its income gearing.
- Gearing is likely to lower the firm's overall cost of capital.
- The increased risks imposed by gearing are likely to cause shareholders to demand a higher rate of return.
- For companies using a mixture of debt and equity, there may be an optimal capital structure at which the overall, or Weighted Average Cost of Capital, is minimized.
- The WACC is found by weighting the cost of each type of finance by its proportionate contribution to overall financing.
- The WACC is the appropriate cut-off rate for new investment so long as the company adheres to the optimal capital proportions.
- When companies deviate from the optimal capital structure, the Marginal Cost of Capital becomes the correct cut-off rate.
- In view of the risks of gearing, an increase in borrowing *may* be a way of signalling to the market greater confidence in the future.

Further reading

A good overview of the theoretical ground can be found in Board's contribution to Firth and Keane (1986). Brealey and Myers (1991) devote two chapters to optimal capital structure at a rather less rigorous level than Copeland and Weston (1988).

It would be useful to look at Rutterford and Carter (1988) for a treatment of practical issues such as restrictive covenants.

Miller (1991) provides an overview of the capital structure debate to date in his Nobel lecture.

Questions

Self-test questions

1. Distinguish between capital gearing and income gearing, suggesting how each can be measured.

2. How is capital gearing similar to operational gearing?
3. How does capital gearing affect earnings per share, share price and hence company value, and the riskiness of shareholder earnings?
4. How is the cost of debt-finance calculated, allowing for tax relief on interest payments?
5. How does gearing affect the required return on investment?
6. What is meant by financial distress? Give five examples of how this can occur.

Exercises

1. Trexon plc is a major oil and gas exploration company which has most of its operations in the Middle East and South East Asia. Recently, the company acquired rights to explore for oil and gas in the Gulf of Mexico. Trexon plc proposes to finance the new operations from the issue of equity shares. At present, the company is financed by a combination of equity capital and loan capital. The equity shares have a nominal value of £0.50 and a current market value of £2.60. The current level of dividend is £0.16 per share and this has been growing at a compound rate of 6 per cent p.a. in recent years. The loan capital issued by the company is irredeemable and has a current market value of £94 per £100 nominal. Interest on the loan capital is at the rate of 12 per cent and interest due at the year end has recently been paid. At present, the company expects 60 per cent of its finance to come from equity capital and the rest from loan capital. In the future, however, the company will aim to finance 70 per cent of its operations from equity capital.

   When the proposal to finance the new operations via the rights issue of shares was announced at the annual general meeting of the company objections were raised by two shareholders present.

   Shareholder A argued:

   'I fail to understand why the company has decided to issue shares to finance the new operation. Surely it would be better to re-invest profit as this is, in effect, a free source of finance to the company.'

   Shareholder B argued:

   'I also fail to understand why the company has decided to issue shares to finance the new operation. However, I do not agree with the suggestion made by Shareholder A. I do not believe that shareholder funds should be used at all to finance the new operation. Instead, the company should issue more loan capital as it is cheap relative to equity capital and would, therefore, reduce the overall cost of capital of the company.'

   Corporation tax is at the rate of 35 per cent.

   Required
   (a) Explain the term 'cost of capital' and state why a company should calculate its cost of capital with care.
   (b) Calculate the weighted average cost of capital of Trexon plc which should be used in future investment decisions.

(c) Comment on the remarks made by:
  (i) Shareholder A; and
  (ii) Shareholder B.

(Certified Diploma, June 1990)

(Solution in Appendix A)

2. The managers of a small company, Capit Ltd, plan to borrow £200,000 to invest in buildings, equipment, and working capital. It will take more than 18 months before significant cash inflows are generated from the investment. The managers are worried about servicing the interest on the borrowed funds for an 18-month period as interest rates have recently been volatile.

  The company's advisers believe that there is an equal chance of interest rates rising or falling by 2 per cent during the first six months. After the first six months there is a 60 per cent chance of rates continuing to move by a further 2 per cent in the same direction as in the first six months in each future six-month period and a 40 per cent chance of a 2 per cent movement in the opposite direction. Interest is payable at the end of each six-month period.

  The managers are undecided whether to borrow the £200,000 in either:

(a) £150,000 short-term floating rate loan at an initial interest rate of 15 per cent p.a. and renewable every six months, plus a £50,000 five-year fixed rate loan at 17 per cent p.a.

(b) £50,000 short-term loan, £150,000 five-year loan, both on the same terms as (a) above.

  All loans are secured. Interest rate reviews for floating rate loans are every six months.

  Issue costs/renewal costs are 1 per cent of the loan size for each short-term loan, and £800 for the five year loan. Issue costs are payable at the end of the previous loan period except for the initial loans where issue costs are payable at the start of the loan period. Tax relief is available on interest payments twelve months after the interest has been paid. No tax relief is available on issue costs. Corporate tax is at the rate of 25 per cent. It is expected that £19,500, £18,500 and £15,500 will be available to service the loans in the first, second and third six month periods respectively. Any unused surplus may be carried forward to the next six-monthly period.

Required

(a) Discuss which form of financing Capit Ltd should use.

(b) Estimate which form of financing is expected to be cheapest for Capit Ltd during the 18-month period. For each financing method calculate the probability of the company being unable to service its interest payments during the eighteen-month period. Assume that financing will continue to be required after the eighteen-month period. The time-value of money, and any possible income from investing surplus cash between six-month periods, may be ignored.

(ACCA Level 3, June 1990)

3. Hargreaves Ltd is a medium-sized textile company supplying items of children's wear to large retail chain stores in the United Kingdom. The company has been operating for many years and is controlled by the Hargreaves family. The accounts of the company for the year ended 31 May 1990 are as follows:

Balance Sheet as at 31 May 1990

	£m	£m	£m
Fixed assets			
Freehold land and buildings at cost			20.1
Plant and machinery at cost		13.2	
Less: Accumulated depreciation		4.6	8.6
			28.7
Current assets			
Stock at cost		14.2	
Debtors		8.1	
Cash		1.0	
		23.3	
Less creditors: Amounts falling due within one year			
Trade creditors	5.7		
Proposed dividend	1.0		
Taxation	3.3	10.0	13.3
			42.0
Less creditors: Amounts falling due beyond one year			
Loans (12%)			10.0
			32.0
Capital and reserves			
Ordinary shares 25p			4.0
Retained profit			28.0
			32.0

Extracts from the profit and loss account for the year ended 31 May 1990

	£m
Turnover	78.4
Profit before interest and taxation	10.5
Interest payable	1.2
Profit before taxation	9.3
Taxation	3.3
Profit after taxation	6.0
Dividends	1.0
Retained profit for the year	5.0

The company has recently secured a large contract to supply a new range of children's wear for one of its major customers. Although new equipment costing £8 million will have to be purchased it is estimated that the profit before interest and taxation will increase by £3.0 million as a result of taking the contract.

Industrial Finance Ltd has offered to finance the expansion in any one of the following ways:

(i) the purchase of 4 million ordinary shares at a premium of £1.75 per share;
(ii) the purchase of £4 million 10% £1 preference shares at par and £4 million $12\frac{1}{2}$% debentures;
(iii) the purchase of two million ordinary shares at a premium of £1.75 per share and £4 million $12\frac{1}{2}$% debentures.

The company expects to maintain dividend per share at its current level for the foreseeable future.

The rate of corporation tax is 35 per cent.

Required

(a) Prepare a profit and loss account for Hargreaves Ltd for the year ended 31 May 1991 for each of the three financing schemes.
(b) Calculate the earnings per share for the year ended 31 May 1991 and the level of gearing at that date under each financing scheme.
(c) Calculate the level of profit before interest and taxation at which the earnings per share under scheme (i) and (iii) are equal.
(d) Briefly assess each of the financing schemes available to Hargreaves Ltd from the viewpoint of an existing shareholder.

(Certified Diploma, June 1990)

Practical assignment

For a company of your choice, undertake an analysis of gearing similar to that conducted in the text for Rolls-Royce. Pay particular attention to the treatment of minority interests, provisions and other components of long-term liabilities. If you decide to include short-term indebtedness in your capital gearing measure, should you not include trade and other creditors as well?

Try to form a view as to whether your company is operating with high or low gearing.

CHAPTER 15

Capital structure: the underlying relationships

WILL GRANADA LIVE AGAIN?

In 1986, the leisure and business services group Rank Organisation bid for Granada, the TV and leisure company best known for producing the long-running soap opera *Coronation Street*. Unlike many takeover bids, this one seemed to have 'industrial logic', due to considerable overlap in the activities of the two enterprises. However, the bid was blocked by the Independent Broadcasting Association as it would have involved transferring the TV franchise to the new owner, thus contravening the terms on which it was awarded.

Free from the threat of takeover, Granada then embarked on a series of adventures, largely financed by borrowing.

First, in an effort to gain primacy in its core TV rental business, it made several acquisitions, whose profits subsequently plunged as the UK economy entered recession.

Second, following the fashion for 'globalization', it sought to export its TV rental concept to Germany and Canada, with little thought to cultural differences, ensuring its failure and significant losses.

Third, it diversified into computer maintenance services, despite having already failed with computer retailing. Again, the results did not justify the huge investment.

Fourth, it invested in 'high-technology' (literally), via its involvement with the satellite joint-venture BSB (subsequently, BSkyB, after the merger with Sky).

These escapades resulted in a fall in pre-tax profits between 1989 and 1990 from £164m to £121m and a further fall in the next half-year profits from £63m to £38m. In May 1991, it reduced the interim dividend from 4.4p per share to 2.5p. More significant, perhaps, was the growth in the group's indebtedness. Granada's debt rose between September 1990 and May 1991 by £140m to £634m, producing gearing of 125 per cent, hence the dividend cut in order to conserve cash resources. The dividend cut was accompanied by a cash call to shareholders via a one-for-three

---

rights issue at 140p, deeply discounting the market price, which promptly dropped from 211p to 184p. In addition, Granada sold one of its main profit-earners, its bingo halls, to the brewers Bass.

It would be fair to say that Granada had lost its way. Its share price at the time of Rank's bid was around £3, but by July 1991 had fallen below 150p. Moreover, several observers suggested that Granada's debt was really much higher than the published figure, mainly due to its BSkyB holding. Granada had made off-balance sheet guarantees of around £130m and faced further commitments of some £25m, having already assumed responsibility for BSkyB's rental and hire purchase accounts.

15.1   Introduction

The Granada episode reveals a company which pursued strategic objectives by the extensive use of debt finance and, in the process, appeared to damage shareholder interests severely. This damage was primarily due to ill-defined and poorly executed strategy, and was aggravated by the over-use of debt, a good example of poor investment decisions, coupled with faulty financing decisions. A *Guardian* writer commented: 'Management theory seems to have been swallowed whole and regurgitated as company strategy without the benefit of digestion by the stomach juices of experience.'

The previous chapter provided a 'traditional' focus on the possible impact of capital structure decisions on company value and shareholder wealth, and it is easy to explain the Granada experience using the 'traditional' approach. For giving prominence to 'tradition' we make no apology, yet we believe, nevertheless, that the reader should be aware of the key features of a substantial body of finance theory initially developed in opposition to the traditional perspective. This was first developed by Modigliani and Miller (MM) in an important paper in 1958. We consider the MM approach in this chapter and discuss some of its recent revisions.

LEARNING OBJECTIVES

This chapter offers a more theoretically-oriented analysis of capital structure decisions. After reading it you should:

* Understand the theoretical underpinnings of 'modern' capital structure theory.
* Appreciate the differences between the 'traditional' view of gearing and the Modigliani–Miller versions.
* Know how to ungear a Beta coefficient.

15.2   The Modigliani–Miller message

To Modigliani and Miller, the traditional perception of the impact and desirability of gearing seemed unsupported by a theoretical framework and hence was suspect. In particular, there seemed little reason, apart from some form of market imperfection such as information deficiency, why a mere alteration in the capital structure of a firm should be expected to alter its value. *After all, neither its earnings stream nor its inherent business risk would alter* – it would remain the same enterprise, operating under the same managers and in the same industry!

If wealth depends on value-creation, then why should merely 'repackaging' the company's income stream into the two components of dividend and interest payments alter the wealth-creating properties of the company's assets. In other words, *MM contended that in a perfect capital market, the value of a company depended simply on its operating income stream and the degree of business risk attaching to this, regardless of the actual capital structure.* Therefore, any imbalance between the value of a geared company and an otherwise identical ungeared company could only be a temporary aberration and would be quickly unwound by market forces. The specific mechanism for equalizing the values of companies, identical except for their gearing, was the process of 'arbitrage', a feature of all developed financial markets which ensures that assets with the same risk-return characteristics sell at the same prices.

To support these contentions, algebraic analysis is required, although readers will find that it is less complex than appears at first sight. However, those who may wish to skip the detailed analysis can jump ahead to the concluding section 15.9.

The analytical framework

No distinction is made between short- and long-term debt and we assume that all borrowing is perpetual. The company is expected to deliver constant and perpetual annual earnings of E, the estimate of which is derived from a normally distributed range of possible outcomes. Investors are assumed to have homogeneous expectations, i.e. they all formulate similar estimates of company earnings. E is thus the Net Operating Income (NOI) before interest and tax, or more simply, revenues less variable costs less fixed operating costs. As we saw in Chapter 14, the NOI corresponds to Earnings Before Interest and Tax (EBIT). It is important to note that we are using the *free cash flow* concept of earnings as explained in Chapter 4, i.e. income net of any investment required to make good wear-and-tear on capital equipment and thus maintain annual earnings at E.

The discount rate applied to the stream of expected earnings depends on the degree of business risk incurred by the enterprise. MM utilized the concept of 'equivalent risk classes', each containing firms whose earnings depend on the same risk factors and from which the market expects the same return. In CAPM terms, this means that the earnings streams from firms in the same risk category are perfectly correlated and member companies have identical Betas.

For consistency, we utilize the same definitions and notation as in Chapter 14. The reader may find it useful to be reminded of the key definitions which appear in Table 15.1.

Table 15.1 Key definitions in capital structure analysis

V_0 = the market value of the whole company
V_S = the value of the shareholders' stake in the company
V_B = the value of the company's outstanding debt
B = the book value of debt (assumed equal to market value)
k_e = the rate of return required by shareholders
k_d = the rate of return required by providers of debt capital
i = the coupon rate on debt
iB = annual interest charges (i.e. payments to lenders)
$k_e V_S$ = payments to shareholders = $(E - iB)$, so that
E = annual net operating income (NOI) = $(iB + k_e V_S)$ = EBIT
It should be stressed that we are assuming no retention of earnings, i.e.
D (dividends) = E, and hence no growth. In terms of the Dividend Growth model, $g = 0$, hence

$$k_e = \frac{D}{V_S} + g$$
$$= \frac{D}{V_S} = \frac{E}{V_S}$$

Allowing for interest payments of IB,
$$k_e = \frac{(E - iB)}{V_S}$$

The overall rate of return the company must achieve to satisfy all stakeholders is the WACC, denoted by k_0. This can be expressed as:

$$k_0 = \left(k_e \times \frac{V_S}{V_0} \right) + \left(k_d \times \frac{V_B}{V_0} \right) = \frac{E}{V_o}$$

The WACC also equals E/V_0 since total operating income is composed of payments to shareholders, $k_e V_S$, plus payments to lenders, iB.

Within this framework of definitions, we now examine the impact of variations in capital structure on V_0 and k_0. The original MM analysis did not apply directly to the UK context, being expressed in terms of substituting debt for equity, i.e. using debt to repurchase ordinary shares. This was not generally possible in the United Kingdom until the Companies Act 1981, which enabled firms, subject to shareholder approval, to undertake such repurchases. Now this is permitted, the original MM analysis is more readily applicable to the capital structure decisions of UK firms. Using debt-for-equity substitution rather than adding debt to equity has the major advantage of enabling us to hold constant both the book values of capital employed and assets and also the EBIT, a device used in the Lindley example in Chapter 14. Any gearing change alters only the company's capital and liabilities with no effect on company size nor on the level and riskiness of earnings. As a result, we can focus directly on the relationship between V_o and k_0.

MM's assumptions

Much criticism of MM's analysis stemmed from failure to understand positive scientific methodology. Their analysis attempted to isolate the critical variables affecting firm value under the restrictive conditions of a perfect capital market. This provided a systematic basis for examining how imperfections in real world markets could influence the links between value and risk. The key assumptions are:

1. All investors are price-takers.
2. All market participants, including firms and investors, can lend or borrow at the same risk-free rate.
3. There are neither personal nor corporate income taxes.
4. There are no brokerage or other transactions charges.
5. Investors are all rational utility-of-expected-wealth-seekers.
6. Firms can be grouped into 'homogeneous risk classes', such that the market seeks the same return from all member firms in each group.
7. Investors formulate similar expectations about future company earnings, which are described by a normal probability distribution.
8. In the event of bankruptcy, assets can be sold at market values.

15.3   MM's propositions

The MM analysis was presented in three propositions, of which the first is the most fundamental.

Proposition I

The central proposition made by MM is that the *WACC is independent of the debt/equity ratio and equal to the cost of capital which the firm would have with no gearing in its capital structure.* In other words, the appropriate capitalization rate for a firm is the rate applied by the market to an ungeared company in the relevant risk category. The arbitrage mechanism will operate to equalize the values of any two companies whose values are temporarily out of line with each other. We use the example of Nogear plc and Higear plc to illustrate this.

Nogear plc and Higear plc

Nogear plc is ungeared, financed by 5 million £1 shares, while Higear plc has a Balance Sheet, or 'book', debt/equity ratio of 25 per cent (4 million £1 shares and 10 per cent debt with a book value of £1m). The two firms are identical in every other respect, including their business risk and level of annual expected earnings (E) of £1m. The market requires a return of 20 per cent for ungeared income streams of this particular risk.

Imagine that, temporarily at least, the market value of Nogear is £4m and that of Higear is £6m, involving gearing at *market* values of £1m/£5m = 20%. These market values correspond to respective share prices of $\frac{£4m}{5m} = 80p$ for Nogear and $\frac{(£6m - £1m)}{4m} = £1.25$ for Higear.

The relative values conform to the traditional relationship, since Higear has a greater value. Also, it appears that Nogear is undervalued by the market, as a 20 per cent capitalization rate should yield a value of £5m. MM argue that such imbalances can only be temporary and the benefit obtained by Higear for its shareholders is largely illusory. It will actually pay them to sell their holdings in the over-valued company and buy stakes in the undervalued one. Specifically, shareholders can achieve a higher return by selling holdings in Higear, and simultaneously, replicate its gearing (MM call this *home-made gearing*) and achieve a higher overall return. This process of arbitrage will exert downward pressure on the value of Higear and upward pressure on Nogear's value, until their values are equalized.

Home-made gearing

Consider the case of an investor with a 1 per cent equity stake in Higear. At present this stake is worth (1% of £5m) = £50,000, attracting an income of 1% of (£1m less interest payments of 10% × £1m), i.e. (1% × £900,000) = £9,000. Such an investor could realize his holdings for £50,000 and duplicate Higear's debt/equity ratio of 20 per cent by borrowing £10,000 at 10 per cent and investing the total stake of £60,000 in Nogear shares. This would buy £60,000/£4m = 1.5% of Nogear's equity, to yield a dividend of (1.5% × £1m) = £15,000. Personal interest commitments amount to (10% × borrowings of £10,000) = £1,000, for a net return of (£15,000 − £1,000) = £14,000. Clearly, it would pay investors to undertake this *arbitrage* exercise, thus pushing down the value of Higear and pushing up the value of Nogear until there was no further scope to exploit such gains. This point would be reached when the values of the two companies were equal and each offered the appropriate 20 per cent return demanded by the market:

$$\text{Value of Nogear} = \text{Value of Higear} = \frac{E}{k_e} = \frac{£1m}{0.2} = £5m$$

At this equilibrium relationship, the share price of each company is £1. For Nogear, the calculation is £5m/5m = £1, while for Higear, the relevant figures are (£5m less £1m debt) divided by 4m shares = £1. *In an MM world, there are no prolonged benefits from gearing and any short-term discrepancies between geared and otherwise identical ungeared companies quickly evaporate. As a result, MM conclude that both company value and the overall required return, k_0, are invariant to capital structure.*

In reality, not all of the conditions required to support the arbitrage process may apply, suggesting that any *observed* benefits may derive from imperfections in the capital market. Moreover, if gearing does result in higher company value, the corollary is that there must have been a wealth transfer, since nothing has occurred to alter the fundamental wealth-creating properties of the company.

Financing Decisions and Policy

Proposition II: the behaviour of the equity cost of capital

Underpinning Proposition I is a statement about the behaviour of the relevant cost of capital concepts, in particular the rate of return required by shareholders, which is expressed in MM's second proposition. This states 'the expected yield of a share of equity is equal to the appropriate capitalization rate, k_e, for a pure equity stream in the class, plus a premium related to the financial risk equal to the debt-to-equity ratio times the spread between k_e and k_d'. This proposition can be expressed as follows:

$$k_{eg} = k_{eu} + (k_{eu} - k_d) \cdot \frac{V_B}{V_S}$$

where k_{eg} and k_{eu} denote the returns required by the shareholders of a geared company and an equivalent ungeared company, respectively. The expression is easily obtained from Proposition I, as shown in Appendix I. It simply tells us that the *rate of return required by shareholders increases linearly as the debt/equity ratio is increased*, i.e. the cost of equity rises exactly in line with any increase in gearing to precisely offset any benefits conferred by the use of apparently cheap debt. The relevant relationships are shown in Figure 15.1.

It should now be appreciated that in the Nogear/Higear example, Higear shareholders were seeking too low a rate of return, i.e. Higear was overvalued, and the market was temporarily offering Nogear's shareholders too high a return, i.e. Nogear was undervalued. Via the process of arbitrage, their values were brought back into line, and appropriate rates of return on equity established, reflecting their respective levels of gearing. The correct rate of return for Higear's equity, in view of its debt/equity ratio of 25 per cent (at equilibrium market values) is:

$$k_{eg} = k_{eu} + (k_{eu} - k_d) \frac{V_B}{V_S} = 20\% + (20\% - 10\%) \frac{V_B}{V_S} = 22.5\%$$

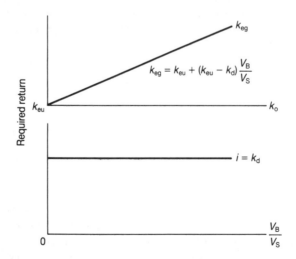

Figure 15.1 MM's Propositions I and II

Proposition III: the cut-off rate for new investment

MM's third proposition asserts that 'the cut-off rate for investment will in all cases be k_0 and will be unaffected by the type of security used to finance the investment'.

To show this, consider a firm whose initial value, V_0, is:

$$V_0 = V_{S0} + V_{B0} = \frac{E_0}{k_0}$$

It contemplates an investment project, with outlay $£I$, involving a perpetual return of R per £ invested. After the investment is accepted, the new value of the firm, V_1, is:

$$V_1 = \frac{E_1}{k_0} = \frac{(E_0 + RI)}{k_0} = V_0 + \frac{RI}{k_0} \tag{A}$$

Assuming the project is debt-financed, the post-project acceptance value of the shares is:

$$V_{S1} = (V_1 - V_{B1}) = V_1 - (V_{B0} + I) \tag{B}$$

Substituting Equation (A) into Equation (B) yields:

$$V_{S1} = V_0 + \frac{RI}{k_0} - V_{B0} - I$$

and since

$$V_{S0} = (V_0 - V_{B0})$$

the change in V_S equals

$$(V_{S1} - V_{S0}) = \frac{RI}{k_0} - I$$

This exceeds zero only if $R > k_0$. Hence, *a firm acting in the best interests of its shareholders should only undertake investments whose returns at least equal k_0, the Weighted Average Cost of Capital, which itself is invariant to gearing according to Proposition I.*

Illustration

Nogear decides to raise £1m via a debt issue at 10 per cent to finance a new project expected to yield an annual return of 15 per cent. Is this an acceptable project? Proposition I tells us that the value of the company (and the equity) prior to the issue is:

$$V_0 = V_{S0} = \frac{£1m}{0.2} = £5m$$

Incorporating the new project's earnings, the post-issue value is:

$$V_1 = \frac{£1m + (15\% \times £1m)}{20\%} = \frac{£1.15m}{0.2} = £5.75m.$$

The new value of the equity is:

$$V_{S1} = V_0 + \frac{RI}{k_0} - V_{B0} - I = \pounds 5\text{m} + \frac{\pounds 0.15\text{m}}{0.2} - 0 - \pounds 1\text{m} = \pounds 4.75\text{m}.$$

The value of the equity falls because the new project's return, although above the interest rate on the debt used to finance it, is less than the capitalization rate applicable to this risk category.

15.4   Impediments to arbitrage

Analysis of the arbitrage process demonstrates that corporate and personal gearing are perfect substitutes in a perfect capital market. The Nogear/Higear example showed how individual investors could duplicate corporate gearing to unwind any transitory premium in the share price of a geared company. Much criticism of MM centres on the perfect capital market assumptions and the extent to which the arbitrage process can be expected to operate in practice.

In reality, brokerage fees discriminate against small investors, and other transaction costs limit the gains from arbitrage. Moreover, if companies can borrow at lower rates than individuals, investors may prefer the equity of geared companies as vehicles for obtaining benefits otherwise denied to them. In the United Kingdom, the Report of the Wilson Committee (1980) produced evidence that, for reasons of size, security and convenience, large firms could borrow at lower rates than small firms and individuals. In addition, some major UK investors, e.g. the pension funds, face restrictions on their borrowing powers, limiting their scope for home-made gearing.

Some authors suggest that such imperfections may foster investor demand for the equity of geared companies. However, to sustain this argument, we would need to produce evidence that relatively (but safely) geared companies are more attractively rated by the market. There is little evidence that such firms sell at relatively high P/E ratios. Indeed, UK investment trust companies, which invest in equities using substantial borrowed capital, typically sell at significant discounts to their net asset values, discounts far higher than can be explained by the transactions costs which would be incurred in liquidating their portfolios.

15.5   MM with corporate income tax

The analysis of MM's three Propositions in section 15.3 is a largely theoretical exercise, designed to isolate the key variables relating company value and gearing. This only becomes operational when 'real-world' complications are introduced. Perhaps the most important of these is corporate taxation. In most economies, interest charges are tax-allowable, providing an incentive for companies to gear their capital structures. In a taxed world, the MM conclusions require significant modification.

Corporation Tax is applied to the stream of earnings after deducting interest charges, so that the value of a geared company's shares is the capitalized value of the after-tax earnings stream (Net Income):

$$V_S = \frac{(E - iB)\ (1 - T)}{k_{eg}}$$

Where:

$$T = \text{the marginal rate of tax on corporate earnings.}$$

Assuming that the book and market values of debt capital coincide, so that the cost of debt, k_d, equates to the coupon rate, i, the value of debt is the discounted interest stream, i.e. $V_B = iB/i$, so the value of the overall company is

$$V_0 = V_S + V_B = \frac{(E - iB).(1 - T)}{k_{eg}} + \frac{iB}{i}$$

It can be shown that geared companies will sell at a premium over equivalent ungeared companies because of the benefits of tax-allowable debt interest. The post-tax annual expected earnings stream, E_T, is comprised of the earnings attributable to shareholders plus the debt interest:

$$E_T = (E - iB)\ (1 - T) + iB$$

This simplifies to:

$$E_T = E(1 - T) + TiB$$

This second expression is very useful: the first element is the Net Income which the shareholders in an equivalent ungeared company would receive, while the second element is the tax benefit afforded by debt interest relief. The total value of the geared company, V_g, is found by capitalizing the first element at the cost of equity capital applicable to an ungeared company (k_{eu}), while the second is capitalized at the cost of debt, which we assume equals the nominal rate of interest, i:

$$V_g = \frac{E(1 - T)}{k_{eu}} + \frac{TiB}{i} = \frac{E(1 - T)}{k_{eu}} + TB = V_u + TB$$

This is a significant result. The expression for the value of the geared company is comprised of the value of an equivalent ungeared company, V_u, plus a premium derived by discounting to perpetuity the stream of tax savings, applicable so long as the company has sufficient taxable capacity, i.e. if $E > iB$. This second element, TB, is called the *Tax Shield*. This is a major modification of MM's Proposition I, as shown in Figure 15.2.

The company value profile now rises continuously with gearing. Proposition II also needs modification. With no corporate tax, this stated that the shareholders in a geared company require a return, k_{eg}, of:

$$k_{eg} = k_{eu} + (k_{eu} - k_d)\ \frac{B}{V_S}$$

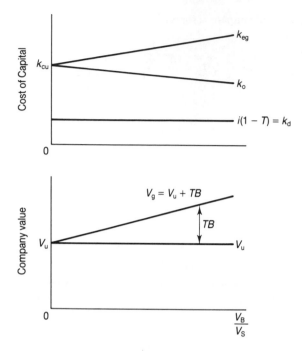

Figure 15.2 The MM thesis with corporate income tax

In a taxed world, the return required by shareholders becomes:

$$k_{eg} = k_{eu} + (k_{eu} - k_d)(1 - T)\frac{B}{V_s}$$

The return required by the geared company's shareholders is the sum of the cost of equity in an identical ungeared company plus a financial risk premium related to the corporate tax rate and the debt/equity ratio.

The premium for financial risk required by shareholders is lower in this version due to the tax deductibility of debt interest. This relationship is also shown by Figure 15.2. Finally, it follows that if, at every level of gearing, the cost of equity is lower and also the cost of debt itself is reduced by interest deductibility, the Weighted Average Cost of Capital is lower at all gearing ratios, and declines as gearing increases. Figure 15.2 shows the resultant *pivoting* in the k_0 profile.

Clearly, there are now significant advantages from gearing with the implication that companies should gear up almost to 100%!

Illustration

It is now helpful to demonstrate these relationships using the examples of Nogear and Higear. Recall that both companies had E of £1m and their equilibrium market values were £5m under the no-tax version of the MM thesis. After taxation, shareholder earnings in Nogear fall to £1m$(1-T)$. With 33 per cent Corporation Tax, net income is £1m $(1-33\%)=$£0.67m. Capitalized at 20 per cent, the value of the ungeared company is:

$$V_u = \frac{£1m(1-33\%)}{k_{eu}} = \frac{£0.67m}{0.2} = £3.35m$$

In the case of Higear, Net Income is given by taxable earnings of $(E-iB)$ less the tax charge of $T(E-iB)$ to yield:

$$NI = (E-iB)(1-T) = [£1m - (10\% \times £1m)].(1-33\%)$$
$$= (£0.9m).(0.67) = £0.603m.$$

This might be capitalized at the geared cost of equity and added to the value of debt to yield the overall company value. However, there is a circular problem here since the calculation of the market value of the shares, V_S, derives from the calculation of k_{eg} which itself depends on V_S! A remedy for this problem is to use the expression $V_g = V_u + TB$. This yields:

$$V_g = V_u + TB = £3.35m + (33\% \times £1m) = £3.35m + £0.33m = £3.68m$$

The geared company clearly has a greater market value – it is worth more due to the value of the Tax Shield. The size of the Tax Shield depends on the gearing ratio, the rate of taxation and the taxable capacity of the enterprise. Returning to the earlier point regarding the largely illusory benefits of gearing, clearly the previous conclusion has to be modified. It is still correct to argue that the wealth-creating properties of the company are unchanged since its trading activities are unaltered, yet gearing has raised company value. To explain this phenomenon, we must look for a *wealth transfer*. Quite simply, the stakeholders of Higear benefit at the expense of the taxpayer due to the tax deductibility of debt interest. (Whether we can say this is desirable or not in a wider context depends on the value of the forgone tax revenues in their alternative use.)

In its tax-adjusted form, the MM thesis looks far more like the traditional version, although it must be emphasized that the benefits from gearing derive from the tax system, rather than from failure of the shareholders to respond to financial risk by seeking higher returns. We will discover that the similarity becomes even closer when we allow for financial distress.

15.6 MM with financial distress

In section 15.5, we saw how including corporate taxation into the MM model implied that companies should gear up to almost 100 per cent. This implication is clearly at odds with observed practice – few companies gear up to extreme levels, through fear of liquidation and its associated costs. It may seem surprising in retrospect that MM should have omitted liquidation costs from their analysis, but this was a logical consequence of their perfect capital market assumptions. In such a market, where investors are numerous and rational, have homogeneous expectations and plentiful access to information, the resale value of assets, even those being sold in a liquidation, will reflect their true economic values. Investors will recognize the worth of such assets as measured by the present values of their future income flows, and be prepared to bid up to this value, so that the price realized by a liquidator should not involve any discount. In other words, the mere event of insolvency is irrelevant, except insofar as it involves a change of ownership.

In effect, liquidation costs and the other *costs of financial distress*, examined in section 14.7, introduce a new imperfection into the analysis of capital structure decisions, namely the actual or expected inability to realize 'full value' for assets in a distress sale and the costs of actions taken to forestall this contingency.

FINANCIAL DISTRESS

Denoting the 'costs of financial distress' by FD, the value of a geared company becomes:

$$V_g = V_u + [TB - FD]$$

From this, we may conclude that the *financial manager should attempt to maximize the gap between tax benefits and financial distress costs, i.e. (TB − FD) and that there exists an optimal capital structure where company value is maximized.* This occurs where the marginal benefit of further tax savings equate to the marginal cost of anticipated financial distress. This occurs at gearing ratio X^* in Figure 15.3.

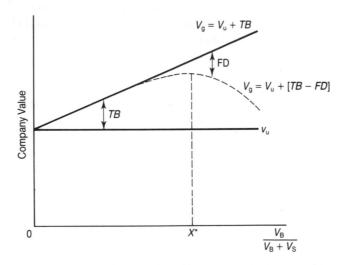

Figure 15.3 Optimal gearing with liquidation costs

The costs of financial distress rise with gearing once the market starts to perceive a substantially increased risk of financial failure. The likelihood of FD being non-zero depends on the probability distribution of the firm's earnings profile. For example, in the Lindley example in Chapter 14, for gearing ratios up to 50 per cent the probability of inability to meet interest payments is zero, but would be 0.25 for any higher gearing ratio. For most companies, the probability, p, of financial distress will increase with the book values of debt, B, so that the FD function increases with gearing. If d denotes the expected percentage discount on the pre-liquidation value in the event of a forced sale, the costs of financial distress are:

$$FD = (pdV_g)$$

and the value of the geared firm is:

$$V_g = V_u + (TB - pdV_g)$$

This suggests that market imperfections can be exploited to raise company value so long as TB exceeds pdV_g. Notice that the inverted 'U'-shaped value profile now appears remarkably similar to the traditional version and, of course, is associated with a mirror-image Weighted Average Cost of Capital schedule.

15.7 Capital structure theory and the CAPM

A feature of MM's initial model was the classification of firms into 'homogeneous risk classes' as a way of controlling for inherent operating or business risk. The modern distinction between systematic and specific risk makes this device unnecessary, as relevant business risk is automatically catered for via the Beta. It is a relatively simple task to integrate the MM analysis with the CAPM. This was first done by Hamada (1969), who demonstrated that the required return on the equity of a geared firm in a CAPM framework is:

$$k_{eg} = R_f + (ER_m - R_f)\beta_u \left[1 + \frac{V_B}{V_s}(1 - T) \right]$$

where β_u is the Beta applicable to the earnings of an ungeared company, or the pure equity Beta. Multiplying out, we derive:

$$k_{eg} = R_f + \beta_u(ER_m - R_f) + (ER_m - R_f)\beta_u \left[\frac{V_B}{V_s}(1 - T) \right]$$

This looks unwieldy, but is a useful vehicle for making the distinction between business and financial risk. Observed Betas such as those recorded by the London Business School, are equity Betas, incorporating elements of both types of risk. From our revised CAPM expression, it can be seen that the observed Beta will be:

$$\beta_g = \beta_u \left[1 + \frac{V_B}{V_s}(1 - T) \right]$$

The ungeared equity Beta is therefore:

$$\beta_u = \frac{\beta_g}{(1 + \frac{V_B}{V_S}(1-T))}$$

Using the relevant tax rate and the company's debt/equity ratio allows us to separate the two premia for business risk and financial risk. To illustrate this concept, consider the example of Langbar plc whose equity Beta is 1.2, and whose debt/equity ratio is 25 per cent. Assume a risk-free return of 10 per cent and an expected market return of 18 per cent. The Corporation Tax rate is 33 per cent.

The basic CAPM equation suggests a required return of:

$$k_{eg} = R_f + \beta_g(ER_m - R_f) = 10\% + 1.2\ (18\% - 10\%) = 19.6\%$$

The ungeared equity Beta is given by:

$$\beta_u = \frac{1.2}{\left[1 + \frac{1}{4}\ (1 - 33\%)\right]} = \frac{1.2}{1.1675} = 1.028$$

The components of the overall required return on Langbar's equity can now be specified. The cost of equity is synthesized as follows:

Cost of equity	=	Risk-free rate	+	Premium for Business Risk	+	Premium for Financial Risk
k_{eg}	=	R_f	+	$(ER_m - R_f)\beta_u$	+	$(ER_m - R_f)\beta_u \dfrac{V_B}{V_S}(1-T)$
			= 10% + (18% − 10%)(1.028) + (18% − 10%)(1.028)(1/4)(1 − 33%)			
		= 10% +	8.2%	+	1.4% = 19.6%	

This is the same result obtained using the usual CAPM formula. The distinction between the geared Beta and the ungeared Beta will be particularly useful in Chapter 18 where we examine the rates of return required for particular activities.

15.8   Allowing for personal taxation: Miller's revision

The MM analysis including corporate earnings taxation still leaves something of a 'puzzle' to solve. The expression for the value of a geared company indicates that the Tax Shield is equal to the tax rate (T) times the book value of corporate debt (B), i.e. TB. With the present (1992–3) UK rate of Corporation Tax of 33 per cent, for every £1 of corporate debt the value of the company would be increased by £0.33. If such tax benefits can stem from corporate gearing, why do we find widely dispersed gearing ratios even in the same industry? And why are some of these so much lower than the MM theory (even allowing for the costs of financial distress) might suggest? According to Miller (1977), the answers to such questions lie in the interaction of the corporate taxation system with the personal taxation system, an issue omitted from the MM analysis.

In seeking to re-establish the irrelevance of gearing for company value, Miller formulated a revised model of company value, based on the value of the combined flows of income to corporate stakeholders after allowing for their personal taxation. These flows comprise the flow of dividend income, taxed at the individual's marginal rate of tax on dividends, t_e, plus the flow of lenders' interest payments, taxed at their marginal rate of taxation on interest payments, t_B:

$$D(1-t_e)+i(1-t_B)B$$

where $D=$ annual dividends and $B=$ the nominal value of debt. With zero retentions, this equals the free cash flow into the firm and its appropriation into interest, taxation and dividends.

Applying the MM procedure of valuing the stream of equity income by discounting at the appropriate risk-adjusted rate and capitalizing the stream of tax savings at the appropriate after-tax cost of debt, the value of a geared company is:

$$V_g = V_u + \left[1 - \frac{(1-T)(1-t_e)}{(1-t_B)} \right] B$$

The value of the Tax Shield per £1 of corporate debt now depends on a complex interrelationship between the various rates of tax. The Tax Shield equals TB as in the MM model when $t_e = t_B$, i.e. when the marginal rates of personal tax applicable to dividends and debt interest are equal. With dividends taxed at the standard rate (t_s), Ashton (1989) shows that the tax advantage per £1 of debt is:

$$\text{Tax Shield per £1 of debt} = 1 - \frac{(1-T)}{(1-t_s)} = \frac{(T-t_s)}{(1-t_s)}$$

The set of rates applicable for 1992–3 under the UK's Imputation Tax system for a basic rate taxpayer (with no further liability to pay income tax on net dividend receipts) are $T=33\%$ and $t_B=t_s=25\%$. This combination of rates suggests the value of the Tax Shield is only about £0.11 per £ of debt compared with that of £0.33 as implied by the MM model. However, this is not a general result. The value of the Tax Shield depends on the particular combination of tax rates applicable to the firm and its stakeholders. In reality, as Ashton also shows, the picture is also complicated by retention of earnings and income from capital gain. In the United Kingdom, many individuals have a definite preference for capital gains because of their relatively favourable tax treatment (first £5,800 of gains exempt, indexation of gains, tax only payable when gains realized).

The relevance of capital structure thus depends on the precise tax position of the company and its shareholders. For a faithful guide to capital structure decisions, the financial manager needs to know stakeholders' marginal tax rates, information which is not easily available. We find ourselves in the same position as in the dividend policy debate where we argued that companies are likely to attract a clientele of shareholders for whom their particular dividend policy is attractive – for dividend policy, simply read 'capital structure'.

The Miller analysis suggests that low-rate taxpayers should be attracted to high-debt companies since they would benefit from a Tax Shield without incurring high personal taxation, while low debt would attract a clientele of high-rate taxpayers. Shareholders in different categories would seek the shares of different companies according to their own tax positions. Moreover, as a result of portfolio reorganization by individuals according to their particular tax positions, it is possible that any tax advantage of corporate debt could disappear in the resulting segmented market, which could explain the variety of observed gearing ratios.

However, with a 'typical' tax advantage of debt equal to $(T-t_s)/(1-t_s)$, we can reformulate several of the above MM expressions. This is done in Appendix I, based on Ashton (1989).

15.9 Summary and conclusions

These two chapters have covered extensive ground attempting to isolate the critical variables relating company value to capital structure. In this process, we have travelled from the lower ground of the somewhat crude 'traditional' version up to the more rarefied heights of the pure and less pure MM and Miller analyses, before arriving at the firmer footing of the model displayed in Figure 15.3. This closely resembles the traditional theory itself, with its U-shaped cost of capital schedule and optimal capital structure. In so doing, however, we have established that the *benefits of debt stem mainly from market imperfections, especially the tax relief on debt interest but that a different type of imperfection, liquidation costs, can offset these tax breaks at higher levels of gearing.* In addition, we have shown that even the tax benefits of gearing are not universally available, as they depend on the particular mix of personal and corporate tax rates faced by the company and its stakeholders.

Key points

- MM argue that as the method of financing a company does not affect its fundamental wealth-creating capacity, the use of debt capital, under perfect market conditions, has no effect on company value.
- Shareholders respond to an increase in the likely variability of earnings, i.e. financial risk, by seeking higher returns to exactly offset the apparent benefits of 'cheap' debt.
- The appropriate cut-off rate for new investment is the rate of return required by shareholders in an equivalent ungeared company.
- When corporate taxation is introduced, the tax deductibility of debt interest creates value for shareholders via the Tax Shield, but this is a wealth transfer from taxpayers.
- The value of a geared company equals the value of an equivalent ungeared company plus the Tax Shield:

$$V_g = V_u + TB$$

- With corporate taxation, the rate of return required by the geared company's shareholders is less than that in the all-equity company, reflecting the tax benefits.
- A further effect of corporation taxation is to lower the overall cost of capital, which appears to fall continuously as gearing increases.
- However, this result relies on the absence of default risk and the consequent costs of financial distress incurred as a company reaches or approaches the point of insolvency.
- A major cost of financial distress is the inability to achieve 'full market value' in a fire sale of assets.
- There is, in theory, an optimal capital structure where the marginal benefit of tax savings equals the marginal cost of financial distress.
- In reality, while companies should balance the benefits of the Tax Shield against the likelihood of financial distress costs, prudence will persuade most financial directors to restrain gearing levels, especially as tax savings are uncertain, depending on fluctuations in corporate earnings.
- The Miller analysis warns us that the tax benefits of debt may not be as high as they appear, since they are influenced by the tax status of the company and its shareholders.

Appendix I   Derivation of MM's Proposition II

Given that:

$$\frac{E}{V_S + V_B} = \frac{E}{V_0} = k_0$$

and

$$k_e = \frac{(E - iB)}{V_S}$$

we may write

$$E = k_0 V_0 = k_0 (V_S + V_B)$$

Substituting for E,

$$k_e = \frac{k_o(V_S + V_B) - iB}{V_S} = \frac{k_0 V_S + k_0 V_B - iB}{V_S} = k_0 + (k_0 - i)\frac{V_B}{V_S}$$

Since Proposition I argues that k_0 equals the return required by shareholders in an equivalent ungeared company, k_{eu}, and so long as book and market values of debt capital coincide, ensuring that $i = k_d$, then this expression may be written

$$k_{eg} = k_{eu} + (k_{eu} - k_d)\frac{V_B}{V_S}$$

as in the text. In other words, the return required by shareholders is a linear function of the company's debt/equity ratio.

Appendix II
Key MM expressions under the imputation tax system

First, the relationship between the values of geared and ungeared companies is given by:

$$V_g = V_u + \frac{(T - t_s)}{(1 - t_s)} B$$

Second, the return required by shareholders becomes:

$$k_{eg} = k_{eu} + [k_{eu} - i(1 - t_s)] \left[\frac{(1 - T)}{(1 - t_s)} \frac{V_B}{V_S} \right]$$

Third, assuming corporate debt can be treated as risk-free, the geared and ungeared Betas are related by:

$$\beta_g = \beta_u \left[1 + \frac{V_B}{V_S} \frac{(1 - T)}{(1 - t_s)} \right]$$

See Ashton (1989) for derivations and explanations of these expressions.

Questions

Self-test questions

1. What are the key assumptions of the basic MM model?
2. List, explain and illustrate graphically the three MM propositions.
3. Why is the value of a geared company higher than that of an equivalent ungeared company in the MM-with-tax model?
4. How would you identify the point beyond which a company would be unable to issue any further debt securities?
5. How can you reconcile the MM models with the 'traditional' view of gearing?

Exercises

1. Slohill plc plans to raise finance sometime within the next few months. Slohill's managing director remembers the stock market crash of October 1987 when share prices fell approximately 30 per cent during one week, and is worried about the possible effects of a further crash on the cost of capital.

Slohill plc
Summarized Balance Sheet as at 31 March 1989

	£ million	£ million
Fixed assets at cost less depreciation		262.20
Current assets		
Stock	69.00	
Debtors	82.80	
Bank	27.60	
	179.40	
Less: Current liabilities		
Creditors	75.31	
Dividend	8.99	
Taxation	26.10	
	110.40	69.00
Less: 11% debenture 2004		138.00
Net assets		193.20
Shareholders' funds		
Ordinary shares (£1 par value)		69.00
Reserves		124.20
		193.20

Five-year Summarized Profit and Loss Account

Year ended 31 March	Turnover £m	Profit before tax £m	Tax £m	Profit after tax £m	Dividend £m
1985	583.7	49.63	19.85	29.78	9.86
1986	644.6	58.42	20.45	37.97	10.94
1987	639.5	59.61	20.86	38.75	12.17
1988	742.3	62.43	21.85	40.58	13.48
1989	810.6	74.57	26.10	48.47	14.98

The company's current share price is 546 pence ex div, and debenture price £93. No new share or debenture capital has been issued during the last five years. Corporate tax is at the rate of 35 per cent.

If another crash were to occur it would lead to increased demand for gilts and other fixed interest stocks and a change of approximately 2 per cent in all interest rates.

Required

(a) Estimate what effect a second stock market crash of the same magnitude as in 1987 might have on Slohill's current weighted average cost of capital if:

(i) The crash has negligible effect on the earnings expectations of the company and on the growth rate of the company's earnings.

(ii) The annual pre-tax growth rate of the company's earnings is expected to fall by 20 per cent.

State clearly any assumptions that you make.

(b) If a second stock market crash were to occur, advise the managing director of the likely effect on the cost of capital of raising a substantial amount of new capital:

(i) If the capital raised is all equity;

(ii) If the capital raised is all debt.

(c) If the capital asset pricing model were to be used to estimate the cost of equity in scenarios (a)(i) and (a)(ii) above explain in which direction the main variables in the model would be likely to move.

(Solution in Appendix A)

2. Hesi Engineering Ltd produces and sells a pocket tape recorder which has been designed for business users. The company has been in operation for four years and has an issued share capital of 800,000 £1 ordinary shares. To date the company has produced only one product. For the year ended 31 May 1991 the company sold 60,000 tape recorders to large retail outlets at a price of £30 per recorder.

The profit and loss account for the year to 31 May 1991 is as follows:

	£000	£000
Sales		1800
Less:		
Variable expenses	720	
Fixed expenses	360	1,080
Net profit before interest and taxation		720
Less interest payable		190
Net profit before taxation		530
Less corporation tax (at 35%)		186
Net profit after taxation		344
Dividend paid		160
Retained profit for the year		184

In recent months the company has been experiencing labour problems and, as a result, has decided to introduce a new highly automated production process in order to improve efficiency. The new production process is estimated to increase fixed costs by £120,000 (including depreciation) but will reduce variable costs by £7 per unit.

The new production process will be financed by the issue of £2,000,000 debentures at an interest rate of 12.5 per cent. If the new production process is introduced immediately the directors believe that sales for the forthcoming year will be the same as for the year ended 31 May 1991. Stocks will remain at the current level throughout the forthcoming year.

Required

(a) Calculate the change in earnings per share if the company introduces the new production process immediately.
(b) Explain what is meant by the terms 'operating gearing' and 'financial gearing'. Why is it important for the directors of a company to consider the levels of operating and financial gearing?
(c) Assuming the company introduces the new production process immediately, compute for the year to 31 May 1992:
  (i) the degree of operating gearing.
  (ii) the degree of financial gearing, and
  (iii) the combined gearing effect.
(d) Briefly explain what is meant by the term 'combined gearing effect'.

(Certified Diploma, June 1991)
(Solution in Appendix A)

3. Santander is an unquoted public limited company which is wholly equity financed at present. The company's current level of earnings before interest and tax is £4 million. This earnings level is expected to be stable for the foreseeable future.

    A major competitor, Bilbao, is a quoted company with a capital structure of shareholder equity valued at £40 million and £10 million 12% unsecured loan stock valued at par. Bilbao's equity Beta is estimated to be 1.25. The business risk of the two companies is similar.

    The rate of return on risk-free assets is at present 10% and the overall return on the market portfolio is 15%. These rates are expected to remain constant for the foreseeable future.

    The directors of Santander are considering introducing debt into the capital structure prior to applying for a stock market quotation. They are examining two options:

  A £5 million 11% Unsecured Loan Stock at Par
  B £10 million 10% Unsecured Loan Stock at £90 per £100 of stock

The Directors estimate that if they proceed with option A the company has a 10% chance of financial distress. If they proceed with option B the chances of financial distress are increased to 20%. The costs associated with financial distress are estimated at £2,500,000 in both cases.

    The rate of corporation tax is expected to remain at 33% and interest on debt is tax-deductible.

Required

(a) Explain why Santander may wish to *raise* its gearing before gaining a quotation.
(b) Calculate the total market values *and* debt/equity ratios of Santander under the two options.
(c) Assuming Santander proceeds with option B, what would its equity Beta be after the issue of debt?

CHAPTER 16

Leasing decisions

LEASING LIBERATES DERELICT SITE

In 1988, five leasing companies formed a syndicate to provide £230m of 'big ticket' lease finance for the Meadowhall Shopping and Leisure Centre located in the east end of Sheffield. Reputedly the largest retailing complex in Europe, Meadowhall provides over 1.5m sq. ft of shopping and leisure space, includes seven department stores and over 200 shops, and expects to attract 30 million visitors annually. It was part of the scheme initiated by the Sheffield Development Corporation to regenerate the City's Don Valley area, devastated during the 1980s by the rationalization of the steel industry, once the region's major employer. Meadowhall progressed from derelict site to opening in under two years and is expected to create over 8,000 new jobs.

Leasing finance here, as in many other cases, has proved a valuable tool for funding much-needed capital investment.

16.1   Introduction

Leasing is a financing vehicle which resembles borrowing in many respects, but it deserves a separate chapter for two reasons.

First, because lease finance is highly significant in size. Following two decades of sustained growth in leasing activity, about a fifth of all capital investment is now financed via leasing contracts. The growth in leasing is indicated in Table 16.1, which shows the amount of leasing undertaken over the period 1975–90 by members of the industry's trade association, the Equipment Leasing Association (ELA).

The data, showing the value of equipment purchased by ELA members for on-leasing to clients (but excluding contracts with purchase options), exhibit substantial growth during the 1970s, a tendency to level off in the early 1980s, and renewed but erratic growth in the

Table 16.1 Assets acquired by Equipment Leasing Association members

Year	Value of Assets Acquired for Leasing Purposes (£m)
1975	340
1977	675
1979	1,802
1980	2,359
1981	2,674
1982	2,834
1983	2,894
1984	4,012
1985	5,757
1986	5,182
1987	6,024
1988	7,836
1989	9,641
1990	10,314

Source: ELA Annual Reports.

later 1980s. The data should be read with caution, both because they are not inflation-adjusted, and because in the earlier years at least, they include the effect of increased membership of the ELA as well as additional activity by existing members. As a result, they may well exaggerate the increase in leasing activity. Nevertheless, they convey a picture of robust growth.

Leasing is also very important in relation to total UK fixed capital investment. In 1978, the ELA claimed that leasing accounted for about 8 per cent of UK investment. This had risen to 15 per cent by 1984 and to as much as 20 per cent by 1990 (28 per cent if leases with purchase options are included). This compares with about 10 per cent penetration for leasing in Japan and 33 per cent in the United States. The Meadowhall complex is one of the biggest lease-financed projects completed in Britain.

The second justification for a detailed examination of leasing is that it provides an example of the interaction between investment and financing decisions, and in particular, an opportunity to demonstrate that DCF principles can be applied to financing as well as investment decisions. (It is also an area where the Adjusted Present Value approach, to be examined in Chapter 18, can be applied.)

What is leasing?

According to the International Accounting Standards Committee:

> A leasing transaction is a commercial arrangement whereby an equipment owner conveys the right to use the equipment in return for payment by the equipment user of a specified rental over a pre-agreed period of time.

This definition provides a concise picture of what a leasing contract involves. It is an alternative way of obtaining the use of items of equipment for companies which, for varying reasons, may wish to avoid acquiring them outright using other financing vehicles. But leasing as a method of finance involves important interactions between the investment and the financing decision. Having defined a lease, we will go on to examine how a lease works, the advantages and disadvantages of different forms of lease contract, how to evaluate the decision as to whether to lease or buy an asset, and the importance of the taxation system in leasing analysis. Finally, we offer practical guidelines regarding the circumstances in which leasing may be more attractive than outright purchase.

LEARNING OBJECTIVES

Leasing is a way of obtaining the use of an asset without having to incur the 'lumpy' up-front cash outlay required to purchase it. After completing this chapter, you should:

- Understand the difference between operating and finance leases.
- Understand how to approach a leasing decision.
- Understand the full range of factors which a finance manager should consider when evaluating a 'lease versus borrow-to-buy' decision.

16.2   How a lease works

Most leasing activity is undertaken by banking and similar institutions, such as Forward Trust Group, a subsidiary of Midland Bank, and Scandinavian Leasing, a subsidiary of Scandinavian Bank. In addition, certain manufacturers, such as IBM and Phillips Electronics, operate leasing companies to market their own products. A company wishing to obtain the use of an asset (*the lessee*), for example, an oil company wishing to lease a tanker, or a Development Corporation, as in the Meadowhall case, wishing to lease property, will approach the leasing specialist (*the lessor*) with its requirements. The deal will involve the lessor purchasing the tanker, or the site, and arranging to rent it out to the lessee in return for a pre-specified series of rental payments over a specific time period.

In the United Kingdom, it is important that the ownership of the asset remains the legal property of the lessor, otherwise certain tax advantages may be lost. At the expiration of the lease contract, the two parties may negotiate a *secondary lease*, or the owner may otherwise dispose of the asset. For assets with long lives, it is not uncommon to find the lessor ignoring the potential resale value of the asset when setting the rentals, on the basis that it is too distant in time to predict accurately. Instead, he may agree to reimburse the lessee with a proportion, often over 90 per cent (but never 100 per cent) of the resale value, an agreement known as a *rebate clause*. Secondary leases are often undertaken at nominal or 'peppercorn' rentals to reflect their bonus nature – the owner will already have received back his outlay plus target profit if the contract has run its full term.

Types of lease

Where the agreed term of the lease approximates to the expected lifetime of the asset, the lessee is clearly using the lease arrangement as an alternative form of finance to outright acquisition. As a result, he avoids having to incur the perhaps substantial outlay required at the outset of the project. Hence, the type of lease which we have described is called a *finance lease* or *capital lease*, or a *full pay-out lease*.

However, not all forms of lease operate over long time periods. The user may not wish to incur the long-term contractual liability to pay rentals, especially if he wishes only to obtain the use of the asset to perform a specific job, e.g. drilling equipment to bore out a specific oil well. Lessors are willing to rent out equipment to such firms on the basis of an *operating lease*. This is usually job-specific and can be easily cancelled, whereas cancellation of a finance lease usually involves financial penalties so severe that termination is rarely worthwhile. The lessor will obviously hope to arrange a series of such contracts in order to recover his capital outlay and to achieve a profit. For this reason, the operating lease is called a *part-pay-out lease*. Unlike the finance lease, where the user bears the full risks both of 'downtime' (inability to use the asset) and also of obsolescence, in an operating lease the owner incurs the brunt of these risks. To compensate for the risk of having a yard full of idle and rusting equipment, the lessor will apply a rental which is higher per unit of time than that for financial lease, thus incorporating a risk premium.

In other words, finance leasing is more risky for the user while the operating lease is more risky for the owner, explaining why the latter is normally considerably more costly per unit of time.

Operating leases have another advantage for lessees. They are usually negotiated on a 'maintenance and insurance' basis, whereby the owner will undertake to insure and service the asset. This is normally the responsibility of the user in the case of the finance lease, although the owner may actually perform the servicing functions for a fee. The suitability of the operating lease for short-term projects explains its popularity in the construction industry under the guise of *plant hire*, and for assets with a rapid rate of technological advance such as photocopiers and computers. To compensate for the risks of leasing out high technology assets, lessors are sometimes able to protect themselves by using specialist computer leasing insurers, although premium rates are generally high.

Sale-and-Leaseback

A variation on the leasing theme illustrating the attraction of leasing to capital-hungry companies is the *Sale-and-Leaseback (SAL)* arrangement. This involves selling assets (usually property) to a financial institution seeking good quality investments with potential for long-term growth in capital value. The seller, while giving up the ownership rights to the property, will then arrange to lease the premises from the new owner. SAL, therefore, is a transfer of ownership with retention of rights to use for a specified period. Its attraction to the vendor is the raising of capital, although its obvious disadvantage is the loss of any entitlement to capital appreciation. However, for a company eager to grow, the return achieved in the early years of projects which exploit that growth potential could outweigh the lost capital gains. This was the reasoning behind the SAL by Tesco, the supermarket chain, of many of its store sites in the 1980s when it was eager to claw back the market share advantage held by Sainsburys. The finance generated by a series of SALs was used to purchase and develop new sites for stores. Access to SAL arrangements was an element vital to Tesco's competitive strategy.

Another SAL involved the raising of some £140m, in May 1990, by Polly Peck International, the electronics and fresh produce group, by selling refrigerated cargo vessels, acquired as part of its purchase of the Del Monte fruit business from RJR Nabisco. Here, the motive was not to obtain finance for expansion, but to lower what later transpired to be a catastrophic level of gearing. The acquirer was a Norwegian consortium of companies, led by Kvaerner, Hafslund Nycomed and an investment group headed by Norse Partners, which undertook to lease back the ships over a ten-year term.

16.3   Profile of leasing activity

The previous section gave a broad indication of some reasons for leasing. In this section, we illustrate, using additional ELA data, the types of equipment which are leased and by whom.

Figure 16.1(a) shows that plant and machinery constitutes the most important category of leased assets, followed by cars and commercial vehicles. The importance of computerization for the UK leasing industry is clear, largely reflecting modernization in the service industries, especially in banking and finance. The importance of transport equipment and the financial services sector for the leasing industry is also shown in Figure 16.1(b), which displays data for assets acquired by ELA members by type of customer, analysed by Standard Industrial Classification categories.

To complete this profile of leasing activity, Figure 16.1(c) shows how the assets acquired were leased out according to primary period. Clearly, the major proportion of leasing activity is to be found over terms of 2–5 years.

16.4   Lease evaluation: a simple case

We can now formally evaluate the decision whether to lease or purchase an asset. We begin by establishing the basic principles.

A lease requires a series of fixed rentals. This is a major appeal of a lease – the lessee can predict with certainty his future lease payments and budget accordingly. Because leasing effectively offers fixed-rate finance, we examine the merits of a lease against the yardstick of the cheapest alternative form of borrowing which would otherwise be used to acquire the asset, normally a bank loan. In other words, *leasing is an alternative to borrowing at the risk-free rate (or, more realistically, the bank's lending rate) in order to buy the asset outright.* Because leasing involves incurring a fixed liability, it is seen by astute lenders as displacing the firm's capacity to borrow, i.e. leases and debts are regarded as substitutes, so that an increase in the former should lead to an exactly compensating decrease in the other. While

Assets Acquired in 1990 by Type of Asset

Note: Ignoring contracts with purchase options

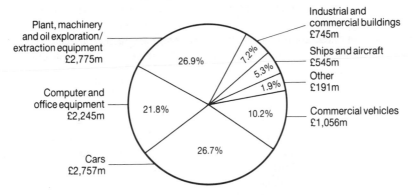

Assets Acquired in 1990 by Type of Customer

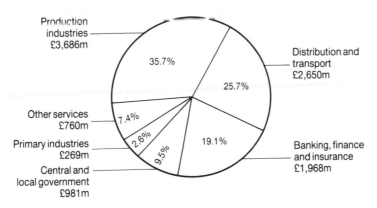

Assets Acquired in 1990 by Primary Period

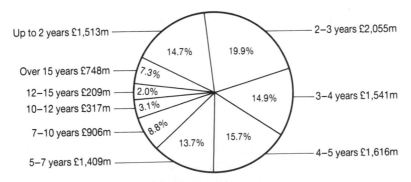

Figure 16.1 Profile of leasing activity. (a) Assets acquired by ELA members, 1990. (b) Customers of ELA members, 1990. (c) Primary period of leases written by ELA members, 1990

this 'one-for-one' debt displacement hypothesis is not universally accepted, we will assume that lenders are astute enough to recognize leasing for what it effectively is. Using this assumption, the leasing decision amounts to evaluating the question: 'Is it preferable to lease or borrow-to-buy?'

The upshot of these comments is that the *appropriate rate of discount to use in lease evaluation is the lessee's cost of borrowing.* This is incorporated into the example of Hardup plc.

Lease evaluation: Hardup plc

Hardup plc wishes to lease an executive jet aircraft from Flush Ltd, the leasing subsidiary of Moneybags Bank plc. The aircraft would otherwise cost £13.75m to purchase via a bank loan at a 12 per cent interest rate. Flush quotes an annual rental of £5m over three years, with the first instalment payable immediately, and thereafter, annually. Should Hardup lease or borrow-to-buy? With a lease, Hardup avoids the immediate cash outlay of £13.75m, but loses out on any resale value (ignoring any rebate clause). *We may assess the value of the lease on an incremental basis, by finding the NPV of the decision to lease rather than borrow-to-buy, sometimes called the Net Advantage of the Lease (NAL).* Table 16.2 sets out the relevant cash flows for this computation. Notice that for the purposes of this simple example, tax has been ignored (although we will later discover that the tax regulations have had an important bearing on the growth of leasing). We also ignore, for simplicity, any resale value.

The incremental cash flow profile shows that, by leasing, Hardup effectively obtains net financing of £8.75m in exchange for debt service costs of £5m in each of the following two years. (Notice that the timing of rental payments conflicts with our usual assumption of year-end payments. The lease rentals are actually paid at the start of Years 1, 2 and 3, respectively, which has negligible impact on the present value computations, but could have important tax implications). After allowing for the 12 per cent cost of borrowing, the positive NPV indicates that the optimal form of financing arrangement is to obtain a lease from Flush. The same result could have been obtained by separately discounting the two cash flow streams and choosing the one with the lowest present value. This is simply a comparison between an outlay of £13.75m and a three-year annuity at 12 per cent, beginning now, of £5m p.a. which has a present value of £13.45m. For many purposes, the incremental layout is easier and clearer, for example, it focuses attention directly on the relative merits of the two options.

An alternative method of evaluation: the Equivalent Loan

Another approach to lease evaluation is to compare the purchase price of the asset concerned with the *Equivalent Loan*, defined as the loan which would involve the same schedule of interest and repayments as the profile of rentals required by the lessor. The lease is adjudged worthwhile if the lease schedule is compatible with a larger loan than is actually required to purchase the asset – in other words, if it provides more finance than the loan which would otherwise be required to obtain the asset by outright purchase. The appeal of this approach is that it emphasizes the financing function of a lease. In the Hardup example, the equivalent

Table 16.2 Hardup plc's leasing analysis

Item of Cash Flow (£m)	0	Year 1	2
Lease			
Rentals	−5.00	−5.00	−5.00
Buy			
Outlay	−13.75		
Incremental Cash Flows	+8.75	−5.00	−5.00
Present value at 12%	+8.75	−4.46	−3.99
Net present value = +0.30			

loan is the maximum loan at 12 per cent which could be supported by a payment of £5m now and two further payments of £5m, after one and two years, respectively. To find the equivalent loan, we simply calculate the present value of a two-year annuity of £5m and add the undiscounted first payment of £5m, yielding a total of:

$$PV = £5m + £5m \ (PVIFA_{(12,2)}) = £5m + £8.45m = £13.45m$$

Table 16.3 shows the behaviour of a loan of this amount, serviced by the same profile of payments entailed by the lease itself.

All we have done here is to express our calculation format in a different way. In so doing, we have found that the equivalent loan is £13.45m, while the lease itself provides the ability to acquire an asset whose price is £13.75m, i.e. for the same profile of payments, the lease allows the firm to 'borrow' an extra £0.30m, which is precisely the Net Advantage of the Lease. We can now see that lease evaluation effectively involves computing a loan equivalent. A lease is worthwhile if the required payments or cash flows could service a loan higher than the outlay required to undertake the project. In other words, a lease is worthwhile if the effective financing obtained is higher than the equivalent loan. Many writers and analysts prefer to evaluate leases in terms of equivalent loans, but, in more realistic cases, the phasing of rental payments, intermingled with tax complications, can make the computation of an equivalent loan highly complex. Generally, we advocate the incremental cash flow approach.

Table 16.3 The behaviour of the equivalent loan (£m)

Year	0	1	2	3
Balance of loan at start of year	13.45	8.45	4.46	0
Interest at 12%	—	1.01	0.54	—
Repayments, of which:	5.00	5.00	5.00	—
interest	—	1.01	0.54	—
capital	5.00	3.99	4.46	—
Balance of loan at end of year	8.45	4.46	0	—

16.5   Leasing as a financing decision: the three-stage approach

In this section, we offer a note of warning. In the Hardup example, we found leasing to be the optimal form of finance, at least in preference to borrowing. However, in many companies, the analysis might not have got this far. For example, had the underlying project (the acquisition of the jet), been revealed as unattractive, the financial manager might not have bothered to undertake a financing analysis. In other words, firms may evaluate decisions in two-stages: first, to assess the basic desirability of the activity; second, if the project is deemed acceptable, to assess the optimal form of financing. The danger in this sequence is that some projects that might be rendered worthwhile by especially favourable financing packages could be rejected. The key point here is that it may make more sense to *evaluate projects as linked investment and financing packages*. To explore this interaction between investment and financing further, we now need to explain the *three-stage approach*.

In the analysis of Hardup's acquisition of the jet, it was implicitly assumed that the investment was inherently worthwhile using the firm's usual financing methods, and that the remaining issue was how best to finance it. Let us now examine the underlying investment decision. Imagine Hardup is all-equity financed and that its shareholders require a return of 15 per cent. Assume further that acquisition of the jet would result in annual benefits (such as savings in executive time and in travel expenses and fees from hiring) of £6m p.a. for three years, treated as year-end lump-sum payments, and which, while uncertain to be realized, are no more risky than existing company operations. Assuming continued equity financing, and applying the 15 per cent discount rate, the NPV of the jet purchase is:

$$\text{NPV} = -£13.75\text{m} + £6\text{m} \ (\text{PVIFA}_{(15,3)}) = -£13.75\text{m} + £13.70\text{m} = -£0.05\text{m}$$

The project would be rejected on the NPV criterion and the issue of how best to finance it might never arise (unless there were non-financial motives, such as corporate prestige, to justify it).

However, it could be acceptable using other methods of finance such as borrowing or leasing. Of these, lease financing appears to be the most attractive because we know the Net Advantage of the Lease (NAL) is £0.30m. In this example, the acquisition should be undertaken, since the NAL exceeds the negative NPV anticipated from all-equity financing. This suggests how and why a three-stage analysis should be applied. The three stages are:

1. Determine whether the project is inherently attractive. Then, even if the NPV is negative,
2. Evaluate the NAL to assess whether to lease or borrow-to-buy.
3. Assess the value of the project with the chosen financing method.

As we found earlier, the answer to stage 2 is a NAL of £0.30m. To examine stage 2, we compare the benefits anticipated from the project, discounted at the 'risky' rate of 15 per cent, with the costs associated with the cheapest financing method, in this case the stream of rental payments.

We have already found the present value of project benefits, i.e. £13.70m. Now applying the 12 per cent cost of debt finance to the rental stream, we have:

$$\text{PV of rentals} = £5\text{m} + £5\text{m}(\text{PVIFA}_{(12,2)}) = £13.45\text{m}$$

Since the project benefits exceed the costs asssociated with the cheapest financing method, the overall investment-cum-financing package is worthwhile. This is an important result. When judged on its intrinsic merits, and evaluated using 'normal' criteria, the project reduces shareholder wealth. Yet when evaluated using alternative financing methods, it becomes worthwhile.

It certainly does not follow that all marginal investment decisions can be turned around by clever financing decisions, but this analysis does suggest that a three-stage approach along these lines can help to avoid rejecting some projects which might be worth undertaking if financed in particular ways. In broader terms, one could be forgiven for asking: 'Since this is essentially a wealth-reducing project and the firm benefits, who loses?' It is possible that the lessor may have applied too low a rental to meet his required return, but net benefits from leasing usually accrue from the tax system, so that the loser in this kind of situation is generally the taxpayer.

With this warning, we will continue to assume that projects are worthwhile in their own right when their benefits are discounted at the appropriate risk-adjusted rate, although it is implicit in our analysis that a three-stage analysis will have been undertaken.

16.6 Motives for leasing

Some writers suggest leasing is undertaken primarily to exploit tax advantages. Large numbers of firms in the 1970s and early 1980s found that their desired capital expenditures exceeded their taxable earnings, and as a result, could not take advantage of the 100 per cent First Year Allowances, at least until their profitability had recovered. Under these circumstances, leasing was often a more cost-effective way of obtaining the use of an asset than borrowing-to-buy.

Many firms possessing taxable capacity set up leasing subsidiaries in order to shelter their own profits from tax by purchasing capital equipment on behalf of tax-exhausted firms. As a result, the ELA membership list included such odd-looking bedfellows as Tesco, Mothercare, Ladbrokes and Marks & Spencers, all highly profitable companies during this period. Such companies were able to obtain the tax benefits from equipment purchase considerably earlier than their tax-exhausted clients could expect to. In effect, lessors bought equipment on behalf of clients, took the tax benefits and passed these on to clients in the form of rentals lower than they would otherwise have been.

The extent to which tax benefits are actually passed on depends on the state of competition in the market for leasing and how near to the end of the lessor's tax year the negotiations take place. Sometimes, very attractive lease terms can be obtained from a lessor anxious to qualify for tax reliefs as soon as possible. In these cases, the lessor can profit from the contract, and the lessee may find leasing more attractive than outright purchase. Therefore, both parties can gain from the arrangement at the expense of the taxpayer.

While tax breaks have been important in explaining the rise of leasing, they do not account for the continuing increase in the popularity of leasing after the abolition of First Year Allowances in 1984. We must look beyond the tax system, at a variety of commonly quoted reasons which have been proposed to explain the rise of leasing.

'Leasing offers an attractive alternative source of funds'

For firms suffering from capital rationing, leasing may offer an attractive means to access capital markets. This applies especially to small, growing businesses which lack a sufficiently impressive track record to satisfy lenders, or which possess inadequate assets upon which to secure a loan. With a lease, no security is required, since if the lessee defaults, the owner simply repossesses the asset and looks for another client. For this reason, it is unusual to find restrictive clauses in lease contracts in contrast with debt covenants where the lender may stipulate, for example, that the borrower should not exceed a specified gearing ratio. In addition, few projects have 100 per cent debt capacity, i.e. few lenders will offer 100 per cent debt financing (except to firms with copper-bottomed financial circumstances which have no need to borrow!). They prefer instead to see the client inject a significant amount of equity. This is not the case with a lease contract, which may thus be seen as a 'back-door' method of obtaining total debt financing for the acquisition of at least the equipment needs of a project.

Some organizations, such as local authorities and government departments, persistently suffer from constraints on capital expenditure and may find leasing an appealing device to overcome these difficulties. In such organizations, there is often a rigid distinction between 'revenue' budgets and 'capital' budgets which can be exploited by managers alert to the leasing alternative. Equipment may be acquired not by using the tightly controlled capital budget, but by undertaking a lease contract where the rentals are paid out of the revenue budget. Indeed, in the short term, leasing may even be presented as a way of 'saving money' by astute managers! People who accept this argument, of course, confuse cash flow with wealth. However, the public sector remains an important source of leasing business, despite the removal in 1979 of the ability of lessors to obtain tax relief on equipment purchase regardless of the tax status of the lessee. From 1979, tax relief has been available only in cases where the lessee is normally liable for Corporation Tax, even if, perhaps temporarily, tax-exhausted.

'Leasing has cash flow advantages'

Leasing, as we have seen, removes the need for a substantial cash outlay at the outset of a project in return for a series of contractually agreed, and therefore, predictable, cash flows over the term of the lease contract. A lease thus has the effect of smoothing out cash flows which facilitates budgetary planning.

'Leasing provided off-balance sheet financing'

Although this point is no longer applicable it was often propounded as a major reason to explain the popularity of leasing in the 1970s. Until the advent of SSAP 21, issued in 1984, made the capitalization of leases mandatory, companies were not required to show lease obligations in their published accounts. This had the effect of disguising their indebtedness by lowering the recorded gearing ratio, and also raising the return on capital employed. However, lease obligations had to be mentioned in the notes to the accounts. But it may have been somewhat fanciful to imagine that lenders (perhaps with their own leasing subsidiaries) were not alert to this form of window-dressing when assessing corporate performance and borrowing levels!

'Leasing is cheaper than other forms of finance'

As well as the pragmatic attractions of leasing, it is often a more cost-effective way of acquiring an asset. We have already seen how leasing can be a profitable alternative to bank borrowing under certain conditions. This is equivalent to saying that the effective rate of interest on a lease contract is lower than that on a bank loan. Indeed, many firms evaluate leases by comparing the bank's effective lending rate with the rate of interest implicit in the lease contract, i.e. the internal rate of return on the profile of lease payments, including the 'up-front' financing. Of particular interest here is the case of an 'end-year lease', written on or just before the end of the lessor's tax year. At this juncture, the lessor is anxious to get the contract drawn up so as to claim the tax relief in the year just ending, rather than having to wait a further year before reaping the tax advantage.

We complete this section by noting a survey of 273 quoted UK companies by Drury and Braund (1990), which found that the cost of leasing, Corporation Tax considerations and, to a lesser extent, conservation of working capital were the most important factors in the lease or borrow-to-buy decision. Their findings are shown in Table 16.4, which lists the factors proposed to executives in order of the importance which they attributed to them.

16.7 Allowing for Corporation Tax in lease evaluation

The evaluation of the Hardup example, while demonstrating the incremental nature of the analysis, omitted the impact of taxation. Lease rentals qualify for tax relief, as do interest

Table 16.4 Reasons for leasing

Rank	Factor
1	Rate of interest implicit in the lease finance compared with borrowing.
2	Corporation Tax considerations.
3	Conservation of working capital.
4	Leasing permits 100 per cent financing – the full cost of the asset is met.
5	Ability of a lease to offer a complete package including, for example, service agreements.
6	Lease finance can be obtained with greater ease and fewer restrictions than with other forms of finance.
7	Leases can be arranged in which the rental payments increase over the lease period, thus enabling low rentals to be charged against profits in the early stages of a project's life.
8	Leasing is easier to arrange, from an administrative point of view, than borrowing.

Source: Drury and Braund (1990).

payments on loans, while expenditures to purchase capital equipment generally attract capital allowances against Corporation Tax. Our omission of taxation is particularly culpable, since the UK tax system was widely believed to be largely responsible for the upsurge in leasing activity which occurred during the past two decades. Indeed, some observers regard the particular quirks of the tax system as the single most important reason for this growth.

Retaining the figures from the Hardup example, we now assume Corporation Tax is paid at 33 per cent with a one-year delay and the availability of a 25 per cent Writing Down Allowance (WDA). Under this regime, a firm with sufficiently high taxable profits, i.e. at least as great as the allowances available, can set off 25 per cent of its outlay on capital equipment against profits in the year of expenditure, and in each subsequent year, based on a reducing balance. Consequently, by careful timing of expenditures, a company with sufficient taxable capacity can qualify for significant tax savings.

Assuming that Hardup is not tax-exhausted, it can shelter its profits from tax by acquiring the aircraft. In effect, the taxpayer subsidizes the required outlay, making equipment purchase a more attractive proposition for the tax-paying enterprise. Conversely, tax relief on rental payments lowers their effective cost. The final tax adjustment is to the discount rate.

THE AFTER-TAX COST OF BORROWING

When interest payments qualify for tax relief, the effective rate of interest, r^*, depends on the rate of tax (T) and the tax delay period:

$$r^* = r\left(1 - \frac{T}{(1+r^*)^D}\right)$$

where r = the nominal or quoted pre-tax interest rate
  D = the delay in tax payment

This is awkward to solve, but may be *approximated* by replacing r^* on the right-hand side by r. For Hardup, facing a pre-tax borrowing rate of 12 per cent, this produces a tax-adjusted effective interest rate of about 8.5 per cent, i.e.

$$r^* = 0.12\left[1 - \frac{0.33}{(1.12)}\right] = 0.085, \text{ i.e. } 8.5\%$$

Retaining our previous incremental format, and allowing for the various tax complications, Table 16.5 shows the relevant cash flows.

The figures indicate that the lease is still worthwhile for the lessee. We could have undertaken a parallel analysis from the lessor's standpoint, to examine whether it was worth his while to purchase the asset for leasing it to Hardup. In fact, the computation has effectively been done for us, because all the cash flows have the same numerical values, except that their signs are reversed. As a result, we would find the NPV of the project to Moneybags would be − £0.13m (assuming that both firms could obtain capital at 12 per cent pre-tax). In other words, if we added together their respective gains from the lease contract, we would

Table 16.5   Hardup's leasing decision with tax

Item of Cash Flow (£m)	0	1	Year 2	3	4
Lease:					
Rental	−5.00	−5.00	−5.00	—	—
Tax saving at 33%*		+1.65	+1.65	+1.65	+1.65
Net lease cash flows (L)	−5.00	−5.00	−3.35	+1.65	—
Borrow-to-buy:					
Outlay	−13.75				
Tax saving**		+1.13	+0.85	+0.64	+1.91
Net purchase cash flows (B)	−13.75	+1.13	+0.85	+0.64	+1.91
Net incremental cash flows (L–B)	+8.75	−6.13	−4.20	+1.01	−0.26
Present value at 8.5%	+8.75	−5.65	−3.57	+0.79	−0.19
Net present value (NAL) =	−0.13				

*Tax savings on the rentals are actually delayed by two years owing to the timing of the rental payments, i.e. on the first day of each of years 1, 2 and 3.
**The profile of tax savings is based on setting the allowable expenditure against profits in year zero and in three subsequent years. The undepreciated balance is set against profits in the last year. No salvage value is assumed. Insurance and maintenance costs are also ignored.

find that leasing contracts between tax-paying companies were zero-sum games. In reality, the lessor is likely to have special advantages, like access to cheaper finance, reducing his required return below that of the lessee, and preferential buying terms, especially if he is able to purchase equipment in bulk. Economies of bulk purchase are common for lessors of motor cars with 40 per cent discounts on list price not unknown.

The relative desirability of leasing and borrowing-to-buy depends largely on the tax regime. In the system operating prior to 1984, it was generally the case that leasing was more attractive for the tax-exhausted company and conversely less attractive for the tax-paying firm. If the company is in a non-tax-paying situation (and expects to be so indefinitely), the lease evaluation should be done on a 'simple' basis, ignoring tax, and conversely, when the potential lessee is a taxpayer.

16.8   Loose ends

In this section, we introduce some 'fiddly bits', deliberately neglected until now to minimize the complexity of the analysis. These issues are in order of treatment: residual values, the riskiness of the tax savings, and the case of temporary *tax-exhaustion*.

Treatment of residual values

The Hardup example ignored any resale or salvage value after the three-year asset lifetime. There can be two justifications for this. First, the salvage value may be difficult to estimate for long-life leases, and can be effectively ignored when its present value is likely to be small. Second, sometimes the bulk of the salvage value is rebated to the lessee as a form of loyalty bonus. However, in the case of relatively short-term leases, the assumption of zero expected resale value is not very satisfactory. It seems likely that lessors will obtain a degree of expertise in 'reading' second-hand markets and assessing possible second-hand values. For instance, in the example of the leasing of a jet aircraft, an asset with a well-developed second-hand market, it seems unrealistic to expect a negligible value after just three years, the term of the lease. In such cases, and where the resale value is not to be rebated, including the resale value may have an important bearing on the terms of the lease, and could reverse the recommendation.

The UK's Corporation Tax regime allows assets to be written down for tax purposes to their disposal values. Including the resale value will lower the tax reliefs available while providing a cash inflow at the time of disposal. In the Hardup example, the effect of disposal for say, £2m, at the end of the third year would have the following effects:

$$\text{Present Value of Disposal Proceeds at } 8.5\% = \frac{£2m}{(1.085)^3} = £1.57m$$

Reduced WDA in Year $3 = £2m$,
resulting in reduced tax saving in Year 4

$$= \frac{0.33 \times £2m}{(1.085)^4} = (£0.48m)$$

Net Benefit	$+£1.09m$

This net gain to the lessor will be reflected in the minimum rental he would have to apply in order to break even and should thus be reflected in the actual rental in a competitive leasing market. In other words, resale values lower rentals and make leasing apparently more attractive. However, the other side of the coin is that borrowing-to-buy also becomes more attractive since the resale value becomes a benefit. Because the net effect in the lease evaluation depends on the figures involved, it is difficult to generalize about the overall benefit.

The riskiness of tax savings

Cash flows in our example have been discounted at the post-tax cost of borrowing, thus effectively treating all cash flows as risk-free. Many people have difficulty in accepting this approach. It seems reasonable to treat the lease rentals as risk-free since they are contractually agreed, but the Tax Shields are a different matter. The timing and magnitude of these depend on the future profitability of the enterprise, which is by no means certain. Should they be discounted at a higher rate to reflect their higher risk? The answer is probably 'yes', but there remains the issue of the appropriate rate of discount to apply. Arguably, they could be treated as a stream of equity earnings and discounted accordingly since they are as risky as the company's underlying assets. However, this seems excessively risk-averse for a financing contract which is inherently low risk. Besides, few concerns, in practice, suffer the sort of profits collapse which would invalidate the assumptions made about future ability to claim tax reliefs. In principle, of course, all items of cash flow should be assessed separately for their degree of risk and discounted appropriately, but the practical difficulties of specifying the relevant set of rates usually preclude this approach.

Temporary tax-exhaustion

Some companies may not be liable for Corporation Tax every year but expect to resume making tax payments eventually. This is referred to as *temporary tax-exhaustion*. It may arise for a number of reasons ranging from a 'hump' in capital expenditure, whereby the WDAs exceed otherwise taxable income, to sheer unprofitability. Again, it is difficult to generalize about the net impact of this, mainly because it depends on the longevity of tax-exhaustion.

From an analytical standpoint, there are two main effects. First, any tax savings are delayed until profitability recovers sufficiently; and second, the relevant discount rate will change. Clearly, if the tax-delay period increases, the value of tax relief on debt interest reduces, so that the after-tax cost of debt rises. The reduction in the value of the WDA is then found by using this rate. The reader will appreciate that the case of temporary tax exhaustion is potentially quite awkward to evaluate since there may be a variety of discount rates to apply depending on the length of the period of tax-exhaustion.

16.9 Policy implications: when should firms lease?

What pointers can be gleaned from examining lease evaluation models? Broadly, there are two lessons to be drawn from this analysis.

First, lease evaluation is simply the analysis of a financing decision. This is borne out by the three-stage analysis. Sometimes, especially favourable financing arrangements, available via a lease contract, may tip the balance between project rejection and acceptance. But these cases are rare and the margin of acceptance offered by the attractive financing will probably be fairly narrow. If the project is only worthwhile because of the financing package, this should be explicitly recognized and the importance of concessionary finance regarded as a 'one-off', which may not be repeated in other cases. It has been argued that if the financing deal is all that makes the project acceptable, then the activity should probably be rejected. This seems unduly purist – few financial managers would or should pass up the opportunity to take advantage of an attractive financing opportunity. *However, we consider that policy is more profitably directed at finding genuinely worthwhile projects, rather than diverting resources to obtaining marginal financing advantages.*

Second, the analysis enables us to pinpoint the factors which suggest the relative attractiveness of leasing as compared to other financing arrangements. We now present a catalogue of factors which impact on the leasing decision, but add the 'health-warning' that these are mainly 'other things being equal' prognoses – 'look before you lease' would seem to be a sensible motto.

Taxable capacity

Leasing is a means whereby lessors can exploit their own taxable capacity and pass on any tax savings to firms in less favourable tax positions. Hence we can say that the greater is the taxable capacity of would-be lessors and the lower that of users of capital equipment, the greater the attractions of leasing.

Competition among lessors

A major factor in the development of the UK leasing market has been the entry of new players, eager to exploit their taxable capacity and thus shelter their profits from Corporation Tax. This has had the effect of increasing competition for available leasing business and reducing the general level of lease rentals. Therefore, we can state that the greater the degree of competition among lessors, the greater the attractiveness of leasing.

Investment incentives

Another major factor in the growth of the leasing industry has been the availability of especially generous inducements to encourage firms to acquire plant, machinery and industrial buildings. Although the present UK incentives are less generous than those existing prior to 1984, there has been no fall-off in leasing evident since the removal of First Year Allowances, probably due to the other attractions of leasing. However, it does seem reasonable to argue that the greater the generosity of the tax authorities, the greater the attractiveness of leasing simply because tax-breaks lower the effective cost of equipment purchase for lessors, who may then pass on the benefits to lessees, whether or not they are tax-exhausted.

Corporation Tax

Investment incentives are most valuable when rates of Corporation Tax are highest, since these in turn raise the value of the tax savings generated. For example, under the pre-1984 regime with 100 per cent FYAs, the total (undiscounted) tax saving with Corporation Tax payable at 52 per cent for a £10m investment was £5.2m, but would fall to £3.3m with a tax rate of 33 per cent (and even lower with 25 per cent WDAs). *The more onerous the rate of corporate profits tax, the more attractive leasing becomes, because lessors can shelter their profits to a greater extent.*

Inflation

Rising price levels reduce the real value of all future payments such as a series of fixed rental payments. Although equipment prices will also rise, including the resale values of leased assets, this is probably insufficient to compensate for the reduced real values of rental payments. Therefore, we suggest that the higher is the rate of inflation expected, the greater is the appeal of leasing. However, some qualifications are in order. The inflation effect will only benefit the lessee if he correctly anticipates a higher rate of inflation than the lessor. As in all contractual arrangements, unanticipated inflation is what does the damage, and it is by no means certain that the lessee will be more successful than the lessor in forecasting inflation. If lessors feel confident in their ability to predict inflation and the rentals they set incorporate their expectations, and if they are more or less correct, the benefits expected by lessees will evaporate. In addition, lease contracts for some items now incorporate some form of inflation adjustment.

Interest rates

The relevant rate of discount in lease evaluation is the rate applicable to the best alternative bank loan. The higher the rate of interest, the greater the discounting effect on all future payments, including contractual lease obligations. Generally, therefore, the higher the interest rate, the more attractive a lease appears, since the present value of a given set of rentals will become lower. However, this effect may become diluted by the impact of lessors applying higher rentals in order to cover their own increased borrowing costs. If there is any tendency for the spread of interest rates to widen at higher levels of interest rates, then this effect may still operate since lessors usually have access to borrowed capital at more advantageous rates than lessees.

In addition, higher interest rates are usually an indication of excess demand for credit in relation to the available supply. We would therefore argue that when interest rates are relatively high, more firms are likely to lease since leasing provides finance.

16.10 Summary

In this chapter, we have explained the various types of lease contract, discussed why leasing has risen in popularity, and analysed the lease or borrow-to-buy decision, with primary emphasis on finance leases.

Key points

- Leasing is a way of obtaining the use of an asset without incurring the initial 'lump' of capital outlay required for outright purchase.
- Leases may be 'job-specific', contracts applicable for periods less than the lifespan of assets (operating leases), or written for periods coinciding with the asset's expected lifetime (financial leases).
- A lease contract normally involves a commitment to pay a series of fixed rental charges, which qualify the lessee for tax relief.

- A financial or capital lease is thus an alternative to borrowing in order to purchase an asset, and the firm should expect its ability to borrow to fall by an equivalent amount.
- A major factor in the growth of UK leasing has been access to generous tax breaks, enabling lessors with taxable capacity to purchase assets for on-leasing to tax-exhausted clients.
- In the United Kingdom, if the ownership of a leased asset should pass to the lessee, the tax breaks are clawed back by the Inland Revenue.
- A further attraction of leasing was the ability to 'hide' the true level of a company's borrowing by treating lease obligations as 'off-Balance Sheet' finance.
- SSAP 21 now precludes this, stipulating that leased assets must be included among fixed assets and that future rental obligations be recorded as liabilities.
- The evaluation of a lease, i.e. whether to lease or to borrow-to-buy, may be undertaken in three equivalent ways:
  1. by comparing the present values of the respective cost streams,
  2. by assessing what equivalent loan could be raised with the same stream of payments entailed by the lease,
  3. by comparing the effective rate of interest payable on the lease with the costs of raising an equivalent loan.
- Lease evaluation usually assumes that the asset is worth obtaining in its own right, regardless of financing mechanism, but it is possible that an unattractive investment could be rendered worth-while by leasing. To ascertain this, a three-stage analysis should be undertaken.
- Leasing is *generally* more attractive:
  - when many lessors have significant taxable capacity,
  - when many lessees are tax-exhausted,
  - when there is strong competition among lessors,
  - when there are generous investment incentives available,
  - the higher the rate of Corporation Tax,
  - the higher the rate of inflation,
  - the higher are interest rates.
- Even though financial criteria may point to a definite preference, consideration of non-financial factors may reverse the lease or borrow-to-buy decision.

Further reading

The classic works on leasing are the text by Clark (1978) and the book by Tomkins, Lowe and Morgan (1979). Rutterford and Carter (1988) give a more up-to-date treatment, while successive annual reports of the Equipment Leasing Association will keep the reader abreast of developments in the field. Drury and Braund (1990) is the most recent empirical work. See also Fawthrop's contribution to Firth and Keane (1986).

Questions

Self-test questions

1. What are the differences between an operating lease and a finance lease?
2. What is meant by the term 'Equivalent Loan'?
3. What is sale-and-leaseback?
4. How is the analysis of the leasing decision affected by Corporation Tax and capital allowances?
5. What is meant by 'tax-exhaustion', and of what relevance is this for leasing decisions?
6. What is a three-stage analysis in relation to lease evaluation?

Exercises

1. Louise is the financial controller of a division of a large manufacturing company listed on the London Stock Exchange. She is currently evaluating whether to lease or buy a specialized machine. If the machine were to be purchased on 1 January 1987 the cash price of £92,000 would be financed by a loan of £100,000 on which interest would be payable at 16 per cent p.a., in six-monthly instalments *in advance*. The capital element of the loan would be repaid in two equal annual instalments on 1 January 1988 and 1 January 1989. The two interest payments in each calendar year would be based on the amount of the loan outstanding at the beginning of that year. The machine would be used until 1 January 1989 when it would be transferred to another division within the company at its tax written-down value.

   If a lease were to be taken out, four rentals of £16,000 would be paid at six-monthly intervals starting on 1 January 1987. The machine would be returned to the lessor on 1 January 1989.

   The company has an accounting reference date of 30 June and Corporation Tax is payable twelve months later. Louise expects that the Corporation Tax rate of 35 per cent will continue and that the machine will be eligible for an annual writing down allowance of 25 per cent. She has calculated that the effective six-monthly after-tax cost of the loan is 6 per cent. Louise expects that the company will have sufficient tax liabilities to absorb allowances generated by either the lease or buy option.

Required

(a) Show whether Louise is correct in her calculation of the effective six-monthly after-tax cost of the loan as 6 per cent.

(b) Using the after-tax cost of the loan of 6 per cent, determine whether the machine should be leased or purchased using the cash raised from the loan.

(c) Determine whether the machine should be leased or purchased if the company were to have no tax liabilities in the foreseeable future (assuming the transfer value of the machine remains unchanged).

(d) Discuss the factors which management should consider when deciding between finance leases and operating leases.

(ICAEW P.E.II, December 1986)

(Solution in Appendix A)

2. Mordred plc has approached Bedevere Leasing Ltd, a wholly-owned subsidiary of Avalon Bank plc for lease finance relating to the acquisition of an executive jet which it wishes to acquire. The outlay involved is £12m and the rentals would be £3m p.a. payable one year in advance over four years. Mordred can borrow at an APR of 10 per cent pre-tax. The Corporation Tax rate is 33 per cent, payable with a one-year delay. The expected resale value of the aircraft is £2m after four years. Bedevere can borrow at 7 per cent post-tax.

Evaluate the net advantage of the lease from Mordred's perspective:

   (i) Assuming Mordred is not expecting to have to pay Corporation Tax for the foreseeable future.

  (ii) Assuming Mordred is currently liable for tax.

 (iii) What would be the break-even rental payment from Bedevere's perspective?

(*Note*: For the purposes of this question, you may assume that capital expenditure may be written off at the rate of 25 per cent p.a. *straight line*.)

3. **(a)** Discuss the relative advantages and disadvantages of operating and financial leases.

   (b) Account for the rise in UK leasing activity over the past two decades.

   (c) Leicester Forest Leasing plc has been approached by Trowell plc with a view to financing the acquisition of a new office photocopier via a lease arrangement. The expenditure required to purchase equipment is £1,000. A 25 per cent writing down allowance is available and the equipment will last for three years and have an expected salvage value of £200. Lease rentals would be paid annually in advance in lump-sum form. Leicester Forest can borrow at an APR of 14.9 per cent. The Corporation Tax rate is 33 per cent (assume no tax delay).

       What rental must Leicester Forest charge in order to at least break even on the agreement?

   (d) Using a rental figure of £350 p.a., determine the NAL to Trowell, using a pre-tax cost of borrowing of 25 per cent, assuming:

    (i) Trowell is currently a taxpayer.

   (ii) Trowell is not expected to pay tax for the foreseeable future.

4. Ayr Credit plc has been approached by a client, Filey plc, to arrange a lease contract for an item of equipment requiring an outlay of £10m and which has a three-year life. A writing-down allowance is available at 25 per cent reducing balance, and estimated scrap value is £2m, 90 per cent of which will be rebated to the lessee. (This arrangement has no effect on Ayr's tax position.) Ayr can borrow at an APR pre-tax of 14 per cent. Corporation Tax is paid at 33 per cent with a one-year delay.

Required

(a) What rental payment will allow Ayr to break even on this contract?

(b) Using your answer to (a), evaluate the net advantage of the lease to Filey:

    (i) assuming Filey is a taxpayer and can borrow at 17 per cent.

    (ii) assuming Filey would only have taxable capacity in the final year of the project.

(c) Under what circumstances would a firm prefer to obtain a financial lease rather than an operating lease?

5. Birkett is a subsidiary of a joint stock bank. It specializes in the provision of leasing finance and has recently been approached by Bovington with a request to provide leasing facilities to finance the acquisition of an item of packing machinery. The equipment will last for two years and is expected to have no scrap value. The required outlay is £10,000 and Birkett quotes a rental of £6,000 p.a. payable as a lump sum in advance.

Further information

(a) A 25 per cent writing down allowance is available.

(b) The Corporation Tax rate is 33 per cent, payable a year in arrears.

(c) You may assume, for the purposes of this question, that tax years coincide with project years, and that Birkett can always take full and immediate advantage of the depreciation allowance.

Required

Evaluate the lease from both lessor and lessee perspectives:

    (i) assuming both firms are currently taxpayers and each can borrow at 12 per cent post-tax.

    (ii) assuming that Birkett can borrow at 8 per cent and that Bovington is tax-exhausted for the foreseeable future.

Practical assignment

Obtain the latest annual report of a company of your choice and calculate the various gearing ratios as explained in Chapter 14. Now consult the notes to the accounts, and obtain information on

1. leased assets,
2. obligations in connection with lease contracts.

Recalculate the gearing ratios excluding the effect of lease contracts, as might have been done prior to the introduction of SSAP21.

You may find it helpful to consult the company's statement of accounting policies, contained in the report, and the relevant accounting standard.

CHAPTER 17
Working capital management and policy

A CREDIT MANAGEMENT CRISIS

After political and economic liberalization in Hungary in 1989, the central bank, Magyar Nemzeti Bank, implemented a tight money policy to control inflationary pressure. In more sophisticated capital markets, various financial securities such as short-term loans, promissory notes and certificates of deposit might have arisen to assist short-term company liquidity. However, Hungarian enterprises reacted with an innovative response – 'debt-queuing', or simply non-payment of bills – so that by late 1991, 150 billion Forints ($2 billion) of inter-company debts were outstanding (equivalent to 15 per cent of the money supply).

Bus manufacturer Ikarus, one of Hungary's most successful companies, had depended on the USSR for much of its sales. When this market collapsed, Ikarus began to postpone payments to creditors resulting in its major supplier, the Csepel Automotive Factory, owing its own suppliers billions of Forints. This intensified use of trade credit, forced loans from suppliers, bankrupted many companies, but probably allowed many more to overcome their own severe short-term liquidity problems.

17.1   Introduction

It is a simple mistake to assume that financial management only concerns long-term financial decisions, such as capital investment, capital structure and dividend policy decisions. In reality, much of financial management addresses issues of a shorter duration, such as short-term financing and working capital management. In this chapter, we examine the more strategic issues surrounding working capital and its funding.

LEARNING OBJECTIVES

Having read this chapter, the reader should have a general appreciation of the importance of working capital in corporate finance and of the basic terminology involved. Specific attention will be paid to:

- The types of working capital policy and their financial effects.
- How to finance working capital and the problem of 'overtrading'.
- Approaches to managing stocks, debtors and cash.

Definitions

Before proceeding further, it is as well to remind ourselves of the need to maintain adequate liquidity. The Hungarian example referred to earlier is not so very different from the United Kingdom.

In 1991, business failures in the United Kingdom reached the highest level on record. Many of these failures can be attributed to the economic recession, but sales decline is not the sole reason for business failure. Analysis of the companies on the Unlisted Securities Market that entered receivership in 1989 and 1990 reveals that 14 per cent had annual sales growth in their final year in excess of 100 per cent, while only 6 per cent experienced sales decline! In the vast majority of cases you do not have to be a financial genius to detect the signals of business failure. These signals come through loud and clear from a straightforward analysis of the accounts.

Let us now clarify the basic terms and ratios employed in this chapter:

Working capital is an often ill-defined term. *Gross working capital* refers to current assets (e.g. stocks, debtors, marketable securities and cash).

Net working capital (or simply working capital) refers to current assets less current liabilities – hence its alternative name of net current assets. Current assets include cash, marketable securities, debtors and stock. Current liabilities are obligations that are expected to be repaid within the year.

Working capital management refers to the financing, investment and control of net current assets within policy guidelines. *Liquidity management* is the planned acquisition and utilization of cash – or near cash – resources to ensure that the company is in a position to meet its cash obligations as they fall due. A vital document in this regard is the *cash budget* which forecasts the expected cash flow on a monthly or weekly basis. Any predicted cash shortfall may lead to the raising of additional finance, disposal of fixed assets or tighter control over working capital requirements in order to avoid a liquidity crisis.

The current ratio is defined as the ratio of current assets to current liabilities. A high ratio (relative to the industry) would suggest that the firm is in a relatively liquid position. However, if much of the current assets are in the form of raw materials and finished stocks, this may not be the case.

The quick or 'acid test' ratio recognizes that stocks may take many weeks before being

Table 17.1 Working capital in large UK companies as percentages of total assets

	All Industry %	Manufacturing %	Drink %	Industry Chemical %	Mechanical & Instrument Engineering %
Stocks	15.6	18.7	14.1	17.6	23.5
Debtors	19.5	21.6	10.4	25.9	36.5
Cash and securities	10.3	13.2	3.3	9.6	10.0
Total current assets	45.4	53.5	27.8	53.1	70.0
Net fixed assets	54.6	46.5	72.2	46.9	30.0
Total assets	100	100	100	100	100
Net working capital	11.0	15.7	3.7	16.0	27.0

Source: Business Monitor M3 (1989 data).

realized in cash terms. Accordingly, it is computed by dividing current liabilities into current assets excluding stock.

Days cash-on-hand ratio. This ratio is found by dividing the cash and marketable securities by projected daily cash operating expenses. As its name implies, it indicates the number of days the firm could continue to meet its cash obligations on the extremely pessimistic assumption that no further cash is received during the period. Daily cash operating expenses should be based on the projected cash flows from the cash budget, but a somewhat cruder approach is found by dividing the annual cost of sales plus selling, administrative and financing costs by 365.

Why working capital matters

Without working capital, a company cannot continue to trade. For most firms, it constitutes a sizeable proportion of total assets employed. Table 17.1 shows the elements of working capital as a percentage of total assets and indicates that, for all large UK manufacturing companies, current assets represent over half of total assets. This proportion varies considerably across firms. In 1989, the drinks industry held only around 28 per cent of its assets in current form, compared with 70 per cent in the mechanical and instrument engineering industry. The importance of trade creditors as a source of finance is seen in the much lower proportion of total assets held as net working capital. For example, while for all UK large companies current assets (or gross working capital) were approximately 45 per cent of total assets, the net working capital position fell to 11 per cent.

17.2   Cash operating cycle

For a typical manufacturing firm there are three primary activities affecting working capital: purchasing resources, manufacturing the product and selling the product. Because these activities are subject to uncertainty (e.g. delivery of materials may come late, manufacturing problems may arise, sales may become sluggish, etc.) the cash flows associated with them are also uncertain. If a firm is to maintain liquidity, it needs to invest funds in working capital and to ensure that the operating cycle is properly controlled.

The cash operating cycle is the length of time between the firm's cash payment for purchases of material and labour and cash receipts from the sale of goods. In other words, it is the length of time the firm has funds tied up in working capital. This is calculated as follows:

Cash operating cycle = stock period + customer credit period − supplier credit period

---

An example will help explain how the cash operating cycle is found.

Briggs plc, a manufacturer of novelty toys, has the following working capital items in its balance sheet at the start and end of its financial year:

	1 January	31 December
Stock	£5,500	£6,500
Debtors	£3,200	£4,800
Creditors	£3,000	£1,500

Turnover for the year is £50,000 and cost of sales is £30,000. For how many days is working capital tied up in each item? What is the cash operating cycle period?

Our first task is to calculate the turnover ratios for each:

Stock turnover $= \dfrac{\text{Cost of sales}}{\text{Average stock}} = \dfrac{£30,000}{£6,000} = 5$ times p.a.

Debtors turnover $= \dfrac{\text{Sales}}{\text{Average Debtors}} = \dfrac{£50,000}{£4,000} = 12.5$ times p.a.

Creditors turnover $= \dfrac{\text{Cost of sales}}{\text{Average Creditors}} = \dfrac{£30,000}{£3,750} = 8$ times p.a.

To find the number of days each item is held in working capital, we divide the turnover calculations into 365 days:

Stock period $= 365/5 = 73$ days
Debtors' (customer credit) period $= 365/12.5 = 29.2$ days
Creditors' (supplier credit) period $= 365/8 = 45.6$ days

The cash operating cycle is therefore:

$$73 + 29.2 - 45.6 = 56.6 \text{ days}$$

This is illustrated as in Figure 17.1.

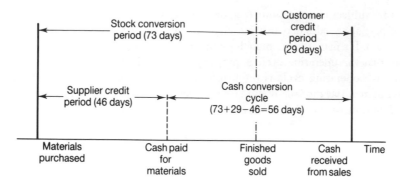

Figure 17.1   Cash conversion cycle

17.3   Working capital policy

The financial manager should ensure that the firm operates sound working capital policies. These policies cover such areas as the levels of cash and stock held, and the credit terms granted to customers and agreed with suppliers. Successful implementation of these policies influences the company's expected future returns and associated risk which, in turn, influence shareholder value.

Failure to adopt sound working capital policies may jeopardize long-term growth and even corporate survival. For example:

- Failure to invest in working capital to expand production and sales may result in lost orders and profits.
- Failure to maintain current assets which can quickly be turned into cash can affect corporate liquidity and may damage the firm's credit rating and increase borrowing costs.
- Poor control over working capital is a major reason for *overtrading* problems, discussed later in this chapter.

Typical questions arising in the working capital management field include:

1. What should be the firm's total level of investment in current assets?
2. What should be the level of investment for each type of current asset?
3. How should working capital be financed?

We now consider how firms establish the level of working capital appropriate for their business, its financing and how the two impact on profitability and risk. The level and nature of working capital within any organization depends on a variety of factors, such as:

- the industry within which the firm operates,
- the type of products sold,

- whether products are manufactured or bought in,
- level of sales,
- stock and credit policies, and
- the efficiency with which working capital is managed.

We saw in Chapter 1 that central to financial management is the relationship between risk and the required financial return. Investment in working capital is no exception. In establishing the planned level of working capital investment, management should assess the level of liquidity risk it is prepared to accept, risk being defined as the possibility that the firm will not be able to meet its financial obligations as they fall due. This is a further dimension of financial risk.

Helsinki plc, a dairy produce distributor, is considering which working capital policy it should adopt.

Figure 17.2 shows the two working capital strategies under consideration. Notice that both schedules are curvilinear, suggesting that economies of scale permit working capital to grow more slowly than sales. A more *aggressive* approach means that the firm operates with lower levels of stock, debtors and cash than with a more relaxed strategy.

A *relaxed*, lower-risk and more flexible policy for working capital means maintaining a larger cash balance and investment in marketable securities that can quickly be turned into cash, granting more generous customer credit terms and investing more heavily in stock. Such a policy may attract more custom, but will usually lead to a reduction in profitability for the business, given the high cost of tying up capital in relatively low profit-generating assets. Conversely, an aggressive policy should increase profitability, at the same time increasing the risk of failing to meet the firm's financial obligations.

This can be seen in Table 17.2. The relaxed working capital strategy involves a further £20 million investment in current assets. The additional stocks and more generous credit facilities enable Helsinki's management to attain an additional £5 million sales with the aggressive policy. This gives a 19.5 per cent return on capital employed and a secure current ratio of 2.7.

A more aggressive working capital strategy would certainly improve the return on capital. In Helsinki's case the rate increases to 30 per cent. But this is achieved by increasing corporate risk. Net working capital falls to only £5 million and the current ratio to 1.3.

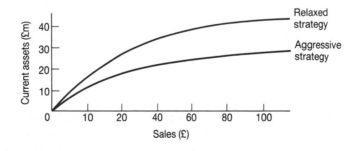

Figure 17.2   Helsinki plc working capital strategies

Table 17.2 Helsinki plc profitability and risk of working capital strategies

	Relaxed (£m)	Aggressive (£m)
Current assets (CA)	40	20
Fixed assets	25	25
Total assets	65	45
Current liabilities (CL)	(15)	(15)
Capital employed (Net Assets)	50	30
Planned Sales	65	60
Planned Profit (15% of sales)	9.75	9.0
Return on capital employed	19.5%	30.0%
Net Working Capital (CA−CL)	£25m	£5m
Current ratio (CA/CL)	2.7	1.3

Working capital costs

Managing working capital involves not only a trade-off between risk and required return, but also between costs that increase and costs that fall with the level of investment. Costs that increase with additional investment are termed *carrying costs*, while costs which fall with increases in investment are termed *shortage costs*. These two types of cost may be found in most forms of current assets, but particularly in stocks and cash.

The main form of carrying costs are opportunity costs associated with the investment.

Bedford auto-vending machine company example

The Bedford Auto-Vending Machine Company is considering how much to invest in current assets:

	Flexible Policy £m	Aggressive Policy £m
Stock	32	25
Debtors	28	22
Cash and Marketable Securities	12	—
	72	47

It will be seen that the flexible policy requires a further £25 million investment in working capital over and above that required for the aggressive policy. What is the cost of carrying this £25 million additional working capital? The main carrying cost is the return that could be earned by investing the additional £25 million in financial assets outside the business. If these could generate 10 per cent p.a. the additional earnings would be £2.5 million (less any interest earned on short-term cash and securities). Other carrying costs include the additional storage and handling costs for stock.

Aggressive or restrictive working capital policies are more susceptible to incurring shortage costs. These costs are usually of two types:

1. *Ordering costs* – costs incurred in placing orders for stock, cash, etc. (in the case of stocks this may also include the production set-up costs). Operating a restrictive policy means ordering stock more regularly and in smaller amounts than for more relaxed policies.
2. *Costs of running out of stock or cash* – the most obvious costs here are costs from the lost business and even the possible liquidation of the firm. Less tangible costs are the lost customer goodwill, the disruption to the production schedule, and the time and cost of negotiating alternative sources of finance.

The trade-off between carrying costs and shortage costs can be shown diagramatically as in Figures 17.3 and 17.4. In Figure 17.3 carrying costs are seen to increase steadily as current assets grow. Conversely, shortage costs fall with the level of investment in current assets. The

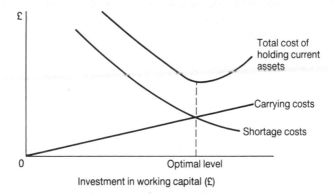

Figure 17.3   Optimal level of working capital for a 'relaxed' strategy

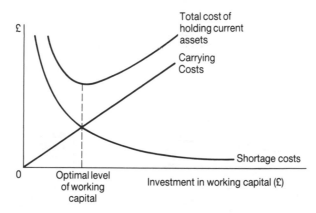

Figure 17.4   Optimal level of working capital for an 'aggressive' strategy

cost of holding current assets is the combined cost of the two, *the minimum point being the optimal amount of current assets held*. For simplicity, we have shown current assets in total, but in practice, it is preferable to consider each element, such as cash or stock, separately.

Different businesses will be more sensitive to certain types of cost. An aggressive policy is more appropriate when carrying costs are high relative to shortage costs, as in Figure 17.4. For example, a major car manufacturer like Ford will not want to hold excessive quantities of raw material stocks, but will buy in materials and parts a short while before they are to be used in car production reflecting the Just-in-Time philosophy (see section 17.6). Often there will be penalty clauses for non-delivery of such materials to the manufacturer by agreed dates. A flexible policy tends to be more suited to low carrying costs relative to shortage costs (see Figure 17.3).

17.4 Financing working capital

Having determined the optimal level of current assets, a firm must then assess how much of the investment is to be financed by short-term and how much by long-term finance. Once again, this involves a trade-off between risk and financial return.

Current assets can be classified into:

1. *Permanent current assets* – those current assets held to meet the firm's long-term requirements. For example, there is a minimum level of cash and stock (often called 'safety stocks') required at any given time, and a minimum level of debtors will always be outstanding.
2. *Fluctuating current assets* – those current assets which change with seasonal or cyclical variations. For example, most retail stores build up considerable stock levels prior to the Christmas period and run down to minimum levels following the January sales.

Figure 17.5 illustrates the nature of fixed assets and permanent and fluctuating current assets for a growing business.

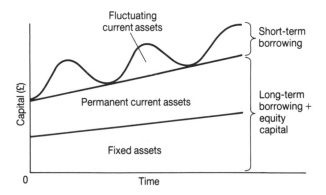

Figure 17.5 Financing working capital: the matching approach

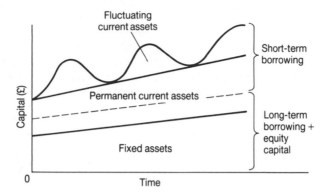

Figure 17.6 Financing working capital needs: an aggressive strategy

How should such investment be funded? There are several approaches to the funding mix problem.

First, there is the *Matching Approach* (Figure 17.5), where the maturity structure of the company's financing exactly matches the type of current asset. Long-term finance is used to fund fixed assets and permanent current assets, while fluctuating current assets are funded by short-term borrowings.

A more aggressive and risky approach to financing working capital is seen in Figure 17.6, using a higher proportion of relatively cheaper short-term finance. Such an approach is more risky because the loan is reviewed by lenders more regularly. For example, a bank overdraft is repayable at any time the bank manager so requires. Finally, a relaxed approach would be a safer, but more expensive strategy. Here, most if not all the seasonal variation in current assets are financed by long-term funding, any surplus cash being invested in short-term marketable securities or placed in a bank deposit.

17.5 Overtrading problems

The question of what is the appropriate long-term capital structure for a business has been discussed in earlier chapters. Here we address the problems arising from carrying on a business with an inappropriate capital structure, a phenomenon known as *overtrading*.

Overtrading arises from at least three serious managerial mistakes:

1. *Initial under-capitalization* Many businesses experience overtrading problems from the very start because they never invested sufficient equity at the time of formation to finance the anticipated level of trading. It is all very well to assume that profits will quickly be achieved to be ploughed back into the business, but experience suggests that the early years of trading are often difficult years, and shareholders will probably want some incentive in the form of dividends.

2. *Over-expansion*   When a business expands to such a degree that its capital base is insufficient to support the new level of activity, the business is overtrading or, to put it another way, under-capitalized. In many cases the business looks to be healthy in that the level of activity is growing and the business is profitable. But unless sufficient cash is generated to finance the anticipated increase in working capital and fixed investment, the business may encounter serious overtrading problems.

3. *Poor utilization of working capital resources*   Even when a business has been adequately capitalized and is not over-expanding its activity, overtrading can still occur in several ways:
   (a) Failure to achieve planned profit and cash flow levels may mean that debt capacity, originally intended for working capital needs, is used to replace lost earnings.
   (b) Cost over-runs on fixed capital projects and other unanticipated capital investment can swallow up finance intended for working capital needs.
   (c) Similarly, strategic decisions, such as a major acquisition, can have adverse effects on working capital finance unless the capital basis is adequately enlarged.
   (d) Higher dividends mean reduced profit retentions, often the major source of finance for working capital.

Consequences and remedies for overtrading

The consequences of overtrading can be extremely serious and possibly fatal. As the pace of activity increases, working capital needs will also increase. Without the necessary capital structure and cash flow, serious liquidity problems will arise. Business life then becomes a matter of crisis management; finding the cash to meet the wage bill, the creditors' claims and the tax charges. Such myopic behaviour takes attention away from the business of creating wealth and will, ultimately, lead to a decline in competitiveness and profitability.

What, then, can management do to remedy the cash flow problems caused through overtrading?

1. The most drastic step is to *reduce the level of business activity*. Profitable orders may be rejected due to insufficient capital to finance additional working capital needs. However, if the alternative is to accept the order and, in so doing, jeopardize the business by exceeding the overdraft limit, a slower rate of growth is the preferred course of action.

2. The most obvious remedy is to *increase the capital base*. Reference back to Figure 17.6 shows that an aggressive strategy for financing working capital operates on a lower long-term capital base, thus making overtrading more likely. Movement towards a matching approach (Figure 17.5) is perhaps called for where permanent increases in current assets are matched by the injection of permanent capital, preferably in the form of equity or long-term loans perhaps with a moratorium on repayments in the early years.

3. Finally, steps should be taken to *maintain tight control over working capital*. Economies of scale should mean that as the business grows, working capital increases more slowly and at a declining growth rate. Constant review of the working capital policy and its cash flow implications can allow the firm to minimize the extra capital resources required to fund expansion.

We now turn our attention to the management of the main elements of working capital: inventory, debtors and cash.

17.6   Inventory management

Inventory (or stock) is the least liquid of current assets and it is therefore vital that it is managed in such a way that it can be converted from raw material to work-in-progress and finished goods over the shortest period of time.

The costs of holding high levels of stocks include the lost interest in tying up capital in such assets, the costs of storing, insuring, managing and protecting stock from pilferage, deterioration, etc., and obsolescence costs. Against this, there are costs involved in holding low levels of stock or running out of stock: loss of goodwill from failure to deliver by the date specified by customers, lost production and disruption due to essential items being unavailable, re-order costs (buyer's and storekeeper's time, telephone, postage, invoice-processing costs, etc.).

A variety of stock management models have been developed to help managers determine the optimal level of stock which balances holding costs against shortage costs. One way of addressing the issue is to determine the *economic order quantity (EOQ)* for the stock required.

We illustrate the graphical approach to determining the optimal level in Figures 17.3 and 17.4 within the context of total working capital. At its simplest, the economic order quantity can be calculated as follows:

$$EOQ = \sqrt{\frac{2AC}{H}}$$

Where:

    C = the cost of placing an order,
    A = the annual usage of the stock, and
    H = the cost of holding a unit of stock for one year.

Ivan plc Example

Ivan plc uses 2,000 units of stock item KPR each year. The costs of holding a single item for a year are £2 and the cost of placing each order is £45. What is the most economical size for each order?

Applying the above formula:

$$EOQ = \sqrt{\frac{2 \times 2,000 \times £45}{£2}} = \sqrt{90,000}$$
$$= 300 \text{ units}$$

Each order will be placed for 300 units, which implies that orders will be placed every 55 days (i.e. $300/2,000 \times 365$).

This simple model has two limitations:

1. Demand, and therefore stock usage, may be seasonal. The constant usage rate for stock assumed here may be unrealistic. Alternatively, demand may be difficult to predict, which necessitates the need for *safety or buffer stocks*, thus calling for a modification of the model.
2. Only the more easily quantifiable costs are included. Many of the other costs referred to earlier (lost goodwill, lost production, etc.) should also be considered.

Just-In-Time

In recent times, managers in some manufacturing firms have been aiming for 'stockless production' and Just In Time (JIT) deliveries. JIT aims towards an 'ideal' level of zero stocks, but with no hold-ups due to stock shortages. Materials and parts are delivered from suppliers only just before they are needed, and products are manufactured only just before they are needed for sale to customers. Where such an operation operates successfully, the consequent reduction in inventory and the cash operating cycle can be very considerable. Indeed, trade creditors can virtually match the current asset investment, thus enabling the business to operate with the minimum of working capital.

17.7   Managing trade credit

Trade credit can be both a source and a use of finance because it can be obtained (via trade creditors or payables) and extended (via trade debtors or receivables). We will concentrate on the extension of trade credit and its management, although many of the issues raised apply also to the receipt of trade credit.

Debtors represent the currently unpaid element of credit sales. While the extension of credit is accepted practice within most industries, credit is essentially an unproductive asset (unless it generates additional business) which both ties up scarce financial resources and is exposed to the risk of default, particularly when the credit period taken by customers is lengthy. Effective management of debtors is therefore an essential element of sound financial management practice.

Effective debtor control policy requires careful consideration of the following: *credit period, credit standards, cost of cash discounts and collection policy*. While the main responsibility for setting credit policy lies within financial management, other functions should be involved, particularly marketing, but all too often this collaboration is lacking.

Credit period

The main factors influencing the period of credit granted to customers are:

1. *The normal terms of trade for the industry*   It would be difficult to operate a trade credit policy where the period offered was considerably below the normal expectation for the

industry unless the company has some other clear competitive advantage, such as recognized better quality product.

2. *The importance of trade credit as a marketing tool*   Determining the optimum credit period requires the finance manager to identify the point where the costs of increased credit are matched by the profits made on the increased sales generated by the additional credit. The more that credit is perceived as being a vital tool in marketing the firm's products, the longer the likely period of credit.

3. *The individual credit ratings of customers*   Most firms operate regular credit terms, for good quality customers, and specific credit terms for higher-risk customers. The credit quality of customers is based on the credit standards addressed in the following section.

Credit standards

We have already noted that granting trade credit is partly a marketing exercise designed to increase sales. However, at the individual customer level, it is essentially a credit assessment and control exercise. In this sense, extending trade credit is no different from a bank granting a loan to a customer. The risk of granting trade credit can be seen when we consider the effect on profit of customer default. If a company sells a product for £1,000 with a 10 per cent net margin, which subsequently becomes a bad debt, the business must make ten similar sales to good customers simply to recover the £1,000 bad debt incurred.

Credit assessment should involve consideration of the following:

1. Prior experience with the particular customer. The credit extended and payment experience in the past is a useful guide, but it should be borne in mind that this may relate to a time when the customer was not experiencing financial difficulty. Even so, it is wise to have more rigorous procedures for assessing new accounts.

2. Analysis of the customer's accounts and credit reports. Profit and Loss Accounts and Balance Sheets are available from the company's registered office. Credit reports include:

   (a) bank references,
   (b) trade references expressing the views of other businesses trading with the customer, and
   (c) credit bureau reports. Credit-reporting agencies (such as Dun & Bradstreet) provide factual data and credit ratings that can be used in credit analysis. It is common practice and makes a lot of sense for firms to offer credit agencies full disclosure of financial and trading information in order to gain a good rating. From an assessment of the customer's credit worthiness, it is possible to establish appropriate credit rules covering:
      (i) the maximum period of credit granted,
      (ii) the maximum amount of credit,
      (iii) the payment terms, including discounts for early payment and interest charges on overdue accounts.

Cash discounts

Cash discounts are financial inducements for customers to pay accounts promptly. Such discounts can be very costly.

Yorko plc example

Yorko plc offers terms of trade which are '2/10 net 30'. This shorthand means that a 2 per cent discount is offered for all accounts settled within ten days, otherwise payment in full is to be made in thirty days. A 2 per cent discount may not seem much until one realizes that this is, in effect, for a payment in advance of just twenty days (i.e. $30 - 10$). The annualized cost is actually over 37 per cent, calculated by the formula below:

$$\text{Cost of Cash Discount} = \frac{\text{Discount \%}}{(100 - \text{Discount \%})} \times \frac{365}{(\text{Final Date} - \text{Discount Period})}$$

In the Yorko plc example, the cost of forgoing the cash discount is:

$$\begin{aligned} \text{Cost} &= \frac{2}{(100-2)} \times \frac{365}{(30-10)} \\ &= 0.0204 \quad \times 18.25 \\ &= 37.23\% \end{aligned}$$

Where such generous terms are available, it probably makes sense for customers to opt for the discount even if it means raising a loan, as long as the cost of finance is clearly below the annualized cost of discount. So why should firms offer such inducements? First, early payment can significantly improve cash flow and reduce bad debt risk. Second, cash discounts can attract new customers who are attracted by the discounts. However, the financial manager should be aware of the true cost of such discounts and be able to justify why terms should be offered costing more than the cost of capital.

Credit collection policy

A good credit collection policy is one where there are clearly defined procedures and where customers know the rules. Debtors who are experiencing financial difficulties will always try to delay payment to companies with poor or relaxed collection procedures. The supplier who insists on payment in accordance with agreed terms, and who is prepared to cut off supplies or take action to recover overdue debts, is most likely to be paid in full and on time.

Using debtors as security

The financing of trade debtors may involve either the assignment of debts (termed *invoice discounting*) or the selling of debts (termed *factoring*). With invoice discounting, the risk of default on the trade debtors pledged remains with the borrower. Factoring, on the other hand, can be and usually is 'without recourse', i.e. the factor bears the loss in the event of a bad debt. Factors provide a wide range of services, the most common of which include:

1. Advancing cash against invoices. Up to 80 per cent of the value of invoices can typically be obtained, repayments (together with interest on the advances) are paid from the subsequent cash collected from debtors.
2. Insurance against bad debts.
3. Administration of the credit control functions. This involves sending out invoices, maintaining the sales ledger and collecting payments.

17.8   Cash management

Throughout this book we have emphasized the importance of cash – rather than profit – in financial management. We now consider why cash has such a vital role to play, and how cash flow forecasts are prepared and used to help manage businesses operating within uncertain environments.

Figure 17.7 illustrates the pivotal role played by cash in a typical firm, first encountered in chapter 1. Attention has already been paid to the cash operating cycle based on working capital requirements. Working capital, together with fixed investment, is financed by two major sources: equity and loan finance, together with less important sources such as the disposal of fixed assets (unless, of course, major parts of the business are sold as in a buy-out).

Corporate liquidity is essential for the firm to be able to mobilize sufficient cash to meet

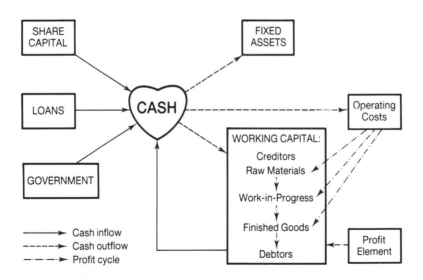

Figure 17.7   Cash – the lifeblood of a business

its financial obligations (suppliers, debenture holders, employees, Inland Revenue, bank, etc.). The financial manager should therefore project forward the firm's ability to finance its operations and to manage corporate cash flow.

Even in well-diversified firms it makes sense to centralize cash management:

1. It allows the treasurer to operate on a larger scale which should give rise to more competitive interest rates and reduced staffing costs.
2. Specialist staff can be employed to work in management.
3. Negative cash flows from one operating unit may be offset by positive cash flows from others, thus avoiding additional financing and loan raising costs. This may well mean that the overall level of cash required to cover unanticipated cash shortfalls is reduced.
4. Banking operations become faster and more efficient, giving rise to advantageous banking arrangements.

Cash flow forecasting

The cash flow forecast, or cash budget, is the primary tool in short-term financial planning. It helps identify short-term financial requirements and surpluses based on the firm's budgeted activities. Cash budgeting is a continuous activity with budgets being rolled forward, usually in weeks or months, as time progresses.

Preparation of the cash budget involves four distinct stages:

1. *Forecast the anticipated cash flows*   The main source of cash is likely to be sales, and the sales forecast will therefore be the primary data source. Sales can be divided into cash sales and credit sales, the cash flow arising from the latter depending on the agreed credit terms. Thus, for example, the sales forecast for January would appear in the cash budget in March as a cash receipt if all sales were on credit terms of 60 days. Other cash inflows would include income on investments, cash from disposal of fixed assets, etc.

2. *Forecast the anticipated cash outflows*   The principal payment is generally the payment of trade purchases. Once again, the credit period taken must be allowed for. Other cash outflows include wages and salaries, administrative costs, taxation, capital expenditure and dividends.

3. Compare the anticipated cash inflows and outflows to determine the *net cash flow* for each period.

4. Calculate the *cumulative cash flow* for each period by adding the opening cash balance to the net cash flow for the period.

Mangle Ltd example

Mangle Ltd produces a single product – a manually operated spindryer. It plans to increase production and sales during the first half of next year; the plans for the next eight months are shown in Table 17.3.

Table 17.3 Mangle Ltd: production and sales

Month	Production	Sales
November	70	70
December	80	80
January	100	80
February	120	100
March	120	120
April	140	130
May	150	140
June	150	160

The selling price is £100, with an anticipated price increase to £110 in June. Raw materials cost £20 per unit, wages and other variable costs are £30 per unit. Other fixed costs are £1,800 a month, rising to £2,200 from May onwards. Forty per cent of sales are for cash, the remainder being paid in full 60 days following delivery. Material purchases are paid one month after delivery and are held in stock one month before entering production. Wages and variable and fixed costs are paid in the month of production.

A new machine costing £10,000 is to be purchased in February to cope with the planned expansion of demand. An advertising campaign is also to be launched, involving payments of £2,000 in January and March. The directors plan to pay a dividend of £1,000 in May. On 1 January the firm expects to have £2,000 in the bank. What will the cash position look like over the following six months?

Table 17.4 Mangle Ltd: cash budget for six months to June

	Jan. (£)	Feb. (£)	Mar. (£)	Apr. (£)	May (£)	June (£)
Inflows						
Receipts from cash sales	3,200	4,000	4,800	5,200	5,600	7,040
Receipts from debtors	4,200	4,800	4,800	6,000	7,200	7,800
(A)	7,400	8,800	9,600	11,200	12,800	14,840
Outflows						
Payments to creditors	2,000	2,400	2,400	2,800	3,000	3,000
Variable costs	3,000	3,600	3,600	4,200	4,500	4,500
Fixed costs	1,800	1,800	1,800	1,800	2,200	2,200
Advertising	2,000		2,000			
Capital expenditure		10,000				
Dividend					1,000	
(B)	8,800	17,800	9,800	8,800	10,700	9,700
Net cash surplus (deficit) in month (A–B)	(1,400)	(9,000)	(200)	2,400	2,100	5,140
Opening cash balance	2,000	600	(8,400)	(8,600)	(6,200)	(4,100)
Closing cash balance	600	(8,400)	(8,600)	(6,200)	(4,100)	1,040

The first step is to determine the actual sales revenue each month. Forty per cent of sales is for cash and is therefore received in the month of sales, while the remaining 60 per cent is received two months after the month of sale. Purchases are made the month prior to entering production, but because a month's credit is taken, the payment to creditors is in the same month as production.

After including all cash flows, the net cash flow for each of the six months shows that in the first three months, Mangle Ltd has a negative cash flow, and a negative cash balance for the February to May period. The company may decide that this is a seasonal business and that it is acceptable to operate with such monthly cash flow figures. In this case, the firm should seek to negotiate a loan to cover the shortfall. However, it would do well to consider ways of minimizing the monthly deficits. For example, could cash receipts from debtors be collected more quickly? Could payment of creditors be deferred for a few weeks? Could the price increase be brought forward? Could payment terms on the capital equipment be extended over a longer period, possibly by leasing the equipment? The cash budget allows finance managers to consider such questions well ahead of actual events. Frequently, such forward planning avoids the need to raise external finance through astute management of working capital.

Short-term investment

When the cash budget indicates a cash surplus, the financial manager needs to consider opportunities for short-term investment. Any cash surplus beyond the immediate needs should be put to work, even if just invested overnight. The following considerations should be made in assessing how to invest short-term cash surpluses:

- The length of time for which the funds are available.
- The amount of funds available.
- The return offered on the investment in relation to the investment involved.
- The risks associated with calling in the investment early (e.g. the need to give three months' notice to obtain the interest).
- The ease of realization.

Examples of short-term investment opportunities include:

1. *Treasury Bills* – issued by the Bank of England and guaranteed by the UK government. No interest as such is paid, but they are issued at a discount and redeemed at par after 91 days. At any time the bills can be sold on the Discount Market.

2. *Bank deposits* – a wide range of financial instruments are available from banks, but the more established investment opportunities are:
   (a) term deposits, where for a fixed period (usually from one month to six years) a fixed rate is given. For shorter periods (typically up to three months) the interest may be at a variable rate based on money market rates.
   (b) Certificates of Deposit, issued by the banks at a fixed interest rate for a fixed term

(usually between three months and five years) but which can be realized on the Discount Market at any time.

3. *Money market accounts* – most major financial institutions offer schemes for investment in the money market at variable rates of interest.

GEC AND THE £1 BILLION CASH MOUNTAIN

General Electric Company (GEC), Britain's largest electrical and electronics manufacturer, was often criticized in the boom years of the 1980s for stockpiling cash. Its managing director, Lord Weinstock, was accused of being a corporate miser with no new ideas and no strategy for growth. While other businesses were investing heavily and making acquisitions, GEC was amassing over £1 billion in cash.

But by 1991, as Britain and much of the rest of Europe slid into deep recession, GEC's strategy to 'stay liquid' was viewed rather differently. With record levels of bankruptcies and many major companies saddled with huge debt repayments created in a dash for growth, GEC had over £800 million in cash and a further £600 million cash in its European joint ventures such as Germany's Siemens and France's Alsthom. This level of liquidity enables GEC to be viewed by shareholders as a 'safe' investment with the flexibility to pursue growth strategies at a time when many other businesses struggle to survive.

17.9 Summary

The management of working capital is a key element in financial management, not least because, for most firms, current assets represent a major proportion of their total investment. Working capital policy is concerned with determining the total amount and the composition of a firm's current assets and current liabilities.

Key points

- Working capital policy trades off expected profitability and risk. Risk in this context refers to the probability that the firm will be unable to meet its financial obligations. An 'aggressive' working capital policy, which seeks to employ the minimum level of net current assets (including cash and marketable securities), will probably achieve a higher return on investment, but may jeopardize the financial health of the business.
- The cash operating cycle (the length of time between cash payment and cash receipt for goods) should be regularly reviewed and controlled.
- The financing and investment of working capital should be considered simultaneously. In general, it is advisable that long-term finance is used to fund both fixed assets and

permanent current assets, fluctuating current assets being funded by short-term borrowing.

- The consequences of overtrading (or under-capitalization) can be extremely serious, if not fatal, for the firm.
- Inventory management involves determining the level of stock to be held, when to place orders, and how many units to order at a time.
- Inventory costs can be classified into carrying or holding costs (which increase as the level of stock rises), and shortage costs (or stock-out costs and ordering costs) which fall as stock levels increase.
- A variety of economic order quantity models are available for determining the order quantity that will minimize total inventory cost. The basic model is:

$$EOQ = \sqrt{\frac{2AC}{H}}$$

Where: C = the cost of placing an order, A = the annual usage of stock, and H = the cost of holding a unit of stock one year.

- A firm's credit policy consists of credit period, credit standards, cost of cash discounts and credit collection policy.
- The cost of cash discounts is given by the formula:

$$\frac{\text{Discount } \%}{100 - \text{Discount } \%} \times \frac{365}{(\text{Final Date} - \text{Discount Period})}$$

- Trade debtors can be used to raise finance through invoice discounting and factoring.

Further reading

Brigham and Gapenski (1991) and Brealey and Myers (1991) provide fuller discussions on the issues addressed in this chapter. Chadwick and Pike (1985) offer a practical guide to the subject.

Questions

Self-test questions

1. Explain why one firm may have a cash operating cycle of only 5 weeks, while another could have a cycle of 25 weeks. What are the financial implications?
2. Define overtrading. How does it arise and what are its consequences?
3. What are the main elements in a firm's credit policy?
4. What do you understand by carrying costs and ordering costs? How do they fit into the economic order quantity formula?
5. Specify the basic formula for calculating the cost of cash discounts.

Exercises

1. Hunslett Express Company specifies payment from its customers at the end of the month following delivery. On average, customers take 70 days to pay. Sales total £8 million per year and bad debts total £40,000 per year.

   The company plans to offer cash discounts for payment within 30 days. It is estimated that 50 per cent of customers will take up the discount but that the remaining customers will take 80 days to pay. The company has an overdraft facility costing 13 per cent p.a. If the proposed scheme is introduced bad debts will fall to £20,000 and savings in credit administration of £12,000 p.a. are expected.

   Required

   (a) Should the company offer the new credit terms?

   (Solution in Appendix A)

2. Salford Engineers Limited, a medium-sized manufacturing company, has discovered that it is holding 180 days' stock while its main competitors are holding only 90 days' stock.

   Required
   (a) Discuss what you consider to be the most important factors which determine the optimum level of stockholding for the company.
   (b) What action would you take if you were asked to investigate the reasons for Salford's high level of stock?

   (Certified Diploma)
   (Solution in Appendix A)

3. Torrance Ltd was formed in 1988 in order to produce a new type of golf putter. The company sells the putter to wholesalers and retailers and has an annual turnover of £600,000. The following data relates to each putter produced:

	£	£
Selling price		36
Variable costs	18	
Fixed cost apportionment	6	24
Net profit		12

   The cost of capital (before tax) of Torrance Ltd is estimated at 15 per cent.

   Torrance Ltd wishes to expand sales of this new putter and believes this can be done by offering customers a longer period in which to pay. The average collection period of the company is currently 30 days. The company is considering three options in order to increase sales. These are as follows:

	Option		
	1	*2*	*3*
Increase in average collection period (days)	10	20	30
Increase in sales (£s)	30,000	45,000	50,000

In addition to reconsidering its policy towards customers, Torrance Ltd is also reconsidering its policy towards trade creditors. In recent months the company has suffered from liquidity problems which it believes can be alleviated by delaying payment to trade creditors. Suppliers offer a 2.5 per cent discount if they are paid within ten days of the invoice date. If they are not paid within ten days suppliers expect the amount to be paid in full within thirty days. Torrance Ltd currently pays suppliers at the end of the ten-day period in order to take advantage of the discounts. However, it is considering delaying payment until either thirty days or forty-five days after the invoice date.

Required
(a) Prepare calculations to show which credit policy the company should offer its customers.
(b) Discuss the advantages and disadvantages of using trade credit as a source of finance.
(c) Prepare calculations to show the implicit annual interest cost associated with each proposal to delay payment to creditors. Discuss your findings.

(Certified Diploma, December 1990)

4. Dalgleish Ltd is a wholesale supplier of stationery. In recent months the company has experienced liquidity problems. The company has an overdraft at the end of November 1991 and the bank has been pressing for a reduction in this overdraft over the next six months. The company is owned by the Dalgleish family who are unwilling to raise finance through long-term borrowing.

The balance sheet of the business as at 30 November 1991 is as follows:

Balance Sheet as at 30 November 1991

	£000	£000	£000
Fixed assets			
Freehold land and premises at cost		250	
Less accumulated depreciation		24	
		—	226
Fixtures and fittings at cost		174	
Less accumulated depreciation		38	
		—	136
			—
			362

Current assets

Stock at cost	142	
Trade debtors	120	
	262	

Less: creditors' amounts due within one year

Trade creditors	145		
Dividends	20		
Corporation tax	24		
Bank overdraft	126	315	(53)
			309

Share capital and reserves

Ordinary £1 shares	200
Profit and loss account	109
	309

The following forecasts for the six months ended 31 May 1992 are available concerning the business:

(i) Sales and purchases for the six months ended 31 May 1992 will be as follows:

	Sales £000	*Purchases* £000
December	160	150
January	220	140
February	240	170
March	150	110
April	160	120
May	200	160

(ii) Seventy per cent of sales are on credit and 30 per cent are cash sales. Credit sales are received in the following month. All purchases are on one month's credit.

(iii) Wages are £40,000 for each of the first three months. However, this will increase by 10 per cent as from March 1992. All wages are paid in the month they are incurred.

(iv) The gross profit percentage on goods sold is 30 per cent.

(v) Administration expenses are expected to be £12,000 in each of the first four months and £14,000 in subsequent months. These figures include a monthly charge of £4,000 in respect of depreciation of fixed assets. Administration expenses are paid in the month they are incurred.

(vi) Selling expenses are expected to be £8,000 per month except for May 1992 when an advertising campaign costing an additional £12,000 will be paid for. The advertising campaign will commence at the beginning of June 1992. Selling expenses are paid in the month they are incurred.

(vii) The dividend outstanding will be paid in December 1991.

(viii) The company intends to purchase, and pay for, new fixtures and fittings at the end of April 1992 for £28,000. These will be delivered in June 1992.

Required

(a) Prepare a cash flow forecast for Dalgleish Ltd for each of the six months to 31 May 1992.

(b) Prepare a forecast profit and loss account for the six month period to 31 May 1992.

(c) Briefly discuss ways in which the company might reduce the bank overdraft as required by the bank.

(Certified Diploma, December 1991)

Practical Assignment

1. Sound credit management can play an important role in the financial success of a business.

Required

(a) Explain the role of the credit manager within a business.

(b) Discuss the major factors a credit manager would consider when assessing the creditworthiness of a particular customer.

(c) Identify and discuss the major sources of information that may be used to evaluate the creditworthiness of a commercial business.

(d) State the basis upon which any proposed changes in credit policy should be evaluated.

(Certified Diploma, June 1980)

2. If you are based in a firm where credit management is important, apply question 1 to your organization.

PART IV

Integrated Topics: Overview

In Part IV, we endeavour to bring together many of the issues and techniques examined in previous chapters. To a degree, we have presented investment and financing decisions as fairly separate issues. It is now necessary to explore some of the interactions between these two key elements in finance.

In Chapter 18, we examine more fully the issue of how to establish the required rate of return for an activity, initially assuming all-equity financing and then considering the complications introduced by mixed financing at three levels: the overall enterprise, the corporate segment and the individual project. In Chapters 19 and 20, we extend our focus to cover international operations and the special risks which international traders and investors, respectively, face in their business decisions. The reader will find a distinctly Eastern European flavour in our treatment of overseas direct investment, for which we offer no apologies – we believe that the more strategically aware companies should be looking eastwards to exploit opportunities in increasingly liberalized countries!

Many corporate decisions bear option-like characteristics. In Chapter 21, we explain how the traded options markets operate and how the methodology of option valuation can be applied to certain business investment and financial decisions.

Finally, in Chapter 22, we examine mergers and takeovers – why they occur, how they are financed, and the effects they have on organizational structure and shareholder wealth. Other forms of restructuring are also examined. This chapter is supplemented by a case study, based on a recent takeover bid that failed, but which raised many interesting issues.

CHAPTER 18

The required rate of return on investment

HOW QUAKER DERIVES ITS COST OF CAPITAL

'Our value driver equation does not end with the cash flow generated by our strong brands. It also includes a financing component that provides us with a discipline to choose our best investment option. Our challenge to be the best directs us to pursue business strategies that will allow us consistently to deliver cash flows to shareholders at rates in excess of our cost of capital and better than our competition. We measure all potential projects by their cash flow merit. We then discount projected cash flows back to present value in order to compare the initial investment cost with a project's future returns to determine if it will add incremental value after compensating for a given level of risk. To arrive at the appropriate discount factor, we calculate our cost of capital as the weighted average of the costs of debt and equity used to finance the company. Given the favourable tax treatment of debt, we have decided to gradually increase, over time, the amount of debt relative to the amount of equity in order to lower our cost of capital.

The two components of cost of capital are the weighted averages of the cost of debt and the cost of equity. Cost of equity is a measure of the minimum return Quaker must earn to properly compensate investors in a stock of comparable risk. It is made up of two prime components: the "risk-free" rate and the "equity risk premium". The risk-free rate is the sum of the expected rate of inflation and a "real" return, above inflation, of 2 to 3 per cent. A commonly used surrogate for the risk-free rate is the rate for US Treasury Bonds, which are unconditional obligations of the government intended to pay a real return of two or three per cent above long-term inflation expectations. For fiscal 1989, the average risk-free rate on these securities was approximately 9 per cent.

For Quaker, a 'risk premium' of about 5.3 per cent is added to the risk-free rate to compensate investors for holding Quaker's stock, the returns of which depend on the future profitability of the Company. To derive Quaker's cost of equity, the risk premium is added to the risk-free rate. In fiscal 1989, the company's average cost of equity was approximately 14.2 per cent.

Just as Quaker's cost of equity is calculated from an investor's viewpoint, the Company's cost of debt is "market-related" and reflects the returns that lenders expect in the marketplace. To arrive at Quaker's cost of debt, we use the current yield offered by long-term US Treasury Bonds plus a spread as our proxy for this return.'

(Quaker Inc. Annual Report, 1989)

18.1   Introduction

The Quaker Annual Report shows the company's keen appreciation of the need to reward all stakeholders. No company can expect prolonged existence without achieving returns which at least compensate investors for their opportunity costs. Failure to meet prior interest payments may result in insolvency, while shareholders who receive a poor rate of return will vote with their wallets, depressing share price. If the share price underperforms the market (allowing for risk), the market is indicating that a company is ripe for reorganization, takeover or both. A management team, motivated if only by job security, must earn acceptable returns for stakeholders. This chapter deals with assessing such rates of return, an issue closely linked to the firm's capital structure. We will also find that there may be different returns required for different activities, according to their riskiness. In this context, we will examine the case of divisionalized companies which operate in a range of often unrelated activities, for which we may have to calculate tailor-made 'divisional cut-off rates' to reflect the risks of particular activities.

In general, as Quaker clearly articulates, the required return depends mainly on two factors:

1. The inherent business risk of the activity.
2. How the company obtains finance, i.e. the appropriate capital structure.

LEARNING OBJECTIVES

This chapter extends the required return concept to cover mixed capital structures. After reading it, you should:

- Grasp the ways of establishing the return required by shareholders.
- Understand that different rates of return may be required at different levels of the organization.
- Appreciate the drawbacks of the WACC as a project cut-off rate.
- Be able to apply the Adjusted Present Value approach.
- Be able to use an ungeared Beta in setting a discount rate.

Initially, however, we study the simplest case of the all-equity company, operating in a single sphere. Two prominent approaches for specifying the shareholder's required return are the Dividend Growth Model (DGM) and the Capital Asset Pricing Model (CAPM), developed in Chapters 4 and 10, respectively.

18.2 The required return in ungeared companies: using the dividend growth model (DGM)

The DGM revisited

In Chapter 4 it was shown that the value of a firm which retains a constant fraction, b, of its earnings to finance investment, expected to achieve a rate of return, R, resulting in a growth rate of $g = bR$, is:

$$V_0 = \frac{D_1}{(k_e - g)} = \frac{D_0(1+g)}{(k_e - g)}$$

Where: D_0 and D_1 represent this year's and next year's dividend respectively, and k_e is the return required by shareholders.

THE COST OF EQUITY IN AN UNGEARED COMPANY

Rearranging the expression, we find the shareholder's required return is:

$$k_e = \frac{D_1}{V_0} + g$$

The shareholders' required return is a compound of two elements, the *prospective* dividend yield and the expected rate of growth in earnings and dividends.

It is important to appreciate that this formula for k_e is based on the current market value of the shares and that it incorporates specific expectations about growth, dependent on assumptions about both the retention ratio, b, and the expected rate of return, R. With b and R constant, the rate of growth, g, is also constant. These are highly restrictive assumptions. Often, the nearest we can get to assessing the likely growth rate is to project the past rate of growth, modifying it if we believe that a faster or slower rate may occur in future.

For example, assume Arthington plc is correctly valued by the market at £3 per share, having recently paid a dividend of 20p per share, and with recent dividend growth of 12 per cent p.a. From this, we can infer that shareholders require a return of 19.5 per cent.

$$k_e = \frac{£0.2(1.12)}{£3} + 0.12 = 0.075 + 0.12 = 0.195, \text{ i.e. } 19.5\%$$

To illustrate this approach with a real company, consider the dividend payment record

Table 18.1 The return on Pilkington shares

Year to 31 March	Dividend (p)	Closing (p)	Share Price High (p)	Low (p)
1981	3.5	101	101	62
1982	3.5	89	119	82
1983	3.5	71	91	47
1984	3.8	108	117	64
1985	4.2	95	111	75
1986	4.5	147	153	83
1987	7.3	263	270	133
1988	8.4	211	354	186
1989	9.5	246	270	192
1990	10.5	211	270	202
1991	10.5	188	214	140

Source; Pilkington Annual Reports

and end-of-financial year share prices for Pilkington plc for the years 1981–91. Also shown in Table 18.1 are share price highs and lows recorded for each year.

The dividend per share (DPS) grew from 3.5p in 1981 to 10.5p by 1991. Using discount tables, we find the average annual compound growth rate is 11.5 per cent.*

Applying this result to the share price of £1.88 ruling at the end of March 1991, Pilkington's year end, we find:

$$k_e = \frac{10.5p(1.115)}{£1.88} + 0.115 = 0.063 + 0.115 = 0.178, \text{ i.e. } 17.8\%$$

Some problems

Apart from the restrictive assumptions of the dividend growth model, some further warnings are in order:

(1) Suppose the growth calculation was conducted over a shorter time period, say, 1986–90, during which DPS rose from 4.5p to 10.5p, reflecting growth of some 23.5 per cent p.a. The

---

* The growth rate, g, is found from the expression:

$$3.5 \, (1+g)^{10} = 10.5p$$

or

$$(1+g)^{10} = 3.0p$$

The growth rate can be found directly from compound interest tables, or by inverting the expression from the present value tables, i.e. $\frac{1}{(1+g)^{10}} = 0.3333$, whence g lies about half-way between 11 per cent and 12 per cent.

formula for k_e would indicate a return of 29 per cent required by Pilkington shareholders, considerably above our first result. Over this particular period, two distorting factors were at work. Pilkington was recovering from the recession years of the early 1980s, and given the tendency for dividend increases to lag behind earnings increases, the 1986 dividend was still low. Also, Pilkington was subject to a takeover bid from BTR in 1986 and one defence tactic was to offer a sharply increased dividend. Once the bidder was safely rebuffed, Pilkington reverted to more sedate dividend growth, albeit above the pre-bid rate. The point, of course, is that the calculation of g, and hence k_e, should be based on a sufficiently long period to allow random distortions to even out. We may still feel that past growth is an unreliable guide to future performance, especially for a company in a mature industry, growing roughly in line with the economy as a whole. If past growth is considered unrepresentative, we may interpose our own forecast, but this would involve second-guessing the market's growth expectations impounded in the current share price.

(2)   The calculated k_e depends on the choice of reference date for measuring share price. Our calculation used the price at the end of the accounting period, but this pre-dates the announcement of the result and payment of dividend. We could use the ex-dividend price, as this values all future dividends, beginning with those payable in one year's time. This would reduce the distortion to share price caused by the pattern of dividend payment, i.e. the share price drops abruptly when it reaches the Record Day beyond which purchasers of the share will not qualify for the declared dividend. However, given the delays in paying dividends, the ex-dividend price may well reflect a different set of expectations than those ruling earlier.

Conversely, we must recognize that in an efficient capital market, share prices gradually increase as the date of dividend payment approaches, so that, especially for companies which pay several dividends each year, there is always likely to be some distorting effect present. Our practical advice is to take the ruling share price as the basis of calculation but to moderate the calculation itself by recognizing that there may be a dividend in the offing. For example, if a 5p dividend is expected in two months' time, a prospective fall in share price of 5p should be allowed for. In our assessment, the error caused by using an out-of-date share price is likely to outweigh that from using a valuation incorporating a forthcoming dividend.

(3)   The calculation is at the mercy of short-term movements in share price. If, as many observers believe, capital markets are becoming more volatile, possibly undermining their efficiency in setting reliable guides as to the fair values of companies, the financial manager may feel disinclined to rely on market prices anyway. Managers are generally reluctant to accept the EMH and commonly feel that the market undervalues their companies. However, there still remains a need for a benchmark return to guide managers. One might examine, over a period of years, the actual returns received by shareholders in the form of both dividends and capital gains. One way of conducting such a calculation is to focus on annual rates of return, based on the analysis adopted in Chapter 10, where we saw such a calculation applied to Pilkington. This generated an annual return of 26.6 per cent, based on the rather artificial assumption of a one-year holding period. Readers are advised to re-examine the figures in Table 10.1, and to digest the wild swings in annual returns. These are food for thought for anyone who doubts the degree of risk involved in short-term equity investment!

18.3 The required return in ungeared companies: using the CAPM

In Chapter 10, we examined how the Security Market Line (SML) traced out the systematic risk/return characteristics of all securities traded in an efficient capital market. The SML equation is:

$$ER_j = R_f + \beta_j (ER_m - R_f)$$

ER_j is the return required on the shares of the company in question, and therefore is the same as k_e, R_f is the risk-free rate of return, and ER_m is the expected return on the market portfolio. We saw in Chapter 10 that, in order to utilize the CAPM, we needed to either measure, or directly make assumptions about, these items. The reader is referred back to the discussion of measurement difficulties and the application to GKN.

However, despite these problems, the CAPM has major advantages over the Dividend Growth Model (DGM). The DGM requires extrapolation of past rates of growth and acceptance of the validity of the market's valuation of the equity at any time. If we have reason to suspect that past growth rates are unlikely to be replicated and/or we suspect that a company's share price is over- or under-valued, we might in turn doubt the validity of an estimate of k_e derived from the DGM.

The CAPM does not require growth projections nor does it totally depend on the instantaneous efficiency of the market. Recall that the Beta is derived from a regression model relating the returns from holding security j to the returns on the market over a lengthy period. Taking, say, monthly observations over five years effectively irons out short-term inefficiencies. This does require semi-strong market efficiency over the period studied and a reasonably consistent relationship between security returns and the returns on the market.

Applying the CAPM to Pilkington

We will now apply the CAPM formula to Pilkington plc to compare the result with that given by the DGM. In Autumn 1991, the return on three-month Treasury Bills was about 10 per cent, and the RMS quoted a Beta for Pilkington of 1.33. Using the historical risk premium on the market portfolio of 9%, we find:

$$ER_{Pilkington} = 0.10 + 1.33(0.09) = 0.10 + 0.12 = 0.22, \text{ i.e. } 22\%$$

This compares with the DGM estimate of about 18%.

Since the two approaches should yield broadly the same result, some reconciliation may be required. The figure of 22% may be an overestimate. At the time of this calculation, market rates of interest were historically high, both in money and real terms, reflecting both inflationary fears and deliberate UK government policy to use high interest rates to squeeze consumer expenditure and protect the exchange rate. In addition, the historical estimate of the market risk premium was taken from a period prior to the market crash of 1987 – updating this might have generated a lower risk premium.

So, as with the DGM, we find our estimate is susceptible to the date of calculation, which is hardly surprising since both expectations and hence market values and required returns are also dynamic variables.

18.4 The required return in a geared company

The main message of Chapters 14 and 15, whichever view of gearing we adopt, is that gearing can be dangerous. There may well be an optimal capital structure, but it is by no means clear at what level of gearing it occurs. Firms should thus aim for some target capital structure which they expect will provoke no adverse capital market reaction and which leaves some spare borrowing capacity in case of emergency. With this view, some form of the Weighted Average Cost of Capital may appear to be the appropriate cut-off rate for new investment projects, at least so long as gearing conforms to the target ratio.

Required conditions for using the WACC

However, there are some major requirements which have to be satisfied before use of the WACC can be justified:

1. The WACC assumes the project is a marginal, scalar addition to the company's existing activities, with no overspill or synergistic impact likely to disturb the current valuation relationships.
2. It assumes that project financing involves no deviation from the current capital structure (otherwise the MCC should be used).
3. Using the WACC implies that any new project lies in the same risk category as the company's existing operations. This is possibly a reasonable assumption for minor projects in existing areas and perhaps replacements, but hardly so for major new product developments.

In the short term, at least, firms are almost certain to deviate from the target structure, especially as market values fluctuate and the financial manager perceives and exploits ephemeral financing bargains, e.g. an arbitrage opportunity in an overseas capital market. It is thus unrealistic to expect the hurdle rate for new investment to be adjusted for every minor deviation from the target gearing ratio. To all intents and purposes, for such a firm, the capital structure is given – only for major divergences from the target gearing ratio should the discount rate be altered. Similarly, even where a project is wholly financed by debt or equity, so long as the project is a minor one with no appreciable impact on the overall gearing ratio, then it is appropriate to use the WACC as the cut-off rate. The following worked example shows how to compute the WACC when the gearing ratio can be regarded as constant.

Example: Saddleback plc

Saddleback is an undiversified producer of animal feedstock. Senior managers are concerned to discover what overall rate of return it should achieve for stakeholders. This rate will be applied as a cut-off rate for all new projects which will be financed in a way replicating the company's existing gearing ratio.

Table 18.2 shows Saddleback's financial statements.

It is important to use market value weights in computing the WACC since the book

Table 18.2   Saddleback plc

Balance Sheet as at 31 December 1992

	£m	£m
Fixed assets (net)	100	
Net current assets	40	140
Issued share capital	70	
Reserves	50	
Long-term loans	20	140

Profit and Loss Account: year ended 31 December 1992

	£m	
Sales		160
Net profit	30	
Interest	(2)	
Tax payable (after allowances)	(5)	
Profits attributable to ordinary shareholders		23

 (i) Par value of ordinary shares = 50p, market value £1.20. The Beta for Saddleback's shares is 1.1.
 (ii) The loan stock, issued in £100 units, is not due for redemption for many years and can be treated as perpetual. The market price is currently £85. Three month Treasury Bills offer a return of 10 per cent. The return on the market portfolio is expected to be 16 per cent after taxes.
(iii) Dividends of £8m have recently been paid. The growth rate in dividends has averaged 10 per cent over the past decade.
(iv) The rate of Corporation Tax is 33 per cent. Assume no delay.

value of capital employed usually reflects the historic cost of the company's assets. Shareholders are concerned not with the return expressed on what may well be an extremely dated measure of the value of their capital but with the return on the market value. It is easy to find examples of companies whose market values are several times their book values. A similar point applies to debt capital. The relevant consideration is not the coupon rate on old debt but the return which the company would have to offer on a fresh issue of debt, as measured by the yield implied by the current market price of its debt. The relevant market values for Saddleback are:

Equity: No. of shares × market price = (70m × 2 × £1.20) = £168m (91%)
Debt : £20m × £85/£100 =   £17m (9%)
                                                              ───────
Total Value =   £185m

The CAPM suggests a required return on equity of:

$$\mathrm{ER}_j = R_f + \beta(\mathrm{ER}_m - R_f)$$
$$= 0.10 + 1.1(0.16 - 0.10) = 0.166, \text{ i.e. } 16.6\%$$

Alternatively, using the dividend growth model, we obtain:

$$k_e = \frac{D_0(1+g)}{V_s} + g = \frac{£8m(1.10)}{£168m} + 0.10 = 0.052 + 0.10 = 0.152, \text{ i.e. } 15.2\%$$

The disparity between these estimates of k_e is not substantial. It could be due to an historically high-level risk-free rate at the time of analysis, or to the shares of Saddleback being temporarily overvalued, or perhaps to expectations that Saddleback will grow faster in the future.

The cost of debt, k_d, may be found by solving a simple perpetuity expression, taking into account the tax relief the firm enjoys on interest payments:*

$$£85 = \frac{10\% \times £100(1-T)}{k_d}$$

For $T=33\%$, the solution for the post-tax cost of debt is 7.9 per cent. We may now complete the calculation of the WACC using the estimate of k_e from the CAPM, by substituting into the usual expression (see Chapters 14 and 15):

$$\text{WACC} = \left(k_e \times \frac{V_S}{V_S + V_B} \right) + \left(k_d(1-T) \times \frac{V_B}{V_S + V_B} \right) = (0.166 \times 0.91) + (0.079 \times 0.09)$$

$$= 0.151 + 0.007 = 0.158,$$
$$\text{i.e. } 15.8\%$$

Using the lower estimate for k_e (15.2 per cent) yielded by the DVM, a WACC of 14.5 per cent would have been obtained. It is largely a question of managerial judgement as to which estimate is based on most reliable data.

In the Saddleback example, no change in gearing was envisaged when financing new projects. However, as we have repeatedly warned, a significant change in gearing affects the market values of both debt and equity capital, e.g. shareholders respond adversely to higher gearing and the financial risk which it entails. Also, the value of debt may be marked down in the market. To compute the WACC, we would have to assess the new return required by shareholders, k_{eg}, given by:

$$k_{eg} = k_{eu} + (k_{eu} - k_d)(1-T)\frac{V_B}{V_S}$$

Where:

$$k_{eu} = R_f + \beta_u(\text{ER}_m - R_f)$$
$$\beta_u = \text{the ungeared Beta coefficient}$$

(See Chapter 15.)

To value the equity, i.e. to derive a measure for V_S, we would need to apply the perpetuity expression for valuing a stream of post-tax geared equity income:

$$V_S = \frac{(E - iB)(1-T)}{k_{eg}}$$

We now encounter a circular problem since the market value depends on k_{eg} and to find k_{eg}, we need to know the market value!

---

*In reality, we should consider the delay in tax payment which lowers the effective rate of Corporation Tax and thus reduces the discrepancy between the pre-tax and post-tax costs of debt (see Chapter 17). For simplicity and convenience, the delay in payment is ignored here.

As it happens, use of the WACC in this situation may be inappropriate anyway since, unless the firm is at and adheres to the target ratio, the WACC and the marginal cost of capital (MCC) will diverge. If the firm is below the optimal capital structure, the MCC is less than WACC, and the MCC exceeds the WACC when it overshoots the optimal gearing ratio. We found, in Chapter 14, that when the firm departs from the optimal gearing ratio, the appropriate required return is the MCC:

THE MARGINAL COST OF CAPITAL

$$\text{MCC} = \frac{\text{Change in required returns}}{\text{Amount available to invest}}$$

$$= \frac{\begin{array}{c}\text{Change in returns required} \\ \text{by shareholders}\end{array} + \begin{array}{c}\text{Change in returns required} \\ \text{by lenders}\end{array}}{\text{Amount available to invest}}$$

However, this does not always help us too much either, since, to calculate the MCC, we again need to know the market values of both equity and debt at the higher level of gearing, i.e. we again encounter the circular problem described earlier. It is clear that the WACC is only suitable for small-scale projects which do not materially disturb the gearing ratio, and that the theoretically more correct MCC is also problematic.

Fortunately, as we shall see in the next section, help is at hand.

18.5   The adjusted present value method

The Adjusted Present Value (APV) of a project is simply the 'essential' worth of the project, adjusted for any financing benefits (or costs) attributable to the particular method of financing it. The rationale for the APV method was provided by Myers (1974), using MM's gearing model with corporate tax, but is only valid so long as the WACC profile is declining due to the value of the Tax Shield. In Chapter 15, we saw that the value of a geared firm, V_g, is the value of an equivalent all-equity-financed company, V_g, plus a Tax Shield, TB, the discounted tax savings resulting from tax-deductibility of debt interest less the costs of financial distress, FD:

$$V_g = V_u + [TB - \text{FD}]$$

This expression can be translated from the value of a firm to the value of an individual project. However, different projects can probably support different levels of debt. For example, they may involve different inputs of easily resaleable fixed assets and have different levels of operational gearing. As a result, it may be more appropriate to evaluate the particular effects of the financing of each project separately.

The APV is calculated in three steps:

Step 1   Evaluate the 'Base Case' NPV, discounting at the rate of return which shareholders would require if the project were financed wholly by equity, derived by ungearing the company's equity Beta.

Step 2　Evaluate separately the cash flows attributable to the financing decision, discounting at the appropriate risk-adjusted rate.

Step 3　Add the present values derived from the two previous stages to obtain the APV. The project is acceptable if the APV is greater than 0.

A simple example will illustrate the use of the APV.

Rigton plc

Rigton plc has a gearing ratio, measured by debt-to-equity at market values, of 20 per cent. The equity Beta is 1.30. The risk-free rate is 10 per cent and a return of 16 per cent is expected from the market portfolio. The rate of Corporation Tax is 33 per cent. Rigton proposes to undertake a project requiring an outlay of £10m, financed partly by equity and partly by debt. The project, which is a perpetuity, is thought to be able to support borrowings of £3m at an interest rate of 12 per cent, thus imposing interest charges of £0.36m. It is expected to generate pre-tax cash flows of £2.5m p.a. Using the formula developed in Chapter 15 for the ungeared Beta.

$$\beta_u = \frac{\beta_g}{1 + \frac{V_B}{V_S}(1-T)} = \frac{1.30}{1 + 0.20(1-0.33)} = \frac{1.30}{1.13} = 1.15$$

This yields a required return on ungeared equity of:

$$ER_j = R_f + \beta_u(ER_m - R_f) = 0.10 + 1.15(0.16 - 0.10) = 0.10 + 0.069$$
$$= 0.169, \text{ i.e. } 16.9\%$$

The Base Case NPV is:

$$NPV = -£10m + \frac{£2.5m(1-0.33)}{0.169} = -£10m + \frac{£1.68m}{0.169}$$
$$= -£10m + £9.91m = -£0.09m$$

The present value of the tax savings, i.e. the Tax Shield, TB, is given by

$$\frac{TiB}{i} = \frac{(0.33)(0.12)(£3m)}{0.12} = £0.99m$$

The Adjusted Present Value is thus:

$$APV = -£0.09m + £0.99m = +£0.90m$$

and the project is clearly worthwhile. The significance of this result is that, although the Base Case NPV is negative, the project is rescued by the Tax Shield of £0.99m. An essentially unattractive project is rendered worthwhile by the generosity of the state taxation system! We have encountered this kind of result already, when we examined leasing decisions. The three-stage analysis of a lease-or-borrow-to-buy decision was effectively an APV calculation – the base case NPV was calculated to determine the underlying profitability of the project, and then the optimal financing arrangements were assessed.

In the Rigton example, the project creates wealth only for the Rigton's shareholders. From the perspective of the overall economy, it is wealth-reducing and, unless there are compelling 'social' reasons to justify it, should not be undertaken. In other words, the project involves a transfer of wealth from taxpayers to Rigton's shareholders. This sort of reasoning led the then Chancellor of the Exchequer, Nigel Lawson, to reduce the rate of Corporation Tax in 1984 in order to lower the tax advantage of debt financing, and hence reduce the extent to which investment decisions were likely to be distorted by the system of tax breaks.

Further aspects

Before leaving the APV, several related issues are worth examining:

(1) The APV in practice is affected by the terms and conditions of a pre-arranged schedule for debt interest and capital repayment and sometimes, the calculations can be exceptionally tedious. Rather than utilize the convenient assumption of perpetual debt financing, let us assume that the debt plus interest must be repaid over two years, with interest and two equal capital payments occurring at end-year. Table 18.3 shows the repayment schedule and the resulting tax savings.

With no tax delay assumed, the present value of the tax savings is:

$$\frac{£0.119m}{(1.12)} + \frac{£0.059m}{(1.12)^2} = £0.106m + £0.047m = £0.153m$$

Obviously, the value of the Tax Shield is much lower with the accelerated payments, and would be lower still with a tax delay.

(2) Although our example focused on the side-effects of debt financing, the APV routine can be easily applied to any other financing costs and benefits, many of which are awkward to handle with the simple WACC. For example, if equity capital is externally raised, normally there are various issuing and underwriting costs to bear. Including these would alter the APV formula as follows:

APV = Base Case NPV + Tax Shield − PV of Issue Costs

A similar treatment would be applied to subsidized borrowing costs, investment grants and to the tax savings from utilizing the investment allowances against corporate taxes which many governments offer.

Table 18.3 The Tax Shield with finite-life debt

Balance of Loan at Start of Year	Interest at 12%	Tax Saving	Repayment	Balance of Loan at End of Year
£3.0m	£0.36m	(33% × £0.36m) = £0.119m	£1.5m	£1.5m
£1.5m	£0.18m	(33% × £0.18m) = £0.059m	£1.5m	0

(3) We ought to recognize that tax savings are not certain because they depend on the inherent profitability of the company. As this is a random variable, the company's ability to set off interest payments (and other tax reliefs) against income is also random. Our examples assume continuous profitability, but if there are periods during which the company is expected to be tax-exhausted, this should be allowed for in the computation of the APV. If the future pattern of liability to tax is uncertain, then it is not appropriate to use a risk-free rate to discount the tax savings. As it happens, in the Rigton example, we have used the company's cost of debt, rather than the totally risk-free rate, reflecting the non-zero risk attached to corporate debt. This is probably a sufficient adjustment for the risk of the Tax Shield.

(4) Finally, we have glossed over the issues which impact on the debt-supporting capacity of particular projects. In principle, the debt capacity of a project is given by the present value of future expected earnings from the firm as a whole, taking into account any existing borrowings. It might seem obvious that more profitable companies are able to borrow relatively more than unprofitable companies. However, this assumes that there are no costs of financial distress. Enhanced borrowing ability for more profitable companies is not universal, since a would-be lender should still look at the break-up value of the enterprise. Failure to do this explains some of the more bizarre lending decisions made by UK banking institutions during the 1980s.

Several subsequently distressed companies, such as British and Commonwealth Holdings, Brent Walker and many of the then fashionable management buy-outs were able to obtain plentiful supplies of borrowed capital. However, this was largely due to abandonment by commercial banks of prudent lending principles, in particular, losing sight of the vulnerability of highly geared clients to business recession and rising interest rates. It is doubtful whether banks in future will be so anxious to lend against earning capacity. In the final analysis, the crucial factor which governs debt capacity is how much can be raised by a distress sale of assets.

18.6 Using 'tailored' discount rates

A further problem with using a uniform discount rate like the WACC is that it implies new projects fall into the same risk category as the company's other operations. This might be a reasonable assumption for minor projects in existing areas and perhaps for replacements, but hardly seems justifiable for major new product developments or acquisitions of companies in unrelated areas. If the expected return is positively related to risk, firms which rely on a single discount rate may tend to over-invest in risky projects to the detriment of less risky though still attractive projects. Many multi-divisional companies are effectively portfolios of diverse activities of different degrees of risk. Each division contributes to the firm's overall business risk in a way similar to how individual shares contribute to the systematic risk of a portfolio of securities. The problem this poses for a uniform discount rate is shown in Figure 18.1.

Figure 18.1 shows the relationship between the rate of return required on a particular project and that expected on the market portfolio, linked by the Beta. The overall portfolio of

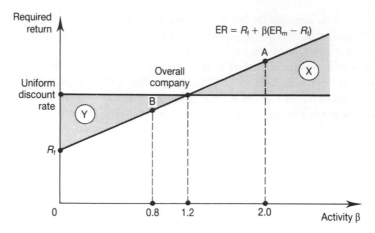

Figure 18.1   Risk premiums for activities of varying risk

company activities may have a Beta of say, 1.2, but this is only a weighted average of the Betas of component activities. For example, activity A has a greater degree of risk with a Beta of 2.0, and thus a higher than average discount rate would be applicable when appraising new projects in this area while the reverse applies for activity B which has a Beta of only 0.8. Clearly, to appraise all new projects using a discount rate based on the overall company Beta of 1.2 would invite serious errors. For example, in area X, application of the uniform discount rate would result in accepting some projects which should be rejected because they offer too low a return for their level of risk, while in area Y, some worthwhile low risk projects would be rejected. To avoid making such errors, firms should use 'tailor-made' cut-off rates for activities involving a degree of risk different from that of the overall company.

There are three levels, or tiers, of risk in the multi-activity enterprise, with each tier requiring a different cut-off rate, for evaluating investment. These are shown in Figure 18.2 and explained below.

The overall company

Company-level risk is a weighted average of all the risks of component operations. Here, the WACC would be used for valuing the income from the company as a whole, but is only relevant as a cut-off rate for projects which replicate the average risk of the company.

The division

Many companies are structured into separate strategic sub-units or divisions, along product or geographical lines. For example, Boots plc has two main activities, retailing and manufacturing pharmaceuticals and toiletries. Intuitively, we may regard these as activities of different degrees of systematic risk, and would suggest differential discount rates to evaluate 'typical' projects within each division, say, 12 per cent, for the relatively low risk activities in retailing and 19 per cent, say, for more risky manufacturing of pharmaceutical products which involve significant risky R & D outlays.

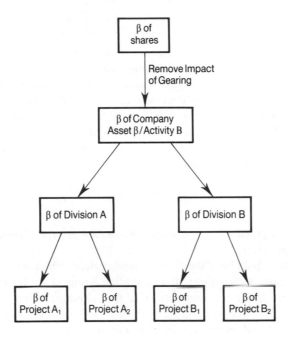

Figure 18.2 The Beta pyramid

Individual projects

However, even within divisions, no two projects have identical risk. Hence, differential discount rates are required when new projects differ in risk from existing divisional activities.

SEGMENTAL BETAS

The company Beta is a weighted average of component divisional Betas. For a company with two divisions, A and B, the overall Beta is given by:

$$\text{Company } \beta = \left(\beta_A \times \frac{V_A}{V_A + V_B} \right) + \left(\beta_B \times \frac{V_B}{V_A + V_B} \right)$$

where the weights V_A and V_B represent the proportion of company value accounted for by each segment. A similar expression would apply for each division, where the corresponding weights would represent the contribution to divisional value accounted for by each activity. Figure 18.2 illustrates these concepts as a Beta pyramid.

We will use the Boots example to illustrate the derivation of the appropriate discount rate at different levels of an organization. In each case, we recommend the APV principle, which involves discounting the operating cash flows at the all-equity rate and adding back any financing benefits, or deducting any financing costs.

The required return for Boots plc

In October 1991, the Risk Measurement Service cited a Beta of 0.90 for Boots. As an equity Beta, this reflects not only the inherent systematic risk of Boots' overall activities, but also the financial risk which Boots' shareholders are required to shoulder, i.e. it must be ungeared to find the inherent systematic risk. The 'Beta ungeared' is also called the *'asset Beta'* or *'activity Beta'* because it reflects the risk of the activity in which the underlying assets are engaged rather than that of the securities which have been used to finance them.

As the traditional accounting equation states that Assets equal Liabilities, i.e. every asset has been financed somehow, we deduce that:

$$\text{Asset } \beta = \text{Liability } \beta = \left(\text{Equity } \beta \times \frac{V_S}{V_S + V_B}\right) + \left(\text{Debt } \beta \times \frac{V_B}{V_S + V_B}\right)$$

where each Beta is weighted according to the contribution its type of finance makes to total financing (at market values).

Quite simply, the 'Asset Beta' equals the 'Liability Beta', which is a weighted average of the component security Betas. Debt Betas are often assumed to be zero, implying that company debt instruments are systematic risk free although some empirical evidence suggests debt Betas of between 0.1 and 0.2. For convenience, we will assume a debt Beta of zero but the reader should appreciate the short-cut involved.

With a debt Beta of zero, the asset Beta is:

$$\beta_u = \left(\text{Equity } \beta \times \frac{V_S}{V_S + V_B}\right)$$

Adjusting for tax relief on debt interest, this becomes $\beta_u = \text{Equity } \beta \times \dfrac{V_S}{V_S + V_B(1-T)}$ which is equivalent to the expression encountered in chapter 15 for Beta ungeared, i.e.:

$$\beta_u = \frac{\beta_g}{1 + \dfrac{V_B}{V_S}(1-T)}$$

At its reporting date Boots had a gearing ratio (long- and short-term debt to market value of equity) of 13 per cent, so that its asset Beta was:

$$\beta_u = \frac{0.90}{1 + 0.13(0.67)} = \frac{0.90}{1.087} = 0.83$$

Taking the historical estimate for the risk premium on the market portfolio of 9 per cent, and using the yield on three-month Treasury Bills as at October 1991 of 10 per cent, the CAPM suggests the following cut-off rate for all-equity financed investment:

$$\text{ER} = 0.10 + 0.83(0.09) = 0.10 + 0.075 = 0.175, \text{ i.e. } 17.5\%$$

Would we apply this rate to all investments undertaken by Boots? Not if we believe there are risk differences between the divisions. If so, we should be looking for tailor-made discount rates.

The divisional cut-off rate

We need now to consider what are suitable Betas for the two main Boots divisions, Retailing and Pharmaceuticals. However, no Betas are recorded for company divisions, simply because no market trades securities representing title to Boots' divisional assets. Instead, we need to look for two surrogate companies and use their ungeared Betas as the 'stand-in' estimates for the Betas of the two Boots divisions. This involves using what Fuller and Kerr (1981) have called the *pure play technique*. This relies on the principle that: 'the risk of a division of a conglomerate company is the same as the risk of an undiversified firm in the same line of business (adjusted for financial risk)'.

Consulting the Risk Measurement Service again, we find geared Betas for Kingfisher, another high street retailer, and for Glaxo, manufacturers of pharmaceuticals, of 0.85 and 1.13, respectively. Accepting these as reasonably close surrogates, and converting to the equivalent ungeared Betas by using their respective gearing ratios (14 per cent and 7 per cent), we derive the following estimates for the divisional cut-off rates:

Required Return	$= R_f + $ Kingfisher Ungeared Beta $\times (ER_m - R_f)$
for Retailing	$= 0.10 + 0.78(0.09) = 0.10 + 0.07 = 0.17$, i.e. 17.0%
Required Return	$= R_f + $ Glaxo Ungeared Beta $\times (ER_m - R_f)$
for Manufacturing	$= 0.10 + 1.08(0.09) = 0.10 + 0.097 = 0.197$, i.e. 19.7%

If these are good surrogates, the value-weighted average Beta should equal the Boots Beta.

The project cut-off rate

We must now address the objection that the required return figures are only relevant for appraising new projects whose systematic risk is identical to that of typical projects already operating within the divisions. If either division undertakes a new venture which takes it outside its existing risk parameters, then we must clearly look for different rates of return – in effect, we need to obtain estimates for individual project Betas. Without having access to internal records, our analysis can only be indicative, but the following principles should guide the analyst in practice.

First, we should look for sources of risk which make the individual project more or less chancy than existing operations. There are two broad reasons why projects have different risks, different revenue sensitivity and different operational gearing.

Revenue sensitivity

Imagine we are dealing with the development of a new retail site. The sales generated by the projected facility may vary with changes in economic activity to a greater or lesser degree than existing sales. For example, we may expect that, for a 10 per cent rise in the level of GDP, whereas overall retail sales of Boots increase by 12 per cent, the sales of the new facility rise by 15 per cent.

THE REVENUE SENSITIVITY FACTOR

This magnifying effect is measured by the *'Revenue Sensitivity Factor' (RSF)*. The RSF is calculated as follows:

$$RSF = \frac{\text{sensitivity of project sales to economic changes}}{\text{sensitivity of divisional sales to economic changes}} = \frac{15\%}{12\%} = 1.25$$

Within Boots, sales of Do–It–Yourself goods are known to be far more responsive to prevailing economic conditions than sales of the toiletries and other goods retailed in High Street outlets, so if the new site will specialize in DIY, it should merit a RSF greater than one.

Operational gearing

The second source of additional project risk lies in the extent to which the project cost structure comprises fixed charges, i.e. the project's *operational gearing*. The higher the proportion of fixed costs in the cost structure, the greater the impact of a change in economic conditions on the net cash flow of the project, thus magnifying the revenue sensitivity effect. Again, the individual project may exhibit a degree of operational gearing different from that of the division as a whole.

To illustrate the impact of operational gearing, consider the figures in Table 18.4, where the firm applies a 50 per cent mark-up on variable cost.

In this example, an increase in sales revenue of 50 per cent will lead to an increase in net cash flow of 66 per cent because of the gearing effect. There is thus a magnifying factor of 1.33 (it is not symmetrical!). This is called the *Project Gearing Factor (PGF)* and may differ from the gearing factor(s) found elsewhere in the division.

OPERATIONAL GEARING

To measure the relative level of gearing, the *Operational Gearing Factor (OGF)* is used. This is defined as:

$$OGF = \frac{\text{Project Gearing Factor}}{\text{Divisional Gearing Factor}}$$

Table 18.4 The effect of operational gearing

Sales	Variable Costs	Fixed Costs	Net Cash Flow
£90	£60	£5	£25
£60	£40	£5	£15

The second step in assessing the project discount rate brings together these two sources of project risk into a Project Risk Factor (PRF).

THE PROJECT RISK FACTOR

The Project Risk Factor is simply the compound of the RSF and OGF:

$$\text{Project Risk Factor} = \text{RSF} \times \text{OGF}$$

In our example this is equal to $(1.25 \times 1.33) = 1.66$. In this case, the project is considerably more risky than the 'average' project within the division and merits the application of a higher Beta. Based on the Boots ungeared retailing Beta, this is given by:

$$\text{Project Beta} = 1.66 \times 0.78 = 1.29$$

The final step calculates the required return using the SML equation:

$$\text{Required return} = 0.10 + 1.29(0.09) = 0.10 + 0.116 = 0.216, \text{ i.e. } 21.6\%$$

Project discount rates in practice

Considering the informational requirements for obtaining reliable tailor-made discount rates for particular investment projects, it is not too surprising that few firms go to these lengths. Instead, a far more common practice is to seek an overall divisional rate of return, which becomes the average cut-off rate, but is then adjusted for risk on a largely intuitive basis according to the perceived degree of risk of the project. For example, many firms group projects into 'risk categories' such as the classification in Table 18.5. For each category, a target or required return is established as the cut-off rate.

Table 18.5 Subjective risk categories

Project Type	Required Return
Replacement	12%
Cost saving/Application of advanced manufacturing technology	15%
'Scale' Projects, i.e. Expansion of existing activities	18%
New Product Development:	
Imitative products	20%
Conceptually new products, i.e. no existing competitors	25%

While this listing is only illustrative, it gives the flavour of the sort of classification procedures often employed in practice. The divisional required return appears to be 18 per cent, the rate applicable to projects involving replicas of the firm's existing activities. Around this benchmark are clustered activities of varying degrees of risk and, as the perceived riskiness increases, the target return rises in tandem.

A final point to stress is that in all these cases, we are discussing a discount rate derived from the ungeared Beta. In other words, we are separating out the inherent profitability of the project from any financing costs and benefits. These can easily be added back by utilizing the APV procedure.

18.7   Problems with 'tailored' discount rates

The pure play technique is an appealing device for estimating discount rates for specific activities but suffers from a number of practical difficulties. Among these are:

Selecting the proxy

To select a proxy, the firm needs to examine the range of apparently similar candidates operating in the relevant sector. However, no two companies have the same business risk due to diversity of markets, management skills and other operating characteristics. How one chooses between a range of 'fairly similar' candidates is essentially an issue of judgement.

Ungearing the Beta

Our method for ungearing Beta uses market values of both equity and debt. If the debt of the surrogate is not traded, one can only use book values. As a result, the business risk element in the Beta has to be approximated.

Divisional interdependencies

In practice, it is difficult to make a rigid demarcation of divisional costs and incomes, since most divisionalized companies share facilities, ranging from the highest decision-making level to joint research and development, joint distribution channels and joint marketing activities. Indeed, access to shared facilities often provides the initial motive for forming a diversified conglomerate, enabling the elimination of duplicated services and the exploitation of scale economies. If carefully evaluated and implemented, the merging of activities should create value and reduce business risk. Only when a merger has no operating impact across divisional lines, can it be suggested that business risk itself is unaffected. Even so, there may well be synergies at the peak decision-making level.

Differential growth opportunities

Using a cut-off rate based on another firm suggests that the division in question has the same growth prospects as the surrogate. However, opportunities to grow are determined by dividend policy, the extent of capital rationing and the interaction between divisions, e.g. competition for perhaps scarce investment capital. In reality, because the firm's own decision processes help to determine the potential for growth, it is not accurate to assume that growth opportunities are externally derived.

Joint ventures

The use of differential discount rates may destroy the incentive to cooperate on projects that straddle divisional boundaries. For example, a joint venture whose expected return lies between the cut-off rates of the two divisions will be attractive to one and unacceptable to the other. Here, some form of mediation is required at peak level, which reassures the 'victim' of the decision that subsequent performance will be assessed after adjusting for having to operate with a project it did not want or without a project which it did wish to undertake.

18.8   A critique of divisional hurdle rates*

Modern strategic planning has developed away from crude portfolio planning devices such as the Boston Consulting Group's market share/market growth matrix towards capital allocation methods which emphasize the creation of shareholder value. Central to value-based approaches is discounting projected cash flows to determine the value to shareholders of business units and their strategies. *A key feature of the DCF-based approach is the recognition that different business strategies involve different degrees of risk and should therefore be discounted at tailored risk-adjusted rates.*

However, critics such as Reimann (1990), suggest that using differential rates may be dysfunctional by increasing the likelihood of internal dissension whereby a manager of a 'penalized' division may resent the requirement to earn a rate of return significantly higher than some of his colleague-competitors. This resentment may be worsened by the observation that longer-term developments, especially in Advanced Manufacturing Technology and other potentially high value-added activities, prospective money-spinners but undeniably risky, may be 'unfairly' discriminated against. As a result, managers may be reluctant to advance some potentially attractive projects.

As we saw in Chapter 8, the use of risk-adjusted discount rates has the effect of compounding risk differences, making ostensibly riskier projects appear to increase in risk over time. One school of thought contends that in order to avoid this risk penalty, the attempt to tailor discount rates to divisions should be modified, if not abandoned. For example,

---

* This section relies heavily on arguments used by Reimann (1990).

instead of using differential discount rates, firms might use a more easily understood and acceptable, company-wide discount rate for projects of 'normal' risk but appraise high risk/high return projects using different approaches.

Underlying these arguments is the familiar assertion that corporate diversification differs crucially from shareholder diversification, so to apply the CAPM to the former could be misleading. If an investor adds a new share to an existing portfolio, the market risk, as indicated by Beta, of the portfolio will alter according to the Beta of the new security. If its Beta is higher than that of the existing portfolio, then the portfolio Beta increases, and vice versa. With corporate diversification, however, we are not dealing with a basket of shares of unrelated companies, which may be freely traded on the market. A firm which diversifies rarely adds *totally* unrelated activities to its core operations. It may add value if the new activity possesses synergy, or detract from value if the market views the combination as merely a bundle of disparate, unwieldy activities.

Market risk can be altered by strategic diversification decisions at two levels. At the corporate level, decisions concerning business and product mixes, operating and financial gearing can affect market risk. The effect of both types of gearing can be magnified by the effect of the business cycle, so that a firm which engages in contra-cyclical diversification may dampen oscillations in shareholder returns and thus reduce market risk. At the business level, market risk can be reduced by tying up outlets and supplier sources, i.e. by increasing market power, and by developing business activities which enjoy important interrelationships such as common skills or technologies, i.e. by exploiting economies of scale.

Many businessmen feel that emphasis on hurdle rates is probably misplaced in so far as accurate cash flow forecasts are more important to creating business value than the particular discount rate applied to them. This probably explains the continuing popularity of the payback method, noted in an earlier chapter, and the reluctance, at least in the United Kingdom, to adopt CAPM-based approaches. In addition, it may explain why so many successful firms place great emphasis on post-auditing capital projects in order to sharpen up the cash flow forecasting and project appraisals of subordinate staff. Furthermore, there is evidence (Pruitt and Gitman 1987; Pohlman *et al.* 1988) that senior managers manifest their suspicion of subordinates' cash flow predictions by deflating the figures presented to them when projects are submitted for approval.

In view of these arguments, there may be a case for reconsidering the merits using certainty equivalents – adjusting not the discount rate but the cash flow estimates and then discounting at the risk-free rate. However, this has not been widely adopted. Apart from the difficulty of specifying the risk-free asset, there is the problem of determining the certainty equivalent factors, which involves specifying the probability of a range of possible cash flows as a basis of assessing their utility values. While there are techniques available for doing this (Swalm 1966; Chesley 1975), this has not proved to be practicable in most firms.

In view of these problems, Reimann (1990) suggests a 'management by exception' approach. The firm should establish and continuously update a corporate cost of capital, based on CAPM principles, which should be applied as a common hurdle rate for the majority of business activities, which he argues, typically exhibit very similar degrees of risk. *At the business level, major emphasis should be given to careful cash flow estimation, based on evaluation of long-term strategic opportunities and competitive advantage.* A key element of this should be a multiple scenario approach, whereby the implications of 'best', 'worst' and 'most likely' states of the world are examined. For projects which, by their very nature, have demonstrably greater level of risk, other procedures may be appropriate. Rather than adjust the corporate discount rate, Reimann suggests the risk adjustment be made to the cash flow estimates by the business unit executives themselves, i.e. those with closest knowledge both of the market and of competitors' behaviour patterns. Again, a multiple-scenario approach should be adopted. This has the key advantage of avoiding the effect of compounding risk differences over time and thus penalizing longer-term projects, which may have a demotivating effect on staff engaged in progressing high-risk activities.

This discussion may seem to downgrade the importance of DCF and CAPM approaches in the appraisal of alternative courses of action. It is not designed to do this. It is intended to warn the reader that apparently neat mathematical models rarely hold out the whole answer. If the rigid application of a numerical routine leads managers to question the basis of the routine itself (which we believe offers powerful guidance in many situations) and to exhibit dysfunctional behaviour, far better to modify the routine itself to reflect real world practicalities.

18.9 Summary

This chapter has considered the relative merits of using the DGM and the CAPM to derive the rate of return required by shareholders, and has examined the appropriate discount rate to apply in geared companies. The case for and against using tailor-made discount rates for particular business segments and projects was also discussed.

Key points

- The return required on new investment depends primarily on two factors, degree of risk and the method of financing the project.
- In ungeared companies, the return required by shareholders can be estimated using either the DGM or the CAPM.
- The DGM relies on several critical assumptions, in particular, sustained and constant growth, and the instantaneous reliability of the share price set by the market.
- The CAPM relies on a Beta estimate obtained after smoothing short-term distortions, but the estimated k_e may be affected by random influences on the risk-free rate.
- In principle, for geared companies, the required return can be derived by combining k_e with the after-tax debt cost to obtain the WACC.
- However, the WACC is only acceptable under restrictive conditions, in particular, when project financing replicates existing gearing, and when project risk is identical to that of existing activities.
- To resolve the problems of the WACC, the Adjusted Present Value can be used. This is the 'basic' worth of the project, i.e. the NPV assuming all-equity financing, adjusted for any financing benefits such as tax savings on debt interest, or costs such as issue expenses.

- To resolve the problem of risk differences between divisions of a company, the Beta of a surrogate firm, adjusted for gearing, can be used to establish divisional cut-off rates.
- If individual projects within the division also differ in risk, the divisional Beta can be adjusted for differences in revenue sensitivity and/or for differences in operating gearing.
- Not all academics and business people accept the need to define discount rates so carefully, preferring instead to concentrate on the problems of cash flow estimation.
- Reimann argues that a divisional cut-off rate should be used as a rough benchmark for projects but alternative methods of risk analysis should be applied to explore more fully the risk characteristics and the acceptability of investment proposals.

Further reading

The chapter in Brealey and Myers (1991) on the interactions between investment and financing decisions is recommended.

The short article by Gregory (1985) provides a clear application of the APV method. Analyses of the 'tailored' discount rate can be found in Dimson and Marsh (1982) and Andrews and Firer (1987). Gup and Norwood (1982) provide a practical illustration of how one US corporation applies divisional discount rates, while Reimann (1990) gives a critique of the whole approach.

Questions

Self-test questions

1. Suggest reasons why the estimate of the shareholders' required return obtained via the DGM may differ from that obtained from the CAPM.
2. Under what conditions is the WACC a valid measure of the rate of return required on new investment projects?
3. Why is the MCC preferable to the WACC but also awkward to apply?
4. What is the APV, and how is it calculated?
5. What are the dangers in applying a uniform discount rate to all investment projects?
6. What information is required to calculate:
   (a) the return which a whole division should achieve?
   (b) the return required on individual projects?

Exercises

1. The managing director of Wemere, a medium-sized private company, wishes to improve the company's investment decision-making process by using discounted cash flow

techniques. He is disappointed to learn that estimates of a company's cost of equity usually require information on share prices which, for a private company, are not available. His deputy suggests that the cost of equity can be estimated by using data for Folten plc, a similar sized company in the same industry whose shares are listed on the USM, and he has produced two suggested discount rates for use in Wemere's future investment appraisal. Both of these estimates are in excess of 17 per cent p.a. which the managing director believes to be very high, especially as the company has just agreed a fixed rate bank loan at 13 per cent p.a. to finance a small expansion of existing operations. He has checked the calculations, which are numerically correct, but wonders if there are any errors of principle.

Estimate 1: *Capital asset pricing model*
Data have been purchased from a leading business school

> Equity Beta of Folten: 1.4
> Market return: 18%
> Treasury Bill yield: 12%

The cost of capital is $18\% + (18\% - 12\%)\ 1.4 = 26.4\%$
This rate must be adjusted to include inflation at the current level of 6%. The recommended discount rate is 32.4 per cent.

Estimate 2: *Dividend valuation model*

	Folten plc	
Year	Average share price (pence)	Dividend per share (pence)
1985	193	9.23
1986	109	10.06
1987	96	10.97
1988	116	11.95
1989	130	13.03

The cost of capital is: $\dfrac{D_1}{P-g}$

Where:

> D_1 is the expected dividend
> P is the market price
> g is the growth rate of dividends (%)
>
> $= \dfrac{14.20\text{p}}{138\text{p} - 9} = 11.01\%$

When inflation is included the discount rate is 17.01 per cent.

Other financial information on the two companies is presented below:

	Wemere £000	Folten £000
Fixed assets	7,200	7,600
Current assets	7,600	7,800
Less: Current liabilities	3,900	3,700
	10,900	11,700
Financed by:		
Ordinary shares (25 pence)	2,000	1,800
Reserves	6,500	5,500
Term loans	2,400	4,400
	10,900	11,700

Notes

1. The current ex-div share price of Folten plc is 138 pence.
2. Wemere's board of directors has recently rejected a take-over bid of £10.6 million.
3. Corporate tax is at the rate of 35 per cent.

Required

(a) Explain any errors of principle that have been made in the two estimates of the cost of capital and produce revised estimates using both of the methods.
    State clearly any assumptions that you make.
(b) Discuss which of your revised estimates Wemere should use as the discount rate for capital investment appraisal.

(ACCA Level 3, June 1990)
(Solution in Appendix A)

2. Lancelot plc is a diversified company with three operating divisions – North, South and West. The operating characteristics of North are 50 per cent more risky than South, while West is 25 per cent less risky than South. In terms of financial valuation, South is thought to have a market value twice that of North, which has the same market value as West.

Lancelot has an observed equity Beta of 1.27 and a ratio of debt to equity of 0.2. The firm's 10 per cent irredeemable debt is valued at par and can be regarded as virtually risk-free. The overall return on the FT All Share Index is 25 per cent, with a standard deviation of 16 per cent.

Recently, South has been underperforming and Lancelot's management plan to sell it and use the entire proceeds to purchase East Ltd, an unquoted company. East is all-equity financed and Lancelot's financial strategists reckon that while East is operating in broadly similar markets and industries as South, East has a revenue sensitivity of 1.4 times that of South, and an operating gearing ratio of 1.6 compared to the current operating gearing in South of 2.0.

Assume: No synergistic benefits from the divestment and acquisition.

Note: You may ignore taxation.

Required

(a) Calculate the asset Betas for the North, South and West divisions of Lancelot. Specify any assumptions which you make.
(b) Calculate the asset Beta for East.
(c) Calculate the asset Beta for Lancelot after the divestment and acquisition.
(d) Calculate the weighted average cost of capital for Lancelot.
(e) What discount rate should be applied to any new investment projects in East division?
(f) Indicate the problems in obtaining a 'tailor-made' project discount rate such as that calculated in section (e).

3. Claxby is an undiversified company operating in light engineering. It is all equity financed with a Beta of 0.6. Total risk is 40 (standard deviation of annual return). Management want to diversify by acquiring Sloothby Ltd, which operates in an industrial sector where the average equity Beta is 1.2 and the average gearing (debt to total capital) ratio is 1:3. The standard deviation of the return on equity (on a book value basis) for Sloothby is 25. The acquisition would increase Claxby's asset base by 40 per cent. The overall return on the market portfolio is expected to be 18% and the current return on risk-free assets is 11 per cent. The standard deviation of the return on the market portfolio is 10. The rate of Corporation Tax is 33 per cent.

Required

(a) What is the asset Beta for Sloothby?
(b) Analyse both Sloothby's and Claxby's total risk into their respective specific and market risk components.
(c) What would be the Beta for the expanded company?
(d) Using the new Beta, calculate the required return on the expanded firm's equity. Under what conditions could this be taken as the cut-off rate for new investment projects?
(e) In the light of the figures in this example, discuss whether the acquisition of Sloothby may be expected to operate in the best interests of Claxby's shareholders.

4. The most recent annual accounts (greatly simplified) for Hassle plc show the following:

Profit and Loss Account for year ended 31 December 1991

	£m
Operating Income	32.77
Debt Interest	2.00
Taxable Profit	30.77
Corporation Tax @ 35 per cent	10.77
Profit After Tax available for Ordinary Shareholders	20.00
Dividends	5.00
Retained Earnings	15.00

Balance Sheet as at 31 December 1991

	£m	£m
Capital Employed:		
Fixed Assets (net)	100	
Net Current Assets	20	
		120
Financed By:		
Ordinary Shares	60	
Reserves	40	
Long-term Debt	20	
		120

Notes

1. Ordinary shares are denominated in 25p units. The present market price is 50p.
2. The Long-term Debt is comprised of a Secured Loan Stock, redeemable in 2002, with a coupon rate of 10 per cent. The present market price of this stock is £80.

   Hassle is contemplating a new capital investment project, which requires an outlay of £10m (this can be financed internally), and promises a perpetual annual cash flow (before tax) of £6.15m. The directors of Hassle are in disagreement about the appropriate discount rate to apply to these cash flows when appraising the project. One group, led by Mr Bother, argues that there is sufficient information in the annual accounts to support a cost of capital calculation, whereas the opposing faction, led by Mr. Aggro, argues that a more sophisticated approach is required, utilizing the Beta coefficient for Hassle (estimated by London Business School at 1.20).

Required

(a) Discuss, with supporting calculations, how the annual accounts may be used by the Bother faction to compute the weighted average cost of capital.
(b) Explain the drawbacks with the various approaches which you suggest in (a).
(c) Explain how the Capital Asset Pricing Model may assist in the estimation of Hassle's cost of capital.

5. The Finance Director of Nebeng Ltd wishes to know whether to install a new machine.

The machine would either be purchased for cash, or on hire-purchase terms, or would be leased through a finance lease agreement. The purchase cost of the machine is £142,500. It has an expected life of four years and, if purchased, will be sold at the end of Year 4 leading to a balancing charge or allowance. The realizable value at the end of four years is expected to be £22,500. The new machine is expected to generate after-tax net cash flows of £40,000 p.a. for four years; this estimate excludes the tax effects of financing and writing-down allowances. If hire-purchase is used, an initial 20 per cent deposit is payable, followed by four equal annual year-end payments covering both the interest and principal elements of the payment. The four equal payments are expected to yield the lessor an interest return of 20 per cent per year in present value terms. Leasing would involve an annual rental payment of £45,000, payable in advance.

The company pays tax at the rate of 35 per cent per year, one year in arrears and a 25 per cent writing-down allowance is available on the machinery, on a reducing balance basis.

Nebeng Ltd would finance the outright purchase of the machine with a loan repayable in full after four years. The 20 per cent initial deposit on the hire-purchase deal would be financed in the same way. The company's cost of debt is estimated to be 16 per cent per year and equity 22 per cent per year. Three per cent of the 22 per cent cost of equity is due to the company's financial risk (gearing), and the current project is of a similar risk to the company's other activities. The risk free rate is 14 per cent per year, and the market return is 21 per cent per year.

Required

(a) Discuss the relative advantages to the lessee or borrower of leasing and hire-purchase.
(b) Using the APV approach, evaluate whether the machine should be installed and, if so, which means of financing should be chosen.
     State clearly any assumptions that you make.

(ACCA Financial Management, June 1991)

Practical assignment

Re-read the exposition of how we obtained tailored discount rates for the two Boots' divisions. How close do you think our two surrogates were?

For another divisionalized company of your choice (try to find a two- or three-division company):

1. Consult the RMS for an up-to-date estimate of the equity Beta, and use the CAPM to assess the shareholders' required rate of return.
2. Estimate discount rates for each division. You will need to select surrogate companies, record their Betas, and obtain an indication of their own asset Betas by ungearing their equity Betas.
3. Determine whether the weighted average Beta for the company corresponds to its ungeared Beta. You will probably have to use weights based on earnings or sales as very few companies report book values (let alone market values!) of their segments.

CHAPTER 19
Managing currency risk

UNFAIR FOREIGN EXCHANGE

Currency management is a hazardous activity, and sometimes things go very badly wrong. Some companies attempt to minimize the risks of foreign exchange exposure by adopting various hedging devices while others treat their foreign currency dealing activities as profit centres. This essentially involves guessing which way the exchange rate between say the Deutschmark and the dollar will move and adopting a 'position'. For example, if you think the US dollar will fall against the Deutschmark, you may sell dollars hoping for a profit when the expected currency realignment occurs.

One company that came badly unstuck in its foreign exchange speculation was Allied Lyons, which lost around £150m in 1991 when it was thought to have gambled on a dollar depreciation against sterling. Quite the reverse happened as the dollar, heavily sold before the Gulf War, recovered sharply following the rapid cessation of hostilities and the news that non-combatant beneficiaries would meet some portion of the cost of the war. The news of Allied's problems slashed £300m (6 per cent) off its market value. Although the loss itself was not disastrous, the revelation that a food and drinks company of Allied's stature could gamble and lose such amounts on the volatile foreign exchange market did considerable damage to the credibility of its management and their control systems.

19.1 Introduction

World trade has grown by a factor of three over the last twenty years. Virtually all companies deal, either as buyer, seller or investor, in foreign currency, making the management of foreign currency a key factor in financial management.

Foreign currency can change in value relative to the home currency by a substantial

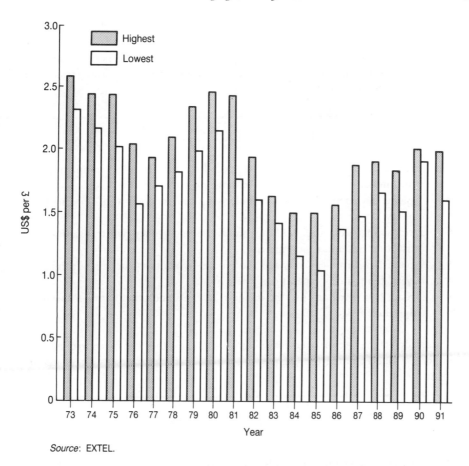

Figure 19.1 Exchange rate between the US$ and sterling, 1973–91 (highest and lowest rate in year)

Source: EXTEL.

margin over a short period of time. Figure 19.1 shows the movement of sterling against the US dollar (US$) over the period 1973–91. We see that the value changed from a high of over 2.5 US$ to £1 in 1973 to a low of 1.08 US$ in 1985. At the beginning of 1991, the rate stood at 1.92 US$ to £1. Yet by August 1991, it had swung back to 1.64 $ to £1, a 15 per cent shift in eight months.

Swings in value of this magnitude can eliminate the profit on a contract and even drive a company into bankruptcy. The UK computer companies Sinclair and Acorn were forced to sell out to other larger companies because they had contracted to buy computer chips from the United States in contracts denominated in dollars at a time when the pound plunged in value against the dollar. The problems surrounding the multinational company Polly Peck in 1990 were as much concerned with currency management as with other unorthodox business practices.

The central issue for the international treasurer is whether to *avoid* exposure to exchange rate risk or to *control* the degree of exposure.

Marks & Spencer in its 1991 annual report stated very clearly its position on managing currency risk: 'The Group's Treasury operates as a profit centre, but within strict risk limits and with a prohibition on speculative activity.'

LEARNING OBJECTIVES

This chapter explains the nature of the special risks incurred by companies who engage in international operations. The aims are to:
- Explain the economic theory underlying the operation of international markets.
- Give you an understanding of the three forms of currency risk: translation risk, transaction risk and economic risk.
- Explain how firms can manage these risks by adopting hedging techniques *internal* to the firms' operations.
- Explain how firms can use the financial markets and other *external* means to hedge these risks.

Knowledge of the risks of overseas operations and how they can be controlled is an important underpinning for Chapter 20, which examines overseas direct investment.

19.2   The structure of exchange rates: spot and forward rates

It is misleading to talk of 'the exchange rate' between currencies because there always exists a spectrum of rates according to when delivery of the currency transacted is required.

The simplest rate to understand is the *spot market* rate which is quoted for 'immediate' (in practice, within two days) delivery. For example, at the close of trading on 16 January 1992, the spot rate for French francs (FF) against sterling was quoted as 9.7075–9.7175 per £1. The spot rate is actually two rates – the first one is the rate at which the financial manager can *purchase* a currency and the higher one is the rate at which he can *sell* it. The difference, or *spread* represents the dealer's profit margin on transactions. At times of great volatility in currency markets, the spread widens to reflect the greater risk in currency trading.

For convenience, we will ignore the spread and work in terms of middle-market rates (i.e. the average of the two rates quoted). On the day cited, the middle-market rate was thus:

$$9.7125 \text{ FF per } £1$$

It is also possible to buy and sell currency for delivery and settlement at specified future points in time. This can be done via the *forward market*, which sets the rate applicable to advance transactions. On the day mentioned above, the following forward rates were quoted (ignoring the spread): for delivery in one and three months, respectively:

1 month: $\frac{1}{2}$ centime premium

3 months: $1\frac{7}{16}$ centimes premium

For both these periods, the forward rates valued the FF at a premium over the spot rate, which suggested that the FF would appreciate against the pound over both of these time periods, i.e. fewer FF would be required to purchase each pound. The associated forward exchange rates are found by deducting the expected premium from the spot rate. Over one month, the FF was expected to appreciate by half a centime (0.005FF) to 9.7075 per £1, while over three months, the FF was expected to appreciate by $1\frac{7}{16}$ centimes (0.0144FF) to 9.6981 to the £1. The opposite interpretation would have applied if the FF/£ rate had involved a discount.

Spot and forward rates for other currencies against sterling are thus connected as follows:

$$\text{Forward Rate} = \text{Spot Rate} \begin{cases} \text{plus forward discount} \\ \text{OR} \\ \text{minus forward premium} \end{cases}$$

Forward rates, therefore, are an assessment of how the currency market expects two currencies to move in relation to each other over a specified time period, and may thus be regarded as a prediction of the future spot rate at the end of that period. As we shall see, this is an important interpretation.

19.3   Foreign exchange exposure

All foreign exchange exposure can be allocated to one of three categories:

1. Transaction exposure.
2. Translation exposure.
3. Economic exposure.

Translation exposure is sometimes called Balance Sheet exposure and economic exposure is sometimes called long-term cash flow exposure.

Transaction exposure is concerned with the exchange risk involved in sending money over a currency frontier. It occurs when cash, denominated in a foreign currency, is contracted to be paid or received at some future date.

For example, a British company might contract to buy US$ 40m worth of computer chips from a US company over a three-year period. When the contract is set up, the rate of exchange between the dollar and the pound is US$ 1.95 to £1, but what will happen in a year or two's time? What if the rate of exchange alters to US$ 1.50 to £1 in a year's time?

The US$ 40 million was equivalent to $40/1.95 = £20.5$ million at the beginning of Year 1, but after the fall in the value of the pound against the dollar, the cost of the contract in pounds rises to $40/1.50 = £26.7$ million. This substantial rise in cost could well place the UK company in financial difficulties.

Similar risks apply regarding expected cash inflows. If the UK company was due to receive $50 million Canadian dollars and the Canadian dollar rose from 2.2 C\$ to £1 to 2.0 C\$ to £1, the UK company would gain £2.28 million on the contract (i.e. the difference between the expected income of £22.72m (50/2.2) and the actual income of £25m (50/2.0)).

We see that unexpected changes in exchange rates can inflict substantial losses (and provide unexpected gains) unless action is taken to control the risk. Short-term cash flow exposure of this nature is called *transaction exposure*.

Translation exposure

Transaction exposure is concerned with the exchange risk involved in sending money over a currency frontier; *translation exposure* is concerned with the value of company assets and liabilities denominated in currencies other than the home currency.

TRANSLATION vs. TRANSACTION EXPOSURE

Translation exposure is concerned with *values* while transaction exposure is concerned with *cash flows*. To put it another way, transaction exposure is concerned with items set out in the Profit and Loss Account while translation exposure is concerned, for the most part, with items set out in the Balance Sheet.

Examples of items, which a treasurer might consider to be subject to translation exposure if denominated in foreign currency, are debts, loans, inventory, shares in foreign companies, land and buildings, plant and equipment.

There can be little argument that if the Canadian dollar falls in value by 3 per cent between the date a contract is signed and the date the dollars are received in the United Kingdom, this represents a real loss to the UK company if no action is taken to hedge the exchange risk. But is a real loss sustained by a UK company if C\$30 million of its inventory or C\$10 million of its bills receivable are being held in Toronto at the time of a devaluation of the C\$ against sterling? This question has been much debated during the last thirty years. We will answer the question later in the chapter.

Economic exposure

A third form of exchange exposure is *economic exposure*. This type of exposure has also been called long-term cash flow exposure. A company trading internationally buys goods and services from abroad and sells its goods or services into foreign markets. If the exchange rate between the pound sterling and the foreign currency shifts over time, then the value of the foreign cash flows in the local currency will alter through time.

In general, a UK company should try to buy goods in currencies which are falling in value against sterling and sell in currencies which are rising in value against sterling. For example, over the period 1987–90, a UK company would have increased its earnings in sterling if it had bought from the United States in US$ and sold into Germany in Deutschmarks.

Even if a UK company denominates all of its contracts in sterling, it cannot avoid the problem of economic exposure. The foreign company will convert the sterling cost of purchases and sales into its own currency for comparison with purchase or sales from companies in other countries using other currencies. Management of economic exposure involves looking at long-term movements in exchange rates and attempting to hedge long-term exchange risk by shifting out of currencies which are moving against the long-term profitability of the company.

19.4   Economic theory and exposure management

The first step in currency management is to identify the transaction, translation and economic exposure to which the company is subject. The second step is to decide how the exposure should be managed. Should the risk be totally hedged, or should some degree of risk be accepted by the company?

The international treasurer must devise a hedging strategy to control exposure to exchange rate changes. The precise strategy adopted by an astute international treasurer is likely to be influenced by certain economic theories which have evolved over the last century, and the extent to which he considers them to be valid. These theories are:

1. The Purchasing Power Parity theory,
2. The Interest Rate Parity theory,
3. The 'Open Fisher' theory,
4. The international version of the Efficient Markets Hypothesis.

We can do no more in this chapter than provide brief sketches of these important contributions to the literature of international economics (See Kindleberger (1978) for an expanded treatment.)

Purchasing Power Parity (PPP)

The Purchasing Power Parity theory claims that the rate of exchange between two currencies depends on relative inflation rates within the respective countries. PPP is based on the *Law of One Price*, which asserts that identical goods must sell at the same price in different markets, after adjusting for the exchange rate. For example, if the market rate of exchange between French francs and sterling is 10FF:£1, a microcomputer could not sell for very long at simultaneous prices of say, £1,200 in London and 8,000FF (i.e. £800) in Paris. The 'correct' prices are those reflecting the 10:1 exchange rate. In this example, people would buy in the 'cheap' market (Paris) and ship the goods to London, thus tending to equilibrate the two prices at, say, a London price of £1,000 and a Paris price of FF10,000 (£1,000). (In reality, transport and other transaction costs would distort this relationship.)

THE LAW OF ONE PRICE

The Law of One Price therefore states that, for *tradeable* goods and services the

£ price of a good × FF/£ exchange rate = FF price of a good.

If relative price levels change, for example, UK prices in general inflate at 10 per cent p.a. and French prices inflate at 3 per cent p.a., the Law of One Price would insist that there should be a fall in the value of the £ against the FF of about 7 per cent.

Taking our microcomputer example, after one year the £ price will rise to £1,000 (1.10) = £1,100 while the FF price becomes FF10,000(1.03) = FF10,300. This implies that the FF/£ exchange rate in the future spot market should move to:

$$\frac{10,300}{1,100} = FF9.36 : £1$$

which represents a depreciation in sterling of 6.4 per cent.

If foreign exchange markets operate freely without government intervention, goods which can be easily traded on international markets, such as oil, are highly likely to obey the Law of One Price, although transport costs between markets may explain a continued price discrepancy. However, not all goods can be easily transported. Most notably, with land and property which are physically impossible to shift, a sustained price discrepancy may apply between markets. In the longer term, however, even these differentials may close as investors and property speculators perceive that one market is cheap relative to the other.

PPP may be expected to operate broadly in the longer term for most goods and services although it can be distorted by government intervention in the foreign exchange markets and the formation of currency blocs such as the European Monetary System, which are designed to frustrate the operation of free market forces. However, while exchange controls and official intervention can *delay* any adjustment necessary to reflect differential rates of inflation, the required change will eventually take place.

The Law of One Price has important implications for the relationship between spot and forward rates of exchange. If people possessed perfect predictive ability, and the rates of inflation in the microcomputer example were *certain*, the market could specify with total precision the appropriate exchange rate between FF and sterling for delivery in the future (i.e., the forward rate of exchange).

More specifically, PPP states that foreign exchange rates may be expected to move in order to adjust for differences in inflation rates and so maintain the Law of One Price:

$$Forward\ Rate = Spot\ Rate \times \frac{(1 + FF\ inflation\ rate)}{(1 + £\ inflation\ rate)}$$

Using expected *annual* inflation rates, this implies that the one year forward rate is given by $\frac{(1.03)}{(1.10)} \times 10FF : £1$ spot rate = FF9.36 : £1, as in the example above.

In this example, the forward rate is predicting the spot rate which should apply in the future. If buyers and sellers of foreign exchange can rely on the currency markets to operate in this way, the risks presented by differential inflation rates could be removed by using the forward market.

The forward rate has been shown to be a poor predictor of the future spot rate. However, it has also been shown to be, for the most part, an *unbiased predictor* of the future spot rate.

By an 'unbiased predictor' we mean that although the forward rate often underestimates the future spot rate and often overestimates the future spot rate, it does not *consistently* do either. In the long run, the differences between the forward rate prediction for a given date and the future spot rate on that date sum to zero. This fact, as we shall see, has important implications for the international treasurer.

Interest Rate Parity (IRP)

The Interest Rate Parity Theory is concerned with the difference between the spot exchange rate (the rate applicable for transactions involving immediate delivery) and the forward exchange rate (the rate applicable for transactions involving delivery at some future specified time) between two currencies. Suppose the spot rate for FF to sterling is 10FF per £1, and the one-year forward rate is 9.36FF per £1. Here, the FF is selling at a 64 centime premium – it will become more expensive in terms of sterling. The currency market thus expects the FF to rise in value by approximately 7 per cent during the year against sterling.

The Interest Rate Parity theory converts this expected rise in the value of the FF against the pound into a difference in the rate of interest in the two countries. The rate of interest on one-year bonds denominated in FF will be lower than bonds otherwise identical in risk but denominated in sterling. The difference will be determined by the premium on the forward exchange rate. If a depreciation of sterling against the French franc is expected, this should be reflected in a roughly comparable interest rate disparity as borrowers in London seek to compensate lenders for exposure to the risk of currency losses. In other words, interest rates offered in different locations tend to become equal, allowing for expected exchange rate movements.

The equilibrium relationship which should operate is given by the expression:

$$\text{Forward Rate} = \text{Spot Rate} \times \frac{(1 + \text{FF interest rate})}{(1 + \text{Sterling interest rate})}$$

For example, if the interest rate available in London is 12 per cent p.a., the figures in our example will indicate a French interest rate as follows:

$$(1 + \text{FF interest rate}) = \frac{9.36}{10.00} \times (1.12)$$
$$= 1.0483$$

so that the French interest rate is 4.83 per cent.

This is an interesting result. A Parisian attracted by higher UK interest, who is tempted to place money on deposit for a year in London, will find that what he gains on the interest rate differential he will lose on the adverse movement of sterling against the FF over the year.

To appreciate this 'swings and roundabouts' argument, consider the following figures:

January – convert FF1,000 into £ → £100
invest for one year in London at 12%
£100 (1.12) → £112
December – convert back to FF at 9.36   → FF 1,048.3

vs.

January – invest FF1,000 in Paris at 4.83% → FF1,048.3

Clearly, the rational investor should be indifferent between these two alternatives, unless he expects interest rates to fall in Paris relative to those in London, or if he believes that the forward rate is not a good predictor of the spot rate in one year's time. One reason why this predictive ability is weakened in practice is intervention in foreign exchange markets by governments. In the absence of such intervention, exchange rates seem to operate so as to smooth out interest rate disparities, but with the creation of artificial market inefficiencies, there often exist opportunities to arbitrage. For example, borrowing money at low interest rates in one market, hoping to repay it before IRP fully exerts itself. However, many UK corporate treasurers have been wrong-footed by borrowing apparently cheap money in Germany or Switzerland but having to repay at exchange rates quite different from those envisaged when raising the loan, because market forces have eventually asserted themselves to remove any interest rate discrepancy.

This equalizing process is effected by financial operators called *arbitrageurs*, who act upon any short-term disparities in these relationships. For example, if in the previous example, the interest rate disparity were 3 per cent, it would pay to borrow in sterling and purchase FF bonds in London.

Open Fisher theory

Another economic theory of use to international treasurers is the 'Open Fisher' theory, sometimes called the 'International Fisher' theory. *The Open Fisher theory claims that the difference between the interest rates offered on identical bonds in different currencies represent the market's estimate of the future changes in the exchange rates over the period of the bond.* The theory is of particular importance in the case of fixed rate bonds having a long life to maturity, say, five to fifteen years' duration.

Let us suppose that an international treasurer wishes to raise £50m for a one-year period. He approaches a bond broker and he is offered the following loan alternatives:

- A sterling loan at 12 per cent p.a.
- A FF loan at 4.83 per cent p.a.

The Open Fisher theory claims that the difference in the interest rate charged on the loan in each currency represents the market's 'best estimate' of the likely future change in the exchange rates between the currencies over the next year. In other words, in broad terms, the Open Fisher theory suggests that the market expects sterling to devalue by around 7 per cent against the French franc over the next year.

To understand this, recall the relationship between 'real' and 'money' interest rates encountered in Chapter 6. The Fisher Effect concerns the relationship between expectations regarding future rates of inflation and domestic interest rates – investors' expectations about future price level changes will be translated directly into nominal market interest rates. In other words, rational lenders will expect compensation not only for waiting for their money but also for the likely erosion in its real purchasing power. For example, if the *real* rate of interest which equilibrates the demand and supply schedules for capital is 5 per cent, and people in general expect inflation of 4 per cent p.a., then the nominal rate of interest will be about 9 per cent. Real and nominal interest rates are connected by the following formula:

$$(1+P)\,(1+I)=(1+M)$$

Where:

$$P = \text{real interest rate}$$
$$I = \text{expected general inflation rate}$$
$$M = \text{market interest rate}$$

The Open Fisher theory asserts that all countries will have the same *real* interest rate, i.e. in real terms, all securities of a given risk will offer the same yield, although nominal or market interest rates may differ due to expected inflation rates.

The Open Fisher theory can be more precisely expressed by an amalgamation of the PPP and IRP theories:

$$\frac{(1+\text{FF interest rate})}{(1+\pounds \text{ interest rate})} \times \text{Spot Rate} = \text{Forward Rate} = \frac{(1+\text{FF inflation rate})}{(1+\pounds \text{ inflation rate})} \times \text{Spot Rate}$$

For example, suppose the London and Paris interest rates are 12 per cent and 4.83 per cent, respectively, as quoted by our bond brokers, above, and the respective expected rates of inflation are 10 per cent and 3 per cent. If the spot rate is FF10.00 to £1, then the Open Fisher theory predicts a depreciation in £ as expressed by the forward rate as follows:

$$\frac{(1.0483)}{(1.12)} \times 10 = 0.936 = \frac{(1.03)}{(1.10)} \times 10$$

In other words, when the spot rate is FF10 per £1, this combination of inflation rates and interest rates is consistent with a forward rate of FF9.36 per £1, as calculated earlier.

The reader will appreciate that these economic theories are interlocking or mutually reinforcing, as shown in Figure 19.2 by an 'equilibrium grid'.

Several other factors, such as the timing of the change, tax and exchange controls, can also affect the relative movement of currencies but the major factor influencing the difference in interest rates is claimed to be the expected future change in exchange rates.

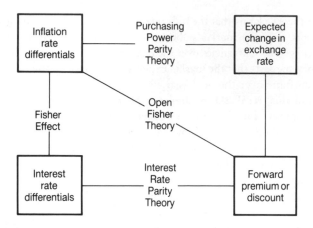

Figure 19.2 Interlocking theories in international economics

The International EMH

The reader will recall that the EMH claims that all publicly available information is very quickly incorporated into the value of any financial instrument traded in the efficient market. In other words, past information is of no use in valuing a financial instrument. Any *change* in value is due to future events which are, by definition, unknowable at the present time. Past trends in exchange rates cannot provide any useful information to assist in predicting future rates.

This theory only applies to information–efficient markets. Currencies operating within a 'currency snake' such as the European exchange rate mechanism (ERM) are operating within a controlled market so the EMH will not fully apply. *Where markets are information-efficient, the EMH casts doubt on the ability of treasurers to make profits out of using exchange rate forecasts.*

This section of the chapter has provided a brief sketch of some economic theories relevant to devising a foreign exchange management strategy. Let us now design such a strategy by applying these theories to the various types of foreign exchange exposure outlined earlier in this chapter.

19.5   Designing a foreign exchange management (FEM) strategy

Hedging translation exposure: Balance Sheet items

We noted earlier in this chapter that total exchange exposure is made up of cash flowing across a national frontier plus the assets and liabilities of the company which are denominated in a foreign currency.

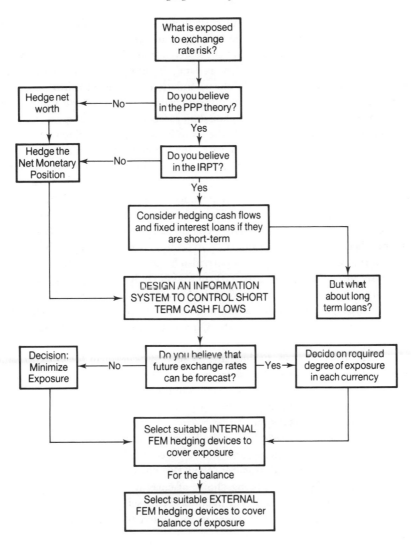

Figure 19.3 Flowchart demonstrating a logical approach towards devising a foreign exchange management strategy

If an international treasurer does not believe the theories outlined in the previous section, he or she might decide to hedge all foreign currency transactions plus the total net worth of all foreign subsidiaries. This strategy is over-elaborate and very expensive, but is adopted by many companies, particularly those dealing in currencies which fluctuate widely in value over short periods.

Figure 19.3 illustrates a more systematic approach to the problem. The basic strategy displayed in Figure 19.3 is to remove from consideration all items which are self-hedging so far as exchange rate risk is concerned and so to concentrate attention on those few cash flows, assets and liabilities which are subject to exchange rate risk in the short term.

We start with a position where all cash flows, assets and liabilities denominated in foreign currency values are assumed to be subject to exposure.

Let us now try to eliminate some of these items from the exposure equation. First, we eliminate all non-monetary assets such as land, buildings and inventory. These non-monetary assets will float in value with internal inflation. The rate of adjustment in value will vary, internationally traded goods will jump in value faster than the value of land, but eventually the prices of all of these non-monetary assets will rise to compensate for the fall in value of the local currency. The PPP theory relates inflation differences to changes in exchange rates. In time, the asset or liability denominated in the foreign currency will rise in value sufficiently to compensate for the fall in the foreign currency value. In other words, there will be more foreign currency units available each of a lesser value than before. The total in terms of home currency will remain unchanged.

Non-monetary assets are thus self-hedging in the long term. If the asset has to be sold in the short term and the foreign cash exchanged into local currency, it is a different story. The amount then becomes a part of transaction exposure. A real loss might be involved.

Short-term loans can, for the most part, also be considered self-hedged. The higher or lower interest rate on the foreign currency loan is a kind of insurance policy against the future fall or rise of the other currency in terms of the home currency. A forward contract could be taken out to cover the risk, but this would be a needless expense since the forward rate is an unbiased predictor of the future spot rate. On average, the forward contracts would make neither a profit nor a loss.

Long-term loans are more problematic. A fervent believer in the Open Fisher would claim that the long-term loan, like the short, is also self-hedged. The interest rate difference is the market's best guess as to the future changes in the value of the currency. A lower-rated loan will generate a higher capital sum to repay in the home currency. A higher-rated loan will generate a smaller capital sum.

Some recent empirical research casts doubt on this hypothesis, suggesting that interest rate differentials, at the very least, are not unbiased predictors of future exchange rate changes. Certainly, international treasurers claim that currency *availability* in the future, not *cost*, is the dominant factor influencing choice of currency in raising foreign loans.

If in doubt about monetary assets or liabilities being self- hedging the best solution is to calculate the 'net monetary asset position' in each currency and make sure it is either in balance or in the 'right' direction.

In other words, if it is predicted that a currency will fall in value against sterling, then make sure you owe money in that currency. If it is predicted that a currency will rise in value against sterling, then make sure you are owed money in that currency.

This might require some juggling with the financing mix of the firm via 'currency swaps', which we discuss later in the chapter.

Transaction exposure: hedging the cash flows

The first step in identifying and hedging cash flow exposure in foreign currency is to set up a *currency information system*. The control of currency is much simplified if this information system is centralized but this is not a necessary condition of efficient currency management.

Figure 19.4 illustrates two reports typical of those used in currency management. One reports on future estimated cash flows, the other on quarterly income statement exposure forecasts.

Once the estimated cash flows in each currency are identified the next step is to consolidate this data. The individual flows are netted to arrive at the estimated net balance in each currency for each forward period. Research suggests that monthly estimates for six months ahead is the most common requirement but large companies holding or trading in many currencies may require weekly or even daily reports (especially if speculative positions are opened).

The next stage is to consider whether the company wishes to follow a risk-minimization policy or a profit-maximization policy. If the company believes that currency forecasting is impossible, or not profitable, then it has to adopt a *risk-minimization policy*. The aim will be to reduce exposure in all currencies to a minimum unless the cost of this policy is prohibitive.

If the company believes that currency forecasting is both possible and profitable it must decide, in the light of current currency forecasts, the degree of imbalance which is desirable in each currency in which it trades. Even if forecasting is thought to be possible and profitable the company might decide to prohibit currency speculation as a matter of principle. Many UK multinationals take this position. In the past, US multinationals have been more willing than similar UK companies to speculate in currency, but recent case study research by Belk and Glaum (1990) suggests that attitudes among UK treasurers are changing.

The next step is to convert the 'natural' exposure position arising from normal trading into the 'desired' exposure position as decided above. The task of converting the 'natural' to the 'desired' position is achieved by using various hedging techniques. Some of these techniques are internal to the firm, and some external. The external hedging techniques are provided by several external currency markets such as the forward, swap and option markets.

The key problem in currency risk management is thus to identify the various types of exposure facing the company and then to hedge any unwanted exposure risks. Non-monetary assets and short-term loans in foreign currency are for the most part self-hedged. The exchange risk involved in financing with foreign loans and bonds is less clear. With regard to transaction exposure, a currency information system needs to be designed and installed to identify estimated short-term cash flow exposure in each currency.

Once this system is in place the company must decide whether it (1) believes that future exchange rates can be forecast, and (2) will permit speculation in currency. If the answer to either question is 'no', then the company must seek to minimize the exposure position in all currencies. If a profit-maximizing strategy is adopted, the company will use currency forecasts to decide on an optimal position in each foreign currency.

The 'natural' exposure position is converted to the 'desirable' position by using various currency hedging devices. Some of these are internal to the firm, others external. Prindl (1978), who introduced the important distinction between internal and external hedging, also pointed out that internal hedging is almost invariably cheaper than external hedging. The

Transactional Exposure Forecast

UNIT __USA Inc__   CURRENCY FORECAST _____£_____   PREPARED BY __D.P.W__ $/£ RATES   SPOT _____2.2100_____

COUNTRY __USA__   FORECAST PERIOD __6 months ending 30 June__   DATE PREPARED __28 December__   at 28 December   1 Month __2.1900__   3 Month __2.1600__

£'000	January	February	March	April	May	June	Six Months Totals
RECEIPTS							
Third party	3.000	3.000	4.000	4.000	4.000	4.000	22.000
Intercompany, unit __UK Ltd__	5.000	5.000	6.000	6.000	6.000	8.000	36.000
Intercompany, unit _____							
Intercompany, unit _____							
TOTAL RECEIPTS	8.000	8.000	10.000	10.000	10.000	12.000	58.000
PAYMENTS							
Third party	2.000	3.000	3.000	4.000	4.000	5.000	21.000
Intercompany, unit __UK Ltd__	1.000	1.000	1.000	1.000	1.000	1.000	6.000
Intercompany, unit _____							
Intercompany, unit _____							
TOTAL PAYMENTS	3.000	4.000	4.000	5.000	5.000	6.000	27.000
NET RECEIPT (PAYMENT)	5.000	4.000	6.000	5.000	5.000	6.000	31.000
FORWARD COVER – Receipts	4.000	3.000	5.000	1.000			13.000
– Payments							
NET EXPOSURE	1.000	1.000	1.000	4.000	5.000	6.000	18.000

FORWARD CONTRACT DETAILS											
Contract date	30.7	20.10	20.10	28.10	15.11	2.12	14.12				
Settlement date	JAN	JAN	FEB	FEB	MARCH	MARCH	APRIL				
Rate	2.2000	2.1500	2.1400	2.1200	2.1300	2.0900	2.0800				
Amount	2000	2000	2000	1000	2000	3000	1000				13.000

Quarterly Income Statement Exposure Forecast

UNIT _____   PREPARED BY _____

UNIT CODE NO. _____   DATE PREPARED _____

LOCATION _____   FORECAST DATE: QUARTER ENDING _____

LOCAL CURRENCY _____

		All amounts in $'000 equivalents, using budget exchange rates issued by corporate treasury				
Income statement line	Income statement item	Items translated at average exchange rates			Items translated at historical exchange rates	TOTAL
		Parent currency (US $)	Local currency	Foreign[a] currency		
	Revenues:					
1	Domestic					
2	Intercompany export					
3	Third party export					
4	Total sales					
	Less Cost of sales:					
5	Domestic					
6	Intercompany import					
7	Third party import					
8	Total cost of sales					
9	Gross profit					
	Less Expenses:					
10	Selling, general, administrative					
11	Depreciation					
12	Other					
13	EBIT[b]					
14	Interest expenses					
15	EBT[c]					
16	Tax expense					
17	NET INCOME					

Notes:

a. Specify foreign currencies
b. EBIT – Earnings Before Interest and Tax
c. EBT – Earnings Before Tax

Figure 19.4   Typical reports required for collecting input data for an efficient foreign exchange management information system

international treasurer should first adjust the 'natural' exposure position using internal techniques and only use the expensive external techniques once the internal hedging possibilities have been exhausted.

19.6   Internal hedging techniques

Figure 19.5 lists techniques commonly used by companies to hedge their risk of loss through changes in currency exchange rates. All of these techniques are internal to the firm.

Netting is a technique whereby the Head Office and its foreign subsidiary net off the intra-organizational debts due at the end of each period. Only the balance exposed to currency risk needs to be hedged.

Matching is a technique whereby the stream of payments in each currency from all sources is centralized and the net balance in each period calculated. Only the net balance needs to be hedged. This technique can involve payments and receipts from third parties.

Devices for Handling Exposure Risk

Some devices INTERNAL to the firm:

- NET INTER-COMPANY DEBTS EACH PERIOD
- MATCH PAYMENTS IN SAME CURRENCY
- LEAD & LAG INTER-COMPANY PAYMENTS
- ADJUST CONTRACT PRICE TO FORWARD RATE
- ALTER CURRENCY OF INVOICING
- JUGGLE MONETARY ASSETS AND LIABILITIES TO REDUCE EXCHANGE RISK

Devices for Handling Exposure Risk

Some devices EXTERNAL to the firm:

- FORWARD CONTRACTS (1, 3, 6, 12 MONTH)
- SHORT-TERM FOREIGN CURRENCY LOANS
- FOREIGN CURRENCY BILLS OF EXCHANGE
- FACTORING FOREIGN CURRENCY DEBTS
- FOREIGN CURRENCY OPTIONS
- INTEREST AND LOAN SWAPS
- CURRENCY COCKTAIL DENOMINATION
- EXCHANGE RATE GUARANTEES

Figure 19.5   Some financial devices available for hedging foreign exchange risk

Leading and lagging is a technique for delaying or speeding up payments when a change in the value of a currency is expected. Where payments are involved, the payment in foreign currency is speeded up if the foreign currency is expected to rise in value and slowed down if the foreign currency is expected to depreciate in value against the home currency. Foreign governments in developing countries scrutinize payment patterns very carefully to prevent leading and lagging, which can cause violent oscillations in the value of a weak currency.

Altering the price of a contract to take into account expected currency changes is another useful way of hedging anticipated exchange rate changes. For example, a UK exporter could use an export price based on the forward rate rather than the spot rate when fixing the price of a contract.

Another possibility is to change the currency in which a contract is denominated. The most likely use of this technique is to switch the contract price from the home currency to the foreign currency. Many transactions which have no connection with the United States are denominated in US dollars, as in oil supply deals between Japan and Saudi Arabia.

19.7   External hedging techniques

The most widely-used hedging technique, which accounts for around 60 per cent of total currency hedging, is the *forward contract*. A UK company expecting 50 million Canadian dollars in six months' time will instruct its bank to sell the C$50 million six months forward at the six-month forward rate.

Many variations are available on the simple forward contract. One of the most popular is the *forward–forward contract*, which allows a company to both buy and sell a fixed amount of currency at some date in the future as a single contract.

The short-term foreign currency loan provides a simple but effective hedging device. A company due to receive FF30 million in one year's time borrows FF30 million immediately and converts the FF30 million to sterling. The money can be invested in liquid UK securities over the intervening year. At the end of the year, the FF loan is repaid out of the proceeds of the FF30 million due on the contract. If the French franc should unexpectedly fall in value during the year against sterling, then lower than expected receipts from the French contract are offset by the lower sterling payment required to repay the French loan.

International factoring is a fast-expanding business. The international factor can provide many services to the small company. One of the services offered is to absorb the exchange rate risk. Once a foreign contract is signed the factor pays, say, 90 per cent of the foreign value to the UK company in sterling. If the exchange rate moves against the interests of the UK company before receipt of the foreign currency, the factor absorbs the loss. In compensation, the factor also takes any gain arising from the change in rates.

Loan swaps can be used to cover large exposure risks. The market for these has expanded massively since 1985. Swapping occurs where a company owing a large amount of money in a foreign currency finds another company which owes an equally large amount in the home currency. The two companies then effect a 'swap' of the obligations on the loans. Swaps can alter currency exposure positions quite dramatically. However, finding a suitable swap partner is not always easy. There is a tendency for all international companies to wish to swap the same way if a particular currency becomes speculative. Swaps are usually noted 'off-Balance Sheet'.

The currency option market has also expanded in recent years. An option confers the right but not the obligation to buy or sell a fixed amount of currency at or between two dates in the future at an agreed exchange rate.

For example a UK company might pay £2,000 for a 'call' (an option to buy) on US$200,000 in six months' time at 1.90 US$ to £1. When the six months are up, if the exchange rate is US$1.84 to £1, the option will be exercised. The option rate is lower than the spot rate. If the spot rate in six months' time is US$ 1.96 to £1 the option is scrapped, it is cheaper to buy the dollars on the spot market. In the former case, the option is said to be 'in the money', and in the latter case, 'out of the money'. Should the spot rate turn out to be 1.90 US dollars to the pound, the UK option would be 'at the money'.

The currency option market is very complex, offering a wide range of products. It is sometimes claimed to be expensive compared to the forward market. It should, however, be remembered that an option is a gambling chip as well as an insurance policy. A traded option can be sold at a profit, unlike a forward contract. A UK currency futures market also exists and has been recently merged with the options market.

Once the currency information system has generated a 'natural' exposure position, the treasurer will wish to alter this to the 'desired' exposure position. The desired position might be a position of minimum exposure risk or alternatively the treasurer, in consultation with the Board of Directors, might decide to seek an unbalanced exposure position. If so, he is speculating in currency.

The change from the natural to the desired position is effected by using various hedging devices. Some of these devices are internal to the firm and some use external markets. The external hedging devices tend to be more expensive to operate than the internal devices.

The prime objective in designing a foreign exchange management strategy is to achieve a desired exposure position in each currency at the end of each period. In other words, the exposure to exchange rate fluctuation should be controlled and not imposed upon the firm by outside forces.

19.8   Conclusions

The globalization of world trade is forcing many financial managers to take a keen interest in currency management. The management of currency is closely bound up with the management of foreign exchange exposure. There are three types of exposure. Transaction exposure, which estimates the flow of cash across a currency frontier, translation exposure, which measures the value of assets and liabilities denominated in a foreign currency, and economic exposure which calculates the impact on long-term cash flows of likely changes in exchange rates.

Not all transactions, assets and liabilities denominated in foreign currencies are necessarily exposed to exchange rate risk. The essential skills required in currency management are to identify those exposures which are at risk and to devise suitable means of hedging the risks. It is important to differentiate between those hedging techniques internal to and those external to the firm. Several financial markets have been developed which allow the international treasurer to hedge foreign exchange risk. Financial instruments such as swaps, options, futures and forwards can be used to hedge foreign exchange risks.

A key question for the international treasurer must be to decide whether or not exchange rates can be forecast with any degree of reliability. With exchange rates floating freely, research suggests that forecasting is not profitable. However when governments begin to interfere with the free market, forecasting has proved to be a profitable activity. Exchange controls and 'currency snakes' may make forecasting worth while.

We conclude that the company's exposure to exchange rate fluctuation must be controlled by the treasurer and not imposed upon the firm by outside forces.

19.9 Summary

This chapter has examined the nature and sources of a company's exposure to the risk of adverse foreign exchange rate movements and has explained a number of widely-used strategies to hedge, or safeguard against these risks, applying techniques both internal to the firm and also available on external capital markets.

Key points

- Corporate profitability can be seriously affected by adverse movements in foreign exchange rates.
- Currency can be transacted for immediate payment on the spot market or for future delivery via the forward market.
- The international treasurer is faced with three kinds of foreign exchange exposure: transaction exposure, translation exposure and economic exposure.
- Transaction exposure generally relates to the likely variability in short-term operating cash flows; for example, the cost of specific imported raw materials and the income from specific exported goods.
- Translation exposure relates to the risk of exchange rate movements reducing the sterling value of assets located overseas or increasing the value of assets located overseas or increasing the sterling value of liabilities due to be settled overseas.
- Economic exposure refers to the ongoing risks incurred by the company in its choice of long-term contractual arrangements such as licensing deals or decisions to invest overseas. These risks are the long-term equivalent of transaction exposure.
- All companies trading internationally must devise a foreign exchange strategy.
- The strategy evolved by the international treasurer depends on the treasurer's belief in the validity of certain international trade theories. The Purchasing Power Parity (PPP) theory, the Interest Rate Parity (IRP) theory, the Unbiased Forward Rate (UFR) theory and the Open Fisher theory.
- PPP states that, having adjusted for the prevailing exchange rate, identical goods must

sell for a common price in different locations. If inflation rates differ in different locations, exchange rates will adjust to preserve the 'Law of One Price'.

• IRP asserts that any differences in international interest rates are a reflection of expected exchange rate movements, so that the interest rate offered in a location whose currency is expected to depreciate will exceed that in an appreciating currency location by the amount of the expected exchange rate movement.

• The forward premium or discount should equal the expected rate of appreciation or depreciation of a currency.

• The Open Fisher theory asserts that different countries will offer the same expected real interest rate, so that differences in their nominal rates of interest can be explained by expected differences in their rates of inflation.

• Once the exposure position of the company is identified and measured the treasurer must devise a hedging strategy to control the foreign exchange risk faced by his/her firm.

• Many apparent exposures are often self-hedging, for example, holdings of plant and machinery which can be traded internationally.

• Generally, internal hedging techniques are cheaper to apply than using the external markets which offer various financial instruments for hedging currency risks.

Further reading

Extensive treatments of foreign exchange exposure and ways of hedging risks can be found in a variety of textbooks on international finance, for example, McRae and Walker (1981), Shapiro (1989) and Eiteman, Stonehill and Moffet (1992). For detailed treatments of the mechanics of the various markets for hedging instruments, see Andersen (1987), Price and Henderson (1988), Koziol (1990) and Ball and Knight (1990). For the underlying economic theory of the operation of currency and other markets, see Prindl (1978) and Kindleberger (1978).

Articles by Rodriguez (1981), Collier and Davies (1985) and Belk and Glaum (1990) report on the currency management practices of US and UK multinational companies.

Questions

Self-test questions

1. Calculate the relevant forward buying and selling rates of exchange at the end of trading on 12 March 1992, when the Deutschmark was quoted as follows against sterling:

Closing rates	One month	Three months
2.8575–2.8625	1/4–1/8 pfpm	3/4–1/2 pfpm

2. Ford Fiesta motor cars sell in Holland for 13,000 Fl, while the UK price is £6,500. The current exchange rate is 3.2 Fl to £1. What is the 'correct' UK price if the foreign currency markets are fully efficient?

3. The respective rates of inflation in Germany and the UK are 2 per cent and 4 per cent. The market rates of interest are 9 per cent and 10 per cent respectively. If the spot rate of exchange is 2.80 DM to £1, what does this suggest about the forward rate?
4. Distinguish between translation, transaction and economic exposures. Is it necessary to actively hedge against all these foreign exchange risks?
5. What is the difference between 'hedging' and 'speculation' on the foreign exchanges?
6. Explain when and how a company would use internal and external hedging techniques, respectively.

Exercises

1. (a) Explain what is meant by the terms foreign exchange translation exposure, transactions exposure and economic exposure.

     What is the significance of these different types of exposure to the financial manager?

   (b) Runswick Ltd is an importer of clock mechanisms from Switzerland. The company has contracted to purchase 3,000 mechanisms at a unit price of 18 Swiss francs. Three months credit is allowed before payment is due.

     Runswick currently has no surplus cash, but can borrow short term at 2 per cent above bank base rate or invest short term at 2 per cent below bank base rate in either the United Kingdom or Switzerland.

Current Exchange Rates

	Swiss Franc/£
Spot	2.97–2.99
1 month forward	$2\frac{1}{2}$–$1\frac{1}{2}$ premium
3 months forward	$4\frac{1}{2}$–$3\frac{1}{2}$ premium

(The premium relates to the Swiss franc.)

Current Bank Base Rates

Switzerland	6% p.a.
United Kingdom	10% p.a.

Required

(a) Explain and illustrate three policies that Runswick Ltd might adopt with respect to the foreign exchange exposure of this transaction. Recommend which policy the company should adopt.

     Calculations should be included wherever relevant.

     Assume that interest rates will not change during the next three months.

(b) If the Swiss supplier were to offer $2\frac{1}{2}$ per cent discount on the purchase price for payment within one month evaluate whether you would alter your recommendation in (a) above.

(ACCA Level 3, June 1986)
(Solution in Appendix A)

2. Two firms, to which you act as advisor, are concerned about their plans for overseas operations.

North

North is about to enter the export market but is uncertain whether its policy should be to invoice export sales in:

(a) North's own domestic currency, or

(b) the currency of the purchaser.

South

South, a UK-based manufacturing company, is about to set up an overseas subsidiary to deal with local manufacturing and sales. South has decided to finance the overseas subsidiary largely by fixed interest debt finance using its own large equity base and small level of existing leverage to justify the large borrowing required for the new subsidiary. South will either borrow the required finance itself or will require its subsidiary to undertake the required borrowing.

The finance director is uncertain whether South's strategy for financing its foreign subsidiary should be:

(a) for South to borrow in the United Kingdom for all financing needs. The subsidiary will then be financed by South:

(b) to require the subsidiary to borrow in the country, and currency, of its operations;

(c) for South to borrow in whatever country, and currency, has the lowest annual interest rate at the time of taking out the loan. South will then finance the subsidiary;

(d) some combination of the above three approaches.

Required

(a) Advise North on the matters to be considered in deciding on the currency in which to invoice export sales.

(b) Advise South on the factors to be considered in deciding on the financing of its foreign subsidiary. Explain the main merits and disadvantages of each of the financing strategies mentioned.

(ACCA Level 3, December 1983)

Practical assignment

Many companies experience accounting problems in recording overseas transactions and in translating foreign currency values into their accounts. Select a company involved in international trade and examine its report and accounts to determine its policy with regard to foreign exchange, and the extent of foreign currency losses or gains for the year concerned. Do you think these were 'real money' losses or gains or merely accounting entries?

CHAPTER 20

The foreign investment decision

EXPEDITIONS TO HUNGARY

British firms have invested significant amounts of capital overseas in 'traditional' locations such as the United States and Australia, and more recently in France and Germany in efforts to 'globalize' their operations. Following liberalization of political and economic systems in Eastern Europe in the 1980s, many far-sighted Western companies, ranging from giant multinationals like BAT to relative minnows like Watmoughs, also began to evaluate the strategic potential of long-term investment in foreign countries like Poland, Czechoslovakia and Hungary.

In 1991, two multinational cigarette manufacturers, fearing a decline in sales for their products in Western Europe and North America, decided to expand their operations into Hungary. Philip Morris purchased Egri Tobacco Factory, the country's largest tobacco company (measured by turnover), while BAT Industries acquired a majority shareholding in Pecsi Tobacco Factory, which produces 40 per cent of the 26 billion cigarettes consumed annually in Hungary. Pecsi Tobacco made profits in 1990 of 266m Forints (Ft) on turnover of Ft 2.5bn, in one of Hungary's most profitable industrial sectors.

In February 1991, Watmoughs, the Bradford-based UK quality printers, acquired a 57 per cent interest in Revai Obuda Nyomda Kft, an established Hungarian printer, for a total consideration of £2.3m. Revai has recently moved to a new purpose-built factory of 55,000 square feet close to the centre of Budapest and has installed its first web offset press, to complement existing facilities serving the high quality publishing and fine art markets.

According to Watmoughs' chairman, this development represented 'a significant opportunity to expand our interests by employing the Group's technological and marketing skills in a country expected to play a leading role in the integration of Western and Eastern European markets'.

20.1 Introduction: what is foreign investment?

Foreign investment may be divided into *direct* and *portfolio* investment. Portfolio investment refers to participation in overseas investment without any control over the running of the business. It involves the purchase of shares or loan stock in an overseas organization. *Foreign direct investment (FDI) is a lasting interest in an enterprise in another economy where the investor's purpose is to have an effective voice in the management of the enterprise.* Such direct investment usually arises from acquisition of an overseas business or from setting up an overseas branch or subsidiary. This definition also extends to the increasingly common cases of joint venture development such as BAT's interest in Pecsi Tobacco and Watmoughs' stake in Revai Obuda.

LEARNING OBJECTIVES

This chapter provides a strategic interpretation of the motives for FDI and examines the special problems which firms face in evaluating overseas projects. The specific aims are to:

- Examine the strategic motives for FDI.
- Explain how firms should evaluate overseas projects.
- Demonstrate how knowledge of the working of international markets can assist this appraisal.
- Explain how the risks, including political ones, of FDI can be managed.

20.2 The multinational corporation

A working definition of a multinational corporation (MNC) is 'a firm that owns production, sales and other revenue-generating assets in a number of countries'. Foreign direct investment by MNCs in the establishment and acquisition of overseas raw material and component operations, production plants and sales subsidiaries occurs because of potentially greater cost-effectiveness and profitability in sourcing inputs and servicing markets through a direct presence in a number of locations rather than relying solely on a single 'home' base and on imports and exports to support their operations.

Foreign direct investment decisions are not fundamentally different from the evaluation of domestic investment projects, although the political structures, economic policies and value systems of the host country may cause certain analytical problems, which are discussed later. There is ample evidence (Robbins and Stobaugh 1973; Wilson 1990; Neale and Buckley 1992) that the majority of multinational corporations (MNCs) use essentially similar methods of evaluating and control of capital investment projects for overseas subsidiaries as for domestic operations, although they may well apply different discount rates.

Pilkington plc is a prime example of a UK-based MNC, exemplifying the extent to

Table 20.1 The globalization of Pilkington

Geographical Analysis of Turnover by Markets

	1980 %	1985 %	1990 %
UK	51	30	19
Europe excluding UK:	18		
– EC	n/a	29	23
–Non-EC	n/a	9	7
North America	8	5	29
Australasia	8	10	11
Africa	5	12	5
South America	6	3	5
Other	4	2	1
	100	100	100

Source: Pilkington Annual Reports.

which many UK companies have globalized their operations in recent years. In the 1980s, Pilkington made major European and North American acquisitions which sharply reduced the proportion of its sales accounted for by its traditional UK base, mainly in St Helens.

Table 20.1 shows a geographical analysis of Pilkington turnover by markets in which the Group's products are sold.

20.3 Factors favouring foreign direct investment

International expansion through FDI is an alternative to growth focused on the firm's domestic market. Thus, a firm may choose to expand horizontally on a global basis by replicating its existing business operations through direct investment in a number of countries, or via international vertical integration, backwards by establishing raw material/ components sources and forwards into final production and distribution. Additionally, firms may choose product diversification as a means of developing their international business interests. Firms may expand internationally by greenfield (new 'start-up') investments in component and manufacturing plants, etc., or takeover of, and merger with, established suppliers, or the establishment of joint ventures with overseas partners. In the case of foreign market servicing, the MNC may also choose to complement direct investment with some exporting and licensing. Foreign direct investment is thus one important means of sustaining the growth impetus of the firm. It also provides added opportunities for establishing cost/price and product differentiation competitive advantages over rival suppliers.

A firm may possess competitive advantages over rival suppliers in the form of patented process technology, know-how and skills, or a unique branded product which it can better exploit and protect by establishing overseas production or sales subsidiaries. A production facility in an overseas market may enable a firm to reduce its distribution costs and keep it in closer touch with local market conditions – changes in customer tastes, competitor's actions, etc. Moreover, direct investment enables a firm to avoid government restrictions on market access such as tariffs and quotas and the problems of currency variation. For example, the growth of protectionism by the European Community bloc and the rising value of the yen have been important factors leading to increased Japanese investment in the EC, in particular in the United Kingdom.

By the same token, firms may be able to benefit from the availability of grants and other subsidies given by 'host' governments to encourage inward investment. Much Japanese investment such as Nissan's car manufacturing plant near Sunderland has been attracted into the United Kingdom by the availability of regional selective assistance. In the case of sourcing, direct investment allows the MNC to take advantage of some countries' lower labour costs or provides them with access to superior technological know-how thereby enhancing their international competitiveness.

Moreover, direct investment, by internalizing input sourcing and market servicing within the one organization, enables the MNC to avoid various transaction costs of using the market. For example, it avoids the costs of finding suppliers and distributors and negotiating contracts with them and the costs associated with imperfect market situations, such as monopoly surcharges imposed by input suppliers, unreliable sources of supply and restrictions on access to distribution channels. It also allows the MNC to take advantage of the internal transfer of resources at prices which enables it to minimize its tax bill or practise price discrimination between markets.

Finally, in the case of some products (for example, flat glass, metal cans, cement) decentralized local production rather than exporting is the only viable way a MNC can supply an overseas market because of the prohibitive costs of transporting a bulky product or one which for competitive reasons, has to be marketed at a low price.

Globalization of production and marketing operations

As noted, MNC's are characterized by foreign direct investment in raw materials, production and sales subsidiaries. FDI, however, needs to be examined alongside a broader-based global strategy for the MNC, which also involves exporting and licensing options as alternative means of servicing international markets.

Exporting involves both the indirect export of products from the 'home' country through independent agents, distributors, merchant houses, trading companies, etc., and the direct export of products through the firm's own export division to overseas markets. *Licensing* involves the assignment of production and selling rights by a firm to producers located in overseas markets in return for royalty payments.

With exports the bulk of value-adding activities takes place in the home country, while licensing and FDI transfer much of the value-adding activities to the host country, the so-called 'location effect'. Licensing is said to have an 'externalization effect' since it represents a market sale of intermediate goods or corporate assets by the firm – the firm sells rights and the use of assets to a licensee. In exporting and FDI, such activities are *internalized*, i.e. retained as functional activities within the firm.

MNCs in practice tend to use various combinations of these modes to supply global markets because of the added scope it gives to their operations. In resource terms, exporting

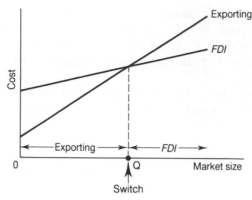

Source: Buckley and Casson (1981).

Figure 20.1   Exporting vs. FDI

from established production plants is a relatively inexpensive way of supplying a foreign market. However, the firm could be put at competitive disadvantage, for example, because of local producers' lower cost structures and control of distribution channels, or because of government tariffs, quotas and other restrictions on imports. Licensing enables a firm to gain rapid penetration into world markets and can be advantageous to a firm lacking the financial resources to set up overseas operations.

FDI is often expensive and risky (although host country governments often offer subsidies etc to attract such inward investment), but in many cases the 'presence effects' of operating locally (familiarity with local conditions and the cultivation of contacts with local distributors and retailers) are important factors in building market share over the long run.

A simple break-even model of a firm facing a significant overseas market is illustrated in Figure 20.1. This model specifies two kinds of relevant costs, fixed and variable, and two forms of foreign market servicing; exporting which, relatively, has low fixed but high variable costs, and FDI which has high fixed but low variable costs. When foreign market size exceeds Q, then the firm will switch its mode of market servicing from exporting to direct investment.

MNC advantages over national firms

The MNC, as distinct from firms that undertake their international operations exclusively from a single 'home' country, may be in a position to enhance its competitive position and profitability in four main ways:

(1) It can take advantage of differences in country-specific circumstances. In a world economy that consists of a spectrum of countries at different stages of economic evolution (some industrially-advanced, others mainly primary producers), certain general country advantages may have knock-on effects in terms of creating or augmenting firm-level competitive advantages which the MNC can exploit on a global basis. For example, the MNC may locate its R & D establishments in a more technologically-advanced country in order to draw on local scientific and technological infrastructure and skills to develop innovative new processes and products. Similarly, MNCs may locate their production plants

in a less developed country in order to take advantage of lower input costs, in particular the availability of cheap labour. Alternatively, the MNC may choose to continue to produce its outputs in its 'home' country but seek to remain competitive by sourcing key components from subsidiary plants based 'off-shore', again taking advantage of lower labour costs.

(2) MNCs benefit from the flexibility of being able to choose an appropriate mode of serving a particular market as between exporting, licensing or direct investment. For example, exporting may provide an entry path into a low-price, commodity-type market, with the MNC taking advantage of marginal pricing and the absence of set-up costs; licensing may be an appropriate mode if market size is limited or market niches are being targeted. Direct investment in production and sales subsidiaries may be a more effective way of capturing a large market share where 'closeness' to customers is an important consideration, or where market access via exporting is limited by impositions such as tariffs. Through these various routes, MNCs are able to pursue a complex global market servicing strategy. For example, Ford makes car engines in its British plants and gearboxes in its German factories, which are then shipped (along with other parts) to Spain for assembly into complete cars. These are then exported to other European markets.

(3) 'Internalization' of the MNC's operations across countries by direct investment provides a unique opportunity for the firm to maximize its global profits by the use of various transfer pricing policies. While a national, vertically integrated firm needs to establish transfer prices for components and finished products being transferred between component and assembly plants and between assembly plants and sales subsidiaries, the greater scale and cross-frontier nature of such transactions by MNCs makes these transfer prices more significant.

(4) Finally, an international network of production plants and sales subsidiaries enables an MNC to introduce a new product simultaneously in a large number of markets (an important consideration in the case of products having a relatively short life-cycle span and/or patent protection) in order to maximize sales potential. Equally importantly, it spreads the risk of consumer rejection across a diversified portfolio of overseas markets so that failure in one market may be offset (or perhaps more than compensated by) rapid acceptance in another. In this respect, transnational product development is an important component of a risk management policy. Additionally, it enables the MNC to develop a 'global brand' identity (as with, for example, Coca-Cola and Foster's lager) or, alternatively, to 'customize' more effectively a product to suit local demand preferences.

20.4 Evaluating the foreign investment decision

Appraising foreign investment involves additional complexities, not encountered in evaluating domestic projects. The main ones are:

1. Fluctuations in exchange rates over lengthy time periods are largely unpredictable. While these may vary in either direction, possibly enhancing the sterling value of project

cash flows, there remains the opposite risk of depreciation of the currency of the host country reducing the sterling proceeds in sterling terms.

2. A foreign investment project may involve quite different levels of systematic risk than the equivalent project undertaken in the domestic economy. This poses the problem of how to estimate a suitable required rate of return.

3. Once up and running, the foreign investment is exposed to variations in economic policy by the host government, for example, tax changes, which may reduce net cash flows.

4. Government intervention may also take the form of blocking the repatriation of profits to the home country. A project which is inherently profitable may not be worth undertaking if the returns cannot be remitted. This raises the issue of whether the evaluation should be conducted from the standpoint of the subsidiary, i.e., the project itself, or from that of the parent company. If however, we maintain the pursuit of shareholder value, this is really a non-issue – the relevant evaluation is from the parent's standpoint.

Some companies have adopted ingenious ways of repatriating profits. Pepsico, which had invested in a bottling plant in Hungary, found it difficult to repatriate profits from this operation. To overcome this problem, it financed the shooting of a motion picture locally and exported the film to the United States.

Evaluation – Sparkes plc and Zoltan Kft

To illustrate the evaluation of a foreign project, consider the case of a UK company, Sparkes plc, investing in the Zoltan consumer electronics factory in Hungary. The project will generate a stream of cash flows in the local currency, Forints, which have to be converted into sterling. There are two possible approaches to evaluating this investment:

Approach A Discount the cash flows from the project, measured in Forints at the locally denominated discount rate. The resulting NPV will then be converted into sterling using the spot rate of exchange.

Approach B Convert the local currency cash flows into sterling at the spot rates expected to rule in each year of the project. The sterling cash flows will then be discounted at the sterling discount rate to produce a sterling NPV, which indicates the worth of the project to the parent company's shareholders.

Both approaches yield precisely the same result. However, they each rely on the operation of the economic theories regarding the relationship between interest rates, exchange rates and inflation rates, discussed in the previous chapter. In particular, we rely on Purchasing Power Parity forcing exchange rates to alter in a predictable fashion if relative inflation rates diverge and on the Open Fisher effect to ensure that the real rate of return, suitably adjusted for risk, is the same in all locations. If these conditions apply, we need not worry about forecasting local rates of inflation – these will be anticipated by the market and be reflected in relative exchange rate movements. Putting this another way, we can evaluate the locally denominated cash flows at constant prices and allow any inflation differentials to be worked out via relative exchange rate movements. The relevant details regarding Sparkes and its proposed investment in Zoltan are given in Table 20.2.

Table 20.2 Sparkes and Zoltan

- Expected net cash flows from Zoltan in millions of Forints:—

Year	0	1	2	3	4
	−700	+420	+420	+420	+420

- The project may operate for a further six years, but the local government has expressed its desire to purchase a 50 per cent stake at the end of Year 4. The purchase price will be based on the net book value of assets.
- The spot rate between sterling and Forints is 140Ft per £1. The present rates of inflation are 30 per cent in Hungary and 5 per cent for the United Kingdom. These rates are expected to persist for the next few years.
- For this level of systematic risk, Sparkes would require a return of 10 per cent in real terms if the project were located in the United Kingdom.

Should Sparkes invest?

First of all, we must consider the time dimension – this project is capable of operating for ten years, but the host government has expressed its desire to buy into the project after four years. This may signal to Sparkes the possibility of more overt intervention, possibly extending to outright nationalization, perhaps by a successor government. Given these risks, it seems prudent to confine the analysis to a four-year period and to include a terminal value for the project based on net book values. If we assume a ten-year life and straight-line depreciation, and assuming no investment in working capital, the NBV after four years will be 60 per cent of 700m Ft = 420m Ft. Half of this can be treated as a cash inflow paid by the host government and half as a (perhaps conservative) assessment of the value of Sparkes' continuing stake in the enterprise.

In practice, we often encounter complications in assessing terminal values. For example, the assets may include land which may appreciate in value at a rate faster than general price inflation. If so, there may be holding gains to consider, gains which may well be taxable by the host government.

Second, what are the relevant exchange rates to use? If PPP holds, then the inflation differential between the UK and Hungary should cause the exchange rate of Forints against sterling to depreciate by around 25 per cent p.a., to preserve the Law of One Price. This rate of depreciation can be calculated using the formula developed in Chapter 19, which links relative inflation rates to the spot and forward exchange rates,

$$\text{Spot Rate} \times \frac{(1 + \text{Hungarian Inflation})}{(1 + \text{UK Inflation})} = \text{Forward Rate}$$

We can assess the appropriate one-year forward rate as follows:

$$\text{Forward Rate} = \frac{1.30}{1.05} \times 140 = 173.33 \text{ Ft per £1}$$

This signifies expected Forint depreciation of 23.8 per cent. There is an element of artificiality here in so far as there is no one-year forward market for currencies of such uncertain value as the Forint. In practice, currency dealers are prepared to quote forward rates beyond six months only for a very limited rate of very solid currencies like the dollar, Deutschmark and the yen. All we can say when dealing with 'exotic' currencies is that if there were an organized forward market extending to a year, PPP would predict a rate of 173.33 Ft against sterling. However, stretching artificiality and foresight a little further, we can predict that if these respective inflation rates persist, the Forint will depreciate by about 23.8 per cent p.a. This yields the following profile of expected exchange rates:

End of Year	Expected Exchange Rate: Ft per £
1	$140\,(1.238) = 173.33$
2	$140\,(1.238)^2 = 214.57$
3	$140\,(1.238)^3 = 265.63$
4	$140\,(1.238)^4 = 328.86$

Third, what is the appropriate discount rate to use? Projects of this degree of systematic risk require a return of 10 per cent when undertaken in the United Kingdom. Assuming an equivalent degree of risk in a Hungarian location, we can find the locally denominated Hungarian discount rate, k_H, by using the Interest Rate Parity (IRP) theorem, i.e.:

$$\text{Spot Rate} \times \frac{(1 + \text{Hungarian Annual Discount Rate})}{(1 + \text{UK Discount Rate})} = \text{Forward Rate}$$

This yields:

$$140 \times \frac{(1 + k_H)}{(1.10)} = 173.33$$

So that:

$$k_H = \left(\frac{173.33}{140} \times 1.10\right) - 1 = 1.362 - 1 = 0.362$$

$$\text{i.e. } 36.2\%$$

We may now illustrate the two basic approaches in Table 20.3, to show that they both yield the same expected NPV, and also recommend acceptance of the project.

Additional complexities

The Sparkes/Zoltan example was relatively simple, but served a purpose in illustrating the equivalance of the two basic approaches. However, it ignored a number of crucial factors such as taxation, both locally and in the parent's own country, investment incentives provided by the host government (for example, in Ireland, the rate of Corporation Tax applicable to inward investors is only 10 per cent), barriers to repatriation of profit and any likely overspill effect on the parent's existing operations. All these factors are brought out in the following example.

Table 20.3 Evaluation of the Zoltan project

Approach A

Year	Ftm	36.2% *Discount Factors*	PV in Ftm
0	−700	1.0000	−700.00
1	+420	0.7342	308.36
2	+420	0.5391	226.41
3	+420	0.3960	166.23
4	+420	0.2906	122.05
4 Terminal value	+420	0.2906	122.05
		NPV =	245.10

Converting the NPV back to sterling at the spot rate yields:

$$\frac{245.1\text{mFt}}{140} = £1.75\text{m}$$

Approach B

Year	Cash Flows in Ftm	Ft/£ Exchange Rate	Cash Flows in £m	10% Discount Factors	PV in £m
0	−700	140	5.00	1.0000	−5.00
1	420	173.33	2.42	0.9091	2.20
2	420	214.57	1.96	0.8264	1.62
3	420	265.63	1.58	0.7513	1.19
4	840	328.86	2.55	0.6830	1.74
				NPV =	£1.75m

Example: Brighteyes plc

Brighteyes plc manufactures optical instruments for sale both in its domestic market and for export. It is currently investigating the possibility of setting up a manufacturing plant in Lastonia. Initial discussions with the Minister of Economic Development have met with a favourable response, providing the project can generate the 10 per cent pre-tax return currently obtained by other firms in that country. The company requires a project of this kind to earn at least a 15 per cent real return.

The planned investment will be partly import substituting, and partly export-based, selling to neighbouring countries. Additionally, the local consumption element has been classified as having a strategic military and special cultural significance. The project has been offered a tax holiday exempting it from all corporate and income taxes for the first ten years, except to the extent that profits and capital receipts are repatriated, in which case a 20 per cent withholding tax will be deducted. A modern factory on a well-serviced industrial estate has been offered at a reasonable rent.

The initial investment will be £10m in plant, machinery and commissioning costs, all payable in hard currency by the parent company. Additional finance will come from a 'balloon' bank loan of 20m Latts (4L = £1) negotiated with a local bank, which applies a concessionary interest rate of 10 per cent p.a. This will be used to finance working capital. Operating cash flows (upon which tax is assumed to be calculated) are estimated to be £10m in Year 1 and L22m thereafter until Year 5. It is proposed that the whole of each year's profit after payment of local interest be repatriated to the United Kingdom. The Lastonia withholding tax will be allowable as a deduction before calculating the Corporation Tax payable to the UK Inland Revenue, currently at the rate of 33 per cent. All such transfers may be treated as arising on the last day of the accounting period to which they relate, when all tax becomes due and payable.

It is expected that the new venture will have a minor 'cannibalizing' effect on the exports which the company would otherwise have made. This will result in £0.5m loss of contribution (after tax) for each of Years 2 to 5.

For planning purposes, it is considered that Year 5 will be the cut-off year. At that time, the realizable value of the plant and equipment may be taken as L24M. The working capital will be realized, subject to losses on stocks of L2m and debtors of L2m. These funds will be used first to pay off the local bank loan. Any balance remaining will be transferred to the United Kingdom without any further tax penalty or restriction. The exchange rate is forecast to remain at $L4 = £1$ until Year 2, when it will change to $L5 = £1$.

Solution

Evaluation of the Brighteyes project can be viewed from a number of different perspectives. We shall consider three:

1. Is the project acceptable as far as the Lastonia economy is concerned?
2. Is it a wealth-creating project from the foreign subsidiary company's viewpoint?
3. Is it wealth-creating for the shareholders of the parent company?

Table 20.4(A) summarizes the cash flows for the three levels, for each of which present values are given in Table 20.4(B). It will be seen that the project meets the country requirement to achieve a 10 per cent return. Discounting the country-level cash flows produces a 'local' NPV of L37.3m. It also achieves a satisfactory L26.6m NPV at the project level in Lastonia after local financing costs when discounted at the appropriate rate. Alas, the project fails to offer an acceptable net present value for the parent company. Why is there such a contrast? Recall that three extra elements were introduced at this stage:

1. Deteriorating exchange rates.
2. UK taxation and withholding taxes.
3. 'Spillover' effects on the whole business in terms of lost exports.

In our example, all three factors work against the project to produce a NPV of −£1.31m. The foreign investment proposal, as it stands, does not make economic sense for the shareholders.

Table 20.4 (A) Brighteyes plc: cash flow profiles

	Year					
	0	1	2	3	4	5
Basic Project (Lm)						
Plant	(40)					
Working capital	(20)					
Operating cash flows		10	22	22	22	22
Realization of plant						24
Realization of working capital (net)						16
Country cash flow	(60)	10	22	22	22	62
Loan and interest	20	(2)	(2)	(2)	(2)	(22)
Project cash flow	(40)	8	20	20	20	40
Withholding tax (20%)		1.6	4	4	4	8
Remitted to United Kingdom	(40)	6.4	16	16	16	32
Exchange rate	4	4	5	5	5	5
Sterling equivalent (£m)	(10)	1.6	3.2	3.2	3.2	6.4
UK tax (net of Lastonia withholding tax)		(0.3)	(0.5)	(0.5)	(0.5)	(1.0)
Post-tax cash flows	(10)	1.3	2.7	2.7	2.7	5.4
Loss in exports (after tax)			(0.5)	(0.5)	(0.5)	(0.5)
Parent company cash flow (£m)	(10)	1.3	2.2	2.2	2.2	4.9

(B) The Value of the Project

Year	Country (Lm)	PV (10%)	Project (Lm)	PV (15%)	Parent Co. £m	PV (15%)
0	(60)	(60)	(40)	(40)	(10)	(10)
1	10	9.1	8	7.0	1.3	1.1
2	22	18.2	20	15.1	2.2	1.7
3	22	16.5	20	13.2	2.2	1.5
4	22	15.0	20	11.4	2.2	1.3
5	62	38.5	40	19.9	4.9	1.3
		NPV 37.3		NPV 26.6		NPV (3.1)

20.5 Required rates of return

Modern capital market theory leads us to conclude that the rate applicable for discounting project cash flows is the required rate of return for the project's degree of market risk. We have already encountered some problems with the practical implementation of this approach. These difficulties are heightened in the case of overseas investments by the different nominal interest rates and market returns obtainable in various countries, the lack of efficient capital markets in certain countries and the segmentation of international capital markets.

One practical approach to estimating the cost of capital for foreign investments is to base it on the local opportunity cost of capital. This is the return currently achieved or required for comparable investments in the same country of operation. If the MNC is prepared to operate at a level of return below the opportunity cost of capital, it would mean that the nation's scarce resources are not being utilized efficiently. In the longer term, this would hinder good relations with the host government and possibly give rise to government interference. This logic does not apply to short-lived investments where there is currently underemployment of national resources.

One reason often cited for investing overseas is that by diversifying corporate assets across a number of different countries, overall business risk is reduced. Domestic investments are all subject to the same underlying economic circumstances. Foreign investments are subject to different economic circumstances, and although the economies of many countries are to some extent positively correlated with each other, this suggests that international diversification can offer significant benefits beyond those offered by diversification within a single country.

A question which logically follows is whether the diversification benefits can legitimately be extended to foreign direct investment. The answer lies, first, in the ability of companies to diversify efficiently direct investments, and secondly, in whether it is desirable. To eliminate most of diversifiable risk requires a portfolio of approximately thirty randomly selected investments. Although some diversification may be achievable, it cannot be as effective as portfolio diversification, as only the large MNCs will invest in a dozen or more countries. Furthermore, most foreign investments are in the same product market as the domestic market and therefore cannot be well diversified. It can also be argued that corporate diversification is not a thing of value. It does nothing that the company's shareholders could not do themselves by holding a well-diversified world portfolio of bonds and stocks. International diversification of direct investments is not necessarily a valid means of reducing risk.

20.6   Investment and financing interactions: using the adjusted present value approach

The analysis of the Brighteyes investment decision was based upon the operation of the key theories of international economics examined in Chapter 19. If these hold, the rate of return required on activities of identical systematic risk, but based in different locations, would be identical, the real rate of interest would be the same regardless of location and differential price level movements would be swiftly translated into exchange rate movements. An important implication of this apparatus is that exchange rate risk can be ignored.

In practice, a host of imperfections limit the applicability of a simple NPV model. For example, government intervention affects tax rates in different locations, the ability to repatriate earnings and also the effective cost of capital expenditures via investment incentives. One such investment incentive is subsidized finance – the host government may offer cheap finance directly or subsidize a local financial institution. Access to such finance is conditional on undertaking the project, and if there is no ceiling on the amount offered, it may pay the MNC to finance the project entirely by local finance. As a result, its overall debt/equity ratio is likely to alter, thus affecting the required return on the project. As we saw in an earlier chapter, this creates the sort of interaction between the investment and the financing decision, which is most conveniently handled by the Adjusted Present Value approach. Lessard (1979) extended the APV model developed by Myers (1974) to include the complexities introduced in evaluating FDI. This involves separating out the individual components of the cash flows accruing to the parent company and discounting each at the appropriate risk-adjusted rate.

For example, imagine the new government of Bielarus wants to attract investment by foreign food processors and distributors. It proposes the following set of incentives and conditions:

1. An initial cash grant.
2. Tax relief on investment (net of grant) for the first five years of the project, based on 20 per cent p.a. reducing balance.
3. Subsidized finance involving a 5 per cent subsidy on local borrowing costs.
4. Tax relief on loan interest.
5. A requirement to invest 10 per cent of profits in local enterprises. Such investment will qualify for a guaranteed interest rate of 10 per cent above the local rate, plus a 20 per cent share in profits from these enterprises, with repatriation blocked for five years.

Clearly, there are different degrees of risk attaching to these items of cash flow. The APV equation would be set up as follows:

$$\text{APV} = \begin{array}{l}\text{P.V. of}\\\text{capital}\\\text{outlays net}\\\text{of grant}\end{array} + \begin{array}{l}\text{P.V. of}\\\text{cash flows}\\\text{from initial}\\\text{project}\end{array} + \begin{array}{l}\text{P.V. of tax}\\\text{relief on}\\\text{investment}\\\text{outlay}\end{array} + \begin{array}{l}\text{P.V. of tax}\\\text{relief on}\\\text{interest}\\\text{payments}\end{array} + \begin{array}{l}\text{P.V. of interest}\\\text{rate subsidy}\end{array}$$

$$+ \begin{array}{l}\text{P.V. of repatriated}\\\text{interest earnings from}\\\text{forced investment}\end{array} + \begin{array}{l}\text{P.V. of repatriated}\\\text{dividends from local}\\\text{enterprise profits}\end{array}$$

Estimation of the relevant discount rates remains a problem but using the APV may provide the discipline required to focus more clearly on the risks of individual items.

20.7 Hedging the risk of foreign projects

Operating a foreign investment involves both translation exposure and economic exposure. The translation risk stems from exposure to unexpected exchange rate movements, for example, a fall in the value of the Australian dollar against sterling will reduce the sterling value of assets appearing in the Australian subsidiary's Balance Sheet. When consolidated into the parent's accounts this will require a write-down of the value of assets in sterling terms. This problem can be avoided if the exposed assets are matched by a corresponding liability. For example, if the initial investment is financed by a loan denominated in A$ then the diminution in the sterling value of assets will be matched by the diminution in the sterling value of the loan.

However, perfect matching of assets and liabilities is not always possible. Many overseas capital markets are not equipped to supply the required capital. Besides, it is probably politic to provide an input of parent company equity to signal commitment to the project, the government and the country. However perfect matching is probably unnecessary since some assets such as machinery can be traded internationally. If so, the cause of the exchange rate depreciation, i.e. higher internal prices, will cause asset prices to rise, and if the Law of One Price holds, this appreciation in the value of locally held assets will compensate for the reduced sterling value of the currency. As a result, the need to match probably only applies to property assets and items of working capital such as debtors, which cannot readily be traded on international markets. (Note the obvious attraction, goodwill considerations aside, of operating with a sizeable volume of short-term creditors, especially at the financial year end!)

The upshot is that so long as the value of assets tradeable on world markets increases to offset the adverse exchange rate movement (and this appreciation is recorded in the local Balance Sheet), local loan financing need only be sought in relation to property and working capital requirements.

Economic exposure is the long-term counterpart of transaction exposure – it applies to a stream of cash inflows and outflows. In theory, the problem of variations in the prices of inputs and outputs should also be solved by the operation of the Law of One Price. For example, local price inflation at a rate above that prevailing in the parent company's country will be exactly offset by depreciation in the local currency, thus maintaining intact the sterling value of locally produced goods.

However, in practice, problems arise when PPP does not apply in the short term and when *project* prices alter at different rates from *prices in general*. The movement in the local price index is only an average price change, hiding a wide spread of higher and lower price variations. In principle, the firm could use the forward market to remove this element of unpredictability in the value of cash flows, but in practice the forward market has a very limited time horizon, or is non-existent for many currencies.

Nevertheless, there are devices which the parent company with widely spread overseas operations can adopt. It can mix the project expected cash flows and outflows with those of other transactions to take advantage of netting and matching opportunities. It can lead and lag payments as appropriate when it expects adverse currency movements, although host governments usually object to this. It can also use third party currencies. For example, if it invests in oil extraction, its output will be priced in dollars and the otherwise exposed cost of inputs may perhaps be sourced or invoiced in dollars or in a currency expected to move in line with the dollar. However, a more aggressive policy might involve invoicing sales in currencies expected to be strong and sourcing in currencies expected to be weak, including perhaps the local one.

Another tactic is to use the foreign project's net cash flows to purchase goods for the host country which are exportable or which can be used as inputs for the parent's own production requirement. This has the effect of converting the foreign currency exposure of the project's cash flow into a world price exposure of the goods traded. This may be desirable if the degree of uncertainty surrounding the relevant exchange rate is greater than that attaching to the relevant product price.

Much world trade is conducted on the stipulation that the exporter accepts payment in goods supplied by the trading partner, or otherwise undertakes to purchase goods and services in the country concerned. This linking of export contracts with reciprocal agreements to import is known as *countertrade*. This is usually found where the importer suffers from a severe shortage of foreign currency or limited access to bank credits.

One form of countertrade is *buyback*, which is a way of financing and operating foreign investment projects. In a buyback, suppliers of plant, equipment or technical know-how agree to take repayment in the form of the future output of the investment concerned. This involves a long-term supply contract with the overseas partner and raises some interesting principal/agent issues, concerning in particular the quality of the output and the management of the operation. Ideally, the output should be an article for which a ready market is available or which the exporter can use in its own production process. The former Soviet Union used to favour long-term buybacks to promote industrial co-operation. For example, Italy sold a $90m acrylic fibre plant to the USSR in return for deliveries of the fibre. However, buybacks between developed nations do occur. Davy Loewy, the steel plant contractor, built a steelworks for a Finnish firm, which undertook to repay in kind. An additional feature of this deal was the provision by Davy of lease finance for its customer, i.e. the lease rentals were paid for in steel ingots.

The advantage of buybacks for a Western company is that it secures long-term supplies and obviates any need to worry about exchange rate movements. The effective cost is the cost incurred in financing the original construction, and perhaps an opportunity cost if world prices of the goods received should fall. It is, therefore, a way of locking into the present world price for the goods transferred, which has some appeal in a market where prices fluctuate widely.

20.8 Political risk

It is hardly surprising that foreign investment by multinational corporations involve strong elements of political and social risk. Their very size and strength in relation to host nations create the possibility of political action, whether favourable (such as granting generous incentives) or adverse (such as expropriation of assets). Where the objectives of the host nation and the MNC are clearly at odds with each other, the political risk is heightened. It is not always easy for corporations to be clear as to their own objectives, but it is considerably more difficult to ascertain the objectives of various countries.

Political risk is heightened where political and social instability prevails. How can such instabilities be defined, identified and predicted? Political and social instability is the result of internal pressures or civil strife which may be caused by such factors as inequalities between various internal factions (whether racial, religious, tribal, etc.), extreme political pro-grammes, recent or forthcoming independence or impending elections.

An MNC considering foreign investment may observe the signals of political instability, but to measure its extent is more complex. A major cause of political and social instability is attributable to economic influences. This has become very apparent for many industrialized as well as developing nations with a series of oil crises and resulting price increases in oil and related imports, deterioration in balance of payments, rampant inflation and sluggish world economic growth.

Economic instability often gives rise to heavy overseas borrowings. The risk of default can be gauged by such factors as the overseas debt service ratio (debt service payments in relation to exports of goods and services), debt age profile, the extent to which such overseas borrowing will finance exports, and the likelihood that domestic savings will eventually replace overseas borrowings. The political risks of such economic pressures will lead to any of the following actions:

1. Exchange controls and currency regulations.
2. Restrictions on registration of foreign companies (e.g. there must be local equity participation).
3. Restrictions on local borrowing.
4. Expropriation or nationalization.
5. Tax discrimination.
6. Import controls.
7. Limitations on access to strategic sectors of industry.

Expropriation (confiscation of corporate assets with or without compensation), asset freezing (loss of control over the management of assets) and nationalization represent the greatest political threat to foreign investors. The major risk is not so much of expropriation *per se*, but the risk that compensation will be inadequate and deferred. Full-scale, or 'creeping', expropriation (where there are increasing restrictions on prices, issuing work permits, transfer of shares, imports and dividends) is more likely to occur where a nation feels threatened by the size and dominance of multinationals. Thus, before deciding to operate in a new country, a pertinent question to ask is whether the company, individually or collectively with other multinationals, will dominate the industry. If this is a strong possibility, then political risk is greater than when penetration is low.

Managing political risk

Managing political risk does not imply that a company can eliminate risk, for risk is largely uncontrollable. What is possible, to a certain extent, is that such risk can be identified, appraised and sometimes reduced. Political risk management is best applied on a project basis, but it is essentially an overall company approach that involves:

1. Dispassionate analysis of the project and its likely results.
2. Identification of all community groups and organizations that will be affected by, and will possibly react in a significant way to, the project.
3. Comparison of objectives and consequences of the project with the aims of local and national government.
4. A carefully organized programme of information and involvement using the whole

company, which is reflected in the way the total organization operates and is therefore much more than just a public relations exercise.

The risk-averse company will want either to avoid any clear political risk, simply by not investing in such countries, or to insure fully against such risks materializing. A number of governments have introduced insurance guarantee programmes, such as the (now partly privatized) Exports Credit Guarantee Department (ECGD) in the United Kingdom, and in addition, private insurance schemes are often available. Most of these guarantee programmes cover risks for direct investments of:

1. Nationalization, expropriation and confiscation.
2. War, revolution and insurrection.
3. Restrictions or delays in repatriation of profits and capital.

Generally, it would be uneconomic to cover such risks in all situations. Premiums on government schemes are usually levied on a uniform basis over a wide spread of countries. It follows, therefore, that relatively risky investments are worth insuring but less risky projects are likely to prove expensive. This third approach to risk management is to accept some degree of political risk after full consideration of the probability and effect of losses being sustained.

A firm is very largely a hostage to future events with no power to influence the future. However, it can so position itself that, should adverse events materialize, it will sustain the minimum of discomfort. This requires the prior agreement of risk-minimizing policies and contingency plans. Take, for example, an MNC that believes it is economically viable to invest in a developing nation which has recently gained independence, or where there is tribal conflict and severe economic pressures in terms of inflation and currency value. How can this high political risk be managed? Table 20.5 shows a suggested risk-management programme.

20.9 Summary

In this chapter we have examined some of the motives underlying decisions by MNCs to expand overseas, shown how the additional complications of overseas operation can be incorporated into project appraisal, and discussed various ways in which the risks of overseas projects can be managed.

Key points

- Foreign direct investment (FDI) may be undertaken for a variety of strategic reasons for example, globalization of component sources or meeting the threat of a competitor already based overseas.
- FDI is generally undertaken when exporting (with relatively high variable costs, but low

Table 20.5   Risk management programme and contingency plan

A.	Reduce Probability of Political Interference	B.	Reduce Financial Consequences of Political Interference
DO			
	Keep informed of social, political and economic developments within the country and of its neighbours and partners		Borrow locally
			Insure risks with insurance guarantee scheme
	Monitor government attitude towards overseas investment		
			Share risks through participation of international agencies in financing
	Understand the role and workings of government		
			Pledge corporate assets as collateral
	Develop links and skills in dealing with government officials		
	Identify with national aspirations and objectives and be a model citizen		
	Develop allies with local employees, suppliers and customers		
	Use local materials and labour wherever possible		
	Train local labour force for technical and managerial positions		
	Co-operate in joint ventures or provide local equity participation (if political benefits outweigh economic drawbacks)		
		C.	Contingency plan in the event of expropriation, etc.
DON'T			
	Antagonize host government by:		Seek meeting with government for rational negotiation
	1. major repatriation of capital or profits		Decide on whether voluntary divestiture of ownership is best policy
	2. unfair competition with local traders, e.g. price subsidies		
	3. ignoring local customs and cultures		Explore legal remedies (locally, overseas or internationally)
	4. maintaining foreign or colonial image		If all else fails, surrender ownership and seek only salvage value
	5. over-partisan involvement		

fixed costs) becomes more expensive than overseas production (with relatively high fixed costs but low variable costs).

- In principle, the evaluation of FDI is similar to the evaluation of 'domestic' investment.
- In practice, FDI may be complicated by factors such as concessionary access to local finance, difficulties in repatriating profits and differential inflation rates.

- The presence of such complications may result in the inherent 'local profitability' of the investment differing from the value of the project to the MNC.
- In theory, if the Open Fisher operates, differential inflation rates should 'come out in the wash' of relative exchange rate movements. If so, no hedging of the income from overseas investment is required.
- If the Open Fisher is not expected to apply, expected cash flows should generally be hedged by internal means such as netting and matching. In addition, it is sensible to borrow in the local currency to finance the project, thus matching assets and liabilities.
- Political risk can be insured against by using various specialist agencies, but this is costly.
- In principle, political risk can be diversified away by investing in many countries, but few companies possess the resources to do this.

Further reading

Two interesting and comprehensive texts on international business strategy and operations are Daniels and Radebaugh (1989) and Rugman, Lecraw and Booth (1985). The texts by Eiteman, Stonehill and Moffet (1992) and Shapiro (1989) both focus more closely on multinational business finance each devoting several chapters to foreign investment. A whole issue of *Managerial Finance* (Wilson 1990) was devoted to the evaluation of overseas investment, while Holland's contribution to Firth and Keane (1986) is clear and concise. Prasad (1987) reports on a survey of MNC motivations to invest in Ireland, while Madura and Whyte (1990) discuss the diversification benefits of foreign direct investment.

Questions

Self-test questions

1. Why do multinational corporations elect to engage in direct foreign investment rather than other forms of market servicing?
2. What are the specific characteristics which distinguish the foreign investment decision from domestic investment?
3. Why 'should' the two basic approaches to evaluating FDI yield the same answer? What assumptions are made about the operation of international markets?
4. In what ways can the *economic* risks of FDI be protected against?
5. What is political risk and how can it be minimized?

Exercises

1. Brookday plc is considering whether to establish a subsidiary in the United States. The subsidiary would cost a total of $20 million, including $4 million for working capital.

A suitable existing factory and machinery have been located and production could commence quickly. A payment of $19 million would be required immediately, with the remainder required at the end of Year 1.

Production and sales are forecast at 50,000 units in the first year and 100,000 units per year thereafter.

The unit price, unit variable cost and total fixed costs in Year 1 are expected to be $100, $40 and $1 million, respectively. After Year 1 prices and costs are expected to rise at the same rate as the previous year's level of inflation in the United States: this is forecast to be 5 per cent p.a. for the next five years. In addition, a fixed royalty of £5 per unit will be payable to the parent company, payment to be made at the end of each year.

Brookday has a four-year planning horizon and estimates that the realizable value of the fixed assets in four years' time will be $20 million.

It is the company's policy to remit the maximum funds possible to the parent company at the end of each year. Assume that there are no legal complications to prevent this.

Brookday currently exports to the United States yielding an after-tax net cash flow of £100,000. No production will be exported to the United States if the subsidiary is established. It is expected that new export markets of a similar worth in southern Europe could replace exports to the United States. UK production is at full capacity and there are no plans for further expansion in capacity.

Tax on the company's profits is at a rate of 50 per cent in both countries, payable one year in arrears. A double taxation treaty exists between the United Kingdom and United States and no double taxation is expected to arise. No withholding tax is levied on royalties payable from the United States to the United Kingdom.

Tax allowable depreciation is at a rate of 25 per cent on a straight-line basis on all fixed assets.

Brookday believes that the appropriate Beta for this investment is 1.2. The after-tax market rate of return is 12 per cent, and the risk-free rate of interest 7 per cent after tax.

The current spot exchange rate is US $1.30/£1, and the pound is expected to fall in value by approximately 5 per cent p.a. relative to the US dollar.

Required

(a) Evaluate the proposed investment from the viewpoint of Brookday plc. State clearly any assumptions that you make.

(b) What further information and analysis might be useful in the evaluation of this project?

(ACCA Level 3, December 1985)
(Solution in Appendix A)

2. You have been appointed by Ranek plc to advise on the price that the company should tender for the construction of a small power station in a foreign country, Zmbland.

The company normally charges a price that gives a 20 per cent markup on all directly attributable costs (which includes leasing and the current written-down value of assets less any residual value of assets expected at the end of the contract but excludes any tax effects of such costs).

The power station will take 15 months to construct. All costs are payable in pounds sterling. Wages totalling £380,000 are payable monthly in arrears in pounds sterling. Materials are purchased two months in advance of the month when they are to be used. One month's credit is taken on all material purchases. Materials usage is expected to be £715,000 per month, payable in sterling. Other direct costs are expected to be £50,000 per month and the company will allocate central overhead to the project at £25,000 per month. No increases in costs are expected during the contract period.

Ranek already owns some plant and equipment that could be used in this project. These assets cost £3 million and have a written-down value of £1.8 million after deduction of tax allowable depreciation at 25 per cent on a reducing balance basis. If the contract is not undertaken the existing plant and equipment will be sold immediately for £2 million. The realizable value of these assets at the end of 15 months is expected to be £900,000. Special equipment for the contract would be obtained through an operating lease at a quarterly cost of £620,000 payable in advance on the first day of the quarter.

Assume that corporate tax in the United Kingdom at the rate of 35 per cent is payable on net cash flows six months after the end of the relevant tax year. No foreign tax liability is expected. Any tax effects associated with the disposal of assets also occur six months after the relevant year end. The end of Ranek's financial year occurs three months after the start of the project.

The tender price for the power station is to be in Zmbland dollars (Z$). Thirty per cent is payable immediately and the balance upon completion. The current exchange rate is Z$45.5–46.0/£ and the Zmbland dollar is expected to steadily depreciate in value relative to the pound by approximately 25 per cent during the next 15 months. No forward foreign exchange market exists.

Ranek's managers estimate that the company's opportunity cost of capital is 1 per cent per month. The company currently has spare capacity.

Required

(a) Estimate the tender price that would result from a 20 per cent markup on sterling direct costs. Ignore the time value of money in the estimate of the required markup.

(b) Estimate the net present value of the proposed project and discuss and recommend the minimum price that the company should tender. State clearly any assumptions that you make.

(ACCA Level 3, June 1990)

3. Lionel plc is a profitable UK conglomerate. It is thinking of undertaking a capital investment in an overseas country whose currency is not convertible, and hence the local government will arrange for payment in US dollars, on a fixed price basis.

The following details are available:

Project Outlay $12m.
Life 3 years.
Scrap Value $3.0m.
Operating cash flow $16m pre-tax.

Finance	All equity financed by capital export by Lionel.
	Lionel's equity Beta = 1.2.
	Lionel's debt/equity ratio = 33.3 per cent.
Risk, etc.	The project has a revenue sensitivity factor of 1.6.
	The project has an operational gearing factor of 1.8 compared to Lionel's 1.2.
	The return on the FTSE Index is 16 per cent.
	The risk-free rate in the United Kingdom is 8 per cent.
Tax, etc.	UK Corporation Tax is paid at 35 per cent, one year in arrears.
	The host country corporation tax rate is 20 per cent, payable at each year-end, without delay. In the host country, straight-line depreciation on historic cost is allowable against tax.
	Overseas investors are allowed to remit only 50 per cent of each year's post-tax income to the home country.
	All blocked funds earn interest at 25 per cent in a special government account and can only be remitted at the end of the project's life.
Exchange rate	The current dollar:pound spot rate is $2 = £1. The dollar is expected to appreciate at the rate of 5 per cent p.a. against sterling over the next few years.

Required

(a) Evaluate the profitability of the project itself, ignoring the restriction on income remittances.

(b) Evaluate the profitability of the project from the stand-point of the parent company's shareholders.

(c) What are the major risks in this project, and how might they be alleviated?

4. The directors of Duschek plc are contemplating undertaking a project in Aloysia, an under-developed country whose currency is the weber. The project requires plant and equipment costing 34 million webers and initial working capital of 2.8 million webers. The working capital required at the beginning of each year is expected to be equal to 10 per cent of that year's pre-tax operating cash surplus. The project has a four-year life and it is expected that all the working capital at the start of the fourth year will be recovered at the end of that year. The project will be taxed in Aloysia at the rate of 25 per cent on the pre-tax operating cash surplus. No capital allowances are given and tax can be assumed to be paid at the end of the year to which it relates.

The directors have estimated that the following pre-tax operating cash surpluses and exchange rates will occur (taking Year 0 as the start of the project):

Year	0	1	2	3	4
Pre-tax operating cash surplus (million webers)	—	28	32	36	33
Rate of exchange of weber/£	16	20	25	30	33

The political situation in Aloysia is uncertain and an election is expected at the end of the second year of the project. There are three parties, A, B and C, which might be elected and each has a different solution to the poor performance of the Aloysian economy:

- Party A, which is currently in power, favours a *laissez-faire* policy on foreign investment and will continue to allow overseas investors unrestricted movement of funds.
- Party B favours expropriating the assets of overseas companies and offering tax-exempt compensation. Duschek plc expects to receive compensation equal to 60 per cent of the initial cost of the plant and equipment, which would be paid at the end of the third year of the project. No compensation for loss of working capital would be given. Duschek plc would be able to repatriate its second year earnings but later earnings would be lost.
- Party C favours the introduction of exchange controls to block any currency being repatriated overseas. The controls would be maintained for two years and then they would be relaxed completely. The second and third year earnings of Duschek plc would thus be frozen, although they would be invested in a local bank to yield an annual after-tax return of 5 per cent.

The directors of Duschek plc have estimated that the three parties have the following probabilities of being elected:

Party	Probability of being elected
A	0.7
B	0.1
C	0.2

The initial capital will be provided from the UK cash reserves of Duschek plc. If possible, Duschek plc will repatriate all its overseas cash surpluses at the end of the year in which they arise. The cost of capital for this type of investment is 20 per cent per annum.

Required

(a) Determine whether Duschek plc should proceed with the proposed investment in Aloysia.
(b) Estimate the sensitivity of the decision to proceed with the proposed investment to a change in the probability of the election of Party C. You should assume that Party A's probability of election is correspondingly changed and Party B's probability is unchanged.
(c) Discuss how a multinational company can structure its overseas investments so as to minimize the risk caused by overseas political events.
Note: Ignore UK taxation.

(ICAEW PE II, December 1986)

Practical assignment

Consider the information given in section 20.1 regarding the international operations of Pilkington, one of many UK companies which 'went international' to a significant degree in the 1980s. For a company of your choice (GMH and BTR are good examples), undertake a similar exercise to the one presented in the text. (You may find difficulty in obtaining accounts reaching back as far as 1980, but examination of a sample should give you a flavour of the company's policy regarding internationalization.)

Look also at the chairman's statements to glean an indication of the importance attached to overseas operations in the company's strategy.

CHAPTER 21
Identifying and valuing options

SPOT THE OPTIONS

An option gives the holder the right to buy or sell something in the future at a fixed price. Spotting options is very important in financial management because options can increase the value of the business. See if you can spot the five options presented in the following case. (The numbered superscripts offer clues!) **Enigma Drugs plc** is an innovative pharmaceutical company. The management team is considering setting up a separate limited company to develop and produce a new drug.

The project is forecast to incur development costs and new plant expenditure totalling £50 million and to break even over the next five years (by which time its competitors are likely to have found a way round the patent rights). Enigma's management is considering deferring the whole decision by two years when the outcome of a major court case with important implications for the drug's success are known.[1]

The risks on the venture are high, but should the project prove unsuccessful, and it has to be abandoned, the 'knowhow' developed from the project can be used inside the group or sold to its competitors for a considerable sum.[2] Enigma's management realizes that there is little or no money to be made in the initial five years, but it should allow them to gain vital expertise for the development of a 'wonder drug' costing £120 million which could be launched in four years' time.[3]

The newly-formed company would be largely funded by borrowing £40 million in the first instance, repayable in total after eight years, unless the company prefers to be 'wound up' for defaulting on the loan.[4] Some of the debt raised will be by 9% Convertible Loan Stock, giving holders the right to convert to equity at any time over the next four years at 360p compared to the current price of 297p.[5] We will reconsider the Enigma case in section 21.4 of this chapter.

21.1 Introduction

Business managers like to 'keep their options open'. Most business decisions involve a combination of closing off certain options while opening up others. For example, the decision by Enigma Drugs plc to launch a new product would tie up considerable finance, denying the option to use the funds in some other way; but it may well open up new options such as follow-on products based on the knowledge and reputation gained from the initial product. Option-like features occur in various aspects of finance and option theory provides a powerful tool for understanding the value of such options.

In finance, *options are contractual arrangements giving the owner the right, but not the obligation, to buy or sell something, at a given price, at some time in the future.* Note the two key elements in options: (1) the right to *choose* whether or not to take up the option, and (2) at an agreed price. It is not a true option if I am free to buy in the future at the *prevailing* market price, or if I am *compelled* to buy at an agreed price. Many securities have option features. For example, we have previously discussed, in Chapter 12, convertible loan stocks and share warrants, where options to convert to, or acquire, equity are given to the owner.

LEARNING OBJECTIVES

By the end of this chapter the reader should possess a clear understanding of:

- The basic types of option and how they are employed.
- The main factors determining option values and how their values can be estimated.
- How option values can be estimated.
- The various applications of options theory to corporate finance.

21.2 Share options

To begin with, we will restrict our attention to share options, where there is a highly active market on the Stock Exchange for traditional and traded options. *Traditional* options are available on most shares and last for three months. A problem with such options is that they are not particularly flexible or negotiable; no mechanism exists for investors to trade their options, they must either *exercise* their option (i.e. buy or sell the underlying share) or allow it to lapse. To overcome these difficulties *Traded Options* markets were established, first in Chicago, then in Amsterdam (The European Options Exchange) and, in 1978, The London Traded Options Market (LTOM) was established for major companies, now called the London International Finance Futures and Options Exchange. *Pure options* are financial instruments created by exchanges (e.g. share options) rather than by the company (e.g. convertible loan stock).

OPTIONS TERMINOLOGY

- A *call option* gives its owner the right to buy specific shares at a fixed price – the *exercise price* or striking price.
- A *put option* gives its owner the right to sell shares at a fixed price.
- A *European option* can only be exercised on a particular day (i.e. the end of their life), while an *American option* may be exercised any time up to the date of expiry. These terms are a little confusing because most options traded in the United Kingdom and the rest of Europe are actually American options.
- The *premium* is the price of the option paid at the outset. Option prices are quoted for shares and traded in *contracts* (or units) of 1,000 shares.
- *In the money* is the term used where the exercise price for a call option is below the current share price. In other words, it makes sense to take up the option.
- *Out of the money* is where the exercise price for a call option is above the current share price.

In return for the option, the purchaser pays a fee or *premium*. The premium costs just a fraction of the share price, and offers holders the opportunity to gain the benefits of investment gearing while limiting their risk to a known amount. The size of premium depends on the expected volatility of shares which, in turn, is a function of the state of the market and the underlying risk of the share. The premium might range from as little as 6 per cent for a well-known share in a 'quiet' market to over 20 per cent for shares of smaller companies in a more volatile market. During the 1987 Stock Market crash, for example, option premiums shot up dramatically. A *call option* gives the purchaser the right to buy a share at a given price within a set period; a *put option* gives the right to sell; a *double* gives the right to do either. As we shall see later, share options can be used either as a form of speculation or insurance.

Table 21.1 shows the prices (or premiums) at which options on BP were traded on 26 February 1992 on the traded options market of the Stock Exchange.

The options are traded over a nine-month period with expiry dates every three months. Two exercise prices are given, the first is below the current share price ('in the money') and the second is above the current price ('out of the money'). Option prices vary both with the agreed exercise price (the lower the exercise price for a call option, the higher the premium) and the exercise date (the longer the period, the higher the premium).

Table 21.1   Option on BP shares (current price 267p)

Exercise Price	Call Option Prices			Put Option Prices		
	April	July	Oct	April	July	Oct
260	15	21	25	5	11	15
280	5	11	16	16	22	25

Source: *Financial Times* (26 February 1992).

Speculative use of options

Kate Casino thinks that there will be a takeover attempt on BP in the coming months and that the share price will move up sharply from its current level of 267p to a level in April sufficiently above the exercise price of 260p to justify the option price of 15p. Kate instructs her broker to purchase a *contract* for 1,000 April call options at a cost of 15p × 1,000 = £150. Let us look at three possible share prices arising in April when the option ends:

If the takeover attempt is made, BP's share price will rise to 330p by April; otherwise it will do no better than 285p and could actually fall as low as 250p. Her profit in each case would be:

	Pence		
Share price in April	330	285	250
Exercise price	260	260	260
Profit on Exercise	70	25	Not exercised
Option premium paid	15	15	15
Profit (Loss)	55	10	(15)

Kate would obviously not exercise her option if the price falls to 250p, so the loss in this case would be restricted to the 15p premium paid. If BP's price does shoot up to 330p she will have made a return of well over 400 per cent in just three months! This compares with a return on the shares (ignoring any dividends) over the three months of 24 per cent ($63 \times 100/267$). Of course, if the share price is below the exercise price she loses 100 per cent of the premium paid, but this is just a fraction of the underlying share price ($15 \times 100/267 = 5.6\%$).

This is illustrated as in Figure 21.1. We saw in Table 21.1 that the call option to buy BP shares at 260p costs 15p with an April expiry date. If the share price does not rise above the exercise price, the option is worthless. The option breaks even at 275p (260p + 15p premium) and the potential profit to be made thereafter is unlimited!

Options as a hedge

While options offer an excellent opportunity to speculate, they are equally useful as a means of risk reduction, insurance or hedging. Rick Aversion is concerned that the current (26 February) share price on his ICI shareholding will fall over the next three months. Because he wants to keep his shares as a long-term investment, he buys a put option, giving the right to sell shares in April at the striking price of 1,250p. This option costs him 55p.

By late March, the shares have fallen to 1,000p, and the option has increased in value to 250p (i.e. 1,250 − 1,000). So Rick sells the option and retains the shares, using the profit on the option to offset the loss on the shares. Such an approach is administratively cheaper and more convenient than selling his shareholding and then buying them back.

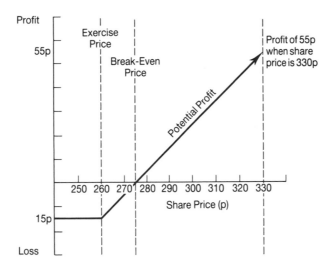

Figure 21.1 BP call option

Doubles – the option to buy or sell a share – also provide a form of insurance. One example is where a company is about to embark on a major project or product launch, the outcome of which could materially affect its future performance. Successful implementation would strongly enhance shareholder value, but failure could spell disaster for the company. Other option combinations, often with intriguing names (e.g. short butterfly, long straddle and bull spread), also enable the treasurer to change the risk-return profile.

Figure 21.2 illustrates in graphical form the four main types of option transactions and the relationship between share price movements and wealth created.

Consider now the implications of buying a call option (a) and selling a put option (c), where the exercise price is the same for both. From Figure 21.2 we can see that the combined effect is a straight line (d), where the loss moves to profit as the underlying share price increases, achieving the same effects as holding the share itself. In other words, *purchasing a share at today's price is equivalent to buying a call option and selling a put option, while placing the remaining sum on deposit to earn a risk-free return over the option period.*

21.3   Option pricing

Option prices are comprised of two elements: *intrinsic value* and *time-value*. Intrinsic value refers to what the option would be worth were it about to expire; it reflects the degree to which an option is 'in the money' – in the case of a call option, the extent to which the exercise price is below the current share price. The time-value element depends on the length of time the option has to run – the longer the period, the better the chance of making a gain on the contract.

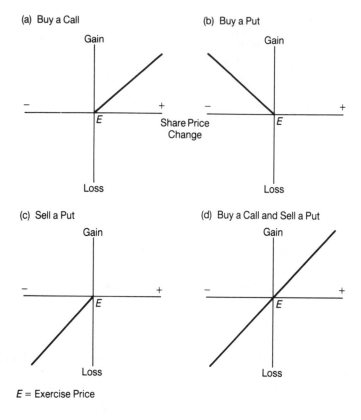

Figure 21.2   Option transactions

Having grasped the basics of options, we can now focus on what determines their value. The following notation is employed with respect to valuing call options:

S_0 = Share price today
S_1 = Share price at expiry date
E = Exercise price on the option
C_0 = Value of call option today
C_1 = Value of call option on expiration date
R_f = Risk-free interest rate

A number of formal statements can be made about call options:

1. *Option prices cannot be negative.* If the share price ends up below the exercise price on the expiration date, the call option is worthless, but no further loss is created beyond that of the initial premium paid. In mathematical terms:

$$C_1 = 0 \text{ if } S_1 \leqslant E \tag{1}$$

This is the case where an option is out of the money on expiry.

2. *An option is worth on expiry the difference between the share price and the exercise price.*

$$C_1 = S_1 - E \text{ if } S_1 > E \tag{2}$$

This is the case where an option is in the money on expiry.

Thus far we have found the intrinsic values of the option – what it would be worth were it about to expire. We have previously noted that options with some time still to run will generally be worth more than that because during that time prices may exceed the share price on expiry.

3. *The maximum value of an option is the share price itself* – it could never sell for more than the underlying share price value.

$$C_0 \leqslant S_o \tag{4}$$

The minimum value of a call today is equal to or greater than the current share price less the exercise price:

$$C_0 \geqslant S_0 - E \text{ if } S_0 > E \tag{5}$$

But the exercise price is at some future point in time. It was shown in the previous section that the pay-offs from a share are identical to the pay-offs from buying a call option and selling a put option and investing the remainder in a risk-free asset which yields the exercise price on the expiry date. In other words, we need to bring the exercise price to its present value by discounting at the risk-free rate of interest. This gives rise to the following revised statement.

4. *The minimum value of an option is the difference between the share price and the present value of the exercise price* (or zero if greater).

$$C_0 \geqslant S_0 - E/(1 + R_f)^t \tag{6}$$

The value of a call option can be observed in Figure 21.3 based on Guinness. This shows how the value of an option to buy Guinness shares at 1,100p moves with the share price. The upper limit to the option price is the share price itself; the lower limit is zero (for share prices up to 1,100p) and the share price minus exercise price when share price moves above 1,100p. In fact, the actual option prices lie between these two extremes, on a curved, upward-sloping line as shown. It rises slowly at first, but then accelerates rapidly.

Let us look at three points on this curve. At point A, at the very start, the option is worthless. If the share price for Guinness remained well below the exercise price, the option would remain worthless. At point B, when the share price has rocketed to 1,400p, the option value approximates the share price minus the present value of the exercise price. At point C, the share price exactly equals the exercise price. If exercised today, the option would be worthless. However, there may still be two months for the option to run, in which time the share price could move up or down. In an efficient market, where share prices follow a random walk, there is a 50 per cent chance that it will move higher and an equal probability that it will go lower. If the share price falls, the option will be worthless, but if it rises, the option will have some value. The value placed on the option at point C depends largely on the likelihood of substantial movements in share price.

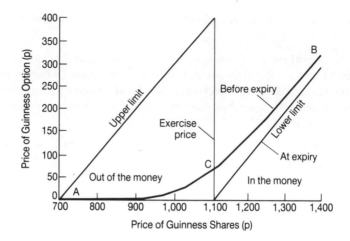

Figure 21.3 Option and share price movements for Guinness (1991)

However, we can say that *the higher the share price relative to the exercise price, the safer the option* (i.e. more valuable).

5. *The value of a call option increases as time and interest rates increase.* From examination of equation (5), we can observe that the value of an option increases as the present value of the exercise price falls. This reduction in present value occurs with increases in the interest rate and/or increases in the time period.

Our final statement concerns risk and how it affects option values. Recall from our chapters on share and capital investment valuation that values fall as risk increases. Quite the opposite occurs with options!

6. *The more risky the underlying share the more valuable the option.* Why should this be if investors are risk-averse? The answer is simple. The greater the variance in the underlying share price, the greater the possibility that prices will exceed the exercise price. But because option values cannot be negative (i.e. the holder would not exercise the option), the 'downside' risk can be ignored.

To summarize, the value of a call option is influenced by:

• *The share price*   The higher the price of the share, the greater will be the value of an option written on it.
• *The exercise price of the option*   The lower the exercise price, the greater the value of the call option.
• *The time to expiry of the option*   As long as investors believe that the share price has a chance of yielding a profit on the option, the option will have a positive value. It therefore follows that the longer the time to expiry, the higher the option price.

- *The risk-free interest rate*   As short-term interest rates rise, the value of a call option also increases.
- *The volatility in the underlying share returns.* The greater the volatility in share price, the more the likelihood that the exercise price will be exceeded and, hence, the option value will rise.
- *Dividends*   The price of a call option will normally fall with the share price as a share goes ex-div (i.e. the next dividend is not received by the buyer).
- *Strong market trends*   Whether moving upwards ('bull' markets) or downwards ('bear' markets) strong market trends generally offer greater scope for making money through options.

A call option is therefore a contingent claim security which depends on the value and riskiness of the underlying share on which it is written.

Black–Scholes pricing model

Black and Scholes (1973) combined the main determinants of option values to develop a model of option pricing, the mathematics of which are somewhat daunting to the non-mathematician. This, however, does not mean that it has no practical application. Every day, dealers in options use specially programmed calculators to determine option prices, just one of many instances where theoretical developments in finance have been put to practical use.

Options can be valued by using the table based on the Black–Scholes formula in Appendix D. We demonstrate how it is used in the following example.

Example of option pricing – Tryella plc

Tryella plc shares currently trade at 150p. You want to purchase a two-year call option on the shares, the exercise price being 180p. The standard deviation on its shares are 30 per cent and the risk-free interest rate is 10 per cent.

Approach

1. Estimate the degree of risk by multiplying the standard deviation of the percentage change in share price (or asset value) by the square root of the time (in years) to expiration of the option.

$$\text{SD} \times \sqrt{t} = 0.3 \times \sqrt{2} = 0.42$$

2. Calculate the relationship between share price and the present value of the exercise price.

$$\frac{\text{Share Price}}{\text{PV (exercise price)}} = \frac{150}{180/(1.1)^2} = \frac{150}{148.76} = 1.01$$

3. Look up the call option value as a percentage of share price in appendix D using the results obtained in stages 1 and 2. The nearest reading is 15.9.

A two-year-old call option on Tryella shares is therefore worth 15.9 per cent of the share price, or 23.85p.

The value of a put option with the same exercise price is found by deducting the share price from the sum of the value of the call and the present value of the exercise price, as below:

	Pence	*Pence*
Value of call	23.85	
PV Exercise price	148.76	172.61
Less:		
Share price		150.00
Value of put		22.61

21.4 Application of option theory to finance

Option theory has implications going far beyond the valuation of traded options. It offers a powerful tool for understanding various other contractual arrangements in finance. Some examples are:

- *Share warrants*, giving the holder the option to buy shares directly from the company at a fixed exercise price for a given period of time.
- *Convertible loan stock*, giving the holder a combination of a straight loan or bond and a call option. On exercising the option, the holder exchanges the loan in exchange for a fixed number of shares in the company.
- *Loan stock* can have a call option attached giving the company the right to repurchase the stock before maturity.
- *Executive share option schemes* are share options issued to company executives as incentives to pursue shareholder goals.
- *Insurance and loan guarantees* are a form of put option. An insurance claim is the exercise of an option. Government loan guarantees are a form of insurance. The government, in effect, provides a put option to the holders of risky bonds so that, if the borrowers default, the bond holders can exercise their option by seeking reimbursement from the government. Underwriting a share issue is a similar type of option.
- *Currency and interest rate options* have been discussed in earlier chapters as ways of hedging or speculating on currency or interest rate movements.
- *Capital investment options* and equity options are two further forms of option discussed in the next sections.

Capital investment options

Capital investment options (sometimes termed *real* options) are option-like features found in capital budgeting decisions. While discounted cash flow techniques are very useful tools of analysis, they are generally more suited to financial assets, because they assume that assets are held rather than managed. The main difference between evaluating financial assets and real assets is that investors in, say, shares, are generally *passive*. Unless they have a fair degree of control, they can only monitor performance and decide whether to hold or sell their shares.

Corporate managers, on the other hand, play a far more *active* role in achieving the planned net present value on a capital project. When a project is slipping behind forecast they can take action in an attempt to achieve the original NPV target. In other words, they can create options – actions to mitigate losses or exploit new opportunities presented by capital investments.

Three such options discussed below are:

1. The abandonment option.
2. The timing option.
3. The strategic opportunity option.

Abandonment option

Major investment decisions involve heavy capital commitments and are largely irreversible; once the initial capital expenditure is incurred, management cannot turn the clock back and do it differently. Because management is committing large sums of money in pursuit of higher, but uncertain, pay-offs, the option to abandon, or 'bail out' should things look grim, can be valuable.

Example: Carling Components

Carling Components Ltd is considering building a new plant to produce components for the nuclear defence industry. Proposal A is to build a custom-designed plant using latest technology, but applicable only to nuclear defence contracts. A less profitable scheme, B, is to build a plant using standard machine tools giving greater flexibility in application.

The outcome of a general election to be held one year hence has a major impact on the decision. If the current government is returned to office, their commitment to nuclear defence is likely to give rise to new orders, making proposal A the better choice. If, however, the current opposition party is elected, its commitment to run down the nuclear defence industry would make proposal B the better course of action. Proposal B has, in effect, a put option attached to it, giving the flexibility to abandon the proposed operation in favour of some other activity.

Timing option

The Carling Components example not only introduces an abandonment option, it also raises the option to wait and see. The management may have viewed the investment as a 'now or never' opportunity, arguing that in highly competitive markets there is no scope for delay; money is made by keeping ahead of the competition. In effect, this amounts to viewing the

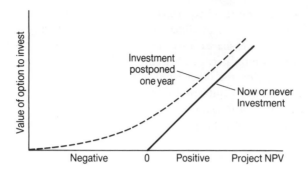

Figure 21.4 The value of the options to delay investment: Carling Components plc

decision as a call option which is about to expire on the new plant for the capital investment outlay. If a positive NPV is expected, the option will be exercised, otherwise the option lapses and no investment is made.

The option to defer the decision by, say, one year until the outcome of the general election is known, makes obvious sense. This may look something like the curved line in Figure 21.4.

An immediate investment would either yield a negative NPV – in which case it would not be taken up – or a positive NPV. Delaying the decision by a year to gain valuable new information (the curved broken line) is a more valuable option. This helps us understand why management sometimes do not take up apparently wealth-creating opportunities; they believe that the option to wait and gather new information is sufficiently valuable to warrant such delay.

Strategic investment options

In Chapter 6, we discussed how certain investment decisions gave rise to follow-on opportunities which are wealth-creating. New technology investment, involving large-scale research and development, is particularly difficult to evaluate. Managers refer to the high level of intangible benefits associated with such decisions. What they really mean is that these investments offer further investment opportunities (e.g. greater flexibility), but at this stage, the precise form of such opportunities cannot be quantified. An example will illustrate how a follow-on option can be valued.

Harlequin plc

Harlequin plc has developed a new form of mobile phone using the latest technology. The company is considering whether to enter this market by investing in equipment costing £400,000 to produce and then market the product in the North of England during the first four years. The expected net present value from this initial project, however, is minus

£25,000. The strategic case for such an investment is that by the end of the project's life sufficient expertise would have been developed to launch an improved product on a larger scale to be distributed throughout Europe. The cost of the second project in four years' time is estimated at £1.32 million. Although there is a reasonable chance of fairly high pay-offs, the expected net present value suggests this project will do little more than break even.

'Obviously, with the two projects combining to produce a negative NPV the whole idea should be scrapped,' remarked the finance director.

Gary Owen, a recent MBA graduate, was less sure that this was the right course of action. He reckoned that the second project was a kind of call option, the initial cost being the exercise price and the present value of its future stream of benefits equivalent to the option's underlying share price. The risks for the two projects looked to be in line with the variability of the company's share price which had a standard deviation of 30 per cent a year.

If, by the end of Year 4, the second project did not suggest a positive NPV, the company could walk away from the decision, the option would lapse and the cost to the company would be the £25,000 negative NPV on the first project (the option premium). But it could be a winner, and only 'upside' risk is considered with call options.

Gary knew that Harlequin's discount rate for such projects was 20 per cent and the risk-free interest rate was 10 per cent. Table 21.2 shows his estimation of the value of the call option.

This shows that the present value of the four-year call option to invest in the follow-on

Table 21.2 Harlequin plc: call option valuation

	(£000)
(A) *Initial Project*	
Cost of Investment	(400)
PV of cash inflows	375
Net present value	(25)
(B) *Follow-on-Project*	
Cost of Investment in Yr. 4	(1320)
PV of cash inflows in Yr. 4	1320
Net present value	—
Combined NPV (A + B)	(25)

Valuing the call option

(C) Standard deviation $\times \sqrt{\text{time}} = .3 \times \sqrt{4} = .6$

(D) $\dfrac{\text{Asset value}}{\text{PV (Exercise Price)}} = \dfrac{\text{PV of cash inflows at Yr.4}/(1+k)^4}{\text{Exercise Price}/(1+R_f)^4}$

$$= \frac{1320/(1.2)^4}{1320/(1.1)^4} = \frac{636}{901} = .7$$

The computed values in C and D gives a call option value of 11.9% of asset value (using Appendix D)

Call option value = £636,000 × .119 = £75,684

project with an exercise price of £1.32 million is worth around £75,000. This value arises because there is a chance that the project could be really profitable, but the company will not know whether this is likely until the outcome of the first project is known. The high degree of risk in the second project actually increases the value of the call option. It seems, therefore, that the initial project launch, which creates an option value of £75,000 for a 'premium' of £25,000 (negative NPV) may make economic as well as strategic sense.

Such valuation calculations applied to strategic investment options are still somewhat crude and raise as many questions as they answer. (For example, is much of the risk for the follow-on project dependent upon the outcome of the initial project?) But option pricing does offer insights into the problem of valuing 'intangibles' in capital budgeting, particularly where they create options not otherwise available to the firm.

Equity as a call option on a company's assets: Bakobright Ltd

Option-like features are found in financially-geared companies. *Equity is, in effect, a call option on the company's assets.* Consider the following example.

Bakobright Ltd has a single £1 million debenture in issue which is due for repayment in one year. The directors, on behalf of the shareholders, have a choice. They can pay off the loan at the year end, thereby having no prior claim on the firm's assets, or they can default on the debenture. If they default, the debenture holders will take charge of the assets to recover the £1 million owing to them.

In such a situation, the shareholders of Bakobright have a call option on the company's assets with an exercise price of £1 million. They can exercise the option by repaying the loan, or they can allow the option to lapse by defaulting on the loan. Their choice depends on the value of the company's assets. If they are worth more than £1 million, the option is 'in the money' and the loan should be repaid. If the option is 'out of the money', because the assets are worth less than £1 million, option theory argues that shareholders would prefer the company to default or enter liquidation. This option-like feature arises because companies have limited liability status, effectively protecting them from having to make good any losses.

Options and moral hazard

Moral hazard is the term given to the risk that the existence of a contract will change the behaviour of one or both parties to the contract.

Option contracts can have moral hazard implications. For example, an insurance policy (a type of put option) may encourage management to take fewer fire precautions because the loss is carried by the insurer. Similar moral hazard aspects can be found in loan guarantee and underwriting contracts. Perhaps the most significant example is that referred to in the previous section: the moral hazard that shareholders in highly-geared companies, where asset values are below the level of borrowings, will allow the default, knowing that the loss will be sustained by the loanstock holders.

While the options literature has developed highly complex models for valuing options, insufficient attention has been paid to *value-creation* through options. This involves a three-stage process by the financial manager.

Table 21.3   Enigma Drugs plc options

Option	Type	Length	Exercise Price
To the company:			
Investment timing (1)	American call	2 years	£50m investment outlay
Abandonment (2)	American put	5 years	Resale value of 'knowhow'
Follow-on-project (3)	European call	4 years	£120m investment
Default on loans (5)	European call	8 years	£40m face value of the loan
To the loanstock holder:			
Convertible loan (4)	American call	4 years	360p

1. *Review all business activities to identify where options with possible financial pay-offs arise.* To do this, the manager needs not only a clear grasp of what an option is, but also needs to view activities within an options framework.

2. Consider all major decisions with risky payoffs to *establish how option-like features could be incorporated.* Option values *increase* with risk and uncertainty, but only if the holder has the right to walk away from the option without incurring additional losses.

3. *Assess the value of such actual or potential options as part of the normal decision-making process.* Other than in the more specialized options markets, such an evaluation will be largely subjective because risk-analysis in decision-making is generally a subjective assessment.

Spot the options in Enigma Drugs plc

The mini-case presented at the start of the chapter incorporated five options. Take another look at the case to identify the type of option, its length and exercise price. Recall that American options offer the holder the right to exercise at any time up to a certain date, while a European option is exercised on one particular date. The solution is given in Table 21.3, the numbers relating to those in the case.

21.5   Summary

Options or option-like features permeate virtually every area of financial management. A better understanding of options and the development of option pricing have made the topic an increasingly important part of financial theory. In this chapter we have sought to increase the reader's awareness of what options are, where they are to be found, and how managers can begin to value them. The topic is still in its infancy and we have probably raised as many problems as we have solved; but its study may yield important insights into financial and investment decisions.

Key points

- Option features are to be found in most areas of finance. For example, convertibles and warrants, insurance, currency and interest rate management, and capital budgeting.
- Pure options are financial instruments created by exchanges (e.g. stock markets) rather than companies.
- The two main types of option are (1) *call options*, giving the holder the right to buy a share (or other asset) at the *exercise* price at some future time, and (2) *put options*, giving the holder the right to sell shares at a given price at some future time.
- The minimum value of a call option is the difference between the share price and the present value of the exercise price.
- The value of call options increase as:
  - Underlying share price increases.
  - The exercise price falls.
  - The time to expiry lengthens.
  - The risk-free interest rate rises.
  - The volatility of the underlying share price increases.
- The Black–Scholes Option Pricing Model can be applied to estimate the value of call options.
- Capital investment decisions may have options attached covering the option to (1) abandon, (2) delay or (3) invest in follow-on opportunities.
- Where the value of a company's assets fall below the value of its borrowings, shareholders may not exercise their option to repay the loan, but prefer the company to default on the debt.

Further reading

A more detailed treatment of options is found in Brealey and Myers (1991) and Brigham and Gapenski (1991). An introduction to options is given by Redhead (1990), while Kester (1984) discusses the topic of real options. Those who like a mathematical challenge may want to try Black and Scholes' (1973) classic paper.

Questions

Self-test questions

1. Define a call option and a put option.
2. What is the basic difference between a European and an American option?
3. Give two examples where companies can issue call options (or something similar).
4. Explain why option value increases with the volatility of the underlying share price.

Exercises

1. On 1 March the ordinary shares of Gaymore plc stood at 469p. The traded options market in the shares quotes April 500p puts at 47p. If the share price falls to 450p, how much, if any, profit would an investor make? What will the option be worth if the share price moves up to 510p?

(Solution in Appendix A)

2. Explain the factors influencing the price of a traded option and whether volatility of a company's share option price is necessarily a sign of financial weakness.

3. Frank purchased a call option on 100 shares in Marmaduke plc six months ago at 10p per share. The share price at the time was 110p and the exercise price was 120p. Just prior to expiry the share price has risen to 135p.

Required

(a) State whether the option should be exercised.
(b) Calculate the profit or loss on the option.
(c) Would Frank have done better by investing the same amount of cash six months ago in a bank offering 10 per cent p.a.?

Practical Assignment

1. Choose two forms of financial contracting arrangement with option features and show how option pricing theory can help in analysing them.

2. Consider a major capital investment recently undertaken or under review. Does it offer an option? Could an option feature be introduced? What would the rough value of the option be?

CHAPTER 22
Acquisitions and restructuring

CAN THE MICHELIN MAN BOUNCE BACK?

In 1989, Michelin, the French motor tyre company, paid $730m to acquire its US competitor Uniroyal-Goodrich, the main supplier to General Motors. In addition, Michelin assumed $800m of U-G's debt, raising the total cost to $1,530m. This raised Michelin's own debts to FF30 billion, producing an interest bill for 1990 of FF3 billion, a major portion of its overall losses of FF5 billion.

Michelin is renowned for the technical excellence of its products, obtained by a policy of ploughing back cash into R & D, but is reputed to have a less accomplished manufacturing and marketing capability. The appeal of the U-G purchase was higher market share and increased production capacity in the United States. The result of the acquisition was to propel Michelin into world market leadership, with around 20 per cent of the world market, and 10 per cent of the increasingly important Japanese market.

However, the acquisition was made just before the world economy in general, and the US automobile market in particular, deflated with a loud hiss. Michelin found itself saddled with worldwide reorganization costs of some FF3.4 billion, of which the United States accounted for about two-thirds. While mostly in the form of provisions and write-offs, the red ink cast doubts on both the wisdom and the timing of the acquisition. Michelin argued that, had it not taken the plunge, a major competitor, such as Goodyear (US) or Bridgestone (Japan), might have done so, although its own move probably contributed to (subsequently aborted) defensive merger talks in 1990–1 between Pirelli (Italy) and Continental (Germany).

22.1   Introduction

Acquisitions of other companies are investment decisions and should be evaluated on essentially the same criteria examined when new items of machinery are obtained. However,

514

there are two important differences between takeovers and many 'standard' investments.

First, because takeovers are frequently contested, (i.e. resisted by the target's incumbent managers), bidders often have little or no access to intelligence about their targets beyond published financial and market data and any inside information which they may glean.

Second, many takeovers are undertaken for longer-term strategic reasons, which are often difficult to quantify. It is common to hear the chairmen of acquiring companies talking of an acquisition opening up a 'strategic window'; what they often do not add is that the window is usually not only shut but has curtains drawn across it or even bars across it! To a large extent, a takeover is a shot in the dark, partly explaining why so many firms which launched giant takeovers in the 1980s came to grief.

But there were other reasons. Targets were often too large in relation to bidders so that any unexpected 'skeletons in the cupboard', integration problems, or excessive borrowings throttled the parent.

An example of a company biting off more than it could chew was the case of the Blue Arrow employment agency, which launched a massive rights issue to finance the acquisition of Manpower, the largest employment agency in the United States. The rights issue was a complete failure, with a high proportion of the shares left in the hands of the advising merchant bank, County Securities, part of NatWest Bank. Failure to disclose the extent of this shareholding led to legal action by the regulatory authorities against NatWest. Meanwhile, merger integration problems rapidly led to the ousting of Tony Berry, head of Blue Arrow, from the Board, and the emergence of Mitchell Fromstein, former head of Manpower, as the head of the expanded group – a case of the bitten biting back!

There are important lessons to be learned here from risk analysis and portfolio theory. When acquisitions have highly uncertain outcomes, the larger they are, the more catastrophic the impact of any adverse outcomes. As a result, it may be rational and less risky to confine takeover activity to small, uncontested bids. Alternatively, a spread of large acquisitions might confer portfolio diversification benefits, so long as they have low cash flow correlation. However, the greater the scale of takeover activity, the greater the resulting financing burden placed on the parent, and the greater the impact of diverting managerial capacity into solving integration problems.

Some of these issues can be seen in Michelin's acquisition of Uniroyal-Goodrich. Michelin eagerly sought market share, yearning for world market leadership, influenced possibly by prevailing marketing wisdom which positively links market share and profitability. Yet, apart from the poor timing of the bid, significant questions arise. It created great financing burdens on a Michelin striving to absorb an enterprise which effectively doubled its size. The Michelin strategy may well pay off, but it has undoubtedly introduced financial pressures which may in time undermine its ability to fund an ongoing R&D programme, the cornerstone of its earlier successes.

The acquisition decision is thus a complex one. It involves significant uncertainties (except in purely asset-stripping takeovers), it often requires substantial funding as few companies can finance acquisitions out of cash balances, and may pose awkward problems of integration if the hoped-for benefits are to accrue. Yet, as some takeover 'kings' like Hanson and BTR have shown, spectacular pay-offs can be achieved. These are some of the themes of this chapter – how to evaluate a takeover, how to finance it and how to integrate it. But first, we examine the remarkable boom in UK takeover activity, which occurred in the 1980s.

LEARNING OBJECTIVES

A major aim of this chapter is to emphasize the strategic aspects of takeovers. Having read it, you should understand:

- Why firms select acquisitions rather than other strategic options.
- How acquisitions can be financed.
- How acquisitions should be integrated.
- How the degree of success of a takeover can be evaluated.
- How corporate restructuring can enhance shareholder value.

Included in the chapter is a full case study, based on BAT Industries plc, designed to illustrate many of the aspects of this chapter and to draw upon key concepts explained earlier in the book.

22.2   The 1980s takeover boom

Although the terms 'takeover' and 'merger' are used as synonyms, there is a technical difference. A takeover is the acquisition by one company of the share capital of another in exchange for cash, ordinary shares, loan stock, or some mixture of these. This results in the identity of the acquiree being absorbed into that of the acquirer (although, of course, the expanded company may continue to utilize the acquiree's brand names and trademarks). A merger is a pooling of the interests of two companies into a new enterprise, requiring the agreement of both sets of shareholders, e.g. the amalgamation of packaging interests by the UK MB (Metal Box) and the French concern Carnaud to form CMB. By definition, mergers involve the friendly (initially, at least) restructuring of assets into a new organization, whereas many takeovers are hotly resisted. In practice, the vast majority of business amalgamations are takeovers rather than mergers. Table 22.1 shows the upsurge in UK takeover activity in the mid-1980s and allows comparison with the previous major takeover boom in the early 1970s.

The figures (although not inflation-adjusted) show how the recent merger boom took off in terms of expenditure in 1984 and in terms of numbers of acquisitions in 1986. On both these criteria, the boom reached higher peaks than the earlier upsurge in activity. In addition, the latest boom lasted far longer than its predecessor. A further interesting aspect is how the pattern of financing varied. As the stock market rose in the 1980s, the use of ordinary share financing became more popular, but fell abruptly after the stock market crash of 1987 as more deals were financed in cash (effectively meaning borrowing for many acquirors).

Among the many explanations for the latest takeover boom, some of the most prominent are:

1. The sharp growth in real company profitability in the mid-1980s increased the ability of companies to finance acquisitions. Emergence from recession is usually heralded by a

Table 22.1 The scale and financing of takeover activity

Year	Number Acquired	Outlay (£m)	Cash	Percentage via: Ordinary Shares	Fixed Interest
1970	793	1,122	22	53	25
1971	884	911	31	48	21
1972	1,210	2,532	19	58	23
1973	1,205	1,304	53	36	11
1974	504	508	68	22	9
1975	315	291	59	32	9
1976	353	448	72	27	2
1977	481	824	62	37	1
1978	567	1,140	57	41	2
1979	534	1,656	56	31	13
1980	469	1,475	52	45	3
1981	452	1,144	68	30	3
1982	463	2,206	58	32	10
1983	447	2,343	44	54	2
1984	568	5,474	54	34	13
1985	474	7,090	40	52	7
1086	842	15,370	26	57	17
1987	1,528	16,539	35	60	5
1988	1,499	22,839	70	22	8
1989	1,337	27,250	82	13	5
1990	776	8,235	77	18	5

Sources: CSO Business Monitor (MQ7) and Financial Statistics.

rising stock market, which increases the ability of companies to finance takeovers by share exchanges or with cash raised from rights issues.

2. The move to deregulation in capital markets led to increasing supplies of debt capital accompanied by a greater readiness of institutions to lend in more novel ways.

3. Companies emerging from the recession with lower gearing ratios were more willing and able to borrow.

4. Takeover booms often begin when market values are low in relation to the replacement cost of assets. The high interest rates of the recession years resulted in heavy discounting of future corporate earnings, so that many asset-rich firms appeared to be undervalued. For acquirors wishing to build capacity ahead of an economic upturn, acquisition of 'cheap' targets provided a lower cost alternative than internal growth.

5. The abolition of 100 per cent First Year Allowances in 1984 weakened the incentive to invest in new capacity rather than buying 'off-the-peg'.

6. Apparently contradicting market efficiency arguments, there may have been a tendency for the rising market to overvalue larger firms relative to small ones, making it easier for the former to acquire the latter.

7. The regulatory environment was generally perceived to be more relaxed. The UK government in 1983, without precedent, reversed the Monopolies and Mergers Commission recommendation regarding the takeover bid by Standard Chartered Bank for Anderson Strathclyde, the Scottish engineers. One year later, in 1984, the Secretary

of State for Trade and Industry, Norman Tebbit, declared that mergers would be judged henceforth *primarily* on competition grounds, rather than on wider public interest grounds.

22.3   Motives for takeover

Managers seeking to maximize the wealth of shareholders should continually seek to exploit value-creating opportunities. There are two occasions when managers feel able to enrich shareholders via takeovers:

1. *When managers believe that the target company can be acquired at less than its 'true value'.* This implies disbelief in the ability of the capital market to consistently value companies correctly. If a company is thought to be undervalued on the market, there may well be opportunities for 'asset-stripping', i.e. selling off the components of the taken-over company for a combined sum greater than the purchase price.
2. *When managers believe that two enterprises will be worth more if merged than if operated as two separate entities.* Thus for two companies, X and Y:

$$V_{X+Y} > V_X + V_Y$$

The principle of value additivity would refute this unless the amalgamation resulted in some form of 'synergy' or more effective utilization of the assets of the combined companies.

In practice, it is very difficult to differentiate between these two explanations for merger, especially as many mergers result in only partial disposals when activities which appear to fit more neatly into existing operations are retained. Companies are valued by the market on the basis of information which their managements release regarding market prospects, value of assets, R & D activity, and so on. Market participants may suspect that an underperforming company could be operated more efficiently by an alternative management team, but until a credible bidder emerges, poor results may simply be reflected in a poor share market rating.

But, conversely, poor results can generate expectations of an imminent bid, raising the share price substantially. In 1989, Jaguar's dire profit figures signalled that it was unlikely to be able to continue as an independent trading entity, thus opening the door to Ford. Jaguar was worth more under a new management better able to market the famous brand name, so in a sense, it was undervalued prior to Ford's bid.

How mergers may increase value

There are solid reasons why amalgamation can enhance value. The more specific reasons cited for launching takeover bids usually reflect the anticipated benefits which a merger is expected to generate:

1. *To exploit scale economies.* Larger size is usually expected to yield production economies if manufacturing operations can be amalgamated, marketing economies if similar

distribution channels can be utilized, and financial economies if size confers access to capital markets on more favourable terms.

2. *To obtain synergy.* This term is often used to include any gains from merger, but strictly, it refers to benefits unrelated to scale. In addition to scale economies, gains may emerge from a particular way of combining resources. One company's managers may be especially suited to operating another company's distribution systems, or the sales staff of one company may be able to sell another company's, perhaps closely related, product as part of a package.

3. *To enter new markets.* For firms which lack the expertise to develop different products, or do not possess the outlets required to access different market segments, takeover may be a simpler, and certainly a quicker, way of expanding. The acquisition in 1987 by Iceland of its frozen food competitor, Bejam, was designed to achieve a greater penetration into the northern half of England, an area where Bejam was particularly strong and Iceland weak.

4. *To provide 'critical mass'.* As many product markets have become more global and the lifespan of products has tended to diminish, greater emphasis has to be placed on R & D activities. In some industries, such as aerospace and telecommunications, it is thought that small-scale enterprises are simply unable to generate the cash flows required to finance R & D and brand investment, a factor partly responsible for the downfall of Jaguar. There is also a credibility effect operating. For example, companies may be unwilling to use small firms as a source of components when their future survival, and hence ability to supply, is suspect.

5. *To impart or restore growth impetus.* Maturing firms whose growth rate is weakening may look to younger, more dynamic companies both to obtain a quick, short-term growth 'fix', and also to utilize their entrepreneurial ideas to achieve higher rates of growth in the longer term. BAT used the substantial cash flows from its mature tobacco business to acquire Allied Dunbar (pensions) and Eagle Star (insurance) to diversify into the financial services sector, which it perceived as a potential growth area.

6. *To acquire market power.* Obtaining higher earnings is easier if there are fewer competitors. Competition-reducing takeovers (horizontal integration), are likely to be investigated by the regulatory authorities, but are often justified by the need to enhance ability to compete internationally on the basis of a securer home market. In addition, 'backward vertical integration', mergers undertaken to capture sources of raw materials, e.g. BP's acquisition of Britoil in order to obtain its oil reserves, and 'forward vertical integration' to secure new outlets for the company's products, have the effect of increasing the firm's grasp over the whole production cycle, and are thus competition-reducing in a wider sense. Many past brewery takeovers were mounted not to obtain production capacity but to secure access to the target's estate of tied public houses, and to acquire brands, as in the case of Scottish and Newcastle's purchase of Theakstons.

7. *To reduce dependence on existing, perhaps volatile activities.* This issue was aired in Chapter 10, where we concluded that risk reduction *per se* as a motive for diversification may be misguided. There is no reason why two enterprises owned by one company should have greater value unless the amalgamation produces scale economies or some other synergies. If shareholder portfolio formation is a substitute for corporate diversification, there is no point in acquiring other companies to reduce risk – rational

shareholders will already have diversified away specific risk and market risk is undiversifiable.

The market for management control

Several of the above motives for merger suggest that some companies can be more efficiently operated by alternative managers. A more general motive for merger is thus to weed out inefficient personnel. There are three ways in which the market mechanism can penalize managerial inefficiency:

1. Bankruptcy, which usually involves significant costs.
2. Shareholder revolt, which is difficult to organize given the diffusion of ownership and the general reluctance of institutional investors to interfere in operational management unless disaster beckons.
3. The takeover process is the commonest way of removing sitting managers. In this respect, the takeover bidding process may be regarded as a 'market for managerial control', where the threat of takeover provides a spur to inefficient managers. Clearing out managerial deadwood has a two-fold effect: it lowers costs and removes barriers to more effective utilization of assets. Theory suggests that incompetently managed firms will be acquired at prices which ensure that the owners of the acquiror suffer no loss in value. If a bid premium over the market price is payable, this should be recoverable from the higher cash flows generated from more efficient asset utilization. To this extent, takeover activity may be seen as a perfectly healthy expression of the workings of the market system.

Managerial motives for takeover

The motive of diversification to reduce risk suggests a second possible explanation for takeover activity. With the divorce of ownership and control, and the consequent high level of managerial autonomy, managers are relatively free to follow activities and policies, including acquisition of other firms, which enhance their own objectives, both in monetary and non-pecuniary forms.

Managerial salaries and perquisites are usually higher in large and growing firms, and since growth by acquisition is usually easier and swifter than organic growth, managers may view acquisition with some eagerness. If acquisitions are 'managerial' in this sense, then acquirors may be prepared to expend 'excessive' amounts to gain ownership of target companies simply to secure deals which promote managerial well-being but at the expense of shareholder value. If this explanation is correct, then acquisitions may result in a transfer of wealth from shareholders of acquiring firms to shareholders of acquired companies, even when presented as promoting the best interests of the former.

Takeovers may also be related to the way managers are remunerated. In the 1980s, UK managers were increasingly paid by results, with the commonest criterion of performance being growth in EPS. This is a notoriously unreliable measure of performance as not only is it dependent on accounting conventions, but it is relatively easy to manipulate. For example, shutting down a loss-making activity, and treating associated costs as extraordinary, will raise EPS.

How to increase EPS by takeover: Hawk takes over Vole

A common means of increasing EPS has been to acquire other companies with lower PE ratios than one's own, these being companies out of favour with the market, either through poor performance or because too little was known about them. It can be shown that the acquisition of such companies, on certain conditions, can raise both EPS and share price. Consider the example in Table 22.2. Hawk, with a PE ratio of 20, reflecting strong growth expectations, contemplates the takeover of Vole, whose PE ratio is only 10. Hawk proposes to make an all-share offer. If it were able to obtain Vole at the market price, it would have to issue 5m shares to Vole's shareholders in exchange for their 20m shares.

Table 22.2 shows the impact of the exchange if the PE ratio of the expanded company were to remain at 20. The new EPS is £22m/105m = 21p, resulting in a post-bid share price of £4.20, and an overall market value of £441m. This apparently magical effect seems to have generated wealth of £21m! If it works out this way, the beneficiaries are the two sets of shareholders: Hawk's existing shareholders find their 100m shares valued at a price higher by 20p, i.e. £20m in total, and Vole's former shareholders find they now hold shares valued at £21m, rather than the value of £20m placed on Vole prior to the bid, i.e.:

Gains to Hawk's shareholders =	£20m
Gains to Vole's shareholders =	£1m
	= £21m

This effect is referred to as 'financial illusion' because it is unlikely to occur quite like this in reality. In particular, it relies on two critical assumptions. First, the absence of a bid premium. In practice, Hawk would have to offer above the market price to tempt Vole's

Table 22.2 Hawk and Vole

	Pre-bid		Post-bid
	Hawk	Vole	Hawk + Vole
Number of shares	100m	20m	100m + 5m = 105m
Earnings after tax	£20m	£2m	£20m + £2m = £22m
EPS	20p	10p	£22m ÷ £105 = 21p
PE ratio	20:1	10:1	20:1
Share price	£4	£1	20 × 21p = £4.20
Capitalization (Market value)	£400m	£20m	105m × £4.20 = £441m

shareholders into selling, thus altering the balance of gain. Second, it assumes that the market applies the same PE ratio to the expanded group as the pre-bid ratio for Hawk. If no operational synergies were expected, then the likely post-bid PE ratio is the weighted average of the two component pre-bid values:

$$\left(\text{Hawk PE ratio} \times \frac{\text{Value of Hawk}}{\text{Total Value}}\right) + \left(\text{Vole PE ratio} \times \frac{\text{Value of Vole}}{\text{Total Value}}\right)$$

$$= \left(20 \times \frac{£400\text{m}}{£420\text{m}}\right) \quad + \left(10 \times \frac{£20\text{m}}{£420\text{m}}\right) = 19.5$$

However, if Hawk is expected to reorganize Vole and imbue it with the same growth impetus expected from Hawk itself, the PE ratio post-bid could exceed the weighted average figure, and approach Hawk's pre-bid value of 20. If this occurred, then both groups of shareholders can enjoy the value created by the expectation of more efficient operation of Vole's assets and henceforth higher cash flows. Conversely, expectations of integration difficulties might offset such gains.

It does not follow that a higher EPS will lead to a higher share price. If the acquisition moved Hawk into a riskier area, its Beta should rise accordingly and the higher cash flows will be discounted at a higher required return. Similarly, if instead of financing the bid by a share exchange, Hawk had borrowed the required £20m, then, despite the higher EPS, the share price might not rise if the greater gearing and accompanying financial risk resulted in a higher equity Beta. Unqualified belief in the 'EPS effect' suggests disbelief in market efficiency and the suspicion remains that many acquisitions, not simply small ones of the Hawk–Vole variety, but some of the 'mega-mergers' of the 1980s, ostensibly undertaken to raise the acquiror's share price were really undertaken for 'manageerial' reasons.

Certainly, the subsequent difficulties experienced in post-merger integration and operation does not support the view that mergers are always in the best interests of shareholders.

22.4   Financing a bid

Table 22.1 shows data on the three main ways of financing takeovers: cash, issue of ordinary shares and fixed interest securities (loan stock, convertibles and preference shares). Clearly, the first two methods predominate, although their relative importance varies over time. As a rule of thumb, share exchange is more favoured when the stock market is high and rising, while cash offers are used to a greater extent when interest rates are relatively low or falling, given that many cash offers are themselves financed by the acquiror's borrowing. Increasingly, however, bidders offer their targets a choice of cash or shares, or even a three-way choice between straight cash vs. cash with shares vs. shares alone.

For example, in 1991, when bidding for its main UK competitor, Tootal, the textile company, Coats Viyella offered two alternatives. Shareholders of Tootal could either opt for a full cash consideration of 80p per share, but which would not qualify them to receive an imminent dividend of 3p per share, or accept 83.3p per share in cash and paper, based on the Coats share price at the date of the offer. The second option involved £51.02 in cash and 23 newly issued Coats shares for every 100 Tootal shares owned.

Such tactics are designed to appeal to the widest possible body of shareholders. Whichever type of package is chosen depends on the balance of relative advantages and disadvantages of the different methods, from both the bidder's and the target shareholder's viewpoints.

Cash

Everyone understands a cash offer. The amount is certain, there being no exposure to the risk of adverse movement in share price during the course of the bid. The targeted shareholder is more easily able to adjust his portfolio than if he receives shares, which involve dealing costs when sold. Because no new shares are issued, there is no dilution of earnings nor change in the balance of control of the bidder (unless, in the case of borrowed capital, creditors insist on restrictive covenants). Moreover, if the return expected on the assets of the target exceeds the cost of borrowing, the EPS of the bidder may increase, although increased perception of financial risk may mitigate this apparent benefit. A disadvantage from the recipient's viewpoint is a possible liability to Capital Gains Tax (CGT).

Share exchanges

Any liability to CGT is delayed with a share offer, and the cash flow cost to the bidder is zero, apart from the administration costs involved. However, equity is more costly to service than debt, especially for a company with taxable capacity, and an issue of new shares may interfere with the firm's gearing ratio. There could be an adverse impact on the balance of control if a major slice of the equity of the bidder came to be held by institutions looking for an opportunity to sell their holdings. The overhanging threat of a substantial share sale may depress the share price of the bidder.

Other methods

The use of other financing instruments is comparatively rare. When fixed interest securities are used, they are usually offered as alternatives to cash and/or ordinary shares. Convertibles have some appeal because any diluting effect is delayed and the interest cost on the security, which qualifies for tax relief, can usually be pitched below the going market rate on loan stock, due to the expectation of capital gain on conversion. Preference share financing in general is comparatively rare due to the lack of tax deductibility of preferred dividends and to restrictions on voting rights.

22.5 The importance of strategy

Considerable evidence has emerged that acquisitions have little better than an even chance of success. Although definitions of 'success' may vary, any activity that fails to enhance shareholder interests is unlikely to be regarded favourably by the capital market. While it is often difficult to assess what would have happened had a company not embarked on the takeover trail, if post-acquisition performance is inferior to pre-acquisition performance, or if the acquisition actually leads to a fall in shareholder wealth, it is difficult to argue that the acquisition has not been a failure.

The McKinsey firm of management consultants studied the 'value-creation perform-ance' of the acquisition programmes of 116 large US and UK companies, using financial measures of performance. The criterion of success used was whether the company earned at least its cost of capital on funds invested in the acquisition process. On this basis, a remarkable 60 per cent of all acquisitions failed, with large unrelated takeovers achieving a failure rate of 86 per cent.

There are numerous reasons why acquisitions fail. One explanation is that acquirors pay too much for their targets, either as a result of a flawed evaluation process which overestimates the likely benefits, or as a result of getting caught up in the 'machismo' of a competitive bidding situation, where to yield is regarded as a sign of corporate weakness.

In 1988, the UK television contractor TVS acquired the US TV programme producer, MTM Entertainments, for £190m. At the date of purchase, MTM sported a record of stagnant earnings for the three previous years. Within a year, a third of the stock market value of TVS was wiped off as the market reacted to news that MTM had been hit by a slump in the US syndication market with small TV stations failing to buy its programmes, resulting in operating losses of around £15m for the year, and in 1991, TVS wrote down the value of MTM by £21m, and announced that it had abandoned attempts to sell it. (TVS subsequently lost its UK franchise in 1992.)

A second reason is the alarming frequency with which 'skeletons' appear in cupboards. The disastrous takeover by Ferranti of International Signal and Control (see Chapter 4) is a good example of a badly researched acquisition which nearly destroyed the acquiror.

A third reason is that acquirors often fail to plan and execute properly the integration of their targets, frequently neglecting the organizational and internal cultural factors. Sometimes, acquirors know too little about the target's business to prepare detailed plans, as in the case of the hostile bid by GEC and Siemens for the defence contractor, Plessey.

Yet many companies have sound acquisition records. Their targets are carefully selected, they rarely get involved in competitive auctions, they often have the sense to walk away from deals when they realize the gravity of the likely integration problems and they seem able quickly and successfully to integrate acquisitions once deals are completed. What these companies have in common is a strategic approach to acquisitions.

22.6 The strategic approach

Most successful acquirors see their acquisitions as part of a long-term strategic process, designed to contribute towards overall corporate development. This requires acquirors to approach acquisitions only after a careful analysis of their own underlying strengths, identification of suitable candidates which satisfy chosen criteria, and most importantly, provide 'strategic fit' with the company's existing activities. In other words, a structured,

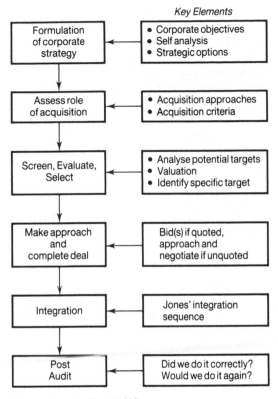

Source: Based on Payne (1985).

Figure 22.1 A strategic framework

coherent approach, while not a guarantee of success, is more likely to avoid the potentially disastrous consequences of many apparently ill-considered takeovers which many firms have come to regret by the early 1990s.

Figure 22.1 displays a simple strategic framework within which a thorough-going acquisition programme might be conducted. The six steps begin with a full strategic review of the company as it stands, and its strategic options, followed by a detailed consideration of the role of acquisitions, i.e. the reasons why an acquisition may be targeted, leading to the process of selecting and bidding for the chosen prey, culminating in the often neglected activities of post-merger integration and post-audit.

Objectives

Formulating strategy should begin with an expression of corporate objectives, concentrating on maximizing shareholder wealth. Many firms now publish 'mission statements', but these are usually somewhat vague expressions of the image which the company would like to portray, often largely for internal consumption in order to motivate staff (Klemm *et al.*, 1991). If in building the desired image, the company's managers fail to earn at least the cost of equity, they will themselves invite the risk of takeover. Strategy concerns the examination of alternative routes to achieving the ultimate aim, and then the optimal way of executing the chosen path. Achieving long-term goals usually involves expansion of the enterprise, a route often preferred by managers for personal motives.

Internal or external growth?

There are two main ways of achieving growth: (1) by self-development of new products, markets and processes (internal growth), and (2) by acquisition (external growth). Although both of these routes are usually expensive in executive time and resources, external growth has the advantage of securing quick access to new markets or productive capacity. However, firms should not overlook intermediate strategies, such as licensing, whereby a royalty is paid to the developer of new technology in exchange for rights to exploit it, or joint ventures, where an existing company could be partially acquired, or a totally new one set up in partnership with another firm.

The decision to grow internally or externally will depend partly on an analysis of the particular strengths, weaknesses, opportunities and threats (SWOTs) of the firm. This self-analysis should make the potential acquiror aware of any competitive advantages it enjoys over rival companies. *Competitive advantage* stems from two sources: *cost advantage*, where products are virtually similar, and *product differentiation*. Exploitation of each of these creates value for shareholders. When areas of competitive advantage have been identified, the company can decide whether to build upon existing strengths or to attempt to develop distinctive competence in areas of perceived weakness. This evaluation may also result in a decision to divest certain activities where no obvious advantage is possessed, or where it is felt that too many resources would be required to sustain this advantage.

In deciding which strategic route to follow, potential acquirors would do well to consider the results of research at Harvard Business School by Porter (1987), who examined the acquisition record of thirty-three large diversified US companies. The criterion for judging 'success' was the subsequent divestment rate of earlier acquisitions. The main finding was that successful acquirors almost invariably diversify into related fields, and vice versa. In other words, diversifications into activities unrelated to the core business of the acquiror carry much greater risks of failure. Even companies with successful 'related diversification' records achieved poor results when they wandered into unrelated fields. Porter concluded that the corporate portfolio strategy of many diversifying companies 'has failed – diversification just doesn't work' because most diversifiers fail 'to think in terms of how they really add value'.

Acquisition criteria

The company should next assess what specific role it hopes the acquisition will perform. Table 22.3, drawn from a publication by 3i (Investors in Industry), which specializes in

Table 22.3 Strategic opportunities

Where you are	▶	How to get to where you want to be
Growing steadily but in a mature market with limited growth prospects.	▶	Acquire a company in a younger market with a higher growth rate.
Marketing an incomplete product range, or having the potential to sell other products or services to your existing customers.	▶	Acquire a company with a complementary product range.
Operating at maximum productive capacity.	▶	Acquire a company making similar products operating substantially below capacity.
Under-utilizing management resources.	▶	Acquire a company into which your talents can extend.
Needing more control of suppliers or customers.	▶	Acquire a company which is, or gives access to, a significant customer or supplier.
Lacking key clients in a targeted sector.	▶	Acquire a company with the right customer profile.
Preparing for flotation but needing to improve your balance sheet.	▶	Acquire a suitable company which will enhance earnings per share.
Needing to increase market share.	▶	Acquire an important competitor.
Needing to widen your capability.	▶	Acquire a company with the key talents and/or technology.

Source: 3i (Investors in Industry).

offering acquisition advice, lists possible strategic reasons for acquisition with suggested routes to achieving the stated aims.

At this stage, the company should reassess the alternatives to merger, in view of the many difficulties involved. Taking over another company is rather like moving to a larger, more expensive house. Mergers involve considerable disruptions during the planning and bidding phase, costs such as legal advice and the printing and publishing of documents, possible exposure to increased financial risk, and the upheavals of integration. Just as some marriages do not survive the strains of house-moving, some companies often fail to recover after the stress of merger. Having identified the specific role of the acquisition, the company can now consider whether this can be achieved in other, perhaps more cost-effective ways.

Harrison (1987) suggests that for every merger motive there are several alternative ways of achieving the same end. For example, if the aim is sales growth, this can be achieved by internal expansion or by a joint venture. If the aim is to improve earnings per share, a loss-making subsidiary can be shut down or efficiency enhancing measures can be instituted. If it is wished to utilize spare cash, this can be invested in marketable securities and trade investments or even returned to shareholders as dividends or in the form of share repurchases. If an improvement in management skills is sought, appropriately skilled personnel can be bought in to replace existing managers, outside consultants can be used for advice, or incentive and bonus schemes can be introduced. In short, if the decision to grow by acquisition is made, the potential acquiror must be very sure that the stipulated aims are unattainable by alternative measures.

Most firms with corporate planning departments exercise a continuous review of the key members of the industry in which they operate and also of related, and often, unrelated areas. Some firms are known to 'track' several dozen potential takeover candidates, assessing their various strengths and weaknesses, and estimating the likely net value obtainable if they were acquired. Such companies are cross-checked against a set of possible acquisition criteria. The following list of key factors is suggested by 3i:

- *Industry*   Are the activities in which possible targets are engaged suitably attractive? What are the strengths and weaknesses of these activities?
- *Geography*   Which areas are attractive, and which should be avoided, or are too distant for effective control?
- *Size*   What is affordable, compared with what is desirable in terms of turnover, net assets, number of employees, sales outlets?
- *Financial condition*   Is it worth considering a loss-maker, or must the target already be financially successful?
- *Level of investment*   How much investment in fixed assets and working capital would be required to sustain and develop the acquired company?
- *Management*   Should the acquisition already have a good management? Is it desirable and feasible to install one's own?
- *Price*   How much capital can be expended either from internal sources or by additional borrowing?

When the decision to expand by acquisition is taken, the corporate planning staff should be able to rapidly provide a short-list of candidates, expressing the SWOTs of each, especially its vulnerability to takeover at that time. It is common for defending managements to dismiss takeover bids as 'opportunistic' in a pejorative way. For an acquisitive company which adopts the strategic approach, this means 'well-timed', as such companies are continually seeking opportune moments to launch a bid, especially when the stock market rating of the target appears low. The joint takeover by GEC and Siemens of Plessey was opportunistic in the sense that the target's return on capital was relatively low due to a substantial investment programme which it had recently completed. Whether the market had correctly valued Plessey is arguable, but the bidders undoubtedly spotted a favourable opportunity to acquire Plessey at a time when its performance looked weak in relation to the market, thus eliminating a major competitor for lucrative British Telecom contracts.

Bidding

Bidding is an exercise in applied psychology. Readiness to bid implies an assessment that the target is either undervalued as it stands or would be worth more under alternative management. In such cases, the bid itself provides new information about prospective value, and the bidder should expect to have to pay above the market price to secure control. However, it is often unclear before the event how much of a bid premium, if any, is already built into the market price as the market attempts to assess the probability of a bidder emerging and succeeding with its offer. The trick in mounting profitable takeover bids is to promise to use assets more effectively in order to entice existing shareholders to sell without making such extravagant claims that the market price moves up too sharply before the acquisition is completed! Conversely, to accentuate the difficulties of reorganizing the target could be regarded as disingenuous or even call into question the wisdom of the bid itself, leading to a fall in the bidder's own share price.

Post-merger activities

Probably the most difficult part of takeover strategy and execution is the integration of the newly acquired company into the parent. In the case of contested bids, the acquiror will normally have only a limited amount of information to guide his integration plans and should not be too shocked to encounter some 'nasties' regarding the quality of the target's assets and personnel. The difficulty of integration depends also on the extent to which the acquiror wants to control the operations of the target. If only limited control is required, as in the case of unrelated acquisitions, the extent of integration is probably restricted to meshing the financial reporting systems of the component companies. Conversely, if full integration of common manufacturing activities is required, integration assumes a different order of complexity.

Jones (1982 and 1986) points out that the degree of complexity of integration depends on the type of acquisition, e.g. whether a horizontal takeover of a very similar company, requiring a detailed plan for integrating supply, production and distribution, or at the other extreme, a purely conglomerate acquisition where there is little or no overlap of functions. The relationship between type of acquisition, type of overlap of activity (split into financial, manufacturing and marketing) and the resulting degree of integrative complexity is shown in Figure 22.2. Because we believe that integration is perhaps the most important part of the acquisition process, we devote the whole of the following section to further analysis of this issue.

Finally, the acquisition should be post-audited. The post-audit team should review both the evaluation phase to assess whether and to what extent the appraisal was under- or

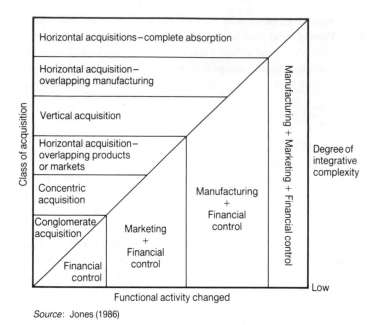

Source: Jones (1986)

Figure 22.2   Type of acquisition and integrative complexity

over-optimistic, and whether appropriate plans were formulated and executed. The emphasis, as in any post-audit, should centre on what lessons can be learned to guide any subsequent acquisition exercise.

22.7   Post-merger integration

Poorly planned and executed integration are two of the commonest reasons for the failure of takeovers. All too often, acquisitive companies focus senior management attention on the next adventure rather than devoting adequate resources to carefully absorbing the newly-acquired firm. Yet it is rash to lay down optimal integration procedures in advance, because to a large degree, the appropriate integration procedures are situation-specific. The 'right' way to approach integration depends on the nature of the company acquired, its internal culture and its strengths and weaknesses.

However, Drucker (1981) contends that there are Five Golden Rules to follow in the integration process. These are:

1. Ensure that acquired companies have a 'common core of unity' with the parent. In his view, mere financial ties between companies are insufficient to obtain a bond. The companies should have significant overlapping characteristics like shared technology or markets in order to exploit synergies.

2. The acquiror should think through what potential skill contribution it can make to the acquiree. In other words, the takeover should be approached not solely with the attitude of 'what's in it for the parent?' but also with the view 'what can we offer them?'
3. The acquiror must respect the products, markets and customers of the acquired company. Disparaging the record and performance of less senior management is likely to sap morale.
4. Within a year, the acquiror should provide appropriately skilled top management for the acquiree.
5. Again within a one-year timespan, the acquiror should make several cross-company promotions.

These are largely common-sense guidelines with a heavy emphasis on behavioural factors but many studies have shown that acquirors fail to follow these apparently obvious principles.

The integration sequence

Jones explains that integration of a new company is a complex mix of corporate strategy, management accounting and applied psychology. Acquirors should follow an 'Integration Sequence', based on five key steps, the relative weight attaching to each step depending on the type of acquisition. The sequence is as follows:

1. Decide upon and communicate initial reporting relationships.
2. Achieve rapid control of key factors.
3. Review the resource base of the acquiree via a 'resource audit'.
4. (Re-)define corporate objectives and develop strategic plans.
5. Revise the organizational structure.

Each of these is now briefly examined.

Reporting relationships

Clear reporting relationships have to be established in order to avoid uncertainty. An important issue is whether to impose reporting lines at the outset or whether to await the new organizational structure. In resolving this issue, it is desirable to avoid managers establishing their own informal relationships and to stress that some changes may only be temporary.

Control of key factors

Control requires access to plentiful and accurate information. To control key factors, acquirors should rapidly, but without damaging motivation, gain control of the information channels which export control messages and import key data about resource deployment. It may sometimes be desirable not to introduce controls identical to those of the parent, first, because group controls may not be appropriate for the acquired company, and second, because those group controls may no longer be appropriate for the revised organization. If the acquiree's existing control systems are thought to be adequate, it may be worth retaining them. Two important financial controls are the setting of clear borrowing limits and an early review of capital expenditure limits and appraisal procedures.

Jones notes that poor financial controls are often found within newly acquired companies, and indeed, have often contributed to their demise. Examples are over-reliance on financial, rather than management, accounting systems (MAS), an MAS which provides inappropriate information in an inappropriate format, poor use of the MAS, and distortions in the overhead allocation mechanism, making it difficult to pinpoint unprofitable products and customers. The net result is often poor budgetary control, inadequate costing systems and an inability to monitor and control cash movements.

Resource audit

The resource audit should examine both physical and human assets to obtain a clear picture of the quality of management at all levels. The extent of the required audit will depend on how much information is made available prior to the acquisition, but auditors should not be surprised if 'skeletons' are found lurking in hidden cupboards, requiring a reappraisal of the value of the acquired firm and possibly a different way of integrating it into the parent's future strategy and plans. For example, a business which was meant to be absorbed into the parent's operations may be divested if its capital equipment is unexpectedly dilapidated.

Corporate objectives and plans

These should be harmonized with those of the parent but should also reflect any differences due to industrial sector, such as different 'normal' rates of return or profit margin in different industrial sectors. Managers of acquired firms should have some freedom to formulate their plans to meet the stated aims, but the degree of freedom should depend on the complexity of the merger. For example, in a conglomerate acquisition, where the primary aim is to secure financial control, it may be appropriate to allow executives to develop a system of management control suitable to their own operating patterns, so long as these are consistent with the aims of the takeover. In cases where cash generation is the main spur, all that may be needed is centralized cash management plus control over capital allocations.

Revising the organizational structure

A discussion of organizational design is outside our scope here, but obviously a demoralized labour force is unlikely to offer optimal performance.

One study found that important factors enhancing the success of the takeover were the thoroughness of the resource audit and the degree of senior management contact in the very

---

THE HUMAN FACTOR

A study of the 'human factor', undertaken by Hunt and Leese of the London Business School and Egon Zehnder Associates (1987) commented:

> unless the human element is managed carefully, there is a serious risk of losing the financial and business advantages which the acquisition could bring to the parent company.

---

early stages of the takeover. Employees of acquired companies seek a rapid resolution of uncertainty, especially regarding how they and their company fit into the future structure and strategy of the acquiror, and how soon the new management team will assume control. Particularly important for morale are the lifting of any previous embargo on capital expenditure and the provision of improved performance incentives, pension schemes and career prospects.

Some of these aspects are illustrated in the following short case, relating to the integration of Dunlop by BTR.

BTR's integration of Dunlop
(based on an article in the Financial Times (1987))

Dunlop had been UK market leader in motor car tyres for several decades, but, despite diversification into promising areas like the Slazenger sports equipment business, had been brought to its knees by the prolonged contraction of the UK motor industry. Prior to its takeover by BTR in 1986, it had already divested the tyre business to Sumitomo of Japan in order to reduce its huge indebtedness.

BTR had grown from humble beginnings into a prominent position in the UK top twenty companies by a policy of acquisition in a diverse range of industrial goods. It had gained a reputation as a shrewd assessor of value and for a highly professional approach to takeover planning and integration. The tale of how Dunlop was integrated gives an insight into BTR's own management systems as well as its post-acquisition philosophy, important factors in BTR's past growth.

BTR takes a strategic view of its businesses and so the first task was to determine how Dunlop's activities fitted into its overall structure. Some activities such as hose and belting fitted naturally into existing BTR operations, while others such as Slazenger required separate treatment due to their size and distinctiveness. The existing Dunlop management was retained intact because 'in every acquisition we have made, we have discovered a wealth of talent at the operational level' (BTR chief of European operations). In order to allay the fears of Dunlop managers, top BTR executives travelled to all Dunlop plants to explain BTR management philosophy and financial control methods.

For many years, Dunlop had been an organization where 'there were financial corners you could hide in'. As a result, the rigorous overhaul of its financial system by BTR proved a 'real culture shock' according to a senior Dunlop manager, 'but it has proved a vigorous and disciplined way of controlling operations'. The cornerstone of BTR policy is heavy stress on return on sales as a performance measure, a ratio chosen because 'it ensures good cash flow'. BTR argues that concentration on return on capital or assets, used by many companies (including Dunlop), lays insufficient emphasis on cash and profits *per se*. The second element in financial planning is strict supervision of working capital controls, even extending to assistance in debt collection by another BTR subsidiary, Clear-a-Debt.

Return on sales targets and working capital controls are built into an annual profits plan drawn up by each subsidiary between August and September in a series of negotiations between line managers and Head Office. The objective behind the profit plan is resolved by BTR's MD, while the plan itself is prepared at the level of the business unit for eventual approval by a committee delegated by the Board. The aim is to establish a set of performance targets for the following year which will stretch the companies. Each group files highly detailed monthly reports to BTR's London Head Office. These are compared against the annual profit plan. In line with BTR's highly centralized system of financial controls, each business unit also prepares a three-year strategic plan which emphasizes the devolution of responsibility for the direction of businesses to managers in the field. As a result, many Dunlop managers felt they had much more freedom than under the old system of interference from a Head Office which 'wanted to know what was going on in all corners of the business'. This was reflected in the removal of the frequent conflicts over capital expenditure which characterized the old Dunlop regime. The lifting of these restrictions meant that many more attractive projects could be developed and promoted so long as the target growth in both profit and sales was achieved. However, ultimate control over project approval remained with Head Office.

The whole process of deciding on the development of a new set of financial controls and the absorption of the old Dunlop into the expanded BTR took only four weeks. By early 1987, the process could be judged a success as measured in terms of the profits of the Slazenger division, up from £9m in 1985 to £16m in 1986, by a significant expansion in advertising budgets for consumer goods activities and by making available more capital to fund long-term investments to provide extra capacity to produce goods hitherto made in the Far East.

22.8   Assessing the impact of mergers

Investigating the effects of merger activity is one of the busiest areas of contemporary applied finance research. There are two main ways of attempting to assess the impact of mergers.

The first is based on examining the key financial characteristics of both acquiring and acquired firms before the takeover to study whether they are more or less profitable than firms not involved in acquisitions, and whether their profitability improves after the acquisition. The second is based on examining the impact of the takeover on the share prices of both acquired and acquiring firms to assess the extent to which expected benefits from merger are impounded in share prices and how these are shared between the two sets of shareholders.

The 'financial characteristics approach' suffers from severe limitations:

1. Different accounting conventions used by different firms, e.g. treatment of extraordinary items, often makes comparisons misleading.
2. Post-acquisition measures of profitability may be distorted due to the application of acquisition accounting procedures. If substantial amounts of goodwill are written off after the takeover, the return on investment may look considerably higher because the capital base is lower.
3. To assess properly the impact of the takeover really requires an extended analysis ranging over, say, five to ten years. Many acquisitions are undertaken for 'strategic' purposes, the benefits of which may only show through after several accounting periods perhaps following lengthy and costly reorganization. Very frequently, when 'efficient' companies take over 'inefficient' companies, their return on net assets and fixed asset turnover ratios automatically fall.
4. Accounting studies are not capable of assessing what the performance of the expanded group would have been in the absence of the merger and are thus unable to assess what improvement in performance (if any) was due to factors beyond the merger *per se*. This problem increases with the time period used for the post-merger investigation.
5. The approach does not allow for risk. If the aim of many mergers is to lower total risk (possibly for managerial reasons), or to shift the company into a lower Beta activity, a lower return post-merger is not especially surprising, since according to the EMH/CAPM, relatively low risk securities offer relatively low returns.

The second method, which we may call the 'capital markets approach', caters for many of these difficulties, and is thus the most frequently used mode of analysis. By adopting a CAPM framework, it enables the returns on shares of acquiring firms to be examined prior to and following the merger. As noted in Chapter 10, the market model indicates that the expected return on any security, j, in any time period t, ER_{jt}, is a linear function of the expected return on the market portfolio:

$$ER_{jt} = \alpha_{jt} + \beta_j ER_{mt}$$

However, the *actual* return in any time period, R_{jt}, results from a compound of market-related factors and company-specific factors:

$$R_{jt} = \alpha_{jt} + \beta_j R_{mt} + u_{jt}$$

u_{jt} is an error term with zero expected value, indicating that random company-specific factors are expected to cancel out over several time periods.

If, over a suitable period of time, we examine the actual pattern of returns, allowing for overall movements in the market, the differences between the expected returns and the actual returns, the ('residuals' or 'abnormal returns'), should sum to zero, i.e. the expected value of the cumulated differences between ER_{jt} and R_{jt} is zero.

A takeover bid is a company-specific event likely to raise share price, and hence the return on holding the shares. When a bid occurs, the increase in returns can be attributed to the market's assessment of the impact of the bid, i.e. the evaluation of its likelihood of success, and if successful, its appraisal of the benefits likely to ensue. Therefore, both in the period

Table 22.4   Pre- and post-bid returns

Kenning Motor Group

Time Period (months)	Share Price (p)	Actual Return (%)	Expected Return (%)	Residual	Cumulated Residual
−3	140	−3.45	−0.29	−3.16	−3.16
−2	160	14.29	1.67	12.61	9.45
−1	158	−1.25	−6.64	−7.89	1.56
0	212	34.18	7.63	26.54	28.10
1	268	26.42	−0.19	26.60	54.70
2	310	15.67	−3.04	18.71	73.41
3	310	0	3.08	−3.08	70.33
Tozer–Kemsley–Milbourn					
−3	66	−2.94	−0.32	−2.62	−2.62
−2	81	22.73	1.87	20.86	18.24
−1	108	33.33	7.42	25.91	44.15
0	136	25.93	8.53	17.39	61.54
1	177	30.15	−0.21	30.36	91.90
2	172	−2.82	−3.40	0.58	92.48
3	180	4.65	3.44	1.21	93.69

Source: Data collected by Krista Bromley.

leading up to the bid, as the potential bidder builds a stake, and also on the day of announcement of the bid, we might expect the residuals to be non-negative. For example, if the market thinks the takeover is a mistake for the acquiror, we may find negative residuals for the bidder, but positive residuals for the target, if, as usually happens, the share price of the target rises sharply. Hence, the cumulated residual returns may be taken as an assessment of the value of the takeover to the shareholders of the acquiror and acquiree companies, respectively.

To illustrate this use of the market model, consider the data in Table 22.4. This relates to the successful takeover bid by the conglomerate Tozer Kemsley Milbourn (TKM), in 1986, of the Kenning Motor Group. There was a degree of industrial logic in this bid as both TKM and Kennings retailed motor cars, and Kennings operated a substantial car hire business. Kennings had attempted in previous years to diversify, but due to the haphazard selection of targets and poorly executed integration, its core business was suffering, reflected in declining profitability and weakening cash flow. The data show the residual returns for both companies in the three months prior to, and also following the bid, while month 0 is the day of the bid, eventually completed at a price of £3.10.

The data clearly show positive residuals for Kennings, both before the bid, on the day of the bid itself, and also in the following periods as TKM raised its bid. In this case, both sets of shareholders enjoyed substantial returns. After allowing for the movement in the market as a whole, the returns on the shares of both companies were substantially positive, indicating market expectations that this merger would be wealth-creating. This proved to be the case, following very swift and effective reorganization of Kenning by TKM.

However, until recently, the bulk of the empirical evidence (e.g. see surveys by Jensen and Ruback 1983; DTI 1988; Mathur 1989) suggested that positive gains from takeovers accrue almost entirely to the shareholders of target firms. While the average abnormal returns (the cumulated residuals for all firms divided by the number of firms examined in the study) recorded in these studies are invariably positive and statistically significant, returns to the shareholders of bidding firms are negative for mergers and not significantly different from zero for takeovers. In other words, *on average*, takeovers and mergers are not wealth-creating, but the acquisition process transfers wealth from the shareholders of acquirors to those of acquirees. These are very important results as they seem to question the judgement or the motives, or both, of the instigators of takeover bids.

However, a more recent and very significant study by Franks and Harris (1989), based on both UK and US data, has contradicted much earlier work in an important respect. The study is especially important for two reasons. First, the authors have taken mergers and takeovers over a much longer period (1955–85) than most other studies; and second, they examined a considerably larger sample than any previous study. For the United Kingdom, 1900 acquisitions involving 1,058 bidders were studied and the US sample was 1,555 acquisitions involving 850 bidders. The targets were all publicly traded, facilitating a capital markets approach. Table 22.5 shows their results in terms of excess stock market returns as compared to the market portfolio, and allowing for systematic risk.

As with earlier studies, these data record a substantial increase in wealth for the shareholders of target firms, but unlike earlier ones, they reveal a relatively smaller, but statistically significant increase in wealth for the shareholders of acquirors over the whole period leading up to and just after the bid.

A subsequent study by Limmack (1991), using only UK data for the period 1977–86, suggests that 'the gains made by target company shareholders are at the expense of shareholders of bidder companies'. He also suggests that the average wealth decreases suffered by the shareholders of bidding companies are mainly confined to the period 1977–80, and that bids made in the years 1981–6 produce no significant wealth decrease for shareholders of bidding firms.

These may prove significant findings as they may imply that bidding firms and the capital market in general may have learned from earlier mistakes and perhaps subsequent studies will show overall net gains. What may prove equally significant would be a study of bids made in the heady years of stock market boom, when one suspects many bids were ill-considered compared to bids made in years of greater stock market stability. However, an alternative methodology might be appropriate to focus the study on the real gains from

Table 22.5 The gains from mergers

	UK Month		US Month	
	0	−4 to +1	0	−4 to +1
Targets	+24%	+31%	+16%	+24%
Bidders	+1%	+8%	+1%	+4%

Source: Franks and Harris (1989).

merger using physical measures, such as productivity improvements, although, of course, these should be translated into share price gains in an efficient capital market.

In the next section, we return to a recurrent theme in this book, the meaning and reliability of the values placed on companies by the stock market.

22.9   Value gaps

Evidence from *some* studies indicates that there may be net gains from merger, while *most* surveys indicate that the shareholders of target companies experience a beneficial wealth effect. The near-certainty that shareholders of targets will benefit suggests that market values typically fall short of the value that potential or actual bidders would place on them. These disparities in value are called *value gaps*.

There are numerous explanations as to how they arise. One explanation is that it 'must' cost more to obtain overall control of a company rather than simply to participate in its profits. Control confers the right to intervene in the operation of the company, to restructure its activities, to integrate some operations with those of the parent, to shut down or sell others, and to introduce a new management team. From the standpoint of the bidders, it is these opportunities to intervene, and their prospective pay-offs, which generate the extra value to justify the acquisition premium.

But this raises an interesting conundrum. If the bidder can perceive the benefits from a different mode of operation, why do existing managers and shareholders (not to mention financial advisers) also not devote attention to alternative *modus operandi* for these companies? Is the persistence of a value gap a reflection of poor 'corporate parenting'? If a bidder can perceive from the outside that it could add value by changes in management and in strategic development, why can the existing parent not arrive at the same conclusion and implement the appropriate policy changes?

Of course, value gaps may be a reflection of the market's inability to value a company's shares correctly. Alternatively, it could be that takeover bidders persistently delude themselves into believing that their targets are worth more than the market suggests, but, if this is correct, why do bidders not learn from experience?

There are perhaps four possible explanations for value gaps.

Poor corporate parenting

Value gaps may arise because some business segments do not make their maximum possible profit contributions to the parent. Ultimately, this is a reflection of poor central management, which is thus failing to add value to the group or actually reducing value. Examples of management deficiencies are:

1. Some assets, such as land and premises, may not be fully exploited by either the parent or its subsidiaries.
2. The parent pursues too many ventures of dubious value, perhaps intending to gain entry into other areas of business, but in which it does not possess appropriate expertise.

3. The HQ may fail to take sufficiently decisive action to prevent or correct poor profitability in business segments.
4. The HQ may indulge in costly central activities or services which are a net burden rather than benefit to business units.
5. Poor group structure may leave business units at a disadvantage compared to competitors. For example, a business unit may be too small to compete effectively in its main markets, or it may be denied sufficient capital resources to develop its activities. As a result, it may have a greater value under alternative, more perceptive management.

Poor financial management

The HQ corporate finance department might have followed a gearing policy which fails to exploit its ability fully to borrow and gear up returns to equity; or alternatively, it may be chronically over-borrowed. Similarly, its past dividend policy may have been over- or under-generous.

Over-enthusiastic bidding

It has been said that takeover bidders' greatest victims are themselves. Many bids are undoubtedly successful, for example, BP's acquisition of Britoil in order to obtain the latter's oil reserves. However, many others, like the Trustee Savings Bank's acquisition of the merchant bank Hill Samuel, are outright failures; and some, such as British and Commonwealth Holdings' purchase of Atlantic Computers, are totally disastrous. Perhaps, at the time of the bid, the assessment of the bidding management was correct, but they were caught out by changed circumstances. A more likely explanation is that they were buoyed-up with excessive enthusiasm about the bid. Although some bidders have the sense to walk away from a bid which they realize is ill-advised (for example, Meggitts' aborted bid for United Scientific Holdings), in too many cases bidders convince themselves that the proposed takeover is vital to the development of the group.

Stock market inefficiency

Does the stock market fail to assess the full value of a business, because it belongs to a sector which is 'out of favour', or because the market adopts too short-term a view of the prospects of the company?

Assessing the relative weights of these arguments is a major challenge for finance and business researchers.

22.10   Corporate restructuring

Acquisitions and mergers are not the only vehicles by which management can enhance shareholder value by changing the ownership structure. *Corporate restructuring*, as it is generally called, is an important strategic topic which we address in this section.

Corporate restructuring involves three key elements:

1. Concentration of equity ownership in the hands of managers or 'inside' investors well-placed to monitor managers' efforts.
2. Substitution of debt for equity.
3. Redefinition of organizational boundaries through mergers, divestment and management buy-outs, etc.

In the dynamic environment within which companies operate, the financial managers should be ever-alert to new and better ways of structuring and financing their businesses. The value-creation process will involve the following:

1. Review the corporate financial structure from the shareholders' viewpoint. Consider whether changes in capital structure, business mix or ownership would enhance value.
2. Increase efficiency and reduce the after-tax cost of capital through the judicious use of borrowing.
3. Improve operating cash flows through focusing on wealth-creating investment opportunities (i.e. having positive net present values), profit improvement and overhead reduction programmes and divestiture.
4. Pursue financially-driven value creation using various new financing instruments and arrangements (i.e. financial engineering).

Types of restructuring

A feature of the 1980s and 1990s has been the development of new and elaborate methods of corporate restructuring. Restructuring can occur at three different levels.

Corporate restructuring refers to changing the ownership structure of the parent company to enhance shareholder value. Such changes can arise through diversification, introducing new types of share, share repurchase, forming strategic alliances, leveraged buy-outs and even liquidation.

Business restructuring considers changing the ownership structure at the strategic business unit level. Examples include acquisitions, joint ventures, divestments and management buy-outs.

Asset restructuring refers to changing the ownership of assets. This can be achieved through sale and leaseback arrangements, offering assets as security, factoring debts and asset disposals.

Most of the above-mentioned restructuring devices have been covered elsewhere in this book. We devote the next section to a brief discussion on share repurchase, divestments and Management Buy-Outs (MBOs) which have received only passing mention to date.

Share repurchase

Until fairly recently it was illegal in the United Kingdom for a company to repurchase its shares in issue. The Companies Act 1981 gave companies the right, subject to fulfilling certain conditions, to buy back some of its shares from willing shareholders. The main benefits of such a scheme include:

1. Increasing earnings per share and share price through a reduction of the number of shares in issue.
2. Enabling companies experiencing a temporary or permanent decline in their business to readjust their equity base to more appropriate levels.
3. Increasing gearing. Where a company wants to become more highly geared without increasing its total long-term funding, share repurchase enables debt-for-equity substitution.

While share repurchase schemes offer certain attractions to companies, the return of monies to some shareholders ahead of lenders and creditors will require certain additional undertakings to be given – for example, lenders may impose additional restrictive covenants in order to safeguard their position and to limit their potential risk.

Divestment

A *divestment* is the opposite of an investment or acquisition; it is the sale of part of a company (e.g. assets, product lines, divisions, brands, etc.) to a third party. The heavy use of divestment as a means of restructuring reflects the continuing efforts by corporate management to adjust to changing economic and political environments.

No management team relishes the prospect of divesting itself of certain business activities, but it is often necessary as the strategic focus changes. Examples of divestment motives include:

1. *Dismantling conglomerates* originally created by merger activity through defensive diversification strategies. One result of the unsuccessful takeover attempt for BAT Industries was that this heavily diversified company was obliged to restructure by divesting a number of its activities.
2. *A change in strategic focus.* This may involve a move away from the core business to new strategic opportunities.
3. *Harvesting past successes*, making cash flow available for new opportunities. Hanson plc has been successful with such a strategy.
4. *Discarding unwanted businesses* following an acquisition. Often such sell-offs are planned at the time of the bid.
5. *Reversing (or learning from) mistakes.*

Divestments enable companies to move their resources to higher-value investment opportunities. They should be evaluated along exactly the same lines as investment decisions, based on the net present value resulting from the divestment.

Management buy-outs

Management buy-outs (MBOs) occur when the management of a company 'buy out' a distinct part of the business which the company is seeking to divest. MBOs usually arise because a parent company decides to divest a subsidiary for strategic reasons. For example, it may decide to exit a certain activity; to sell off an unwanted subsidiary acquired by a takeover of the parent company; to improve the strategic fit of its various business units, or simply to concentrate on its core activities. MBOs can also be purchaser-driven, where the management recognizes that the business has greater potential than the parent company management realizes.

The growth in MBOs has been made possible by the ability of managers to raise large sums of capital through borrowings (leveraged buy-outs), particularly mezzanine finance (a cross between debt and equity) offering lenders a high coupon rate and, frequently, the right to convert to equity should the company achieve a quotation. The Finance Act 1981 gave considerable help here by allowing finance raised to be secured on the acquired assets.

How does restructuring enhance shareholder value? We suggest four ways in which value can be created.

Business fit and focus

As we saw with divestments, a business unit may 'fit' one company better than another. Management should review its strategy, i.e. business units, and ask whether it operates best under its present ownership or whether it would create more value under some other ownership through an external acquisition or management buy-out. When unrelated activities have been divested, management has a much better focus on its core businesses and can concentrate on pursuing wealth-creating investment opportunities and improving efficiencies.

Eliminate sub-standard investment

Managers commonly enter into investments which do not enhance shareholder value.

- Heavy reliance on a single business may lead to diversification. Quite apart from the additional overheads that may be created from diversification and the lack of managerial expertise, such diversification may do no real favours for shareholders. As we saw in Chapters 9 and 10, shareholders can often achieve the same, if not better, risk-reduction effects by creating diversified portfolios.
- Pursuit of growth in sales and earnings brings power and, possibly, protection from takeover, but does little for shareholders. Rather than pay out larger dividends, management may be tempted to reinvest in projects or acquisitions which do not add value.
- While a strategic business unit may be profitable, it is often an amalgamation of profitable and unprofitable projects, the former subsidizing the latter. Restructuring the business creates a leaner operation with no room for cross-subsidization.

Judicious use of debt

Cautious managers argue that borrowing should be minimized as it increases financial risk and leaves little room for errors. Aggressive managers take a very different view.

The requirement to repay debt provides a powerful incentive to improve performance and minimize errors. Few people thought 'Just-in-Time' production processes or 'zero-defects' possible – but the Japanese showed otherwise. By deliberately taking the slack from the system, the operation becomes more efficient. The same applies to debt finance. The consequences of management's successes and mistakes are magnified through gearing, leaving little room for error. Managerial mediocrity is no longer acceptable. Debt is hard and unforgiving. Cash flow – not profit – becomes the all-important yardstick, for it is cash flow that must be generated to service the debt and meet repayment schedules. In this report, incurring debt obligations may provide an important signal to the market concerning the resolve of the management team.

Furthermore, debt is a cheaper source of finance because interest is tax-deductible, while dividends on equity are not. Restructuring the balance sheet by substituting debt for equity, within acceptable gearing limits, creates a Tax Shield and increases the company's market value.

Incentives

Raising debt to realize equity can be a powerful incentive to both shareholders and managers. Equity is concentrated in the hands of fewer shareholders, providing a greater incentive to monitor managerial actions. This often leads to the creation of managerial incentives to enhance shareholder value, through executive share option or profit-sharing schemes, giving managers an equity stake in the company. Remuneration packages may increase profit-related pay at the expense of salaries and wages. This will also benefit loan stock holders who have priority ahead of profit sharing but after employees' wages and salaries.

22.11   Summary

In this chapter, we have explored various motives for merger and takeover activity, and argued the importance of a coherently structured strategic approach to acquisitions, which incorporates a planned integration process emphasizing human and organizational factors. Finally, we briefly discussed some examples of 'corporate restructuring'.

Key points

- The decision to acquire another company is an investment decision and requires evaluation on similar criteria to the purchase of other assets.
- Added complications are the resistance of incumbent managers in the case of hostile bids and the presence of long-term strategic factors.
- The takeovers most likely to succeed are those approached with a strategic focus, incorporating a detailed analysis of the objectives of the takeover, the possible alternatives and how the acquiree can be integrated into the new parent.

- If the takeover mechanism works well, it is an effective and valuable way of clearing out managerial dead wood.
- Many takeovers appear to be launched for 'managerial' motives such as personal and financial aggrandisement.
- The main reasons for failure of takeovers are poor motivation and evaluation, excessive outlays, often with borrowed capital, and poorly planned and executed integration.
- The complexity of takeover integration is related to the motive for the takeover itself, ranging from cash generation, requiring only a loose control over operations, to economies of scale, requiring highly detailed integration.
- The impact of mergers can be studied by comparing the financial characteristics of merger-active and merger-inactive firms to assess any performance differentials, but this approach suffers from many problems.
- The main alternative is a capital market-based approach to assess how the market judges a merger in terms of share price movements.
- The available evidence suggests that the bulk of the gains from mergers accrue to shareholders of acquired companies, although evidence is emerging that shareholders of acquirors can also share in the benefits, presumably if the takeover is well considered.
- Corporate restructuring enhances shareholder value through (i) improving the business fit and focus, (ii) judicious use of debt, and (iii) providing incentives for management.

22.12   Case study: BAT Industries plc

Introduction

In July 1989, a consortium assuming the name Hoylake announced a bid of £13.4 billion for the conglomerate BAT (British American Tobacco) Industries plc. As BAT was then the third largest corporation in the United Kingdom, this event shattered the illusion held by many directors that size alone was a guarantee of immunity from assault by takeover raiders. The motive for the proposed takeover was to 'unbundle' BAT's assets, which, according to Hoylake, were undervalued by the market. Unbundling is a latter-day euphemism for 'asset-stripping' or breaking up the target company in order to resell the component segments at an overall profit.

A remarkable bid

The bid was significant for a number of reasons, apart from its sheer size.

(1) It was launched by a company formed specifically for the purpose of mounting the bid. The founders of Hoylake were three wealthy financiers: the Australian media tycoon Kerry Packer, retailing entrepreneur Sir James Goldsmith and merchant banker Jacob Rothschild.

(2) It was to be financed, not by a cash offer, but by an issue of 'junk bonds', the first time this financing vehicle had been used in the United Kingdom, at least on anywhere like this

scale. Junk bonds are essentially IOUs, which issuers intend to redeem using the proceeds from selling the assets of the dismembered firm. They involve high risks partly because suitable buyers for the unbundled assets may be difficult to find at the right price (although skilled junk-financed takeover exponents are careful to line up buyers prior to bidding). They are also exposed to interest rate increases, which undermine their value. Due to these risks, high yields have to be offered in order to encourage the equity holders of the target to accept 'junk' in exchange for their shares. Previously, most successful asset-stripping, such as the takeover by Hanson of Imperial Tobacco, had been financed by share exchange or a combination of shares and cash/borrowing, exerting less pressure on the bidder-stripper to dispose of assets in a hurry.

(3) The unbundling motivation behind the bid indicated a belief that BAT had a break-up value considerably above its market capitalization. This aspect was especially significant as it threw into question both the wisdom of BAT's past diversification strategy and also raised doubts about the efficiency of the market's valuation of BAT. Clearly, the identity of potential bidders cannot often be predicted, but perhaps the market might have identified BAT as a potential takeover target, especially as bigger (i.e. more expensive) bids had already been successfully mounted in the United States, e.g. the junk-financed bid by Kohlberg–Kravis–Roberts for RJR Nabisco.

(4) The BAT defence strategy, as revealed in its defence document *Building Shareholder Value*, was a novel mixture of tactical devices. In many respects, it amounted to a volte face of both prior financial and business strategies.

(5) Because of BAT's overseas ramifications, the bid raised important issues relating to regulation of takeover activity, and the ownership of major financial services concerns.

BAT's financial record: implications for diversification

More generally, the bid raised issues about the rationality of conglomerate diversification. BAT had historically derived the bulk of its profits and cash flow from overseas tobacco operations, in which it possessed virtual monopolies in many markets. However, acknowledging the accumulation of medical evidence on the harmful effects of smoking, BAT increasingly perceived tobacco as a declining market, at least in Western and more health-conscious societies. Consequently, it decided to use the strong and continuing cash flows from this source to buy into other activities, most notably, retailing, paper and packaging, cosmetics and, eventually, financial services. Many of these diversifications, such as Macfisheries (later known as International Stores), the Yardley cosmetics business and the Mardon packaging operation were disappointing and were subsequently sold off.

By the late 1980s, BAT's profits were earned from six areas, including its share of associated company earnings. Exhibit I shows key financial data for the 'old' BAT group over the period 1984–9 from both the Income Statements and also the Balance Sheets. Exhibit II shows the performance of the individual divisions in terms of turnover and operating profits, and also gives the asset base for each segment. Exhibit III shows the segmental contributions for the years 1986–1990, restated to reflect the post-bid restructuring.

Exhibit I   (A) BAT income statement, 1984–9

	Year ending 31 December:					
	1984	1985	1986	1987	1988	1989
Turnover (£m)	18,203	17,051	19,167	17,208	17,653	21,636
Operating profit (£m)	1,465	1,287	1,483	1,396	1,604	2,197
Profit after tax (£m)	873	736	869	868	1,038	1,271
Attributable to						
BAT shareholders	784	673	793	787	949	1,172
Extraordinary items	64	(34)	75	(36)	15	123
Profit for the year	848	639	868	751	965	1,295
Dividends (net)	151	179	209	248	299	443
Dividend per share (p)	10.30	12.10	14.30	16.90	20.10	30.00
EPS (p)	53.60	45.72	53.51	52.78	62.81	76.75

Source: BAT Annual Report 1989.

Exhibit I   (B) Balance Sheets, 1984–9

31 December Balance Sheet	1984	1985	1986	1987	1988	1989
Tangible fixed assets	2,820	2,482	2,524	2,178	2,257	2,659
Investments in financial						
services subsidiaries	941	1,142	1,482	1,503	3,583	4,229
Other fixed assets	1,034	719	588	488	560	570
Stocks	2,640	2,238	2,146	1,810	1,939	2,235
Other current assets	2,629	2,244	2,635	2,542	1,575	1,862
Total assets	10,064	8,825	9,375	8,521	9,914	11,555
BAT Industries' shareholders'						
funds	4,276	3,660	4,174	3,946	3,601	4,683
Interest of minority shareholders	422	347	413	347	340	406
Shareholders' funds	4,698	4,007	4,587	4,293	3,941	5,089
Provisions for liabilities						
and charges	518	656	683	629	684	748
Borrowings – due beyond one year	1,986	1,453	1,338	1,171	2,089	2,374
Borrowings – due within one year	555	577	551	300	572	340
Other creditors	2,307	2,132	2,216	2,128	2,628	3,004
Total funds employed	10,064	8,825	9,375	8,521	9,914	11,555

Source: BAT Annual Report 1989

Exhibit II   Segmental performance, 1984–9 (old group)

		(all figures are %s of the relevant totals)				
		1984	*1985*	*1986*	*1987*	*1988*	*1989*
A	TURNOVER						
	Tobacco	38	37	38	35	34	33
	Retailing	25	23	21	19	19	18
	Paper	8	8	9	9	9	8
	Other trading activities	8	7	4	3	3	3
	Commercial activities	79	75	72	66	65	62
	Financial services	6	12	15	20	18	22
	Share of associated companies	15	13	13	14	17	16
	Total sales	100	100	100	100	100	100
B	OPERATING PROFITS						
	Tobacco	48	50	46	46	41	38
	Retailing	15	11	12	13	10	8
	Paper	10	12	14	13	12	9
	Other trading activities	5	4	I	1	1	1
	Commercial activities	78	77	73	73	64	56
	Financial services	9	10	18	16	24	33
	Share of associated companies	13	13	9	11	12	11
	Operating profits	100	100	100	100	100	100
C	OPERATING ASSETS						
	Tobacco	32	30	32	30	23	25
	Retailing	30	31	24	22	17	17
	Paper	10	11	12	14	11	10
	Other trading activities	10	7	9	8	6	5
	Commercial activities	82	79	77	74	57	57
	Financial services	10	14	18	22	39	39
	Share of associated companies	8	7	5	4	4	4
	Operating assets	100	100	100	100	100	100

Source: BAT Annual Reports (1984–9).

Exhibit III Segmental contributions 1986–90 (continuing group)

			(all figures are %s of relevant totals)		
A	Turnover (including Associated companies)	*1986*	*1987*	*1988*	*1989*	*1990*

		1986	*1987*	*1988*	*1989*	*1990*
	Financial Services:					
	General business	13	14	18	21	20
	Life business	13	16	14	17	16
	Commercial activities:					
	Tobacco	64	60	58	54	57
	Other trading activities	10	10	10	8	7
	Continuing Group	100	100	100	100	100
B	Operating Profit					
	Financial services:					
	General business:	20	17	27	34	(3)
	Life business	8	10	10	13	21
	Commercial activities:					
	Tobacco	70	72	62	53	85
	Other trading activities	5	5	5	3	1
	Share of associates' net interest	(3)	(4)	(4)	(3)	(4)
	Operating profit: continuing group	100	100	100	100	100

Source: BAT Annual Report (1990).

Exhibit IV (A) BAT share price movements relative to FTSE 100 Share Index

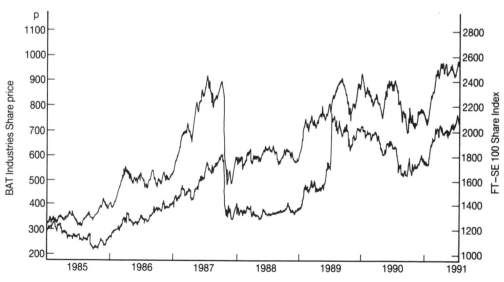

Source: Extel Financial Microview.

Exhibit IV   (B) BAT Beta values

As at October 1985	0.98
,, ,, ,, 1986	0.93
,, ,, ,, 1987	0.95
,, ,, ,, 1988	1.14
,, ,, ,, 1989	1.19
,, ,, ,, 1990	1.12
,, ,, ,, 1991	1.15

Source: LBS Risk Measurement Service.

Exhibit I suggests that the old conglomeration of activities was not especially profitable. Over the period 1984–8, nominal operating profit grew erratically at an average annual rate of about 2.5 per cent, EPS growth was equally sluggish at about 4 per cent on average, while sales actually fell. Poor bottom-line performance was also reflected in below par share price performance in the rising markets of the 1980s.

Exhibit IV (A) shows the movement of the BAT ordinary share price in relation to the FTSE 100 Index over the period 1985–91, underperforming the market prior to the bid and outperforming it following the bid. Beta values for BAT for the same period are also given in Exhibit IV (B).

The valuation of BAT: dividend policy and investment strategy

While it is commonplace for bidders to offer above the market price for their targets, the magnitude of the bid – £13.4 billion – surprised many observers when the market value was only around £8.5 billion. This prompted numerous attempts to assess the 'true' value of BAT. For example, stockbrokers Hoare-Govett reckoned that BAT's components could be sold for some £16.7 billion.

A distinction ought to be made between 'sum-of-the-parts' valuations, which place a value on each segment of the company assuming that the individual units are quoted as separate entities, and 'break-up' valuations, which assume that the individual parts are each sold off to the highest bidders. However, most 'after-the-event' observers were agreed that BAT had in some sense been undervalued by the market, but there was less agreement as to why.

Intimately connected with the issue of whether the market had correctly valued BAT was the relationship between dividend policy and the financing of corporate diversification strategy. In a letter to *The Financial Times* (penned well before the publication of BAT's defence document), a unit trust manager attempted to explain why BAT was apparently undervalued and why a shift in dividend policy was required. The writer forcefully argued that past failure to pay higher dividends was responsible for the apparent undervaluation:

> profits are not being distributed on sufficient a scale to the shareholders; they
> may be merely piling up in cash or equivalent form, or being ploughed back
> into acquisitions at prices which absorb much of the cash flow.

He went on to state:

> Distributing more of your profits to shareholders raises your share price. There
> may be limits of prudence here, but these limits are nowhere near tested by
> most companies. The standard defence against high distribution – the need for
> re-investment for future growth – is also greatly overplayed. If assets are
> profitable they can be financed by many other means than retentions.
> Companies fool themselves if they think that retentions are 'cheap finance'.
> They are not. They ultimately cost the standard rate, the cost of capital, which
> is partly a function of the company's actual share price. High retentions
> depress share prices.

In its defence document, *Building Shareholder Value*, highlights of which are shown in
Exhibit V, the BAT board recognized that BAT was a conglomerate which had grown
beyond its optimum size and was insufficiently 'focused' on its core activities of tobacco and
financial services. It undertook to divest various assets, including VG Instruments, retail
stores in the United States, France and West Germany, to give away shares in Argos and
Wiggins-Teape-Appleton and also to pay higher dividends in the future. The defence
document declared:

> The 1989 dividend payout will be significantly increased through the proposed
> second interim dividend of 10.3p and the proposed final dividend of 10.4p. As
> a result, dividend cover will be reduced from 3.1 times in 1988 to around 2.6

Exhibit V   Highlights of the BAT defence

BAT INDUSTRIES

Building Shareholder Value

An outstanding 1989

■ Forecast pre-tax profits of approximately £2 billion
   – up 22 per cent
■ Forecast earnings per share of approximately 76.5 p
   – up 22 per cent
■ Proposed further dividends of 20.7 p
   Total for the year of 30 pence – up 49 per cent

An outstanding future

■ A group focused on financial services and tobacco with forecast 1989 pre-tax profits
   of approximately £1.64 billion
   – equal to the entire Group in 1988
■ A direct stake in:
   – Argos, one of the UK retailing success stories of the decade, with forecast 1989
      trading profits of approximately £63 million
   – Wiggins Teape and Appleton, a combined international force in specialist paper
      and pulp, with forecast 1989 trading profits of approximately £212 million
■ A higher dividend payout ratio starting in 1989
■ Proposals to authorize the buy-back of up to 10 per cent of the company's shares
■ The orderly divestment of US retailing and certain other businesses

---

times in 1989. The strong cash flow and the quality of earnings of the continuing group should enable us to increase the level of payout further, reducing cover to 2.0–2.5 times in future years.

Clearly, this was a major shift in dividend policy reflecting a great belief (or hope) in the power of dividend payouts to increase share price and secure shareholder loyalty.

Attitudes of the regulatory authorities

A further complication in the BAT episode was the interaction between UK takeover regulations and the complexity introduced by BAT's ownership of the Farmers insurance company, acquired only in 1988, as part of its strategy of diversification into financial services. Under UK regulations, a bid must be completed within 60 days (unless another bidder emerges). US insurance industry regulations require investigation by, and the approval of, state insurance commissioners before an insurance company can change hands. The required procedures are extremely tortuous, as BAT had itself found when it acquired Farmers, having to fight off objections in state after state in which Farmers operated. Because of the expected length of the forthcoming proceedings, the UK Take-Over Panel granted BAT an extension of the bid until the US authorities had pronounced. In effect, the UK takeover rules were being bent to accommodate the requirements of an extra-territorial authority.

Meanwhile, the Secretary of State for Trade and Industry, Nicholas Ridley, had decided not to refer the bid to the Monopolies and Mergers Commission for investigation, as it appeared to raise no issues relating to competition, the major criterion by which the merits of takeovers and mergers were appraised at this time. Many observers felt that there were, however, broader public interest issues involved in the bid relating to the proposed method of financing.

During the US hearings, it transpired that Hoylake had lined up a buyer for Farmers, should the bid succeed, namely, the French insurance company, Axa-Midi (which had also undertaken to pay the bulk of the US legal fees, amounting to over £60m). As a result, the US regulators were now deliberating the merits of not one, but two changes of ownership.

In the event, despite the accommodating stance of the UK authorities, the bid foundered before the insurance commissioner for California, Roxani Gillespie, who apparently was concerned by Axa-Midi's proposed method of financing. The French firm intended to borrow some $4.5 billion to finance the Farmers purchase. This was regarded as likely to leave Axa-Midi with an excessively high gearing level, especially at a time when the whole US financial system was already reeling from the failure of the Savings and Loans Associations (the US equivalent of building societies).

The bid was also killed by the collapse in junk-bond financing in the US due to rising interest rates and a series of scandals involving market manipulation by certain junk-bond dealers. Interest rate increases squeezed junk bond issuers in two ways. First, the return they had to pay increased substantially, as many such bonds were linked to underlying interest rates. Second, the higher interest rates made it harder to sell assets quickly for the handsome prices required to redeem the debt obligations.

Exhibit VI BAT's main divestments

Disposals:	VG Instruments	£186m
	Breuners Retail	$92.5m
	Breuners Rental	$15m
	Marshall Fields	$1.1bn
	Saks Fifth Avenue	$1.5bn
	Ivey's	$110m
	Eurotec	£155m
	Horten AG	£140m
Flotations:	Argos	£600m
	Wiggins Teape	£1.05bn

Exhibit VII Bid timetable

1989

11 July	Launch of £13.4 billion bid by Hoylake.
31 July	Californian regulators insist on scrutinizing the effect of the bid on the Farmers insurance subsidiary.
8 August	The Hoylake offer document accuses BAT of failing in its past business strategy.
23 August	Hoylake agrees sale of Farmers for £3 billion to Axa-Midi if US authorities agree change of ownership.
15 September	Hoylake wins extension of bid timetable.
21 September	Hoylake bid cleared by Monopolies and Mergers Commission
23 September	BAT announces break-up plans.

1990

13 February	California hearings begin.
15 March	Details of Argos demerger announced: one free Argos share for every five BAT shares held.
21 March	BAT reports 24 per cent profits increase and dividend increase of 49 per cent.
6 April	Argos chain of discount stores floated.
10 April	California rules against Hoylake bid.
19 April	Marshall Fields sold for $1.1 bn.
23 April	Hoylake abandons bid.
25 April	Sale of Saks Fifth Avenue to Investcorp announced.
10 May	Details of Wiggins-Teape demerger announced: one free Wiggins Teape share for every three BAT shares held.
31 May	Disposal of Eurotec announced to Klockner Werke AG.
3 December	Sale of Horten AG announced for £140m to Westdeutsche Landesbank.

The impact of the bid

Meanwhile, by 1990, BAT profitability had improved rapidly (as predicted in the defence document), and it was clear that any new bid would have to be considerably higher, and made in cash form. The major impact of the whole saga was the realization of significant benefits for BAT shareholders. While the US authorities were deliberating, BAT proceeded to sell off many of its now apparently superfluous activities in an effort to focus itself into a two-core business, tobacco and financial services. Not too surprisingly, the BAT chairman, Patrick Sheehy, declared that it was BAT's strategy to do this anyway, decided far in advance of the Hoylake bid.

Whether due to panic response or the product of mature consideration, BAT was widely thought to have realized very fair values for most of its disposals (shown in Exhibit VI), while the proceeds for the US retail operations, Saks Fifth Avenue and Marshall Field were considerably higher than many expected. Indeed, Sir James was moved to admit that the disposal proceeds were around the top end of Hoylake's own valuations. As well as the disposals, shareholders were given free shares in the discount retail chain, Argos, which realized a flotation value of around £600m, and in the paper concern, Wiggins-Teape-Appleton, which floated at £1.05 billion. Analysts reckoned that the BAT financial services interests were worth over £7 billion, while the tobacco business was valued at about £5 billion. The overall value of disposals and the market values of flotations plus the estimated value of the remaining core significantly exceeded both the offer of £13.4 billion and the pre-bid market value of £8.5 billion.

Discussion questions

Now consider the following questions:

1. What light does the BAT experience shed on the arguments for and against corporate diversification?
2. Consider the BAT defence strategy. What implications do these tactics have for BAT's financial strategy, especially its dividend policy, both in its acquisitive phase and also its unbundling phase?
3. If it makes sense for BAT to spin off its stores and other divisions, why should it retain two apparently diverse remnants, tobacco and financial services?
4. To what extent does the BAT episode cast doubt on the validity of the Efficient Markets Hypothesis?

Further reading

Cooke (1986) offers a primer on the various steps in takeover strategy from strategic evaluation to post-audit; similar ground is covered by Payne (1987). The two books by Jones (1982 and 1983) are useful, both as general reference works and for analyses of the integration process. A treatment of the relative importance of different methods of takeover financing can be found in Franks and Harris (1989), while defences against takeover are examined by Ruback (1988) and Gluck (1988). Jensen (1984) analyses the validity of contemporary criticisms of the takeover mechanism. Gray and McDermott (1989) provide an interesting set of case studies of 'mega'-UK takeover battles: see especially that on BTR/Pilkington as an example of one that got away.

For a summary of corporate restructuring and buy-outs in the UK and the rest of Europe see Wright and Robbie (1991) and Walters (1991).

Questions

Self-test questions

1. How does a merger differ from a takeover?
2. Suggest and explain some possible 'managerial motives' for mergers.
3. Why may shareholders prefer to receive a bid via cash rather than in other forms?
4. What are the common causes of failure for takeovers? How would you judge success or failure in this context?
5. What are the key elements in a coherent acquisition strategy?
6. How is the type and motive for takeover related to the likely complexity of integrating the new acquisition?
7. Distinguish between corporate, business and asset restructuring. Give examples of each.
8. Discuss how corporate restructuring can enhance shareholder value.

Exercises

1. As a defence against a possible takeover bid the managing director proposes that Woppit make a bid for Grapper plc, in order to increase Woppit's size and, hence, make a bid for Woppit more difficult. The companies are in the same industry.

   Woppit's equity Beta is 1.2 and Grapper's is 1.05. The risk-free rate and market return are estimated to be 10 per cent and 16 per cent p.a. respectively. The growth rate of after-tax earnings of Woppit in recent years has been 15 per cent p.a. and of Grapper 12 per cent p.a. Both companies maintain an approximately constant dividend payout ratio.

   Woppit's directors require information about how much premium above the current market price to offer for Grapper's shares. Two suggestions are:

   (a) The price should be based upon the Balance Sheet net worth of the company, adjusted for the current value of land and buildings, plus estimated after tax profits for the next five years.
   (b) The price should be based upon a valuation using the dividend valuation model, using existing growth rate estimates.

Summarized financial data for the two companies are shown below:

Most Recent Balance Sheets

		£ million		
		Woppit	Grapper	
Land and buildings (net)[1]		560		150
Plant and machinery (net)		720		280
Stock	340		240	
Debtors	300		210	
Bank	20		40	
	—	660	—	490
Less: Trade creditors	200		110	
Overdraft	30		10	
Tax payable	120		40	
Dividends payable	50		40	
	—	400	—	200
Total assets less current liabilities		1,540		720
Financed by:				
Ordinary shares[2]		200		100
Share premium		420		220
Other reserves		400		300
		1,020		620
Loans due after one year		520		100
		1,540		720

1. Woppit's land and buildings have been recently revalued. Grapper's have not been revalued for four years, during which time the average value of industrial land and buildings has increased by 25 per cent p.a.
2. Woppit 10p par value, Grapper 25p par value

Most Recent Profit and Loss Accounts

	£ million	
	Woppit	Grapper
Turnover	3,500	1,540
Operating profit	700	255
Net interest	120	22
Taxable profit	580	233
Taxation	203	82
Profit attributable to shareholders	377	151
Dividends	113	76
Retained profit	264	75

The current share price of Woppit is 310 pence and of Grapper 470 pence.

Required

(a) Calculate the premium per share above Grapper's current share price that would result from the two suggested valuation methods. Discuss which, if either, of these values should be the bid price.

State clearly any assumptions that you make.

(b) Assess the managing director's strategy of seeking growth by acquisition in order to make a bid for Woppit more difficult.

(c) Illustrate how Woppit might achieve benefits through improvements in operational efficiency if it acquires Grapper.

(ACCA Level 3, December 1990)

(Solution in Appendix A)

2. The board of directors of Oxclose plc is considering making an offer to purchase Satac Ltd, a private limited company in the same industry. If Satac is purchased it is proposed to continue operating the company as a going concern in the same line of business.

Summarized details from the most recent financial accounts of Oxclose and Satac are shown below:

	Oxclose plc Balance Sheet as at 31 March (*£ millions*)		*Satac Ltd* Balance Sheet as at 31 March (*£000s*)	
Freehold property		33		460
Plant and equipment (net)		58		1,310
Stock	29		330	
Debtors	24		290	
Cash	3		20	
Less: Current liabilities	(31)	25	(518)	122
		116		1,892
Financed by				
Ordinary shares[1]		35		160
Reserves		43		964
Shareholders' equity		78		1,124
Medium term bank loans		38		768
		116		1,892

Notes:

1. Oxclose plc 50p ordinary shares, Satac Ltd 25p ordinary shares.

| | *(£ millions)* | | *(£000s)* | |
Year[2]	Profit after tax	Dividend	Profit after tax	Dividend
t − 5	14.30	9.01	143	85
t − 4	15.56	9.80	162	93.5
t − 3	16.93	10.67	151	93.5
t − 2	18.42	11.60	175	102.8
t − 1	20.04	12.62	183	113.1

2. t − 5 is five years ago, t − 1 the most recent year, etc.

Satac's shares are owned by a small number of private individuals. The company is dominated by its managing director who receives an annual salary of £80,000, double the average salary received by managing directors of similar companies. The managing director would be replaced if the company is purchased by Oxclose.

The freehold property of Satac has not been revalued for several years and is believed to have a market value of £800,000.

The Balance Sheet value of plant and equipment is thought to fairly reflect its replacement cost, but its value if sold is not likely to exceed £800,000. Approximately £55,000 of stock is obsolete and could only be sold as scrap for £5,000.

The ordinary shares of Oxclose are currently trading at 430p ex-div. It is estimated that because of differences in size, risk and other factors the required return on equity by shareholders of Satac is approximately 15 per cent higher than the required return on equity of Oxclose's shareholders (i.e. 115 per cent of Oxclose's required return). Both companies are subject to Corporate Taxation at a rate of 40 per cent.

Required

(a) Prepare estimates of the value of Satac using three different methods of valuation, and advise the board of Oxclose plc as to the price, or possible range of prices, that it should be prepared to offer to purchase Satac's shares.

(b) Briefly discuss the theoretical and practical problems of the valuation methods that you have chosen.

(c) Discuss the advantages and disadvantages of the various terms that might be offered to the shareholders of a potential 'victim' company in a takeover situation.

(ACCA Level 3, December 1986)

3. Craig plc is considering the purchase of 100 per cent of the share capital of the all-equity-financed Earl plc. Earl operates in two divisions – Red and Blue – and a head office. The divisions operate independently of each other, the only joint costs of Earl, not attributable directly to either division, are those of the head office. Earl's management

are currently committed to operating both divisions for four years and have estimated operating cash flows, and the taxable operating profits of each division as:

	Operating Cash Flows			Taxable Operating Profits		
	Division		Divisional	Division		Divisional
	Red	Blue	Total	Red	Blue	Total
Year	(£'000s)	(£'000s)	(£'000s)	(£'000s)	(£'000s)	(£'000s)
1	600	600	1,200	400	600	1,000
2	600	400	1,000	600	400	1,000
3	800	400	1,200	800	400	1,200
4	1,000	200	1,200	1,200	200	1,400

The above figures exclude:

(a) Head Office costs of £200,000 p.a.

(b) Planned capital expenditure by Red division in Year 1 of £400,000 and its tax consequences. This capital expenditure is necessary for Red division's continued operations and the above figures assume it will be undertaken.

(c) The salvage values of Earl's assets. Salvage values will be received at Year 4 and are estimated at:

	£'000s
Red division	1,200
Blue division	600

Equipment used at head office is all rented on short term operating leases and therefore has no salvage value to Earl at any time.

(d) Earl's current tax liability of £600,000 which is due for payment at Year 1.

The above details are widely known and would continue to apply to Earl after any takeover except that:

(i) some of Earl's administrative activities would be undertaken by Craig resulting in savings of head office costs of 50 per cent in Years 1 and 2 and 75 per cent in Years 3 and 4;

(ii) at Year 4 Red division's assets would be used by Craig to substitute for capital expenditure of £1.4 million planned for Year 4.

Craig's Corporate Planning manager has suggested that if the takeover is completed then various options are available to Craig. He has detailed the options but has made no attempt to appraise their financial desirability. The details are:

(a) Early termination of Blue division's operations. This would change the estimated salvage values which would be realized immediately on termination of the division's activities. Early termination would also enable operating cash flows, and taxable profits, to be increased by a constant amount for each year of the division's revised life, the level of the constant increase being dependent upon the date of termination. The revised figures are:

Blue Division

Operations terminated at end of year	Revised salvage Value	Increase in Annual Cash Flows for each year until termination
	(£'000s)	(£'000s)
2	1,000	200
3	800	150

(b) Craig's own transport department could be used to carry out Red division's deliveries thereby saving the division £30,000 per annum in transport costs. However, this policy would cause Craig's transport department to modify its planned replacement cycle and expenditure of £80,000, scheduled for both Year 3 and Year 5, would be increased to £100,000 and would occur earlier, in Year 1 and Year 4. Thereafter all planned replacements would be unchanged.

(c) By incurring additional advertising of £180,000 in Year 1, sales of Red division would increase producing additional profit, and cash flow, of £120,000 for each of Years 3 and 4.

Craig's financial director believes that an appropriate *after-tax* discount rate to be applied to all cash flows relating to the consequences of the proposed acquisition is 18 per cent.

The tax rate is 50 per cent and the tax delay is one year. All capital expenditure is eligible for 100 per cent First Year Allownces and sales of assets would be subject to tax. Assume all cash flows occur on the last day in each year.

Required

Using 18 per cent as the appropriate after tax discount rate:

(a) Determine the market value of Earl plc in the absence of any takeover possibilities.
(b) Advise Craig on the maximum amount it should be prepared to pay for Earl if the Corporate Planning manager's suggestions are completely ignored.
(c) Determine which of the Corporate Planning manager's suggestions should be undertaken and specify the optimum life of Blue division. Advise Craig of the maximum amount it should now be prepared to pay for Earl.

(ACCA Level 3, December 1983)

4. The Board of Directors of Rundum plc are contemplating a takeover bid for Carbo Ltd, an unquoted company which operates in both the packaging and building materials industries. If the offer is successful, there are no plans for a radical restructuring or divestment of Carbo's assets.

Carbo's Balance Sheet for the year ending 31 December 1991 shows the following:

Assets employed:		£m
Freehold property		4.0
Plant and equipment		2.0
Current assets:		
stocks	1.5	
debtors	3.0	
cash	0.1	4.6
Total assets		10.6
Creditors payable within one year		3.0
Total assets less current liabilities		7.6
Creditors payable after one year		1.0
Net assets		6.6
Financed by:		
Ordinary share capital (25p units)		2.5
Revaluation reserve		0.5
Profit and loss account		3.6
Shareholders' funds		6.6

Further information

(a) Carbo's pre-tax earnings for the year ended 31 December 1991 were £2m.

(b) Corporation Tax is payable at 33 per cent.

(c) Depreciation provisions were £0.5m. This was exactly equal to the funding required to replace worn-out equipment.

(d) Carbo has recently tried to grow sales by extending more generous trade credit terms. As a result, about a third of its debtors have only a 50 per cent likelihood of paying.

(e) About half of Carbo's stocks are probably obsolete with a resale value as scrap of only £50,000.

(f) Carbo's assets were last revalued in 1980.

(g) If the bid succeeds, Rundum will pay off the presently highly overpaid managing director of Carbo for £200,000 and replace him with one of its own 'high-flyers'. This will generate pre-tax annual savings of £60,000 p.a.

(h) Carbo's two divisions are roughly equal in size. The industry P:E ratio is 8:1 for packaging and 12:1 for building materials.

Required

(a) Value Carbo using a net asset valuation approach, based on the accounts.

(b) Value Carbo using a price-earnings ratio approach.

(c) Calculate the rate of return achieved by Carbo for its shareholders.

(d) The average Beta for the packaging industry is 1.15 and 0.85 for building materials. The risk-free interest rate is currently 10 per cent and historically the market portfolio has yielded an overall return of 18 per cent.

Assess the value of Carbo using a Capital Asset Pricing model approach. (You may assume that Carbo has a perpetual life-span.)

(e) Explain why the valuations attained by the above three methods are likely to differ. How much would you offer for Carbo?

Practical assignment

Select one of the merger/takeover situations which has been given prominence recently in the media. Analyse your selected case under the following headings (indicative guidelines are provided).

1. *Strategy* – How does the 'victim' appear to fit into the acquirer's long-term strategy?
2. *Valuation and bid tactics* – Has the acquirer bid or paid 'over the odds'? Should it have done? What were the pros and cons of the financing package?
3. *Defence tactics* – Were the tactics employed sensible ones? Were the managers of the target company genuinely resisting or simply seeking to squeeze out a higher offer?
4. *Impact* – Will the acquireee be difficult to integrate? Are any sell-offs likely?

References

Allen, D., R. Day, I. Hirst and J. Kwiatkowski (1987) 'Equity, Gilts, Treasury Bills and Inflation', *The Investment Analyst*, January, No. 83.

Altman, E. I. (1968) 'Financial Ratios, Discriminant Analysis and the Prediction of Corporate Bankruptcy', *Journal of Finance*, September.

Andersen, J. A. (1987) *Currency and Interest Rate Hedging* (Prentice Hall).

Andrews, G. S. and C. Firer (1987) 'Why Different Divisions Require Different Hurdle Rates', *Long Range Planning*, October.

Ashton, D. J. (1989) 'Textbook Formulae and UK Taxation: Modigliani and Miller revisited', *Accounting and Business Research*, Summer.

Ball, J. (1991) 'Short Termism – Myth or Reality', *National Westminster Bank Quarterly Review*, August.

Ball, J. and M. Knight (eds.) (1990) 'A Guide to Export Finance', *Euromoney Publications*.

Belk, P. A. and M. Glaum (1990) 'The Management of Foreign Exchange Risk in UK Multinationals: An Empirical Investigation', *Accounting and Business Research*, Winter.

Bhattacharya, M. (1979) 'Imperfect Information, Dividend Policy and the Bird-in-the-Hand Fallacy', *Bell Journal of Economics and Management Science*, Spring.

Bierman Jr, H. and J. E. Hass (1973) 'Capital Budgeting under Uncertainty: A Reformulation', *Journal of Finance*, March.

Black, F. and M. Scholes (1973) 'The Pricing of Options and Corporate Liabilities', *Journal of Political Economy*, May–June.

Brealey, R. A. and S. C. Myers (1991) *Principles of Corporate Finance*, (McGraw-Hill).

Brennan, M. (1971) 'A Note on Dividend Irrelevance and the Gordon Valuation Model', *Journal of Finance*, December.

Brigham, E. F. and L. C. Gapenski (1991) *Financial Management Theory and Practice* (Dryden).

Bromwich, M. and A. Bhimani (1991) 'Strategic Investment Appraisal', *Management Accounting*, March.

Brown, B. (1986) *The Forward Market in Foreign Exchange* (Croom Helm).

Buckley, P. J. and M. Casson (1981) 'The Optimal Timing of a Foreign Direct Investment', *Economic Journal*, Vol. 92, No. 361, March.

Chesley, G. R. (1975) 'Elicitation of Subjective Probabilities: A Review', *Accounting Review*, April.

Clark, T. M. (1978) *Leasing* (McGraw-Hill).

Collier, P. and E. W. Davies (1985) 'The Management of Currency Transaction Risk by UK Multinational Companies', *Accounting and Business Research*, Autumn.

Cooke, T. E. (1986) *Mergers & Acquisitions* (Blackwell).

Cooper, D. J. (1975) 'Rationality and Investment Appraisal', *Accounting and Business Research*, Summer.

Copeland, T. E., T. Koller and J. Murrin (1990) *Measuring and Managing the Value of Companies* (Wiley).

Copeland, T. E. and J. F. Weston (1988) *Financial Theory and Corporate Policy*, 3rd edn (Reading, Mass., Addison-Wesley).

Daniels, J. D. and L. H. Radebaugh (1989) *International Business: Environments and Operations* (Reading, Mass., Addison-Wesley).

Department of Trade and Industry (1988) *Mergers Policy* (HMSO).

Department of Trade and Industry (1990) *Innovation: City Attitudes and Practices* (HMSO).

Dickson, M. (1987) 'A Culture Shock that won Ardent Converts', *Financial Times*, 13 January.

Dimson, E. and R. A. Brealey (1978) 'The Risk Premium on UK Equities', *The Investment Analyst*, December.

Dimson, E. and P. Marsh (1982) 'Calculating the Cost of Capital', *Long Range Planning*, April.

Drucker, P. F. (1981) 'Five Rules for Successful Acquisition', *Wall Street Journal*, 15 October.

Drury, J. C. and S. Braund (1990) 'The Leasing Decision: A Comparison of Theory and Practice', *Accounting and Business Research*, Summer.

Eiteman, D. K., A. I. Stonehill and M. H. Moffet (1992) *Multinational Business Finance* (Reading, Mass., Addison-Wesley).

Elton, E. J. (1970) 'Capital Rationing and External Discount Rates', *Journal of Finance*, June.

Elton, E. J. and M. Gruber (1970) 'Marginal Stockholder Tax Rates and the Clientele Effect', *Review of Economics and Statistics*, February.

Fairburn, J. A. and J. A. Kay (eds.) (1989) *Mergers & Merger Policy* (Oxford University Press).

Fama, E. F. (1970) 'Efficient Capital Markets. A Review of Theory and Empirical Work', *Journal of Finance*, May.

Fama, E. F. and M. H. Miller (1972) *The Theory of Finance* (Holt, Rinehart and Winston).

Ferguson, A. (1989) 'Hostage to the Short Term', *Management Today*, March.

Firth, M. and S. Keane (1986) *Issues in Finance* (Philip Allan).

Foley, B. J. (1991) *Capital Markets* (Macmillan).

Fosback, N. (1985) 'Stock Market Logic', *The Institute for Econometric Research*, (Fort Lauderdale).

Franks, J. R., R. S. Harris and C. Mayer (1988) 'Means of Payment in Take-overs: Results from the UK and US', in A. J. Auerbach (ed.), *Corporate Takeovers: Causes and Consequences* (National Bureau of Economic Research, Chicago Press).

Franks, J. R. and R. S. Harris (1989) 'Shareholder Wealth Effects of Corporate Takeovers: The UK Experience 1955–85', *Journal of Financial Economics*, Vol. 23.

Friedman, M. (1953) 'The Methodology of Positive Economics', in *Essays in Positive Economics* (The University of Chicago Press).

Fuller, R. J. and H. S. Kerr (1981) 'Estimating the Divisional Cost of Capital: An Analysis of the Pure-Play Technique', *Journal of Finance*, December.

Gale, B. T. and D. J. Swire (1988) 'Business Strategies that Create Wealth', *Planning Review*, March–April.

Ghosh, C. and J. Woolridge (1989) 'Stock Market Reaction to Growth – Induced Dividend Cuts: Are Investors Myopic?' *Managerial & Decision Economics*, March.

Gluck, F. W. (1988) 'The Real Take-over Defense', *The McKinsey Quarterly*, Winter.

Gordon, M. (1959) 'Dividends, Earnings and Financing Policy', *Review of Economics and Statistics*, May.

Gordon, M. (1963) 'Optimal Investment and Financing Policy', *Journal of Finance*.

Graham, B., D. Dodd and S. Cottle (1962) *Security Analysis: Principles and Techniques (4th edn)* (McGraw-Hill).

Graves, S. B. (1988) 'Institutional Ownership and Corporate R & D in the Computer Industry', *Academy of Management Journal*, Vol. 31.

Gray, S. J. and M. C. McDermott (1989) *Mega-Merger Mayhem* (Paul Chapman Publishing).

Gregory, A. (1985) 'Appraising the Effect of Different Financing Methods', *Management Accounting*, November.

Gup, B. E. and S. W. Norwood (1982) 'Divisional Cost of Capital: A Practical Approach', *Financial Management*, Spring.

Hamada, R. S. (1969) 'Portfolio Analysis: Market Equilibrium and Corporate Finance', *Journal of Finance*, March.

Harrison, J. S. (1987) 'Alternatives to Merger – Joint Ventures and Other Strategies', *Long Range Planning*, December.

Harvey-Jones, J. (1989) *Making It Happen – Reflections on Leadership* (Fontana).

Hayes, R. H. and D. A. Garvin (1982) 'Managing as if Tomorrow Mattered', *Harvard Business Review*, May–June.

Hertz, D. B. (1964) 'Risk Analysis in Capital Investment', *Harvard Business Review*, January–February.

Hirshleifer, J. (1958) 'On the Theory of Optimal Investment Decision', *Journal of Political Economy*, Vol. 66.

Hodder, J. E. (1986) 'Evaluation of Manufacturing Investments: A Comparison of U.S. and Japanese Practices', *Financial Management*, Spring.

Hunt, J. and S. Leese (1987) *Acquisition – the Human Factors* (London Business School and Egon Zehnder Associates).

Ibbotson Associates (1990) *Stocks, Bonds, Bills and Inflation, 1990 Yearbook* (Ibbotson Associates).

Jensen, M. C. (1984) 'Take-overs: Folklore and Science', *Harvard Business Review*, November/December.

Jensen, M. C. and W. H. Meckling (1976) 'Theory of the Firm: Managerial Behaviour, Agency Costs and Ownership Structure', *Journal of Financial Economics*, October.

Jensen, M. C. and R. S. Ruback (1983) 'The Market for Corporate Control: The Scientific Evidence', *Journal of Financial Economics*, April.

Jones, C. S. (1982) *Successful Management of Acquisitions* (Derek Beattie Publishing).

Jones, C. S. (1983) *The Control of Acquired Companies* (Chartered Institute of Cost and Management Accountants).

Jones, C. S. (1986) 'Integrating Acquired Companies', *Management Accounting*, April.

Kaplan, R. S. (1986) 'Must CIM be Justified by Faith Alone?' *Harvard Business Review*, March/April.

Keane, S. (1974) 'Dividends and the Resolution of Uncertainty', *Journal of Business Finance and Accountancy*, Autumn.

Kester, W. C. (1984) 'Today's Options for Tomorrow's Growth', *Harvard Business Review*, March–April.

Kindleberger, C. P. (1978) *International Economics* (Irwin).

King, P. (1975) 'Is the Emphasis of Capital Budgeting Misplaced?' *Journal of Business Finance and Accounting*, Spring.

Klemm, M., S. Sanderson and G. Luffman (1991) 'Mission Statements: Selling Corporate Values to Employees', *Long-Range Planning*, June.

Koziol, J. D. (1990) *Hedging: Principles, Practices and Strategies* (John Wiley).

Lambert, R. A. and D. F. Larcker (1985) 'Executive Compensation, Corporate Decision-making and Shareholder Wealth: A Review of the Evidence', *Midland Corporate Finance Journal*, Winter.

Larcker, D. F. (1983) 'Association between Performance Plan Adoption and Capital Investment', *Journal of Accounting and Economics*, April.

Lessard, D. R. (1979) 'Evaluating Foreign Projects: An Adjusted Present Value Approach', in D. R. Lessard, *International Financial Management Theory and Application* (Warren, Gorham and Lamont).

Levy, H. and M. Sarnat (1990) *Capital Investment and Financial Decisions*, (Prentice Hall).

Limmack, R. J. (1991) 'Corporate Mergers and Shareholder Wealth Effects: 1977–1986', *Accounting and Business Research*, Summer.

Lorie, J. H. and L. J. Savage (1955) 'Three Problems in Capital Rationing', *Journal of Business*, October.

Lumby, S. (1991) *Investment Appraisal and Financing Decisions* (Chapman and Hall).

Madura, J. and A. M. Whyte (1990) 'Diversification Benefits of Direct Foreign Investment', *Management International Review*, Vol. 30, No. 1.

Mao, J. C. T. and J. F. Helliwell (1969) 'Investment Decisions under Uncertainty: Theory and Practice', *Journal of Finance*, May.

Marais, D. (1982) 'Corporate Financial Strength', *Bank of England Quarterly Bulletin*, June.

Markowitz, H. M. (1952) 'Portfolio Selection', *Journal of Finance*, March.

Markowitz, H. M. (1991) 'Foundations of Portfolio Theory', *Journal of Finance*, June.

Marsh, P. (1991) *Short-termism on Trial* (International Fund Managers Association).

Mathur, I. (1989) 'A Review of the Theories of and Evidence on Returns Related to Mergers and Takeovers', *Managerial Finance*, Vol. 15, No. 4.

McDaniel, W. R., D. E. McCarty and K. A. Jessell (1988) 'Discounted Cash Flow with Explicit Reinvestment Rates: Tutorial and Extension', *The Financial Review*, August.

McGowan, C. B. and J. C. Francis (1991) 'Arbitrage Pricing Theory Factors and their Relationship to Macro-economic Variables', in C. F. Lee, T. J. Frecka and L. O. Scott (eds.), *Advances in Quantitative Analysis of Finance and Accounting* (JAI Press).

McIntyre, A. D. and N. J. Coulthurst (1985) 'Theory and Practice in Capital Budgeting', *British Accounting Review*, Autumn.

McLaney, E. J. (1991) *Business Finance for Decision Makers* (Pitman).

McRae, T. W. and D. Walker (1981) *Foreign Exchange Management* (Prentice Hall).

Miller, M. (1977) 'Debt and Taxes', *American Economic Review*, May.

Miller, M. (1986) 'Behavioural Rationality in Finance: the Case of Dividends', *Journal of Business*.

Miller, M. H. (1991) 'Leverage', *Journal of Finance*, June.

Miller, M. H. and F. Modigliani (1961) 'Dividend Policy and the Valuation of Shares', *Journal of Business*, October.

Mills, R. W. (1988) 'Capital Budgeting Techniques Used in the UK and USA', *Management Accounting*, January.

Mittra, S. and C. Gassen (1981) *Investment Analysis and Portfolio Management* (Harcourt Brace Jovanovich).

Modigliani, F. and M. Miller (1958) 'The Cost of Capital, Corporation Finance and the Theory of Investment', *American Economic Review*, June.

Mossin, J. (1966) 'Equilibrium in a Capital Assets Market', *Econometrica*, October.

Myers, S. C. (1974) 'Interactions of Corporate Financing and Investment Decisions – Implications for Capital Budgeting', *Journal of Finance*, March.

Neale, C. W. and P. J. Buckley (1992) 'Differential British and US Adoption Rates of Investment Project Post-Completion Auditing', *Journal of International Business Studies*.

Neale, C. W. and D. E. A. Holmes (1988) 'Post-Completion Audits: The Costs and Benefits', *Management Accounting*, Vol. 66, No. 3.

Neale, C. W. and D. E. A. Holmes (1991) *Post-Completion Auditing* (Pitman).

O'Shea, D. (1986) *Investing for Beginners*, Financial Times Business Information.

Payne, A. F. (1987) 'Approaching Acquisitions Strategically', *Journal of General Management*, Winter.

Peters, E. E. (1991) *Chaos and Order in the Capital Markets* (John Wiley)

Peters, T. and R. Waterman (1982) *In Search of Excellence* (Harper & Row).

Pike, R. H. (1982) *Capital Budgeting in the 1980s* (Chartered Institute of Management Accountants).

Pike, R. H. (1983) 'The Capital Budgeting Behaviour and Corporate Characteristics of Capital-Constrained Firms', *Journal of Business Finance and Accounting*, Summer.

Pike, R. H. (1988) 'An Empirical Study of the Adoption of Sophisticated Capital Budgeting Practices and Decision-Making Effectiveness', *Accounting and Business Research*, Autumn.

Pike, R. H. (1992) 'Capital Budgeting Survey: An Update', *Bradford University Discussion Paper*.

Pike, R. H. and S. M. Ho (1991) 'Risk Analysis Techniques in Capital Budgeting Contexts', *Accounting and Business Research*, Vol. 21, No. 83.

Pike, R. H. and T. S. Ooi (1989) 'The Impact of Corporate Investment Objectives and Constraints on Capital Budgeting Practices', *British Accounting Review*, August.

Pike, R. H. and M. Wolfe (1988) *Capital Budgeting in the 1990s* (Chartered Institute of Management Accountants).

Pinches, G. (1982) 'Myopic Capital Budgeting and Decision-Making', *Financial Management*, Vol. 11, No. 3.

Pohlman, R. A., E. S. Santiago and F. L. Markel (1988) 'Cash Flow Estimation Practices of Large Firms', *Financial Management*, Summer.

Porter, M. E. (1980) *Competitive Strategy* (Free Press).

Porter, M. E. (1985) *Competitive Advantage* (Free Press).

Porter, M. E. (1987) 'From Competitive Advantage to Corporate Strategy', *Harvard Business Review*, May–June.

Prasad, S. B. (1987) 'American and European Investment Motives in Ireland', *Management International Review* (Third quarter).

Price, J. and S. K. Henderson (1988) *Currency and Interest Rate Swaps* (Butterworths).

Prindl, A. (1978) *Currency Management* (John Wiley).

Pruitt, S. W. and L. J. Gitman (1987) 'Capital Budgeting Forecast Biases: Evidence from the Fortune 500', *Financial Management*, Spring.

Rappaport, A. (1987) 'Stock Market Signals to Managers', *Harvard Business Review* November/December.

Redhead, K. (1990) *Introduction to Financial Futures and Options* (Woodhead-Faulkner).

Reimann, B. C. (1980) 'Why Bother with Risk Adjusted Hurdle Rates?', *Long Range Planning*, June.

Risk Measurement Service, London Business School.

Robbins, S. and R. Stobaugh (1973) 'The Bent Measuring Stick for Foreign Subsidiaries', *Harvard Business Review*, September/October.

Robichek, A. and S. Myers (1965) *Optimal Financing Decisions* (Prentice Hall).

Rodriguez, R. M. (1981) 'Corporate Exchange Risk Management: Theme and Aberrations', *Journal of Finance*, May.

Roll, R. (1977) 'A Critique of the Asset Pricing Theory's Tests; Part I: On Past and Potential Testability of the Theory', *Journal of Financial Economics*, March.

Ross, S. A. (1976) 'The Arbitrage Theory of Capital Asset Pricing', *Journal of Economic Theory*, Vol. 13, No. 3.

Ross, S. A. (1977) 'The Determination of Financial Structure: the Incentive Signalling Approach', *Bell Journal of Economics*, Spring.

Ruback, R. S. (1988) 'An Overview of Takeover Defenses', in A. J. Auerbach (ed.), *Mergers & Acquisitions* (University of Chicago Press).

Rugman, A. M., D. J. Lecraw and L. D. Booth (1985) *International Business, Firm and Environment* (McGraw-Hill).

Rutterford, J. and D. Carter (1988) *Handbook of UK Corporate Finance* (Butterworths).

Shapiro, A. C. (1989) *Multinational Financial Management* (Allyn and Bacon).

Sharpe, W. F. (1964) 'Capital Asset Prices – A Theory of Market Equilibrium under Conditions of Risk', *Journal of Finance*, September.

Sharpe, W. (1981) *Investments* (Prentice Hall).

Stock Exchange Fact Book, *The International Stock Exchange* (annually).

Swalm, R. O. (1966) 'Utility Theory – Insights into Risk-taking', *Harvard Business Review*, November/December.

Taffler, R. (1991) 'Z-Scores: An Approach to the Recession', *Accountancy*, July.

3i *Making an Acquisition*.

Tobin, J. (1958) 'Liquidity Preference as Behaviour Towards Risk', *Review of Economic Studies*, February.

Tomkins, C. R., J. F. Lowe and E. J. Morgan (1979) *An Economic Analysis of the Financial Leasing Industry* (Saxon House).

Van Horne, J. (1975) 'Corporate Liquidity and Bankruptcy Costs', Research Paper 205, Stanford University.

Van Horne, J. (1986) *Financial Management and Policy* (Prentice Hall).

Walters, A. (1991) *Corporate Credit Analysis* (Euromoney Publications).

Wearing, R. T. (1989) 'Cash Flow and the Eurotunnel', *Accounting & Business Research*, Winter.

Weaver, S. C., D. Peters, R. Cason and J. Daleiden (1989) 'Capital Budgeting', *Financial Management*, Spring.

Weingartner, H. (1977) 'Capital Rationing: Authors in Search of a Plot', *Journal of Finance*, December.

Weston, J. F. and T. E. Copeland (1988) *Managerial Finance* (Cassell).

Wilson, M. (1990) 'Capital Budgeting for Foreign Direct Investments', *Managerial Finance*, Vol. 16, No. 2.

Wright, M. and K. Robbie (1991) 'Corporate Restructuring, Buy-Outs and Managerial Equity: The European Dimension', *Journal of Applied Corporate Finance*, Winter.

APPENDIX A
Suggested solutions to selected end-of-chapter questions

Chapter 1

Question 1

The goal of maximizing owners' wealth is the normally accepted economic objective for resource allocation decisions. Rather than concentrate on the organization it evaluates investments from the viewpoint of the organization's owners – usually shareholders. Any investment that increases their stock of wealth (the present value of future cash flows) is economically acceptable.

In practice, many of the assumptions underlying this goal do not always hold (e.g. shareholders are only interested in maximizing the market value of their shareholdings). In addition, owners are often far removed from managerial decision-making where capital investment takes place. Accordingly, it is common to find that more easily measurable criteria are used, such as profitability and growth goals. There are also non-economic considerations, such as employee welfare and managerial satisfaction which can be important for some decisions.

Chapter 2

Question 1

UK taxation policy influences financial management decisions in three main areas:

1. *Raising finance.*   Interest on borrowing attracts tax relief whereas dividends on equity do not attract relief. The tax system is therefore biased in favour of borrowing.

2. *Investment.* Some forms of investment (e.g. industrial plant and machinery, industrial buildings and vehicles) attract a form of tax relief termed capital allowances. These are, in effect, cash incentives to tax-paying firms, as their tax bill is reduced through such investment.

3. *Dividend payment.* While the UK taxation system is more neutral than in some other countries, it is still slightly biased towards a low dividend policy. Advance Corporation Tax (ACT) is payable at the time of dividend payment, this bringing forward part of the tax bill. Where a company has insufficient profits to recover the ACT paid, this can be particularly costly.

The above issues have considered only Corporation Tax, but personal taxes on investors can also affect corporate financing decisions, and firms should seek to discover the tax status of its major shareholders.

Chapter 3

Question 1

$$PV = \frac{£623}{(1.07)^8} + \frac{£1092}{(1.07)^{16}} = £732$$

Question 2

Using the table in Appendix C, the annuity factor for ten years and $i = 20\%$ is 4.1925

$$PV = £100 \times 4.1925 = £419.25$$

Question 3

Using the tables:

$$PV = £250 \times 8.0751 + £1,200 \times 0.10067 = £2,140$$

Question 4

Savings	£5000 × 3.7908	£18,954
Residual value	£1000 × 0.62092	£621
		£19,575
less:		
Initial Cost		£20,000
NPV		£(425)

The NPV is negative. Recommend the project is rejected.

Question 5

(a) The firm should invest $£6,000 - £4,000 = £2,000$
(b) Market rate of interest $= £10,000/£80,000 = 1.25$, i.e. 25%
(c) Average return on investment $= \dfrac{£5,000}{£2,000} \times 100 = 250\%$
(d) Present value of an investment of $£2,000 = 5,000/1.25 = £4,000$
    $NPV = £4,000 - £2,000 = £2,000$
(e) Value of firm after investment $= £6,000 + £2,000 = £8,000$

(f) If a dividend of £3,000 is paid now, a further £1,000 will be invested on the capital market (there being no internal projects offering a better return). This will give cash next year of £1,000 × 1.25 = £1,250 from external investment plus £5,000 from internal investment, a total dividend of £6,250.

Students should be aware of the assumptions for the two-period investment model:

(a) Only the present and subsequent periods are considered.
(b) Investors are wealth-maximizers.
(c) All decisions – relevant information is known with certainty.
(d) Investment projects are entirely independent of each other and are divisible.
(e) No capital markets.
(f) The firm is owner-managed.

The last two assumptions can be dealt with by adjusting the basic model.

Chapter 4

Question 1

Cogburn

(a) P:E ratio for Pepper = 8:1
Pepper's profit after tax (PAT) = £1.5m (after deducting the extraordinary item)

Hence, market value = 8 × £1.5m = £12m
The price per share is £12m/(£10m × 2) = 60p

Since the last dividend was paid 'about a year ago' this appears to be a cum-dividend share price.

Last year's dividend per share was $\left[\dfrac{£0.5m}{2 \times £10m}\right] = 2.5p$

Given 12 per cent growth, *this* year's dividend would be 2.5p (1.12) = 2.8p. Therefore, the ex-dividend price would be about 57p.
(b) Book value is based on historic cost. Market value depends on earning power. Values stated in the accounts may be suspect (e.g.) fixed assets under-valued, stocks over-valued.
(c) Book value of net assets = £13m.
Shareholder earnings after tax = £1.5m (see above)

$\text{Return on book value} = \dfrac{£1.5m}{£13m} = 11.5\%$

Alternatively,

$\text{Return on market value} = \dfrac{£1.5m}{£12m} = 12.5\%$

(Which figure is more useful as a guide to the return required by shareholders?)

(d) *Using the CAPM*

$$ER_j = ke_j = R_f + \beta_j \, [ER_m - R_f]$$

$\beta_j = 1.2$

$R_j = 10\%$

ER_m is not given but $[ER_m - R_f] = 9\%$

Therefore, required return $= 10\% + 1.2\,[9\%] = 20.8\%$

(e) Pepper's 'normal' cash flow
$= (PAT - \text{extraordinary item} + \text{depreciation})$
$= £2.0m - £0.5m + £2m = £3.5m$
- What lifetime to assume?
- What rate of growth to assume?
- What is Cogburn's required return?
- Are there ongoing investment requirements?

Assume

- Infinite life, i.e. use perpetuity formula
- no growth
- k_e for Cogburn given by CAPM $= 20.8\%$
- Annual *replacement* investment for Pepper $=$ depreciation charge of £2m

Allowing for operating savings of £0.5m,

$$\text{free cash flow} = £3.5m - £2m + £0.5m = £2m \text{ p.a.}$$

With no growth, value of Pepper $= \left[\dfrac{£2m}{20.8\%} \right] = £9.6m$

How acceptable are the assumptions, especially regarding company life-span and growth?

(f)
- Net Asset Value
- Using P:E ratio for a surrogate (i.e. very similar, comparable company)
- Using discounted cash flow approach (as in (e))

Chapter 5

Question 1

Microtic Ltd

		Project A (£)		Project B (£)
1.	*Payback Period*			
	Outlay/annual flow	1,616/500 =		556/200 =
		3.2 years		2.8 years
2.	*Net present value* (15%)			
	Annual cash flow five years £500 × 3.352	1,676,000	200 × 3.352	670,400
	Scrap value £301 × 0.497	149,600	56 × 0.497	27,800
	Outlay	(1,616,000)		(556,000)
	NPV	209,600		142,200

3. *Internal rate of return*

	try 20%		try 25%
(use trial and error to obtain NPV of zero)			
Annual cash flow 500 × 2.991	1,495,500	200 × 2.689	537,800
Scrap value 301 × 0.402	121,000	56 × 0.328	18,400
Outlay	(1,616,000)		(556,000)
NPV	500		200

4. *Accounting rate of return*

Average profit before depreciation	500,000		200,000
Depreciation (1616 − 301)/5	263,000	(556 − 56)/5	100,000
	237,000		100,000
Average capital employed (1616 + 301)/2	958,500	(556 + 56)/2	306,000
Rate	24.7%		32.7%

Investment Advice

All appraisal methods apart from the NPV approach recommend acceptance of Project B. This is because it generates a higher return for every £1 invested. The question is, however, which of the two projects creates most wealth for the owners. Clearly, the much larger Project A has the higher NPV. Unless the firm is experiencing severe capital rationing problems, Project A should be accepted.

Question 2

Mace Ltd (£000)

Project	NPV per £ Outlay	Ranking	Fraction Accepted	Required Capital (£)	NPV (£)
1	1.6/60 = 0.027	4	0	—	—
2	1.3/30 = 0.043	3	1/3	10	0.43
3	8.3/40 = 0.207	1	1	40	8.3
4				0	0.9
5	7.9/50 = 0.158	2	1	50	7.9
				100	17.53

Chapter 6

Question 1

Bramhope Manufacturing

(i)(a) Additional investment: £123,500 − £15,000 = £108,500
Additional annual inflow =   £24,300 (see below)
Therefore payback period =   £108,500/£24,300 = 4.5 years

(b)

Time	Cash Flow (£)	DF at 15%	PV (£)	DF at 17%	PV (£)
0	(108,500)	1	(108,500)	1	(108,500)
1–8	24,300	4.48732	109,042	4.20716	102,234
8	20,500	0.32690	6,701	0.28478	5,838
			7,243		(428)

(c) NPV AT 15% = £7,243
     IRR   = approx 17%

        Workings:
        Existing project's annual cash inflow:
        £200,000 × (0.95 − 0.12 − 0.48) = £70,000

        New project's annual cash inflow:
        £230,000 × (0.95 − 0.08 − 0.46) = £94,300

        Incremental cash flow:
        £94,300 − £70,000   = £24,300

(ii) The project appears to offer a positive net present value and should be accepted. However, an NPV of £7,000 on a project costing £123,500 is relatively small, and questions should be asked as to how sensitive the key assumptions are to uncertainty. For example, is it realistic that the additional capacity can be sold at the current price? Will there really be no increase in fixed overheads? If an advanced machine has been developed after just two years, is an eight-year economic life optimistic?

Chapter 7

Question 1

(a) Payback = four years. The reciprocal is 25 per cent which is the IRR for a project of infinite life.
(b) For a 20-year life, IRR = 24%
     For an 8-year life, IRR = 19%
(c) When the annual cash flows are approximately the same for a long-lived project, the payback reciprocal is a reasonable proxy for the IRR. The actual IRR is always something less than that given by the payback reciprocal.

Question 2

The preference for IRR in practice is because:

(a) It is easier to understand (this is debatable),
(b) It is useful in ranking projects (although not always accurate),
(c) Lower-level managers do not need to know the discount rate. Where a risk-adjusted hurdle rate is used, there may be considerable negotiation over the appropriate rate.
(d) Psychological. Managers prefer a percentage.

Chapter 8

Question 1

Woodpulp Project

Year	CE	NCF(£)	ENCF(£)	10%	PV(£)
1	0.90	8,000	7,200	0.90	6,480
2	0.85	7,000	5,959	0.83	4,938
3	0.80	7,000	5,600	0.75	4,200
4	0.75	5,000	3,750	0.68	2,550
5	0.70	5,000	3,500	0.62	2,170
6	0.65	5,000	3,250	0.56	1,820
7	0.60	5,000	3,000	0.51	1,530
				PV	23,688

$NPV = £23,688 - £13,000 = £10,688$. Accept the project.

Question 2

Mystery Enterprises

Expected Value Year 1 $(£) = 0.2(400) + 0.3(500) + 0.3(600) + 0.2(700)$
$$= £550$$

Variance $(£)$ $\qquad = 0.2(400{-}550)^2 + 0.3(500{-}550)^2 + 0.3(600{-}550)^2 + 0.2(700{-}550)^2$
$$= £10,500$$

Standard deviation $\qquad = £102$

Expected Value Year 2 $(£) = 0.2(300) + 0.3(400) + 0.3(500) + 0.2(600)$
$$= £450$$

Variance $(£)$ $\qquad = 0.2(300{-}450)^2 + 0.3(400{-}450)^2 + 0.3(500{-}450)^2 + 0.2(600{-}450)^2$

Standard deviation $\qquad = £102$

Assuming a discount rate of 10 per cent and independent cash flows

$$NPV = \frac{£550}{1.1} + \frac{£450}{(1.1)^2} - £800 = £71$$

$$SD = \frac{(£102)^2}{(1.1)^2} + \frac{(£102)^2}{(1.1)} = £125$$

$$\text{Coefficient of variation} = \frac{£125}{£71} = 1.76$$

Chapter 9

Question 1 Nissota

(a) EIRE:—EV of $IRR = (0.3 \times 20\%) + (0.3 \times 10\%) + (0.4 \times 15\%)$
$$= 6\% + 3\% + 6\% = 15\%$$

and

(b)

Outcome %	Deviation	Sq'd Dev.	p	Sq'd Dev. $\times p$
20	$+5$	25	0.3	7.5
10	-5	25	0.3	7.5
15	0	0	0.4	
				Total $\overline{15}$

Variance $= 15$ $\sigma = 3.87$

HUMBERSIDE:— EV of IRR $= (0.3 \times 10\%) + (0.3 \times 30\%) + (0.4 \times 20\%)$
$= 3\% + 9\% + 8\% = 20\%$

Outcome %	Deviation	Sq.d Dev.	p	Sq'd Dev. $\times p$
10	-10	100	0.3	30
30	$+10$	100	0.3	30
20	0	0	0.4	0
				Total $\overline{60}$

Variance $= 60$ $\sigma = 7.75$

(c) **(i)** For a 50/50 Split investment
EV of IRR $= (0.5 \times 15\%) + (0.5 \times 20\%)$ $= 17.5\%$
$\sigma = \sqrt{(0.5)^2(15) + (0.5)^2(60) + 2(0.5)(0.5)\ 0.(3.87)(7.75)}$
   $= \sqrt{3.75 + 15}$ $= \sqrt{18.75}$ $= 4.33$

(ii) 75/25 Split
EV $= (0.75 \times 15\%) + (0.25 \times 20\%) = 11.25\% + 5\% = 16.25\%$
$\sigma = \sqrt{(0.75)^2(15) + (0.25)^2(60)}$
   $= \sqrt{8.44 + 3.75}$ $= \sqrt{12.19}$ $= 3.49$

Chapter 10

Question 1

Megacorp

(i) EV of return $= (0.6 \times 10\%) + (0.4 \times 20\%) = 14\%$

Outcome	Deviation	Squared deviation	prob	sq'd dev $\times p$
10%	-4%	16	0.6	9.6
20%	$+6\%$	36	0.4	14.4
			Total	$\overline{24.0}$
				$\sigma = 4.9$

(ii) Megacorp   ER $= 30\%$ $\sigma = 14\%$ $\alpha = 0.8$
Erewhon   ER $= 14\%$ $\sigma = 4.9\%$ $\alpha = 0.2$

$$\text{ER}_{MG} = (0.8 \times 30\%) + (0.2 \times 14\%) = 24\% + 2.8\% = 26.8\%$$

$$\sigma_{MG} = \sqrt{(0.8)^2(14)^2 + (0.2)^2(4.9)^2 + 2(0.8)(0.2)(-0.36)(30)(4.9)}$$
$$= \sqrt{109.47} = 10.46$$

(iii) The present Beta $= 1.20$

$$\text{Beta of project} = \frac{\text{cov}_{jm}}{\sigma^2_{m}} = \frac{r_{jm}\sigma_j\sigma_m}{\sigma^2_{m}} = \frac{r_{jm}\sigma_j}{\sigma_m}$$

What is the risk of the market (σ_m)?

$$\text{Rearranging, } \sigma_m = \frac{\sigma_j r_{jm}}{\text{Beta}_j} \qquad \text{For Megacorp } \sigma_m = \frac{(14)(0.8)}{1.2} = 9.33$$

$$\text{Project Beta} = \frac{(-0.1)(4.9)}{9.33} = -\frac{0.49}{9.33} = -0.05$$

New Beta for Megacorp $= (0.8 \times 1.2) + (0.2 \times -0.05) = 0.95$
Therefore, the new project lowers Megacorp's Beta.

(iv) • Management have selected lower risk profile for company as a whole.
   • This interferes with shareholder preferences.
   • Have the management gone for lower overall/total risk?
   • Arguably, shareholders could equally well formulate a portfolio with Beta $= 0.95$ by share purchase.
   • Only desirable if shareholders unable to engage in efficient portfolio formation.

Chapter 11

Question 1

Bias and forecasting errors creep into proposals once they begin to gain support by interested parties, or when staff are under pressure to achieve targets. Audit reviews can sometimes assist in identifying systematically over- or under-optimistic forecasts. Where managers are rewarded on the basis of investment results it is in their best interests to provide accurate estimates.

Question 2

It is rarely possible to separate the person sponsoring the proposal from the proposal itself. Success or failure may depend on the sponsor's enthusiasm and expertise in creating and implementing the proposal. Top managers frequently prefer to back the judgement of lower-level managers rather than reject proposals.

Chapter 12

Question 1

Anglia Paper Company

	Pence
3 old shares prior to rights issue at 320p	960
1 new share at £2	200
4 shares worth	1,160
1 share therefore worth 1160/4	290

Value of the rights is the difference between the pre-rights share price and the ex-rights price:

320p − 290p = 30p for every share held before the issue.

Alternatively, it is 290p − 200p = 90p for every new share issued.

Question 2

Cambridge Castings Ltd
Proposed Preference Share Issue

(i) *Benefits to the company*
   • Dividends are only paid if funds are available.
   • No asset security required as with some loans.
   • Lower risk than for ordinary share capital, giving a cheaper source of finance.
   • Suitable when a company does not want to increase the number of ordinary shares but is concerned that its gearing is already high.
   Drawbacks to the company
   • Cost of preference shares is usually higher than for debentures because the risks are greater.
   • No tax relief on the dividends (unlike loan interest).

(ii) *Benefits to the investor*
   • Should produce a higher yield than fixed interest securities.
   • Lower risk than ordinary shares.
   • Redeemable preference shares provide a means of liquidating the investment where markets are thin or non-existent.
   Drawbacks to the investor
   • Unable to participate fully in the profits.
   • Not usually secured.
   • No guaranteed dividend.

Many of the drawbacks can be overcome where preference shares are cumulative, participating, redeemable and convertible into equity if desired.

Chapter 13

Question 1 Galahad

(a) The price per share is given by:

$$P_0 = \frac{D_1}{(k_e - g)}$$

Where:

D_1 = next year's dividend
k_e = the shareholder's required return
g = the expected rate of growth in dividends

The growth rate can be found from the expression:
$5.0\text{p}(1+g)^4 = 7.3\text{p}$ where g = the past (compound) growth rate.

$$(1+g)^4 = \frac{7.3\text{p}}{5.0\text{p}} = 1.46$$

or $\dfrac{1}{(1+g)^4}$ $= 0.6849$

From the present value tables, $g = 10\%$ whence:

$$P_0 = \frac{7.3\text{p}(1.1)}{(16\% - 10\%)} = \frac{8.03\text{p}}{0.06} = £1.34$$

(b) With D_1 at just 5.0p, using managerial expectations for the investment:

$$P_0 = \frac{5.0\text{p}}{(16\% - 14\%)} = \frac{5.0\text{p}}{0.02} = £2.50$$

(c) To break even, share price must not fall below £1.34,

$$\text{i.e. } £1.34 = \frac{5.0\text{p}}{(16\% - g)}$$

Solving for g, $g = 12.3\%$, marginally above the assessment of the more pessimistic managers.

(d) Until 1990, Galahad has pursued a policy of distributing 40–50 per cent of profit after tax as dividend. Each year, it has offered a steady dividend increase even in 1989 when its earnings actually fell. This was presumably out of reluctance to lower the dividend, fearing an adverse market reaction, and reflecting a belief that the earnings shortfall was a temporary phenomenon. In 1990 it offered a 12 per cent dividend increase, the highest percentage increase in the time series, possibly to compensate shareholders for the relatively small increase (only 8 per cent) in 1989. It would appear that Galahad has either built up a clientele of investors whose interests it is trying to safeguard, or that it is trying to do so.

　　The proposed dividend cut to 5.0p per share would represent a sharply increased dividend cover of 3.5, on the assumption that EPS also grows at 10 per cent p.a. Such a sharp rise in the dividend safety margin is likely to be construed by the market as implying that Galahad's managers expect earnings to be depressed in the future, especially as it follows a year of record dividend increase. Such an abrupt change in dividend policy is thus likely to offend its clientele of shareholders at best, and at worst, to alarm the market as to the reliability of future earnings.

In an efficient capital market, with homogeneous investor expectations, the share price would increase by the amount calculated in (b), at least, if the market agreed with the managers' views about the attractions of the projected expenditure. However, in view of the information content of dividends, Galahad's board will have to be very confident of its ability to persuade the market of the inherent desirability of the proposed investment programme. This may well be a difficult task, especially given the stated doubts of some of its managers. The board will have to explain why they feel internal financing is preferable to raising capital externally, either by a rights issue, or by raising further debt finance. While the level of indebtedness of Galahad is not given, the implication is that it is unacceptably high so as to obviate the issue of additional borrowing instruments. If this is the case, then it seems doubly risky to propose a dividend cut, as it may signal fears regarding Galahad's ability to service a high level of debt.

If the dividend cut is greeted adversely, then the ability of the shareholder clientele to home-make dividends will be impaired since, apart from the transactions costs involved, there will perhaps be no capital gain to realize. Any significant selling to convert capital into income will further depress share price.

If the investment programme is truly worthwhile, Galahad's managers perhaps should not shrink from offering a rights issue, since, despite the costs of such issues, shareholders will eventually reap the benefits in the form of higher future earnings and dividends. However, this might suggest a short-term reduction in share price which may penalize short-term investors, but who still have the option of protecting their interests by selling their rights.

Chapter 14

Question 1 Trexon

- The cost of equity is found from:
(b)
$$k_e = \frac{D_1}{P_0} + g = \frac{D_0(1+g)}{P_0} + g$$
$$= \frac{(16p \times 1.06)}{260} + 6\% = 12.5\%$$

- The cost of debt is found from:
$$£94 = \frac{£12\ (1-35\%)}{k_d}$$

Whence $k_d = 8.3\%$

- Capital structure weightings stem from target debt to total capital of 70 per cent:
Hence the WACC is:
$$WACC = \left(12.5\% \times \frac{70}{100}\right) + \left(8.3 \times \frac{30}{100}\right)$$
$$= 8.75\% + 2.5\% = 11.3\%$$

(c) Shareholder A is incorrect – retained earnings do *not* represent free finance – a decision to retain denies shareholders the opportunity to invest in some other venture. They will expect the managers to earn a return on such funds at least as great as they could otherwise obtain. In other words, the cost of retained earnings equals the normal cost of equity. However, in practice, market imperfections like transactions costs and differential taxes as between dividend income and capital gains may reduce the effective cost.

Shareholder B appears to support the traditional view of gearing, i.e. that up to a critical level of gearing a company can raise the value of its shares and lower the overall cost of capital. In fact, so long as the company is still below the critical gearing level, further use of debt finance will involve a marginal cost of finance lower than the (falling) WACC, thus opening up the scope for further worthwhile investment. (This effect is enhanced by the impact of tax relief on debt interest.) The marginal cost of finance can still fall even if the cost of debt begins to rise although the company should heed the warning signals.

Chapter 15

Question 1 Slohill

(a) The dividend valuation model can be used to assess Slohill's cost of equity, viz.

$$k_e = \frac{D_1}{P_0} + g$$

Dividends have grown at around 11 per cent p.a. over the past four years. The current dividend per share is

$$\frac{14.98p}{69m} = 21.71p$$

D_1 is predicted as $21.71p \ (1.11) = 24.10p$

$$\text{Hence } k_e = \frac{24.10p}{546p} + 0.11 = 0.154, \text{ i.e. } 15.4\%$$

The debentures are fifteen years from maturity, so treating these as perpetual, k_d can be approximated from:

$$\pounds 93 = \frac{11p \ (1-35\%)}{k_d} \quad \text{(i.e.) } k_d = 7.7\%$$

(More accurately, k_d is the solution to a fifteen-year IRR expression. The approximation used in the solution is close to the correct answer of 8%.)

The WACC can be found once we know the respective debt and equity weightings.

Market value of debt (m) $= (0.93 \times \pounds 138) = \pounds 128.34$, i.e. 25.4% of total

Market value of equity (m) $= (69 \times 546p) = \dfrac{\pounds 376.74}{\pounds 505.08m}$, i.e. 74.6% of total

Hence, WACC

$$\begin{aligned} &= (74.6\% \times 15.4\%) + (25.4\% \times 7.7\%) \\ &= \quad 11.5\% \quad + \quad 2\% \ = 13.5\% \end{aligned}$$

(i) A second crash will lower the share price to

$$(0.7 \times 546p) = 382p$$

and k_e will rise to $\dfrac{24.10p}{382p} + 11\% = 17.3\%$

Greater demand for gilts will lead to a fall in interest rates of about 2% $(1-35\%)=1.3\%$. The new post-tax debt cost will be 6.4%. This is associated with a rise in market value to

$$\frac{£11(1-35\%)}{6.4\%}=£111.7$$

The new market values are:

Debt $(£111.7 \times £138m)=£154.15$, i.e. 36.9% of total

Equity $(382p \quad \times \quad 69m) \quad \dfrac{£263.58}{£417.73}$, i.e. 63.1% of total

The new WACC $=(36.9\% \times 6.4\%)+(63.1\% \times 17.3)$
$$= \quad 2.4\% \quad +10.9\%=13.3\%$$

(ii) With earnings growth lower by 20 per cent, dividend growth is likely to fall to a similar extent. (Both have grown at around the same rate in recent years.)

Hence, g becomes 11% $(0.8)=8.8\%$
D_1 is predicted at 21.71p $(1.088)=23.62p$
$$k_e=\frac{23.62p}{382p}+8.8\%=15\%$$

Using the same results for k_d and market value of debt as in (a) (i),

WACC is now $=(36.9\% \times 6.4\%)+(63.1\% \times 15\%)$
$$= \quad 2.3\%+9.5\%=11.8\%$$

(b) If only equity finance is raised and expected earnings remain unaltered, the cost of equity will increase, due to the fall in share price, and the WACC will probably rise. At the existing gearing level, the WACC would be expected to remain almost constant, but the higher equity weighting post-issue is likely to push up the WACC since k_e exceeds k_d.

If earnings expectations decline, and the expected annual growth in dividends declines similarly, the cost of equity and debt will fall. The WACC could move either way depending on the size of the new equity issue but it would require an equity issue larger than the company's existing equity base to *raise* the WACC.

If debt is used in both cases, a fall in the WACC is likely since a higher proportion of relatively cheap debt is used in the capital structure. (This assumes that neither k_e nor k_d rise appreciably due to the greater financial risk at the higher level of gearing.)

(c) According to the CAPM, shareholders' required return is given by:

$$ER_j=R_f+\beta_j\,(ER_m-R_f)$$

If interest rates fall, then clearly R_f will also fall. ER_m may rise under scenario (i), as shares fall in price, the expected return in the market portfolio will increase. Under scenario (ii), ER_m could rise or fall according to the extent to which the market's earnings are expected to decline after the crash.

Beta indicates the systematic risk of the company's shares in relation to the overall market. With no change in either the company's or the market's expected earnings, and if market values and the company's share price fell to a similar extent, the company's Beta is likely to remain constant.

If differential earnings expectations occur, the return on the company's shares could be more or less volatile relative to market returns, and the equity Beta could rise or fall.

Chapter 16

Question 1   Louise

(a) If Louise is correct in her calculation of the effective six-monthly after-tax cost of the loan, the borrowing flows will have a net present value equal to the amount of the loan, when discounted at the calculated rate of 6%:

Denote 1 January 1987 as Time 0, etc.

Time will be measured in six-monthly periods:

	11/1/87 Time 0	1/7/87 Time 1	1/1/88 Time 2	1/7/88 Time 3	1/1/89 Time 4	1/7/89 Time 5	1/7/90 Time 7
Interest ($£$)	(8,000)	(8,000)	(4,000)	(4,000)			
Tax relief ($£$)				2,800		4,200	1,400
Repayments ($£$)			(50,000)		(50,000)		
Net cash flow ($£$)	(8,000)	(8,000)	(54,000)	(1,200)	(50,000)	4,200	1,400
PVIF at 6%	1	0.94	0.89	0.84	0.79	0.75	0.66
Present value ($£$)	(8,000)	(7,520)	(48,060)	(1,008)	(39,500)	3,150	924

Net present value $= £(100,014)$

Thus Louise is correct in her calculations as this effectively equals the amount of the loan ($£100,000$).

Explanatory notes

1.   Interest and tax relief
Year ended 31 December 1987
Interest: $£100,000 \times 16\% = £16,000$, paid in two equal instalments

$£8,000$ 1.1.1987 (Time 0)
$£8,000$ 1.7.1987 (Time 1)

Tax relief: $£8,000 \times 35\% = £2,800$ per instalment.

1.1.1987 instalment: deductible against tax liability for y/e 30.6.1987
effect on cash flows 30.6.1988 (Time 3)
1.7.1987 instalments: deductible against tax liability for y/e 30.6.88
effect on cash flows 30.6.1989 (Time 5)

Year ended 31 December 1988
Interest: $£50,000 \times 16\% = £8,000$, paid $£4,000$ 1.1.1988 (Time 2)
$£4,000$ 1.7.1988 (Time 3)
Tax relief: $£4,000 \times 35\% = £1,400$ per instalment.
1.1.1988 instalment: effect on cash flows 30.6.1989 (Time 5)
1.7.1988 instalment: effect on cash flows 30.6.1990 (Time 7)

Summary	Time	Interest ($\pounds$)		Tax relief ($\pounds$)
	0	(8,000)		
	1	(8,000)		
	2	(4,000)		
	3	(4,000)		2,800
	5		$2,800 + 1,400 =$	4,200
	7			1,400

(b) To evaluate the lease, the lease flows may be discounted at the post-tax cost of borrowing:

	T_0	T_1	T_2	T_3	T_4	T_5	T_6
Rentals ($\pounds$)	(16,000)	(16,000)	(16,000)	(16,000)			
Tax relief ($\pounds$)				5,600		11,200	5,600
Lost CAs ($\pounds$)				(8,050)		(6,038)	
Lost disposal proceeds ($\pounds$)					(51,750)		
Net cash flow ($\pounds$)	(16,000)	(16,000)	(16,000)	(18,450)	(51,750)	5,162	5,600
PVIF AT 6%	1	0.94	0.89	0.84	0.79	0.75	0.66
Present value ($\pounds$)	(16,000)	(15,040)	(14,240)	(15,498)	(40,883)	3,872	3,696

Net present value = $\pounds$(94,093)

Leasing is equivalent to borrowing $\pounds$94,093 at 6 per cent, making the option of borrowing $\pounds$92,000 and buying preferable.

Explanatory notes

2   Tax relief on lease payments

Payment date	Accounting y/e	Cash flow effect of tax relief	Time	$\pounds$
1.1.1987	30.6.1987	30.6.1988	3	5,600
1.7.1987 and 1.1.1988	30.6.1988	30.6.1989	5	11,200
1.7.1988	30.6.1989	30.6.1990	7	5,600

3.   Capital allowances

			Tax relief	Time
1.1.1987	Purchase	$\pounds$92,000		
30.6.1987	WDA (25%)	($\pounds$23,000) × 35%	$\pounds$8,050	3
		$\pounds$69,000		
30.6.1988	WDA (25%)	($\pounds$17,250) × 35%	$\pounds$6,038	5
		$\pounds$51,750		
1.1.1989	Disposal	$\pounds$51,750		4
		0		

(c) To evaluate the lease for the non-taxpayer, it is necessary to use the pre-tax cost of borrowing since, by definition, no tax relief is available.

To find the effective cost of borrowing:
Calculate the IRR from stream of borrowing costs (ignoring tax, of course).

	T_0	T_1	T_2	T_3	T_4	T_5	T_7
Interest ($£$)	$-8,000$	$-8,000$	$-4,000$	$-4,000$	—	—	—
Repayments ($£$)	—	—	$-50,000$	—	$-50,000$	—	—
Net Cash Flows ($£$)	$-8,000$	$-8,000$	$-54,000$	$-4,000$	$-50,000$		
NPV at 9% $=$	$-8,000$	$-7,339$	$-45,452$	$-3,098$	$-35,420$		
$= -£99,300$							
NPV at 8% $=$	$-8,000$	$-7,407$	$-46,296$	$-3,175$	$-36,750$		
$= (£101,628)$							
and IRR $=$ 8.75%							

	T_0	T_1	T_2	T_3	T_4	T_5	T_7
Buy ($£$)	$-92,000$				$+51,750$		
Lease ($£$)	$-16,000$	$-16,000$	$-16,000$	$-16,000$	—		—
Buy $-$ Lease ($£$)	$-76,000$	$+16,000$	$+16,000$	$+16,000$	$+51,750$ —		—
NPV ($£$) $=$	$-76,000$	$+14,713$	$+13,529$	$+12,441$	$+37,260$		
$= -76,000$	$+77,943$						
$= +£1,943$							

Hence, borrow-to-buy is the recommended alternative.

Chapter 17

Question 1

Hunslett Express Co.

	$£000$
Average level of debtors – current policy	
$70/365 \times £8m$ =	1,534
Average level of debtors – proposed policy	
$50\% \times 30/365 \times £8m$	329
$50\% \times 80/365 \times £8m$	876
	1,205
Reduction in debtors under new policy	329
Financial Cost Savings ($13\% \times £329,000$)	43
Bad debt savings	20
Administration cost savings	12
	75

Cost of cash discounts
      50% × £8m × 2%   80
                                                          ———

      Estimated cost of scheme   5
The net cost of the proposed scheme is £5,000

Question 2

Salford Engineers Limited

(a) The optimum stockholding level is a trade-off between the cost of holding stocks and the cost of *not* holding stock.

Stockholding costs include:
  (i) *Storage costs.* Where stock is valuable these costs can be large.
  (ii) *Financing costs.* Excessive stock requires unnecessary and expensive working capital.
  (iii) *Insurance costs* against theft or damage.
  (iv) *Obsolescence costs.* Stock held for long periods of time may become obsolete through new products coming to the market.

Costs of holding too little stock include:
  (i) *Loss of customer goodwill and business* through not being able to supply goods on time.
  (ii) *Production stoppages.* A 'stockout' can mean costly and harmful disruptions to the production process.
  (iii) *Lost flexibility.* Shortage of stock makes it difficult for a firm to respond to unexpected demand or to extended production runs.

(b) In investigating the reasons for large stock levels for Salford Engineering, the following action should be taken:

  (i) Examine the stock re-order levels for each stock line.
  (ii) Examine how the optimum stock level is determined. Is any technique for assessing the optimum level employed?
  (iii) Are stock requirements carefully budgeted?
  (iv) Are ratios used (e.g. stock turnover) to monitor stock levels in total and by stock lines?
  (v) Are stock records reliable and adequate?

Chapter 18

Question 1   *Wemere*

(a) *CAPM*
  ● The stated Beta is an equity Beta so that the required return on equity
      $= R_f + \beta \, (ER_m - R_f)$
      $= 12\% + 1.4(18\% - 12\%) = 20.4\%$
  ● This is unsuitable as a discount rate because:
   (i) It is the required return on equity rather than the required return on the overall company.
   (ii) The equity of 1.4 reflects the financial risk of Folten's equity. Wemere's gearing differs from that of Folten, hence their equity Betas will differ.

- The inflation adjustment is unnecessary since ER_m and R_f already incorporate the expected impact of inflation.
- The equity Beta for Wemere can be estimated by ungearing Folten's equity Beta and regearing to reflect the financial risk of Wemere.

The market value-weighted gearing figures are:

Folten
Equity (138p × 7.2m shares) = £9.936m, i.e. 69.3% of total
Debt   = £4,400m, i.e. 30.7% of total

Wemere
Equity (using the take-over bid offer) = £10.6m, i.e. 81.5% of total
Debt   = £2.4m, i.e. 18.5% of total

Assuming corporate debt is risk-free, the ungeared equity Beta

$$\beta_u = \beta_g \times \frac{1}{1 + \frac{V_B}{V_S}(1-T)} = 1.4 \times \frac{1}{1 + (0.44)(1-35\%)}$$

$$= 1.089$$

Regearing Beta for Wemere,

$$\beta_g = \beta_u (1 + \frac{V_B}{V_S}(1-T))$$
$$= 1.089\ [1 + 0.23\ (1-35\%)]$$
$$= 1.25$$

- The cost of equity for Wemere is thus:

$$12\% + 1.25\ [18\% - 12\%] = 19.5\%$$

- Given the cost of debt is 13%

$$\text{WACC} = [13\%\ (1-35\%) \times 18.5\%] + [19.5\% \times 81.5\%]$$
$$= 17.5\%$$

- However, the WACC is only suitable as a discount rate if the systematic risk of the new investment is similar to that of the company as a whole.

Dividend Valuation Model
- The expression for this model relates to the cost of equity not the overall cost of capital.

$$\text{i.e. } k_e = \frac{D_1}{P_0} + g = \frac{14.20p}{138p} + 9\% = 19.3\%$$

- No inflation adjustment is required.
  The WACC is: $[13\%\ (1-35\%) \times 18.5\%] + [19.3\% \times 81.5\%]$
  $$= 19.3\%$$

(b) Neither method is problem-free. The surrogate company is unlikely to have identical characteristics, either at an operating level or in terms of financial characteristics. For example, the cost of equity in the dividend valuation model is derived from a different set of data regarding dividend policy, growth and share prices.

Folten's managers may have different capabilities, and the company may face different growth opportunities. Before using the estimated WACC, Wemere must be confident that the two companies are a sufficiently close fit.

Even so, the calculated WACC is inappropriate if the systematic risk of any new project differs from that of the company as a whole, and/or if project financing involves moving to a new capital structure.

Chapter 19

Question 1

(b) Runswick could adopt a number of policies:

(i) *Do nothing*

In this case, it accepts the foreign exchange risk and will have to purchase Swiss francs at the spot rate ruling on the foreign exchange market when it requires the currency, i.e. in three months.

(ii) *Forward foreign exchange market cover*

This would require buying Swiss francs at today's price on the forward market for delivery at a fixed date in future, i.e. three months' time. The contract for 54,000 Swiss francs can be covered by buying three months forward at a rate of 2.925 per £, i.e. $2.970 - 0.045$, the cost will be $\frac{54,000 \text{ SF}}{2.925} = £18,462$.

If the Swiss franc strengthens by less than implied in the forward exchange rate, Runswick will make an opportunity loss, and vice versa.

(iii) *Lead payment*

With the Swiss franc strengthening against sterling, it may be beneficial to make payment earlier than required rather than risk having to pay over a greater amount in sterling on the required date. Leading the payment, i.e. paying now will involve a cost of:

$$\frac{54,000 \text{ SF}}{2.970} = £18,182$$

In addition, there is a borrowing cost to include. This will be $(£18,182 \times 12\% \times 3/12) = £545$, making a total cost of £18,727.

(iv) *Money market cover*

This would require borrowing in one country, exchanging the borrowed funds at the spot rate into the currency in which payment is required, and investing in the country in whose currency payment is required. The total proceeds can then be used to pay for the goods.
This tactic requires:

> Borrow £18,002 for three months at 12 per cent
> Convert to Swiss francs at 2.97 per £1 = 53,466 SF
> Invest 53,466 SF for three months at 4 per cent to yield
>   53,466 SF (1.04) = 54,000 SF in three months

This involves an interest cost of:

$(£18,002 \times 12\% \times 3/12) = £540$, to yield a total cost of £18,542.

(v) If the discount is taken, the cost of the goods will be 52,650SF.

- Forward market cover will cost $\frac{52,650 \text{ SF}}{2.945} = £17,878$

Borrowing this amount for two months at 12 per cent costs £357, to give a total cost of £18,235.

- If payment is led, the cost is $\dfrac{52{,}650 \text{ SF}}{2.97} = £17{,}727$

Borrowing costs for three months = £532, to yield a total cost of £18,259.

- Money market cover involves borrowing £17,668 for three months at 12 per cent, converting at the spot rate of 2.970 to yield 52,475SF. Investing this amount at 4 per cent for one month yields a total of 52,650SF, enough to pay for the goods. The total cost is:

$$£17{,}668 \text{ plus interest of } £530 = £18{,}198.$$

From these alternatives, the cheapest option is to take the discount and undertake money market cover.

Chapter 20

Question 1   Brookday

(a) To maximize shareholder wealth, Brookday will remit maximum possible funds to the parent company. The project is worthwhile if the NPV to the parent company is positive.
(i) *Predicted Earnings for the US Subsidiary* ($000)

Item/Year	0	1	2	3	4	5
Price		100	105	110.25	115.8	
Volume (000)		50	100	100	100	
Sales revenue		*5,000*	*10,500*	*11,025*	*11,580*	
Variable costs		2,000	4,200	4,410	4,630	
Fixed costs		1,000	1,050	1,102	1,158	
Royalty		309	586	557	529	
Depreciation		*4,000*	*4,000*	*4,000*	*4,000*	
		(7,309)	(9,836)	(10,069)	(10.317)	
Taxable profit		(2,309)	664	956	1,263	
US tax		—	—	—	—	(287)
PAT		(2,309)	664	956	1,263	(287)

(ii) *Predicted Cash Flow for the US Subsidiary* ($000)

Year	0	1	2	3	4	5
PAT		(2,309)	664	956	1,263	(287)
Depreciation		4,000	4,000	4,000	4,000	
Initial Outlay	(19,000)					
Additional Capital		(1,000)				
Residual value of Assets					20,000	
Tax on residual value						(10,000)
Working capital release					4,000	
Cash flow attributable to parent	(19,000)	691	4,664	4,956	29,263	(10,287)

(iii) *Predicted Cash Flow to Parent Company* (£000)

Year	0	1	2	3	4	5
Cash flow available	(14,615)	559	3,976	4,445	27,633	(10,226)
Royalty		250	500	500	500	
UK Tax on Royalty			(125)	(250)	(250)	(250)
Net cash flow	(14,615)	809	4,351	4,695	27,883	(10,476)
P.V. at 13%	(14,615)	716	3,407	3,254	17,092	(5,688)

$$NPV = £4,166,000$$

Notes and Assumptions

1. The royalty is payable in £ and depends on the $/£ exchange rate. As sterling is expected to depreciate by 5 per cent p.a. against US$:

Year	1	2	3	4	5
Expected exchange rate $/£	1.235	1.173	1.115	1.059	1.006
Royalty (£000)	250	500	500	500	
Royalty ($000)	309	586	557	529	

2. The loss of exports to the United States if the project is undertaken is not a relevant cash flow.
3. All losses are carried forward and set against subsequent profits for taxation purposes.
4. The company's planning horizon is only four years, and because the subsidiary will operate beyond that, a residual or terminal value must be estimated. Tax will be payable as the assets have been depreciated in full.

5.   There is assumed to be no double taxation on cash flows remitted from the United States. The royalty has not been taxed in the United States and will bear UK tax.

6.   The discount rate of 13 per cent is found as follows:

$$\text{ER from project} = R_f + \text{Project } \beta \ (\text{ER}_m - R_f)$$
$$= 7\% + 1.2 \ (12\% - 7\%)$$
$$= 13\%$$

Information required for further analysis

(i)   Why is a four-year planning horizon used? How does the NPV alter for an extended working life of the project?

(ii) How has the residual value been assessed?

(iii) How has the project Beta been assessed? Has account been taken of the degree of correlation between the two economies? Have any other techniques of risk analysis, such as sensitivity analysis been applied?

(iv) How susceptible are the project cash flows to US political factors regarding, for example, exchange controls and tax? How can these risks be managed?

Chapter 21

Question 1   Gaymore

Traded options give the holder the right, but not the obligation, to buy (a call option) or sell (a put option) a quantity of shares at a fixed price on an exercise date in the future. They are usually in contracts of 1,000 shares and for three, six or nine months.

Holders of a put option in Gaymore plc have the right to sell shares in April at 500p. For this right they currently have to pay a premium of 47p, or £470 on a contract of 1,000 shares.

If the share price falls below 453p (i.e. 500p − 47p), the shares become profitable and the holder is 'in the money'. So if they fall to 450p, the investor can buy shares at this price, and exercise his put option to sell shares for 500p. A profit of 50p per share which, after the initial cost of the option gives a net profit 3p per share or £30 on the contract.

If the share price moves up to 510p by April, the option becomes worthless, and the investor loses his 47p premium.

Options such as this one can be used to either speculate or hedge on share price changes for a relatively low premium.

Chapter 22

Question 1   Grapper

(a)   The balance sheet net asset value is total assets minus total liabilities, i.e. £620m. Land and buildings have an estimated value of £150m × (1.25)^4 = £366m, i.e. £216m higher than the book value. Hence, the adjusted NAV is £836m.

Applying Grapper's 12 per cent growth rate, estimated PAT for the coming five years is:

$$£151(1.12) + £151(1.12)^2, \text{ etc.} = £1,074\text{m}$$

This yields total value of $£836\text{m} + £1,074\text{m} = £1,910\text{m}$

Grapper's market value is currently (400m shares $\times$ share price 470p) $= £1,880\text{m}$

The premium is thus $£30\text{m}$ or 7.5p per share.

This is not a sound basis for valuation as it ignores the time value of money. The premium of 1.6 per cent above the current market price is very small compared to those achieved in many 'real' bids.

Using the dividend valuation model:

$$P_0 = \frac{D_1}{k_e - g} = \frac{D_0 \ (1+g)}{k_e - g}$$

$$\text{Current dividend per share} = \frac{£76\text{m}}{400\text{m}} = 19\text{p}$$

Hence $D_1 = 19\text{p}(1.12) = 21.3\text{p}$

From the CAPM,

$$k_e = \text{ER} = R_f + \beta(\text{ER}_m - R_f) = 10\% + 1.05 \ (16\% - 10\%) = 16.3\%$$

Thus, $P_0 = \dfrac{21.3\text{p}}{16.3\% - 12\%} = 495\text{p}$, i.e. 5.3 per cent above the market price.

Restrictive assumptions underlying such a valuation include a constant growth rate, and an unchanged dividend policy. It is more rational to assess the value of Grapper incorporating post-merger rationalization.

(b) The post-merger sales revenue of Woppit will be over $£5,000\text{m}$, a size which could deter other takeover raiders, at least from the United Kingdom. However, bids from American and European sources should not be ruled out. In addition, debt-financed bids from consortia like Hoylake (which bid for BAT) show that size alone is not an adequate protection against a takeover bid.

(c) An indication of the scope for improving Grapper's efficiency can be obtained by examination of key financial ratios.

	Woppit	Grapper
Operating Profit Margin (EBIT/Sales)	20%	16.6%
Asset Turnover (Sales/Total Assets)	1.80	1.36
Debtors' Collection Period	31 days	50 days
Stock Turnover	10.3	6.4
Current Ratio	1.65:1	2.45:1

There are clear opportunities to improve Grapper's performance by rationalization and restructuring of activities. For example:

- Grapper's operating profit margin could be brought into line with Woppit's by a price increase and/or cost reduction.
- Grapper's stock level looks high by comparison. There could well be stockholding economies in an expanded operation.
- Grapper's cash holdings look excessive – again, centralized cash management may generate economies.

- Grapper's asset turnover is relatively low. Some assets could well be sold and others worked more intensively.
- Grapper seems to have scope for reducing its investment in debtors.

Introduction of such economies may well close the gap between Woppit's return on assets of 36 per cent and Grapper's present 22.5 per cent.

APPENDIX B

Present value of £1.00 due at the end of n Years

n	1%	2%	3%	4%	5%	6%	7%	8%	9%	10%	n
1	0.99010	0.98039	0.97007	0.96154	0.95238	0.94340	0.93458	0.92593	0.91743	0.90909	1
2	0.98030	0.96117	0.94260	0.92456	0.90703	0.89000	0.87344	0.85734	0.84168	0.82645	2
3	0.97059	0.94232	0.91514	0.88900	0.86384	0.83962	0.81630	0.79383	0.77218	0.75131	3
4	0.96098	0.92385	0.88849	0.85480	0.82270	0.79209	0.76290	0.73503	0.70843	0.68301	4
5	0.95147	0.90573	0.86261	0.82193	0.78353	0.74726	0.71299	0.68058	0.64993	0.62092	5
6	0.94204	0.88797	0.83748	0.79031	0.74622	0.70496	0.66634	0.63017	0.59627	0.56447	6
7	0.93272	0.87056	0.81309	0.75992	0.71068	0.66506	0.62275	0.58349	0.54703	0.51316	7
8	0.92348	0.85349	0.78941	0.73069	0.67684	0.62741	0.58201	0.54027	0.50187	0.46651	8
9	0.91434	0.83675	0.76642	0.70259	0.64461	0.59190	0.54393	0.50025	0.46043	0.42410	9
10	0.90529	0.82035	0.74409	0.67556	0.61391	0.55839	0.50835	0.46319	0.42241	0.38554	10
11	0.89632	0.80426	0.72242	0.64958	0.58468	0.52679	0.47509	0.42888	0.38753	0.35049	11
12	0.88745	0.78849	0.70138	0.62460	0.55684	0.49697	0.44401	0.39711	0.35553	0.31863	12
13	0.87866	0.77303	0.68095	0.60057	0.53032	0.46884	0.41496	0.36770	0.32618	0.28966	13
14	0.86996	0.75787	0.66112	0.57747	0.50507	0.44230	0.38782	0.34046	0.29925	0.26333	14
15	0.86135	0.74301	0.64186	0.55526	0.48102	0.41726	0.36245	0.31524	0.27454	0.23939	15
16	0.85282	0.72845	0.62317	0.53391	0.45811	0.39365	0.33873	0.29189	0.25187	0.21763	16
17	0.84438	0.71416	0.60502	0.51337	0.43630	0.37136	0.31657	0.27027	0.23107	0.19784	17
18	0.83602	0.70016	0.58739	0.49363	0.41552	0.35034	0.29586	0.25025	0.21199	0.17986	18
19	0.82774	0.68643	0.57029	0.47464	0.39573	0.33051	0.27651	0.23171	0.19449	0.16351	19
20	0.81954	0.67297	0.55367	0.45639	0.37689	0.31180	0.25842	0.21455	0.17843	0.14864	20
21	0.81143	0.65978	0.53755	0.43883	0.35894	0.29415	0.24151	0.19866	0.16370	0.13513	21
22	0.80340	0.64684	0.52189	0.42195	0.34185	0.27750	0.22571	0.18394	0.15018	0.12285	22
23	0.79544	0.63414	0.50669	0.40573	0.32557	0.26180	0.21095	0.17031	0.13778	0.11168	23
24	0.78757	0.62172	0.49193	0.39012	0.31007	0.24698	0.19715	0.15770	0.12640	0.10153	24
25	0.77977	0.60953	0.47760	0.37512	0.29530	0.23300	0.18425	0.14602	0.11597	0.09230	25

n	11%	12%	13%	14%	15%	16%	17%	18%	19%	20%	n
1	0.90090	0.89286	0.88496	0.87719	0.86957	0.86207	0.85470	0.84746	0.84034	0.83333	1
2	0.81162	0.79719	0.78315	0.76947	0.75614	0.74316	0.73051	0.71818	0.70616	0.69444	2
3	0.73119	0.71178	0.69305	0.67497	0.65752	0.64066	0.62437	0.60863	0.59342	0.57870	3
4	0.65873	0.63552	0.61332	0.59208	0.57175	0.55229	0.53365	0.51579	0.49867	0.48225	4
5	0.59345	0.56743	0.54276	0.51937	0.49718	0.47611	0.45611	0.43711	0.41905	0.40188	5
6	0.53464	0.50663	0.48032	0.45559	0.43233	0.41044	0.38984	0.37043	0.35214	0.33490	6
7	0.48166	0.45235	0.42506	0.39964	0.37594	0.35383	0.33320	0.31392	0.29592	0.27908	7
8	0.43393	0.40388	0.37616	0.35056	0.32690	0.30503	0.28487	0.26604	0.24867	0.23257	8
9	0.39092	0.36061	0.33288	0.30751	0.28426	0.26295	0.24340	0.22546	0.20897	0.19381	9
10	0.35218	0.32197	0.29459	0.26974	0.24718	0.22668	0.20804	0.19106	0.17560	0.16151	10
11	0.31728	0.28748	0.26070	0.23662	0.21494	0.19542	0.17781	0.16192	0.14756	0.13459	11
12	0.28584	0.25667	0.23071	0.20756	0.18691	0.16846	0.15197	0.13722	0.12400	0.11216	12
13	0.25751	0.22917	0.20416	0.18207	0.16253	0.14523	0.12989	0.11629	0.10420	0.09346	13
14	0.23199	0.20462	0.18068	0.15971	0.14133	0.12520	0.11102	0.09855	0.08757	0.07789	14
15	0.20900	0.18270	0.15989	0.14010	0.12289	0.10793	0.09489	0.08352	0.07359	0.06491	15
16	0.18829	0.16312	0.14150	0.12289	0.10686	0.09304	0.08110	0.07078	0.06184	0.05409	16
17	0.16963	0.14564	0.12522	0.10780	0.09393	0.08021	0.06932	0.05998	0.05196	0.04507	17
18	0.15282	0.13004	0.11081	0.09456	0.08080	0.06914	0.05925	0.05083	0.04367	0.03756	18
19	0.13768	0.11611	0.09806	0.08295	0.07026	0.05961	0.05064	0.04308	0.03669	0.03130	19
20	0.12403	0.10367	0.08678	0.07276	0.06110	0.05139	0.04328	0.03651	0.03084	0.02608	20
21	0.11174	0.09256	0.07680	0.06383	0.05313	0.04430	0.03699	0.03094	0.02591	0.02174	21
22	0.10067	0.08264	0.06796	0.05599	0.04620	0.03819	0.03162	0.02622	0.02178	0.01811	22
23	0.09069	0.77379	0.06014	0.04911	0.04017	0.03292	0.02702	0.02222	0.01830	0.01509	23
24	0.08170	0.06588	0.05322	0.04308	0.03493	0.02838	0.02310	0.01883	0.01538	0.01258	24
25	0.07361	0.05882	0.04710	0.03779	0.03038	0.02447	0.01974	0.01596	0.01292	0.01048	25

n	21%	22%	23%	24%	25%	26%	27%	28%	29%	30%	n
1	0.82645	0.81967	0.81301	0.80645	0.80000	0.79365	0.78740	0.78125	0.77519	0.76923	1
2	0.68301	0.67186	0.66098	0.65036	0.64000	0.62988	0.62000	0.61035	0.60093	0.59172	2
3	0.56447	0.55071	0.53738	0.52449	0.51200	0.49991	0.48819	0.47684	0.46583	0.45517	3
4	0.46651	0.45140	0.43690	0.42297	0.40960	0.39675	0.38440	0.37253	0.36111	0.35013	4
5	0.38554	0.37000	0.35520	0.34111	0.32768	0.31488	0.30268	0.29104	0.27993	0.26933	5
6	0.31863	0.30328	0.28878	0.27509	0.26214	0.24991	0.23833	0.22737	0.21700	0.20718	6
7	0.26333	0.24859	0.23478	0.22184	0.20972	0.19834	0.18766	0.17764	0.16822	0.15937	7
8	0.21763	0.20376	0.19088	0.17891	0.16777	0.15741	0.14776	0.13878	0.13040	0.12259	8
9	0.17986	0.16702	0.15519	0.14428	0.13422	0.12493	0.11635	0.10842	0.10109	0.09430	9
10	0.14864	0.13690	0.12617	0.11635	0.10737	0.09915	0.09161	0.08470	0.07836	0.07254	10
11	0.12285	0.11221	0.10258	0.09383	0.08590	0.07869	0.07214	0.06617	0.06075	0.05580	11
12	0.10153	0.09198	0.08339	0.07567	0.06872	0.06245	0.05680	0.05170	0.04709	0.04292	12
13	0.08391	0.07539	0.06780	0.06103	0.05498	0.04957	0.04472	0.04039	0.03650	0.03302	13
14	0.06934	0.06180	0.05512	0.04921	0.04398	0.03934	0.03522	0.03155	0.02830	0.02540	14
15	0.05731	0.05065	0.04481	0.03969	0.03518	0.03122	0.02773	0.02465	0.02194	0.01954	15
16	0.04736	0.04152	0.03643	0.03201	0.02815	0.02478	0.02183	0.01926	0.01700	0.01503	16
17	0.03914	0.03403	0.02962	0.02581	0.02252	0.01967	0.01719	0.01505	0.01318	0.01156	17
18	0.03235	0.02789	0.02408	0.02082	0.01801	0.01561	0.01354	0.01175	0.01022	0.00889	18
19	0.02673	0.02286	0.01958	0.01679	0.01441	0.01239	0.01066	0.00918	0.00792	0.00684	19
20	0.02209	0.01874	0.01592	0.01354	0.01153	0.00983	0.00839	0.00717	0.00614	0.00526	20
21	0.01826	0.01536	0.01294	0.01092	0.00922	0.00780	0.00661	0.00561	0.00476	0.00405	21
22	0.01509	0.01259	0.01052	0.00880	0.00738	0.00619	0.00520	0.00438	0.00369	0.00311	22
23	0.01247	0.01032	0.00855	0.00710	0.00590	0.00491	0.00410	0.00342	0.00286	0.00239	23
24	0.01031	0.00846	0.00695	0.00573	0.00472	0.00390	0.00323	0.00267	0.00222	0.00184	24
25	0.00852	0.00693	0.00565	0.00462	0.00378	0.00310	0.00254	0.00209	0.00172	0.00152	25

n	31%	32%	33%	34%	35%	36%	37%	38%	39%	40%
1	0.76336	0.75758	0.75188	0.74627	0.74074	0.73529	0.72993	0.72464	0.71942	0.71429
2	0.58272	0.57392	0.56532	0.55692	0.54870	0.54066	0.53279	0.52510	0.51757	0.51020
3	0.44482	0.43479	0.42505	0.41561	0.40644	0.39754	0.38890	0.38051	0.37235	0.36443
4	0.33956	0.32939	0.31959	0.31016	0.30107	0.29231	0.28387	0.27573	0.26788	0.26031
5	0.25920	0.24953	0.24029	0.23146	0.22301	0.21493	0.20720	0.19980	0.19272	0.18593
6	0.19787	0.18904	0.18067	0.17273	0.16520	0.15804	0.15124	0.14479	0.13865	0.13281
7	0.15104	0.14321	0.13584	0.12890	0.12237	0.11621	0.11040	0.10492	0.09975	0.09486
8	0.11530	0.10849	0.10214	0.09620	0.09064	0.08545	0.08058	0.07603	0.07176	0.06776
9	0.08802	0.08219	0.07680	0.07179	0.06714	0.06283	0.05882	0.05509	0.05163	0.04840
10	0.06719	0.06227	0.05774	0.05357	0.04973	0.04620	0.04293	0.03992	0.03714	0.03457
11	0.05129	0.04717	0.04341	0.03998	0.03684	0.03397	0.03134	0.02893	0.02672	0.02469
12	0.03915	0.03574	0.03264	0.02984	0.02729	0.02498	0.02287	0.02096	0.01922	0.01764
13	0.02989	0.02707	0.02454	0.02227	0.02021	0.01837	0.01670	0.01519	0.01383	0.01260
14	0.02281	0.02051	0.01845	0.01662	0.01497	0.01350	0.01219	0.01101	0.00995	0.00900
15	0.01742	0.01554	0.01387	0.01240	0.01109	0.00993	0.00890	0.00798	0.00716	0.00643
16	0.01329	0.01177	0.01043	0.00925	0.00822	0.00730	0.00649	0.00578	0.00515	0.00459
17	0.01015	0.00892	0.00784	0.00691	0.00609	0.00537	0.00474	0.00419	0.00370	0.00328
18	0.00775	0.00676	0.00590	0.00515	0.00451	0.00395	0.00346	0.00304	0.00267	0.00234
19	0.00591	0.00512	0.00443	0.00385	0.00334	0.00290	0.00253	0.00220	0.00192	0.00167
20	0.00451	0.00388	0.00333	0.00287	0.00247	0.00213	0.00184	0.00159	0.00138	0.00120
21	0.00345	0.00294	0.00251	0.00214	0.00183	0.00157	0.00135	0.00115	0.00099	0.00085
22	0.00263	0.00223	0.00188	0.00160	0.00136	0.00115	0.00098	0.00084	0.00071	0.00061
23	0.00201	0.00169	0.00142	0.00119	0.00101	0.00085	0.00072	0.00061	0.00051	0.00044
24	0.00153	0.00128	0.00107	0.00089	0.00074	0.00062	0.00052	0.00044	0.00037	0.00031
25	0.00117	0.00097	0.00080	0.00066	0.00055	0.00046	0.00038	0.00032	0.00027	0.00022

Present value of annuity of £1.00 for *n* Years

n	1%	2%	3%	4%	5%	6%	7%	8%	9%	10%	n
1	0.9901	0.9804	0.9709	0.9615	0.9524	0.9434	0.9346	0.9259	0.9174	0.9091	1
2	1.9704	1.9416	1.9135	1.8861	1.8594	1.8334	1.8080	1.7833	1.7591	1.7355	2
3	2.9410	2.8839	2.8286	2.7751	2.7232	2.6730	2.6243	2.5771	2.5313	2.4868	3
4	3.9020	3.8077	3.7171	3.6299	3.5459	3.4651	3.3872	3.3121	3.2397	3.1699	4
5	4.8535	4.7134	4.5797	4.4518	4.3295	4.2123	4.1002	3.9927	3.8896	3.7908	5
6	5.7955	5.6014	5.4172	5.2421	5.0757	4.9173	4.7665	4.6229	4.4859	4.3553	6
7	6.7282	6.4720	6.2302	6.0020	5.7863	5.5824	5.3893	5.2064	5.0329	4.8684	7
8	7.6517	7.3254	7.0196	6.7327	6.4632	6.2098	5.9713	5.7466	5.5348	5.3349	8
9	8.5661	8.1622	7.7861	7.4353	7.1078	6.8017	6.5152	6.2469	5.9852	5.7590	9
10	9.4714	8.9825	8.5302	8.1109	7.7217	7.3601	7.0236	6.7101	6.4176	6.1446	10
11	10.3677	9.7868	9.2526	8.7604	8.3064	7.8868	7.4987	7.1389	6.8052	6.4951	11
12	11.2552	10.5753	9.9539	9.3850	8.8632	8.3838	7.9427	7.5361	7.1607	6.8137	12
13	12.1338	11.3483	10.6349	9.9856	9.3935	8.8527	8.3576	7.9038	7.4869	7.1034	13
14	13.0038	12.1062	11.2960	10.5631	9.8986	9.2950	8.7454	8.2442	7.7861	7.3667	14
15	13.8651	12.8492	11.9379	11.1183	10.3796	9.7122	9.1079	8.5595	8.0607	7.6061	15
16	14.7180	13.5777	12.5610	11.6522	10.8377	10.1059	9.4466	8.8514	8.3125	7.8237	16
17	15.5624	14.2918	13.1660	12.1656	11.2740	10.4772	9.7632	9.1216	8.5436	8.0215	17
18	16.3984	14.9920	13.7534	12.6592	11.6895	10.8276	10.0591	9.3819	8.7556	8.2014	18
19	17.2261	15.6784	14.3237	13.1339	12.0853	11.1581	10.3356	9.6036	8.9501	8.3649	19
20	18.0457	16.3514	14.8774	13.5903	12.4622	11.4699	10.5940	9.8181	9.1285	8.5136	20
21	17.8571	17.0111	15.4149	14.0291	12.8211	11.7640	10.8355	10.0168	9.2922	8.6487	21
22	19.6605	17.6580	15.9368	14.4511	13.1630	12.0416	11.0612	10.2007	9.4424	8.7715	22
23	20.4559	18.2921	16.4435	14.8568	13.4885	12.3033	11.2722	10.3710	9.5802	8.8832	23
24	21.2435	18.9139	16.9355	15.2469	13.7986	12.5503	11.4693	10.5287	9.7066	8.9847	24
25	22.0233	19.5234	17.4131	15.6220	14.0939	12.7833	11.6536	10.6748	9.8226	9.0770	25

n	11%	12%	13%	14%	15%	16%	17%	18%	19%	20%
1	0.9009	0.8929	0.8850	0.8772	0.8696	0.8621	0.8547	0.8475	0.8403	0.8333
2	1.7125	1.6901	1.6681	1.6467	1.6257	1.6052	1.5852	1.5656	1.5465	1.5278
3	2.4437	2.4018	2.3612	2.3216	2.2832	2.2459	2.2096	2.1743	2.1399	2.1065
4	3.1024	3.0373	2.9745	2.9137	2.8550	2.7982	2.7432	2.6901	2.6486	2.5887
5	3.6959	3.6048	3.5172	3.4331	3.3522	3.2743	3.1993	3.1272	3.0576	2.9906
6	4.2305	4.1114	3.9976	3.8887	3.7845	3.6847	3.5892	3.4976	3.4098	3.3255
7	4.7122	4.5638	4.4226	4.2883	4.1604	4.0386	3.9224	3.8115	3.7057	3.6046
8	5.1461	4.9676	4.7988	4.6389	4.4873	4.3436	4.2072	4.0776	3.9544	3.8372
9	5.5370	5.3282	5.1317	4.9464	4.7716	4.6065	4.4506	4.3030	4.1633	4.0310
10	5.8892	5.6502	5.4262	5.2161	5.0188	4.8332	4.6586	4.4941	4.3389	4.1925
11	6.2065	5.9377	5.6869	5.4527	5.2337	5.0286	4.8364	4.6560	4.4865	4.3271
12	6.4924	6.1944	5.9176	5.6603	5.4206	5.1971	4.9884	4.7932	4.6105	4.4392
13	6.7499	6.4235	6.1218	5.8424	5.5931	5.3423	5.1183	4.9095	4.7147	4.5327
14	6.9819	6.6282	6.3025	6.0021	5.7245	5.4675	5.2293	5.0081	4.8023	4.6106
15	7.1909	6.8109	6.4624	6.1422	5.8474	5.5755	5.3242	5.0916	4.8759	4.6755
16	7.3792	6.9740	6.6039	6.2651	5.9542	5.6685	5.4053	5.1624	4.9377	4.7296
17	7.5488	7.1196	6.7291	6.3729	6.0472	5.7487	5.4746	5.2223	4.9897	4.7746
18	7.7016	7.2497	6.8399	6.4674	6.1280	5.8178	5.5339	5.2732	5.0333	4.8122
19	7.8393	7.3658	6.9380	6.5504	6.1982	5.8775	5.5845	5.3162	5.0700	4.8435
20	7.9633	7.4694	7.0248	6.6231	6.2593	5.9288	5.6278	5.3527	5.1009	4.8696
21	8.0751	7.5620	7.1016	6.6870	6.3125	5.9731	5.6648	5.3837	5.1268	4.8913
22	8.1757	7.6446	7.1695	6.7429	6.3587	6.0113	5.6964	5.4099	5.1486	4.9094
23	8.2664	7.7184	7.2297	6.7921	6.3988	6.0442	5.7234	5.4321	5.1668	4.9245
24	8.3481	7.7843	7.2829	6.8351	6.4338	6.0726	5.7465	5.4509	5.1822	4.9371
25	8.4217	7.8431	7.3300	6.8729	6.4641	6.0971	5.7662	5.4669	5.1951	4.9476

n	30%	29%	28%	27%	26%	25%	24%	23%	22%	21%	n
1	0.7692	0.7752	0.7813	0.7874	0.7937	0.8000	0.8065	0.8130	0.8197	0.8264	1
2	1.3609	1.3761	1.3916	1.4074	1.4235	1.4400	1.4568	1.4740	1.4915	1.5095	2
3	1.8161	1.8420	1.8684	1.8956	1.9234	1.9520	1.9813	2.0114	2.0422	2.0739	3
4	2.1662	2.2031	2.2410	2.2800	2.3202	2.3616	2.4043	2.4483	2.4936	2.5404	4
5	2.4356	2.4830	2.5320	2.5827	2.6351	2.6893	2.7454	2.8035	2.8636	2.9260	5
6	2.6427	2.7000	2.7594	2.8210	2.8850	2.9514	3.0205	3.0923	3.1669	3.2446	6
7	2.8021	2.8682	2.9370	3.0087	3.0833	3.1611	3.2423	3.3270	3.4155	3.5079	7
8	2.9247	2.9986	3.0758	3.1564	3.2407	3.3289	3.4212	3.5179	3.6193	3.7256	8
9	3.0190	3.0997	3.1842	3.2728	3.3657	3.4631	3.5655	3.6731	3.7863	3.9054	9
10	3.0915	3.1781	3.2689	3.3644	3.4648	3.5705	3.6819	3.7993	3.9232	4.0541	10
11	3.1473	3.2388	3.3351	3.4365	3.5435	3.6564	3.7757	3.9018	4.0354	4.1769	11
12	3.1903	3.2859	3.3868	3.4933	3.6060	3.7251	3.8514	3.9852	4.1274	4.2785	12
13	3.2233	3.3224	3.4272	3.5381	3.6555	3.7801	3.9124	4.0530	4.2028	4.3624	13
14	3.2487	3.3507	3.4587	3.5733	3.6949	3.8241	3.9616	4.1082	4.2646	4.4317	14
15	3.2682	3.3726	3.4834	3.6010	3.7261	3.8593	4.0013	4.1530	4.3152	4.4890	15
16	3.2832	3.3896	3.5026	3.6228	3.7509	3.8874	4.0333	4.1894	4.3567	4.5364	16
17	3.2948	3.4028	3.5177	3.6400	3.7705	3.9099	4.0591	4.2190	4.3908	4.5755	17
18	3.3037	3.4130	3.5294	3.6536	3.7861	3.9279	4.0799	4.2431	4.4187	4.6079	18
19	3.3105	3.4210	3.5386	3.6642	3.7985	3.9424	4.0967	4.2627	4.4415	4.6346	19
20	3.3158	3.4271	3.5458	3.6726	3.8083	3.9539	4.1103	4.2786	4.4603	4.6567	20
21	3.3198	3.4319	3.5514	3.6792	3.8161	3.9631	4.1212	4.2916	4.4756	4.6750	21
22	3.3230	3.4356	3.5558	3.6844	3.8223	3.9705	4.1300	4.3021	4.4882	4.6900	22
23	3.3254	3.4384	3.5592	3.6885	3.8273	3.9764	4.1371	4.3106	4.4985	4.7025	23
24	3.3272	3.4406	3.5619	3.6918	3.8312	3.9811	4.1428	4.3176	4.5070	4.7128	24
25	3.3286	3.4423	3.5640	3.6943	3.8342	3.9849	4.1474	4.3232	4.5139	4.7213	25

n	31%	32%	33%	34%	35%	36%	37%	38%	39%	40%	n
1	0.7634	0.7576	0.7519	0.7463	0.7407	0.7353	0.7299	0.7246	0.7194	0.7143	1
2	1.3461	1.3315	1.3172	1.3032	1.2894	1.2760	1.2627	1.2497	1.2370	1.2245	2
3	1.7909	1.7663	1.7423	1.7188	1.6959	1.6735	1.6516	1.6302	1.6093	1.5889	3
4	2.1305	2.0957	2.0618	2.0290	1.9969	1.9658	1.9355	1.9060	1.8772	1.8492	4
5	2.3897	2.3452	2.3021	2.2604	2.2200	2.1807	2.1427	2.1058	2.0699	1.9352	5
6	2.5875	2.5342	2.4828	2.4331	2.3852	2.3388	2.2936	2.2506	2.2086	2.1680	6
7	2.7386	2.6775	2.6187	2.5620	2.5075	2.4550	2.4043	2.3555	2.3083	2.2628	7
8	2.8539	2.7860	2.7208	2.6582	2.5982	2.5404	2.4849	2.4315	2.3801	2.3306	8
9	2.9419	2.8681	2.7976	2.7300	2.6653	2.6033	2.5437	2.4866	2.4317	2.3790	9
10	3.0091	2.9304	2.8553	2.7836	2.7150	2.6495	2.5867	2.5265	2.4689	2.4136	10
11	3.0604	2.9776	2.8987	2.8236	2.7519	2.6834	2.6180	2.5555	2.4956	2.4383	11
12	3.0995	3.0133	2.9314	2.8534	2.7792	2.7084	2.6409	2.5764	2.5148	2.4559	12
13	3.1294	3.0404	2.9559	2.8757	2.7994	2.7268	2.6576	2.5916	2.5286	2.4685	13
14	3.1522	3.0609	2.9744	2.8923	2.8144	2.7403	2.6698	2.6026	2.5386	2.4775	14
15	3.1696	3.0764	2.9883	2.9047	2.8255	2.7502	2.6787	2.6106	2.5457	2.4839	15
16	3.1829	3.0882	2.9987	2.9140	2.8337	2.7575	2.6852	2.6164	2.5509	2.4885	16
17	3.1931	3.0971	3.0065	2.9209	2.8398	2.7629	2.6899	2.6202	2.5546	2.4918	17
18	3.2008	3.1039	3.0124	2.9260	2.8443	2.7668	2.6934	2.6236	2.5573	2.4941	18
19	3.2067	3.1090	3.0169	2.9299	2.8476	2.7697	2.6959	2.6258	2.5592	2.4958	19
20	3.2112	3.1129	3.0202	2.9327	2.8501	2.7718	2.6977	2.6274	2.5606	2.4970	20
21	3.2174	3.1158	3.0227	2.9349	2.8519	2.7734	2.6991	2.6285	2.5616	2.4979	21
22	3.2173	3.1180	3.0246	2.9365	2.8533	2.7746	2.7000	2.6294	2.5623	2.4985	22
23	3.2193	3.1197	3.0260	2.9377	2.8543	2.7754	2.7008	2.6300	2.5628	2.4989	23
24	3.2209	3.1210	3.0271	2.9386	2.8550	2.7760	2.7013	2.6304	2.5632	2.4992	24
25	3.2220	3.1220	3.0279	2.9392	2.8556	2.7765	2.7017	2.6307	2.5634	2.4994	25

APPENDIX D
Call option values as per cent of share price

Standard deviation multiplied by square root of time	Share Price Divided by Present Value of Exercise Price							
	0.50	0.60	0.70	0.80	0.85	0.90	0.95	1.00
0.10	0.0	0.0	0.0	0.0	0.2	0.8	2.0	4.0
0.15	0.0	0.0	0.1	0.5	1.1	2.2	3.8	6.6
0.20	0.0	0.0	0.4	1.5	2.5	4.0	5.7	8.0
0.25	0.0	0.2	1.0	2.8	4.2	5.9	7.8	9.9
0.30	0.1	0.7	2.0	4.4	6.0	7.8	9.8	11.9
0.35	0.4	1.4	3.3	6.2	9.8	9.8	11.8	13.9
0.40	0.9	2.4	4.8	8.0	9.4	11.7	13.8	15.9
0.45	1.7	3.7	6.5	9.9	11.8	13.7	15.7	17.8
0.50	2.6	5.1	8.2	11.8	13.8	15.7	17.7	19.7
0.55	3.8	6.6	10.0	13.8	15.7	17.7	19.7	21.7
0.60	5.1	8.3	11.9	15.8	17.7	19.7	21.6	23.6
0.65	6.5	10.0	13.8	17.8	19.7	21.7	23.6	25.5
0.70	8.1	11.9	15.8	19.8	21.7	23.6	25.5	27.4
0.75	9.8	13.7	17.8	21.8	23.7	25.6	27.4	29.2
0.80	11.5	15.7	19.8	23.7	25.7	27.5	29.3	31.1
0.85	13.3	17.6	21.8	25.7	27.6	29.4	31.2	32.9
0.90	15.2	19.6	23.8	27.7	29.5	31.3	33.0	34.7
0.95	17.1	21.6	25.7	29.6	31.4	33.2	34.9	36.5
1.00	19.1	23.6	27.7	31.6	33.3	35.1	36.7	38.3
1.10	23.0	27.5	31.6	35.4	37.0	38.7	40.3	41.8
1.20	27.0	31.5	35.5	39.1	40.7	42.3	43.7	45.1
1.30	31.0	35.4	39.3	42.7	44.2	45.7	47.1	48.4
1.40	34.9	39.2	42.9	46.2	47.6	49.0	50.3	51.6
1.50	38.8	42.9	46.5	49.6	50.9	52.3	53.5	54.7
1.60	42.6	46.5	49.9	52.8	54.1	55.4	56.1	57.6

		Share Price Divided by Present Value of Exercise Price								
		1.05	1.10	1.15	1.20	1.25	1.30	1.40	1.50	2.00
Standard deviation multiplied by square root of time	0.10	6.5	10.0	13.4	16.8	20.0	23.1	28.6	33.3	60.0
	0.15	8.5	11.4	14.4	17.4	20.4	23.3	28.6	33.3	60.0
	0.20	10.4	13.0	15.7	18.5	21.2	23.9	28.9	35.5	60.0
	0.25	12.3	14.7	17.2	19.8	22.3	24.7	29.4	33.8	60.0
	0.30	14.1	16.5	18.8	21.2	23.5	25.8	30.2	34.3	60.0
	0.35	16.0	18.3	20.5	22.7	24.9	27.1	31.2	35.1	60.0
	0.40	17.9	20.1	22.2	24.3	26.4	28.4	32.3	36.0	60.1
	0.45	19.8	21.9	23.9	25.9	27.9	29.8	33.5	37.0	60.2
	0.50	21.7	23.7	25.7	27.6	29.5	31.3	34.8	38.1	60.4
	0.55	23.6	25.5	27.4	29.2	31.0	32.8	36.1	39.2	60.7
	0.60	23.4	27.3	29.1	30.9	32.6	34.3	37.5	40.4	61.0
	0.65	27.3	29.1	30.8	32.6	34.2	35.8	38.9	41.7	61.4
	0.70	29.1	30.9	32.6	34.2	35.8	37.3	40.3	43.0	61.9
	0.75	30.9	32.7	34.3	35.9	37.4	38.9	41.7	44.3	62.4
	0.80	32.7	34.4	36.0	37.5	39.0	40.4	43.1	45.6	63.0
	0.85	34.5	36.2	37.7	39.2	40.6	41.9	44.5	46.9	63.6
	0.90	36.3	37.9	39.3	40.8	42.1	43.5	46.0	48.3	64.3
	0.95	38.1	39.6	41.0	42.4	43.7	45.0	47.4	49.6	65.0
	1.00	39.8	41.2	42.6	44.0	45.2	46.5	48.8	50.9	65.7
	1.10	43.1	44.5	45.8	47.1	48.3	49.4	51.6	53.5	67.2
	1.20	46.5	47.8	48.9	50.1	51.3	52.3	54.3	56.1	68.8
	1.30	49.6	50.9	52.0	53.1	54.1	55.1	57.0	58.7	70.4
	1.40	52.8	53.9	55.0	56.10	56.9	57.9	59.6	61.2	71.9
	1.50	55.8	56.8	57.8	58.8	59.7	60.5	62.1	63.6	73.5
	1.60	58.8	59.6	60.5	61.4	62.3	63.1	64.5	65.9	75.1

Index